Dodge Pick-ups Automotive Repair Manual

by Mike Stubblefield and John H Haynes

Member of the Guild of Motoring Writers

Models covered:
All Dodge Full-size Pick-ups
1994 through 1996

(2Z1 - 30041)

ABCDE
FGHIJ
KLMNO
PQRS

Haynes Publishing Group
Sparkford Nr Yeovil
Somerset BA22 7JJ England

Haynes North America, Inc
861 Lawrence Drive
Newbury Park
California 91320 USA

Acknowledgements

We are grateful to the Chrysler Corporation for providing technical information and certain illustrations. Special thanks to Bill Bunce, diesel technician at Crown Dodge of Ventura, CA. Technical writers who contributed to this project include Rob Maddox, Jay Storer and Larry Warren.

© **Haynes North America, Inc. 1996**

With permission from J.H. Haynes & Co. Ltd.

A book in the Haynes Automotive Repair Manual Series

Printed in the U.S.A.

ISBN 1 56392 171 5

Library of Congress Catalog Card Number 95-80968

96-384

Contents

WI

Haynes mechanic, author and photographer with 1995 Dodge Ram pickup

About this manual

Its purpose

The purpose of this manual is to help you get the best value from your vehicle. It can do so in several ways. It can help you decide what work must be done, even if you choose to have it done by a dealer service department or a repair shop; it provides information and procedures for routine maintenance and servicing; and it offers diagnostic and repair procedures to follow when trouble occurs.

We hope you use the manual to tackle the work yourself. For many simpler jobs, doing it yourself may be quicker than arranging an appointment to get the vehicle into a shop and making the trips to leave it and pick it up. More importantly, a lot of money can be saved by avoiding the expense the shop must pass on to you to cover its labor and overhead costs. An added benefit is the sense of satisfaction and accomplishment that you feel after doing the job yourself.

Using the manual

The manual is divided into Chapters. Each Chapter is divided into numbered Sections, which are headed in bold type between horizontal lines. Each Section consists of consecutively numbered paragraphs.

At the beginning of each numbered Section you will be referred to any illustrations which apply to the procedures in that Section. The reference numbers used in illustration captions pinpoint the pertinent Section and the Step within that Section. That is, illustration 3.2 means the illustration refers to Section 3 and Step (or paragraph) 2 within that Section.

Procedures, once described in the text, are not normally repeated. When it's necessary to refer to another Chapter, the reference will be given as Chapter and Section number. Cross references given without use of the word "Chapter" apply to Sections and/or paragraphs in the same Chapter. For example, "see Section 8" means in the same Chapter.

References to the left or right side of the vehicle assume you are sitting in the driver's seat, facing forward.

Even though we have prepared this manual with extreme care, neither the publisher nor the author can accept responsibility for any errors in, or omissions from, the information given.

NOTE

A **Note** provides information necessary to properly complete a procedure or information which will make the procedure easier to understand.

CAUTION

A **Caution** provides a special procedure or special steps which must be taken while completing the procedure where the Caution is found. Not heeding a Caution can result in damage to the assembly being worked on.

WARNING

A **Warning** provides a special procedure or special steps which must be taken while completing the procedure where the Warning is found. Not heeding a Warning can result in personal injury.

Introduction to the Dodge Ram pick-up

Dodge Ram pick-ups are available in standard and club-cab body styles. All cabs are single welded unit construction and bolted to the frame. Ram pick-ups are available in short-bed and long-bed models. All models are available in two-wheel drive (2WD) and four-wheel drive (4WD) versions.

Powertrain options include a 5.9L inline six-cylinder diesel engine and 3.9L V6, 5.2L V8, 5.9L V8 and 8.0L V10 gasoline engines. Transmissions used are either a five-speed manual, three-speed automatic or four-speed automatic.

Chassis layout is conventional, with the engine mounted at the front and the power being transmitted through either the manual or automatic transmission to a driveshaft and solid rear axle. On 4WD models a transfer case also transmits power to the front axle by way of a driveshaft.

The front suspension on light duty 2WD models features an independent coil spring, upper and lower A-arm type front suspension, while 4WD and heavy duty 2WD models use coil springs and a solid axle located by four links. All models have a solid axle and leaf springs at the rear.

All models are equipped with power assisted disc front brakes and drum rear brakes. Rear Wheel Anti-Lock (RWAL) brakes are standard with a four-wheel Anti-lock Braking System (ABS) used on some models.

Vehicle identification numbers

Modifications are a continuing and unpublicized process in vehicle manufacturing. Since spare parts manuals and lists are compiled on a numerical basis, the individual vehicle numbers are essential to correctly identify the component required.

Vehicle Identification Number (VIN)

This very important identification number is stamped on a plate attached to the left side of the dashboard just inside the windshield on the driver's side of the vehicle (see illustration). The VIN also appears on the Vehicle Certificate of Title and Registration. It contains information such as where and when the vehicle was manufactured, the model year and the body style.

VIN year and engine codes

Two particularly important pieces of information located in the VIN are the model year and engine codes. Counting from the left, the engine code is the eighth digit and the model year code is the 10th digit.

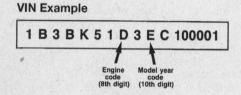

VIN Example

Engine code (8th digit)
Model year code (10th digit)

On the models covered by this manual the engine codes are:

C	5.9L inline 6-cylinder diesel
W	8.0L V10
X	3.9L V6
Y	5.2L V8
Z	5.9L V8 light duty
5	5.9L V8 heavy duty

On the models covered by this manual the model year codes are:

R	1994
S	1995
T	1996

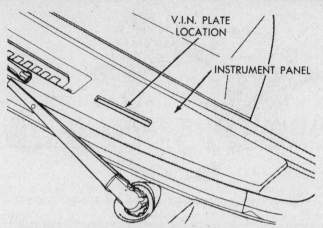

The VIN is visible from the outside of the vehicle, through the driver's side of the windshield

Equipment identification plate

This plate is located on the inside of the hood. It contains valuable information concerning the production of the vehicle as well as information on all production or special equipment.

Safety Certification label

The Safety Certification label is affixed to the left front door pillar. The plate contains the name of the manufacturer, the month and year of production, the Gross Vehicle Weight Rating (GVWR) and the safety certification statement. This label also contains the paint code. It is especially useful for matching the color and type of paint during repair work.

Engine identification number

The engine ID number on V6, V8 and V10 gasoline engines is located next to the left engine mount (see illustration). On diesel engines, the engine data plate is located on the left (driver's) side of the engine in front of the fuel injection pump.

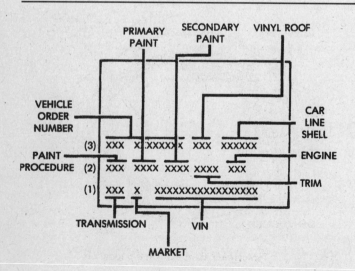

Typical Safety Certification label

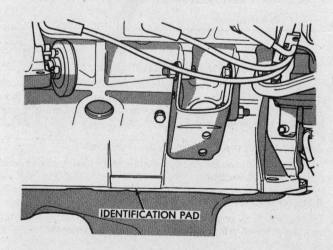

On gasoline engines the identification number is located on a pad near the left side engine mount

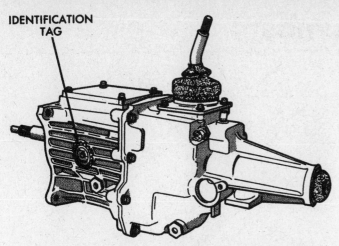

Typical manual transmission identification number location

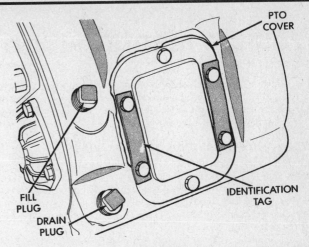

On NV-4500 transmissions the identification tag is attached to the PTO cover

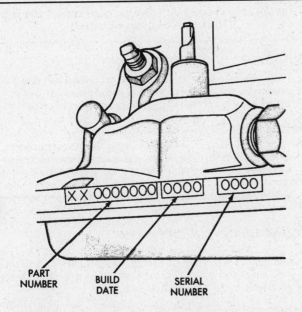

Automatic transmission identification number pad location

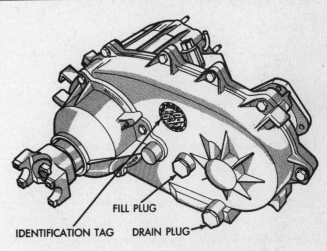

Typical transfer case identification tag location

Transmission identification number

The ID number on manual transmissions is located on the left side of the case (see illustrations). On automatic transmissions, the number is stamped on the left side of the transmission case above the oil pan flange (see illustration).

Transfer case identification number

The transfer case identification plate is attached to the rear side of the case (see illustration).

Axle identification numbers

On both front and rear axles the identification number is located on a tag attached to the differential cover (see illustration).

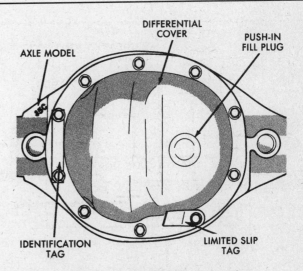

Typical axle identification tag location

Buying parts

Replacement parts are available from many sources, which generally fall into one of two categories - authorized dealer parts departments and independent retail auto parts stores. Our advice concerning these parts is as follows:

Retail auto parts stores: Good auto parts stores will stock frequently needed components which wear out relatively fast, such as clutch components, exhaust systems, brake parts, tune-up parts, etc. These stores often supply new or reconditioned parts on an exchange basis, which can save a considerable amount of money. Discount auto parts stores are often very good places to buy materials and parts needed for general vehicle maintenance such as oil, grease, filters, spark plugs, belts, touch-up paint, bulbs, etc. They also usually sell tools and general accessories, have convenient hours, charge lower prices and can often be found not far from home.

Authorized dealer parts department: This is the best source for parts which are unique to the vehicle and not generally available elsewhere (such as major engine parts, transmission parts, trim pieces, etc.).

Warranty information: If the vehicle is still covered under warranty, be sure that any replacement parts purchased - regardless of the source - do not invalidate the warranty!

To be sure of obtaining the correct parts, have engine and chassis numbers available and, if possible, take the old parts along for positive identification.

Maintenance techniques, tools and working facilities

Maintenance techniques

There are a number of techniques involved in maintenance and repair that will be referred to throughout this manual. Application of these techniques will enable the home mechanic to be more efficient, better organized and capable of performing the various tasks properly, which will ensure that the repair job is thorough and complete.

Fasteners

Fasteners are nuts, bolts, studs and screws used to hold two or more parts together. There are a few things to keep in mind when working with fasteners. Almost all of them use a locking device of some type, either a lockwasher, locknut, locking tab or thread adhesive. All threaded fasteners should be clean and straight, with undamaged threads and undamaged corners on the hex head where the wrench fits. Develop the habit of replacing all damaged nuts and bolts with new ones. Special locknuts with nylon or fiber inserts can only be used once. If they are removed, they lose their locking ability and must be replaced with new ones.

Rusted nuts and bolts should be treated with a penetrating fluid to ease removal and prevent breakage. Some mechanics use turpentine in a spout-type oil can, which works quite well. After applying the rust penetrant, let it work for a few minutes before trying to loosen the nut or bolt. Badly rusted fasteners may have to be chiseled or sawed off or removed with a special nut breaker, available at tool stores.

If a bolt or stud breaks off in an assembly, it can be drilled and removed with a special tool commonly available for this purpose. Most automotive machine shops can perform this task, as well as other repair procedures, such as the repair of threaded holes that have been stripped out.

Flat washers and lockwashers, when removed from an assembly, should always be replaced exactly as removed. Replace any damaged washers with new ones. Never use a lockwasher on any soft metal surface (such as aluminum), thin sheet metal or plastic.

Fastener sizes

For a number of reasons, automobile manufacturers are making wider and wider use of metric fasteners. Therefore, it is important to be able to tell the difference between standard (sometimes called U.S. or SAE) and metric hardware, since they cannot be interchanged.

All bolts, whether standard or metric, are sized according to diameter, thread pitch and length. For example, a standard 1/2 - 13 x 1 bolt is 1/2 inch in diameter, has 13 threads per inch and is 1 inch long. An M12 - 1.75 x 25 metric bolt is 12 mm in diameter, has a thread pitch of 1.75 mm (the distance between threads) and is 25 mm long. The two bolts are nearly identical, and easily confused, but they are not interchangeable.

In addition to the differences in diameter, thread pitch and length, metric and standard bolts can also be distinguished by examining the bolt heads. To begin with, the distance across the flats on a standard bolt head is measured in inches, while the same dimension on a metric bolt is sized in millimeters (the same is true for nuts). As a result, a standard wrench should not be used on a metric bolt and a metric wrench should not be used on a standard bolt. Also, most standard bolts have slashes radiating out from the center of the head to denote the grade or strength of the bolt, which is an indication of the amount of torque that can be applied to it. The greater the number of slashes, the greater the strength of the bolt. Grades 0 through 5 are commonly used on automobiles. Metric bolts have a property class (grade) number, rather than a slash, molded into their heads to indicate bolt strength. In this case, the higher the number, the stronger the bolt. Property class numbers 8.8, 9.8 and 10.9 are commonly used on automobiles.

Strength markings can also be used to distinguish standard hex nuts from metric hex nuts. Many standard nuts have dots stamped into one side, while metric nuts are marked with a number. The greater the number of dots, or the higher the number, the greater the strength of the nut.

Metric studs are also marked on their ends according to property class (grade). Larger studs are numbered (the same as metric bolts), while smaller studs carry a geometric code to denote grade.

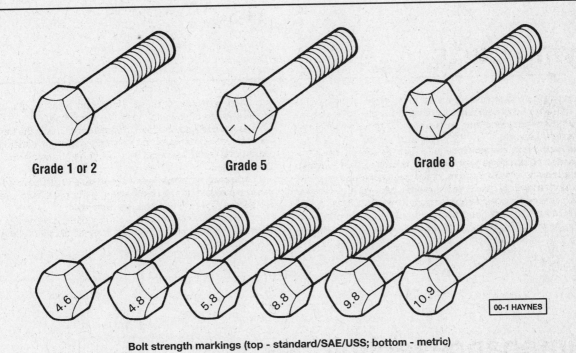

Bolt strength markings (top - standard/SAE/USS; bottom - metric)

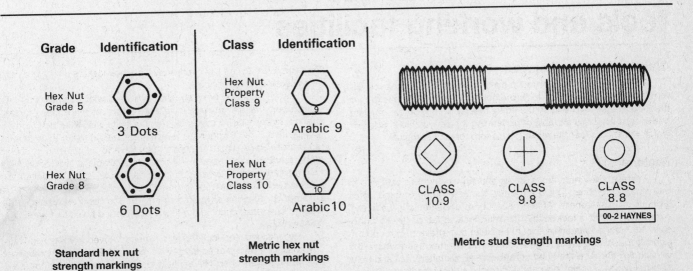

Standard hex nut strength markings

Metric hex nut strength markings

Metric stud strength markings

It should be noted that many fasteners, especially Grades 0 through 2, have no distinguishing marks on them. When such is the case, the only way to determine whether it is standard or metric is to measure the thread pitch or compare it to a known fastener of the same size.

Standard fasteners are often referred to as SAE, as opposed to metric. However, it should be noted that SAE technically refers to a non-metric fine thread fastener only. Coarse thread non-metric fasteners are referred to as USS sizes.

Since fasteners of the same size (both standard and metric) may have different strength ratings, be sure to reinstall any bolts, studs or nuts removed from your vehicle in their original locations. Also, when replacing a fastener with a new one, make sure that the new one has a strength rating equal to or greater than the original.

Tightening sequences and procedures

Most threaded fasteners should be tightened to a specific torque value (torque is the twisting force applied to a threaded component such as a nut or bolt). Overtightening the fastener can weaken it and cause it to break, while undertightening can cause it to eventually come loose. Bolts, screws and studs, depending on the material they are made of and their thread diameters, have specific torque values, many of which are noted in the Specifications at the beginning of each Chapter. Be sure to follow the torque recommendations closely. For fasteners not assigned a specific torque, a general torque value chart is presented here as a guide. These torque values are for dry (unlubricated) fasteners threaded into steel or cast iron (not aluminum). As was previously mentioned, the size and grade of a fastener determine the amount of torque that can safely be applied to it. The figures listed

Metric thread sizes	Ft-lbs	Nm
M-6	6 to 9	9 to 12
M-8	14 to 21	19 to 28
M-10	28 to 40	38 to 54
M-12	50 to 71	68 to 96
M-14	80 to 140	109 to 154

Pipe thread sizes		
1/8	5 to 8	7 to 10
1/4	12 to 18	17 to 24
3/8	22 to 33	30 to 44
1/2	25 to 35	34 to 47

U.S. thread sizes		
1/4 - 20	6 to 9	9 to 12
5/16 - 18	12 to 18	17 to 24
5/16 - 24	14 to 20	19 to 27
3/8 - 16	22 to 32	30 to 43
3/8 - 24	27 to 38	37 to 51
7/16 - 14	40 to 55	55 to 74
7/16 - 20	40 to 60	55 to 81
1/2 - 13	55 to 80	75 to 108

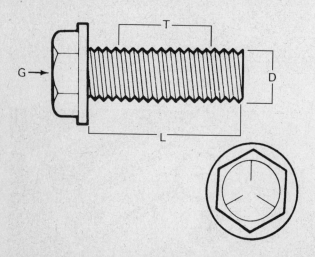

Standard (SAE and USS) bolt dimensions/grade marks

G	Grade marks (bolt strength)
L	Length (in inches)
T	Thread pitch (number of threads per inch)
D	Nominal diameter (in inches)

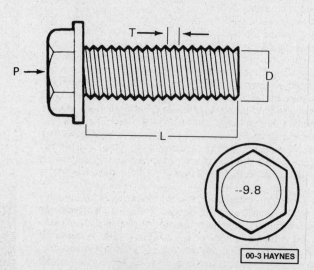

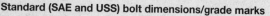

Metric bolt dimensions/grade marks

P	Property class (bolt strength)
L	Length (in millimeters)
T	Thread pitch (distance between threads in millimeters)
D	Diameter

here are approximate for Grade 2 and Grade 3 fasteners. Higher grades can tolerate higher torque values.

Fasteners laid out in a pattern, such as cylinder head bolts, oil pan bolts, differential cover bolts, etc., must be loosened or tightened in sequence to avoid warping the component. This sequence will normally be shown in the appropriate Chapter. If a specific pattern is not given, the following procedures can be used to prevent warping.

Initially, the bolts or nuts should be assembled finger-tight only. Next, they should be tightened one full turn each, in a criss-cross or diagonal pattern. After each one has been tightened one full turn, return to the first one and tighten them all one-half turn, following the same pattern. Finally, tighten each of them one-quarter turn at a time until each fastener has been tightened to the proper torque. To loosen and remove the fasteners, the procedure would be reversed.

Component disassembly

Component disassembly should be done with care and purpose to help ensure that the parts go back together properly. Always keep track of the sequence in which parts are removed. Make note of special characteristics or marks on parts that can be installed more than one way, such as a grooved thrust washer on a shaft. It is a good idea to lay the disassembled parts out on a clean surface in the order that they were removed. It may also be helpful to make sketches or take instant photos of components before removal.

When removing fasteners from a component, keep track of their locations. Sometimes threading a bolt back in a part, or putting the washers and nut back on a stud, can prevent mix-ups later. If nuts and bolts cannot be returned to their original locations, they should be kept in a compartmented box or a series of small boxes. A cupcake or muffin tin is ideal for this purpose, since each cavity can hold the bolts and nuts from a particular area (i.e. oil pan bolts, valve cover bolts, engine mount bolts, etc.). A pan of this type is especially helpful when working on assemblies with very small parts, such as the carburetor, alternator, valve train or interior dash and trim pieces. The cavities can be marked with paint or tape to identify the contents.

Whenever wiring looms, harnesses or connectors are separated, it is a good idea to identify the two halves with numbered pieces of masking tape so they can be easily reconnected.

Gasket sealing surfaces

Throughout any vehicle, gaskets are used to seal the mating surfaces between two parts and keep lubricants, fluids, vacuum or pressure contained in an assembly.

Many times these gaskets are coated with a liquid or paste-type gasket sealing compound before assembly. Age, heat and pressure can sometimes cause the two parts to stick together so tightly that they are very difficult to separate. Often, the assembly can be loosened by striking it with a soft-face hammer near the mating surfaces. A regular hammer can be used if a block of wood is placed between the hammer and the part. Do not hammer on cast parts or parts that could be easily damaged. With any particularly stubborn part, always recheck to make sure that every fastener has been removed.

Avoid using a screwdriver or bar to pry apart an assembly, as they can easily mar the gasket sealing surfaces of the parts, which must remain smooth. If prying is absolutely necessary, use an old broom handle, but keep in mind that extra clean up will be necessary if the wood splinters.

After the parts are separated, the old gasket must be carefully scraped off and the gasket surfaces cleaned. Stubborn gasket material can be soaked with rust penetrant or treated with a special chemical to soften it so it can be easily scraped off. A scraper can be fashioned from a piece of copper tubing by flattening and sharpening one end. Copper is recommended because it is usually softer than the surfaces to be scraped, which reduces the chance of gouging the part. Some gaskets can be removed with a wire brush, but regardless of the method used, the mating surfaces must be left clean and smooth. If for some reason the gasket surface is gouged, then a gasket sealer thick enough to fill scratches will have to be used during reassembly of the components. For most applications, a non-drying (or semi-drying) gasket sealer should be used.

Hose removal tips

Warning: *If the vehicle is equipped with air conditioning, do not disconnect any of the A/C hoses without first having the system depressurized by a dealer service department or a service station.*

Hose removal precautions closely parallel gasket removal precautions. Avoid scratching or gouging the surface that the hose mates against or the connection may leak. This is especially true for radiator hoses. Because of various chemical reactions, the rubber in hoses can bond itself to the metal spigot that the hose fits over. To remove a hose, first loosen the hose clamps that secure it to the spigot. Then, with slip-joint pliers, grab the hose at the clamp and rotate it around the spigot. Work it back and forth until it is completely free, then pull it off. Silicone or other lubricants will ease removal if they can be applied between the hose and the outside of the spigot. Apply the same lubricant to the inside of the hose and the outside of the spigot to simplify installation.

As a last resort (and if the hose is to be replaced with a new one anyway), the rubber can be slit with a knife and the hose peeled from the spigot. If this must be done, be careful that the metal connection is not damaged.

If a hose clamp is broken or damaged, do not reuse it. Wire-type clamps usually weaken with age, so it is a good idea to replace them with screw-type clamps whenever a hose is removed.

Tools

A selection of good tools is a basic requirement for anyone who plans to maintain and repair his or her own vehicle. For the owner who has few tools, the initial investment might seem high, but when compared to the spiraling costs of professional auto maintenance and repair, it is a wise one.

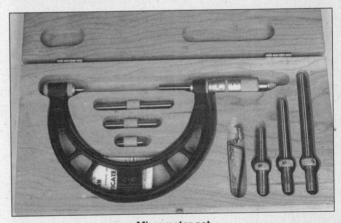

Micrometer set

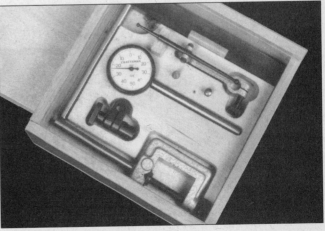

Dial indicator set

Dial caliper

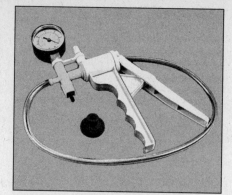

Hand-operated vacuum pump

Timing light

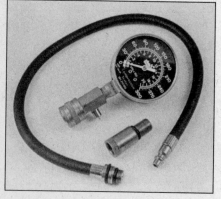

Compression gauge with spark plug
hole adapter

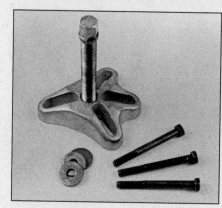

Damper/steering wheel puller

General purpose puller

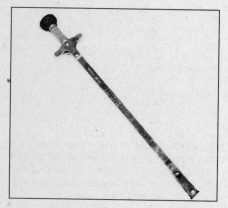

Hydraulic lifter removal tool

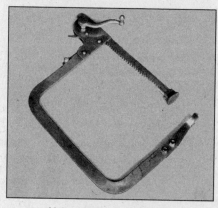

Valve spring compressor

Valve spring compressor

Ridge reamer

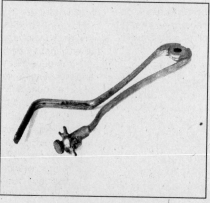

Piston ring groove cleaning tool

Ring removal/installation tool

Ring compressor

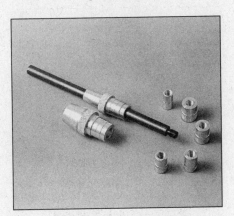

Cylinder hone

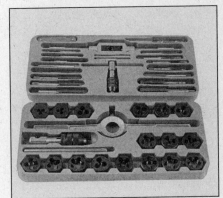

Brake hold-down spring tool

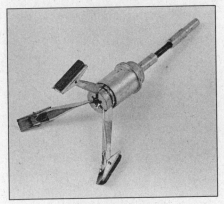

Brake cylinder hone

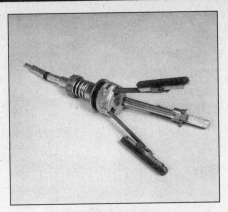

Clutch plate alignment tool

Tap and die set

To help the owner decide which tools are needed to perform the tasks detailed in this manual, the following tool lists are offered: *Maintenance and minor repair, Repair/overhaul* and *Special.*

The newcomer to practical mechanics should start off with the *maintenance and minor repair* tool kit, which is adequate for the simpler jobs performed on a vehicle. Then, as confidence and experience grow, the owner can tackle more difficult tasks, buying additional tools as they are needed. Eventually the basic kit will be expanded into the *repair and overhaul* tool set. Over a period of time, the experienced do-it-yourselfer will assemble a tool set complete enough for most repair and overhaul procedures and will add tools from the special category when it is felt that the expense is justified by the frequency of use.

Maintenance and minor repair tool kit

The tools in this list should be considered the minimum required for performance of routine maintenance, servicing and minor repair work. We recommend the purchase of combination wrenches (box-end and open-end combined in one wrench). While more expensive than open end wrenches, they offer the advantages of both types of wrench.

Combination wrench set (1/4-inch to 1 inch or 6 mm to 19 mm)
Adjustable wrench, 8 inch
Spark plug wrench with rubber insert
Spark plug gap adjusting tool
Feeler gauge set
Brake bleeder wrench
Standard screwdriver (5/16-inch x 6 inch)
Phillips screwdriver (No. 2 x 6 inch)
Combination pliers - 6 inch
Hacksaw and assortment of blades
Tire pressure gauge
Grease gun

Oil can
Fine emery cloth
Wire brush
Battery post and cable cleaning tool
Oil filter wrench
Funnel (medium size)
Safety goggles
Jackstands (2)
Drain pan

Note*: If basic tune-ups are going to be part of routine maintenance, it will be necessary to purchase a good quality stroboscopic timing light and combination tachometer/dwell meter. Although they are included in the list of special tools, it is mentioned here because they are absolutely necessary for tuning most vehicles properly.*

Repair and overhaul tool set

These tools are essential for anyone who plans to perform major repairs and are in addition to those in the maintenance and minor repair tool kit. Included is a comprehensive set of sockets which, though expensive, are invaluable because of their versatility, especially when various extensions and drives are available. We recommend the 1/2-inch drive over the 3/8-inch drive. Although the larger drive is bulky and more expensive, it has the capacity of accepting a very wide range of large sockets. Ideally, however, the mechanic should have a 3/8-inch drive set and a 1/2-inch drive set.

Socket set(s)
Reversible ratchet
Extension - 10 inch
Universal joint
Torque wrench (same size drive as sockets)
Ball peen hammer - 8 ounce
Soft-face hammer (plastic/rubber)
Standard screwdriver (1/4-inch x 6 inch)

Standard screwdriver (stubby - 5/16-inch)
Phillips screwdriver (No. 3 x 8 inch)
Phillips screwdriver (stubby - No. 2)
Pliers - vise grip
Pliers - lineman's
Pliers - needle nose
Pliers - snap-ring (internal and external)
Cold chisel - 1/2-inch
Scribe
Scraper (made from flattened copper tubing)
Centerpunch
Pin punches (1/16, 1/8, 3/16-inch)
Steel rule/straightedge - 12 inch
Allen wrench set (1/8 to 3/8-inch or 4 mm to 10 mm)
A selection of files
Wire brush (large)
Jackstands (second set)
Jack (scissor or hydraulic type)

Note: *Another tool which is often useful is an electric drill with a chuck capacity of 3/8-inch and a set of good quality drill bits.*

Special tools

The tools in this list include those which are not used regularly, are expensive to buy, or which need to be used in accordance with their manufacturer's instructions. Unless these tools will be used frequently, it is not very economical to purchase many of them. A consideration would be to split the cost and use between yourself and a friend or friends. In addition, most of these tools can be obtained from a tool rental shop on a temporary basis.

This list primarily contains only those tools and instruments widely available to the public, and not those special tools produced by the vehicle manufacturer for distribution to dealer service departments. Occasionally, references to the manufacturer's special tools are included in the text of this manual. Generally, an alternative method of doing the job without the special tool is offered. However, sometimes there is no alternative to their use. Where this is the case, and the tool cannot be purchased or borrowed, the work should be turned over to the dealer service department or an automotive repair shop.

Valve spring compressor
Piston ring groove cleaning tool
Piston ring compressor
Piston ring installation tool
Cylinder compression gauge
Cylinder ridge reamer
Cylinder surfacing hone
Cylinder bore gauge
Micrometers and/or dial calipers
Hydraulic lifter removal tool
Balljoint separator
Universal-type puller
Impact screwdriver
Dial indicator set
Stroboscopic timing light (inductive pick-up)
Hand operated vacuum/pressure pump
Tachometer/dwell meter
Universal electrical multimeter
Cable hoist
Brake spring removal and installation tools
Floor jack

Buying tools

For the do-it-yourselfer who is just starting to get involved in vehicle maintenance and repair, there are a number of options available when purchasing tools. If maintenance and minor repair is the extent of the work to be done, the purchase of individual tools is satisfactory. If, on the other hand, extensive work is planned, it would be a good idea to purchase a modest tool set from one of the large retail chain stores. A set can usually be bought at a substantial savings over the individual tool prices, and they often come with a tool box. As additional tools are needed, add-on sets, individual tools and a larger tool box can be purchased to expand the tool selection. Building a tool set gradually allows the cost of the tools to be spread over a longer period of time and gives the mechanic the freedom to choose only those tools that will actually be used.

Tool stores will often be the only source of some of the special tools that are needed, but regardless of where tools are bought, try to avoid cheap ones, especially when buying screwdrivers and sockets, because they won't last very long. The expense involved in replacing cheap tools will eventually be greater than the initial cost of quality tools.

Care and maintenance of tools

Good tools are expensive, so it makes sense to treat them with respect. Keep them clean and in usable condition and store them properly when not in use. Always wipe off any dirt, grease or metal chips before putting them away. Never leave tools lying around in the work area. Upon completion of a job, always check closely under the hood for tools that may have been left there so they won't get lost during a test drive.

Some tools, such as screwdrivers, pliers, wrenches and sockets, can be hung on a panel mounted on the garage or workshop wall, while others should be kept in a tool box or tray. Measuring instruments, gauges, meters, etc. must be carefully stored where they cannot be damaged by weather or impact from other tools.

When tools are used with care and stored properly, they will last a very long time. Even with the best of care, though, tools will wear out if used frequently. When a tool is damaged or worn out, replace it. Subsequent jobs will be safer and more enjoyable if you do.

Working facilities

Not to be overlooked when discussing tools is the workshop. If anything more than routine maintenance is to be carried out, some sort of suitable work area is essential.

It is understood, and appreciated, that many home mechanics do not have a good workshop or garage available, and end up removing an engine or doing major repairs outside. It is recommended, however, that the overhaul or repair be completed under the cover of a roof.

A clean, flat workbench or table of comfortable working height is an absolute necessity. The workbench should be equipped with a vise that has a jaw opening of at least four inches.

As mentioned previously, some clean, dry storage space is also required for tools, as well as the lubricants, fluids, cleaning solvents, etc. which soon become necessary.

Sometimes waste oil and fluids, drained from the engine or cooling system during normal maintenance or repairs, present a disposal problem. To avoid pouring them on the ground or into a sewage system, pour the used fluids into large containers, seal them with caps and take them to an authorized disposal site or recycling center. Plastic jugs, such as old antifreeze containers, are ideal for this purpose.

Always keep a supply of old newspapers and clean rags available. Old towels are excellent for mopping up spills. Many mechanics use rolls of paper towels for most work because they are readily available and disposable. To help keep the area under the vehicle clean, a large cardboard box can be cut open and flattened to protect the garage or shop floor.

Whenever working over a painted surface, such as when leaning over a fender to service something under the hood, always cover it with an old blanket or bedspread to protect the finish. Vinyl covered pads, made especially for this purpose, are available at auto parts stores.

Jacking and towing

Jacking

The jack supplied with the vehicle should only be used for raising the vehicle when changing a tire or placing jackstands under the frame. NEVER work under the vehicle or start the engine when the vehicle supported only by a jack.

The vehicle should be parked on level ground with the wheels blocked, the parking brake applied and the transmission in Park (automatic) or Reverse (manual). If the vehicle is parked alongside the roadway, or in any other hazardous situation, turn on the emergency hazard flashers. If a tire is to be changed, loosen the lug nuts one-half turn before raising off the ground.

Place the jack under the vehicle in the indicated positions **(see illustrations)**. Operate the jack with a slow, smooth motion until the wheel is raised off the ground. Remove the lug nuts, pull off the wheel, install the spare and thread the lug nuts back on with the beveled side facing in. Tighten the lug nuts snugly, lower the vehicle until some weight is on the wheel, tighten them completely in a criss-cross pattern and remove the jack. Note that some spare tires are designed for temporary use only - don't exceed the recommended speed, mileage or other restriction instructions accompanying the spare.

Towing

Equipment specifically designed for towing should be used and attached to the main structural members of the vehicle. Optional tow hooks may be attached to the frame at both ends of the vehicle; they are intended for emergency use only, for rescuing a stranded vehicle. Do not use the tow hooks for highway towing. Stand clear when using tow straps or chains, they may break causing serious injury.

Safety is a major consideration when towing and all applicable state and local laws must be obeyed. In addition to a tow bar, a safety chain must be used for all towing.

Two-wheel drive vehicles with automatic transmission may be towed with four wheels on the ground for a distance of 15 miles or less, as long as the speed doesn't exceed 30 mph. If the vehicle has to be towed more than 15 miles, place the rear wheels on a towing dolly.

Two-wheel drive vehicles with manual transmission can be towed without restrictions for a distance of 50 miles with the ignition lock in

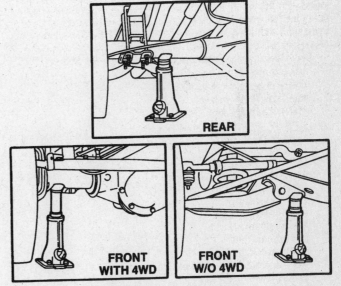

Front and rear jacking points

the Off position and the transmission in Neutral.

Four-wheel drive vehicles should be towed on a flatbed or with all four wheels off the ground to avoid damage to the transfer case.

Vehicles equipped with the NV-021 PTO adapter must be towed with the transfer case and transmission in Neutral with the rear wheels off the ground to avoid drivetrain damage.

If any vehicle is to be towed with the front wheels on the ground and the rear wheels raised, the ignition key must be turned to the OFF position to unlock the steering column and a steering wheel clamping device designed for towing must be used or damage to the steering column lock may occur.

Booster battery (jump) starting

Observe these precautions when using a booster battery to start a vehicle:

a) *Before connecting the booster battery, make sure the ignition switch is in the Off position.*

b) *Turn off the lights, heater and other electrical loads.*

c) *Your eyes should be shielded. Safety goggles are a good idea.*

d) *Make sure the booster battery is the same voltage as the dead one in the vehicle.*

e) *The two vehicles MUST NOT TOUCH each other!*

f) *Make sure the transaxle is in Neutral (manual) or Park (automatic).*

g) *If the booster battery is not a maintenance-free type, remove the vent caps and lay a cloth over the vent holes.*

Connect the red jumper cable to the positive (+) terminals of each battery **(see illustration). Note:** *On diesel models, the connections must be made to the left (driver's side) battery.*

Connect one end of the black jumper cable to the negative (-) terminal of the booster battery. The other end of this cable should be connected to a good ground on the vehicle to be started, such as a bolt or bracket on the body.

Start the engine using the booster battery, then, with the engine running at idle speed, disconnect the jumper cables in the reverse order of connection.

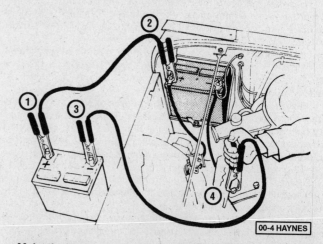

00-4 HAYNES

Make the booster battery cable connections in the numerical order shown (note that the negative cable of the booster battery is NOT attached to the negative terminal of the dead battery)

Automotive chemicals and lubricants

A number of automotive chemicals and lubricants are available for use during vehicle maintenance and repair. They include a wide variety of products ranging from cleaning solvents and degreasers to lubricants and protective sprays for rubber, plastic and vinyl.

Cleaners

Carburetor cleaner and choke cleaner is a strong solvent for gum, varnish and carbon. Most carburetor cleaners leave a dry-type lubricant film which will not harden or gum up. Because of this film it is not recommended for use on electrical components.

Brake system cleaner is used to remove grease and brake fluid from the brake system, where clean surfaces are absolutely necessary. It leaves no residue and often eliminates brake squeal caused by contaminants.

Electrical cleaner removes oxidation, corrosion and carbon deposits from electrical contacts, restoring full current flow. It can also be used to clean spark plugs, carburetor jets, voltage regulators and other parts where an oil-free surface is desired.

Demoisturants remove water and moisture from electrical components such as alternators, voltage regulators, electrical connectors and fuse blocks. They are non-conductive, non-corrosive and non-flammable.

Degreasers are heavy-duty solvents used to remove grease from the outside of the engine and from chassis components. They can be sprayed or brushed on and, depending on the type, are rinsed off either with water or solvent.

Lubricants

Motor oil is the lubricant formulated for use in engines. It normally contains a wide variety of additives to prevent corrosion and reduce foaming and wear. Motor oil comes in various weights (viscosity ratings) from 5 to 80. The recommended weight of the oil depends on the season, temperature and the demands on the engine. Light oil is used in cold climates and under light load conditions. Heavy oil is used in hot climates and where high loads are encountered. Multi-viscosity oils are designed to have characteristics of both light and heavy oils and are available in a number of weights from 5W-20 to 20W-50.

Gear oil is designed to be used in differentials, manual transmissions and other areas where high-temperature lubrication is required.

Chassis and wheel bearing grease is a heavy grease used where increased loads and friction are encountered, such as for wheel bearings, balljoints, tie-rod ends and universal joints.

High-temperature wheel bearing grease is designed to withstand the extreme temperatures encountered by wheel bearings in disc brake equipped vehicles. It usually contains molybdenum disulfide (moly), which is a dry-type lubricant.

White grease is a heavy grease for metal-to-metal applications where water is a problem. White grease stays soft under both low and high temperatures (usually from -100 to +190-degrees F), and will not wash off or dilute in the presence of water.

Assembly lube is a special extreme pressure lubricant, usually containing moly, used to lubricate high-load parts (such as main and rod bearings and cam lobes) for initial start-up of a new engine. The assembly lube lubricates the parts without being squeezed out or washed away until the engine oiling system begins to function.

Silicone lubricants are used to protect rubber, plastic, vinyl and nylon parts.

Graphite lubricants are used where oils cannot be used due to contamination problems, such as in locks. The dry graphite will lubricate metal parts while remaining uncontaminated by dirt, water, oil or acids. It is electrically conductive and will not foul electrical contacts in locks such as the ignition switch.

Moly penetrants loosen and lubricate frozen, rusted and corroded fasteners and prevent future rusting or freezing.

Heat-sink grease is a special electrically non-conductive grease that is used for mounting electronic ignition modules where it is essential that heat is transferred away from the module.

Sealants

RTV sealant is one of the most widely used gasket compounds. Made from silicone, RTV is air curing, it seals, bonds, waterproofs, fills surface irregularities, remains flexible, doesn't shrink, is relatively easy to remove, and is used as a supplementary sealer with almost all low and medium temperature gaskets.

Anaerobic sealant is much like RTV in that it can be used either to seal gaskets or to form gaskets by itself. It remains flexible, is solvent resistant and fills surface imperfections. The difference between an anaerobic sealant and an RTV-type sealant is in the curing. RTV cures when exposed to air, while an anaerobic sealant cures only in the absence of air. This means that an anaerobic sealant cures only after the assembly of parts, sealing them together.

Thread and pipe sealant is used for sealing hydraulic and pneumatic fittings and vacuum lines. It is usually made from a Teflon compound, and comes in a spray, a paint-on liquid and as a wrap-around tape.

Chemicals

Anti-seize compound prevents seizing, galling, cold welding, rust and corrosion in fasteners. High-temperature ant-seize, usually made with copper and graphite lubricants, is used for exhaust system and exhaust manifold bolts.

Anaerobic locking compounds are used to keep fasteners from vibrating or working loose and cure only after installation, in the absence of air. Medium strength locking compound is used for small nuts, bolts and screws that may be removed later. High-strength locking compound is for large nuts, bolts and studs which aren't removed on a regular basis.

Oil additives range from viscosity index improvers to chemical treatments that claim to reduce internal engine friction. It should be noted that most oil manufacturers caution against using additives with their oils.

Gas additives perform several functions, depending on their chemical makeup. They usually contain solvents that help dissolve gum and varnish that build up on carburetor, fuel injection and intake parts. They also serve to break down carbon deposits that form on the inside surfaces of the combustion chambers. Some additives contain upper cylinder lubricants for valves and piston rings, and others contain chemicals to remove condensation from the gas tank.

Miscellaneous

Brake fluid is specially formulated hydraulic fluid that can withstand the heat and pressure encountered in brake systems. Care must be taken so this fluid does not come in contact with painted surfaces or plastics. An opened container should always be resealed to prevent contamination by water or dirt.

Weatherstrip adhesive is used to bond weatherstripping around doors, windows and trunk lids. It is sometimes used to attach trim pieces.

Undercoating is a petroleum-based, tar-like substance that is designed to protect metal surfaces on the underside of the vehicle from corrosion. It also acts as a sound-deadening agent by insulating the bottom of the vehicle.

Waxes and polishes are used to help protect painted and plated surfaces from the weather. Different types of paint may require the use of different types of wax and polish. Some polishes utilize a chemical or abrasive cleaner to help remove the top layer of oxidized (dull) paint on older vehicles. In recent years many non-wax polishes that contain a wide variety of chemicals such as polymers and silicones have been introduced. These non-wax polishes are usually easier to apply and last longer than conventional waxes and polishes.

Conversion factors

Length (distance)

Inches (in)	X	25.4	= Millimetres (mm)	X 0.0394	= Inches (in)
Feet (ft)	X	0.305	= Metres (m)	X 3.281	= Feet (ft)
Miles	X	1.609	= Kilometres (km)	X 0.621	= Miles

Volume (capacity)

Cubic inches (cu in; in³)	X	16.387	= Cubic centimetres (cc; cm³)	X 0.061	= Cubic inches (cu in; in³)
Imperial pints (Imp pt)	X	0.568	= Litres (l)	X 1.76	= Imperial pints (Imp pt)
Imperial quarts (Imp qt)	X	1.137	= Litres (l)	X 0.88	= Imperial quarts (Imp qt)
Imperial quarts (Imp qt)	X	1.201	= US quarts (US qt)	X 0.833	= Imperial quarts (Imp qt)
US quarts (US qt)	X	0.946	= Litres (l)	X 1.057	= US quarts (US qt)
Imperial gallons (Imp gal)	X	4.546	= Litres (l)	X 0.22	= Imperial gallons (Imp gal)
Imperial gallons (Imp gal)	X	1.201	= US gallons (US gal)	X 0.833	= Imperial gallons (Imp gal)
US gallons (US gal)	X	3.785	= Litres (l)	X 0.264	= US gallons (US gal)

Mass (weight)

Ounces (oz)	X	28.35	= Grams (g)	X 0.035	Ounces (oz)
Pounds (lb)	X	0.454	= Kilograms (kg)	X 2.205	= Pounds (lb)

Force

Ounces-force (ozf; oz)	X	0.278	= Newtons (N)	X 3.6	= Ounces-force (ozf; oz)
Pounds-force (lbf; lb)	X	4.448	= Newtons (N)	X 0.225	= Pounds-force (lbf; lb)
Newtons (N)	X	0.1	= Kilograms-force (kgf; kg)	X 9.81	= Newtons (N)

Pressure

Pounds-force per square inch (psi; lbf/in²; lb/in²)	X	0.070	= Kilograms-force per square centimetre (kgf/cm²; kg/cm²)	X 14.223	= Pounds-force per square inch (psi; lbf/in²; lb/in²)
Pounds-force per square inch (psi; lbf/in²; lb/in²)	X	0.068	= Atmospheres (atm)	X 14.696	= Pounds-force per square inch (psi; lbf/in²; lb/in²)
Pounds-force per square inch (psi; lbf/in²; lb/in²)	X	0.069	= Bars	X 14.5	= Pounds-force per square inch (psi; lbf/in²; lb/in²)
Pounds-force per square inch (psi; lbf/in²; lb/in²)	X	6.895	= Kilopascals (kPa)	X 0.145	= Pounds-force per square inch (psi; lbf/in²; lb/in²)
Kilopascals (kPa)	X	0.01	= Kilograms-force per square centimetre (kgf/cm²; kg/cm²)	X 98.1	= Kilopascals (kPa)

Torque (moment of force)

Pounds-force inches (lbf in; lb in)	X	1.152	= Kilograms-force centimetre (kgf cm; kg cm)	X 0.868	= Pounds-force inches (lbf in; lb in)
Pounds-force inches (lbf in; lb in)	X	0.113	= Newton metres (Nm)	X 8.85	= Pounds-force inches (lbf in; lb in)
Pounds-force inches (lbf in; lb in)	X	0.083	= Pounds-force feet (lbf ft; lb ft)	X 12	= Pounds-force inches (lbf in; lb in)
Pounds-force feet (lbf ft; lb ft)	X	0.138	= Kilograms-force metres (kgf m; kg m)	X 7.233	= Pounds-force feet (lbf ft; lb ft)
Pounds-force feet (lbf ft; lb ft)	X	1.356	= Newton metres (Nm)	X 0.738	= Pounds-force feet (lbf ft; lb ft)
Newton metres (Nm)	X	0.102	= Kilograms-force metres (kgf m; kg m)	X 9.804	= Newton metres (Nm)

Power

Horsepower (hp)	X	745.7	= Watts (W)	X 0.0013	= Horsepower (hp)

Velocity (speed)

Miles per hour (miles/hr; mph)	X	1.609	= Kilometres per hour (km/hr; kph)	X 0.621	= Miles per hour (miles/hr; mph)

Fuel consumption*

Miles per gallon, Imperial (mpg)	X	0.354	= Kilometres per litre (km/l)	X 2.825	= Miles per gallon, Imperial (mpg)
Miles per gallon, US (mpg)	X	0.425	= Kilometres per litre (km/l)	X 2.352	= Miles per gallon, US (mpg)

Temperature

Degrees Fahrenheit $= (°C \times 1.8) + 32$

Degrees Celsius (Degrees Centigrade; °C) $= (°F - 32) \times 0.56$

*It is common practice to convert from miles per gallon (mpg) to litres/100 kilometres (l/100km), where mpg (Imperial) x l/100 km = 282 and mpg (US) x l/100 km = 235

Safety first

Regardless of how enthusiastic you may be about getting on with the job at hand, take the time to ensure that your safety is not jeopardized. A moment's lack of attention can result in an accident, as can failure to observe certain simple safety precautions. The possibility of an accident will always exist, and the following points should not be considered a comprehensive list of all dangers. Rather, they are intended to make you aware of the risks and to encourage a safety conscious approach to all work you carry out on your vehicle.

Essential DOs and DON'Ts

DON'T rely on a jack when working under the vehicle. Always use approved jackstands to support the weight of the vehicle and place them under the recommended lift or support points.

DON'T attempt to loosen extremely tight fasteners (i.e. wheel lug nuts) while the vehicle is on a jack - it may fall.

DON'T start the engine without first making sure that the transmission is in Neutral (or Park where applicable) and the parking brake is set.

DON'T remove the radiator cap from a hot cooling system - let it cool or cover it with a cloth and release the pressure gradually.

DON'T attempt to drain the engine oil until you are sure it has cooled to the point that it will not burn you.

DON'T touch any part of the engine or exhaust system until it has cooled sufficiently to avoid burns.

DON'T siphon toxic liquids such as gasoline, antifreeze and brake fluid by mouth, or allow them to remain on your skin.

DON'T inhale brake lining dust - it is potentially hazardous (see *Asbestos* below).

DON'T allow spilled oil or grease to remain on the floor - wipe it up before someone slips on it.

DON'T use loose fitting wrenches or other tools which may slip and cause injury.

DON'T push on wrenches when loosening or tightening nuts or bolts. Always try to pull the wrench toward you. If the situation calls for pushing the wrench away, push with an open hand to avoid scraped knuckles if the wrench should slip.

DON'T attempt to lift a heavy component alone - get someone to help you.

DON'T rush or take unsafe shortcuts to finish a job.

DON'T allow children or animals in or around the vehicle while you are working on it.

DO wear eye protection when using power tools such as a drill, sander, bench grinder, etc. and when working under a vehicle.

DO keep loose clothing and long hair well out of the way of moving parts.

DO make sure that any hoist used has a safe working load rating adequate for the job.

DO get someone to check on you periodically when working alone on a vehicle.

DO carry out work in a logical sequence and make sure that everything is correctly assembled and tightened.

DO keep chemicals and fluids tightly capped and out of the reach of children and pets.

DO remember that your vehicle's safety affects that of yourself and others. If in doubt on any point, get professional advice.

Asbestos

Certain friction, insulating, sealing, and other products - such as brake linings, brake bands, clutch linings, torque converters, gaskets, etc. - contain asbestos. Extreme care must be taken to avoid inhalation of dust from such products, since it is hazardous to health. If in doubt, assume that they do contain asbestos.

Fire

Remember at all times that gasoline is highly flammable. Never smoke or have any kind of open flame around when working on a vehicle. But the risk does not end there. A spark caused by an electrical short circuit, by two metal surfaces contacting each other, or even by static electricity built up in your body under certain conditions, can ignite gasoline vapors, which in a confined space are highly explosive. Do not, under any circumstances, use gasoline for cleaning parts. Use an approved safety solvent.

Always disconnect the battery ground (-) cable at the battery before working on any part of the fuel system or electrical system. Never risk spilling fuel on a hot engine or exhaust component. It is strongly recommended that a fire extinguisher suitable for use on fuel and electrical fires be kept handy in the garage or workshop at all times. Never try to extinguish a fuel or electrical fire with water.

Fumes

Certain fumes are highly toxic and can quickly cause unconsciousness and even death if inhaled to any extent. Gasoline vapor falls into this category, as do the vapors from some cleaning solvents. Any draining or pouring of such volatile fluids should be done in a well ventilated area.

When using cleaning fluids and solvents, read the instructions on the container carefully. Never use materials from unmarked containers.

Never run the engine in an enclosed space, such as a garage. Exhaust fumes contain carbon monoxide, which is extremely poisonous. If you need to run the engine, always do so in the open air, or at least have the rear of the vehicle outside the work area.

If you are fortunate enough to have the use of an inspection pit, never drain or pour gasoline and never run the engine while the vehicle is over the pit. The fumes, being heavier than air, will concentrate in the pit with possibly lethal results.

The battery

Never create a spark or allow a bare light bulb near a battery. They normally give off a certain amount of hydrogen gas, which is highly explosive.

Always disconnect the battery ground (-) cable at the battery before working on the fuel or electrical systems.

If possible, loosen the filler caps or cover when charging the battery from an external source (this does not apply to sealed or maintenance-free batteries). Do not charge at an excessive rate or the battery may burst.

Take care when adding water to a non maintenance-free battery and when carrying a battery. The electrolyte, even when diluted, is very corrosive and should not be allowed to contact clothing or skin.

Always wear eye protection when cleaning the battery to prevent the caustic deposits from entering your eyes.

Household current

When using an electric power tool, inspection light, etc., which operates on household current, always make sure that the tool is correctly connected to its plug and that, where necessary, it is properly grounded. Do not use such items in damp conditions and, again, do not create a spark or apply excessive heat in the vicinity of fuel or fuel vapor.

Secondary ignition system voltage

A severe electric shock can result from touching certain parts of the ignition system (such as the spark plug wires) when the engine is running or being cranked, particularly if components are damp or the insulation is defective. In the case of an electronic ignition system, the secondary system voltage is much higher and could prove fatal.

Troubleshooting

Contents

This section provides an easy reference guide to the more common problems which may occur during the operation of your vehicle. These problems and possible causes are grouped under various components or systems; i.e. Engine, Cooling System, etc., and also refer to the Chapter and/or Section which deals with the problem.

Remember that successful troubleshooting is not a mysterious black art practiced only by professional mechanics. It's simply the result of a bit of knowledge combined with an intelligent, systematic approach to the problem. Always work by a process of elimination, starting with the simplest solution and working through to the most complex - and never overlook the obvious. Anyone can forget to fill the gas tank or leave the lights on overnight, so don't assume that you are above such oversights.

Finally, always get clear in your mind why a problem has occurred and take steps to ensure that it doesn't happen again. If the electrical system fails because of a poor connection, check all other connections in the system to make sure that they don't fail as well. If a particular fuse continues to blow, find out why - don't just go on replacing fuses. Remember, failure of a small component can often be indicative of potential failure or incorrect functioning of a more important component or system.

Engine

1 Engine will not rotate when attempting to start

1 Battery terminal connections loose or corroded. Check the cable terminals at the battery. Tighten the cable or remove corrosion as necessary.
2 Battery discharged or faulty. If the cable connections are clean and tight on the battery posts, turn the key to the On position and switch on the headlights and/or windshield wipers. If they fail to function, the battery is discharged.
3 Automatic transmission not completely engaged in Park or Neutral or clutch pedal not completely depressed.
4 Broken, loose or disconnected wiring in the starting circuit. Inspect all wiring and connectors at the battery, starter solenoid and ignition switch.
5 Starter motor pinion jammed in flywheel ring gear. If manual transmission, place transmission in gear and rock the vehicle to manually turn the engine. Remove starter and inspect pinion and flywheel at earliest convenience (Chapter 5).
6 Starter solenoid faulty (Chapter 5).
7 Starter motor faulty (Chapter 5).
8 Ignition switch faulty (Chapter 12).

2 Engine rotates but will not start

1 Fuel tank empty, fuel filter plugged or fuel line restricted.
2 Fault in the fuel injection system (Chapter 4).
3 Battery discharged (engine rotates slowly). Check the operation of electrical components as described in the previous Section.
4 Battery terminal connections loose or corroded (see previous Section).
5 Fuel pump faulty (Chapter 4).
6 Excessive moisture on, or damage to, ignition components (see Chapter 5).
7 Worn, faulty or incorrectly gapped spark plugs (Chapter 1).
8 Broken, loose or disconnected wiring in the starting circuit (see previous Section).
9 Broken, loose or disconnected wires at the ignition coil (Chapter 5).
10 Broken, loose or disconnected wires at the fuel shutdown solenoid (diesel) (Chapter 4).
11 Air in the fuel system or defective fuel injection pump or injector

(diesel) (Chapter 4).
12 Incorrect fuel injection pump timing (diesel) (Chapter 4).
13 Contaminated fuel.

3 Starter motor operates without rotating engine

1 Starter pinion sticking. Remove the starter (Chapter 5) and inspect.
2 Starter pinion or flywheel teeth worn or broken. Remove the flywheel/driveplate access cover and inspect.

4 Engine hard to start when cold

1 Battery discharged or low. Check as described in Section 1.
2 Fault in the fuel or electrical systems (Chapters 4 and 5).
3 Fault in the intake manifold heater or fuel heater systems (diesel) (Chapter 4).
4 Air in the fuel system or defective fuel injection pump or injector (diesel) (Chapter 4).
5 Incorrect fuel injection pump timing (diesel) (Chapter 4).

5 Engine hard to start when hot

1 Air filter clogged (Chapter 1).
2 Fault in the fuel or electrical systems (Chapters 4 and 5).
3 Fuel not reaching the injectors (see Chapter 4).
4 Air in the fuel system or defective fuel injection pump or injector (diesel) (Chapter 4).
5 Low cylinder compression (Chapter 2).
6 Incorrect fuel injection pump timing (diesel) (Chapter 4).

6 Starter motor noisy or excessively rough in engagement

1 Pinion or flywheel gear teeth worn or broken. Remove the cover at the rear of the engine (if equipped) and inspect.
2 Starter motor mounting bolts loose or missing.

7 Engine starts but stops immediately

1 Loose or faulty electrical connections at distributor, coil or alternator.
2 Fault in the fuel or electrical systems (Chapters 4 and 5).
3 Vacuum leak at the gasket surfaces of the intake manifold or throttle body. Make sure all mounting bolts/nuts are tightened securely and all vacuum hoses connected to the manifold are positioned properly and in good condition.
4 Restricted intake or exhaust systems (Chapter 4)
5 Fault in the fuel heater system (diesel) (Chapter 4).
6 Air in the fuel system or defective fuel injection pump or injector (diesel) (Chapter 4).
7 Contaminated fuel.

8 Engine lopes while idling or idles erratically

1 Vacuum leakage. Check the mounting bolts/nuts at the throttle body and intake manifold for tightness. Make sure all vacuum hoses are connected and in good condition. Use a stethoscope or a length of fuel hose held against your ear to listen for vacuum leaks while the engine is running. A hissing sound will be heard. A soapy water solution will also detect leaks.

2   Fault in the fuel or electrical systems (Chapters 4 and 5).
3   Plugged PCV valve or hose (see Chapters 1 and 6).
4   Air filter clogged (Chapter 1).
5   Fuel pump not delivering sufficient fuel to the fuel injectors (see Chapter 4).
6   Leaking head gasket. Perform a compression check (Chapter 2).
7   Camshaft lobes worn (Chapter 2).
8   Air in the fuel system or defective fuel injection pump or injector (diesel) (Chapter 4).
9   Incorrect fuel injection pump timing (diesel) (Chapter 4).

9   Engine misses at idle speed

1   Spark plugs worn, fouled or not gapped properly (Chapter 1).
2   Fault in the fuel or electrical systems (Chapters 4 and 5).
3   Faulty spark plug wires (Chapter 1).
4   Vacuum leaks at intake or hose connections. Check as described in Section 8.
5   Uneven or low cylinder compression. Check compression as described in Chapter 2.
6   Air in the fuel system or defective fuel injection pump or injector (diesel) (Chapter 4).
7   Incorrect fuel injection pump timing (diesel) (Chapter 4).

10   Engine misses throughout driving speed range

1   Fuel filter clogged and/or impurities in the fuel system (Chapter 1).
2   Faulty or incorrectly gapped spark plugs (Chapter 1).
3   Fault in the fuel or electrical systems (Chapters 4 and 5).
4   Defective spark plug wires (Chapter 1).
5   Faulty emissions system components (Chapter 6).
6   Low or uneven cylinder compression pressures. Remove the spark plugs and test the compression with a gauge (Chapter 2).
7   Weak or faulty ignition system (Chapter 5).
8   Vacuum leaks at the throttle body, intake manifold or vacuum hoses (see Section 8).
9   Air in the fuel system or defective fuel injection pump or injector (diesel) (Chapter 4).
10   Incorrect fuel injection pump timing (diesel) (Chapter 4).

11   Engine stalls

1   Idle speed incorrect. Refer to the VECI label.
2   Fuel filter clogged and/or water and impurities in the fuel system (Chapter 1).
3   Fault in the fuel system or sensors (Chapters 4 and 6).
4   Faulty emissions system components (Chapter 6).
5   Faulty or incorrectly gapped spark plugs (Chapter 1). Also check the spark plug wires (Chapter 1).
6   Vacuum leak at the throttle body, intake manifold or vacuum hoses. Check as described in Section 8.
7   Air in the fuel system or defective fuel injection pump or injector (diesel) (Chapter 4).

12   Engine lacks power

1   Fault in the fuel or electrical systems (Chapters 4 and 5).
2   Faulty or incorrectly gapped spark plugs (Chapter 1).
3   Faulty coil (Chapter 5).
4   Brakes binding (Chapter 1).
5   Automatic transmission fluid level incorrect (Chapter 1).
6   Clutch slipping (Chapter 8).
7   Fuel filter clogged and/or impurities in the fuel system (Chapter 1).
8   Emissions control system not functioning properly (Chapter 6).

9   Use of substandard fuel. Fill the tank with the proper fuel.
10   Low or uneven cylinder compression pressures. Test with a compression tester, which will detect leaking valves and/or a blown head gasket (Chapter 2).
11   Air in the fuel system or defective fuel injection pump or injector (diesel) (Chapter 4).
12   Incorrect fuel injection pump timing (diesel) (Chapter 4).
13   Defective turbocharger or wastegate (diesel) (Chapter 4).
14   Restriction in the intake or exhaust system (Chapter 4).

13   Engine backfires

1   Emissions system not functioning properly (Chapter 6).
2   Fault in the fuel or electrical systems (Chapters 4 and 5).
3   Faulty secondary ignition system (cracked spark plug insulator or faulty plug wires) (Chapters 1 and 5).
4   Fuel injection system in need of adjustment or worn excessively (Chapter 4).
5   Vacuum leak at the throttle body, intake manifold or vacuum hoses. Check as described in Section 8.
6   Valves sticking (Chapter 2).
7   Crossed plug wires (Chapter 1).

14   Pinging or knocking engine sounds during acceleration or uphill

1   Incorrect grade of fuel. Fill the tank with fuel of the proper octane rating.
2   Fault in the fuel or electrical systems (Chapters 4 and 5).
3   Improper spark plugs. Check the plug type against the VECI label located in the engine compartment. Also check the plugs and wires for damage (Chapter 1).
4   Faulty emissions system (Chapter 6).
5   Vacuum leak. Check as described in Section 9.

15   Engine continues to run after switching off

1   Idle speed too high. Refer to (Chapter 4).
2   Fault in the fuel or electrical systems (Chapters 4 and 5).
3   Excessive engine operating temperature. Probable causes of this are a low coolant level (see Chapter 1), malfunctioning thermostat, clogged radiator or faulty water pump (see Chapter 3).
4   Defective fuel shutdown solenoid (diesel) (Chapter 4).

Engine electrical system

16   Battery will not hold a charge

1   Alternator drivebelt defective or not adjusted properly (Chapter 1).
2   Electrolyte level low or battery discharged (Chapter 1).
3   Battery terminals loose or corroded (Chapter 1).
4   Alternator not charging properly (Chapter 5).
5   Loose, broken or faulty wiring in the charging circuit (Chapter 5).
6   Short in the vehicle wiring causing a continuous drain on the battery (refer to Chapter 12 and the Wiring Diagrams).
7   Battery defective internally.

17   Ignition light fails to go out

1   Fault in the alternator or charging circuit (Chapter 5).
2   Alternator drivebelt defective or not properly adjusted (Chapter 1).

18 Ignition light fails to come on when key is turned on

1   Instrument cluster warning light bulb defective (Chapter 12).
2   Alternator faulty (Chapter 5).
3   Fault in the instrument cluster printed circuit, dashboard wiring or bulb holder (Chapter 12).

Fuel system

19 Excessive fuel consumption

1   Dirty or clogged air filter element (Chapter 1).
2   Emissions system not functioning properly (Chapter 6).
3   Fault in the fuel or electrical systems (Chapters 4 and 5).
4   Low tire pressure or incorrect tire size (Chapter 1).
5   Restricted exhaust system (Chapter 4).

20 Fuel leakage and/or fuel odor

1   Leak in a fuel feed or vent line (Chapter 4).
2   Tank overfilled. Fill only to automatic shut-off.
3   Evaporative emissions system canister clogged (Chapter 6).
4   Vapor leaks from system lines (Chapter 4).

Cooling system

21 Overheating

1   Insufficient coolant in the system (Chapter 1).
2   Water pump drivebelt defective or not adjusted properly (Chapter 1).
3   Radiator core blocked or radiator grille dirty and restricted (see Chapter 3).
4   Thermostat faulty (Chapter 3).
5   Fan blades broken or cracked (Chapter 3).
6   Radiator cap not maintaining proper pressure. Have the cap pressure tested by a gas station or repair shop.

22 Overcooling

1   Thermostat faulty (Chapter 3).
2   Inaccurate temperature gauge (Chapter 12).

23 External coolant leakage

1   Deteriorated or damaged hoses or loose clamps. Replace hoses and/or tighten the clamps at the hose connections (Chapter 1).
2   Water pump seals defective. If this is the case, water will drip from the weep hole in the water pump body (Chapter 3).
3   Leakage from the radiator core or side tank(s). This will require the radiator to be professionally repaired (see Chapter 3 for removal procedures).
4   Engine drain plug(s) leaking (Chapter 1) or water jacket core plugs leaking (see Chapter 2).

24 Internal coolant leakage

Note: *Internal coolant leaks can usually be detected by examining the oil. Check the dipstick and inside of the valve cover for water deposits and an oil consistency like that of a milkshake.*

1   Leaking cylinder head gasket. Have the cooling system pressure tested.
2   Cracked cylinder bore or cylinder head. Dismantle the engine and inspect (Chapter 2).
3   Leaking intake manifold gasket (gasoline engines).

25 Coolant loss

1   Too much coolant in the system (Chapter 1).
2   Coolant boiling away due to overheating (see Section 15).
3   External or internal leakage (see Sections 23 and 24).
4   Faulty radiator cap. Have the cap pressure tested.

26 Poor coolant circulation

1   Inoperative water pump. A quick test is to pinch the top radiator hose closed with your hand while the engine is idling, then let it loose. You should feel the surge of coolant if the pump is working properly (see Chapter 1).
2   Restriction in the cooling system. Drain, flush and refill the system (Chapter 1). If necessary, remove the radiator (Chapter 3) and have it reverse flushed.
3   Water pump drivebelt defective or not adjusted properly (Chapter 1).
4   Thermostat sticking (Chapter 3).
5   Drivebelt incorrectly routed, causing the pump to turn backwards (Chapter 1).

Clutch

27 Fails to release (pedal pressed to the floor - shift lever does not move freely in and out of Reverse)

1   Leak in the clutch hydraulic system. Check the master cylinder, slave cylinder and lines (Chapters 1 and 8).
2   Clutch plate warped or damaged (Chapter 8).

28 Clutch slips (engine speed increases with no increase in vehicle speed)

1   Clutch plate oil soaked or lining worn. Remove clutch (Chapter 8) and inspect.
2   Clutch plate not seated. It may take 30 or 40 normal starts for a new one to seat.
3   Pressure plate worn (Chapter 8).

29 Grabbing (chattering) as clutch is engaged

1   Oil on clutch plate lining. Remove (Chapter 8) and inspect. Correct any leakage source.
2   Worn or loose engine or transmission mounts. These units move slightly when the clutch is released. Inspect the mounts and bolts (Chapter 2).
3   Worn splines on clutch plate hub. Remove the clutch components (Chapter 8) and inspect.
4   Warped pressure plate or flywheel. Remove the clutch components and inspect.

30 Squeal or rumble with clutch fully engaged (pedal released)

1   Release bearing binding on transmission bearing retainer. Remove clutch components (Chapter 8) and check bearing. Remove any burrs or nicks; clean and relubricate bearing retainer before installing.

31 Squeal or rumble with clutch fully disengaged (pedal depressed)

1   Worn, defective or broken release bearing (Chapter 8).
2   Worn or broken pressure plate springs (or diaphragm fingers) (Chapter 8).

32 Clutch pedal stays on floor when disengaged

1   Linkage or release bearing binding. Inspect the linkage or remove the clutch components as necessary.
2   Make sure proper pedal stop (bumper) is installed.

Manual transmission

Note: *All the following references are in Chapter 7, unless noted.*

33 Noisy in Neutral with engine running

1   Input shaft bearing worn.
2   Damaged main drive gear bearing.
3   Worn countershaft bearings.
4   Worn or damaged countershaft endplay shims.

34 Noisy in all gears

1   Any of the above causes, and/or:
2   Insufficient lubricant (see the checking procedures in Chapter 1).

35 Noisy in one particular gear

1   Worn, damaged or chipped gear teeth for that particular gear.
2   Worn or damaged synchronizer for that particular gear.

36 Slips out of high gear

1   Transmission loose on clutch housing.
2   Dirt between the transmission case and engine or misalignment of the transmission (Chapter 7).

37 Difficulty in engaging gears

1   Clutch not releasing completely (see clutch adjustment in Chapter 1).
2   Loose, damaged or out-of-adjustment shift linkage. Make a thorough inspection, replacing parts as necessary (Chapter 7).

38 Oil leakage

1   Excessive amount of lubricant in the transmission (see Chapter 1

for correct checking procedures). Drain lubricant as required.
2   Transmission oil seal or speedometer oil seal in need of replacement (Chapter 7).

Automatic transmission

Note: *Due to the complexity of the automatic transmission, it's difficult for the home mechanic to properly diagnose and service this component. For problems other than the following, the vehicle should be taken to a dealer service department or a transmission shop.*

39 General shift mechanism problems

1   Chapter 7 deals with checking and adjusting the shift linkage on automatic transmissions. Common problems which may be attributed to poorly adjusted linkage are:
   a)   *Engine starting in gears other than Park or Neutral.*
   b)   *Indicator on shifter pointing to a gear other than the one actually being selected.*
   c)   *Vehicle moves when in Park.*
2   Refer to Chapter 7 to adjust the linkage.

40 Transmission will not downshift with accelerator pedal pressed to the floor

Throttle valve (TV) cable misadjusted.

41 Transmission slips, shifts rough, is noisy or has no drive in forward or reverse gears

1   There are many probable causes for the above problems, but the home mechanic should be concerned with only one possibility - fluid level.
2   Before taking the vehicle to a repair shop, check the level and condition of the fluid as described in Chapter 1. Correct fluid level as necessary or change the fluid and filter if needed. If the problem persists, have a professional diagnose the probable cause.
3   If the transmission shifts late and the shifts are harsh, suspect a faulty vacuum diaphragm (Chapter 7).

42 Fluid leakage

1   Automatic transmission fluid is a deep red color. Fluid leaks should not be confused with engine oil, which can easily be blown by air flow to the transmission.
2   To pinpoint a leak, first remove all built-up dirt and grime from around the transmission. Degreasing agents and/or steam cleaning will achieve this. With the underside clean, drive the vehicle at low speeds so air flow will not blow the leak far from its source. Raise the vehicle and determine where the leak is coming from. Common areas of leakage are:
   a)   **Pan:** *Tighten the mounting bolts and/or replace the pan gasket as necessary (see Chapter 7).*
   b)   **Filler pipe:** *Replace the rubber seal where the pipe enters the transmission case.*
   c)   **Transmission oil lines:** *Tighten the connectors where the lines enter the transmission case and/or replace the lines.*
   d)   **Vent pipe:** *Transmission overfilled and/or water in fluid (see checking procedures, Chapter 1).*
   e)   **Speedometer connector:** *Replace the O-ring where the speedometer sensor enters the transmission case (Chapter 7).*

Transfer case

43 Transfer case is difficult to shift into the desired range

1   Speed may be too great to permit engagement. Stop the vehicle and shift into the desired range.
2   Shift linkage loose, bent or binding. Check the linkage for damage or wear and replace or lubricate as necessary (Chapter 7).
3   If the vehicle has been driven on a paved surface for some time, the driveline torque can make shifting difficult. Stop and shift into two-wheel drive on paved or hard surfaces.
4   Insufficient or incorrect grade of lubricant. Drain and refill the transfer case with the specified lubricant. (Chapter 1).
5   Worn or damaged internal components. Disassembly and overhaul of the transfer case may be necessary (Chapter 7).

44 Transfer case noisy in all gears

Insufficient or incorrect grade of lubricant. Drain and refill (Chapter 1).

45 Noisy or jumps out of four-wheel drive Low range

1   Transfer case not fully engaged. Stop the vehicle, shift into Neutral and then engage 4L.
2   Shift linkage loose, worn or binding. Tighten, repair or lubricate linkage as necessary.
3   Shift fork cracked, inserts worn or fork binding on the rail. Disassemble and repair as necessary (Chapter 7).

46 Lubricant leaks from the vent or output shaft seals

1   Transfer case is overfilled. Drain to the proper level (Chapter 1).
2   Vent is clogged or jammed closed. Clear or replace the vent.
3   Output shaft seal incorrectly installed or damaged. Replace the seal and check contact surfaces for nicks and scoring.

Driveshaft

47 Oil leak at seal end of driveshaft

Defective transmission or transfer case oil seal. See Chapter 7 for replacement procedures. While this is done, check the splined yoke for burrs or a rough condition which may be damaging the seal. Burrs can be removed with crocus cloth or a fine whetstone.

48 Knock or clunk when the transmission is under initial load (just after transmission is put into gear)

1   Loose or disconnected rear suspension components. Check all mounting bolts, nuts and bushings (see Chapter 10).
2   Loose driveshaft bolts. Inspect all bolts and nuts and tighten them to the specified torque.
3   Worn or damaged universal joint bearings. Check for wear (see Chapter 8).

49 Metallic grinding sound consistent with vehicle speed.

Pronounced wear in the universal joint bearings. Check as described in Chapter 8.

50 Vibration

Note: *Before assuming that the driveshaft is at fault, make sure the tires are perfectly balanced and perform the following test.*
1   Install a tachometer inside the vehicle to monitor engine speed as the vehicle is driven. Drive the vehicle and note the engine speed at which the vibration (roughness) is most pronounced. Now shift the transmission to a different gear and bring the engine speed to the same point.
2   If the vibration occurs at the same engine speed (rpm) regardless of which gear the transmission is in, the driveshaft is NOT at fault since the driveshaft speed varies.
3   If the vibration decreases or is eliminated when the transmission is in a different gear at the same engine speed, refer to the following probable causes.
4   Bent or dented driveshaft. Inspect and replace as necessary (see Chapter 8).
5   Undercoating or built-up dirt, etc. on the driveshaft. Clean the shaft thoroughly and recheck.
6   Worn universal joint bearings. Remove and inspect (see Chapter 8).
7   Driveshaft and/or companion flange out of balance. Check for missing weights on the shaft. Remove the driveshaft (see Chapter 8) and reinstall 180-degrees from original position, then retest. Have the driveshaft professionally balanced if the problem persists.

Axles

51 Noise

1   Road noise. No corrective procedures available.
2   Tire noise. Inspect tires and check tire pressures (Chapter 1).
3   Rear wheel bearings loose, worn or damaged (Chapter 8).

52 Vibration

See probable causes under *Driveshaft*. Proceed under the guidelines listed for the driveshaft. If the problem persists, check the rear wheel bearings by raising the rear of the vehicle and spinning the rear wheels by hand. Listen for evidence of rough (noisy) bearings. Remove and inspect (see Chapter 8).

53 Oil leakage

1   Pinion seal damaged (see Chapter 8).
2   Axleshaft oil seals damaged (see Chapter 8).
3   Differential inspection cover leaking. Tighten the bolts or replace the gasket as required (see Chapters 1 and 8).

Brakes

Note: *Before assuming that a brake problem exists, make sure that the tires are in good condition and inflated properly (see Chapter 1), that the front end alignment is correct and that the vehicle is not loaded with weight in an unequal manner.*

54 Vehicle pulls to one side during braking

1   Defective, damaged or oil contaminated disc brake pads or shoes on one side. Inspect as described in Chapter 9.

2   Excessive wear of brake shoe or pad material or drum/disc on one side. Inspect and correct as necessary.

3   Loose or disconnected front suspension components. Inspect and tighten all bolts to the specified torque (Chapter 10).

4   Defective drum brake or caliper assembly. Remove the drum or caliper and inspect for a stuck piston or other damage (Chapter 9).

5   Inadequate lubrication of front brake caliper slide rails. Remove caliper and lubricate slide rails (Chapter 9).

55   Noise (high-pitched squeal with the brakes applied)

1   Disc brake pads worn out. The noise comes from the wear sensor rubbing against the disc (does not apply to all vehicles) or the actual pad backing plate itself if the material is completely worn away. Replace the pads with new ones immediately (Chapter 9). If the pad material has worn completely away, the brake discs should be inspected for damage as described in Chapter 9.

2   Missing or damaged brake pad insulators (disc brakes). Replace pad insulators (see Chapter 9).

3   Linings contaminated with dirt or grease. Replace pads or shoes.

4   Incorrect linings. Replace with correct linings.

56   Excessive brake pedal travel

1   Partial brake system failure. Inspect the entire system (Chapter 9) and correct as required.

2   Insufficient fluid in the master cylinder. Check (Chapter 1), add fluid and bleed the system if necessary (Chapter 9).

3   Rear brakes not adjusting properly. Make a series of starts and stops while the vehicle is in Reverse. If this does not correct the situation, remove the drums and inspect the self-adjusters (Chapter 9).

57   Brake pedal feels spongy when depressed

1   Air in the hydraulic lines. Bleed the brake system (Chapter 9).

2   Faulty flexible hoses. Inspect all system hoses and lines. Replace parts as necessary.

3   Master cylinder mounting bolts/nuts loose.

4   Master cylinder defective (Chapter 9).

58   Excessive effort required to stop vehicle

1   Power brake booster or vacuum pump (diesel models) not operating properly (Chapter 9).

2   Excessively worn linings or pads. Inspect and replace if necessary (Chapter 9).

3   One or more caliper pistons or wheel cylinders seized or sticking. Inspect and rebuild as required (Chapter 9).

4   Brake linings or pads contaminated with oil or grease. Inspect and replace as required (Chapter 9).

5   New pads or shoes installed and not yet seated. It will take a while for the new material to seat against the drum (or disc).

59   Pedal travels to the floor with little resistance

1   Little or no fluid in the master cylinder reservoir caused by leaking wheel cylinder(s), leaking caliper piston(s), loose, damaged or disconnected brake lines. Inspect the entire system and correct as necessary.

2   Worn master cylinder seals (Chapter 9).

60   Brake pedal pulsates during brake application

1   Caliper improperly installed. Remove and inspect (Chapter 9).

2   Disc or drum defective. Remove (Chapter 9) and check for excessive lateral runout and parallelism. Have the disc or drum resurfaced or replace it with a new one.

Suspension and steering systems

61   Vehicle pulls to one side

1   Tire pressures uneven (Chapter 1).

2   Defective tire (Chapter 1).

3   Excessive wear in suspension or steering components (Chapter 10).

4   Front end in need of alignment.

5   Front brakes dragging. Inspect the brakes as described in Chapter 9.

62   Shimmy, shake or vibration

1   Tire or wheel out-of-balance or out-of-round. Have professionally balanced.

2   Loose, worn or out-of-adjustment front wheel bearings (Chapter 1).

3   Shock absorbers and/or suspension components worn or damaged (Chapter 10).

63   Excessive pitching and/or rolling around corners or during braking

1   Defective shock absorbers. Replace as a set (Chapter 10).

2   Broken or weak springs and/or suspension components. Inspect as described in Chapter 10.

64   Excessively stiff steering

1   Lack of fluid in power steering fluid reservoir (Chapter 1).

2   Incorrect tire pressures (Chapter 1).

3   Lack of lubrication at steering joints (see Chapter 1).

4   Front end out of alignment.

5   Lack of power assistance (see Section 66).

65   Excessive play in steering

1   Loose front wheel bearings (Chapters 1 and 10).

2   Excessive wear in suspension or steering components (Chapter 10).

3   Steering gearbox damaged or out of adjustment (Chapter 10).

66   Lack of power assistance

1   Steering pump drivebelt faulty or not adjusted properly (Chapter 1).

2   Fluid level low (Chapter 1).

3   Hoses or lines restricted. Inspect and replace parts as necessary.

4   Air in power steering system. Bleed the system (Chapter 10).

67 Excessive tire wear (not specific to one area)

1   Incorrect tire pressures (Chapter 1).
2   Tires out-of-balance. Have professionally balanced.
3   Wheels damaged. Inspect and replace as necessary.
4   Suspension or steering components excessively worn (Chapter 10).

68 Excessive tire wear on outside edge

1   Inflation pressures incorrect (Chapter 1).
2   Excessive speed in turns.
3   Front end alignment incorrect. Have professionally aligned.
4   Suspension arm bent or twisted (Chapter 10).

69 Excessive tire wear on inside edge

1   Inflation pressures incorrect (Chapter 1).
2   Front end alignment incorrect. Have professionally aligned.
3   Loose or damaged steering components (Chapter 10).

70 Tire tread worn in one place

1   Tires out-of-balance.
2   Damaged or buckled wheel. Inspect and replace if necessary.
3   Defective tire (Chapter 1).

Notes

Chapter 1
Tune-up and routine maintenance

Contents

Specifications

Recommended lubricants and fluids

Engine oil type
    Gasoline engine .... API grade SH or SH/CD multigrade and fuel-efficient engine oil
    Diesel engine .... API grade CE or CE/SG multigrade and low sulfated ash limit engine oil

Engine oil viscosity .... See accompanying charts

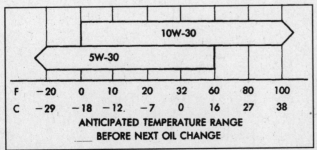

			10W-30						
	5W-30								
F	−20	0	10	20	32	60	80	100	
C	−29	−18	−12	−7	0	16	27	38	

ANTICIPATED TEMPERATURE RANGE
BEFORE NEXT OIL CHANGE

AMERICAN PETROLEUM INSTITUTE
FOR GASOLINE ENGINES
CERTIFIED

Engine oil viscosity chart for gasoline engines - for best fuel economy and cold starting, select the lowest SAE viscosity grade for the expected temperature range

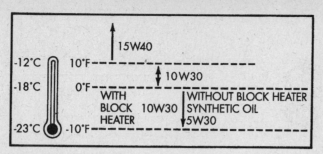

Engine oil viscosity chart for diesel engines - for best fuel economy and cold starting, select the lowest SAE viscosity grade for the expected temperature range

Recommended lubricants and fluids (continued)

Automatic transmission fluid type	Mopar type 7176 ATF Plus or Dexron II or III automatic transmission fluid
Manual transmission lubricant type	
NV3500	Mopar manual transmission lubricant part no. 4761526, or equivalent
NV4500	SAE 75W-90 Mopar manual transmission fluid 4637579 or Castrol Syntorq synthetic gear lubricant
Transfer case lubricant type	Dexron II automatic transmission fluid
Differential lubricant type	SAE 90W GL-5 gear lubricant
Limited slip differential	Add Chrysler Friction Modifier 4318060, or equivalent to the specified lubricant
Brake fluid type	DOT 3 brake fluid
Power steering fluid	Chrysler power steering fluid or equivalent
Manual steering gear lubricant type	SAE 90 GL-5 hypoid gear lubricant
Chassis grease type	NLGI no. 2 EP chassis grease
Front wheel bearing grease	NLGI no. 2 EP high-temperature wheel bearing grease

Capacities (approximate)

Cooling system	
V6 and V8	20.0 qts
Diesel	26.0 qts
V10	24.0 qts
Engine oil (with filter change)	
V6	4.0 qts
V8	5.0 qts
Diesel	
1994	10.0 qts
1995 and later	11.0 qts
V10	7.0 qts
Automatic transmission	
Drain and refill	4.0 qts
Dry fill	9.0 to 16.5 qts (depending on model and options)
Manual transmission	
NV3500	2.2 qts
NV4500	4.0 qts
Transfer case	
NV231 HD	2.5 pts
NV241	5.0 pts
NV241 HD	6.5 pts
NV241 HD w/PTO	9.0 pts
Rear axle	
9-1/4 inch	4.8 pts
Dana 60	6.3 to 7.3 pts*
Dana 70	7.0 to 7.8 pts*
Dana 80	6.8 to 10.1 pts*

*add 8 fl oz of friction modifier if equipped with limited slip differential

Ignition system

Spark plug type	
V6 and V8 engines	Champion RC12YC or equivalent
V10 engine	
1995 and earlier	Champion RC9MC4 or equivalent
1996	Champion QC9MC4 or equivalent
Spark plug gap	
V6 and V8 engines	0.035 inch
V10 engine	0.045 inch

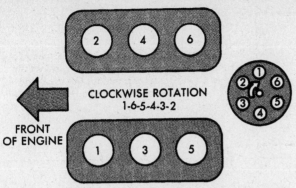

V6 engine cylinder location and distributor rotation diagram

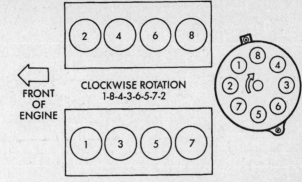

V8 engine cylinder location and distributor rotation diagram

V10 cylinder and coil terminal location diagram

FIRING ORDER
1-10-9-4-3-6-5-8-7-2

FRONT

Firing order

V6 and V8 engines	1-6-5-4-3-2
V8 engine	1-8-4-3-6-5-7-2
V10 engine	1-10-9-4-3-6-5-7-2

General

Valve clearance - diesel engine (cold)	
Intake	0.010 inch
Exhaust	0.020 inch
Disc brake pad lining thickness (minimum)	5/16 inch
Drum brake shoe lining thickness (minimum)	1/16 inch

Automatic transmission band adjustment

1994	
Front band	Tighten to 72 in-lb, back off 2-1/2 turns
Rear band	
32/42RH	Tighten to 72 in-lb, back off 4 turns
36/37/46/47RH	Tighten to 72 in-lb, back off 2 turns
1995	
Front band	
42RH	Tighten to 72 in-lb, back off 2-1/4 turns
46RH	Tighten to 72 in-lb, back off 2-7/8 turns
47RH	Tighten to 72 in-lb, back off 1-7/8 turns
Rear band	
42RH	Tighten to 72 in-lb, back off 4 turns
46RH	Tighten to 72 in-lb, back off 2 turns
47RH	Tighten to 72 in-lb, back off 3 turns
1996	
Front band	Tighten to 72 in-lb, back off 2-7/8 turns
Rear band	Tighten to 72 in-lb, back off 2 turns

Torque specifications

	Ft-lb
Automatic transmission band adjusting screw locknut	
Front band	30
Rear band	25
Automatic transmission pan bolts	13
Differential cover bolts	35
Transfer case drain/fill plug	35
Manual transmission drain/fill plug	
NV3500	20
NV4500	35
Spark plugs	30
Engine oil drain plug	
Gasoline engines	25
Diesel engine	60
Oxygen sensor	20
Wheel lug nuts	
5 stud	95
8 stud single wheel	135
8 stud dual wheel	145

1

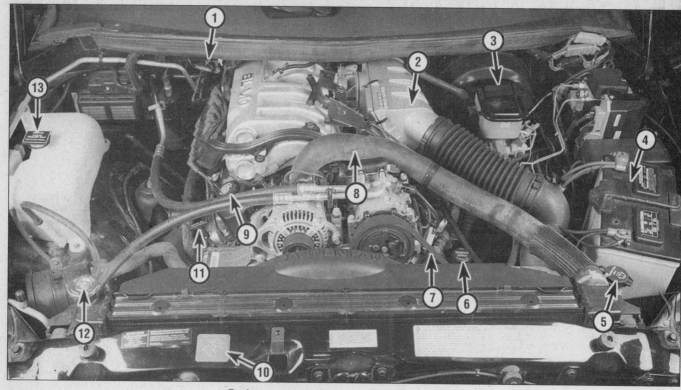

Engine compartment components (V10 engine)

1	Automatic transmission fluid dipstick	6	Power steering fluid reservoir	10	Serpentine drivebelt routing decal
2	Air filter housing	7	Drivebelt	11	Engine oil dipstick
3	Brake fluid reservoir	8	Upper radiator hose	12	Radiator cap
4	Battery	9	Engine oil filler cap	13	Coolant reservoir
5	Windshield washer fluid reservoir				

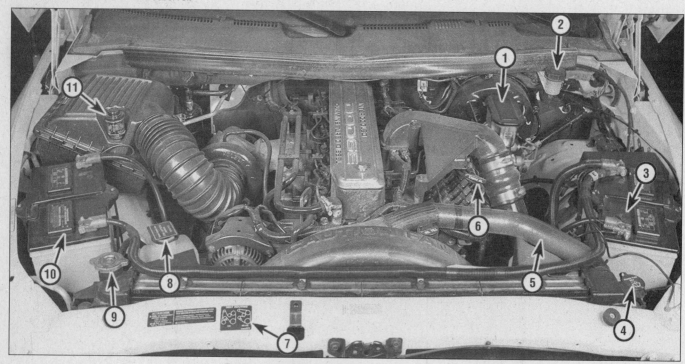

Engine compartment components (diesel engine)

1	Brake fluid reservoir	5	Upper radiator hose	9	Radiator cap
2	Clutch fluid reservoir	6	Engine oil dipstick	10	Battery
3	Battery	7	Serpentine drivebelt routing decal	11	Air filter housing
4	Windshield washer fluid reservoir	8	Coolant reservoir		

Typical engine compartment underside components (diesel engine)

1   Idler arm grease fitting
2   Engine oil filter
3   Tie-rod end

4   Balljoint
5   Fuel filter drain location
6   Transmission

7   Engine oil pan drain plug
8   Exhaust system

Typical rear underside components

1	Rear shock absorber	3	Exhaust system	5	Fuel tank
2	Universal joint	4	Differential check/fill plug		

1 Dodge Ram pick-up Maintenance schedule

The following maintenance intervals are based on the assumption that the vehicle owner will be doing the maintenance or service work, as opposed to having a dealer service department do the work. Although the time/mileage intervals are loosely based on the manufacturers recommendations, most have been shortened to ensure, for example, that such items as lubricants and fluids are checked/changed at intervals that promote maximum engine/driveline service life. Also, subject to the preference of the individual owner interested in keeping his or her vehicle in peak condition at all times, and with the vehicle's ultimate resale in mind, many of the maintenance procedures may be performed more often than recommended in the following schedule. We encourage such owner initiative.

When the vehicle is new it should be serviced initially by a factory authorized dealer service department to protect the factory warranty. In many cases the initial maintenance check is done at no cost to the owner (check with your dealer service department for more information).

Every 250 miles or weekly, whichever comes first

Check the engine oil level (Section 4)
Check the engine coolant level (Section 4)
Check the windshield washer fluid level (Section 4)
Check the brake and clutch fluid levels (Section 4)
Check the tires and tire pressures (Section 5)
Check and replace, if necessary, the air filter (diesel engine) (Section 6)
Drain the fuel filter (diesel engine) (Section 7)
Check the automatic transmission fluid level (Section 8)

Every 3000 miles or 3 months, whichever comes first

All items listed above, plus . . .
Check the power steering fluid level (Section 9)
Change the engine oil and filter (Section 10)
Check and service the battery (Section 11)
Check the cooling system (Section 12)
Inspect and replace, if necessary, all underhood hoses (Section 13)
Inspect and replace, if necessary, the windshield wiper blades (Section 14)

Every 6000 miles or 6 months, whichever comes first

Inspect the suspension and steering components
   (Section 15)
Inspect the exhaust system (Section 16)
Check the manual transmission lubricant level (Section 17)
Check the transfer case lubricant level (Section 18)
Check the differential lubricant level (Section 19)
Rotate the tires(Section 20)
Check the brakes (Section 21) *
Inspect the fuel system (gasoline engine - Section 22)
   (diesel engine - Section 23)
Check the engine drivebelt (Section 24)
Check the seat belts (Section 25)
Check the neutral start switch (automatic transmission
   equipped models only) (Section 26)
Lubricate the chassis components (Section 27) *

Every 24,000 miles or 24 months, whichever comes first

All items listed above, plus . . .
Check and adjust if necessary, the valve clearances (diesel
   engine) (Section 28)
Replace the engine drivebelt (diesel engine) (Section 24)
Inspect the fan hub, damper and water pump (diesel
   engine) (Section 29)
Replace the fuel filter and bleed the system (diesel engine)
   (Section 30)**
Replace the air filter (gasoline engine) (Section 31)
Change the automatic transmission fluid and filter
   (Section 32)**
Adjust the automatic transmission bands (Section 33)**
Change the manual transmission lubricant (Section 34)
Change the transfer case lubricant (Section 35)
Change the differential lubricant (Section 36)

Every 30,000 miles or 30 months, whichever comes first

All items listed above, plus . . .
Check and repack the front wheel bearings (2WD models)
   (Section 37)**
Service the cooling system (drain, flush and refill)
   (Section 38)
Clean the crankcase inlet filter (Section 39)**
Check the Positive Crankcase Ventilation (PCV) system
   (Section 40)
Check the evaporative emissions control system
   (Section 41)
Replace the spark plugs ((Section 42)**
Inspect the spark plug wires, distributor cap and rotor
   (Section 43)

*   This item is affected by "severe" operating conditions,
    as described below. If the vehicle is operated under
    severe conditions, perform all maintenance indicated
    with an asterisk (*) at 3000 mile/three-month intervals.
    Severe conditions exist if you mainly operate the
    vehicle . . .

   in dusty areas
   towing a trailer
   idling for extended periods
   driving at low speeds when outside temperatures
      remain below freezing and most trips are less than
      four miles long

** Perform this procedure every 15,000 miles if operated
    under one or more of the following conditions:

   in heavy city traffic where the outside temperature
      regularly reaches 90-degrees F or higher
   in hilly or mountainous terrain
   frequent trailer pulling

1

2   Introduction

This Chapter is designed to help the home mechanic maintain the Dodge Ram pickup truck with the goals of maximum performance, economy, safety and reliability in mind.

Included is a master maintenance schedule, followed by procedures dealing specifically with each item on the schedule. Visual checks, adjustments, component replacement and other helpful items are included. Refer to the accompanying illustrations of the engine compartment and the underside of the vehicle for the locations of various components.

Servicing your vehicle in accordance with the mileage/time maintenance schedule and the step-by-step procedures will result in a planned maintenance program that should produce a long and reliable service life. Keep in mind that it's a comprehensive plan, so maintaining some items but not others at the specified intervals will not produce the same results.

As you service your vehicle, you will discover that many of the procedures can - and should - be grouped together because of the nature of the particular procedure you're performing or because of the close proximity of two otherwise unrelated components to one another.

For example, if the vehicle is raised for chassis lubrication, you should inspect the exhaust, suspension, steering and fuel systems while you're under the vehicle. When you're rotating the tires, it makes good sense to check the brakes since the wheels are already removed. Finally, let's suppose you have to borrow or rent a torque wrench. Even if you only need it to tighten the spark plugs, you might as well check the torque of as many critical fasteners as time allows.

The first step in this maintenance program is to prepare yourself before the actual work begins. Read through all the procedures you're planning to do, then gather up all the parts and tools needed. If it looks like you might run into problems during a particular job, seek advice from a mechanic or an experienced do-it-yourselfer.

3   Tune-up general information

The term tune-up is used in this manual to represent a combination of individual operations rather than one specific procedure that will maintain a gasoline engine in proper tune.

If, from the time the vehicle is new, the routine maintenance schedule is followed closely and frequent checks are made of fluid levels and high wear items, as suggested throughout this manual, the engine will be kept in relatively good running condition and the need for additional work will be minimized.

More likely than not, however, there will be times when the engine

4.2 The engine oil dipstick is clearly marked

is running poorly due to lack of regular maintenance. This is even more likely if a used vehicle, which has not received regular and frequent maintenance checks, is purchased. In such cases, an engine tune-up will be needed outside of the regular routine maintenance intervals.

The first step in any tune-up or diagnostic procedure to help correct a poor running engine is a cylinder compression check. A compression check (see Chapter 2C) will help determine the condition of internal engine components and should be used as a guide for tune-up and repair procedures. If, for instance, the compression check indicates serious internal engine wear, a conventional tune-up won't improve the performance of the engine and would be a waste of time and money. Because of its importance, the compression check should be done by someone with the right equipment and the knowledge to use it properly.

The following procedures are those most often needed to bring a generally poor running engine back into a proper state of tune.

Minor tune-up

Check all engine related fluids (Section 4)
Clean, inspect and test the battery (Section 11)
Check the cooling system (Section 12)
Check all underhood hoses (Section 13)
Check and adjust the drivebelts (Section 24)
Check the air filter (Section 31)
Check the PCV valve (Section 39)
Replace the spark plugs (Section 41)
Inspect the spark plug and coil wires (Section 41)
Inspect the distributor cap and rotor (Section 41)

Major tune-up

All items listed under Minor tune-up, plus . . .
Check the fuel system (Section 22)
Replace the air filter (Section 31)
Replace the spark plug wires (Section 42)
Replace the distributor cap and rotor (Section 42)
Check the ignition system (Chapter 5)
Check the charging system (Chapter 5)

4   Fluid level checks (every 250 miles or weekly)

Note: *The following are fluid level checks to be done on a 250 mile or weekly basis. Additional fluid level checks can be found in specific maintenance procedures which follow. Regardless of intervals, be alert to fluid leaks under the vehicle which would indicate a fault to be corrected immediately.*

1   Fluids are an essential part of the lubrication, cooling, brake, clutch and windshield washer systems. Because the fluids gradually become depleted and/or contaminated during normal operation of the vehicle, they must be periodically replenished. See *Recommended lubricants and fluids* at the beginning of this Chapter before adding fluid to any of the following components. **Note:** *The vehicle must be on level ground when fluid levels are checked.*

Engine oil

Refer to illustrations 4.2, 4.4 and 4.6
2   The engine oil level is checked with a dipstick that extends through a tube and into the oil pan at the bottom of the engine **(see illustration)**.
3   The oil level should be checked before the vehicle has been driven, or about 15 minutes after the engine has been shut off. If the oil is checked immediately after driving the vehicle, some of the oil will remain in the upper engine components, resulting in an inaccurate reading on the dipstick.
4   Pull the dipstick out of the tube and wipe all the oil from the end with a clean rag or paper towel. Insert the clean dipstick all the way back into the tube, then pull it out again. Note the oil at the end of the dipstick. Add oil as necessary to keep the level between the MIN and

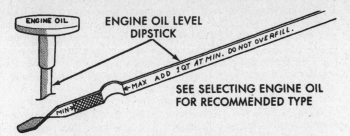

4.4 The oil level must be maintained between the marks at all times - it takes one quart of oil to raise the level from the MIN to MAX mark

MAX marks or within the SAFE zone on the dipstick (see illustration).

5 Do not overfill the engine by adding too much oil since this may result in oil fouled spark plugs, oil leaks or oil seal failures.

6 Oil is added to the engine after unscrewing a cap from the valve cover (see illustration). A funnel may help to reduce spills.

7 Checking the oil level is an important preventive maintenance step. A consistently low oil level indicates oil leakage through damaged seals, defective gaskets or past worn rings or valve guides. If the oil looks milky or has water droplets in it, the cylinder head gasket(s) may be blown or the head(s) or block may be cracked. The engine should be checked immediately. The condition of the oil should also be checked. Whenever you check the oil level, slide your thumb and index finger up the dipstick before wiping off the oil. If you see small dirt or metal particles clinging to the dipstick, the oil should be changed (see Section 10).

Engine coolant

Refer to illustrations 4.8 and 4.9

Warning: *Do not allow antifreeze to come in contact with your skin or painted surfaces of the vehicle. Flush contaminated areas immediately with plenty of water. Don't store new coolant or leave old coolant lying around where it's accessible to children or pets - they're attracted by its sweet smell. Ingestion of even a small amount of coolant can be fatal! Wipe up garage floor and drip pan coolant spills immediately. Keep antifreeze containers covered and repair leaks in the cooling system as soon as they are noted.*

8 Most vehicles covered by this manual are equipped with a pressurized coolant recovery system. A white plastic coolant reservoir located in the engine compartment is connected by a hose to the radiator filler neck (see illustration). If the engine overheats, coolant escapes through a valve in the radiator cap and travels through the hose into the reservoir. As the engine cools, the coolant is automatically drawn back into the cooling system to maintain the correct level. **Warning:** *Do not remove the radiator cap to check the coolant level when the engine is warm.*

9 The coolant level in the reservoir should be checked regularly. The level in the reservoir varies with the temperature of the engine. When the engine is cold, the coolant level should be below the FULL mark on the reservoir. Once the engine has warmed up, the level should be at or near the FULL mark. If it isn't, allow the engine to cool, then remove the cap from the reservoir and add a 50/50 mixture of ethylene glycol-based antifreeze and water (see illustration).

10 Drive the vehicle and recheck the coolant level. If only a small amount of coolant is required to bring the system up to the proper level, water can be used. However, repeated additions of water will dilute the antifreeze and water solution. In order to maintain the proper ratio of antifreeze and water, always top up the coolant level with the correct mixture. Do not use rust inhibitors or additives.

11 If the coolant level drops consistently, there may be a leak in the system. Inspect the radiator, hoses, filler cap, drain plugs and water pump (see Section 12). If no leaks are noted, have the radiator cap pressure tested.

12 If you have to remove the radiator cap, wait until the engine has cooled, then wrap a thick cloth around the cap and turn it to the first stop. If coolant or steam escapes, let the engine cool down longer, then remove the cap.

13 Check the condition of the coolant as well. It should be relatively clear. If it's brown or rust colored, the system should be drained, flushed and refilled. Even if the coolant appears to be normal, the corrosion inhibitors wear out, so it must be replaced at the specified intervals.

Windshield washer fluid

14 Fluid for the windshield washer system is located in a plastic reservoir in the left side of engine compartment.

15 In milder climates, plain water can be used in the reservoir, but it should be kept no more than 2/3 full to allow for expansion if the water freezes. In colder climates, use windshield washer system antifreeze, available at any auto parts store, to lower the freezing point of the fluid. Mix the antifreeze with water in accordance with the manufacturer's directions on the container. **Caution:** *Don't use cooling system antifreeze - it will damage the vehicle's paint.*

16 To help prevent icing in cold weather, warm the windshield with the defroster before using the washer.

Battery electrolyte

Refer to illustration 4.17

17 These vehicles are equipped with a battery which is permanently sealed (except for vent holes) and has no filler caps. Water doesn't

4.6 Oil is added to the engine after unscrewing the oil filler cap - always make sure the area around the opening is clean before removing the cap to prevent dirt from contaminating the engine

4.8 The coolant reservoir is located in the right side of the engine compartment - keep the level near the Full mark (arrow) of the reservoir

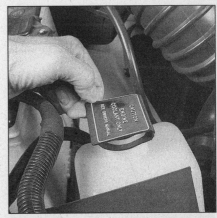

4.9 Coolant can be added after flipping up the reservoir cap

have to be added to these batteries at any time. If a maintenance-type battery is installed, the caps on the top of the battery should be removed periodically to check for a low electrolyte level **(see illustration)**. This check is most critical during the warm summer months.

Brake and clutch fluid

Refer to illustrations 4.19a and 4.19b

18   The brake master cylinder is mounted on the upper left of the engine compartment firewall. The clutch cylinder used on later manual transmission models is mounted next to the master cylinder.

19   The translucent plastic reservoir allows the fluid inside to be checked without removing the cover or cap **(see illustrations)**. Note that the clutch system is a sealed unit and it shouldn't be necessary to add fluid under most conditions (see Chapter 8 for more information). Be sure to wipe the top of either reservoir cover with a clean rag to prevent contamination of the brake and/or clutch system before removing the cover.

20   When adding fluid, pour it carefully into the reservoir to avoid spilling it on surrounding painted surfaces. Be sure the specified fluid is used, since mixing different types of brake fluid can cause damage to the system. See *Recommended lubricants and fluids* at the front of this Chapter or your owner's manual. **Warning:** *Brake fluid can harm your eyes and damage painted surfaces, so use extreme caution when handling or pouring it. Do not use brake fluid that has been standing open or is more than one year old. Brake fluid absorbs moisture from*

the air. Moisture in the system can cause a dangerous loss of brake performance.

21   At this time, the fluid and master cylinder can be inspected for contamination. The system should be drained and refilled if deposits, dirt particles or water droplets are seen in the fluid.

22   After filling the reservoir to the proper level, make sure the cover or cap is on tight to prevent fluid leakage.

23   The brake fluid level in the master cylinder will drop slightly as the pads at the front wheels wear down during normal operation. If the master cylinder requires repeated additions to keep it at the proper level, it's an indication of leakage in the brake system, which should be corrected immediately. Check all brake lines and connections (see Section 21 for more information).

24   If, upon checking the master cylinder fluid level, you discover one or both reservoirs empty or nearly empty, the brake system should be bled (Chapter 9) and thoroughly inspected.

5   Tire and tire pressure checks (every 250 miles or weekly)

Refer to illustrations 5.2, 5.3, 5.4a, 5.4b and 5.8

1   Periodic inspection of the tires may spare you the inconvenience of being stranded with a flat tire. It can also provide you with vital information regarding possible problems in the steering and suspension systems before major damage occurs.

2   The original tires on this vehicle are equipped with 1/2-inch wear bands that will appear when tread depth reaches 1/16-inch, but they don't appear until the tires are worn out. Tread wear can be monitored with a simple, inexpensive device known as a tread depth indicator **(see illustration)**.

3   Note any abnormal tread wear **(see illustration)**. Tread pattern irregularities such as cupping, flat spots and more wear on one side than the other are indications of front end alignment and/or balance problems. If any of these conditions are noted, take the vehicle to a tire shop or service station to correct the problem.

4   Look closely for cuts, punctures and embedded nails or tacks. Sometimes a tire will hold air pressure for a short time or leak down very slowly after a nail has embedded itself in the tread. If a slow leak persists, check the valve stem core to make sure it's tight **(see illustration)**. Examine the tread for an object that may have embedded itself in the tire or for a "plug" that may have begun to leak (radial tire punctures are repaired with a plug that's installed in a puncture). If a puncture is suspected, it can be easily verified by spraying a solution of soapy water onto the puncture area **(see illustration)**. The soapy solution will bubble if there's a leak. Unless the puncture is unusually large, a tire shop or service station can usually repair the tire.

5   Carefully inspect the inner sidewall of each tire for evidence of

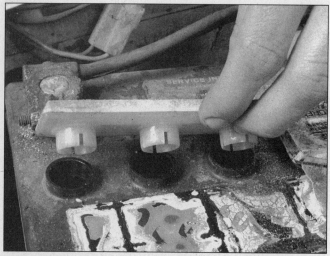

4.17 Remove the cell caps to check the electrolyte level in the battery - if the level is low, add distilled water only

4.19a The brake fluid level should be kept at the top of the slotted window - never let it drop below the MIN mark; flip up the reservoir cover to add fluid

4.19b The clutch fluid level should be kept at the top of the slotted window - never let it drop below the MIN mark; remove the reservoir cover to add fluid

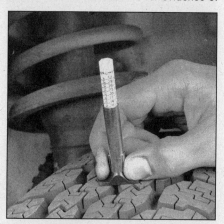

5.2 Use a tire tread depth indicator to monitor tire wear - they are available at auto parts stores and service stations and cost very little

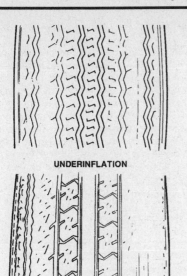

UNDERINFLATION

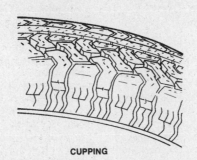

CUPPING

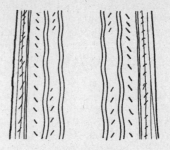

OVERINFLATION

UNDERINFLATION AND/OR MECHANICAL
IRREGULARITIES SUCH AS OUT-OF-BALANCE
CONDITION OF WHEEL AND/OR TIRE, AND BENT
OR DAMAGED WHEEL.
POSSIBLE LOOSE OR WORN STEERING TIE-ROD
OR STEERING IDLER ARM.
POSSIBLE LOOSE, DAMAGED OR WORN FRONT
SUSPENSION PARTS.

INCORRECT TOE-IN OR EXTREME CAMBER

FEATHERING DUE TO MISALIGNMENT

1-b HAYNES

**5.3 This chart will help you determine the condition of the tires, the probable cause(s) of abnormal wear
and the corrective action necessary**

brake fluid leakage. If you see any, inspect the brakes immediately.

6   Correct air pressure adds miles to the lifespan of the tires, improves mileage and enhances overall ride quality. Tire pressure cannot be accurately estimated by looking at a tire, especially if it's a radial. A tire pressure gauge is essential. Keep an accurate gauge in the vehicle. The pressure gauges attached to the nozzles of air hoses at gas stations are often inaccurate.

7   Always check tire pressure when the tires are cold. Cold, in this case, means the vehicle has not been driven over a mile in the three hours preceding a tire pressure check. A pressure rise of four to eight pounds is not uncommon once the tires are warm.

8   Unscrew the valve cap protruding from the wheel or hubcap and push the gauge firmly onto the valve stem **(see illustration)**. Note the reading on the gauge and compare the figure to the recommended tire pressure shown on the placard on the driver's side door pillar. Be sure to reinstall the valve cap to keep dirt and moisture out of the valve stem mechanism. Check all four tires and, if necessary, add enough air

to bring them up to the recommended pressure.

9   Don't forget to keep the spare tire inflated to the specified pressure (refer to your owner's manual or the tire sidewall).

6   Air filter check and replacement (diesel engine) (every 250 miles or weekly)

Refer to illustrations 6.2, 6.4a and 6.4b

Check

1   Since the supply of air is crucial to the operation of a diesel engine, these models have an air restriction gauge built into the air filter housing to monitor the condition of the filter element. This gauge should be checked periodically to determine if the element is restricted with dirt.

5.4a If a tire loses air on a steady basis, check the valve stem core first to make sure it's snug (special inexpensive wrenches are commonly available at auto parts stores)

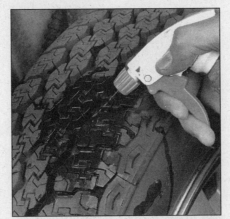

5.4b If the valve stem core is tight, raise the corner of the vehicle with the low tire and spray a soapy water solution onto the tread as the tire is turned slowly - leaks will cause small bubbles to appear

5.8 To extend the life of the tires, check the air pressure at least once a week with an accurate gauge (don't forget the spare!)

6.2   When the yellow disc drops into the red zone (arrow) on the graduated scale, the air filter must be replaced with a new one

2   The gauge has a yellow disc inside a graduated scale that remains at the highest point of restriction when the engine is shut off. With the engine off, check the position of the disc to see if it moved to within the red zone **(see illustration)**. If it has, replace the air filter element.

Replacement

3   The air filter is located inside the air filter housing mounted in the right front corner of the engine compartment.

4   Detach the two clips, separate the housing halves and lift the filter out **(see illustrations)**.

5   Wipe out the inside of the air filter housing with a clean rag.

6   Place the new filter in the air filter housing. Make sure it seats properly, seat the two halves together and secure them with the clips.

7   After installation, press the button on the top of the gauge to reset it.

7   Fuel filter draining (diesel engine) (every 250 miles or weekly)

Refer to illustration 7.3

1   The diesel engine fuel filter incorporates a water separator that removes and traps water in the fuel. This water must be drained from the filter at the specified intervals or when the Water In Fuel (WIF) light is on.

2   Place a small container under the filter drain tube (diesel fuel can

6.4b   . . . then raise the cover and lift the filter element out

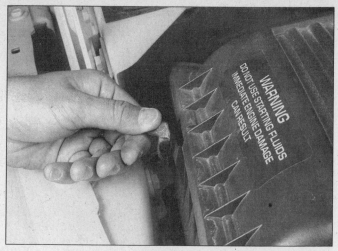

6.4a   Detach the air filter housing clips . . .

damage asphalt paving).

3   With the engine off, reach up under the filter and push up on the collar to release the valve, allowing the accumulated water to drain out **(see illustration)**. Repeat the procedure until clean fuel issues from the filter drain, then release the valve.

4   Remove the container and dispose of the fuel/water mixture properly.

8   Automatic transmission fluid level check (every 250 miles or weekly)

Refer to illustrations 8.3 and 8.6

1   The automatic transmission fluid level should be carefully maintained. Low fluid level can lead to slipping or loss of drive, while overfilling can cause foaming and loss of fluid.

2   With the parking brake set, start the engine, then move the shift lever through all the gear ranges, ending in Park. The fluid level must be checked with the vehicle level and the engine running at idle. **Note:** *Incorrect fluid level readings will result if the vehicle has just been driven at high speeds for an extended period, in hot weather in city traffic, or if it has been pulling a trailer. If any of these conditions apply, wait until the fluid has cooled (about 30 minutes).*

3   With the transmission at normal operating temperature, remove the dipstick from the filler tube. The dipstick is located at the rear of the engine compartment on the passenger's side **(see illustration)**.

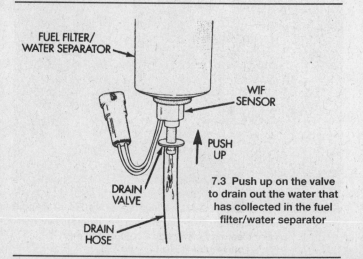

FUEL FILTER/
WATER SEPARATOR

WIF
SENSOR

PUSH
UP

DRAIN
VALVE

DRAIN
HOSE

7.3   Push up on the valve to drain out the water that has collected in the fuel filter/water separator

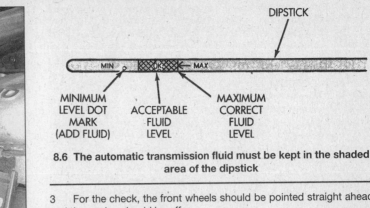

8.6 The automatic transmission fluid must be kept in the shaded area of the dipstick

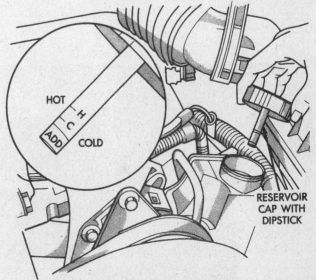

8.3 The automatic transmission dipstick (arrow) is located at the rear of the engine compartment, on the right (passenger's) side

4   Wipe the fluid from the dipstick with a clean rag and push it back into the filler tube until the cap seats.
5   Pull the dipstick out again and note the fluid level.
6   If the fluid is warm, the level should be between the two dimples **(see illustration)**. If it's hot, the level should be in the crosshatched area, near the MAX line. If additional fluid is required, add it directly into the tube using a funnel. It takes about one pint to raise the level from the bottom of the crosshatched area to the MAX line with a hot transmission, so add the fluid a little at a time and keep checking the level until it's correct.
7   The condition of the fluid should also be checked along with the level. If the fluid at the end of the dipstick is a dark reddish-brown color, or if it smells burned, it should be changed. If you are in doubt about the condition of the fluid, purchase some new fluid and compare the two for color and smell.

9   Power steering fluid level check (every 3000 miles or 3 months)

Refer to illustrations 9.2 and 9.6
1   Unlike manual steering, the power steering system relies on fluid which may, over a period of time, require replenishing.
2   The fluid reservoir for the power steering pump is located on the pump body at the front of the engine **(see illustration)**.

3   For the check, the front wheels should be pointed straight ahead and the engine should be off.
4   Use a clean rag to wipe off the reservoir cap and the area around the cap. This will help prevent any foreign matter from entering the reservoir during the check.
5   Twist off the cap and check the temperature of the fluid at the end of the dipstick with your finger.
6   Wipe off the fluid with a clean rag, reinsert the dipstick, then withdraw it and read the fluid level. The fluid should be at the proper level, depending on whether it was checked hot or cold **(see illustration)**. Never allow the fluid level to drop below the lower mark on the dipstick.
7   If additional fluid is required, pour the specified type directly into the reservoir, using a funnel to prevent spills.
8   If the reservoir requires frequent fluid additions, all power steering hoses, hose connections, steering gear and the power steering pump should be carefully checked for leaks.

10   Engine oil and filter change (every 3000 miles or 3 months)

Refer to illustrations 10.3, 10.9a, 10.9b, 10.14 and 10.18
1   Frequent oil changes are the most important preventive maintenance procedures that can be done by the home mechanic. As engine oil ages, it becomes diluted and contaminated, which leads to premature engine wear.
2   Although some sources recommend oil filter changes every other oil change, we feel that the minimal cost of an oil filter and the relative

9.2 The power steering fluid dipstick (arrow) is located in the power steering pump reservoir - turn the cap counterclockwise to remove it

9.6 The power steering fluid dipstick has marks on it so the fluid can be checked hot or cold

ease with which it is installed dictate that a new filter be installed every time the oil is changed.

3   Gather together all necessary tools and materials before beginning this procedure **(see illustration)**.

4   You should have plenty of clean rags and newspapers handy to mop up any spills. Access to the under side of the vehicle may be improved if the vehicle can be lifted on a hoist, driven onto ramps or supported by jackstands. **Warning:** *Do not work under a vehicle which is supported only by a bumper, hydraulic or scissors-type jack.*

5   If this is your first oil change, familiarize yourself with the locations of the oil drain plug and the oil filter.

6   Warm the engine to normal operating temperature. If the new oil or any tools are needed, use this warm-up time to gather everything necessary for the job. The correct type of oil for your application can be found in *Recommended lubricants and fluids* at the beginning of this Chapter.

7   With the engine oil warm (warm engine oil will drain better and more built-up sludge will be removed with it), raise and support the vehicle. Make sure it's safely supported!

8   Move all necessary tools, rags and newspapers under the vehicle. Set the drain pan under the drain plug. Keep in mind that the oil will initially flow from the pan with some force; position the pan accordingly.

9   Being careful not to touch any of the hot exhaust components, use a wrench to remove the drain plug near the bottom of the oil pan **(see illustrations)**. Depending on how hot the oil is, you may want to wear gloves while unscrewing the plug the final few turns.

10   Allow the oil to drain into the pan. It may be necessary to move the pan as the oil flow slows to a trickle.

11   After all the oil has drained, wipe off the drain plug with a clean rag. Small metal particles may cling to the plug and would immediately contaminate the new oil.

12   Clean the area around the drain plug opening and reinstall the plug. Tighten the plug securely with the wrench. If a torque wrench is available, use it to tighten the plug to the torque listed in this Chapter's Specifications.

13   Move the drain pan into position under the oil filter.

14   Use the oil filter wrench to loosen the oil filter **(see illustration)**.

15   Completely unscrew the old filter. Be careful; it's full of oil. Empty the oil inside the filter into the drain pan, then lower the filter (gasoline engines) or lift the filter out from above (diesel engine).

16   Compare the old filter with the new one to make sure they're the same type.

17   Use a clean rag to remove all oil, dirt and sludge from the area where the oil filter mounts to the engine. Check the old filter to make sure the rubber gasket isn't stuck to the engine. If the gasket is stuck to the engine (use a flashlight if necessary), remove it.

18   Apply a light coat of clean oil to the rubber gasket on the new oil filter **(see illustration)**.

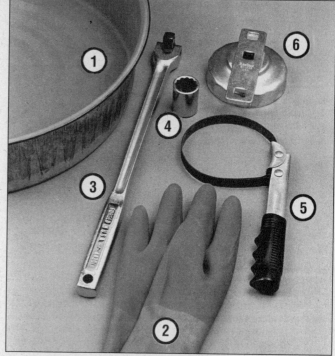

10.3 These tools are required when changing the engine oil and filter

1   *Drain pan - It should be fairly shallow in depth, but wide to prevent spills*

2   *Rubber gloves - When removing the drain plug and filter, you will get oil on your hands (the gloves will prevent burns)*

3   *Breaker bar - Sometimes the oil drain plug is tight, and a long breaker bar is needed to loosen it*

4   *Socket – To be used with the breaker bar or a ratchet (must be the correct size to fit the drain plug - six-point preferred)*

5   *Filter wrench - This is a metal band-type wrench, which requires clearance around the filter to be effective*

6   *Filter wrench - This type fits on the bottom of the filter and can be turned with a ratchet or breaker bar (different-size wrenches are available for different types of filters)*

19   Attach the new filter to the engine, following the tightening directions printed on the filter canister or packing box. Most filter manufacturers recommend against using a filter wrench due to the possibility of

10.9a On gasoline engines, use a proper size box-end wrench or socket to remove the oil drain plug and avoid rounding it off

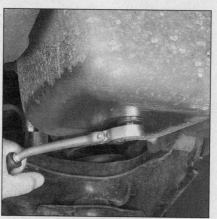

10.9b On diesel engines, remove the oil drain plug with a 3/8-inch drive breaker bar or ratchet

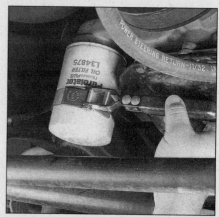

10.14 Since the oil filter is on very tight, you'll need a special wrench for removal - DO NOT use the wrench to tighten the new filter

10.18 Lubricate the oil filter gasket with clean engine oil before installing the filter on the engine

overtightening and damage to the seal.

20   Remove all tools, rags, etc. from under the vehicle, being careful not to spill the oil in the drain pan, then lower the vehicle.

21   Move to the engine compartment and locate the oil filler cap.

22   Pour the fresh oil through the filler opening. A funnel may be helpful.

23   Refer to the engine oil capacity in this Chapter's Specifications and add the proper amount of fresh oil into the engine. Wait a few minutes to allow the oil to drain into the pan, then check the level on the oil dipstick (see Section 4 if necessary). If the oil level is above the hatched area (gasoline) or ADD mark (diesel), start the engine and allow the new oil to circulate.

24   Run the engine for only about a minute and then shut it off. Immediately look under the vehicle and check for leaks at the oil pan drain plug and around the oil filter.

25   With the new oil circulated and the filter now completely full, recheck the level on the dipstick and add more oil as necessary.

26   During the first few trips after an oil change, make it a point to check frequently for leaks and proper oil level.

27   The old oil drained from the engine cannot be reused in its present state and should be disposed of. Check with your local refuse disposal company, disposal facility or environmental agency to see if they will accept the oil for recycling. After the oil has cooled it can be drained into a container (capped plastic jugs, topped bottles, milk cartons, etc.) for transport to one of these disposal sites. Don't dispose of the oil by pouring it on the ground or down a drain!

11   Battery check, maintenance and charging (every 3000 miles or 3 months)

Refer to illustrations 11.1, 11.6a, 11.6b, 11.7a and 11.7b

Warning: *Certain precautions must be followed when checking and servicing the battery. Hydrogen gas, which is highly flammable, is always present in the battery cells, so keep lighted tobacco and all other open flames and sparks away from the battery. The electrolyte inside the battery is actually dilute sulfuric acid, which will cause injury if splashed on your skin or in your eyes. It will also ruin clothes and painted surfaces. When removing the battery cables, always detach the negative cable first and hook it up last!*

1   A routine preventive maintenance program for the battery in your vehicle is the only way to ensure quick and reliable starts. But before performing any battery maintenance, make sure that you have the proper equipment necessary to work safely around the battery **(see illustration)**.

2   There are also several precautions that should be taken whenever

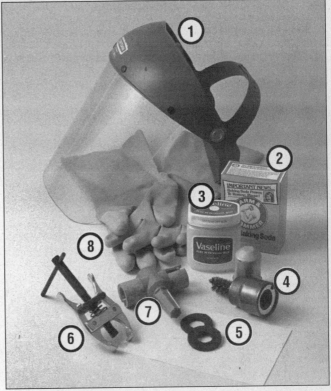

11.1 Tools and materials required for battery maintenance

1   **Face shield/safety goggles** - *When removing corrosion with a brush, the acidic particles can easily fly up into your eyes*

2   **Baking soda** - *A solution of baking soda and water can be used to neutralize corrosion*

3   **Petroleum jelly** - *A layer of this on the battery posts will help prevent corrosion*

4   **Battery post/cable cleaner** - *This wire brush cleaning tool will remove all traces of corrosion from the battery posts and cable clamps*

5   **Treated felt washers** - *Placing one of these on each post, directly under the cable clamps, will help prevent corrosion*

6   **Puller** - *Sometimes the cable clamps are very difficult to pull off the posts, even after the nut/bolt has been completely loosened. This tool pulls the clamp straight up and off the post without damage*

7   **Battery post/cable cleaner** - *Here is another cleaning tool which is a slightly different version of Number 4 above, but it does the same thing*

8   **Rubber gloves** - *Another safety item to consider when servicing the battery; remember that's acid inside the battery!*

battery maintenance is performed. Before servicing the battery, always turn the engine and all accessories off and disconnect the cable from the negative terminal of the battery.

3   The battery produces hydrogen gas, which is both flammable and explosive. Never create a spark, smoke or light a match around the battery. Always charge the battery in a ventilated area.

4   Electrolyte contains poisonous and corrosive sulfuric acid. Do not allow it to get in your eyes, on your skin or on your clothes. Never ingest it. Wear protective safety glasses when working near the battery. Keep children away from the battery.

5   Note the external condition of the battery. If the positive terminal and cable clamp on your vehicle's battery is equipped with a rubber protector, make sure that it's not torn or damaged. It should completely cover the terminal. Look for any corroded or loose connections, cracks in the case or cover or loose hold-down clamps. Also check the entire length of each cable for cracks and frayed conductors.

11.6a Battery terminal corrosion usually appears as light, fluffy powder

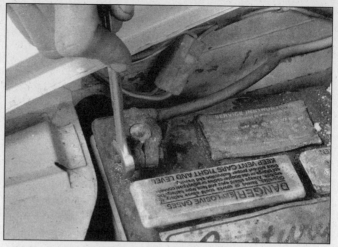

11.6b Removing the cable from a battery post with a wrench - sometimes special battery pliers are required for this procedure if corrosion has caused deterioration of the nut hex (always remove the ground cable first and hook it up last!)

6   If corrosion, which looks like white, fluffy deposits is evident, particularly around the terminals, the battery should be removed for cleaning **(see illustration)**. Loosen the cable clamp bolts with a wrench, being careful to remove the ground cable first, and slide them off the terminals **(see illustration)**. Then disconnect the hold-down clamp bolt and nut, remove the clamp and lift the battery from the engine compartment.

7   Clean the cable clamps thoroughly with a battery brush or a terminal cleaner and a solution of warm water and baking soda **(see illustration)**. Wash the terminals and the top of the battery case with the same solution but make sure that the solution doesn't get into the battery. When cleaning the cables, terminals and battery top, wear safety goggles and rubber gloves to prevent any solution from coming in contact with your eyes or hands. Wear old clothes too - even diluted, sulfuric acid splashed onto clothes will burn holes in them. If the terminals have been extensively corroded, clean them up with a terminal cleaner **(see illustration)**. Thoroughly wash all cleaned areas with plain water.

8   Make sure that the battery tray is in good condition and the hold-down clamp bolts are tight. If the battery is removed from the tray, make sure no parts remain in the bottom of the tray when the battery is reinstalled. When reinstalling the hold-down clamp bolts, do not overtighten them.

9   Any metal parts of the vehicle damaged by corrosion should be covered with a zinc-based primer, then painted.

10   Information on removing and installing the battery can be found in Chapter 5. Information on jump starting can be found at the front of this manual. For more detailed battery checking procedures, refer to the *Haynes Automotive Electrical Manual*.

Charging

Warning: *When batteries are being charged, hydrogen gas, which is very explosive and flammable, is produced. Do not smoke or allow open flames near a charging or a recently charged battery. Wear eye protection when near the battery during charging. Also, make sure the charger is unplugged before connecting or disconnecting the battery from the charger.*

Note: *The manufacturer recommends the battery be removed from the vehicle for charging because the gas that escapes during this procedure can damage the paint. Fast charging with the battery cables connected can result in damage to the electrical system.*

11   Slow-rate charging is the best way to restore a battery that's discharged to the point where it will not start the engine. It's also a good way to maintain the battery charge in a vehicle that's only driven a few miles between starts. Maintaining the battery charge is particularly important in the winter when the battery must work harder to start the engine and electrical accessories that drain the battery are in greater use.

11.7a When cleaning the cable clamps, all corrosion must be removed (the inside of the clamp is tapered to match the taper on the post, so don't remove too much material)

11.7b Regardless of the type of tool used on the battery posts, a clean, shiny surface should be the result

ALWAYS CHECK FOR CHAFED OR BURNED AREAS THAT MAY CAUSE AN UNTIMELY AND COSTLY FAILURE.

SOFT HOSE INDICATES INSIDE DETERIORATION. THIS DETERIORATION CAN CONTAMINATE THE COOLING SYSTEM AND CAUSE PARTICLES TO CLOG THE RADIATOR.

HARDENED HOSE CAN FAIL AT ANY TIME. TIGHTENING HOSE CLAMPS WILL NOT SEAL THE CONNECTION OR STOP LEAKS.

SWOLLEN HOSE OR OIL SOAKED ENDS INDICATE DANGER AND POSSIBLE FAILURE FROM OIL OR GREASE CONTAMINATION. SQUEEZE THE HOSE TO LOCATE CRACKS AND BREAKS THAT CAUSE LEAKS.

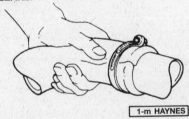

1-m HAYNES

12.4 Hoses, like drivebelts, have a habit of failing at the worst possible time - to prevent the inconvenience of a blown radiator or heater hose, inspect them carefully as shown here

12   It's best to use a one or two-amp battery charger (sometimes called a "trickle" charger). They are the safest and put the least strain on the battery. They are also the least expensive. For a faster charge, you can use a higher amperage charger, but don't use one rated more than 1/10th the amp/hour rating of the battery. Rapid boost charges that claim to restore the power of the battery in one to two hours are hardest on the battery and can damage batteries not in good condition. This type of charging should only be used in emergency situations.

13   The average time necessary to charge a battery should be listed in the instructions that come with the charger. As a general rule, a trickle charger will charge a battery in 12 to 16 hours.

14   Remove all the cell caps (if equipped) and cover the holes with a clean cloth to prevent spattering electrolyte. Disconnect the negative battery cable and hook the battery charger cable clamps up to the battery posts (positive to positive, negative to negative), then plug in the charger. Make sure it is set at 12-volts if it has a selector switch.

15   If you're using a charger with a rate higher than two amps, check the battery regularly during charging to make sure it doesn't overheat. If you're using a trickle charger, you can safely let the battery charge overnight after you've checked it regularly for the first couple of hours.

16   If the battery has removable cell caps, measure the specific gravity with a hydrometer every hour during the last few hours of the charg-

ing cycle. Hydrometers are available inexpensively from auto parts stores - follow the instructions that come with the hydrometer. Consider the battery charged when there's no change in the specific gravity reading for two hours and the electrolyte in the cells is gassing (bubbling) freely. The specific gravity reading from each cell should be very close to the others. If not, the battery probably has a bad cell(s).

17   Some batteries with sealed tops have built-in hydrometers on the top that indicate the state of charge by the color displayed in the hydrometer window. Normally, a bright-colored hydrometer indicates a full charge and a dark hydrometer indicates the battery still needs charging.

18   If the battery has a sealed top and no built-in hydrometer, you can hook up a digital voltmeter across the battery terminals to check the charge. A fully charged battery should read 12.6 volts or higher.

19   Further information on the battery and jump starting can be found in Chapter 5 and at the front of this manual.

12   Cooling system check (every 3000 miles or 3 months)

Refer to illustration 12.4

1   Many major engine failures can be attributed to a faulty cooling system. If the vehicle is equipped with an automatic transmission, the cooling system also cools the transmission fluid and thus plays an important role in prolonging transmission life.

2   The cooling system should be checked with the engine cold. Do this before the vehicle is driven for the day or after it has been shut off for at least three hours.

3   Remove the radiator cap by turning it to the left until it reaches a stop. If you hear a hissing sound (indicating there is still pressure in the system), wait until this stops. Now press down on the cap with the palm of your hand and continue turning to the left until the cap can be removed. Thoroughly clean the cap, inside and out, with clean water. Also clean the filler neck on the radiator. All traces of corrosion should be removed. The coolant inside the radiator should be relatively transparent. If it is rust colored, the system should be drained and refilled (see Section 38). If the coolant level is not up to the top, add additional antifreeze/coolant mixture (see Section 4).

4   Carefully check the large upper and lower radiator hoses along with the smaller diameter heater hoses which run from the engine to the firewall. Inspect each hose along its entire length, replacing any hose which is cracked, swollen or shows signs of deterioration. Cracks may become more apparent if the hose is squeezed **(see illustration)**. Regardless of condition, it's a good idea to replace hoses with new ones every two years.

5   Make sure all hose connections are tight. A leak in the cooling system will usually show up as white or rust colored deposits on the areas adjoining the leak. If wire-type clamps are used at the ends of the hoses, it may be a good idea to replace them with more secure screw-type clamps.

6   Use compressed air or a soft brush to remove bugs, leaves, etc. from the front of the radiator or air conditioning condenser. Be careful not to damage the delicate cooling fins or cut yourself on them.

7   Every other inspection, or at the first indication of cooling system problems, have the cap and system pressure tested. If you don't have a pressure tester, most repair shops will do this for a minimal charge.

13   Underhood hose check and replacement (every 3000 miles or 3 months)

General

Caution: *Replacement of air conditioning hoses must be left to a dealer service department or air conditioning shop that has the equipment to depressurize the system safely. Never remove air conditioning components or hoses until the system has been depressurized.*

1   High temperatures in the engine compartment can cause the deterioration of the rubber and plastic hoses used for engine, accessory and emission systems operation. Periodic inspection should be

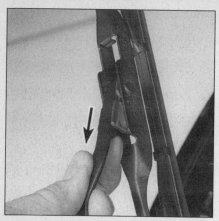

14.3 Depress the release lever and slide the wiper assembly down the wiper arm and out of the hook in the end of the arm

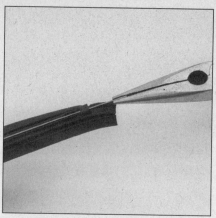

14.4 Detach the end of the element and use needle nose pliers to pull out the support rods

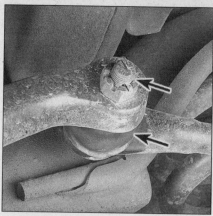

15.4a Check the steering linkage for torn boots and loose fasteners (arrows)

made for cracks, loose clamps, material hardening and leaks. Information specific to the cooling system hoses can be found in Section 12.
2   Some, but not all, hoses are secured to the fittings with clamps. Where clamps are used, check to be sure they haven't lost their tension, allowing the hose to leak. If clamps aren't used, make sure the hose has not expanded and/or hardened where it slips over the fitting, allowing it to leak.

Vacuum hoses

3   It's quite common for vacuum hoses, especially those in the emissions system, to be color coded or identified by colored stripes molded into them. Various systems require hoses with different wall thickness, collapse resistance and temperature resistance. When replacing hoses, be sure the new ones are made of the same material.
4   Often the only effective way to check a hose is to remove it completely from the vehicle. If more than one hose is removed, be sure to label the hoses and fittings to ensure correct installation.
5   When checking vacuum hoses, be sure to include any plastic T-fittings in the check. Inspect the fittings for cracks and the hose where it fits over the fitting for distortion, which could cause leakage.
6   A small piece of vacuum hose (1/4-inch inside diameter) can be used as a stethoscope to detect vacuum leaks. Hold one end of the hose to your ear and probe around vacuum hoses and fittings, listening for the "hissing" sound characteristic of a vacuum leak. **Warning:** *When probing with the vacuum hose stethoscope, be very careful not to come into contact with moving engine components such as the drivebelt, cooling fan, etc.*

Fuel hose

Warning: *There are certain precautions which must be taken when inspecting or servicing fuel system components. Work in a well ventilated area and do not allow open flames (cigarettes, appliance pilot lights, etc.) or bare light bulbs near the work area. Mop up any spills immediately and do not store fuel soaked rags where they could ignite. On fuel-injected models, the fuel system is under high pressure, so if any fuel lines are to be disconnected, the pressure in the system must be relieved first (see Chapter 4A for more information).*
7   Check all rubber fuel lines for deterioration and chafing. Check especially for cracks in areas where the hose bends and just before fittings, such as where a hose attaches to the fuel filter.
8   High quality fuel line, usually identified by the word *Fluoroelastomer* printed on the hose, should be used for fuel line replacement. Never, under any circumstances, use unreinforced vacuum line, clear plastic tubing or water hose for fuel lines.
9   Spring-type clamps are commonly used on fuel lines. These clamps often lose their tension over a period of time, and can be "sprung" during removal. Replace all spring-type clamps with screw clamps whenever a hose is replaced.

Metal lines

10   Sections of metal line are routed along the frame, between the fuel tank and the engine. Check carefully to be sure the line has not been bent or crimped and that cracks have not started in the line.
11   If a section of metal fuel line must be replaced, only seamless steel tubing should be used, since copper and aluminum tubing don't have the strength necessary to withstand normal engine vibration.
12   Check the metal brake lines where they enter the master cylinder and brake proportioning unit for cracks in the lines or loose fittings. Any sign of brake fluid leakage calls for an immediate thorough inspection of the brake system.

---

14   Wiper blade inspection and replacement (every 3000 miles or 3 months)

Refer to illustrations 14.3 and 14.4
1   The windshield wiper blade elements should be checked periodically for cracks and deterioration.
2   Lift the wiper blade assembly away from the glass.
3   Press the release lever and slide the blade assembly out of the hook in the end of the wiper arm **(see illustration)**.
4   Use needle-nose pliers to extract the two metal rods, then slide the element out of the frame **(see illustration)**.
5   Slide the new element into the frame and insert the two metal rods to lock it in place.
6   Installation is the reverse of removal.

---

15   Suspension and steering check (every 6000 miles or 6 months)

Refer to illustrations 15.4a, 15.4b, 15.4c, 15.4d and 15.5
1   Indications of a fault in the suspension or steering systems include:

a) *excessive play in the steering wheel before the front wheels react*
b) *excessive sway around corners*
c) *body movement over rough roads*
d) *binding at some point as the steering wheel is turned.*

2   Raise the front of the vehicle periodically and visually check the suspension and steering components for wear. Make sure the vehicle is supported securely and cannot fall from the stands.
3   Check the wheel bearings. Do this by spinning the front wheels. Listen for any abnormal noises and watch to make sure the wheel spins true (doesn't wobble). Grab the top and bottom of the tire and pull in-and-out on it. Notice any movement which would indicate a

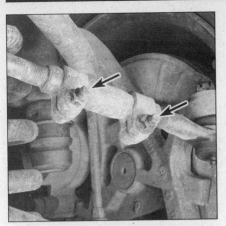

15.4b Make sure the steering tie-rod clamp nuts are tight (arrows)

15.4c Inspect the steering gear for leaks and make sure the nut is tight (arrows)

15.4d Check the rear axle U-bolts and nuts for damage (arrows)

loose wheel bearing assembly. If the bearings are suspect, refer to Section 37 and Chapter 10 for more information.

4   From under the vehicle, check for loose bolts, broken or disconnected parts and deteriorated rubber bushings on all suspension and steering components **(see illustrations)**. Look for fluid leaking from the steering gear assembly. Check the power steering hoses, belts and connections for leaks.

5   Inspect the shock absorbers for fluid leaks, indicating the need for replacement **(see illustration)**. Never replace just one shock absorber; always replace them in sets.

6   Have an assistant turn the steering wheel from side-to-side and check the steering components for free movement, chafing and binding. If the steering doesn't react with the movement of the steering wheel, try to determine where the slack is located.

16 Exhaust system check (every 6000 miles or 6 months)

Refer to illustration 16.2

1   With the engine cold (at least three hours after the vehicle has been driven), check the complete exhaust system from the manifold to the end of the tailpipe. Be careful around the catalytic converter, which may be hot even after three hours. The inspection should be done with the vehicle on a hoist to permit unrestricted access. If a hoist isn't available, raise the vehicle and support it securely on jackstands.

2   Check the exhaust pipes and connections for signs of leakage and/or corrosion indicating a potential failure. Make sure that all brackets and hangers are in good condition and tight **(see illustration)**.

3   Inspect the underside of the body for holes, corrosion, open seams, etc. which may allow exhaust gasses to enter the passenger compartment. Seal all body openings with silicone sealant or body putty.

4   Rattles and other noises can often be traced to the exhaust system, especially the hangers, mounts and heat shields. Try to move the pipes, mufflers and catalytic converter. If the components can come in contact with the body or suspension parts, secure the exhaust system with new brackets and hangers.

17 Manual transmission lubricant level check (every 6000 miles or 6 months)

Refer to illustration 17.2

1   The manual transmission has a filler plug which must be removed to check the lubricant level. If the vehicle is raised to gain access to the plug, be sure to support it safely on jackstands - DO NOT crawl under a vehicle which is supported only by a jack! Be sure the vehicle is level or the check may be inaccurate.

2   Using the appropriate wrench, unscrew the plug from the transmission; some models require an Allen wrench **(see illustration)**.

3   Use your little finger to reach inside the housing to feel the lubricant level. The level should be at or near the bottom of the plug hole. If it isn't, add the recommended lubricant through the plug hole with a syringe or squeeze bottle.

4   Install and tighten the plug. Check for leaks after the first few miles of driving.

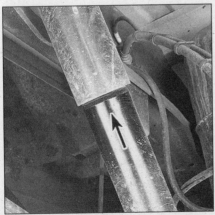

15.5 Check the shock absorbers for leaking fluid in this area (arrow)

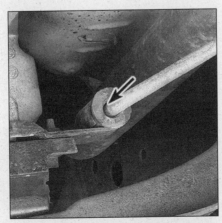

16.2 Inspect the rubber exhaust system mounts for damage (arrow)

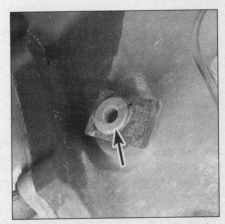

17.2 The manual transmission fill plug is located on the side of the case (arrow)

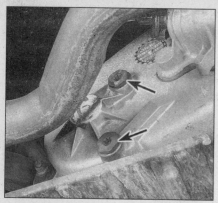

18.1 The 4WD transfer case fill plug (upper arrow) and drain plug (lower arrow) are located on the rear side of the housing

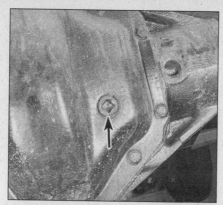

19.2 On most differentials, the fill plug (arrow) is removed by unscrewing it from the differential case using a 3/8-inch drive breaker bar or ratchet

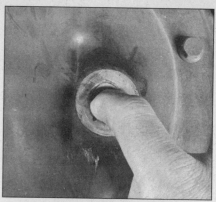

19.3 Use your finger as a dipstick to check the lubricant level

18   Transfer case lubricant level check (4WD models) (every 6000 miles or 6 months)

Refer to illustration 18.1

1   The transfer case lubricant level is checked by removing the upper plug located at the rear of the case **(see illustration)**.

2   After removing the plug, reach inside the hole. The lubricant level should be just at the bottom of the hole. If not, add the appropriate lubricant through the opening.

19   Differential lubricant level check (every 6000 miles or 6 months)

Refer to illustrations 19.2 and 19.3

Note: *4WD vehicles have two differentials - one in the center of each axle. 2WD vehicles have one differential - in the center of the rear axle. On 4WD vehicles, be sure to check the lubricant level in both differentials.*

1   The filler plug on all front and most rear differentials is a threaded metal type while the rear differential on some models may have a rubber press-in filler plug which must be removed to check the lubricant level. If the vehicle is raised to gain access to the plug, be sure to support it safely on jackstands - DO NOT crawl under the vehicle when it's supported only by the jack. Be sure the vehicle is level or the check may not be accurate.

2   Remove the plug from the filler hole in the differential housing or cover **(see illustration)**.

3   The lubricant level should be at the bottom of the filler hole **(see illustration)**. If not, use a pump or squeeze bottle to add the recommended lubricant until it just starts to run out of the opening. On some models a tag is located in the area of the plug which gives information regarding lubricant type.

4   Install the plug securely into the filler hole.

20   Tire rotation (every 6000 miles or 6 months)

Refer to illustrations 20.2a and 20.2b

1   The tires should be rotated at the specified intervals and whenever uneven wear is noticed.

2   Refer to the **accompanying illustrations** for the preferred tire rotation pattern.

3   Refer to the information in *Jacking and towing* at the front of this manual for the proper procedures to follow when raising the vehicle and changing a tire. If the brakes are to be checked, don't apply the parking brake as stated. Make sure the tires are blocked to prevent the vehicle from rolling as it's raised.

4   Preferably, the entire vehicle should be raised at the same time.

This can be done on a hoist or by jacking up each corner and then lowering the vehicle onto jackstands placed under the frame rails. Always use four jackstands and make sure the vehicle is safely supported.

5   After rotation, check and adjust the tire pressures as necessary. Tighten the lug nuts to the torque listed in this Chapter's Specifications.

21   Brake check (every 6000 miles or 6 months)

Warning: *Brake system dust may contain asbestos, which is hazardous to your health. DO NOT blow it out with compressed air, inhale it or use gasoline or solvents to remove it. Use brake system cleaner only.*
Note: *For detailed photographs of the brake system, refer to Chapter 9.*

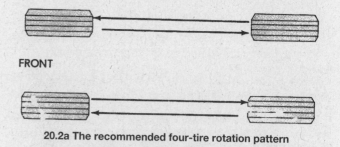

FRONT

20.2a The recommended four-tire rotation pattern

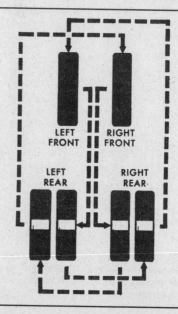

20.2b Six-tire rotation pattern for models with dual rear wheels

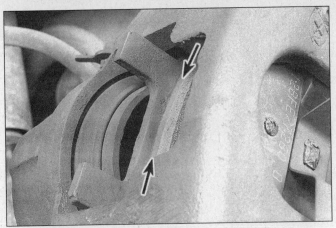

21.5 Look into the inspection hole in the calipers to check the pad the thickness of remaining pad material (arrow)

1   In addition to the specified intervals, the brakes should be inspected every time the wheels are removed or whenever a defect is suspected.
2   To check the brakes, raise the vehicle and place it securely on jackstands. Remove the wheels (see *Jacking and towing* at the front of the manual, if necessary).

Disc brakes

Refer to illustration 21.5

3   Disc brakes are used on the front wheels of all models covered by this manual. Extensive disc damage can occur if the pads are not replaced when needed.
4   The disc brake calipers, which contain the pads, are visible with the wheels removed. There is an outer pad and an inner pad in each caliper. All pads should be inspected.
5   Each caliper has a "window" or opening to inspect the pads. Check the thickness of the pad lining by looking through the inspection window at the top of the housing **(see illustration)**. If the pad material has worn to approximately 5/16-inch or less, the pads should be replaced.
6   If you're unsure about the exact thickness of the remaining lining material, remove the pads for further inspection or replacement (refer to Chapter 9).
7   Before installing the wheels, check for leakage and/or damage (cracks, splitting, etc.) around the brake hose connections. Replace the hose or fittings as necessary, referring to Chapter 9.
8   Check the condition of the disc. Look for score marks, deep scratches and burned spots. If these conditions exist, the hub/disc assembly should be removed for servicing (see Section 37).

Drum brakes

Refer to illustrations 21.11, 21.13 and 21.15

9   Remove the drum by pulling it off the axle and brake assembly. If

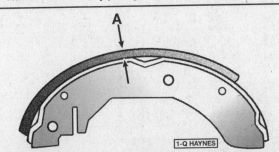

21.13 If the lining is bonded to the brake shoe, measure the lining thickness from the outer surface to the metal shoe, as shown here; if the lining is riveted to the shoe, measure from the lining outer surface to the rivet head

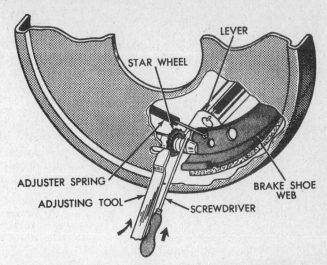

21.11 Use a thin screwdriver to push the lever away, then use an adjusting tool or another screwdriver to back off the star wheel

this proves difficult, make sure the parking brake is released, then squirt penetrating oil around the center hub areas. Allow the oil to soak in and try to pull the drum off again.
10   If the drum still cannot be pulled off, the parking brake lever will have to be lifted slightly off its stop. This is done by first removing the small plug from the backing plate.
11   With the plug removed, insert a thin screwdriver and lift the adjusting lever off the star wheel, then use an adjusting tool or screwdriver to back off the star wheel several turns **(see illustration)**. This will move the brake shoes away from the drum. If the drum still won't pull off, tap around its inner circumference with a soft-face hammer.
12   With the drum removed, do not touch any brake dust (see the **Warning** at the beginning of this Section).
13   Note the thickness of the lining material on both the front and rear brake shoes. If the material has worn away to within 1/16-inch of the recessed rivets or metal backing, the shoes should be replaced **(see illustration)**. The shoes should also be replaced if they're cracked, glazed (shiny surface) or contaminated with brake fluid.
14   Make sure that all the brake assembly springs are connected and in good condition.
15   Check the brake components for any signs of fluid leakage. Carefully pry back the rubber cups on the wheel cylinders located at the top of the brake shoes **(see illustration)**. Any leakage is an indication that the wheel cylinders should be overhauled immediately (see Chapter 9). Also check brake hoses and connections for signs of leakage.

21.15 To check for wheel cylinder leakage, use a small screwdriver to pry the boot away from the cylinder

16   Wipe the inside of the drum with a clean rag and brake system cleaner. Again, be careful not to breathe the dangerous asbestos dust.
17   Check the inside of the drum for cracks, score marks, deep scratches and hard spots, which will appear as small discolorations. If these imperfections cannot be removed with fine emery cloth, the drums must be taken to an automotive machine shop for resurfacing.
18   If after the inspection process all parts are in good working condition, reinstall the brake drum.
19   Install the wheels and lower the vehicle.

Parking brake

20   The parking brake is operated by a foot pedal and locks the rear brake system. The easiest, and perhaps most obvious method of periodically checking the operation of the parking brake assembly is to stop the vehicle on a steep hill with the parking brake set and the transmission in Neutral. If the parking brake cannot prevent the vehicle from rolling, adjust it (see Chapter 9).

22   Fuel system check (gasoline engines) (every 6000 miles or 6 months)

Warning: *Gasoline is extremely flammable, so take extra precautions when working on any part of the fuel system. Don't smoke or allow open flames or bare light bulbs in or near the work area, and don't work in a garage where a natural gas-type appliance (such as a water heater or clothes dryer) with a pilot light is present. Since gasoline is carcinogenic, wear latex gloves when there's a possibility of being exposed to fuel, and, if you spill fuel on your skin, rinse it off immediately with soap and water. Have a Class B fire extinguisher on hand.*
1   The fuel tank is located under the rear of the vehicle.
2   The fuel system is most easily checked with the vehicle raised on a hoist so the components underneath the vehicle are readily visible and accessible.
3   If the smell of gasoline is noticed while driving or after the vehicle has been in the sun, the system should be thoroughly inspected immediately.
4   Remove the gas tank cap and check for damage, corrosion and an unbroken sealing imprint on the gasket. Replace the cap with a new one if necessary.
5   With the vehicle raised, check the fuel tank and filler neck for punctures, cracks and other damage. The connection between the filler neck and the tank is especially critical. Sometimes a rubber filler neck will leak due to loose clamps or deteriorated rubber; problems a home mechanic can usually rectify. **Warning:** *Do not, under any circumstances, try to repair a fuel tank.*
6   Carefully check all rubber hoses and metal lines leading away from the fuel tank. Look for loose connections, deteriorated hoses, crimped lines and other damage. Follow the lines to the front of the vehicle, carefully inspecting them all the way. Repair or replace damaged sections as necessary.
7   If a fuel odor is still evident after the inspection, refer to Section 41.

23   Fuel system check (diesel engine) (every 6000 miles or 6 months)

1   Make sure the Water In Fuel (WIF) sensor electrical connector is secure and that the system is drained of water (see Section 7).
2   The fuel system is most easily checked with the vehicle raised on a hoist so the components underneath the vehicle are readily visible and accessible.
3   If the smell of diesel fuel is noticed while driving or after the vehicle has been in the sun, the system should be thoroughly inspected immediately.
4   Remove the fuel tank cap and check for damage, corrosion and an unbroken sealing imprint on the gasket. Replace the cap with a new one if necessary.
5   With the vehicle raised, check the fuel tank and filler neck for

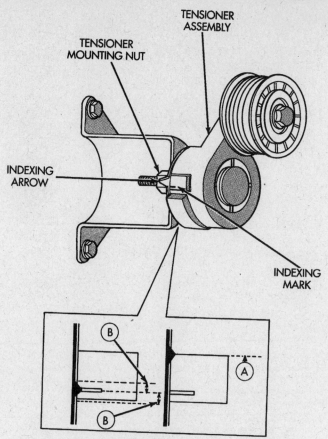

24.4 The serpentine drivebelt tensioner used on V6 and V8 models automatically applies the proper tension on the drivebelt, but it does have limits - the indexing arrow on the tensioner housing (B) must not move beyond point A on the tensioner assembly

punctures, cracks and other damage. The connection between the filler neck and the tank is especially critical. Sometimes a rubber filler neck will leak due to loose clamps or deteriorated rubber; problems a home mechanic can usually rectify. **Warning:** *Do not, under any circumstances, try to repair a fuel tank yourself (except rubber components). A welding torch or any open flame can easily cause the fuel vapors to explode if the proper precautions are not taken!*
6   Carefully check all rubber hoses and metal lines leading away from the fuel tank. Look for loose connections, deteriorated hoses, crimped lines and other damage. Follow the lines to the front of the vehicle, carefully inspecting them all the way. Repair or replace damaged sections as necessary.
7   If a fuel odor is still evident after the inspection, refer to Chapter 4.

24   Drivebelt check, adjustment and replacement (every 6000 miles or 6 months)

Refer to illustrations 24.4, 24.5a, 24.5b, 24.5c and 24.7
1   A single serpentine drivebelt is located at the front of the engine and plays an important role in the overall operation of the engine and its components. Due to its function and material make up, the belt is prone to wear and should be periodically inspected. The serpentine belt drives the alternator, power steering pump, water pump and air conditioning compressor.
2   With the engine off, open the hood and use your fingers (and a flashlight, if necessary), to move along the belt checking for cracks and separation of the belt plies. Also check for fraying and glazing, which

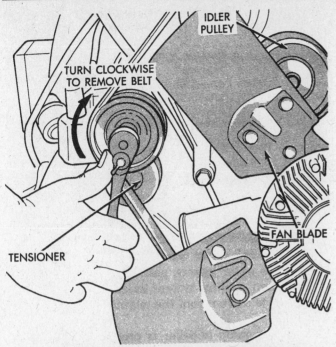

24.5a On standard duty **V6 and V8 models**, release the belt tension by rotating the tensioner clockwise using a wrench on the tensioner bolt

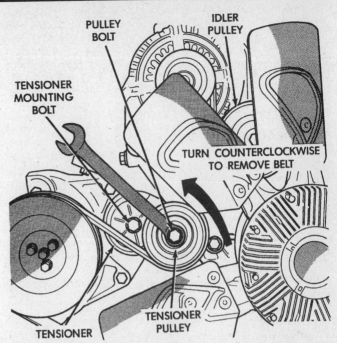

24.5b On heavy duty **V8 and V10 models**, release the belt tension by rotating the tensioner counterclockwise using a wrench on the tensioner bolt

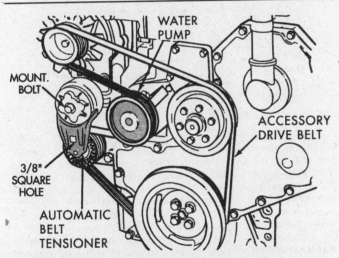

24.5c To release the belt tension on models equipped with a diesel engine, insert a 3/8-inch drive breaker bar or ratchet onto the tensioner arm and rotate it counterclockwise

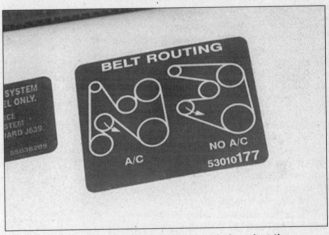

24.7 The drivebelt routing diagram is found on the radiator support

7 Route the new belt over the various pulleys, again rotating the tensioner to allow the belt to be installed, then release the belt tensioner. **Note:** *A drivebelt routing decal is located on the radiator support to help during drivebelt installation* **(see illustration).**

25 Seat belt check (every 6000 miles or 6 months)

1 Check the seat belts, buckles, latch plates and guide loops for any obvious damage or signs of wear.
2 Make sure the seat belt reminder light comes on when the key is turned on.
3 The seat belts are designed to lock up during a sudden stop or impact, yet allow free movement during normal driving. The retractors should hold the belt against your chest while driving and rewind the belt when the buckle is unlatched.
4 If any of the above checks reveal problems with the seat belt system, replace parts as necessary.

gives the belt a shiny appearance. Both sides of the belt should be inspected, which means you will have to twist the belt to check the underside.
3 Check the ribs on the underside of the belt. They should all be the same depth, with none of the surface uneven.
4 The tension of the belt is maintained by a spring loaded tensioner assembly and isn't adjustable. On gasoline engines, the belt should be replaced when the indexing arrow is lined up with the indexing mark A on the tensioner assembly **(see illustration).** On diesel engines, replace the belt according to the maintenance schedule at the front of this chapter, or if it is damaged or worn.
5 To replace the belt, rotate the tensioner to release belt tension **(see illustrations).**
6 Remove the belt from the tensioner and auxiliary components and slowly release the tensioner.

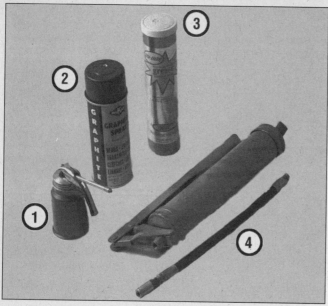

27.1 Materials required for chassis and body lubrication

1 *Engine oil* - *Light engine oil in a can like this can be used for door and hood hinges*
2 *Graphite spray* - *Used to lubricate lock cylinders*
3 *Grease* - *Grease, in a variety of types and weights, is available for use in a grease gun. Check the Specifications for your requirements*
4 *Grease gun* - *A common grease gun, shown here with a detachable hose and nozzle, is needed for chassis lubrication. After use, clean it thoroughly!*

26 Neutral start switch check (models with automatic transmission) (every 6000 miles or 6 months)

Warning: *During the following checks there is a chance the vehicle could lunge forward, possibly causing damage or injuries. Allow plenty of room around the vehicle, apply the parking brake firmly and hold-down the regular brake pedal during the checks.*
1 The neutral start switch prevents the engine from being started unless the gear selector is in Park or Neutral.
2 Try to start the vehicle in each gear. The engine should crank only in Park or Neutral. If it cranks in any other gear, the neutral start switch is faulty or in need of adjustment (see Chapter 7B).
3 Make sure the steering column lock allows the key to go into the Lock position only when the shift lever is in Park.
4 The ignition key should come out only in the Lock position.

27 Chassis lubrication (every 6000 miles or 6 months)

Refer to illustration 27.1 and 27.2
1 Refer to *Recommended lubricants and fluids* at the front of this Chapter to obtain the necessary grease, etc. You'll also need a grease gun **(see illustration)**. Occasionally plugs will be installed rather than grease fittings. If so, grease fittings will have to be purchased and installed.
2 Look under the vehicle and locate the grease fittings **(see illustration)**. Some models with manual transmissions have grease fittings on the shift linkage which should be lubricated whenever the chassis is lubricated.
3 For easier access under the vehicle, raise it with a jack and place jackstands under the frame. Make sure it's safely supported by the stands. If the wheels are to be removed at this interval for tire rotation or brake inspection, loosen the lug nuts slightly while the vehicle is still on the ground.

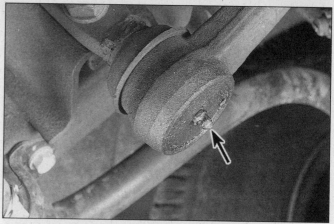

27.2 Wipe the dirt from the grease fittings before pushing the grease gun nozzle onto the fitting

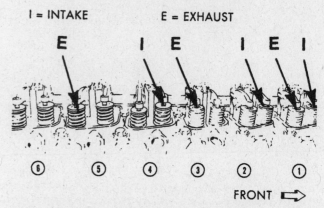

28.3 With the no. 1 piston at TDC on the compression stroke, check and adjust the clearance of the indicated valves

4 Before beginning, force a little grease out of the nozzle to remove any dirt from the end of the gun. Wipe the nozzle clean with a rag.
5 With the grease gun and plenty of clean rags, crawl under the vehicle and begin lubricating the components.
6 Wipe one of the grease fitting nipples clean and push the nozzle firmly over it. Pump the gun until the component is completely lubricated. On balljoints, stop pumping when the rubber seal is firm to the touch. Do not pump too much grease into the fitting as it could rupture the seal. For all other suspension and steering components, continue pumping grease into the fitting until it oozes out of the joint between the two components. If it escapes around the grease gun nozzle, the nipple is clogged or the nozzle is not completely seated on the fitting. Resecure the gun nozzle to the fitting and try again. If necessary, replace the fitting with a new one.
7 Wipe the excess grease from the components and the grease fitting. Repeat the procedure for the remaining fittings.
8 Clean the fitting and pump grease into the driveline universal joints until the grease can be seen coming out of the contact points.
9 Also clean and lubricate the parking brake cable, along with the cable guides and levers. This can be done by smearing some of the chassis grease onto the cable and its related parts with your fingers.

28 Valve clearance check and adjustment (diesel engine) (every 24,000 miles or 24 months)

Refer to illustrations 28.3, 28.4 and 28.6
1 Make sure the engine is cold before beginning this procedure (below 140-degrees F).

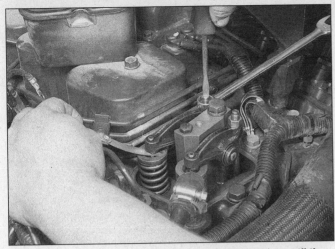

28.4 Loosen the locknut and turn the adjusting screw until the feeler gauge slips between the valve stem tip and rocker arm with a slight amount of drag

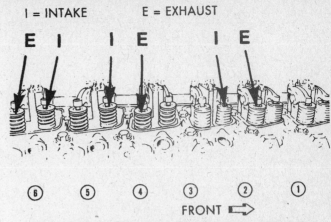

I = INTAKE   E = EXHAUST

E I I E I I E

6 5 4 3 2 1

FRONT ⇨

28.6 Rotate the crankshaft 360-degrees from no. 1 TDC, then check and adjust the clearance of the indicated valves

2   Refer to Chapter 2B and remove the valve cover, then use the timing pin to position the number one piston at TDC on the compression stroke (see Chapter 2B, Section 3). Disengage the timing pin after locating TDC.
3   With the crankshaft at number one TDC, measure the clearance of the indicated valves **(see illustration)**. Insert a feeler gauge of the specified thickness (see this Chapter's Specifications) between the valve stem tip and the rocker arm. The feeler gauge should slip between the valve stem tip and rocker arm with a slight amount of drag.
4   If the clearance is incorrect (too loose or too tight), loosen the locknut and turn the adjusting screw slowly until you can feel a slight drag on the feeler gauge as you withdraw it from between the valve stem tip and the rocker arm **(see illustration)**.
5   Once the clearance is adjusted, hold the adjusting screw with a screwdriver (to keep it from turning) and tighten the locknut to the torque listed in this Chapter's Specifications. Recheck the clearance to make sure it hasn't changed after tightening the locknut.
6   Make a mark on the crankshaft pulley and an adjacent mark on the front cover. Rotate the crankshaft one complete revolution (360-degrees) and realign the marks (make sure the timing pin is removed before rotating the crankshaft). Check the clearance of the remaining valves **(see illustration)**.
7   If necessary, repeat the adjustment procedure described in Steps 3, 4 and 5 until all the valves are adjusted to specifications.
8   Install the valve covers.

29 Fan hub, damper and water pump inspection (diesel engine) (every 24,000 miles or 24 months)

Refer to illustration 29.2
1   At the specified intervals, the fan hub, engine damper and the water pump should be inspected for damage.
2   Check the fan hub, blades and attaching bolts for cracks, damage and loose fasteners **(see illustration)**.
3   Inspect the front engine pulley and damper for damage.
4   Inspect the area below the water pump for signs of coolant leakage, indicating that the pump should be replaced (see Chapter 3).

30 Fuel filter replacement and system bleeding (diesel engine) (every 24,000 miles or 24 months)

Refer to illustrations 30.3, 30.4, 30.5, 30.14 and 30.15
1   At the specified intervals, the fuel filter canister (which incorporates a water separator) should be replaced with a new one.

Removal
2   Drain any water from the filter (see Section 7).
3   Unplug the Water In Filter (WIF) sensor, detach the drain tube, then unscrew the filter canister from the housing **(see illustration)**. An oil filter wrench may be helpful in loosening the filter.

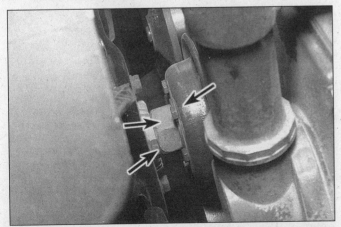

29.2 Inspect the diesel engine fan, hub and bolts (arrows) plus the water pump and crankshaft pulley damper for cracks, leaks and other damage

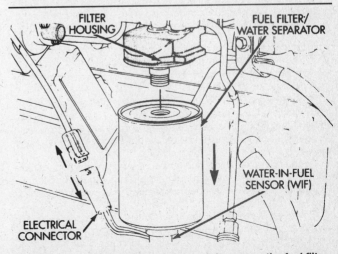

30.3 Unplug the electrical connector and unscrew the fuel filter

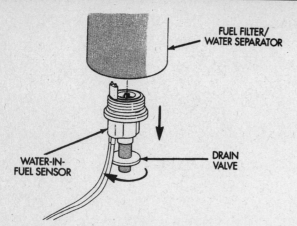

30.4 Remove the WIF sensor by unscrewing it from the fuel filter assembly

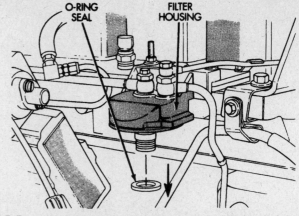

30.5 Be sure to remove the old O-ring seal from the filter housing and replace it with a new one

4   Unscrew the WIF sensor from the old filter and install it on the new one **(see illustration)**.
5   Remove the O-ring seal from the housing and discard it **(see illustration)**.
6   Carefully clean the filter housing contact area and WIF sensor probes.

Installation

7   Fill the new filter with clean fuel. **Caution:** *If the filter isn't filled with fuel, air could be trapped in the system and cause rough running.*
8   Install a new O-ring seal in the filter housing.
9   Lubricate the contact surface of the new filter with clean engine oil.
10   Apply a light coat of clean oil to the rubber gasket on the new filter.

11   Attach the new filter to the housing and tighten it one half turn by hand only. Don't use a filter wrench due to the possibility of overtightening and damage to the seal.
12   Plug in the WIF electrical connector and install the hose on the drain valve.

Bleeding

13   Should some air enter the system during the above procedure, it can be bled out through the filter housing bleed bolt.
14   With the engine off and cold, loosen the bleed bolt on the top of the filter housing **(see illustration)**.
15   Pump the rubber primer button on the fuel transfer pump until clean, bubble free fuel issues from the bleed bolt, then tighten the bolt securely **(see illustration)**.

31   Air filter replacement (gasoline engines) (every 24,000 miles or 24 months)

Refer to illustrations 31.3 and 31.9
1   At the specified intervals, the air filter element should be replaced with a new one.

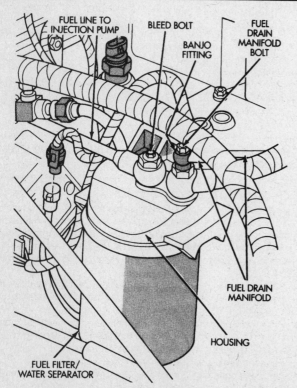

30.14 Loosen the bleed bolt located in the top of the filter housing

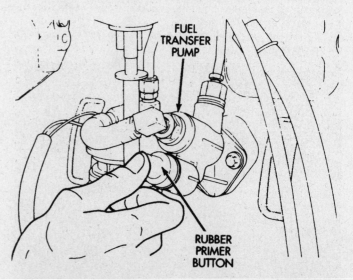

30.15 Continue to press the rubber primer button on the fuel transfer pump until bubble-free fuel comes out of the bleed bolt

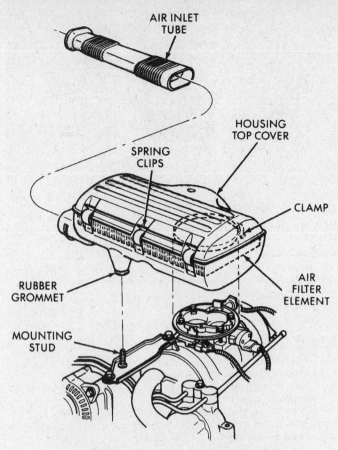

31.3 V6 and V8 engine air filter housing details

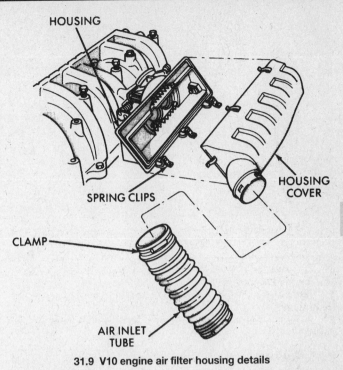

31.9 V10 engine air filter housing details

V6 and V8 engines

2   The filter housing is located on top of the throttle body.

3   Remove the air inlet tube, loosen the housing to throttle body clamp screw, then lift the assembly up and off the mounting stud **(see illustration)**. On some models it will be necessary to detach the air pump hose from the air filter.

4   Detach the spring clips and rotate the housing cover rearward, then lift the air filter element out of the housing. Wipe out the inside of the air filter housing with a clean rag.

5   While the housing is off, be careful not to drop anything down into the throttle body.

6   Place the new filter element in the air filter housing. Make sure it seats properly in the bottom of the housing.

7   Installation is the reverse of removal.

V10 engine

8   The filter is mounted on the side of the throttle body.

9   Use adjustable pliers to loosen the clamps and remove the air inlet tube, detach the spring clips and rotate the housing cover off, then lift the air filter element out of the housing **(see illustration)**. Wipe out the inside of the air filter housing with a clean rag.

10   While the housing cover is off, be careful not to drop anything down into the throttle body.

11   Place the new filter element in the air filter housing. Make sure it seats properly in the bottom of the housing.

12   Installation is the reverse of removal.

32   Automatic transmission fluid and filter change (every 24,000 miles or 24 months)

Refer to illustrations 32.6, 32.9, 32.11a and 32.11b

1   At the specified intervals, the transmission fluid should be drained and replaced. Since the fluid will remain hot long after driving, perform this procedure only after the engine has cooled down completely. The manufacturer also recommends adjusting the transmission bands at this time, since this procedure requires removing the fluid pan (see Section 33).

2   Before beginning work, purchase the specified transmission fluid (see *Recommended lubricants and fluids* at the front of this Chapter) and a new filter.

3   Other tools necessary for this job include a floor jack, jackstands to support the vehicle in a raised position, a drain pan capable of holding at least four quarts, newspapers and clean rags.

4   Raise the vehicle and support it securely on jackstands.

5   Place the drain pan underneath the transmission pan. Remove the rear and side pan mounting bolts, but only loosen the front pan bolts approximately four turns.

6   Carefully pry the transmission pan loose with a screwdriver, allowing the fluid to drain **(see illustration)**.

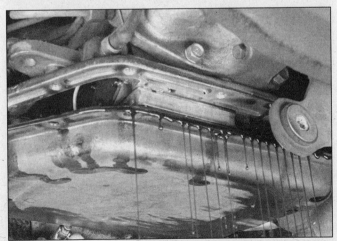

32.6 With the front bolts in place but loose, pull the rear of the pan down to drain the fluid

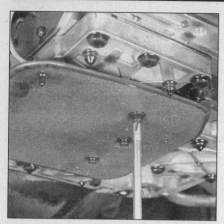

32.9 Remove the filter screws - a special Torx-head wrench is necessary

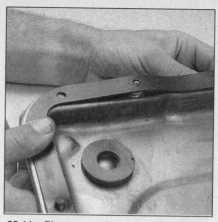

32.11a Place a new gasket in position on the pan and install the bolts to hold it in place

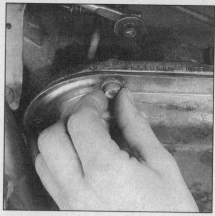

32.11b Hold the pan in place and install all of the bolts snugly before tightening them fully

7   Remove the remaining bolts, pan and gasket. Carefully clean the gasket surface of the transmission to remove all traces of the old gasket and sealant.

8   Drain the fluid from the transmission pan, clean the pan with solvent and dry it with compressed air, if available.

9   Remove the filter from the valve body inside the transmission **(see illustration)**. Use a gasket scraper to remove any traces of old gasket material that remain on the valve body. **Note:** *Be very careful not to gouge the delicate aluminum gasket surface on the valve body.*

10   Install a new gasket and filter. On many replacement filters, the gasket is attached to the filter to simplify installation.

11   Make sure the gasket surface on the transmission pan is clean, then install a new gasket on the pan **(see illustration)**. Put the pan in place against the transmission and, working around the pan, tighten each bolt a little at a time to the torque listed in this Chapter's Specifications **(see illustration)**.

12   Lower the vehicle and add approximately 3-1/2 quarts of the specified type of automatic transmission fluid through the filler tube (see Section 8).

13   With the transmission in Park and the parking brake set, run the engine at a fast idle, but don't race it.

14   Move the gear selector through each range and back to Park. Check the fluid level. It will probably be low. Add enough fluid to bring the level between the two dimples on the dipstick.

15   Check under the vehicle for leaks during the first few trips. Check the fluid level again when the transmission is hot (see Section 8).

33   Automatic transmission band adjustment (every 24,000 miles or 24 months)

Refer to illustrations 33.2 and 33.7

1   The transmission bands should be adjusted at the specified interval when the transmission fluid and filter are being replaced (see Section 32).

Front (kickdown) band

2   The front band adjusting screw is located on the left side of the transmission **(see illustration)**.

3   Raise the front of the vehicle and support it securely on jackstands.

4   Loosen the adjusting screw locknut approximately five turns, then loosen the adjusting screw a few turns. Make sure the adjusting screw turns freely, with no binding; lubricate it with penetrating oil if necessary.

5   Tighten the adjusting screw to 72 in-lbs of torque, then back it off the number of turns listed in this Chapter's Specifications. Hold the adjusting screw from turning, then tighten the locknut to the torque listed in this Chapter's Specifications.

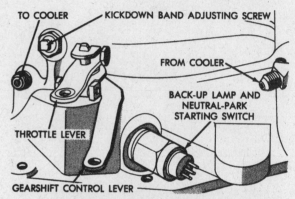

33.2 Location of the front (kickdown) band adjusting screw

33.7 Loosen the rear band locknut so the adjusting screw can be turned

Rear (low-reverse) band

6   To gain access to the rear band, the fluid pan must be removed (see Section 32).

7   Loosen the adjusting screw locknut and back it off four turns **(see illustration)**. Make sure the screw turns freely in the lever.

8   Tighten the adjusting screw to 72 in-lbs of torque, then back it off the number of turns listed in this Chapter's Specifications. Hold the screw from turning, then tighten the locknut to the torque listed in this Chapter's Specifications.

9   Install the transmission fluid pan and refill the transmission (see Section 32).

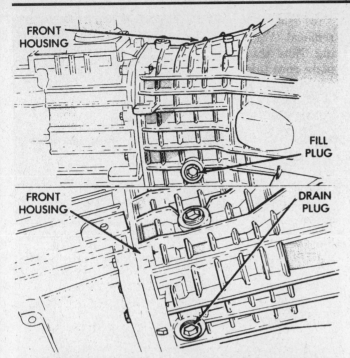

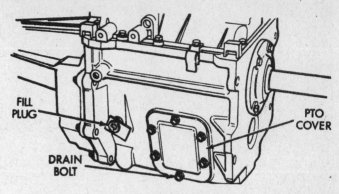

34.3b On the NV4500 transmission, the lower bolt of the PTO cover is the drain plug

5   Remove the fill plug from the side of the transmission case. Using a hand pump, syringe or funnel, fill the transmission with the specified lubricant until it begins to leak out through the hole. Reinstall the fill plug and tighten it securely.
6   Lower the vehicle.
7   Drive the vehicle for a short distance, then check the drain and fill plugs for leakage.

35   Transfer case lubricant change (4WD models) (every 24,000 miles or 24 months)

1   This procedure should be performed after the vehicle has been driven so the lubricant will be warm and therefore will flow out of the transfer case more easily.
2   Raise the vehicle and support it securely on jackstands.
3   Remove the filler plug from the case **(see illustration 18.1)**.
4   Remove the drain plug from the lower part of the case and allow the lubricant to drain completely.
5   After the case is completely drained, carefully clean and install the drain plug. Tighten the plug securely.
6   Fill the case with the specified lubricant until it is level with the lower edge of the filler hole.
7   Install the filler plug and tighten it securely.
8   Drive the vehicle for a short distance and recheck the lubricant level. In some instances a small amount of additional lubricant will have to be added.

34.3a NV3500 transmission drain and fill plug locations

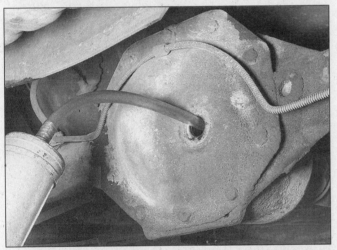

36.3 This is the easiest way to remove the lubricant: work the end of the hose to the bottom of the differential housing and draw out the old lubricant with a hand pump

36   Differential lubricant change (every 24,000 miles or 24 months)

Refer to illustration 36.3, 36.4a, 36.4b, 36.4c and 36.6
1   This procedure should be performed after the vehicle has been driven so the lubricant will be warm and therefore will flow out of the differential more easily.
2   Raise the vehicle and support it securely on jackstands. If the differential has a bolt-on cover at the rear, it is usually easiest to remove the cover to drain the lubricant (which will also allow you to inspect the differential). If there's no bolt-on cover, look for a drain plug at the bottom of the differential housing. If there's not a drain plug and no cover, you'll have to remove the lubricant through the filler plug hole with a suction pump. If you'll be draining the lubricant by removing the cover or a drain plug, move a drain pan, rags, newspapers and wrenches under the vehicle.
3   Remove the filler plug from the differential (see Section 19). If a suction pump is being used, insert the flexible hose. Work the hose down to the bottom of the differential housing and pump the lubricant out **(see illustration)**. If you'll be draining the lubricant through a drain plug, remove the plug and allow it to drain into the pan, then reinstall the drain plug.

34   Manual transmission lubricant change (every 24,000 miles or 24 months)

Refer to illustrations 34.3a and 34.3b
1   This procedure should be performed after the vehicle has been driven so the lubricant will be warm and therefore will flow out of the transmission more easily. Raise the vehicle and support it securely on jackstands.
2   Move a drain pan, rags, newspapers and wrenches under the transmission.
3   Remove the transmission drain plug at the bottom of the case and allow the lubricant to drain into the pan **(see illustration)**. The NV4500 transmission has no drain plug; remove the lower PTO cover bolt to drain the lubricant **(see illustration)**.
4   After the lubricant has drained completely, reinstall the plug and tighten it securely.

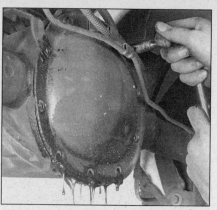

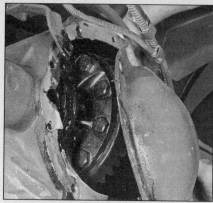

36.4a Remove the bolts from the lower edge of the cover . . .

36.4b . . . then loosen the top bolts and allow the lubricant drain out

36.4c After the lubricant has drained, remove the remaining bolts and the cover

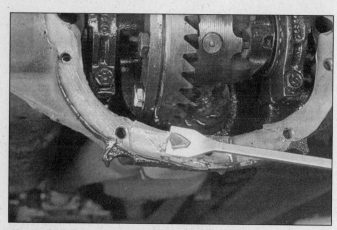

36.6 Carefully scrape the old gasket material off to ensure a leak-free seal

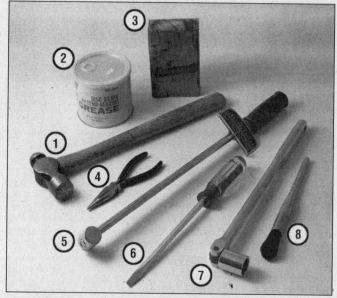

37.1 Tools and materials needed for front wheel bearing maintenance

4   If the differential is being drained by removing the cover plate, remove the bolts on the lower half of the plate. Loosen the bolts on the upper half and use them to keep the cover loosely attached. Allow the oil to drain into the pan, then completely remove the cover **(see illustrations)**.

5   Using a lint-free rag, clean the inside of the cover and the accessible areas of the differential housing. As this is done, check for chipped gears and metal particles in the lubricant, indicating that the differential should be more thoroughly inspected and/or repaired.

6   Thoroughly clean the gasket mating surfaces of the differential housing and the cover plate. Use a gasket scraper or putty knife to remove all traces of the old gasket **(see illustration)**.

7   Apply a thin layer of RTV sealant to the cover flange, then press a new gasket into position on the cover. Make sure the bolt holes align properly.

8   Place the cover on the differential housing and install the bolts. Tighten the bolts securely.

9   Use a hand pump, syringe or funnel to fill the differential housing with the specified lubricant until it's level with the bottom of the plug hole.

10   Install the filler plug and make sure it is secure.

37   Front wheel bearing check, repack and adjustment (2WD models) (every 30,000 miles or 30 months)

Refer to illustrations 37.1, 37.6, 37.7, 37.8, 37.9, 37.10, 37.12, 37.15, 37.19 and 37.22

1   In most cases the front wheel bearings will not need servicing until the brake pads are changed. However, the bearings should be checked whenever the front of the vehicle is raised for any reason.

1   *Hammer - A common hammer will do just fine*
2   *Grease - High-temperature grease that is formulated for front wheel bearings should be used*
3   *Wood block - If you have a scrap piece of 2x4, it can be used to drive the new seal into the hub*
4   *Needle-nose pliers - Used to straighten and remove the cotter pin in the spindle*
5   *Torque wrench - This is very important in this procedure; if the bearing is too tight, the wheel won't turn freely - if it's too loose, the wheel will "wobble" on the spindle. Either way, it could mean extensive damage*
6   *Screwdriver - Used to remove the seal from the hub (a long screwdriver is preferred)*
7   *Socket/breaker bar - Needed to loosen the nut on the spindle if it's extremely tight*
8   *Brush - Together with some clean solvent, this will be used to remove old grease from the hub and spindle*

Several items, including a torque wrench and special grease, are required for this procedure **(see illustration)**.

2   With the vehicle securely supported on jackstands, spin each wheel and check for noise, rolling resistance and freeplay.

3   Grasp the top of each tire with one hand and the bottom with the other. Move the wheel in-and-out on the spindle. If there's any noticeable movement, the bearings should be checked and then repacked

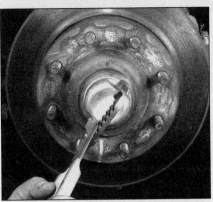

37.6 You may be able to use large pliers to grasp the grease cap securely and work it out of the hub - if it's stuck, you'll have to use a hammer and chisel to detach it

37.7 Remove the cotter pin

37.8 Remove the nut lock and nut

1

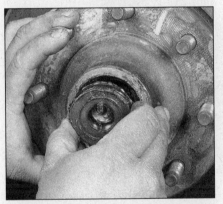

37.9 Pull the hub out to dislodge the outer wheel bearing and washer

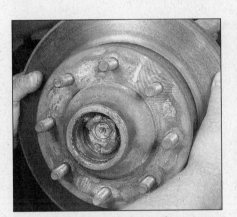

37.10 Reinstall the hub nut, then grasp the hub securely and pull out sharply to dislodge the inner bearing and seal against the back of the nut

37.12 Slide the inner bearing and seal assembly off the spindle

with grease or replaced if necessary.

4   Remove the wheel.

5   Remove the brake caliper (see Chapter 9) and hang it out of the way on a piece of wire. A wood block can be slid between the brake pads to keep them separated, if necessary.

6   Remove the dust cap using large pliers or by prying it out of the hub using a hammer and chisel **(see illustration)**.

37.15 Work the grease completely into the bearing rollers - if you don't like getting greasy, special bearing packing tools that work with a common grease gun are available inexpensively from auto parts stores

7   Straighten the bent ends of the cotter pin, then pull the cotter pin out of the nut lock **(see illustration)**. Discard the cotter pin and use a new one during reassembly.

8   Remove the nut lock, nut and washer from the end of the spindle **(see illustration)**.

9   Pull the hub/disc assembly out slightly, then push it back into its original position. This should force the outer bearing off the spindle enough so it can be removed **(see illustration)**.

10   Temporarily reinstall the hub/disc assembly and spindle nut. Dislodge the inner bearing and seal by grasping the assembly and pulling out sharply **(see illustration)**.

11   Once the bearing and seal are free, remove the hub/disc assembly from the spindle.

12   Remove the inner wheel bearing and seal from the spindle, noting how the seal is installed **(see illustration)**.

13   Use solvent to remove all traces of the old grease from the bearings, hub and spindle. A small brush may prove helpful; however make sure no bristles from the brush embed themselves inside the bearing rollers. Allow the parts to air dry.

14   Carefully inspect the bearings for cracks, heat discoloration, worn rollers, etc. Check the bearing races inside the hub for wear and damage. If the bearing races are defective, the hubs should be taken to a machine shop with the facilities to remove the old races and press new ones in. Note that the bearings and races come as matched sets and old bearings should never be installed on new races.

15   Use high-temperature front wheel bearing grease to pack the bearings. Work the grease completely into the bearings, forcing it between the rollers, cone and cage from the back side **(see illustration)**.

37.19 Use a block of wood and a hammer to tap the inner bearing seal evenly into the hub

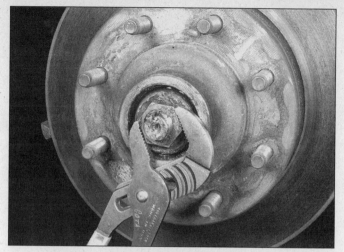

37.22 Seat the bearings by spinning the hub while tightening the hub nut

16   Apply a thin coat of grease to the spindle at the outer bearing seat, inner bearing seat, shoulder and seal seat.

17   Put a small quantity of grease inboard of each bearing race inside the hub. Using your finger, form a dam at these points to provide extra grease availability and to keep thinned grease from flowing out of the bearing.

18   Place the grease-packed inner bearing into the rear of the hub and put a little more grease outboard of the bearing.

19   Place a new seal over the inner bearing and tap the seal evenly into place with a hammer and blunt punch until it's flush with the hub **(see illustration)**.

20   Carefully place the hub assembly onto the spindle and push the grease-packed outer bearing into position.

21   Install the washer and spindle nut. Tighten the nut only slightly (no more than 12 ft-lbs of torque).

22   Spin the hub in a forward direction while tightening the spindle nut to approximately 20 ft-lbs to seat the bearings and remove any grease or burrs which could cause excessive bearing play later **(see illustration)**.

23   Loosen the spindle nut 1/4-turn, then using your hand (not a wrench of any kind), tighten the nut until it's snug. Install the nut lock and a new cotter pin through the hole in the spindle and the slots in the nut lock. If the nut lock slots don't line up, remove the nut lock and turn it slightly until they do.

24   Bend the ends of the cotter pin until they're flat against the nut. Cut off any extra length which could interfere with the dust cap.

25   Install the dust cap, tapping it into place with a hammer.

26   Place the brake caliper near the rotor and carefully remove the wood spacer. Install the caliper (see Chapter 9).

27   Install the wheel on the hub and tighten the lug nuts.

28   Grasp the top and bottom of the tire and check the bearings in the manner described earlier in this Section.

29   Lower the vehicle.

38 Cooling system servicing (draining, flushing and refilling) (every 30,000 miles or 30 months)

Refer to illustrations 38.3 and 38.4

Warning: *Do not allow antifreeze to come in contact with your skin or painted surfaces of the vehicle. Rinse off spills immediately with plenty of water. Antifreeze is highly toxic if ingested. Never leave antifreeze lying around in an open container or in puddles on the floor; children and pets are attracted by it's sweet smell and may drink it. Check with local authorities about disposing of used antifreeze. Many communities have collection centers which will see that antifreeze is disposed of safely.*

38.3 The radiator drain (arrow) is located at the corner of the radiator

1   Periodically, the cooling system should be drained, flushed and refilled to replenish the antifreeze mixture and prevent formation of rust and corrosion, which can impair the performance of the cooling system and cause engine damage. When the cooling system is serviced, all hoses and the radiator cap should be checked and replaced if necessary.

2   Apply the parking brake and block the wheels. **Warning:** *If the vehicle has just been driven, wait several hours to allow the engine to cool down before beginning this procedure.*

3   Move a large container under the radiator drain to catch the coolant. The drain plug is located on the lower left side of the radiator **(see illustration)**. Attach a 3/8-inch diameter hose to the drain fitting (if possible) to direct the coolant into the container, then open the drain fitting (a pair of pliers may be required to turn it). Remove the radiator cap.

4   After coolant stops flowing out of the radiator, move the container under the engine block drain plugs (gasoline engines only) - there's one on each side of the block **(see illustration)**. Remove the plugs and allow the coolant in the block to drain. **Note:** *Frequently, the coolant will not drain from the block after the plug is removed. This is due to a rust layer that has built up behind the plug. Insert a Phillips screwdriver into the hole to break the rust barrier.*

5   While the coolant is draining, check the condition of the radiator hoses, heater hoses and clamps (refer to Section 12 if necessary).

6   Replace any damaged clamps or hoses.

7   Once the system is completely drained, flush the radiator with

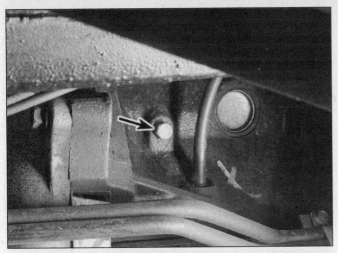

38.4 Gasoline engine cylinder block drain location - there is one on each side of the block

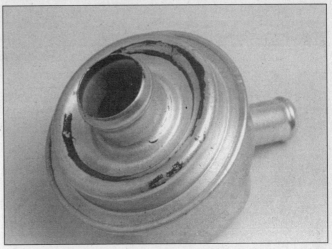

39.4 Lubricate the filter by pouring clean engine oil into the large opening until it drains out the smaller opening

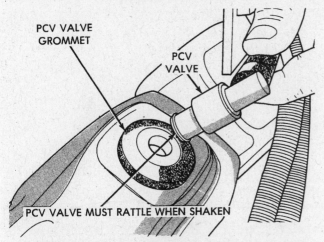

40.2 The PCV valve is pressed into a rubber grommet in the valve cover

fresh water from a garden hose until it runs clear at the drain. The flushing action of the water will remove sediments from the radiator but will not remove rust and scale from the engine and cooling tube surfaces.

8   A limited amount of deposits can be removed with a chemical cleaner. Follow the procedure outlined in the manufacturer's instructions. If the radiator is severely corroded, damaged or leaking, it should be removed (see Chapter 3) and taken to a radiator repair shop.

9   Remove the overflow hose from the coolant reservoir and flush the reservoir with clean water, then reconnect the hose.

10   Close and tighten the radiator drain fitting. Install and tighten the block drain plugs, if equipped.

11   Place the heater temperature control in the maximum heat position.

Diesel engine

12   Fill the system with coolant (a 50/50 mixture of water and antifreeze) and install the radiator cap. The diesel cooling system features a one-way valve that vents air as coolant is added. Consequently it isn't necessary to run the engine to vent air from the cooling system as is required with a gasoline engine.

Gasoline engines

13   Slowly add coolant (a 50/50 mixture of water and antifreeze) to the radiator until it's full. Add coolant to the reservoir up to the lower mark.

14   Leave the radiator cap off and run the engine in a well-ventilated area until the thermostat opens (coolant will begin flowing through the radiator and the upper radiator hose will become hot).

15   Turn the engine off and let it cool. Add more coolant mixture to bring the level back up to the lip on the radiator filler neck.

16   Squeeze the upper radiator hose to expel air, then add more coolant mixture if necessary. Replace the radiator cap.

39   Crankcase inlet filter cleaning (every 30,000 miles or 30 months)

Refer to illustration 39.4

1   The crankcase inlet filter, used on V6 and V8 engines, must be cleaned at the specified intervals.

2   Disconnect the hose and pull the crankcase inlet filter out of the valve cover.

3   Wash the inside of the filter with solvent.

4   Lubricate the filter by pouring clean engine oil into the large opening and allowing into to drain out through the smaller (inlet) opening **(see illustration)**.

5   Reinstall the filter in the valve cover and connect the hose.

40   Positive Crankcase Ventilation (PCV) valve check and replacement (every 30,000 miles or 30 months)

Refer to illustration 40.2

1   The PCV valve is located in the valve cover.

2   With the engine idling at normal operating temperature, pull the valve (with hose attached) from the rubber grommet in the cover **(see illustration)**.

3   Place your finger over the valve opening. If there's no vacuum at the valve, check for a plugged hose, manifold port, or the valve itself. Replace any plugged or deteriorated hoses.

4   Turn off the engine and shake the PCV valve, listening for a rattle. If the valve doesn't rattle, replace it with a new one.

5   To replace the valve, pull it from the end of the hose, noting its installed position.

6   When purchasing a replacement PCV valve, make sure it's for your particular vehicle and engine size. Compare the old valve with the new one to make sure they're the same.

7   Push the valve into the end of the hose until it's seated.

8   Inspect the rubber grommet for damage and hardening. Replace it with a new one if necessary.

9   Push the PCV valve and hose securely into position.

41.2 The evaporative emissions canister is located under the left front of the engine compartment - check the hoses and connections (arrows) for damage

41   Evaporative emissions control system check (every 30,000 miles or 30 months)

Refer to illustration 41.2

1   The function of the evaporative emissions control system used on gasoline engines is to draw fuel vapors from the gas tank and fuel system, store them in a charcoal canister and route them to the intake manifold during normal engine operation.

2   The most common symptom of a fault in the evaporative emissions system is a strong fuel odor in the engine compartment. If a fuel odor is detected, inspect the charcoal canister, located on the frame rail under the left side of the vehicle **(see illustration)**. Check the canister and all hoses for damage and deterioration.

3   The evaporative emissions control system is explained in more detail in Chapter 6.

42   Spark plug check and replacement (every 30,000 miles or 30 months)

Refer to illustrations 42.2, 42.5a, 42.5b, 42.6a, 42.6b, 42.8, 42.10 and 42.12

1   The spark plugs are threaded into the sides of the cylinder heads, adjacent to the exhaust ports.

2   In most cases, the tools necessary for spark plug replacement include a spark plug socket which fits onto a ratchet (spark plug sockets are padded inside to prevent damage to the porcelain insulators on the new plugs), various extensions and a gap gauge to check and adjust the gaps on the new plugs **(see illustration)**. A special plug wire removal tool is available for separating the wire boots from the spark plugs, but it isn't absolutely necessary. A torque wrench should be used to tighten the new plugs.

3   The best approach when replacing the spark plugs is to purchase the new ones in advance, adjust them to the proper gap and replace them one at a time. When buying the new spark plugs, be sure to obtain the correct plug type for your particular engine. This information can be found on the *Emission Control Information* label located under the hood, in the factory owner's manual and the Specifications at the front of this Chapter. If differences exist between the plug specified on the emissions label and in the owner's manual, assume that the emissions label is correct.

4   Allow the engine to cool completely before attempting to remove any of the plugs. While you're waiting for the engine to cool, check the new plugs for defects and adjust the gaps.

5   The gap is checked by inserting the proper-thickness gauge

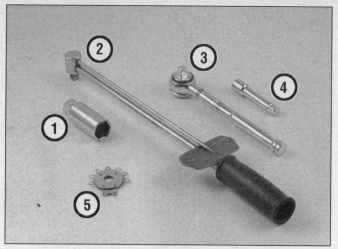

42.2 Tools required for changing spark plugs

1   **Spark plug socket** - This will have special padding inside to protect the spark plug's porcelain insulator
2   **Torque wrench** - Although not mandatory, using this tool is the best way to ensure the plugs are tightened properly
3   **Ratchet** - Standard hand tool to fit the spark plug socket
4   **Extension** - Depending on model and accessories, you may need special extensions and universal joints to reach one or more of the plugs
5   **Spark plug gap gauge** - This gauge for checking the gap comes in a variety of styles. Make sure the gap for your engine is included

between the electrodes at the tip of the plug **(see illustration)**. The gap between the electrodes should be the same as the one specified on the *Emissions Control Information* label or in this Chapter's Specifications. The wire should just slide between the electrodes with a slight amount of drag. If the gap is incorrect, use the adjuster on the gauge body to bend the curved side electrode slightly until the proper gap is obtained **(see illustration)**. If the side electrode is not exactly over the center electrode, bend it with the adjuster until it is. Check for cracks in the porcelain insulator (if any are found, the plug should not be used).

6   With the engine cool, remove the spark plug wire from one spark plug. Pull only on the boot at the end of the wire - do not pull on the wire **(see illustration)**. A plug wire removal tool should be used if available **(see illustration)**.

7   If compressed air is available, use it to blow any dirt or foreign material away from the spark plug hole. A common bicycle pump will also work. The idea here is to eliminate the possibility of debris falling into the cylinder as the spark plug is removed.

8   Place the spark plug socket over the plug and remove it from the engine by turning it in a counterclockwise direction **(see illustration)**.

9   Compare the spark plug with the chart on the inside back cover of this manual to get an indication of the general running condition of the engine.

10   Thread one of the new plugs into the hole until you can no longer turn it with your fingers, then tighten it with a torque wrench (if available) or the ratchet. It might be a good idea to slip a short length of rubber hose over the end of the plug to use as a tool to thread it into place **(see illustration)**. The hose will grip the plug well enough to turn it, but will start to slip if the plug begins to cross-thread in the hole - this will prevent damaged threads and the accompanying repair costs.

11   Before pushing the spark plug wire onto the end of the plug, inspect it following the procedures outlined in Section 43.

12   Attach the plug wire to the new spark plug, again using a twisting motion on the boot until it's seated on the spark plug. On V6 and V8 engines, make sure there is an air gap between the lip of the boot and the top of the metal spark plug heat shields **(see illustration)**.

13   Repeat the procedure for the remaining spark plugs, replacing them one at a time to prevent mixing up the spark plug wires.

42.5a Spark plug manufacturers recommend using a wire-type gauge when checking the gap - if the wire does not slide between the electrodes with a slight drag, adjustment is required

42.5b To change the gap, bend the side electrode only, as indicated by the arrows, and be very careful not to crack or chip the porcelain insulator surrounding the center electrode

42.6a When removing the spark plug wires, twist it back-and-forth and pull only on the boot

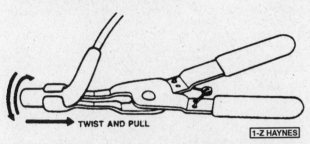

42.6b A tool like this one makes the job of removing the spark plug boot easier

42.8 Use a socket and extension to unscrew the spark plugs

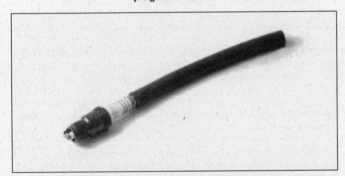

42.10 A length of 3/8-inch ID rubber hose will save time and prevent damaged threads when installing the spark plugs

43 Spark plug wires and distributor cap and rotor - check and replacement (every 30,000 miles or 30 months)

Refer to illustrations 43.10 and 43.13
Note: *V10 engines are equipped with a distributorless ignition system. The spark plug wires are connected directly to the ignition coils. The distributor used on the V6 and V8 engines is mounted at the rear of the block.*

1   The spark plug wires should be checked at the recommended intervals and whenever new spark plugs are installed in the engine.
2   The wires should be inspected one at a time to prevent mixing up the order, which is essential for proper engine operation.
3   Disconnect the plug wire from one spark plug. To do this, grab the rubber boot, twist slightly and pull the wire free. Do not pull on the wire itself, only on the rubber boot.
4   Check inside the boot for corrosion, which will look like a white

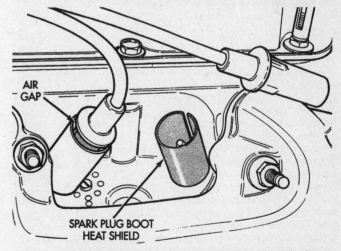

42.12 Make sure there is an air gap between the lip of the boot and the top of the metal spark plug heat shield used on V6 and V8 engines

crusty powder. Push the wire and boot back onto the end of the spark plug. It should be a tight fit on the plug. If it isn't, remove the wire and use a pair of pliers to carefully crimp the metal connector inside the boot until it fits securely on the end of the spark plug.

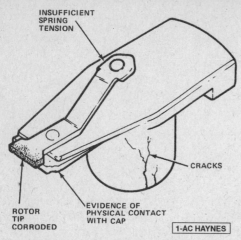

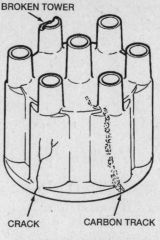

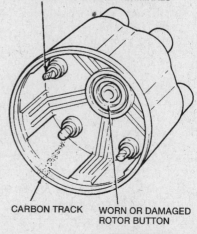

43.10 The ignition rotor should be checked for wear and corrosion as indicated here (if in doubt about its condition, buy a new one)

5   Using a clean rag, wipe the entire length of the wire to remove any built-up dirt and grease. Once the wire is clean, check for holes, burned areas, cracks and other damage. Don't bend the wire excessively or the conductor inside might break.

6   Disconnect the wire from the distributor cap. Pull the wire straight out of the cap. Pull only on the rubber boot during removal. Check for corrosion and a tight fit in the same manner as the spark plug end. Reattach the wire to the distributor cap.

7   Check the remaining spark plug wires one at a time, making sure they are securely fastened at the distributor and the spark plug when the check is complete.

8   If new spark plug wires are required, purchase a new set for your specific engine model. Wire sets are available pre-cut, with the rubber boots already installed. Remove and replace the wires one at a time to avoid mix-ups in the firing order. The wire routing is extremely important, so be sure to note exactly how each wire is situated before removing it.

9   Remove the distributor cap screws. Pull up on the cap, with the wires attached, to separate it from the distributor, then position it to one side.

10   The rotor is now visible on the end of the distributor shaft. Check it carefully for cracks and carbon tracks. Make sure the center terminal spring tension is adequate and look for corrosion and wear on the rotor tip **(see illustration)**. If in doubt about its condition, replace it with a new one.

11   If replacement is required, detach the rotor from the shaft and install a new one. The rotor is a press fit on the shaft and can be pried or pulled off.

12   The rotor is indexed to the shaft so it can only be installed one way. It has an internal key that must line up with a slot in the end of the shaft (or vice versa).

13   Check the distributor cap for carbon tracks, cracks and other damage. Closely examine the terminals on the inside of the cap for excessive corrosion and damage **(see illustration)**. Slight deposits are normal. Again, if in doubt about the condition of the cap, replace it with a new one. Be sure to apply a small dab of silicone dielectric grease to each terminal before installing the cap. Also, make sure the carbon brush (center terminal) is correctly installed in the cap - a wide gap between the brush and rotor will result in rotor burn-through and/or damage to the distributor cap.

14   To replace the cap, simply separate it from the distributor and transfer the spark plug wires, one at a time, to the new cap. Be very careful not to mix up the wires!

15   Reattach the cap to the distributor, then install the screws to hold it in place.

43.13 Shown here are some of the common defects to look for when inspecting the distributor cap (if in doubt about its condition, install a new one)

44   Emissions Maintenance (MAINT REQD) Reminder light

General information

Note: *The Maintenance Reminder light is used on Heavy Duty 5.9L V8 and 8.0L V10 gasoline powered models only.*

The Emissions Maintenance Reminder (EMR) light is designed as a reminder that the vehicle emissions control systems requires maintenance. It is not a warning, only a reminder to service the emissions system. The PCM will illuminate the MAINT REQD light after a predetermined mileage has elapsed. The light will stay on until the emissions service is performed and the light reset. The components that require servicing are the EGR system, PCV system, EVAP system, and the oxygen sensor. Refer to the *Maintenance Schedule* and the appropriate sections of this Chapter for details on checking and replacing the components, if necessary.

Resetting the EMR light requires a special tool (Chrysler DRB-II tester, or equivalent). After performing the emissions service, take the vehicle to a Chrysler dealership service department or other properly equipped repair facility to have the light reset. Resetting the light without performing the required emissions service may be a violation of federal law.

Chapter 2 Part A
Gasoline engines

Contents

Specifications

Bore and stroke

3.9L V6 (239 cubic inches)	3.91 x 3.31 inches
5.2L V8 (318 cubic inches)	3.91 x 3.31 inches
5.9L V8 (360 cubic inches)	4.00 x 3.58 inches
8.0L V10 (488 cubic inches)	4.00 x 3.88 inches

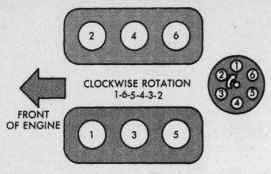

Cylinder location and distributor rotation - V6 engine

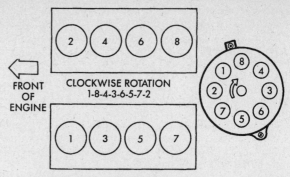

Cylinder location and distributor rotation - V8 engines

General

Cylinder numbers (front-to-rear)	
V6	
Left (driver's) side..........................	1-3-5
Right side..........................	2-4-6
Firing order..........................	1-6-5-4-3-2
V8	
Left (driver's) side..........................	1-3-5-7
Right side..........................	2-4-6-8
Firing order..........................	1-8-4-3-6-5-7-2
V10	
Left (driver's) side..........................	1-3-5-7-9
Right side..........................	2-4-6-8-10
Firing order..........................	1-10-9-4-3-6-5-8-7-2
Distributor rotation (V6 and V8) (viewed from above).........	Clockwise
Minimum compression..........................	100 psi
Maximum variation between cylinders..........................	40 psi

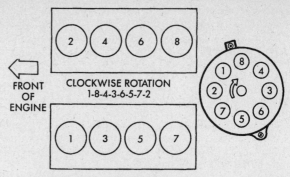

Cylinder and coil terminal locations - V10 engine

Camshaft

Journal diameters	
V6	
No. 1..........................	1.998 to 1.999 inches
No. 2..........................	1.982 to 1.983 inches
No. 3..........................	1.951 to 1.952 inches
No. 4..........................	1.5605 to 1.5615 inches
V8	
No. 1..........................	1.998 to 1.999 inches
No. 2..........................	1.982 to 1.983 inches
No. 3..........................	1.967 to 1.968 inches
No. 4..........................	1.951 to 1.952 inches
No. 5..........................	1.5605 to 1.5615 inches
V10	
No. 1..........................	2.091 to 2.092 inches
No. 2..........................	2.0745 to 2.0755 inches
No. 3..........................	2.059 to 2.060 inches
No. 4..........................	2.043 to 2.044 inches
No. 5..........................	2.027 to 2.028 inches
No. 6..........................	1.917 to 1.918 inches
Endplay	
V6 and V8..........................	0.002 to 0.010 inch
V10..........................	0.005 to 0.015 inch

Valve lift

V6 and 5.2L V8, intake and exhaust..........................	0.432 inch
5.9L V8, intake and exhaust..........................	0.410 inch
V10	
Intake..........................	0.390 inch
Exhaust..........................	0.407 inch

Oil pump

Minimum pressure at curb idle..........................	8 psi
Operating pressure..........................	30 to 80 psi at 2000 rpm
Outer rotor thickness limit	
V6 and V8..........................	0.825 inch minimum
V10..........................	0.5876 inch minimum

Outer rotor diameter limit	
V6 and V8	2.469 inches minimum
V10	3.246 inches minimum
Inner rotor thickness limit	
V6 and V8	0.825 inch minimum
V10	0.5876 to 0.5886 inch minimum
Clearance over rotors	
V6 and V8	0.004 inch maximum
V10	0.0075 inch maximum
Outer rotor clearance limit	
V6 and V8	0.014 inch maximum
V10	0.006 inch maximum
Rotor tip clearance limit	
V6 and V8	0.008 inch maximum
V10	0.0230 inch maximum

Torque specifications*

Ft-lbs (unless otherwise indicated)

Camshaft sprocket bolt	
V6 and V8	50
V10	55
Camshaft thrust plate bolts	
V6 and V8	210 in-lbs
V10	192 in-lbs
Crankshaft pulley bolts	200 in-lbs
Cylinder head bolts	
V6 and V8	
First step	50
Second step	105
V10	
First step	43
Second step	105
Engine mount-to-block bolts	60
Engine mount through-bolt nuts	75
Exhaust manifold bolts/nuts	
V6 and V8	25
V10	192 in-lbs
Exhaust pipe flange nuts	24
Flywheel/driveplate bolts	55
Intake manifold bolts	
V6 and V8	
Step 1	72 in-lbs
Step 2	72 in-lbs
Step 3	144 in-lbs
Step 4	144 in-lbs
V10	
Lower manifold	40
Upper manifold	200 in-lbs
Intake plenum pan bolts (V6 and V8)	
Step 1	24 in-lbs
Step 2	48 in-lbs
Step 3	84 in-lbs
Oil pan bolts/studs	
V6 and V8	200 in-lbs
V10	144 in-lbs
Oil pump cover bolts	
V6 and V8	95 in-lbs
V10	125 in-lbs
Oil pump mounting bolts (V6 and V8)	30
Rocker arm bolts	
V6 and V8	200 in-lbs
V10	21
Timing chain cover bolts	
V6 and V8	30
V10	35
Rear oil seal retainer bolts (V10)	192 in-lbs
Valve cover nuts/studs	
V6 and V8	95 in-lbs
V10	144 in-lbs
Vibration damper-to-crankshaft bolt	135
Water pump-to-cover bolts	30

*Note: Refer to Part C for additional specifications

2A

3.4 Mark the base of the distributor below the number one spark plug terminal

3.6 Align the full-width groove on the damper with the "0" or "TDC" marks on the timing cover

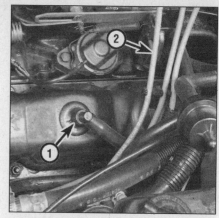

4.3 Remove the PCV valve or breather tube and move the spark plug wires aside

1   *PCV valve*
2   *Spark plug wires*

1   General information

This part of Chapter 2 is devoted to in-vehicle repair procedures for V6, V8 and V10 engines. All information concerning engine removal and installation and engine block and cylinder head overhaul can be found in Part C of this Chapter.

Since the repair procedures included in this Part are based on the assumption that the engine is still installed in the vehicle, if they are being used during a complete engine overhaul (with the engine already out of the vehicle and on a stand) many of the steps included here will not apply.

The specifications included in this Part of Chapter 2 apply only to the procedures found here. The specifications necessary for rebuilding the block and cylinder heads are included in Part C.

Though the engines covered vary greatly in displacement, they all share the same basic design. The 5.2L and 5.9L V8's have been in the corporate line for decades, and the V6 is basically the same design without two of the cylinders, while the V10 shares most characteristics, but with two more cylinders added to the V8 design.

2   Repair operations possible with the engine in the vehicle

Many major repair operations can be accomplished without removing the engine from the vehicle.

Clean the engine compartment and the exterior of the engine with some type of pressure washer before any work is done. A clean engine will make the job easier and will help keep dirt out of the internal areas of the engine.

Depending on the components involved, it may be a good idea to remove the hood to improve access to the engine as repairs are performed (refer to Chapter 11 if necessary).

If oil or coolant leaks develop, indicating a need for gasket or seal replacement, the repairs can generally be made with the engine in the vehicle. The oil pan gasket (the exception is the V10, which requires engine removal to remove the oil pan), the cylinder head gaskets, intake and exhaust manifold gaskets, timing chain cover gaskets and the crankshaft oil seals are all accessible with the engine in place.

Exterior engine components, such as the water pump, the starter motor, the alternator, the distributor and the fuel injection components, as well as the intake and exhaust manifolds, can be removed for repair with the engine in place.

Since the cylinder heads can be removed without removing the engine, valve component servicing can also be accomplished with the engine in the vehicle.

Replacement of, repairs to or inspection of the timing chain and sprockets and the oil pump are all possible with the engine in place.

In extreme cases caused by a lack of necessary equipment, repair or replacement of piston rings, pistons, connecting rods and rod bearings is possible with the engine in the vehicle. However, this practice is not recommended because of the cleaning and preparation work that must be done to the components involved.

3   Top Dead Center (TDC) for number one piston - locating

Refer to illustrations 3.4 and 3.6

1   Top Dead Center (TDC) is the highest point in the cylinder that each piston reaches as it travels up-and-down when the crankshaft turns. Each piston reaches TDC on the compression stroke and again on the exhaust stroke, but TDC generally refers to piston position on the compression stroke. The timing marks are referenced to the number one piston at TDC on the compression stroke.

2   Positioning the pistons at TDC is an essential part of many procedures such as camshaft removal, timing chain replacement and distributor removal.

3   In order to bring any piston to TDC, the crankshaft must be turned using one of the methods outlined below. When looking at the front of the engine, normal crankshaft rotation is clockwise. **Warning:** *Before beginning this procedure, be sure to place the transmission in Neutral (manual) or Park (automatic), apply the parking brake and block the wheels. On V6 and V8 engines disable the ignition system by disconnecting the coil wire from the distributor cap and grounding it on the engine block. On the V10 engine, there is no distributor. Disable the ignition by removing the IGN-RUN fuse from the Power Distribution Center (see Chapter 12).*

4   On V6 and V8 engines, scribe or paint a small mark on the distributor body directly below the number one spark plug wire terminal in the distributor cap **(see illustration)**.

5   Remove the distributor cap as described in Chapter 1.

6   Turn the crankshaft with a large socket and breaker bar attached to the large bolt that is threaded into the damper until the line on the vibration damper is aligned with the zero or "TDC" mark on the timing indicator **(see illustration)**.

7   The rotor should now be pointing directly at the mark on the distributor base. If it is 180-degrees off, the piston is at TDC on the exhaust stroke.

8   If the rotor is 180-degrees off, turn the crankshaft one complete turn (360-degrees) clockwise. The rotor should now be pointing at the mark. When the rotor is pointing at the number one spark plug wire terminal in the distributor cap (which is indicated by the mark on the dis-

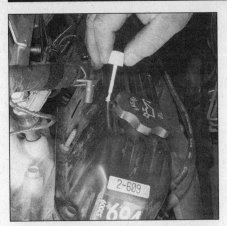

4.5a Remove the valve cover mounting nuts - some fasteners have studs, so mark their locations before removal

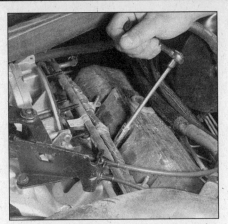

4.5b After removing the air cleaner cover and housing, the left valve cover on V10 engines is accessible

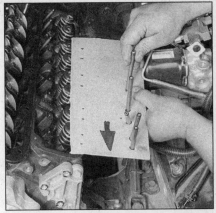

5.3 A perforated sheet of cardboard can be used to store the pushrods to ensure that they're reinstalled in their original locations - note the arrow indicating the front of the engine

2A

tributor body) and the timing marks are aligned, the number one piston is at TDC on the compression stroke.

9   After the number one piston has been positioned at TDC on the compression stroke, TDC for any of the remaining cylinders can be located by rotating the crankshaft, in the normal direction of rotation, until the distributor rotor is pointing to the distributor cap spark plug wire terminal and following the firing order. **Note:** *You can also mark the vibration damper every 120-degrees (V6) or 90-degrees (V8) from TDC. After TDC for number 1 is found, rotate the crankshaft to the first mark to located TDC for the next cylinder in the firing order, etc.*

10   On the V10 engine, there is an alternative method (this method can also be used on the other engines). Remove the number 1 spark plug. Disable the ignition as described in Step 3. Place a finger over the number 1 spark plug hole and rotate the crankshaft with a breaker bar until compression pressure is felt being expelled from the spark plug hole. Continue rotating the crankshaft until the TDC mark lines up. This will be TDC for number 1 piston.

4   Valve covers - removal and installation

Removal

Refer to illustrations 4.3, 4.5a and 4.5b

1   Disconnect the battery cable from the negative battery terminal.
2   Remove the air cleaner assembly (see Chapter 4A).
3   Remove the breather tube or PCV valve and hose **(see illustration)**.
4   Disconnect the evaporative emissions hoses.
5   Remove the valve cover mounting bolts **(see illustrations)**. **Note:** *On the V10 engine, the upper intake manifold will have to be removed to service the right valve cover. Also, note the location of any studs on the V10 covers.*
6   Remove the valve cover. **Note:** *If the cover is stuck to the head, bump the cover with a block of wood and a hammer to release it. If it still will not come loose, try to slip a flexible putty knife between the head and cover to break the seal. Don't pry at the cover-to-head joint, as damage to the sealing surface and cover flange will result and oil leaks will develop.*

Installation

7   The mating surfaces of each cylinder head and valve cover must be perfectly clean when the covers are installed. Use a gasket scraper to remove all traces of sealant or old gasket, then wipe the mating surfaces with a cloth saturated with lacquer thinner or acetone. If there is sealant or oil on the mating surfaces when the cover is installed, oil leaks may develop.

8   Make sure any threaded holes are clean. Run a tap into them to remove corrosion and restore damaged threads.
9   The gaskets are steel-backed silicone material, and are reusable unless damaged in removal. On V10 models, position the gasket with the numbered tab UP.
10   Carefully position the cover on the head and install the nuts/bolts. **Note:** *On the V10 engine, the valve covers are made of cast magnesium, and have specially plated fasteners to prevent corrosion of the magnesium. Do not use substitute bolts on these valve covers.*
11   Tighten the bolts in three steps to the torque listed in this Chapter's Specifications. **Caution:** *DON'T over-tighten the valve cover bolts.*
12   The remaining installation steps are the reverse of removal.
13   Start the engine and check carefully for oil leaks as the engine warms up.

5   Rocker arms and pushrods - removal, inspection and installation

Removal

Refer to illustration 5.3

1   Refer to Section 4 and detach the valve covers from the cylinder heads.
2   Loosen the rocker arm pivot bolts one at a time and detach the rocker arms, bolts, pivots and retainer/guide plate. Keep track of the rocker arm positions, since they must be returned to the same locations. Store each set of rocker components separately in a marked plastic bag to ensure that they're reinstalled in their original locations.
3   Remove the pushrods and store them separately to make sure they don't get mixed up during installation **(see illustration)**.

Inspection

4   Check each rocker arm for wear, cracks and other damage, especially where the pushrods and valve stems contact the rocker arm.
5   Check the pivot seat in each rocker arm and the pivot faces. Look for galling, stress cracks and unusual wear patterns. If the rocker arms are worn or damaged, replace them with new ones and install new pivots or shafts as well. **Note:** *Keep in mind that there is no valve adjustment on these engines, so excessive wear or damage in the valve train can easily result in excessive valve clearance, which in turn will cause valve noise when the engine is running.*
6   Make sure the hole at the pushrod end of each rocker arm is open.
7   Inspect the pushrods for cracks and excessive wear at the ends. Roll each pushrod across a piece of plate glass to see if it's bent (if it wobbles, it's bent).

5.9 Lubricate the pushrod ends and the valve stems with engine assembly lube before installing the rocker arms

5.11 Align the "V6" or "V8" neutral mark before tightening rocker arms

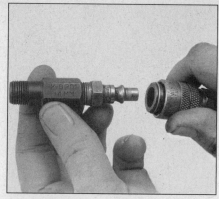

6.5 This is what the air hose adapter that fits into the spark plug hole looks like - they're commonly available from auto parts stores

Installation

Refer to illustrations 5.9 and 5.11

8   Lubricate the lower end of each pushrod with clean engine oil or engine assembly lube and install them in their original locations. Make sure each pushrod seats completely in the lifter socket.

9   Apply engine assembly lube to the ends of the valve stems, the upper ends of the pushrods and to the pivot faces to prevent damage to the mating surfaces on initial start-up **(see illustration)**.

10   Install the rocker arms, pivots, retainers and bolts, but do not tighten the bolts.

11   The rocker arms must be tightened at a "neutral" position in the engine's rotation, to prevent valve-to-piston clearance problems, especially when the lifters have been unloaded. On V6 engines, rotate the crankshaft damper until the "V6" mark on the damper lines up with the TDC or Zero mark on the timing cover. This represents the point at which the rocker arms can be tightened. On V8 engines, turn the engine until the "V8" mark lines up before tightening the rocker arms **(see illustration)**. **Caution:** *Do not rotate the engine at all after matching these marks. Once the rockers are all bolted down, allow at least five minutes for the hydraulic lifters to "bleed down" before turning or starting the engine.*

12   Tighten the rocker arm bolts to the torque listed in this Chapter's Specifications. As the bolts are tightened, make sure the pushrods seat properly in the rocker arms.

13   Refer to Section 4 and install the valve covers. Start the engine, listen for unusual valve train noses and check for oil leaks at the valve cover gaskets.

6   Valve springs, retainers and seals - replacement

Refer to illustrations 6.5, 6.7, 6.14, 6.16 and 6.18

Note: *Broken valve springs and defective valve stem seals can be replaced without removing the cylinder head. Two special tools and a compressed air source are normally required to perform this operation, so read through this Section carefully and rent or buy the tools before beginning the job.*

1   Remove the valve covers (see Section 4).

2   Remove the spark plugs (see Chapter 1).

3   Rotate the crankshaft until the number one piston is at top dead center on the compression stroke (see Section 3).

4   Remove the rocker arms for the number 1 piston.

5   Thread an adapter into the spark plug hole and connect an air hose from a compressed air source to it **(see illustration)**. Most auto parts stores can supply the air hose adapter. **Note:** *Many cylinder compression gauges utilize a screw-in fitting that may work with your air hose quick-disconnect fitting.*

6   Apply compressed air to the cylinder. The valves should be held in place by the air pressure. **Warning:** *If the cylinder isn't exactly at*

TDC, air pressure may force the piston down, causing the engine to quickly rotate. DO NOT leave a wrench on the vibration damper bolt or you may be injured by the tool.

7   Stuff shop rags into the cylinder head holes around the valves to prevent parts and tools from falling into the engine, then use a valve-spring compressor to compress the spring. Remove the keepers with small needle-nose pliers or a magnet **(see illustration)**. **Note:** *Several different types of tools are available for compressing the valve springs with the head in place. One type, shown here, grips the lower spring coils and presses on the retainer as the knob is turned, while the lever-type utilizes the rocker arm bolt for leverage. Both types work very well, although the lever type is usually less expensive.*

8   Remove the valve spring and retainer. **Note:** *If air pressure fails to retain the valve in the closed position during this operation, the valve face or seat may be damaged. If so, the cylinder head will have to be removed for repair.*

9   Remove the old valve stem seals, noting differences between the intake and exhaust seals.

10   Wrap a rubber band or tape around the top of the valve stem so the valve won't fall into the combustion chamber, then release the air pressure.

11   Inspect the valve stem for damage. Rotate the valve in the guide and check the end for eccentric movement, which would indicate that the valve is bent.

12   Move the valve up-and-down in the guide and make sure it does not bind. If the valve stem binds, either the valve is bent or the guide is damaged. In either case, the head will have to be removed for repair.

13   Reapply air pressure to the cylinder to retain the valve in the closed position, then remove the tape or rubber band from the valve stem.

14   If you're working on an exhaust valve, install the new exhaust valve seal on the valve stem and push it down to the top of the valve guide **(see illustration)**.

15   If you're working on an intake valve, install a new intake valve stem seal over the valve stem and press it down over the valve guide. Don't force the intake valve seal against the top of the guide. **Caution:** *Do not install an exhaust valve seal on an intake valve, as high oil consumption will result. On the V10 engine, the intake valve seals are black, and the exhaust valve seals brown.*

16   Install the spring and retainer in position over the valve **(see illustration)**.

17   Compress the valve spring assembly only enough to install the keepers in the valve stem.

18   Position the keepers in the valve stem groove. Apply a small dab of grease to the inside of each keeper to hold it in place if necessary **(see illustration)**. Remove the pressure from the spring tool and make sure the keepers are seated.

19   Disconnect the air hose and remove the adapter from the spark plug hole.

20   Repeat the above procedure on the remaining cylinders, following

6.7 Once the spring is depressed, the keepers can be removed with a small magnet or needle-nose pliers (a magnet is preferred to prevent dropping the keepers)

6.14 Be sure to install the seals on the correct valve stems

1   *Exhaust valve seal*
2   *Intake valve seal*

6.16 Install the seal, spring and retainer

2A

the firing order sequence (see this Chapter's Specifications). Bring each piston to top dead center on the compression stroke before applying air pressure (see Section 3).

21   Reinstall the rocker arm assemblies and the valve covers (see Sections 4 and 5).

22   Allow the engine to sit for five minutes before starting to allow the lifters to "bleed down." Start the engine, then check for oil leaks and unusual sounds coming from the valve cover area. Allow the engine to idle for at least five minutes before revving the engine.

7   Intake manifold - removal and installation

Removal

Refer to illustrations 7.4, 7.11 and 7.12

1   Disconnect the negative battery cable.

2   Pry the accessory belt tensioner over enough to slip the serpentine belt off the idler pulley (see Chapter 1) and remove the belt.

3   Refer to Chapter 4A and relieve the fuel system pressure. Disconnect the electrical connectors at each injector, remove the fuel rails and injectors, and disconnect the throttle body linkage.

4   Remove the air cleaner (refer to Chapter 1), and remove the alternator (refer to Chapter 5). **Note:** *On the V10 engine, remove the intake manifold-to-alternator brace as well* **(see illustration).**

5   Refer to Chapter 1 and disconnect the spark plug wires from the spark plugs. If there is any danger of mixing the plug wires up, it's recommended that they be labeled with pieces of numbered tape. On V6 and V8 engines, remove the distributor cap with the spark plug wires

attached. On the V10 engine, unbolt the coil assembly and remove it along with the spark plug wires.

6   Refer to Chapter 1 and drain the cooling system.

7   On the V10 engine, refer to Chapter 3 and remove the air conditioning compressor-to-intake manifold brace and the compressor mounting bolts. Set the compressor aside, leaving the lines connected. **Warning:** *The air conditioning system is under high pressure. DO NOT loosen any fittings unless the system has been discharged. Air conditioning refrigerant should be properly discharged into an EPA-approved recovery container at a dealer service department or an automotive air conditioning facility. Always wear eye protection when disconnecting air conditioning system fittings.*

8   Disconnect the coolant temperature sending unit and the upper radiator hose from the engine, and the heater hose and water pump bypass hose from the intake manifold.

9   Refer to Chapter 6 and disconnect the PCV and EVAP components connected to or mounted on the intake manifold.

10   On the V10 engine, remove the bolts securing the upper intake manifold to the lower intake manifold and lift off the upper intake manifold.

11   Loosen the intake manifold mounting bolts in 1/4-turn increments until they can be removed by hand. The manifold will probably be stuck to the cylinder heads and force may be required to break the gasket seal. A pry bar can be positioned to pry up a casting projection at the front of the manifold to break the bond made by the gasket **(see illustration). Caution:** *Do not pry between the block and manifold or the heads and manifold or damage to the gasket sealing surfaces may result and vacuum leaks could develop.*

12   Remove the intake manifold **(see illustration).** As the manifold is

6.18 Apply small dab of grease to each keeper as shown here before installation - it'll hold them in place on the valve stem as the spring is released

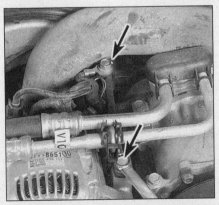

7.4 On the V10 engine, remove the two bolts (arrows) and the brace between the alternator and intake manifold

7.11 Pry the intake manifold up only where there is a casting protrusion, not between the gasket surfaces

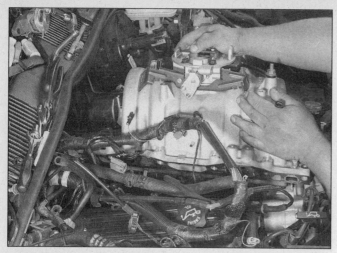

7.12 Get a good grip when pulling up the large intake manifold (V8 shown) - make sure there are no wires or hoses connected

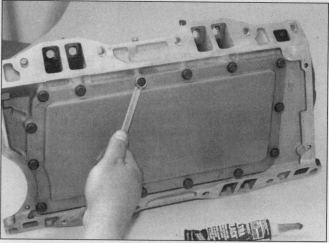

7.15 Remove the plenum pan from under the manifold, clean the gasket surfaces, and replace the gasket, using RTV sealant (V6 and V8 engines only)

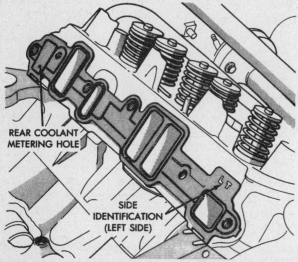

REAR COOLANT METERING HOLE

SIDE IDENTIFICATION (LEFT SIDE)

7.17 The gaskets must be installed on the proper side; they should be marked, as shown, but you'll need to line up the holes with the ports on the head to be sure they're installed correctly

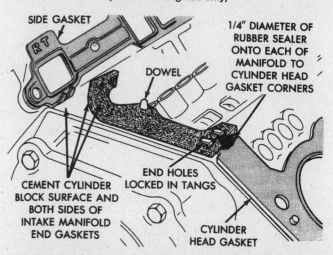

SIDE GASKET

DOWEL

1/4" DIAMETER OF RUBBER SEALER ONTO EACH OF MANIFOLD TO CYLINDER HEAD GASKET CORNERS

CEMENT CYLINDER BLOCK SURFACE AND BOTH SIDES OF INTAKE MANIFOLD END GASKETS

END HOLES LOCKED IN TANGS

CYLINDER HEAD GASKET

7.18 Fit the end seals over the dowels and engage the end tangs with the holes - apply a bead of RTV sealant to each of the four corners where the manifold gaskets and end seals meet

lifted from the engine, be sure to check for and disconnect anything still attached to the manifold.

Installation

Refer to illustrations 7.15, 7.17, 7.18, 7.20a, 7.20b, 7.20c and 7.21
Note: *The mating surfaces of the cylinder heads, block and manifold must be perfectly clean when the manifold is installed. Gasket removal solvents in aerosol cans are available at most auto parts stores and may be helpful when removing old gasket material that is stuck to the heads and manifold. Be sure to follow the directions printed on the container.*

13   Remove carbon deposits from the exhaust crossover passages. Use a gasket scraper to remove all traces of sealant and old gasket material, then wipe the mating surfaces with a cloth saturated with lacquer thinner or acetone. If there is old sealant or oil on the mating surfaces when the manifold is installed, oil or vacuum leaks may develop. Cover the lifter valley with shop rags to keep debris out of the engine. Use a vacuum cleaner to remove any gasket material that falls into the intake ports in the heads.

14   Use a tap of the correct size to chase the threads in the bolt holes, then use compressed air (if available) to remove the debris from the holes. **Warning:** *Wear safety glasses or a face shield to protect your eyes when using compressed air.*

15   On V6 and V8 engines, the intake manifold has a stamped, sheet-

metal pan on the bottom, called the plenum pan **(see illustration)**. If you have the intake manifold off for any reason, it's a good idea to replace the gasket under this pan. Use RTV sealant on the gasket and tighten the bolts to the torque listed in this Chapter's Specifications from the center out to the ends, in three steps.

16   Apply a thin coat of RTV sealant to the cylinder-head side of the new intake manifold side gaskets.

17   Position the side gaskets on the cylinder heads. Note that the gaskets are marked LT for left or RT for right **(see illustration).** On V6 and V8 engines, the words "Manifold Side" may appear, If so, this will ensure proper installation. Make sure they are installed on the correct side and all intake port openings, coolant passage holes and bolt holes are aligned correctly. Gasket/manifold alignment dowels are on the heads for all engines.

18   Install the front and rear end seals on the block. Apply a thin, uniform coating of quick-dry gasket cement to the intake manifold end seals and the cylinder block contact surfaces. Engage the dowels (if equipped) and the end tangs **(see illustration).** Refer to the instructions with the gasket set for further information. Apply RTV sealant at the four corners where the gaskets meet. **Note:** *On the V10 engine, the front and rear end seals have a peel-off backing over a self-stick adhesive. The front seal has a brown peel-off and the rear has a blue peel-off.*

19   Carefully set the manifold in place. **Caution:** *Do not disturb the gaskets and DO NOT move the manifold fore-and-aft after it contacts*

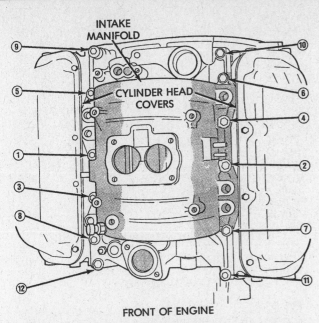

7.20a Intake manifold bolt-tightening sequence - V6 engine

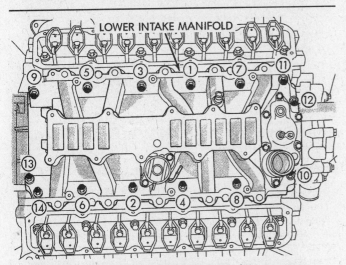

7.20c Lower intake manifold bolt-tightening sequence - V10 engine

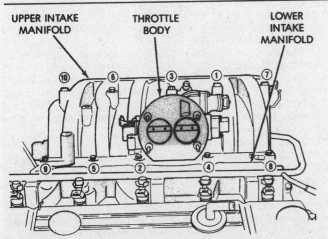

7.21 Upper intake manifold bolt-tightening sequence - V10 engine

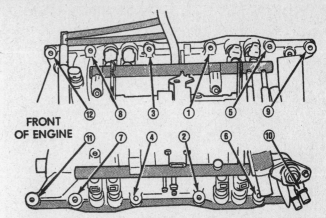

7.20b Intake manifold bolt-tightening sequence - V8 engines

2A

the front and rear seals or the gaskets will be pushed out of place and you may not notice the problem until you see the oil leak.

20 Install the intake manifold bolts and tighten the bolts following the recommended sequence **(see illustrations)**, to the torque listed in this Chapter's Specifications. Do not overtighten the bolts or gasket leaks may develop. **Caution:** *The manufacturer recommends that the intake manifold be installed and bolted down within three minutes of applying the RTV sealant at the four corners.*

21 The remaining installation steps are the reverse of removal. On the V10 engine, use a new gasket between the upper and lower intake manifolds and tighten the bolts in the proper sequence **(see illustration)** to the torque listed in this Chapter's Specifications. Change the engine oil and filter. Add coolant. Start the engine and check carefully for oil, vacuum and coolant leaks at the intake manifold joints.

8 Exhaust manifolds - removal and installation

Removal

Refer to illustrations 8.3, 8.4a, and 8.4b

Warning: *Allow the engine to cool completely before performing this procedure.*

1 Disconnect the battery cable from the negative battery terminal.

2 Disconnect the spark plug wires and remove the spark plugs (see Chapter 1). If there is any danger of mixing the plug wires up, it's recommended that they be labeled with pieces of numbered tape.

3 Raise the vehicle and support it securely on jackstands. Disconnect the exhaust pipe-to-manifold connections **(see illustration)**. Its a good idea to apply penetrating oil on the studs/bolts and let it soak 10 minutes before attempting to remove them.

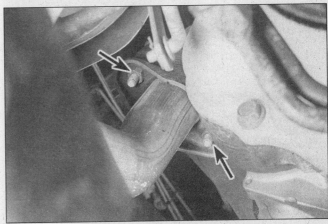

8.3 Remove the exhaust pipe-to-manifold nuts (arrows)

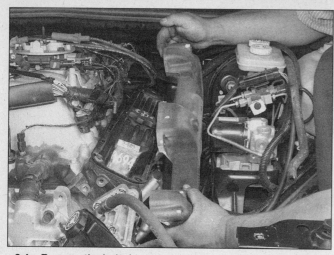

8.4a   Remove the bolts/nuts and separate the exhaust manifold from the cylinder head

4   Lower the vehicle and remove the bolts and nuts retaining the exhaust manifold to the cylinder head **(see illustration)**. On the V10 engine the exhaust heat shield must be removed before detaching the manifold; on V6 and V8 engines the heat shield comes off *after* the manifold is removed **(see illustration)**. **Note:** *If any of the studs come out of the head while removing the manifolds, use new studs on reassembly. The coarse-threaded ends of the studs should be coated with a non-hardening sealant such as Permatex #2 to prevent the possibility of water leaks from the cylinder head.*

5   Remove the manifold(s). On the V10 engine, the EGR tube must be unbolted from the right manifold **(see illustration 8.4b)**.

Installation

6   Installation is the reverse of the removal procedure. Clean the manifold and head gasket surfaces and check for cracks and flatness. On the V10 engine, replace the exhaust manifold gaskets (V6 and V8 engines do not have exhaust manifold gaskets).

7   Install the manifold(s) and fasteners. Tighten the bolts/nuts to the torque listed in this Chapter's Specifications. Work from the center to the ends and approach the final torque in three steps. Install the heat shields first on V6 and V8 engines, and last on the V10 engine. On the V10 engine, use a new EGR pipe gasket on the right manifold.

8   Apply anti-seize compound to the exhaust manifold-to-exhaust pipe bolts and tighten them securely. Also apply anti-seize compound to the EGR pipe bolts on the right V10 manifold.

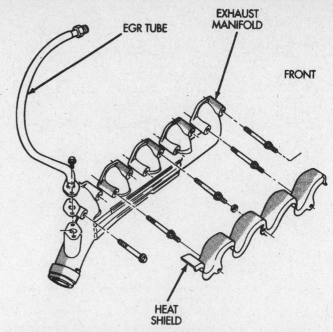

8.4b   On the V10 engine, remove the nuts and the heat shield, then remove the remainder of the manifold bolts - on the right V10 manifold, remove the two bolts on the EGR tube at the rear of the manifold

9   Crankshaft front oil seal - replacement

Refer to illustrations 9.3, 9.5a, 9.5b, 9.6, 9.7, 9.9 and 9.10

1   Disconnect the battery cable from the negative battery terminal.

2   Refer to Chapter 3 and remove the engine cooling fan, then refer to Chapter 1 and remove the drive belt.

3   On V6 and V8 engines, remove the bolts and separate the crankshaft pulley from the vibration damper **(see illustration)**.

4   Remove the large vibration damper-to-crankshaft bolt. To keep the crankshaft from turning, remove the starter (see Chapter 5) and have an assistant wedge a large screwdriver against the ring gear teeth.

5   Using the proper puller (commonly available from auto parts stores), detach the vibration damper **(see illustrations)**. **Caution:** *On V6 and V8 engines, do not use a puller with jaws that grip the outer edge of the damper. The puller must be the type that utilizes bolts to apply force to the damper hub only.*

9.3   Remove the crankshaft pulley bolts (arrows) and separate the pulley from the vibration damper (V6 and V8 engines)

9.5a   Use a bolt-type puller to remove the vibration damper on V6 and V8 engines

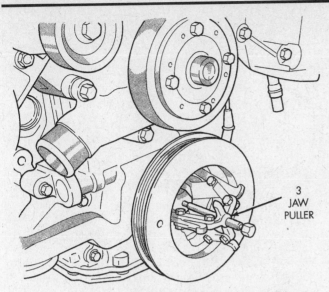

9.6 Drive the old seal out of the cover with a hammer and punch, being careful to strike the seal and not gouge the housing

2A

9.5b Use a three-jaw puller to remove the vibration damper on a V10 engine

6   If the seal is being replaced with the timing chain cover removed, support the cover on top of two blocks of wood and drive the seal out from the backside with a hammer and punch **(see illustration)**. **Caution:** *Be careful not to scratch, gouge or distort the area that the seal fits into or a leak will develop.*

7   If the seal is being removed while the cover is still attached to the engine block, carefully pry the seal out of the cover with a seal removal tool or a large screwdriver **(see illustration)**. **Caution:** *Be careful not to scratch, gouge or distort the area that the seal fits into or an oil leak will develop.*

8   Clean the bore to remove any old seal material and corrosion. Position the new seal in the bore with the seal lip (usually the side with the spring) facing IN (toward the engine). A small amount of oil applied to the outer edge of the new seal will make installation easier - but don't overdo it!

9   Drive the seal into the bore with a large socket and hammer until it's completely seated **(see illustration)**. Select a socket that's the same outside diameter as the seal and make sure the new seal is pressed into place until it bottoms against the cover flange.

10   Check the surface of the damper that the oil seal rides on. If the surface has been grooved from long-time contact with the seal, a press-on sleeve may be available to renew the sealing surface **(see illustration)**. This sleeve is pressed into place with a hammer and a

block of wood and is commonly available from auto parts stores.

11   Lubricate the seal lips with engine oil and reinstall the vibration damper. Use a vibration damper installation tool to press the damper onto the crankshaft.

12   Install the vibration damper-to-crankshaft bolt and tighten it to the torque listed in this Chapter's Specifications. On V6 and V8 engines, install the crankshaft pulley and tighten the bolts to the torque listed in this Chapter's Specifications.

13   The remainder of installation is the reverse of the removal process.

---

10   Timing chain cover, chain and sprockets - removal, inspection and installation

---

Timing chain slack check (cover on engine, V6 and V8 engines)

Note: *This procedure will allow you to check the amount of slack in the timing chain without removing the timing chain cover from the engine. This check cannot be performed on the V10 engine because it has no distributor.*

1   Disconnect the negative battery cable from the battery.

2   Place the engine at TDC (Top Dead Center) (see Section 3).

3   Keeping the piston on the compression stroke, place the number one piston about 30-degrees before TDC (BTDC).

4   Remove the distributor cap (see Chapter 1).

9.7 If you're replacing the seal with the timing chain cover installed, pry it out with a seal removal tool

9.9 Use a seal driver or large-diameter pipe to drive the new seal into the cover

9.10 If the sealing surface of the damper hub has a wear groove from contact with the seal, repair sleeves are available from auto parts stores

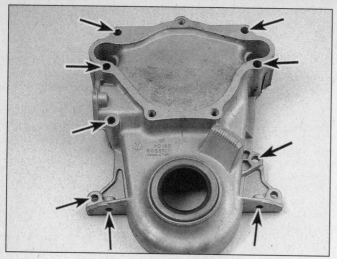

10.15a Timing chain cover bolt hole locations on V6 and V8 engines

10.15b Remove the cover from the engine to get at the chain and gears

5   You must rotate the crankshaft very slowly by hand for accuracy on this check, so get a 1/2-inch drive breaker bar, extension and correct-size socket to use on the large bolt in the center of the crankshaft pulley.

6   Turn the crankshaft clockwise until the number one piston is at TDC. This will take up the slack on the left side of the timing chain.

7   Mark the position of the distributor rotor on the distributor housing.

8   Slowly turn the crankshaft counterclockwise until the slightest movement is seen at the distributor rotor. Stop and note how far the number one piston has moved away from the TDC mark by looking at the ignition timing marks.

9   If the mark has moved more than 10-degrees, the timing chain is probably worn excessively. Remove the timing chain cover for a more accurate check.

Cover removal

Refer to illustrations 10.15a and 10.15b

10   Remove the fan assembly (see Chapter 3) and the crankshaft pulley and damper (see Section 9).

11   Refer to Chapter 1 and drain the cooling system.

12   Remove the water pump (see Chapter 3). On the V10 engine, remove the air conditioning compressor, without disconnecting the refrigerant lines, and set the compressor aside (see Chapter 3).

13   Remove and set aside the power steering pump with the lines still connected (see Chapter 10). On the V10 engine, remove the alternator and the mounting bracket (see Chapter 5).

14   Loosen the oil pan bolts and remove the front two oil pan bolts, that thread into the timing chain cover - they're most easily accessed from below. **Note:** *Even though this procedure can be done without the removal of the oil pan, it is difficult on some models and oil pan removal may actually simplify the job (see Section 13).*

15   Remove the cover mounting bolts and separate the timing chain cover from the block and oil pan **(see illustrations)**. The cover may be stuck; if so, use a putty knife to break the gasket seal. The cover is easily damaged, so DO NOT attempt to pry it off. **Caution:** *Remove the cover as carefully as possible, so as not to tear the one-piece oil pan gasket. If the gasket becomes torn, the oil pan will have to be removed and a new gasket installed.*

Timing chain and sprocket inspection (cover removed, all engines)

Refer to illustration 10.16

16   Attach a socket and torque wrench to the camshaft sprocket bolt and apply force in the normal direction of crankshaft rotation (30 ft-lbs if the cylinder heads are still in position complete with rocker arms,

or 15 ft-lbs if the cylinder heads have been removed). Don't allow the crankshaft to rotate. If necessary, wedge a screwdriver into the flywheel ring gear teeth (with the starter removed) so that it can't move. Using a ruler, note the amount of movement of the chain **(see illustration)**. If it exceeds 1/8-inch, a new timing chain will be required. **Note:** *Whenever a new timing chain is required, the entire set (chain, camshaft and crankshaft sprockets) must be replaced as an assembly.*

17   Inspect the camshaft sprocket for damage or wear. The camshaft sprocket on some models is steel, but most original-equipment cam sprockets will be an aluminum sprocket with a nylon coating on the teeth. This nylon coating may be cracked or be breaking off in small pieces. These pieces tend to end up in the oil pan and may eventually plug the oil pump pickup screen. If the pieces have come off the camshaft sprocket, the oil pan should be removed to properly clean or replace the oil pump pickup screen.

18   Inspect the crankshaft sprocket for damage or wear. The crankshaft sprocket is a steel sprocket, but the teeth can be grooved or worn enough to cause a poor meshing of the sprocket and the chain.

Chain and sprocket removal

Refer to illustrations 10.19, 10.20a and 10.20b

19   Be sure the timing marks are aligned **(see illustration)**. Hold a prybar through one of the camshaft sprocket holes to prevent the camshaft from turning. Remove the bolt from the camshaft sprocket.

20   The sprockets on the camshaft and crankshaft can be removed

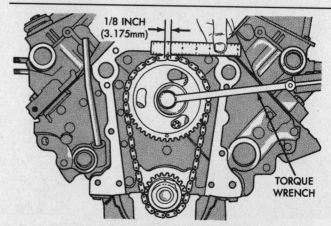

10.16 Position a ruler over the chain to measure slack while applying pressure with a torque wrench to the camshaft sprocket bolt

10.19 With the timing marks aligned, remove the camshaft sprocket bolt

1 Timing marks
2 Camshaft sprocket bolt

20 The sprockets on the camshaft and crankshaft can be removed with a two or three-jaw puller or by using two screwdrivers **(see illustrations)**, but be careful not to damage the threads in the end of the crankshaft. **Note:** If the timing chain cover oil seal has been leaking, refer to Section 9 and install a new one.

Installation

Refer to illustration 10.23

21 Use a gasket scraper to remove all traces of old gasket material and sealant from the cover and engine block. Stuff a shop rag into the opening at the front of the oil pan to keep debris out of the engine. Wipe the cover and block sealing surfaces with a cloth saturated with lacquer thinner or acetone.

22 If you're installing a new crankshaft sprocket, be sure to align the keyway in the crankshaft sprocket with the Woodruff key in the end of the crankshaft. **Note:** *Timing chains must be replaced as a set with the camshaft and crankshaft sprockets. Never put a new chain on old sprockets.* Align the sprocket with the Woodruff key and press the sprocket onto the crankshaft with the vibration damper bolt, a large socket and some washers or tap it gently into place until it is completely seated. **Caution:** *If resistance is encountered, do not hammer the sprocket onto the crankshaft. It may eventually move onto the shaft, but it may be cracked in the process and fail later, causing extensive*

engine damage.

23 Loop the new chain over the camshaft sprocket, then turn the sprocket until the timing mark is at the bottom **(see illustration)**. Mesh the chain with the crankshaft sprocket and position the camshaft sprocket on the end of the camshaft. If necessary, turn the camshaft so the key fits into the sprocket keyway with the timing mark in the 6 o'clock position **(see illustration 10.19)**. When the chain is installed, the timing marks MUST align as shown.

24 Apply a thread locking compound to the camshaft sprocket bolt threads and tighten the bolt to the torque listed in this Chapter's Specifications.

25 Lubricate the chain with clean engine oil.

26 Check for cracks and deformation of the oil pan gasket before installing the timing cover. If the gasket has deteriorated or is damaged, it must be replaced before reinstalling the timing chain cover.

27 Apply a thin layer of RTV sealant to both sides of the new cover gasket and the corners of the pan and block, then position the new cover gasket on the engine. The sealant will hold it in place.

28 Install the timing chain cover on the block and tighten the bolts, a little at a time, until you reach the torque listed in this Chapter's Specifications.

29 Install the two oil pan bolts, bringing the oil pan up against the timing chain cover, and tighten the rest of the pan bolts, if they were previously loosened.

30 Lubricate the oil seal contact surface of the vibration damper hub with clean engine oil, then install the damper on the end of the crankshaft. The keyway in the damper must be aligned with the Woodruff key in the crankshaft nose. If the damper cannot be seated by hand, slip the large washer over the bolt, install the bolt and tighten it to pull the damper into place. Tighten the bolt to the torque listed in this Chapter's Specifications.

31 The remaining installation steps are the reverse of removal.

32 Add coolant and check the oil level. Run the engine and check for oil and coolant leaks.

11 Camshaft and lifters - removal, inspection and installation

Camshaft lobe lift check

Refer to illustration 11.3

1 In order to determine the extent of cam lobe wear, the lobe lift should be checked prior to camshaft removal.

2 Remove the valve covers (see Section 4).

3 Beginning with the number one cylinder, mount a dial indicator on the engine and position the plunger against the top surface of the first rocker arm. Set the number one cylinder at TDC on the compression

10.20a The sprocket on the crankshaft can be removed with a two or three-jaw puller . . .

10.20b . . . or with two screwdrivers

10.23 Slip the chain and camshaft sprocket in place over the crankshaft sprocket with the timing mark (arrow) at the bottom

2A

11.3 When checking the camshaft lobe lift, the dial indicator plunger must be positioned directly above and in-line with the pushrod

11.12a Arrange a method of storing the lifters in order before removing them - a divided cardboard box handy for storage of the lifters

stroke (see Section 3). The plunger should be directly above and in line with the pushrod **(see illustration)**.

4   Zero the dial indicator, then very slowly turn the crankshaft in the normal direction of rotation (clockwise) until the indicator needle stops and begins to move in the opposite direction. The point at which it stops indicates maximum camshaft lobe lift.

5   Record this figure for future reference, then reposition the piston at TDC on the compression stroke.

6   Move the dial indicator to the next rocker arm and repeat the check. Be sure to record the results for each valve.

7   Repeat the check for the remaining valves. Since each piston must be at TDC on the compression stroke for this procedure, work from cylinder-to-cylinder following the firing order sequence. For instance, after checking the number one cylinder rocker arms, turn the engine slowly until the next cylinder in the firing order sequence is at TDC (number six on V6 engines, number eight on V8's, and number ten on the V10 engine).

8   After the check is complete, multiply all the recorded figures by 1.5 to obtain the total valve lift for each valve (the rocker arms have a 1.5:1 ratio). Compare the results to the specifications in this Chapter. If the valve lift is 0.003 inch less than specified, cam lobe wear has occurred and a new camshaft should be installed.

Removal

Refer to illustrations 11.12a, 11.12b, 11.12c, 11.13 and 11.15

9   Refer to the appropriate Sections and remove the intake manifold, rocker arms, pushrods and the timing chain and camshaft sprockets.

10   Remove the distributor on V6 and V8 engines (see Chapter 1). Also remove the radiator and air conditioning condenser (see Chapter 3).

11   There are several ways to extract the lifters from the bores. A special tool designed to grip and remove lifters is manufactured by many tool companies and is widely available, but it may not be required in every case. On newer engines without a lot of varnish buildup, the lifters can often be removed with a small magnet or even with your fingers. A machinist's scribe with a bent end can be used to pull the lifters out by positioning the point under the retainer ring inside the top of each lifter. **Caution:** *Do not use pliers to remove the lifters unless you intend to replace them with new ones (along with the camshaft). The pliers will damage the precision machined and hardened lifters, rendering them useless. Do not attempt to withdraw the camshaft with the lifters in place.*

12   Before removing the lifters and yokes, arrange to store them in a clearly labeled box to ensure that they are reinstalled in their original locations **(see illustration)**. The roller-type lifters should have paint dabs showing which side of the lifter faces the lifter "valley." If they aren't marked, apply some paint dabs before removing the yokes **(see illustration)**. The lifters must be installed the same way to aim the oil feed holes properly. Remove the lifter yoke retainer and yokes and withdraw the lifters **(see illustrations)**. Store the lifters where they will not get dirty. **Note:** *On the V10 engine, the four corner lifters cannot be removed with the cylinder heads in place. If it's necessary to replace the lifters, remove the cylinder heads (see Section 12). If the original camshaft and lifters are to be reused, place a small hose clamp over each lifter, pull the lifter up as far as possible and tighten the hose*

11.12b Note the paint marks (arrows) that indicate which side of the roller lifters face the valley - apply marks if none are visible

11.12c Remove the yoke retainer bolts (arrows) and remove the retainer

11.12d Remove the lifter yoke (arrow) and lifters and store them in order

11.13 Remove the camshaft thrust plate and oil tab

| 1 | Oil tab bolt | 2 | Thrust plate bolts |

11.15 Thread a long bolt into the camshaft sprocket bolt hole to use as a handle - as the camshaft is being removed, support it near the block so the lobes do not nick the bearings

clamp securely around the lifter body. This will support the lifter so the camshaft can be withdrawn.

13   Unbolt and remove the camshaft thrust plate **(see illustration)**. Note how it is installed so you can return it to its original location on reassembly.

14   Thread a long bolt into the camshaft sprocket bolt hole to use as a handle when removing the camshaft from the block.

15   Carefully pull the camshaft out. Support the cam near the block so the lobes do not nick or gouge the bearings as it is withdrawn **(see illustration)**.

Inspection

Refer to illustrations 11.17 and 11.22

16   After the camshaft has been removed from the engine, cleaned with solvent and dried, inspect the bearing journals for uneven wear, pitting and evidence of seizure. If the journals are damaged, the bearing inserts in the block are probably damaged as well. Both the camshaft and bearings will have to be replaced. **Note:** *Camshaft bearing replacement requires special tools and expertise that place it beyond the scope of the average home mechanic. The tools for bearing removal and installation are available at stores that carry automotive tools, possibly even found at a tool rental business. It is advisable though, if bearings are bad and the procedure is beyond your ability, remove the engine block and take it to an automotive machine shop to ensure that the job is done correctly.*

17   Measure the bearing journals with a micrometer to determine if they are excessively worn or out-of-round **(see illustration)**.

18   Check the camshaft lobes for heat discoloration, score marks, chipped areas, pitting and uneven wear. If the lobes are in good condition and if the valve lift measurements recorded earlier are as specified, the camshaft can be reused.

19   Clean the lifters with solvent and dry them thoroughly without mixing them up.

20   Check each lifter wall, pushrod seat and foot for scuffing, score marks and uneven wear. If the lifter walls are damaged or worn (which is not very likely), inspect the lifter bores in the engine block as well. If the pushrod seats are worn, check the pushrod ends.

21   If new lifters are being installed, a new camshaft must also be installed. If a new camshaft is installed, then use new lifters as well. Never install used lifters unless the original camshaft is used and the lifters can be installed in their original locations. **Caution:** *When replacing any of the valvetrain components on V6 engines, make sure the replacement parts are for the exact year of your engine. Match the design of the replacement part to your old part when making any replacement, or serious oiling problems could develop.*

22   Check the rollers carefully for wear and damage and make sure they turn freely without excessive play **(see illustration)**.

Installation

Refer to illustration 11.23

23   Lubricate the camshaft bearing journals and cam lobes with camshaft assembly lube **(see illustration)**.

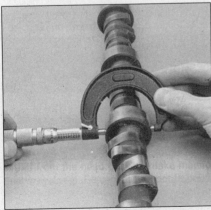

11.17 Check the diameter of each camshaft bearing journal to pinpoint excessive wear and out-of-round conditions

11.22 The roller on the roller lifters must turn freely - check for wear and excessive play as well

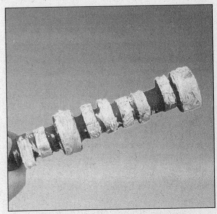

11.23 Be sure to apply camshaft assembly lube to the cam lobes and bearing journals before installing the camshaft

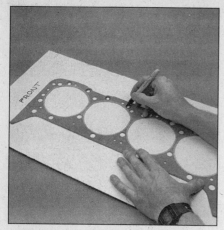

12.6 To avoid mixing up the head bolts, use a new gasket to transfer the bolt pattern to a piece of cardboard, then punch holes to accept the bolts

12.7a Pry on a casting protrusion to break the head loose

12.7b Once loose, get a good hold on the cylinder head and remove it from the engine block

24   Slide the camshaft slowly and gently into the engine. Support the cam near the block and be careful not to scrape or nick the bearings. Only install the camshaft far enough to install the camshaft thrust plate. Pushing it in too far could dislodge the camshaft plug at the rear of the engine, causing an oil leak. Make sure the timing chain oil tab (V6 and V8 engines) is installed with the thrust plate as it was originally **(see illustration 11.13)**.

25   Install the timing chain and sprockets (see Section 10). Align the timing marks on the crankshaft and camshaft sprockets.

26   Lubricate the lifters with clean engine oil and install them in the block. If the original lifters are being reinstalled, be sure to return them to their original locations, and with the paint marks facing the valley and the oil-feed holes on the side of the lifter body facing UP, away from the crankshaft. Install the lifter yokes and the lifter yoke retainer. **Note:** *The lifter yokes must be installed with their arrows pointing toward the camshaft.*

27   The remaining installation steps are the reverse of removal.

28   Change the oil, add Mopar Crankcase Conditioner part no. 3419130, or equivalent, and install a new oil filter (see Chapter 1).

29   Start the engine and check for oil pressure and leaks. **Caution:** *Do not run the engine above a fast idle until all the hydraulic lifters have filled with oil and become quiet again.*

30   If a new camshaft and lifters have been installed, the engine should be brought to operating temperature and run at a fast idle for 15 to 20 minutes to "break in" the new components. Change the oil and filter again after 500 miles of operation.

12   Cylinder heads - removal and installation

Removal

Refer to illustrations 12.6, 12.7a and 12.7b

1   Disconnect the negative battery cable from the battery and drain the cooling system (see Chapter 1).

2   Remove the valve covers (see Section 4).

3   Remove the intake manifold (see Section 7).

4   Detach both exhaust manifolds from the cylinder heads (see Section 8).

5   Remove the rocker arms and pushrods (see Section 5). **Caution:** *Again, as mentioned in Section 5, keep all the parts in order so they are reinstalled in the same location.*

6   Loosen the head bolts in 1/4-turn increments until they can be removed by hand. **Note:** *There will be different-length head bolts for different locations, so store the bolts in a cardboard holder or some type of container as they are removed* **(see illustration)**. *This will*

ensure that the bolts are reinstalled in their original holes.

7   Lift the heads off the engine. If resistance is felt, do not pry between the head and block as damage to the mating surfaces will result. To dislodge the head, place a block of wood against the end of it and strike the wood block with a hammer, or lift on a casting protrusion **(see illustrations)**. Store the heads on blocks of wood to prevent damage to the gasket sealing surfaces. **Warning:** *On the V10 engine, the heads are heavier and more awkward to handle; have an assistant help you lift them off.*

8   Cylinder head disassembly and inspection procedures are covered in detail in Chapter 2, Part C.

Installation

Refer to illustrations 12.10, 12.12, 12.13, 12.16a, 12.16b and 12.16c

9   The mating surfaces of the cylinder heads and block must be perfectly clean when the heads are installed. Gasket removal solvents are available at auto parts stores and may prove helpful.

10   Use a gasket scraper to remove all traces of carbon and old gasket material **(see illustration)**, then wipe the mating surfaces with a cloth saturated with lacquer thinner or acetone. If there is oil on the mating surfaces when the heads are installed, the gaskets may not seal correctly and leaks may develop. When working on the block, cover the lifter valley with shop rags to keep debris out of the engine. Use a vacuum cleaner to remove any debris that falls into the cylinders.

11   Check the block and head mating surfaces for nicks, deep scratches and other damage. If damage is slight, it can be removed with emery cloth. If it is excessive, machining may be the only alternative.

12   Use a tap of the correct size to chase the threads in the head bolt holes in the block. Mount each bolt in a vise and run a die down the threads to remove corrosion and restore the threads **(see illustration)**. Dirt, corrosion, sealant and damaged threads will affect torque readings.

13   Position the new gaskets over the dowels in the block **(see illustration)**.

14   Carefully position the heads on the block without disturbing the gaskets.

15   Before installing the head bolts, coat the threads with a non-hardening sealant such as Permatex No. 2.

16   Install the bolts in their original locations and tighten them finger tight. Following the recommended sequence **(see illustrations)**, tighten the bolts in several steps to the torque listed in this Chapter's Specifications.

17   The remaining installation steps are the reverse of removal.

18   Add coolant and change the oil and filter (see Chapter 1). Start the engine and check for proper operation and coolant or oil leaks.

12.10 Remove all traces of old gasket material

12.12 A die should be used to remove sealant and corrosion from the bolt threads prior to installation

12.13 Install the new head gasket over the dowels (arrow); there is a dowel at each end of the cylinder head

2A

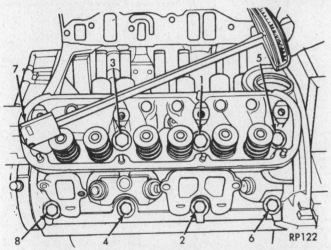

12.16a Cylinder head tightening sequence - V6 engine

12.16b Cylinder head tightening sequence - V8 engines

12.16c Cylinder head tightening sequence - V10 engine

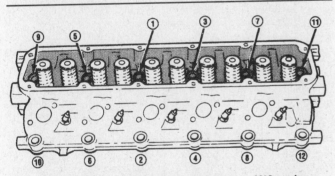

13.6 Remove the bolts around the perimeter of the oil pan - remove and note the location of the transmission cooler line retainers (arrows)

13 Oil pan - removal and installation

Removal

Refer to illustrations 13.6

1   Disconnect the battery cable from the negative battery terminal. Raise the vehicle and support it securely on jackstands (see Chapter 1).

2   Drain the engine oil and replace the oil filter (see Chapter 1). Remove the engine oil dipstick.

3   Unbolt and remove the engine-to-transmission support struts, if equipped.

4   On V6 and V8 engines, disconnect and lower the exhaust pipe **(see illustration 8.3)**.

5   Support the engine from above with an engine hoist, take a little weight off the engine with the hoist, and remove the through-bolts from the engine mounts (see Section 17). Now raise the engine further.

6   Remove all the oil pan bolts **(see illustration)**, then lower the pan from the engine. The pan will probably stick to the engine, so strike the pan with a rubber mallet until it breaks the gasket seal. **Caution:** *Before using force on the oil pan, be sure all the bolts have been removed.* Carefully slide the oil pan out, to the rear.

14.2 Remove the bolts (arrows) and lower the oil pump

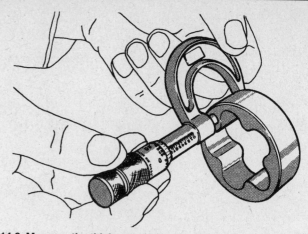

14.6 Measure the thickness of the oil-pump rotors and compare it to the Specifications

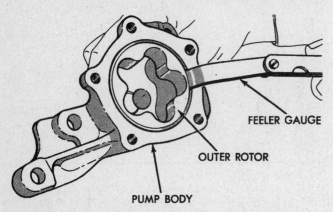

14.7a Measure the clearance between the outer rotor and the pump body. . .

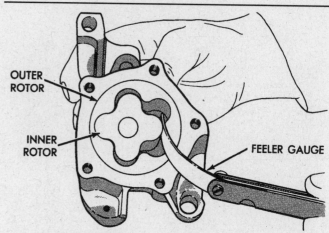

14.7b . . .between the inner and outer rotor tips. . .

Installation

7   Wash out the oil pan with solvent.

8   Thoroughly clean the mounting surfaces of the oil pan and engine block of old gasket material and sealer. If the oil pan is distorted at the bolt-hole areas, straighten the flange by supporting it from below on a 1x4 wood block and tapping the bolt holes with the rounded end of a ball-peen hammer. Wipe the gasket surfaces clean with a rag soaked in lacquer thinner or acetone.

9   Apply some RTV to the corners where the front cover meets the block and at the rear where the rear main cap meets the block; or on the V10 engine, where the rear main oil seal retainer plate meets the block. Then attach the one-piece oil pan gasket to the engine block with contact-cement-type gasket adhesive.

10   Prepare four pan alignment dowels from 5/16-inch bolts 1.5-inches long. Cut off the bolt heads and slot the ends with a hacksaw.

11   Install the four alignment dowels into the frontmost and rearmost pairs of pan bolt holes in the block.

12   Lift the pan into position, slipping it over the alignment dowels and being careful not to disturb the gasket, install several bolts finger tight.

13   Check that the gasket isn't sticking out anywhere around the block's perimeter. When all the bolts are in place, replace the alignment dowels with four pan bolts.

14   Starting at the ends and alternating from side-to-side towards the center, tighten the bolts to the torque listed in this Chapter's Specifications.

15   The remainder of the installation procedure is the reverse of removal.

16   Add the proper type and quantity of oil (see Chapter 1), start the engine and check for leaks before placing the vehicle back in service.

14   Oil pump - removal, inspection and installation

V6 and V8 engines

Refer to illustration 14.2

Removal

1   Remove the oil pan (see Section 13).

2   While supporting the oil pump, remove the oil pump mounting bolts **(see illustration)**.

3   Lower the pump and pickup screen assembly from the vehicle.

Inspection

Refer to illustrations 14.6, 14.7a, 14.7b and 14.7c

4   Remove the oil pump cover and withdraw the rotors from the pump body. Clean the components with solvent, dry them thoroughly and inspect for any obvious damage.

5   Place a straightedge across the inner surface of the oil pump cover and try to insert a .0015-inch feeler gauge under it. If the gauge fits, the oil pump assembly should be replaced.

6   Measure the thickness of the inner and outer rotor with a micrometer **(see illustration)**. If either is less than the minimum thickness listed in this Chapter's Specifications, the pump assembly should be replaced.

7   Install the rotors into the pump body and measure the clearance between the outer rotor and the body, between the inner and outer rotors, and the clearance over the rotors **(see illustrations)**. Compare these measurements to this Chapter's Specifications. If any components are scored, scratched or worn beyond the Specifications,

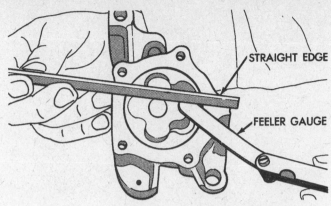

14.7c ... and over the rotors with a straightedge

14.10 Inspect the end of the driveshaft (arrow) for excessive wear and replace it, if necessary, then make sure it is aligned with the pump

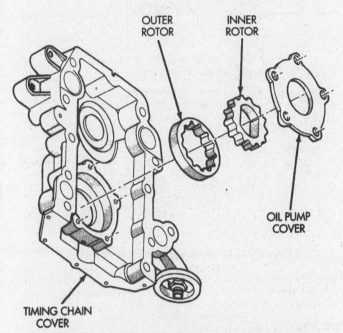

14.15 Remove the five Torx fasteners to remove the oil pump cover on a V10 engine

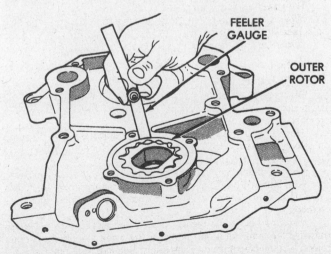

14.19a Measure the outer rotor clearance in the oil pump cavity

replace the oil pump assembly. If the parts are serviceable, replace the cover and tighten the bolts to the torque listed in this Chapter's Specifications.

Installation
Refer to illustration 14.10

8   If removed, thread the oil pickup tube and screen into the oil pump and tighten it. **Caution:** *Be absolutely certain that the pickup screen is properly tightened so that no air can be sucked into the oiling system at this connection.*

9   Prime the pump by pouring clean motor oil into the pickup tube, while turning the pump by hand.

10   Position the pump on the engine with a new gasket, if required. Make sure the pump driveshaft is aligned with the oil pump **(see illustration)**.

11   Install the mounting bolts and tighten them to the torque listed in this Chapter's Specifications.

12   Install the oil pan and add oil.

13   Run the engine and check for oil pressure and leaks.

V10 engine

Removal
Refer to illustration 14.15

14   Refer to Section 10 and remove the timing chain cover. The V10 oil pump is a gerotor-type pump mounted on the back of the front cover and driven by two flats on the crankshaft snout. The oil pan does not have to be removed to service the oil pump.

15   Remove the oil pump cover and the inner and outer rotors **(see illustration)**.

Inspection
Refer to illustrations 14.19a, 14.19b and 14.19c

16   Clean all of the pump components in solvent and inspect them for signs of unusual wear or scoring, be sure to check the oil pump cavity in the timing chain cover.

17   Place a straightedge across the inner surface of the oil pump cover and try to insert a .003-inch feeler gauge under it. If the gauge fits, the cover should be replaced.

18   Using a micrometer, measure the thickness of the inner and outer rotors **(see illustration 14.6)**.

19   Install the rotors in the oil pump cavity and using feeler gauges, measure the outer rotor-to-pump body clearance, the rotor tip clearance and the clearance over the rotors. Compare your measurements to this Chapter's Specifications **(see illustrations)**. If the rotors are scored, damaged or worn beyond the limits, replace the rotors as a set. If the oil pump cavity is scored, damaged or excessively worn, replace the timing cover.

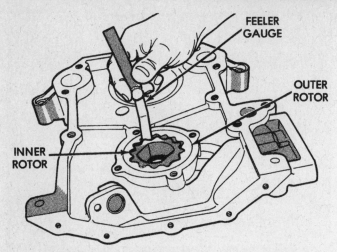

14.19b Measure the clearance between the inner and outer rotor tips

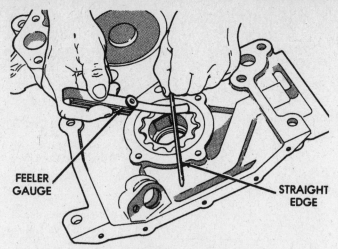

14.19c Using a straightedge placed over the oil pump cavity, check the clearance over the rotors

15.4 Remove the bolts (arrows) and detach the rear main bearing cap from the engine

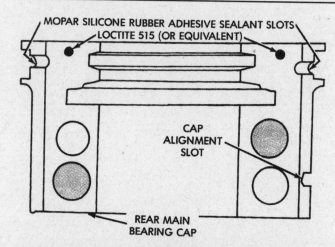

15.10 Apply a small drop of Loctite 515, or equivalent, to either side of the cap in the locations shown - apply RTV to the bearing cap-to-block joints

Installation

20   Pack the oil pump cavity with petroleum jelly, install the pump cover and tighten the bolts to the torque listed in this Chapter's Specifications.

21   Reinstall the front cover, making sure the two flats on the oil pump inner rotor align with the two flats on the crankshaft.

22   Replace the oil filter and add the proper type and quantity of oil (see Chapter 1).

23   Run the engine and check for oil pressure and leaks.

15   Rear main oil seal - replacement

V6 and V8 engines

Refer to illustrations 15.4 and 15.10

Note: *If you're installing a new seal during a complete engine overhaul, ignore the steps in this procedure that concern removal of external parts. Also, since the crankshaft is already removed, it's not necessary to use any special tools to remove the upper seal half; remove and install the upper seal half the same way as the lower seal half.*

1   Remove the oil pan (see Section 13).

2   Remove the oil pump (see Section 14).

3   The rear main seal can be replaced with the engine in the vehicle. The rear main seal is a two-piece design, made from Viton rubber.

4   Remove the bolts and detach the rear main bearing cap from the engine **(see illustration)**.

5   Remove the lower half of the oil seal from the bearing cap and the upper half from the block. **Note:** *It may be easier to remove the upper rear seal when the two main bearing caps ahead of the rear cap are loosened slightly. ALL the main bearing caps should be retightened to Specifications after the new seal and rear cap are installed.*

6   Clean the bearing cap and engine block surfaces carefully to degrease them and remove any sealant.

7   Lightly oil the lips of the new crankshaft seals. **Caution:** *Always wipe the crankshaft surface clean. then oil it lightly before installing a new seal.*

8   Rotate a new seal half into cylinder block with the paint stripe (yellow on some models, white on others) toward the rear of the engine. **Caution:** *Hold your thumb firmly against the outside diameter of the seal as you're rotating it into place. This will prevent the seal outside diameter from being shaved from contact with the sharp edge of the engine block. If the seal gets shaved, you may wind up with an oil leak.*

9   Place the other seal half in the bearing cap with the paint stripe toward the rear.

10   Apply a drop of Loctite 515 or equivalent on either side of the cap, and a small amount of RTV sealant at the cap-to-block joints **(see illustration)**. Install the cap quickly after applying the Loctite and

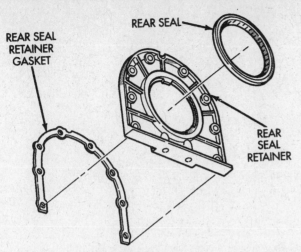

15.15 On the V10 engine, the rear seal is mounted in a retainer at the back of the block

15.16 With the retainer on a flat surface, drive the new seal squarely into the bore using a wood block - check that it is positioned evenly all the way around and driven in to the exact depth as the original

2A

16.2 Before removing the flywheel, mark its relationship to the crankshaft

sealant. Tighten the rear main bearing cap (and ALL the other bearing caps if you loosened any of the others) to the torque listed in Chapter 2C Specifications.

11   Install the oil pump and oil pan.

12   The remainder of installation is the reverse of removal. Fill the pan with oil, run the engine and check for leaks.

V10 engine

Refer to illustrations 15.15 and 15.16

13   Refer to Chapter 7 and remove the transmission. Refer to Section 16 of this Chapter and remove flywheel/driveplate.

14   Refer to Section 13 and remove the oil pan.

15   Unbolt and remove the rear oil seal retainer **(see illustration)**. Clean the gasket from the retainer and the back of the block.

16   Using a blunt punch or screwdriver, drive the old seal out of the retainer. Using a wood block, drive the new seal squarely into the retainer to the same distance as the original seal **(see illustration)**.

17   Reinstall the retainer to the block with a new gasket and tighten the bolts to the torque listed in this Chapter's Specifications.

18   Before reinstalling the oil pan, apply a small amount of RTV sealant to the retainer-to-block joints.

19   The remainder of installation is the reverse of removal.

20   Refill the engine with new oil, start the engine and check for oil leaks.

16   Flywheel/driveplate - removal and installation

Refer to illustration 16.2

1   Remove the transmission (see Chapter 7). If your vehicle has a manual transmission, the pressure plate and clutch will also have to be removed (see Chapter 8).

2   Wedge a large screwdriver in the starter ring gear teeth or driveplate hole to keep the crankshaft from turning, then remove the mounting bolts. Mark the flywheel relationship to the crankshaft for later alignment **(see illustration)**. Since it's fairly heavy, support the flywheel as the last bolt is removed. **Warning:** *The ring-gear teeth may be sharp, wear gloves to protect your hands.*

3   Pull straight back on the flywheel/driveplate to detach it from the crankshaft. On some models there may be a thin spacer installed between the driveplate and crankshaft. Automatic transmission equipped models may have a retainer ring between the bolts and the driveplate.

4   On manual transmission equipped models, check the pilot bushing and replace it if necessary (see Chapter 8). Clean the flywheel with lacquer thinner, especially around the mounting area, and clean the rear flange of the crankshaft.

5   Installation is the reverse of removal. Be sure to align the marks made during removal. Use Locktite on the bolt threads and tighten them to the torque listed in this Chapter's Specifications in a criss-cross pattern.

17   Engine mounts - check and replacement

Refer to illustrations 17.5a and 17.5b

Warning: *Improper lifting methods or devices are hazardous and could result in severe injury or death. DO NOT place any part of your body under the engine/transmission when it's supported only by a jack. Failure of the lifting device could result in serious injury or death.*

1   If the rubber mounts have hardened, cracked or separated from the metal backing plates, they must be replaced. This operation may be carried out with the engine/transmission still in the vehicle.

2   Disconnect the negative cable from the battery.

3   Raise the front of the vehicle and support it securely on jackstands.

4   Support the engine with a lifting device from above. **Caution:** *Do not connect the lifting device to the intake manifold.* Raise the engine just enough to take the weight off the engine mounts.

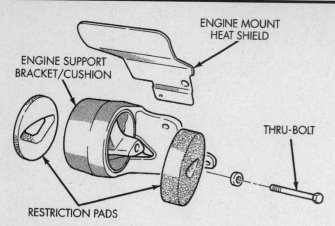

ENGINE MOUNT
HEAT SHIELD

ENGINE SUPPORT
BRACKET/CUSHION

THRU-BOLT

RESTRICTION PADS

17.5a Typical engine mount installation details

17.5b Remove the nut from the engine mount through-bolt (arrow) and withdraw the through-bolt from the mount

5   Remove the engine mount through-bolt and the rubber restriction pads **(see illustrations)**.

6   Remove the mount-to-engine block bolts, then remove the mount. **Note:** *Some models may have a sheetmetal heat shield over the engine mount.*

7   Place the new mount in position, install the mount-to-engine block bolts and tighten the bolts to the torque listed in this Chapter's Specifications. Reinstall the heat shield, if equipped.

8   Install the through-bolt and the rubber restrictors.

9   Lower the engine while guiding the engine mount and through-bolt into the support bracket. Install the through-bolt nut and tighten it to the torque listed in this Chapter's Specifications.

10   Remove the engine hoist.

11   Remove the jackstands and lower the vehicle.

Chapter 2 Part B
Diesel engine

Contents

Specifications

General

Displacement	5.9L (360 cu. in.)
Cylinder numbers (front to rear)	1-2-3-4-5-6
Firing order	1-5-3-6-2-4

Camshaft

Journal diameter, minimum	2.1245 inches
Lobe height, minimum	
Intake	1.852 inches
Exhaust	1.841 inches
Fuel pump lobe	1.398 inches
Endplay	0.006 to 0.010 inch
Gear backlash	0.003 to 0.013 inch

Oil pump

Oil pressure, minimum	
Idle	10 psi
2,500 rpm	30 psi
Gerotor-to-planetary tip clearance, maximum	0.007 inch
Gerotor planetary-to-body clearance, maximum	0.015 inch
Gerotor-to-back plate clearance, maximum	0.005 inch
Gear backlash	0.003 to 0.013 inch

Torque Specifications

Ft-lbs (unless otherwise indicated)

Alternator mounting bolts	30
Camshaft thrust plate bolts	210 in-lbs
Crankshaft damper bolt	135
Cylinder head bolts (in sequence - **see illustration 11.20**)	
Step 1, all bolts	66
Step 2, long bolts	89
Step 3, all bolts	Turn an additional 90-degrees
Engine mount through-bolt nuts....................................	75
Engine mount-to-block bolts..	60
Exhaust manifold bolts	32
Flywheel bolts..	101
Flywheel housing adapter...	57
Gear housing bolts	216 in-lbs
Gear housing cover bolts	216 in-lbs
Intake manifold cover bolts	216 in-lbs
Oil cooler mounting bolts	216 in-lbs
Oil pan drain plug	60
Oil pan bolts..	216 in-lbs
Oil pressure regulator plug	60
Oil pump mounting bolts	216 in-lbs
Rocker arm bolts	
12 mm	Use cylinder head bolt torque specification (and sequence shown in illustration 5.11)
8 mm	216 in-lbs
Valve cover bolts	216 in-lbs

1   General information

This part of Chapter 2 is devoted to in-vehicle repair procedures for the 5.9L Cummins inline six-cylinder diesel engine. All information concerning engine removal and installation and engine block and cylinder head overhaul can be found in Part C of this Chapter.

Since the repair procedures included in this Part are based on the assumption that the engine is still installed in the vehicle, if they are being used during a complete engine overhaul (with the engine already out of the vehicle and on a stand) many of the steps included here will not apply.

The specifications included in this Part of Chapter 2 apply only to the procedures found here. The specifications necessary for rebuilding the block and cylinder heads are included in Part C.

The 5.9L diesel engine is of an extremely rugged, proven design, incorporating a turbocharger and intercooler for efficient power production and low-end torque for all towing applications, when kept in its proper operating rpm range.

2   Repair operations possible with the engine in the vehicle

Many major repair operations can be accomplished without removing the engine from the vehicle.

Clean the engine compartment and the exterior of the engine with some type of pressure washer before any work is done. A clean engine will make the job easier and will help keep dirt out of the internal areas of the engine.

Depending on the components involved, it may be a good idea to remove the hood to improve access to the engine as repairs are performed (refer to Chapter 11 if necessary).

If oil or coolant leaks develop, indicating a need for gasket or seal replacement, the repairs can generally be made with the engine in the vehicle. The cylinder head gasket, intake and exhaust manifold gaskets, gear cover gaskets and the crankshaft oil seals are all accessible with the engine in place. The oil pan gasket, however, does require disconnecting the engine mounts and raising the engine.

Exterior engine components, such as the water pump, the starter motor, the alternator, turbocharger and the fuel injection components, as well as the intake (cover) and exhaust manifold, can be removed for repair with the engine in place.

Since the cylinder head can be removed without pulling the engine, valve component servicing can also be accomplished with the engine in the vehicle.

Replacement of, repairs to or inspection of the gear case components and the oil pump are all possible with the engine in place.

3   Top Dead Center (TDC) - locating (with timing pin)

Refer to illustrations 3.1, 3.2, 3.3a and 3.3b

1   The timing pin is located on the back of the gear case, below the injection pump and above the power steering pump **(see illustration)**. It is normally pulled out, but when timing the engine, it is pushed in until it contacts a hole in the camshaft gear, locking the camshaft gear in the TDC position.

3.1 Location of the timing pin (arrow)

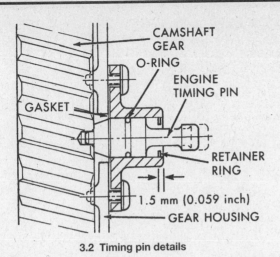

3.2 Timing pin details

3.3a The special barring tool, Chrysler tool no. 7471B, is also available from specialty tool manufacturers

2   If the timing pin itself is to be removed, use a small screwdriver to remove the snap-ring, and pull out the timing pin **(see illustration)**. When installing the timing pin, use a new O-ring.

3   To find TDC, remove the fuel injector nozzles (see Chapter 4, Part B) to allow the engine to rotate smoothly. Remove the timing pin as described in Step 2. Use a breaker bar and a large socket on the crankshaft damper bolt to turn the engine over, while watching through the timing pin hole (use a small bright flashlight and a small mirror) until the hole in the back of the camshaft gear is visible through the hole. **Note:** *A special "barring" tool, available from specialty tool manufacturers, fits into a hole in the bellhousing and engages the flywheel ring-gear teeth* **(see illustrations)**. *Remove the rubber plug from the bellhousing, insert the tool, and the engine can be turned slowly and precisely with the tool, a ratchet and an extension.*

4   When the gear hole appears directly in line with the timing pin hole, push the timing pin back in to lock the camshaft in the TDC position. **Caution:** *Do not attempt to rotate the engine while the timing pin is pushed in.*

3.3b Remove the rubber plug and insert the special barring tool into the bellhousing (arrow) - used in conjunction with a ratchet and extension, the engine can be rotated by hand

4   Valve covers - removal and installation

Refer to illustrations 4.1 and 4.2

1   Remove the two bolts and remove the plastic decorative panel over the valve covers **(see illustration)**.

2   There is an individual valve cover for every cylinder of the engine,

six in all. Remove the bolt and pull off the valve cover for one or all of the cylinders, as necessary **(see illustration)**. **Caution:** *Do not pry between the valve cover and the cylinder head. If the cover sticks, tap it with a rubber mallet or a hammer and block of wood.*

3   The original gaskets are steel-backed silicone and are reusable,

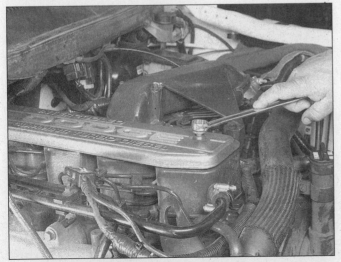

4.1 Remove the plastic cover over the individual valve covers

4.2 Each of the individual valve covers is retained by one bolt

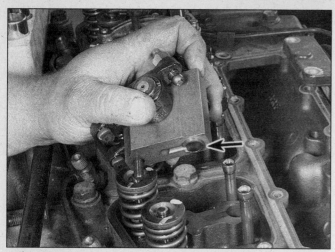

5.3 Remove the bolts and the rocker arm/pedestal assembly - arrow indicates the locating dowel ring on the bottom of the pedestal

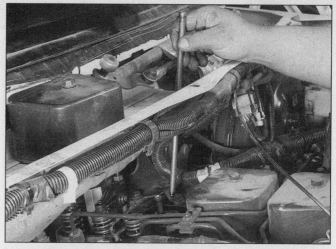

5.4 The pushrods for the two rearmost cylinders must be removed through holes in the cowl above the rear of the engine

unless damaged. Place the gasket on the valve cover, install the valve cover on the cylinder head and tighten the bolt to the torque listed in this Chapter's Specifications.

5   Rocker arms and pushrods - removal, inspection and installation

Removal

Refer to illustrations 5.3 and 5.4
Note: *The following procedure should be performed on a cold engine.*
1   Disconnect the negative cables from both batteries. Remove the valve covers (see Section 4).
2   Loosen the rocker arm adjusting nuts and back out the adjusting screws until they stop.
3   Remove the rocker arm pedestal bolts (which are also cylinder head bolts) and remove the rocker arm/pedestal assemblies **(see illustration)**. **Note:** *Keep the rocker arm/pedestal assemblies in order so they can be installed in their original locations - do not detach the rocker arms from the pedestals unless they are being replaced.*
4   Remove the pushrods. Keep the pushrods in order so they can be installed in their original locations. Remove the rubber access plugs and withdraw the pushrods and long pedestal bolts for the two rearmost cylinders through holes in the cowl panel directly above the rear section of the engine **(see illustration)**.

Inspection

Refer to illustration 5.5
5   Check each rocker arm for wear, cracks and other damage, especially where the pushrods and valve stems contact the rocker arm faces. Also check the rocker arm shafts for wear. If the rocker arms are disassembled from the pedestal shafts, mark the rocker arms first so they can be installed in their original locations. The rocker arms can be removed by removing the snap-ring and thrust washer at each end of the shaft **(see illustration)**.
6   Make sure the oil feed holes in each rocker arm shaft are not plugged so that each rocker arm gets proper lubrication.
7   Check each rocker arm pivot area and wear area on the shaft for excessive wear, scoring, cracks and galling. If the rocker arms or shafts are worn or damaged, replace them with new ones.
8   Inspect the pushrods for cracks and excessive wear at the ends. Roll each pushrod across a piece of plate glass to see if it is bent (if it wobbles, it is bent). Replace the pushrods if any of these conditions are present.

Installation

Refer to illustration 5.11
9   Reinstall the pushrods in their original locations.
10   If the rocker arms were removed from their shafts, lube the shafts with engine assembly lube and reinstall the rocker arms, thrust washers and snap-rings.
11   Place the rocker arm/pedestal assemblies onto the cylinder head, making sure that the dowel rings on the bottom of the pedestals locate properly into the cylinder head holes **(see illustration 5.3)**. Tighten the long bolts to the torque listed in this Chapter's Specifications for the cylinder head bolts, in the proper sequence **(see illustration)**. Tighten the smaller rocker arm bolts to the torque listed in this Chapter's Specifications. **Note:** *If a pedestal will not sit flush against the cylinder head*

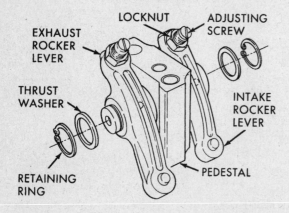

5.5 Rocker arm, shaft and pedestal installation details

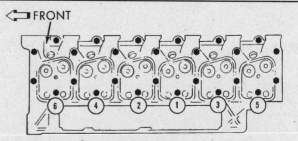

5.11 Tightening sequence for the long rocker arm pedestal retaining bolts (which are also cylinder head bolts)

6.1 Remove the two fuel line brackets (arrows)

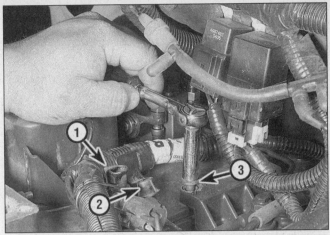

6.6a At the rear of the intake manifold cover, disconnect the charge air temperature sensor (1), pull the wiring harness clip (2) from the fuel filter bolt (3), and remove the fuel filter bolt and stud

before tightening the bolt, rotate the crankshaft to relieve pressure from the pushrod and tighten the bolt to Specifications.

12   Refer to Section 3 to locate the engine at TDC for number 1 piston. Be sure to pull the timing pin back out after locating TDC.
13   Refer to Chapter 1 and adjust the valve clearance.
14   Install the valve covers.
15   The remainder of installation is the reverse of removal. Don't forget to plug the holes in the cowl.

6   Intake manifold cover - removal and installation

Refer to illustrations 6.1, 6.6a and 6.6b

1   The intake manifold on the diesel engine is cast integral with the cylinder head and not removable. The only service procedures are replacement of the air intake heating element and the intake manifold cover gasket. Refer to Chapter 4, Part B and remove the high-pressure fuel lines that cross over the intake manifold. Remove the fuel line retaining brackets **(see illustration)**.
2   Loosen the clamp and disconnect the duct from the intercooler to the intake manifold (see Chapter 4 Part B).
3   Mark the two air intake heater wires with tape so they can be installed in their original locations and remove the nuts and wires from the studs. Unbolt the oil dipstick bracket from the air intake.
4   Refer to Chapter 6, and disconnect the wire to the charge air temperature sensor and disconnect the air temperature switch.
5   Remove the four bolts retaining the air intake housing and gasket

from the manifold cover. Avoid dropping gasket pieces or foreign matter into the manifold.
6   Two of the cover fasteners are a stud and bolt retaining the fuel filter to the intake cover **(see illustration)**. Pull the heating element from the manifold, then unbolt the intake manifold cover and gasket **(see illustration)**.
7   Stuff the intake manifold with rags to keep debris from falling into the manifold and scrape the sealing surface clean. Clean the bottom of the intake manifold cover as well.
8   Install the new gasket and the intake manifold cover, using liquid Teflon sealant on all the bolt threads. Tighten the bolts to the torque listed in this Chapter's Specifications.
9   Install the heating element and a new gasket for the air inlet housing. The remainder of installation is the reverse of removal. Install the high-pressure fuel lines and bleed the fuel system (see Chapter 4, Part B).

7   Exhaust manifold - removal and installation

Refer to illustrations 7.2, 7.3 and 7.5

1   Refer to Chapter 4, Part B and remove the turbocharger.
2   Remove the bolts and brackets retaining the heater lines to the exhaust manifold **(see illustration)**.
3   Remove the exhaust manifold bolts, exhaust manifold and gaskets **(see illustration)**.

6.6b Remove the remaining bolts retaining the intake manifold cover and remove the cover

7.2 Remove the bolt (arrow) retaining the heater hoses to the exhaust manifold

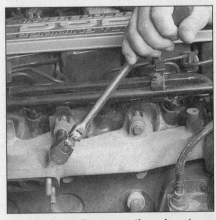

7.3 Carefully remove the exhaust manifold bolts

2B

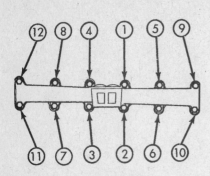

7.5 Exhaust manifold bolt tightening sequence

8.3 Remove the four bolts retaining the vibration damper to the crankshaft

8.4 Use paint to mark the damper's relationship to both the crankshaft and the sensor (above)

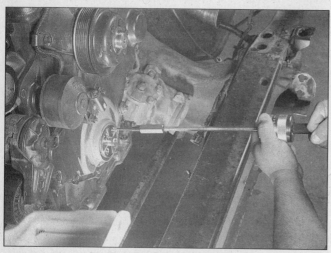

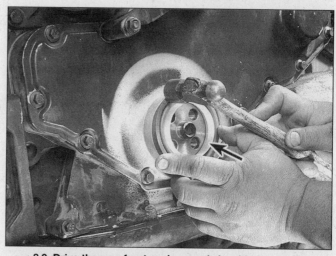

8.6 Use sheetmetal screws and a small slide-hammer to pull the front seal out of the housing

8.9 Drive the new front seal squarely in with the plastic alignment/installation tool (arrow) provided with the new seal

4   Clean the mounting surfaces of the manifold and the cylinder head, and clean the threads of the exhaust manifold mounting bolts.

5   Install the manifold using a new gasket and anti-seize compound on the bolt threads. Tighten the manifold bolts to the torque listed in this Chapter's Specifications in the proper sequence **(see illustration)**.

6   The remainder of installation is the reverse of removal.

8   Crankshaft front oil seal - replacement

Refer to illustrations 8.3, 8.4, 8.6 and 8.9

1   Disconnect the negative cables from both batteries.

2   Refer to Chapter 1 and remove the drivebelt.

3   Remove the bolts retaining the damper to the crankshaft **(see illustration)**.

4   Mark the relationship of the damper to the crankshaft and to the crankshaft position sensor **(see illustration)**. Remove the crankshaft damper - a puller is not necessary.

5   Using an electric drill with an 1/8-inch bit, drill two holes opposite each other in the front seal.

6   Using a slide-hammer with a #10 sheetmetal screw, thread the screw into each of the holes and pull out on the seal **(see illustration)**. Alternate pulling on each hole until the seal is free from the housing.

7   Clean the sealing surface of the crankshaft snout thoroughly.

There should be no oil on the sealing surface or the new seal may leak.

8   Apply Loctite 277 to the outer diameter of the new seal.

9   Using the plastic alignment/installation tool included with the new seal, drive the seal into the housing until it is seated to the same depth as the original seal **(see illustration)**.

10   Reinstall the crankshaft damper, tighten the bolts securely, but do not tighten them to Specifications until after the drivebelt is installed.

11   Install the drivebelt (refer to Chapter 1). Use the barring tool **(see illustration 3.3a)** to hold the flywheel stationary and tighten the crankshaft damper bolts to the torque listed in this Chapter's Specifications.

9   Gear housing cover - removal and installation

Removal

Refer to illustrations 9.3a, 9.3b, 9.3c, 9.5a, 9.5b, 9.6 and 9.7

1   Disconnect the negative cables from both batteries.

2   Refer to Chapters 1 and 3 and remove the drivebelt, belt tensioner, cooling fan and fan shroud.

3   Remove the oil filler tube and elbow from the gear housing cover **(see illustrations)**.

4   Refer to Section 8 and remove the crankshaft damper.

5   Remove the fan drive pulley and the fan drive assembly **(see illus-**

9.3a Loosen the clamp bolt (right arrow) on the oil filler tube, then remove the bolt retaining the clamp to the engine (left arrow)

9.3b Twist the upper portion of the oil filler tube and unscrew it from the lower elbow (arrow)

9.3c The oil filler elbow can now be twisted counterclockwise out of the front cover - note that the elbow covers the nut on the fuel injection pump

2B

9.5a Use large pliers to grip the fan drive pulley while removing the bolts

9.5b Remove the three bolts (arrows) and remove the fan drive assembly

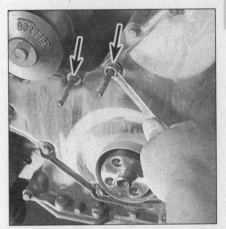

9.6 Remove the crankshaft position sensor and the two studs (arrows), then remove the rest of the cover bolts

5   Remove the fan drive pulley and the fan drive assembly **(see illustrations)**.

6   Remove the crankshaft position sensor and the bolts retaining the cover to the gear housing **(see illustration)**. Carefully pry the cover off. **Note:** *Be careful not to damage the gasket sealing areas of the cover or the gear housing or oil leaks may result.*

Installation

7   Visually inspect the camshaft, crankshaft and oil pump drive gears for excessive wear, chips or cracks **(see illustration)**. If any gears are damaged, refer to the appropriate Section for gear replacement procedures.

8   Pry the original front seal from the cover. Clean the mounting surfaces of the cover and gear housing. Clean the front seal area of the crankshaft, completely, or the new front seal may leak. Lubricate the gear train with clean engine oil.

9   Install the cover, with a new gasket, onto the gear housing. Install the bolts, but leave them slightly loose. Insert the front seal alignment/installation tool (provided with a new front seal) into the seal bore to align the front cover with the crankshaft. Tighten the cover bolts to the torque listed in this Chapter's Specifications, with the alignment tool in place.

10   Remove the alignment/installation tool and install the crankshaft front seal (see Section 9).

11   The remainder of the installation is the reverse of the removal procedure.

9.7 Inspect all of the gears in the case with the cover off

1	Oil pump gear	5	Vacuum pump/power
2	Idler gear		steering pump gear
3	Crankshaft gear	6	Fuel injection pump
4	Camshaft gear		gear

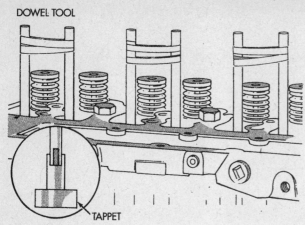

10.7 Long dowels must be prepared or purchased that just fit snugly into the top of the tappets - pull up on each pair of dowels for a cylinder pair and tie them together with heavy rubber bands so the side tension retains the tappets at the top of their travel

10 Camshaft and tappets - removal, inspection and replacement

Note: *Camshaft and tappet replacement in the diesel engine is a very involved process. The diesel engine tappets have a head larger than the tappet body and must be inserted into their bores from the bottom of the bore. This results in a specialized procedure which requires several special tools. There are two methods of retaining the tappets for camshaft removal; read through the entire Section and obtain the special tools before beginning the procedure.*

1   Disconnect both negative battery cables.
2   Refer to Sections 9 and 10 and remove the crankshaft damper and gear housing cover.
3   Refer to Chapter 4, Part B and remove the fuel transfer pump from the left side of the block.
4   Refer to Section 3 and position the engine at TDC.
5   Refer to Sections 4 and 5 and remove the valve covers, rocker arms and pushrods.

Tappet retention
Refer to illustrations 10.7, 10.9a, 10.9b and 10.10

6   The tappets must be retained up in their bores, away from the camshaft lobes, in order to facilitate camshaft removal. A set of 12

10.9a Remove the crankcase vent tube, the two screws and pull the plastic cover off (arrow)

wooden dowels, four inches longer than the pushrods and the correct diameter to just fit snugly into the top of the tappets, will be necessary for the procedure. If you make your own and size them to fit, make sure that they are well-sanded with fine sandpaper and cleaned of sanding residue before use, so that no wood chips or sawdust contaminates the engine.

7   Insert the dowels down through the pushrod holes until they lodge firmly in the tappets. For each cylinder, pull up the two dowels (intake and exhaust) and secure them to each other with large rubber bands **(see illustration)**. There must be enough tension on the rubber bands to keep the tappets raised as far as they can go up in their bores.

8   When all of the tappets are secured at the top of their bores, the camshaft can be removed.

9   A somewhat easier method of tappet retention can be accomplished if the engine is out of the vehicle for overhaul, or in-vehicle, if the fuel filter/water separator and fuel injection pump are removed (see Chapter 4, Part B) allowing removal of the engine side cover **(see illustrations)**.

10   Slip a small hose clamp over each tappet. Pull up the tappet to the top of its travel with a magnetic tool and tighten the hose clamp to keep the tappet at the top of its bore. Repeat this procedure for all of the tappets, tightening the clamps only enough to retain them at the top **(see illustration)**.

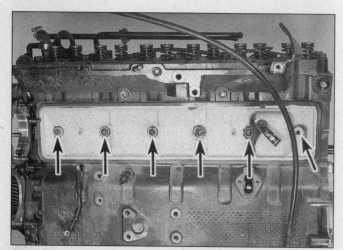

10.9b Remove these six bolts and pull off the stamped-metal side cover and its gasket

10.10 With the side cover off, use a magnetic tool to lift each tappet up, then tighten a small hose clamp around the tappet to keep it there

10.11 Remove the two bolts (arrows) retaining the camshaft thrust plate to the gear housing

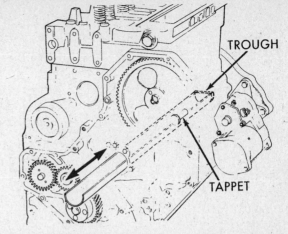

10.13 A long trough-like tool, that may be purchased or fabricated, fits into the camshaft bore and is used to remove and install the tappets

Camshaft removal

Refer to illustration 10.11

11   With the engine positioned at TDC, remove the two bolts retaining the camshaft thrust plate to the block **(see illustration)**.

12   Pull the camshaft out as straight as possible. Be very careful not to nick any of the camshaft bearings in the block with the lobes or journals. Work slowly, its a long and heavy camshaft. **Note:** *Refer to Chapter 3 for removal of the radiator, intercooler and air conditioning condenser and Chapter 11 for removal of the grille to allow room for camshaft extraction.*

Tappet removal

Refer to illustrations 10.13 and 10.14

13   A special tool is necessary to extract the tappets from the block. The tool is a long 1/2-section of pipe slightly smaller than the camshaft bore. The top of the pipe is removed, lengthwise, and one end capped **(see illustration)**.

14   Insert the trough-like tool the full length of the camshaft bore, with the open side up **(see illustration)**. Remove the rubber bands from two of the dowels, pull the dowel out of one tappet, and retie the other dowel with rubber bands to the valve spring or other nearby component. As the dowel is pulled out, that tappet will fall into the trough. Look through the trough with a flashlight to ensure that the tappet is laying on its side in the trough. If not, jiggle the trough to make it fall over and then extract the trough with the tappet.

15   Repeat the procedure for each tappet, keeping them in order so they can be reinstalled in their original locations, until all of the tappets have been removed for inspection.

Inspection

Refer to illustrations 10.17 and 10.19

16   After the camshaft has been removed from the engine, cleaned with solvent and dried, inspect the bearing journals for uneven wear, pitting and evidence of seizure. If the journals are damaged, the bearing inserts in the block are probably damaged as well. Both the camshaft and bearings will have to be replaced. **Note:** *Camshaft bearing replacement requires special tools and expertise that place it beyond the scope of the average home mechanic. Although the tool for bearing removal/installation is available at stores that carry automotive tools and possibly even found at a tool rental business, if the bearings are bad and bearing replacement is beyond your ability, remove the engine and take the block to an automotive machine shop to ensure that the job is done correctly.*

17   Measure the bearing journals with a micrometer to determine if they are excessively worn or out-of-round. Measure the camshaft lobe height **(see illustration)**. Compare your measurements with this chapter's specifications to determine if the camshaft is worn.

10.14 Insert the trough-like tool into the camshaft bore with the open side up - then pull the dowels, or as shown, release the hose clamp from one tappet at a time until it falls into the trough and can be withdrawn from the engine

10.17 Measure the camshaft lobe at its greatest dimension to determine the lobe height

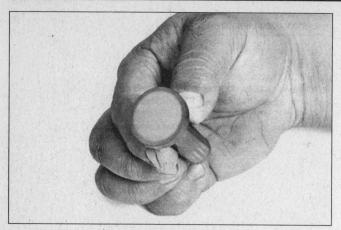

10.19 Examine the foot of the tappet for uneven wear or pitting - it should be perfectly flat

10.22 Drop the tappet retrieval tool down through one of the pushrod holes, pull it out with the trough, and attach it to a tappet - our trough was made from a length of copper pipe, and the retrieval tool is a short section of hose that just fits into the tappet and attached to a long piece of wire

18   Check the camshaft lobes for heat discoloration, score marks, chipped areas, pitting and uneven wear. If the lobes are in good condition and if the journal diameters and lobe height measurements are as specified, the camshaft can be reused.

19   Check each tappet wall, pushrod seat and foot for scuffing, score marks and uneven wear. Each tappet foot (the surface that rides on the cam lobe) should be perfectly flat, although it may be slightly concave in normal wear **(see illustration)**. If there are signs of uneven wear or scoring, the tappets and camshaft must be replaced. If the tappet walls are damaged or worn (which is not very likely), inspect the tappet bores in the engine block as well, using a small inspection mirror with a long handle. If the pushrod seats are worn, check the pushrod ends.

20   If new tappets are being installed, a new camshaft must also be installed. If a new camshaft is installed, then use new tappets as well. Never install used tappets unless the original camshaft is used and the tappets can be installed in their original locations.

Camshaft and tappet installation

Refer to illustrations 10.22, 10.26 and 10.27

21   Another special tool is required to "fish" the new tappets up into their bores before the camshaft is installed. The tool is basically a long wire attached to a short plug that fits inside the tappet. The other end of the long wire is attached to a handle of some kind.

22   Insert the tappet trough tool fully into the camshaft bore and drop the tappet retrieval tool down through the pushrod hole from above until it hits the trough. Carefully draw the trough out of the engine until the tool is exposed, then push the tool into the tappet **(see illustration)**. Lubricate the sides and foot of the tappet with engine assembly

lube.

23   Push the trough back into the engine fully and from above, pull up on the wire until the tappet is at the top of it's bore.

24   Now rotate the trough around until its closed side is UP, which will keep the tappet from falling out of its bore. The "fishing" tool can now be pulled out of the tappet and the dowel inserted and secured, retaining that tappet in place. If the side cover is off, secure the tappet with a hose clamp, as in Step 10.

25   Repeat Steps 22 to 24 for the remaining tappets until all are held high in their proper bores with the dowels and rubber bands, or hose clamps.

26   Lubricate the camshaft lobes and journals thoroughly with camshaft installation lubricant **(see illustration)** and insert the camshaft into the block, again being careful to insert it straight without nicking the bearings with the lobes or journals.

27   As the camshaft is close to being fully inserted, align the timing marks on the camshaft gear with the timing mark on the crankshaft gear **(see illustration)**. When the camshaft is fully inserted and the gears properly meshed, install the camshaft thrust plate bolts and tighten them to the torque listed in this Chapter's Specifications **(see illustration 10.8)**. **Caution:** *Do not push the camshaft any further into the block than is necessary, or the camshaft plug at the back of the block could be loosened, creating an oil leak.*

28   All of the tappet retaining dowels or clamps may now be

10.26 Lube the camshaft thoroughly with camshaft installation lube

10.27 Align the timing marks (arrows) on the crankshaft and camshaft gears

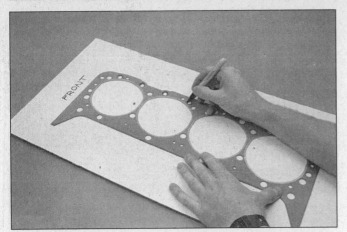

11.7 Use a new head gasket to trace the bolt pattern on a piece of cardboard - punch holes for the head bolts and use the cardboard to keep track of the locations of the three sizes of head bolts

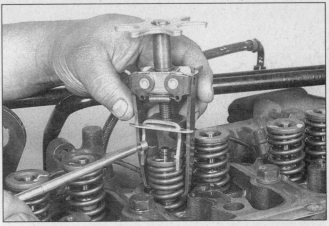

11.10 Compress the valve spring to release the retainer then use needle-nose pliers or a magnet to remove the keepers

removed, and the pushrods, rocker arms and other components installed. Adjust the valve clearance as described in Section 5.

29   The remainder of the installation is the reverse of the removal procedure. If the side cover had been removed, install it with a new gasket. Change the engine oil and oil filter (see Chapter 1).

11   Cylinder head - removal and installation

Caution 1: *If the cylinder head is damaged and must be replaced, the replacement cylinder head must have been originally designed for the newer model intercooled engine. The earlier model cylinder head, designed for a non-intercooled engine, cannot be used on an intercooled engine or vice versa.*
Caution 2: *Make sure the engine is completely cool before beginning this procedure.*

Removal

Refer to illustration 11.7

1   Disconnect both negative battery cables.
2   Refer to Chapter 1, drain the engine coolant and remove the drivebelt.
3   Refer to Sections 4 and 5 and remove the valve covers, rocker arms and pushrods.
4   Refer to Chapter 4, Part B and remove the turbocharger. Refer to Sections 6 and 7 and remove the exhaust manifold, air intake duct and intake manifold cover.
5   Refer to Chapter 3 and remove the heater hoses and radiator hose.
6   Refer to Chapter 4, Part B and remove the fuel filter/water separator.
7   Using a new head gasket, make a template of the bolt hole locations on a piece of cardboard **(see illustration)**. There are three sizes of head bolts, so as each head bolt is removed, insert it into its location on the cardboard template.
8   Carefully pry on a casting protrusion between the cylinder head and the block to break the head gasket seal. The cylinder head is quite heavy, so have an assistant help you lift it off the engine.

Valve seal replacement

Refer to illustration 11.10

9   The cylinder head is a vital part of the engine's efficiency. If you have gone to the trouble to remove it and the engine has accumulated many, many miles, consider having the valves and seats refaced at an automotive machine shop to restore full sealing of the valves. The following procedures involve disassembling the valves for inspection and

11.14 Use a gasket scraper and gasket removing solvent to clean the cylinder head and block sealing surfaces

replacement of the valve guide seals. See Part C of this Chapter for more details on cylinder head inspection procedures.

10   Using a valve spring compressor, compress the first valve spring for the number 1 cylinder and while it is compressed, use needle-nose pliers or a magnet to extract the keepers **(see illustration)**. Slowly release the valve spring compressor.
11   Remove the valve guide seal and install the new seal. Install the valve spring and retainer, compress the spring and install the keepers. Use a dab of grease on the keepers to hold them in place while the compressor is slowly released. **Note:** *The seals are the same for both intake and exhaust valves.*
12   Repeat the procedure for the remaining valves.

Installation

Refer to illustrations 11.14, 11.15, 11.16, 11.17 and 11.20

13   The mating surfaces of the cylinder head and block must be perfectly clean when the heads are installed. Gasket removal solvents are available at auto parts stores and may prove helpful.
14   Use a gasket scraper to remove all traces of carbon and old gasket material **(see illustration)**, then wipe the mating surfaces with a cloth saturated with lacquer thinner or acetone. If there is oil on the mating surfaces when the head is installed, the gasket may not seal correctly and leaks may develop. When working on the block, fill the cylinders with shop rags to keep debris out of the engine. Use a vacuum cleaner to remove any debris that falls into the cylinders. **Note:** *Clean any carbon from the injector nozzle seats with a brass or nylon brush.*

2B

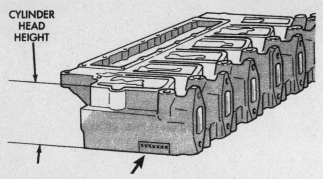

CYLINDER
HEAD
HEIGHT

11.15 If a cylinder head is warped, it must be machined - this pad (arrow) at the rear of the head indicates if the head has been machined before and how much

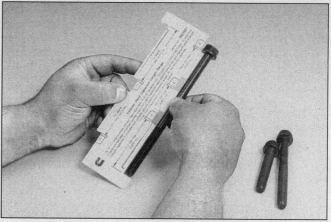

11.16 A head bolt stretch gauge (included with the gasket set) is used to determine if the cylinder heads bolts can be reused

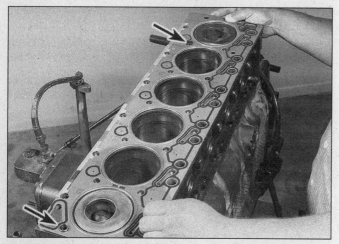

11.17 Position the new head gasket over the dowels in the block - note any markings on the gasket that indicate Top or Front

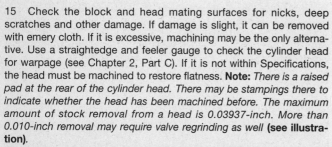

11.20 Cylinder head bolt tightening sequence

15   Check the block and head mating surfaces for nicks, deep scratches and other damage. If damage is slight, it can be removed with emery cloth. If it is excessive, machining may be the only alternative. Use a straightedge and feeler gauge to check the cylinder head for warpage (see Chapter 2, Part C). If it is not within Specifications, the head must be machined to restore flatness. **Note:** *There is a raised pad at the rear of the cylinder head. There may be stampings there to indicate whether the head has been machined before. The maximum amount of stock removal from a head is 0.03937-inch. More than 0.010-inch removal may require valve regrinding as well* **(see illustration)**.

16   Use a tap of the correct size to chase the threads in the head bolt holes in the block. Mount each bolt in a vise and run a die down the threads to remove corrosion and restore the threads. Dirt, corrosion, sealant and damaged threads will affect torque readings. Most engine gaskets sets will include a bolt stretch gauge for the head bolts **(see illustration)**. If the head bolts are longer than indicated on the gauge, they are stretched and must be replaced with new bolts.

17   Position the new gasket over the dowels in the block **(see illustration)**.

18   Carefully position the cylinder head on the block without disturbing the gaskets.

19   Apply engine oil to the threads and underneath the bolt heads.

20   Install the bolts in their original locations and tighten them finger tight. Following the recommended sequence **(see illustration)**, tighten the bolts in several steps to the torque listed in this Chapter's Specifications.

21   The remainder of the installation is the reverse of the removal procedure. Refer to Chapter 1 and change the oil and filter and refill the cooling system.

12 Oil pump - removal, inspection and installation

Refer to illustrations 12.3, 12.4, 12.5, 12.6, 12.7a, 12.7b and 12.7c

1   Disconnect the negative cables from both batteries. Refer to Chapter 1 and drain the engine oil.

2   Refer to Section 9 and remove the gear housing cover.

3   Measure the backlash between the gears using a dial indicator. Install the dial indicator tip against one of the teeth on the idler gear and twist the idler gear back and forth **(see illustration)**. This will give the backlash measurement between the crankshaft gear and the idler gear. Compare it to this Chapter's Specifications.

4   Place the dial indicator tip on the oil pump drive gear and check the backlash between it and the idler gear while securely holding the idler gear from moving **(see illustration)**. If the backlash is greater than that listed in this Chapter's Specifications for either gear, the gears must be replaced.

5   Remove the four mounting bolts and remove the oil pump assembly from the gear case **(see illustration)**.

6   Remove the back plate of the oil pump assembly. Clean the top of the gerotor planetary of oil and mark it with the word TOP with a felt pen or paint **(see illustration)**.

7   Remove the components, clean them with solvent and dry them thoroughly. Assemble the components back in the oil pump housing. **Note:** *The chamfer on the outside diameter of the gerotor planetary must face down, into the housing.* Using a feeler gauge measure the planetary-to-body clearance, the tip clearance and the gerotor-to-back plate clearance **(see illustrations)**. If any clearance is beyond that listed in this Chapter's Specifications, replace the oil pump assembly.

8   If the original pump is being reused, fill the pump cavity with

12.3 With the dial indicator tip positioned against the idler gear (arrow), rotate the idler gear and compare its backlash to the Specifications

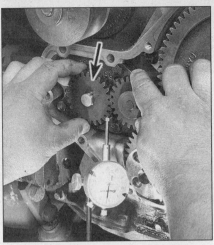

12.4 Check the backlash at the drive gear (arrow) while holding the idler gear

12.5 Remove the four mounting bolts (arrows) to remove the oil pump from the gear case

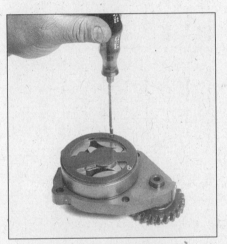

12.6 Remove the two screws on the back plate, then mark the top of the gerotor planetary with a felt marker

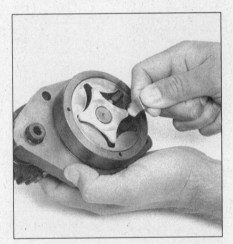

12.7a Measure the gerotor-to-planetary tip clearance with a feeler gauge

12.7b Measure the gerotor planetary-to-body clearance

engine oil and reinstall the back cover, then install the pump assembly in the gear case and tighten the mounting bolts to the torque listed in this Chapter's Specifications.

9   The remainder of the installation is the reverse of the disassembly procedure. Refill the crankcase with oil, start the engine, check for leaks and proper oil pressure.

13   Oil pan - removal and installation

Refer to illustrations 13.2, 13.4 and 13.5

Removal

1   Disconnect the negative cables from both batteries. Refer to Chapter 1 and drain the engine oil.

2   Attach an engine hoist to the engine lift brackets, raise the engine slightly and remove the through-bolts from the engine mounts (see Section 17). Continue to raise the engine until the engine mounts clear the brackets, then remove the engine mounts. **Caution:** *Check the clearance of the engine components as you raise the engine, If necessary remove the cooling fan and fan shroud.* Place two large wood blocks on the frame rails and lower the weight of the engine onto the wood blocks

12.7c Using the feeler gauge and a straightedge, measure the gerotor-to-back plate clearance

13.2 Support the engine with an engine hoist, two large wood blocks (arrows), and place a floor jack under the transmission

13.4 With the engine safely supported, remove the oil pan bolts

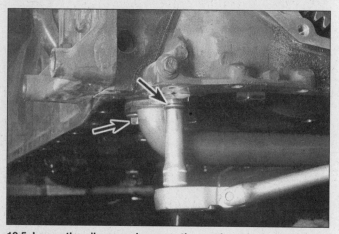

13.5 Lower the oil pan and remove the suction tube bolts (arrows) at the front of the engine

(see illustration). Support the transmission with a floor jack.

3   If equipped with an automatic transmission, disconnect the transmission oil cooler line clips at the oil pan.

4   Remove the oil pan bolts and use a putty knife between the block and the pan to break the gasket seal (see illustration). Caution: *Do not gouge the sealing surfaces with a screwdriver or pry tool.*

5   Lower the pan to access and remove the two bolts retaining the

oil suction tube near the front of the block (see illustration). Lower the suction tube into the oil pan and remove the oil pan and suction tube together.

Installation

6   Clean the interior of the oil pan with rags and solvent and clean the oil suction tube, blowing it out with compressed air if available. Also clean the pan mounting surface of the block of any sealant, gasket material or oil.

7   On the engine, apply a small bead of RTV sealant to the block and front cover joints, and the block and the rear seal retainer joints.

8   Attach a new gasket to the oil suction tube mounting flange and place the suction tube into the pan, with the mounting flange at the front.

9   Raise the oil pan up next to the block and attach the oil suction tube to the block. Install the oil pan. Tighten the bolts, starting in the center and working towards the ends, to the torque listed in this Chapter's Specifications.

10   Install the oil pan drain plug with a new sealing washer and tighten it to the torque listed in this Chapter's Specifications.

11   Refill the engine with new oil (see Chapter 1). The remainder of installation is the reverse of removal. Start the engine and check for oil leaks.

14   Oil filter bypass valve - replacement

Refer to illustrations 14.2a, 14.2b and 14.4

1   Disconnect the negative cables from both batteries.

14.2a Remove the bolts (arrows) retaining the oil cooler cover to the block

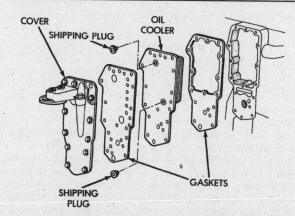

14.2b Engine oil cooler installation details

14.4 Tap the new bypass valve in place with a socket, just until the valve bottoms in the cavity

15.1 There are eight bolts retaining the flywheel on the diesel engine and the pilot bearing is pressed into the center of the flywheel - Mark the flywheel's UP orientation before removal

2B

2   Refer to Chapter 1 and remove the oil filter, then remove the oil cooler cover **(see illustrations)**.
3   Remove the oil filter bypass valve from the oil cooler cover, using locking pliers.
4   Tap the new bypass valve in place with a small hammer and a socket until it seats against its bore in the cover **(see illustration)**. Do not tap further once the valve reaches bottom.
5   Reinstall the oil cooler cover with a new gasket. Tighten the bolts to the torque listed in this Chapter's Specifications.

15 Flywheel/driveplate - removal and installation

Refer to illustration 15.1

Flywheel/driveplate removal and installation for the diesel engine is principally the same as for the gasoline engines **(see illustration)**. Refer to Section 16 of Part A of this Chapter for procedures, but use the torque Specifications in this Chapter's Specifications. Always use new flywheel bolts when the flywheel is reinstalled, and apply Loctite 242 on the threads. **Note:** *The pilot bearing (on manual transmission models) is pressed into the center of the flywheel. If the pilot bearing is worn or has been damaged in transmission removal, refer to Chapter 8 for replacement.*

16.3a Remove these eight bolts to remove the engine-to-transmission adapter . . .

16 Rear main oil seal - replacement

Refer to illustrations 16.3a and 16.3b

1   Rear seal removal and installation for the diesel engine is princi-pally the same as for the gasoline engines (refer to Chapter 2, Part A).
2   The rear seal can be removed with the rear seal retainer plate in place, or by removing the retainer plate and replacing the seal off the engine. If the seal is replaced with the retainer plate still on the engine, an alternate method may be used to remove it; drill holes in the seal and use a slide-hammer as described in Section 8.
3   If the rear seal retainer plate is to be removed, the engine-to-transmission adapter must be removed first **(see illustrations)**.
4   There are two types of rear seals. On seals with a rubber outer diameter, use soapy water around the outside during installation into the retainer plate. The seals without a rubber edge should be installed with Loctite 277 around the outer diameter. **Caution:** *DO NOT use oil on the seal lip or crankshaft during installation - the crankshaft sealing surface and the oil seal must be clean and dry or oil leaks may result.*

16.3b . . . for access to the rear main seal retainer (arrow), held to the block with six bolts

17 Engine mounts - replacement

Refer to illustrations 17.1

Refer to Chapter 2, Part A for this procedure, but use the torque Specifications in this Chapter's Specifications and the accompanying illustration for the engine mount location **(see illustration)**. **Note:** *Align the restriction pads with the projections on the insulator before installing and tightening the through-bolt.*

17.1 Remove these bolts (arrows) to remove the mount from the engine

Chapter 2 Part C
General engine overhaul procedures

Contents

Specifications

Gasoline engines

General

Oil pressure, V6 and V8	
Idle	6 psi minimum
3000 rpm	30 to 80 psi
Oil pressure, V10	
Idle	12 to 25 psi
3000 rpm	50 to 60 psi
Cylinder compression	
V6 and V8	100 psi minimum; no more than 40 psi variation among cylinders
V10	170 to 190 psi

Cylinder block

Cylinder bore diameter (standard)	
V6, 5.2L V8	3.910 to 3.912 inches
5.9L V8	4.000 to 4.002 inches
V10	3.910 to 3.912 inches
Taper limit	0.010 inch
Out-of-round limit	0.005 inch
Deck (head gasket surface) warpage limit	0.00075 inch times the span length of the deck (maximum)

Pistons and rings

Piston-to-cylinder bore clearance (at top of skirt)	0.0005 to 0.0015 inch
Piston ring side clearance	
V6 and V8	
Compression rings	0.0015 to 0.0030 inch
Oil ring (steel rails)	0.002 to 0.008 inch
V10	
Compression rings	0.0029 to 0.0038 inch
Oil ring (steel rails)	0.0073 to 0.0097 inch
Piston ring end gap	
Compression rings	0.010 to 0.020 inch
Oil ring (steel rails)	
V6 and V8	0.010 to 0.050 inch
V10	0.015 to 0.055 inch

Crankshaft and connecting rods

Crankshaft main journal	
Diameter (standard)	
V6, 5.2L V8	2.4995 to 2.5005 inches
5.9L V8	2.8095 to 2.8105 inches
V10	2.9995 to 3.0005 inches
Out-of-round/taper limit	0.001 inch
Main bearing oil clearance	
V6	
Number 1	0.0005 to 0.0015 inch
Numbers 2, 3, and 4	0.0005 to 0.0020 inch
V8	
Number 1	0.0005 to 0.0015 inch
Numbers 2, 3, 4 and 5	0.0005 to 0.0020 inch
V10	0.0002 to 0.0023 inch
Service limit, all	0.0025 inch
Crankshaft connecting rod journal	
Diameter	2.124 to 2.125 inches
Out-of-round/taper limit	0.001 inch
Standard bearing oil clearance	
V6 and V8	0.0005 to 0.0022 inch
V10	0.0002 to 0.0029 inch
Oil clearance service limit	0.003 inch
Connecting rod side clearance	
V6 and V8	0.006 to 0.014 inch
V10	0.010 to 0.018 inch
Crankshaft endplay	
V6 and V8	0.0002 to 0.007 inch
V10	0.003 to 0.012 inch

Cylinder head and valve train

Head gasket surface warpage limit	0.00075 inch times the span length of the head (maximum)
Valve margin, minimum	0.047 inch
Valve stem diameter (standard)	
V6, 5.2L V8, V10	0.311 to 0.312 inch
5.9L V8	
Intake	0.372 to 0.373 inch
Exhaust	0.371 to 0.372 inch
Valve stem-to-guide clearance	
Standard	
V6, 5.2L V8, V10	0.001 to 0.003 inch
5.9L V8	
Intake	0.001 to 0.003 inch
Exhaust	0.002 to 0.004 inch
Service limit (rocking method)	0.017 inch
Valve spring free length	1-31/32 inches
Valve spring installed height	1-41/64 inches
Valve seat width	
V6 and V8	
Intake	0.040 to 0.060 inch
Exhaust	0.060 to 0.080 inch
V10, intake and exhaust	0.040 to 0.060 inch

Torque specifications*   **Ft-lbs** (unless otherwise indicated)

Main bearing cap bolts
    Step 1 20
    Step 2 85
Connecting rod cap bolts 45

***Note:** Refer to Part A for additional torque specifications.*

5.9L diesel engine

General

Oil pressure
    Idle .... 10 psi
    2500 rpm .... 30 psi

Cylinder block

Cylinder bore diameter .... 4.0203 inches
Taper limit .... 0.003 inch
Out-of-round limit .... 0.0015 inch
Deck (head gasket surface) warpage limit .... 0.003 inch

Pistons and rings

Piston-to-cylinder bore clearance .... 0.0005 to 0.0015 inch
Piston skirt diameter (1/2-inch up from bottom) .... 4.0110 to 4.0088 inches
Piston ring side clearance
    Middle ring .... 0.006 inch (maximum)
    Oil ring (steel rails) .... 0.005 inch (maximum)
Piston ring end gap
    Top ring .... 0.016 to 0.0275 inch
    Intermediate ring .... 0.010 to 0.0215 inch
    Oil ring (steel rails) .... 0.010 to 0.0215 inch

Crankshaft and connecting rods

Main journal
    Diameter .... 3.2662 to 2.5005 inches
    Taper limit .... 0.0005 inch
    Out-of-round limit .... 0.002 inch
Main bearing oil clearance, maximum .... 0.0047 inch
Connecting rod journal
    Diameter .... 2.7150 inches
    Taper limit .... 0.0005 inch
    Out-of-round limit .... 0.002 inch
Connecting rod bearing oil clearance .... 0.0035 inch
Connecting rod side clearance .... 0.004 to 0.012 inch
Crankshaft endplay .... 0.004 to 0.017 inch

Cylinder head and valve train

Head gasket surface warpage limit .... 0.012 inch maximum overall, or 0.004 inch variation in any 2-inch area
Cylinder head minimum height .... 3.7008 inches
Maximum head thickness removal (machining) .... 0.03937 inch
Valve margin, minimum .... 0.031 inch
Valve stem diameter (standard) .... 0.3126 to 0.3134 inch
Valve stem-to-guide clearance .... 0.0031 to 0.0051 inch
Valve spring free length .... 2.36 inches
Valve spring pressure, minimum .... 81 lbs at 1.94 inches
Valve seat width
    Minimum .... 0.060 inch
    Maximum .... 0.080 inch

Torque specifications*   **Ft-lbs** (unless otherwise indicated)

Main bearing cap bolts
    Step 1 45
    Step 2 88
    Step 3 129
Connecting rod cap bolts
    Step 1 26
    Step 2 51
    Step 3 73

***Note:** Refer to Part B for additional torque specifications.*

2C

1   General information

Included in this portion of Chapter 2 are the general overhaul procedures for cylinder heads and internal engine components. The information ranges from advice concerning preparation for an overhaul and the purchase of replacement parts to detailed, step-by-step procedures covering removal and installation of internal engine components and the inspection of parts.

The following Sections have been written based on the assumption that the engine has been removed from the vehicle. For information concerning in-vehicle engine repair, as well as removal and installation of the external components necessary for the overhaul, see Parts A and B of this Chapter and Section 8 of this Part.

The Specifications included here in Part C are only those necessary for the inspection and overhaul procedures which follow. Refer to Parts A and B for additional specifications.

2   Engine removal - methods and precautions

If you have decided that an engine must be removed for overhaul or major repair work, several preliminary steps should be taken.

Locating a suitable work area is extremely important. A shop is, of course, the most desirable place to work. Adequate work space, along with storage space for the vehicle, will be needed. If a shop or garage is not available, at the very least a flat, level, clean work surface made of concrete or asphalt is required.

Cleaning the engine compartment and engine before beginning the removal procedure will help keep tools clean and organized.

An engine hoist or A-frame will be needed. Make sure that the equipment is rated in excess of the combined weight of the engine and its accessories, especially when working with the 5.9L diesel engine, which is heavier than most. Safety is of primary importance, considering the potential hazards involved in lifting the engine out of the vehicle.

If the engine is being removed by a novice, a helper should be available. Advice and aid from someone more experienced would also be helpful. There are many instances when one person cannot simultaneously perform all of the operations required when lifting the engine out of the vehicle.

Plan the operation ahead of time. Arrange for or obtain all of the tools and equipment you will need prior to beginning the job. Some of the equipment necessary to perform engine removal and installation safely and with relative ease are (in addition to an engine hoist) a heavy duty floor jack, complete sets of wrenches and sockets as described in the front of this manual, wooden blocks and plenty of rags and cleaning solvent for mopping up spilled oil, coolant and gasoline. If the hoist is to be rented, make sure that you arrange for it in advance and perform beforehand all of the operations possible without it. This will save you money and time.

Plan for the vehicle to be out of use for a considerable amount of time. A machine shop will be required to perform some of the work which the do-it-yourselfer cannot accomplish due to a lack of special equipment. These shops often have a busy schedule, so it would be wise to consult them before removing the engine in order to accurately estimate the amount of time required to rebuild or repair components that may need work.

Always use extreme caution when removing and installing the engine. Serious injury can result from careless actions. Plan ahead, take your time and a job of this nature, although major, can be accomplished successfully.

3   Engine overhaul - general information

Refer to illustrations 3.4a, 3.4b, 3.4c and 3.4d

It is not always easy to determine when, or if, an engine should be completely overhauled, as a number of factors must be considered.

High mileage is not necessarily an indication that an overhaul is

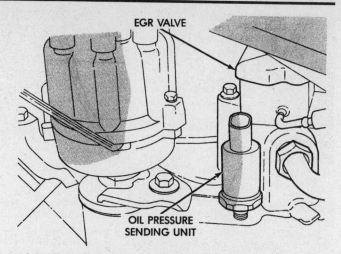

3.4a The oil pressure sending unit on V6 and V8 engines is located at the rear of the engine, just behind the intake manifold (adjacent to the distributor)

needed, while low mileage does not preclude the need for an overhaul. Frequency of servicing is probably the most important consideration. An engine that has had regular and frequent oil and filter changes, as well as other required maintenance, will most likely give many thousands of miles of reliable service. Conversely, a neglected engine may require an overhaul very early in its life.

Excessive oil consumption is an indication that piston rings and/or valve guides are in need of attention. Make sure that oil leaks are not responsible before deciding that the rings and/or guides are bad. Test the cylinder compression (see Section 4) or have a leak-down test performed by an experienced tune-up mechanic to determine the extent of the work required.

If the engine is making obvious knocking or rumbling noises, the connecting rod and/or main bearings are probably at fault. To accurately test oil pressure, temporarily connect a mechanical oil pressure gauge in place of the oil pressure sending unit **(see illustrations)**. Compare the reading to the pressure listed in this Chapter's Specifications. If the pressure is extremely low, the bearings and/or oil pump are probably worn out.

Loss of power, rough running, excessive valve train noise and high fuel consumption rates may also point to the need for an overhaul, especially if they are all present at the same time. If a complete tune-up does not remedy the situation, major mechanical work is the only solution.

An engine overhaul involves restoring the internal parts to the specifications of a new engine. During an overhaul, the piston rings are replaced and the cylinder walls are reconditioned (rebored and/or honed). If a re-bore is done, new pistons are required. The main bearings, connecting rod bearings and camshaft bearings are generally replaced with new ones and, if necessary, the crankshaft may be reground to restore the journals. Generally, the valves are serviced as well, since they are usually in less-than-perfect condition at this point. While the engine is being overhauled, other components, such as the distributor, starter and alternator, can be rebuilt as well. The end result should be a like-new engine that will give many thousands of trouble-free miles. **Note:** *Critical cooling system components such as the hoses, the drivebelts, the thermostat and the water pump MUST be replaced with new parts when an engine is overhauled. The radiator should be checked carefully to ensure that it isn't clogged or leaking. If in doubt, replace it with a new one. Some engine rebuilding companies will not guarantee their short-blocks or long-blocks unless you have proof that a new or reconditioned radiator was installed at the time the engine was exchanged. Also, we do not recommend overhauling the oil pump - always install a new one when an engine is rebuilt.*

Before beginning the engine overhaul, read through the entire procedure to familiarize yourself with the scope and requirements of the job. Overhauling an engine is not difficult if you take your time and follow all procedures carefully. But it is time consuming. Plan on the

3.4b The oil pressure sending unit (arrow) on the V10 engine is below the starter and at the top of the oil filter housing

3.4c The oil pressure sending unit (arrow) on the diesel engine is on the block, just to the rear of the power steering pump

3.4d Unscrew the oil pressure sending unit and install a pressure gauge in its place

2C

vehicle being tied up for a minimum of two weeks, especially if parts must be taken to an automotive machine shop for repair or reconditioning. Check on availability of parts and make sure that any necessary special tools and equipment are obtained in advance. Most work can be done with typical hand tools, although a number of precision measuring tools are required for inspecting parts to determine if they must be replaced. Often an automotive machine shop will handle the inspection of parts and offer advice concerning reconditioning and replacement. **Note:** *Always wait until the engine has been completely disassembled and all components, especially the engine block, have been inspected before deciding what service and repair operations must be performed by an automotive machine shop.* Since the block's condition will be the major factor to consider when determining whether to overhaul the original engine or buy a rebuilt one, never purchase parts or have machine work done on other components until the block has been thoroughly inspected. As a general rule, time is the primary cost of an overhaul, so it does not pay to install worn or substandard parts.

As a final note, to ensure maximum life and minimum trouble from a rebuilt engine, everything must be assembled with care in a spotlessly clean environment.

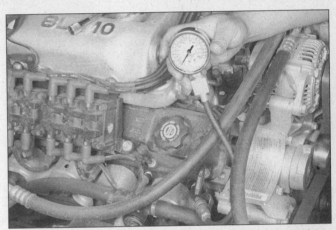

4.4 A compression gauge with a threaded fitting for the spark plug hole is preferred over the type that requires hand pressure to maintain the seal - be sure to open the throttle valve as far as possible during the compression check

4   Compression check

Gasoline engines

Refer to illustration 4.4

1   A compression check will tell you what mechanical condition the pistons, rings, valves and head gaskets of your engine are in. Specifically, it can tell you if the compression is down due to leakage caused by worn piston rings, defective valves and seats or a blown head gasket. **Note:** *The engine must be at normal operating temperature for this check and the battery must be fully charged.*

2   Begin by cleaning the area around the spark plugs before you remove them (compressed air works best for this). This will prevent dirt from getting into the cylinders as the compression check is being done. Remove all of the spark plugs from the engine.

3   Block the throttle wide open and disconnect the primary wires from the coil.

4   With the compression gauge in the number one spark plug hole, crank the engine over at least four compression strokes and watch the gauge **(see illustration)**. The compression should build up quickly in a healthy engine. Low compression on the first stroke, followed by gradually increasing pressure on successive strokes, indicates worn piston rings. A low compression reading on the first stroke, which does not build up during successive strokes, indicates leaking valves or a blown head gasket (a cracked head could also be the cause). Record the highest gauge reading obtained.

5   Repeat the procedure for the remaining cylinders and compare the results to the Specifications.

6   Add some engine oil (about three squirts from a plunger-type oil can) to each cylinder, through the spark plug hole, and repeat the test.

7   If the compression increases after the oil is added, the piston rings are definitely worn. If the compression does not increase significantly, the leakage is occurring at the valves or head gasket. Leakage past the valves may be caused by burned valve seats and/or faces or warped, cracked or bent valves.

8   If two adjacent cylinders have equally low compression, there is a strong possibility that the head gasket between them is blown. The appearance of coolant in the combustion chambers or the oil would verify this condition. Generally, coolant will cause the oil on the dipstick to look light-colored (milky).

9   If the compression is unusually high, the combustion chambers are probably coated with carbon deposits. If that is the case, the cylinder head(s) should be removed and decarbonized.

10   If compression is way down or varies greatly between cylinders, it would be a good idea to have a leak-down test performed by an automotive repair shop. This test will pinpoint exactly where the leakage is occurring and how severe it is.

Diesel engine

Refer to illustration 4.12

11   To test the compression on the diesel engine, the fuel injectors must be removed and the fuel supply disabled (see Chapter 4B). Block the throttle wide open.

4.12 On diesel engines, a special adapter (arrow) must be installed in the cylinder head in place of a fuel injector

5.4 Connect a vacuum gauge to a port on the intake manifold, and plug the disconnected vacuum hose during the test

12   The special compression tester must be tapped into the injector hole for the cylinder being tested, then a compression gauge can be attached **(see illustration)**. **Note:** *The gauge must be made for diesel applications and capable of reading at least 500 psi pressure.*
13   Crank the engine for at least six compression strokes or "puffs" and watch the gauge.
14   Repeat the procedure for the remaining cylinders. **Caution:** *Unlike testing gasoline engines, never add oil to the cylinders during a compression test of a diesel engine. Severe engine damage could result.*
15   The analysis of the compression readings will be similar to Steps 4 and 8 through 10.

5   Vacuum gauge diagnostic checks (gasoline engines)

Refer to illustration 5.4

A vacuum gauge provides valuable information about what is going on in the engine at a low cost. You can check for worn rings or cylinder walls, leaking head or intake manifold gaskets, incorrect carburetor adjustments, restricted exhaust, stuck or burned valves, weak valve springs, improper ignition or valve timing and ignition problems.

Unfortunately, vacuum gauge readings are easy to misinterpret, so they should be used in conjunction with other tests to confirm the diagnosis.

Both the gauge readings and the rate of needle movement are important for accurate interpretation. Most gauges measure vacuum in inches of mercury (in-Hg). As vacuum increases (or atmospheric pressure decreases), the reading will increase. Also, for every 1,000-foot increase in elevation above sea level, the gauge readings will decrease about one inch of mercury.

Connect the vacuum gauge directly to intake manifold vacuum, not to ported (carburetor) vacuum **(see illustration)**. Be sure no hoses are left disconnected during the test or false readings will result.

Before you begin the test, allow the engine to warm up completely. Block the wheels and set the parking brake. With the transmission in Park, start the engine and allow it to run at normal idle speed. **Warning:** *Carefully inspect the fan blades for cracks or damage before starting the engine. Keep your hands and the vacuum tester clear of the fan and do not stand in front of the vehicle or in line with the fan when the engine is running.*

Read the vacuum gauge; an average, healthy engine should normally produce about 17 to 22 inches of vacuum with a fairly steady needle. Refer to the following vacuum gauge readings and what they indicate about the engines condition:
1   A low, steady reading usually indicates a leaking gasket between the intake manifold and carburetor or throttle body, a leaky vacuum hose, late ignition timing or incorrect camshaft timing. Check ignition

timing with a timing light and eliminate all other possible causes, utilizing the tests provided in this Chapter before you remove the timing chain cover to check the timing marks.
2   If the reading is three to eight inches below normal and it fluctuates at that low reading, suspect an intake manifold gasket leak at an intake port.
3   If the needle has regular drops of about two to four inches at a steady rate, the valves are probably leaking. Perform a compression or leak-down test to confirm this.
4   An irregular drop or down-flick of the needle can be caused by a sticking valve or an ignition misfire. Perform a compression or leak-down test and read the spark plugs.
5   A rapid vibration of about four inches-Hg vibration at idle combined with exhaust smoke indicates worn valve guides. Perform a leak-down test to confirm this. If the rapid vibration occurs with an increase in engine speed, check for a leaking intake manifold gasket or head gasket, weak valve springs, burned valves or ignition misfire.
6   A slight fluctuation, say one inch up and down, may mean ignition problems. Check all the usual tune-up items and, if necessary, run the engine on an ignition analyzer.
7   If there is a large fluctuation, perform a compression or leak-down test to look for a weak or dead cylinder or a blown head gasket.
8   If the needle moves slowly through a wide range, check for a clogged PCV system, incorrect idle fuel mixture, carburetor/throttle body or intake manifold gasket leaks.
9   Check for a slow return after revving the engine by quickly snapping the throttle open until the engine reaches about 2,500 rpm and let it shut. Normally the reading should drop to near zero, rise above normal idle reading (about 5 in-Hg over) and then return to the previous idle reading. If the vacuum returns slowly and doesn't peak when the throttle is snapped shut, the rings may be worn. If there is a long delay, look for a restricted exhaust system (often the muffler or catalytic converter). An easy way to check this is to temporarily disconnect the exhaust ahead of the suspected part and re-test.

6   Engine rebuilding alternatives

The do-it-yourselfer is faced with a number of options when performing an engine overhaul. The decision to replace the engine block, piston/connecting rod assemblies and crankshaft depends on a number of factors, with the number one consideration being the condition of the block. Other considerations are cost, access to machine shop facilities, parts availability, time required to complete the project and the extent of prior mechanical experience on the part of the do-it-yourselfer.

Some of the rebuilding alternatives include:
Individual parts - If the inspection procedures reveal that the engine block and most engine components are in reusable condition,

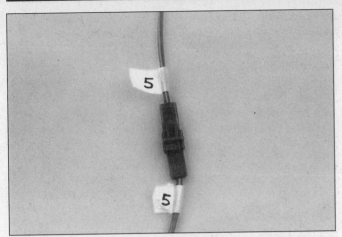

7.12 Label each wire before unplugging the connector

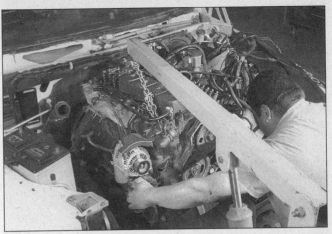

7.21 Lift the engine carefully up and forward with the engine hoist - here the chain is attached to the engine lifting brackets front and rear on this diesel engine

2C

purchasing individual parts may be the most economical alternative. The block, crankshaft and piston/connecting rod assemblies should all be inspected carefully. Even if the block shows little wear, the cylinder bores should be surface honed.

Crankshaft kit - This rebuild package consists of a reground crankshaft and a matched set of pistons and connecting rods. The pistons will already be installed on the connecting rods. Piston rings and the necessary bearings will be included in the kit. These kits are commonly available for standard cylinder bores, as well as for engine blocks which have been bored to a standard oversize.

Short block - A short block consists of an engine block with a camshaft, timing chain and gears, crankshaft and piston/connecting rod assemblies already installed. All new bearings are incorporated and all clearances will be correct. The existing cylinder head(s), valve train components and external parts can be bolted to the short block with little or no machine shop work necessary.

Long block - A long block consists of a short block plus an oil pump, cylinder head(s) and valve train components. All components are installed with new bearings, seals and gaskets incorporated throughout. The installation of manifolds and external parts is all that is necessary.

Give careful thought to which alternative is best for you and discuss the situation with local automotive machine shops, auto parts dealers or parts store personnel before ordering or purchasing replacement parts.

7 Engine - removal and installation

Refer to illustrations 7.12 and 7.21

Warning: *Gasoline and diesel fuel are extremely flammable, so take extra precautions when disconnecting any part of the fuel system. Don't smoke or allow open flames or bare light bulbs in or near the work area and don't work in a garage where a natural gas appliance (such as a clothes dryer or water heater) is installed. If you spill fuel on your skin, rinse it off immediately. Have a fire extinguisher rated for gasoline fires handy and know how to use it! Also, the air conditioning system is under high pressure - have a dealer service department or service station discharge the system before disconnecting any of the hoses or fittings.*

Note: *Read through the following steps carefully and familiarize yourself with the procedure before beginning work.*

Removal

1   On air-conditioned models, have the system discharged by a dealer or service station (see **Warning** above).

2   If you're working on a gasoline-powered model, relieve the fuel system pressure (see Chapter 4, Part A), then disconnect the cable(s) from the negative terminal(s) of the battery (batteries). Remove the hood (see Chapter 11).

3   Remove the air cleaner assembly and all hoses connected to it (see Chapter 4).

4   Drain the cooling system and remove the drivebelts (see Chapter 1).

5   Remove the radiator, shroud and fan (see Chapter 3). Also remove the radiator support (see Chapter 4B).

6   Detach the radiator and heater hoses from the engine.

7   If equipped, remove the air conditioning condenser and automatic transmission oil cooler (see Chapter 3).

8   On diesel engines, remove the intercooler (see Chapter 4B).

9   Disconnect the accelerator cable (see Chapter 4A or 4B) and throttle valve cable (automatic transmission only - see Chapter 7B).

10   Remove the power steering pump and brackets (if equipped) without disconnecting the hoses and tie it out of the way (see Chapter 10).

11   Remove the alternator (see Chapter 5).

12   Label and disconnect all wires from the engine **(see illustration)**. Masking tape and/or a touch-up paint applicator work well for marking items. **Note:** *Take instant photos or sketch the locations of components and brackets to help with reassembly.*

13   Disconnect the fuel lines at the engine (see Chapter 4A or 4B) and plug the lines to prevent fuel loss.

14   Label and remove all vacuum lines from the intake manifold.

15   Raise the vehicle and support it securely on jackstands.

16   Drain the engine oil (see Chapter 1).

17   Disconnect the exhaust pipe(s) from the exhaust manifold(s). On some models, it may be easier to remove the exhaust manifolds also (see Chapter 2A or 2B).

18   Disconnect the wires from the starter solenoid and remove the starter (see Chapter 5).

19   Support the engine from above with a hoist and remove the transmission (see Chapter 7A or 7B). **Caution:** *Do not lift the engine by the intake manifold.*

20   Use the hoist to take the weight off the engine mounts, and remove the engine mount through-bolts or stud nuts (see Chapter 2A or 2B). On diesel engines, remove the oil pan (see Chapter 2B).

21   Check to make sure everything is disconnected, then lift the engine out of the vehicle **(see illustration)**. The engine will probably need to be tilted and/or maneuvered as it's lifted out, so have an assistant handy. **Warning:** *Do not place any part of your body under the engine when it is supported only by a hoist or other lifting device.*

22   Remove the flywheel/driveplate and mount the engine on an engine stand or set the engine on the floor and support it so it doesn't tip over. Then disconnect the engine hoist.

Installation

23   Check the engine mounts. If they're worn or damaged, replace them.

24   On manual transmission models, inspect the clutch components (see Chapter 8). On automatic transmission-equipped models, inspect

the converter seal and bushing.

25   Apply a dab of grease to the pilot bushing on manual transmission models.

26   Attach the hoist to the engine, remove the engine from the engine stand and install the flywheel (see Chapter 2A).

27   Carefully guide the engine into place, lowering it slowly and moving it back into the engine compartment until the engine mounts can be secured.

28   With the engine still supported by the hoist, use a jack with a piece of wood on top to support the oil pan, allowing you control of the angle of the rear of the engine for alignment with the transmission. Refer to Chapter 7A or 7B and reinstall the transmission and rear mount.

29   Tighten all the bolts on the engine mounts and remove the hoist and jack.

30   Reinstall the remaining components in the reverse order of removal.

31   Add coolant, oil, power steering and transmission fluid as needed (see Chapter 1).

32   Run the engine and check for proper operation and leaks. Shut off the engine and recheck the fluid levels.

8   Engine overhaul - disassembly sequence

1   It is much easier to disassemble and work on the engine if it is mounted on a portable engine stand. These stands can often be rented quite cheaply from an equipment rental yard. Before the engine is mounted on a stand, the flywheel/driveplate should be removed from the engine (refer to Chapter 2A or 2B). **Note:** *When overhauling the diesel engine, an engine hoist may be needed again to help in removing the very heavy crankshaft.*

2   If you are going to obtain a rebuilt engine, all external components must come off first, if not already removed. These will be transferred to the replacement engine, just as they will if you are doing a complete engine overhaul yourself. These include:

Alternator and brackets
Emissions control components
Distributor, spark plug wires and spark plugs
Thermostat and housing cover
Water pump
Intake/exhaust manifolds
Engine mounts
Clutch and flywheel/driveplate

Note: *When removing the external components from the engine, pay close attention to details that may be helpful or important during installation. Note the installed position of gaskets, seals, spacers, pins, washers, bolts and other small items.*

3   If you are obtaining a short block, which consists of the engine block, crankshaft, pistons and connecting rods all assembled, then the cylinder heads, oil pan and oil pump will have to be removed as well. See *Engine rebuilding alternatives* for additional information regarding the different possibilities to be considered.

4   If you are planning a complete overhaul, the engine must be disassembled and the internal components removed in the following general order:

Gasoline engines
Valve cover
Intake and exhaust manifolds
Rocker arms and pushrods
Valve lifters
Cylinder head
Oil pan
Timing chain cover
Timing chain and sprockets
Oil pump
Camshaft
Piston/connecting rod assemblies
Crankshaft and main bearings

Diesel engines
Valve covers
Rocker arms and pushrods
Turbocharger and exhaust manifold
High pressure fuel lines
Fuel injection pump
Water pump
Gearcase front cover
Fuel filter
Fuel transfer pump
Fuel heater
Fan drive assembly
Front cover
Oil pump
Timing gears
Cylinder head
Camshaft and tappets
Oil pan
Connecting rods and pistons
Crankshaft

5   Critical cooling system components such as the hoses, the drive-belts, the thermostat and the water pump MUST be replaced with new parts when an engine is overhauled. Also, we do not recommend overhauling the oil pump - always install a new one when an engine is rebuilt.

6   Before beginning the disassembly and overhaul procedures, make sure the following items are available:

Common hand tools
Small cardboard boxes or plastic bags for storing parts
Gasket scraper
Ridge reamer
Vibration damper puller
Micrometers
Telescoping gauges
Dial indicator set
Valve spring compressor
Cylinder surfacing hone
Piston ring groove cleaning tool
Electric drill motor
Tap and die set
Wire brushes
Oil gallery brushes
Cleaning solvent

9   Cylinder head - disassembly

Refer to illustrations 9.2, 9.3a and 9.3b

Note: *New and rebuilt cylinder heads are commonly available for most engines at dealerships and auto parts stores. Due to the fact that some specialized tools are necessary for the disassembly and inspection procedures, and replacement parts may not be readily available, it may be more practical and economical for the home mechanic to purchase replacement heads rather than taking the time to disassemble, inspect and recondition the originals.*

1   Cylinder head disassembly involves removal of the intake and exhaust valves and related components. If they are still in place, remove the rocker arms. Label the parts or store them separately so they can be reinstalled in their original locations.

2   Before the valves are removed, arrange to label and store them, along with their related components, so they can be kept separate and reinstalled in the same valve guides they are removed from **(see illustration)**.

3   Compress the springs on the first valve with a spring compressor and remove the keepers **(see illustration)**. Carefully release the valve spring compressor and remove the retainer and (if used) rotators, the shield, the springs and the spring seat or shims (if used). Remove the oil seal(s) from the valve stem and the umbrella-type seal from over the guide boss (if used), then pull the valve from the head. If the valve binds in the guide (won't pull through), push it back into the head and

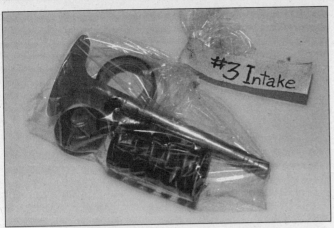

9.2 A small plastic bag, with an appropriate label, can be used to store the valve train components so they can be kept together and reinstalled in their original positions

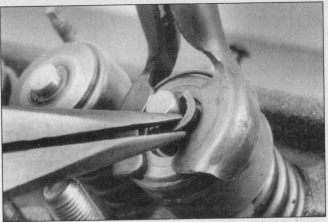

9.3a Use a valve spring compressor to compress the spring, then remove the keepers from the valve stem with a magnet or needle-nose pliers

9.3b If the valve won't pull through the guide, deburr the edge of the stem end and the area around the top of the keeper groove with a file or whetstone

10.11 Check the cylinder head gasket surface for warpage by trying to slip a feeler gauge under the straightedge (see this Chapter's Specifications for the maximum warpage allowed and use a feeler gauge of that thickness)

deburr the area around the keeper groove with a fine file or whetstone **(see illustration)**.

4   Repeat the procedure for the remaining valves. Remember to keep all the parts for each valve together so they can be reinstalled in the same locations.

5   Once the valves and related components have been removed and stored in an organized manner, the head should be thoroughly cleaned and inspected. If a complete engine overhaul is being done, finish the engine disassembly procedures before beginning the cylinder head cleaning and inspection process.

10   Cylinder head - cleaning and inspection

1   Thorough cleaning of the cylinder heads and related valve train components, followed by a detailed inspection, will enable you to decide how much valve service work must be done during the engine overhaul.

Cleaning

2   Scrape away all traces of old gasket material and sealing compound from the head gasket, intake manifold and exhaust manifold sealing surfaces. Be very careful not to gouge the cylinder head. Special gasket removal solvents, which soften gaskets and make removal much easier, are available at auto parts stores.

3   Remove any built up scale from the coolant passages.

4   Run a stiff wire brush through the various holes to remove any deposits that may have formed in them.

5   Run an appropriate-size tap into each of the threaded holes to remove any corrosion and thread sealant that may be present. If compressed air is available, use it to clear the holes of debris produced by this operation.

6   Check the condition of the spark plug threads.

7   Clean the cylinder head with solvent and dry it thoroughly. Compressed air will speed the drying process and ensure that all holes and recessed areas are clean. **Note:** *Decarbonizing chemicals are available and may prove very useful when cleaning cylinder heads and valve train components. They are very caustic and should be used with caution. Be sure to follow the instructions on the container.*

8   Clean all the valve springs, shields, keepers and retainers with solvent and dry them thoroughly. Do the components from one valve at a time to avoid mixing up the parts.

9   Scrape off any heavy deposits that may have formed on the valves, then use a wire brush mounted in a drill motor to remove deposits from the valve heads and stems. Again, make sure the valves do not get mixed up.

Inspection

Cylinder head

Refer to illustrations 10.11 and 10.13

10   Inspect the head very carefully for cracks, evidence of coolant leakage and other damage. If cracks are found, a new cylinder head should be obtained.

11   Using a straightedge and feeler gauge, check the head gasket mating surface for warpage **(see illustration)**. If the warpage exceeds the limit specified in this Chapter, it can be resurfaced at an automotive

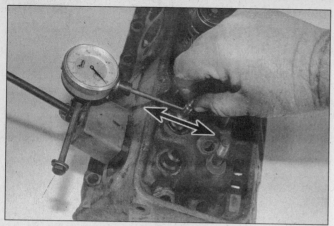

10.13 A dial indicator can be used to determine the valve stem-to-guide clearance - move the valve stem as indicated by the arrows

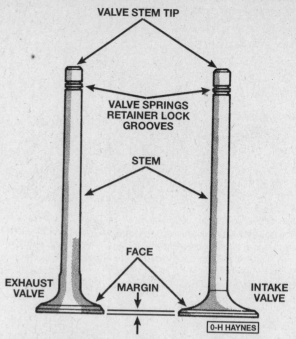

10.14 Check for valve wear at the points shown here

machine shop.

12   Examine the valve seats in each of the combustion chambers. If they are pitted, cracked or burned, the head will require valve service with special equipment that is beyond the scope of most home mechanics, especially from an equipment stand point.

13   Check the valve stem-to-guide clearance by measuring the lateral movement of the valve stem with a dial indicator attached securely to the head **(see illustration)**. The valve must be in the guide and approximately 1/16-inch off the seat. The total valve stem movement indicated by the gauge needle must be divided by two to obtain the actual clearance. After this is done, if there is still some doubt regarding the condition of the valve guides they should be checked by an automotive machine shop (the cost should be minimal).

Valves

Refer to illustrations 10.14 and 10.15

14   Carefully inspect each valve face for uneven wear **(see illustration)**, deformation, cracks, pits and burned spots. Check the valve stem for scuffing and galling and the neck for cracks. Rotate the valve and check for any obvious indication that it is bent. Look for pits and excessive wear on the end of the stem. The presence of any of these conditions indicates the need for valve service by an automotive machine shop.

15   Measure the margin width on each valve. Any valve with a margin that is narrower than what is indicated by the Specifications at the beginning of this Chapter will have to be replaced with a new one **(see illustration)**.

Valve components

Refer to illustrations 10.16 and 10.17

16   Check each valve spring for wear (on the ends) and pits. Measure the free length and compare it to the Specifications in this Chapter **(see illustration)**. Any springs that are shorter than specified have sagged and should not be reused. The tension of all springs should be checked with a special fixture before deciding that they are suitable for use in a rebuilt engine (take the springs to an automotive machine shop for this check).

17   Stand each spring on a flat surface and check it for squareness **(see illustration)**. If any of the springs are distorted or sagged, replace all of them with new parts.

18   Check the spring retainers and keepers for obvious wear and cracks. Any questionable parts should be replaced with new ones, as extensive damage will occur if they fail during engine operation.

Rocker arm components

19   Check the rocker arm faces (the areas that contact the pushrod ends and valve stems) for pits, wear, galling, score marks and rough spots. Check the rocker arm pivot contact areas and shafts. Look for cracks in each rocker arm.

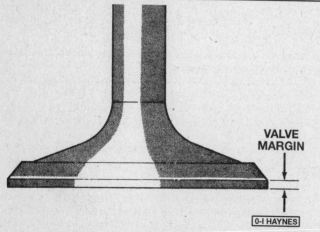

10.15 The margin width on each valve must be as specified (if no margin exists, the valve cannot be reused)

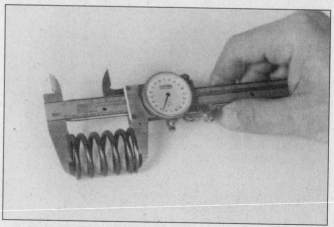

10.16 Measure the free length of each valve spring with a dial or vernier caliper

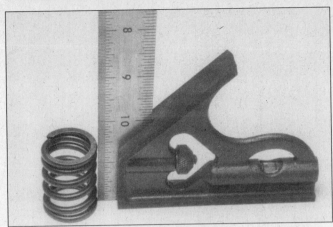

10.17 Check each valve spring for squareness - if it is bent, it should be replaced

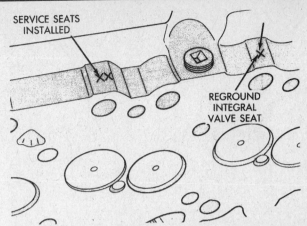

11.5 One X on the diesel cylinder head indicates that the original valve seats have been ground once - two XXs indicates that seat inserts have been installed

20   Inspect the pushrod ends for scuffing and excessive wear. Roll each pushrod on a flat surface, such as plate glass, to determine if it is bent.

21   Check the rocker arm bolt holes in the cylinder heads for damaged threads.

22   On diesel engines, remove the rocker arms from their shafts (do only one pair at a time, to avoid mixing them up) and inspect the shafts. Also inspect the dowels at the bottom of each rocker arm pedestal.

23   Any damaged or excessively worn parts must be replaced with new ones.

24   If the inspection process indicates that the valve components are in generally poor condition and worn beyond the limits specified in this Chapter, which is usually the case in an engine that is being overhauled, reassemble the valves in the cylinder head and refer to Section 11 for valve servicing recommendations.

11   Valves - servicing

Refer to illustration 11.5

1   Because of the complex nature or the job and the special tools and equipment needed, servicing of the valves, the valve seats and the valve guides (commonly known as a "valve job") is best left to a professional. Any complete overhaul of an engine with high mileage should include having the valves and seats ground at a machine shop.

2   The home mechanic can remove and disassemble the heads, do the initial cleaning and inspection, then reassemble and deliver the heads to a dealer service department or an automotive machine shop for the actual valve servicing.

3   The dealer service department, or automotive machine shop, will remove the valves and springs, recondition or replace the valves and valve seats, recondition the valve guides, check and reinstall the valve springs, spring retainers and keepers, replace the valve seals with new ones, reassemble the valve components and make sure the installed spring height is correct. The cylinder head gasket surface will also be resurfaced if it is warped.

4   After the valve job has been performed by a professional, the head will be in like-new condition. When the head is returned, be sure to clean it again before installation on the engine to remove any metal particles and abrasive grit that may still be present from the valve service or head resurfacing operations. Use compressed air, if available, to blow out all the oil holes and passages.

5   On diesel engines, the cylinder head is factory-hardened in the valve seat area. This hardening process is only deep enough to allow one valve job. When one valve job has been performed on the head, the machinist will make a mark on a pad on the outside of the head (see illustration). On the next rebuild, hardened seat inserts will have to be installed in the heads at a machine shop, where the machinist will make another mark to indicate that "service" seats have been installed. The hardened seat inserts can accept numerous valve jobs.

6   The thickness of the diesel cylinder head, and the depth that the valves sit down into the head is critical. When the cylinder head has been resurfaced for flatness, the machinist should stamp the amount of material removed on a pad at the rear of the head, and each time the head is resurfaced, the new amount must be added to the stamped identification. The total amount of material machined from the head must not exceed the Specification. If the head needs more machining, there may be special service head gaskets available from Cummins that are thicker, in oversizes of 0.010-inch and 0.020-inch, to restore the proper compression ratio and valve-to-piston clearances.

12   Cylinder head - reassembly

Refer to illustrations 12.5, 12.6 and 12.8

1   Regardless of whether or not the heads were sent to an automotive machine shop for valve servicing, make sure they are clean before beginning reassembly.

2   If the heads were sent out for valve servicing, the valves and related components will already be in place. Begin the reassembly procedure with Step 8.

3   Beginning at one end of the head, lubricate and install the first valve. Apply moly-base grease or clean engine oil to the valve stem.

4   Different types of oil seals are used on the intake and exhaust valve stems. On some applications, an umbrella type seal which extends down over the valve guide boss is used over the valve stem.

5   Drop the spring seat or shim(s), if used, over the valve guide and set the valve spring and retainer in place (see illustration).

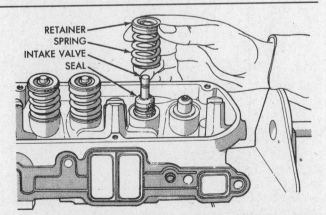

12.5 Push the valve stem seal down onto the guide, then install the spring and retainer

12.6 Apply a small dab of grease to each keeper as shown here before installation - it'll hold them in place on the valve stem as the spring is released

12.8 Valve spring installed height is the distance from the spring seat on the head to the top of the spring

13.1 A ridge reamer is required to remove the ridge from the top of each cylinder - do this before removing the pistons!

6   Compress the springs with a valve spring compressor. Position the keepers in the upper groove, then slowly release the compressor and make sure the keepers seat properly. Apply a small dab of grease to each keeper to hold it in place if necessary **(see illustration)**.

7   Repeat the procedure for the remaining valves. Be sure to return the components to their original locations - do not mix them up!

8   Check the installed valve spring height with a ruler graduated in 1/32-inch increments **(see illustration)** or a dial caliper. If the heads were sent out for service work, the installed height should be correct (but don't automatically assume that it is). The measurement is taken from the top of each spring seat or shim(s) to the bottom of the retainer/rotator. If the height is greater than listed in this Chapter's specifications, shims can be added under the springs to correct it. **Caution:** *Do not, under any circumstances, shim the springs to the point where the installed height is less than specified. A condition called "coil bind" will be caused when the spring is compressed.*

13   Piston/connecting rod assembly - removal

Refer to illustrations 13.1, 13.3a, 13.3b, 13.4 and 13.5

Note: *Prior to removing the piston/connecting rod assemblies, remove the cylinder head(s), the oil pan and the oil pump, if it is mounted in the crankcase, and the oil pump pickup screen assembly by referring to the appropriate Sections in Chapter 2, Part A or Part B.*

1   Completely remove the ridge at the top of each cylinder with a ridge reaming tool **(see illustration)**. Follow the manufacturer's instructions provided with the tool. Failure to remove the ridge before attempting to remove the piston/connecting rod assemblies will result

in piston breakage.

2   After the cylinder ridges have been removed, turn the engine upside-down so the crankshaft is facing up.

3   Before the connecting rods are removed, check the endplay (side clearance) with feeler gauges. Slide them between the first connecting rod and the crankshaft throw until the play is removed **(see illustration)**. The endplay is equal to the thickness of the feeler gauge(s). If the endplay exceeds the service limit listed in this Chapter's Specifications, new connecting rods will be required. If new rods (or a new crankshaft) are installed, the endplay may fall under the specified minimum. If it does, the rods will have to be machined to restore it - consult an automotive machine shop for advice if necessary. Repeat the procedure for the remaining connecting rods. **Note:** *On the diesel engine, the rod big end and cap are slightly offset. The side clearance can only be measured between the rod and the crankshaft, not between the cap and the crankshaft* **(see illustration)**.

4   Check the connecting rods and caps for identification marks **(see illustration)**. If they are not plainly marked, use a small center-punch to make the appropriate number of indentations on each rod and cap.

5   Loosen each of the connecting rod cap nuts 1/2-turn at a time until they can be removed by hand. Remove the number one connecting rod cap and bearing insert. Do not drop the bearing insert out of the cap. Slip a short length of plastic or rubber hose over each connecting rod cap bolt to protect the crankshaft journal and cylinder wall when the piston is removed **(see illustration)**. Push the connecting rod/piston assembly out through the top of the engine. Use a wooden hammer handle to push on the upper bearing insert in the connecting rod. If resistance is felt, double-check to make sure that all of the ridge was removed from the cylinder.

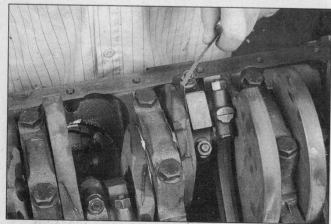

13.3a Check the connecting rod side clearance (endplay) with a feeler gauge as shown here

13.3b On the diesel engine, check the connecting rod side clearance between the body of the rod and the crank, not between the cap and the crank

13.4 The connecting rods should be marked with numbers at the parting line of each rod and cap - the number corresponds to the engine cylinder number - on reassembly, be sure the numbers are on the same side, facing each other, as shown, and the rod/piston goes back into the correct cylinder

6   Repeat the procedure for the remaining cylinders. After removal, reassemble the connecting rod caps and bearing inserts in their respective connecting rods and install the cap nuts finger tight. Leaving the old bearing inserts in place until reassembly will help prevent the connecting rod bearing surfaces from being accidentally nicked or gouged.

14 Crankshaft - removal

Refer to illustrations 14.2, 14.3, 14.4a and 14.4b

Note: *The crankshaft can be removed only after the engine has been removed from the vehicle. It is assumed that the flywheel or driveplate, vibration damper or crankshaft pulley, timing chain, oil pan, oil pump, rear seal retainer plate and piston/connecting rod assemblies have already been removed. On the diesel engine, the front gearcase must also be removed. To remove the gearcase, refer to Chapter 2B and remove the camshaft, gears, oil pump and fuel injection pump, then unbolt the gearcase from the block.*

1   Before the crankshaft is removed, check the endplay. Mount a dial indicator with the stem in line with the crankshaft and touching one of the crank throws.

2   Push the crankshaft all the way to the rear and zero the dial indicator. Next, pry the crankshaft to the front as far as possible and check the reading on the dial indicator **(see illustration)**. The distance that it moves is the endplay. If it is greater than the maximum listed in this Chapter's Specifications, check the crankshaft thrust surfaces for wear. If no wear is evident, new main bearings should correct the endplay.

3   If a dial indicator is not available, feeler gauges can be used. Gently pry or push the crankshaft all the way to the front of the engine. Slip feeler gauges between the crankshaft and the front face of the thrust main bearing to determine the clearance **(see illustration)**.

4   Check the main bearing caps to see if they are marked to indicate their locations. They should be numbered consecutively from the front of the engine to the rear **(see illustration)**. If they aren't, mark them with number stamping dies or a center-punch **(see illustration)**.

13.5 To prevent damage to the crankshaft journals and cylinder walls, slip sections of hose over the rod bolts before removing the piston/rod assemblies

14.2 Checking crankshaft endplay with a dial indicator

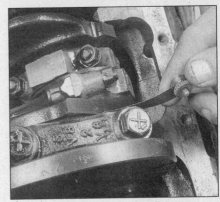

14.3 Checking crankshaft endplay with a feeler gauge

14.4a The main bearing caps are marked to indicate their locations (arrows) - they should be numbered consecutively from the front of the engine to the rear

14.4b If the main cap marks aren't clear, mark the caps with number stamping dies or a center-punch

2C

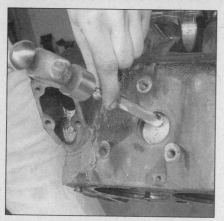

15.1a A hammer and a large punch can be used to knock the core plugs sideways in their bores

15.1b Pull the core plugs from the block with pliers

15.4 Remove all the oil galley plugs/bolts (arrows) to more thoroughly clean all debris from the oiling system (typical galley plugs shown)

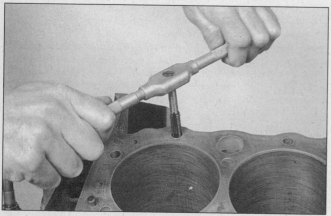

15.8 All bolt holes in the block - particularly the main bearing cap and head bolt holes - should be cleaned and restored with a tap (be sure to remove debris from the holes after this is done)

5   Loosen each of the main bearing cap bolts 1/4-turn at a time each, until they can be removed by hand.

6   Gently separate the main caps from the engine block, using the bolts as levers to remove the caps. Try not to drop the bearing inserts if they come out with the caps. **Note:** *On the diesel engine, the caps have tubular dowels to locate them to the block. Do not use a hammer to tap the caps loose.*

7   Carefully lift the crankshaft out of the engine. It is a good idea to have an assistant available, since the crankshaft is quite heavy. On diesel engines, it is recommended to remove and install the crankshaft with a hoist, using a cloth sling. With the bearing inserts in place in the engine block and main bearing caps, return the caps to their respective locations on the engine block and tighten the bolts finger tight.

15   Engine block - cleaning

Refer to illustrations 15.1a, 15.1b, 15.4, 15.8 and 15.10

1   Using the wide end of a punch **(see illustration)** tap in on the outer edge of the core plug to turn the plug sideways in the bore. Then, using a pair of pliers, pull the core plug from the engine block **(see illustration)**. Don't worry about the condition of the old core plugs as they are being removed because they will be replaced on reassembly with new plugs. **Note:** *On diesel engines, don't overlook the core plug at the top front of the block; it is only revealed when the fan drive assembly is taken off.*

2   Using a gasket scraper, remove all traces of gasket material from the engine block.

3   Remove the main bearing caps and separate the bearing inserts from the caps and the engine block. Tag the bearings, indicating which

cylinder they were removed from and whether they were in the cap or the block, then set them aside.

4   Remove all of the threaded oil gallery plugs from the block **(see illustration)**. The plugs are usually very tight - they may have to be drilled out and the holes retapped. If drilled out or damaged during removal, use new plugs when the engine is reassembled.

5   If the engine is extremely dirty it should be taken to an automotive machine shop to be steam cleaned or hot tanked.

6   After the block is returned, clean all oil holes and oil galleries one more time. Brushes specifically designed for this purpose are available at most auto parts stores. Flush the passages with warm water until the water runs clear, dry the block thoroughly and wipe all machined surfaces with a light, rust preventive oil. If you have access to compressed air, use it to speed the drying process and to blow out all the oil holes and galleries. **Warning:** *Wear eye protection when using compressed air!*

7   If the block isn't extremely dirty or sludged up, you can do an adequate cleaning job with hot soapy water and a stiff brush. Use very hot water and strong laundry detergent, taking plenty of time to do a thorough job. Regardless of the cleaning method used, be sure to clean all oil holes and galleries very thoroughly, dry the block completely and coat all machined surfaces with light oil.

8   The threaded holes in the block must be clean to ensure accurate torque readings during reassembly. Run the proper size tap into each of the holes to remove rust, corrosion, thread sealant or sludge and restore damaged threads **(see illustration)**. If possible, use compressed air to clear the holes of debris produced by this operation. Now is a good time to clean the threads on the head bolts and the main bearing cap bolts as well.

9   Reinstall the main bearing caps and tighten the bolts finger tight.

10   After coating the sealing surfaces of the new core plugs with Permatex no. 2 sealant, install them in the engine block **(see illustration)**. Make sure they're driven in straight or leakage could result. Special tools are available for this purpose, but a large socket, with an outside diameter that will just slip into the core plug, a 1/2-inch drive extension and a hammer will work just as well.

11   Apply non-hardening sealant (such as Permatex no. 2 or Teflon tape) to the new oil gallery plugs and thread them into the holes in the block. Make sure they're tightened securely.

12   If the engine isn't going to be reassembled right away, cover it with a large plastic trash bag to keep it clean.

16   Engine block - inspection

Refer to illustrations 16.4a, 16.4b and 16.4c

1   Before the block is inspected, it should be cleaned (see Section 15).

15.10 A large socket on an extension can be used to drive the new core plugs into the bores

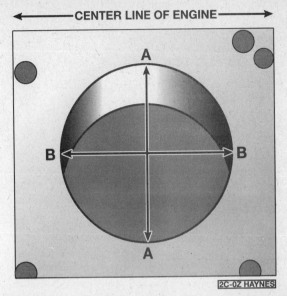

16.4a Measure the diameter of each cylinder at a right angle to the engine centerline (A), and parallel to the engine centerline (B) - out-of-round is the difference between A and B; taper is the difference between the diameter at the top of the cylinder and the diameter at the bottom of the cylinder

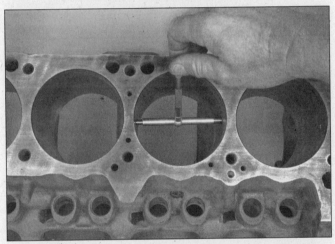

16.4b The ability to "feel" when the telescoping gauge is at the correct point will be developed over time, so work slowly and repeat the check until you're satisfied the bore measurement is accurate

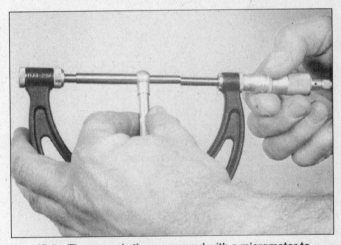

16.4c The gauge is then measured with a micrometer to determine the bore size

2   Visually check the block for cracks, rust and corrosion. Look for stripped threads in the threaded holes. It's also a good idea to have the block checked for hidden cracks by an automotive machine shop that has the special equipment to do this type of work. If defects are found, have the block repaired, if possible, or replaced.

3   Check the cylinder bores for scuffing and scoring.

4   Measure the diameter of each cylinder at the top (just under the ridge area), center and bottom of the cylinder bore, parallel to the crankshaft axis **(see illustrations)**.

5   Measure the diameter of each cylinder at the top (just under the ridge area), center and bottom of the cylinder bore, parallel to the crankshaft axis.

6   Next, measure each cylinder's diameter at the same three locations perpendicular to the crankshaft axis.

7   The taper of each cylinder is the difference between the bore diameter at the top of the cylinder and the diameter at the bottom. The out-of-round specification of the cylinder bore is the difference between the parallel and perpendicular readings. Compare your results to this Chapter's Specifications.

8   Repeat the procedure for the remaining pistons and cylinders.

9   If the cylinder walls are badly scuffed or scored, or if they're out-of-round or tapered beyond the limits given in the Specifications, have the engine block rebored and honed at an automotive machine shop. If a rebore is done, oversize pistons and rings will be required.

10   Using a precision straightedge and a feeler gauge, check the

block deck (the surface that mates with the cylinder head) the same way the cylinder head was checked for distortion (see Section 10). If it's distorted beyond the specified limit, it can be resurfaced by an automotive machine shop.

11   If the cylinders are in reasonably good condition and not worn to the outside of the limits, and if the piston-to-cylinder clearances can be maintained properly, then they don't have to be rebored. Honing is all that's necessary (see Section 17).

17   Cylinder honing

Refer to illustrations 17.3a and 17.3b

1   Prior to engine reassembly, the cylinder bores must be honed so the new piston rings will seat correctly and provide the best possible combustion chamber seal. **Note:** *If you do not have the tools or do not want to tackle the honing operation, most automotive machine shops will do it for a reasonable fee.*

2   Before honing the cylinders, install the main bearing caps and tighten the bolts to the specified torque.

17.3a A "bottle brush" hone will produce better results if you've never honed cylinders before

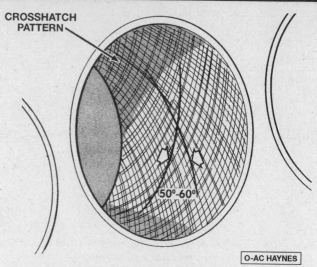

17.3b The cylinder hone should leave a smooth, crosshatch pattern with the lines intersecting at approximately a 60-degree angle (30 to 50-degrees for the diesel engine)

3   Two types of cylinder hones are commonly available - the flex hone or "bottle brush" type and the more traditional surfacing hone with spring-loaded stones. Both will do the job, but for the less experienced mechanic the "bottle brush" hone will probably be easier to use. You will also need plenty of light oil or honing oil, some rags and an electric drill motor. Proceed as follows:

a) *Mount the hone in the drill motor, compress the stones and slip it into the first cylinder (see illustration).*

b) *Lubricate the cylinder with plenty of oil, turn on the drill and move the hone up-and-down in the cylinder at a pace which will produce a fine crosshatch pattern on the cylinder walls. Ideally, the crosshatch lines should intersect at approximately a 60-degree angle (see illustration). Be sure to use plenty of lubricant and do not take off any more material than is absolutely necessary to produce the desired finish. Note: Piston ring manufacturers may specify a smaller crosshatch angle than the traditional 60-degrees, typically 45-degrees, so read and follow any instructions printed on the piston ring packages. On the diesel engine, the factory recommends a crosshatch of 30 to 50-degrees, which will require a slightly slower honing speed than for gasoline engines.*

c) *Do not withdraw the hone from the cylinder while it is running. Instead, shut off the drill and continue moving the hone up-and-down in the cylinder until it comes to a complete stop, then compress the stones and withdraw the hone. If you are using a "bottle brush" type hone, stop the drill motor, then turn the chuck in the normal direction of rotation while withdrawing the hone from the cylinder.*

d) *Wipe the oil out of the cylinder and repeat the procedure for the remaining cylinders.*

4   After the honing job is complete, chamfer the top edges of the cylinder bores with a small file so the rings will not catch when the pistons are installed. Be very careful not to nick the cylinder walls with the end of the file.

5   The entire engine block must be washed again very thoroughly with hot, soapy water to remove all traces of the abrasive grit produced during the honing operation. **Note:** *The bores can be considered clean when a white cloth - dampened with clean engine oil - used to wipe down the bores does not pick up any more honing residue, which will show up as gray areas on the cloth. Be sure to run a brush through all oil holes and galleries and flush them with running water.*

6   After rinsing, dry the block and apply a coat of light rust preventive oil to all machined surfaces. Wrap the block in a plastic trash bag to keep it clean and set it aside until reassembly.

18   Piston/connecting rod assembly - inspection

Refer to illustrations 18.4a, 18.4b and 18.10

1   Before the inspection process can be carried out, the piston/connecting rod assemblies must be cleaned and the original piston rings removed from the pistons. **Note:** *Always use new piston rings when the engine is reassembled.*

2   Using a piston ring installation tool, carefully remove the rings from the pistons. Be careful not to nick or gouge the pistons in the process.

3   Scrape all traces of carbon from the top of the piston. A handheld wire brush or a piece of fine emery cloth can be used once the majority of the deposits have been scraped away. Do not, under any circumstances, use a wire brush mounted in a drill motor to remove deposits from the pistons. The piston material is soft and may be eroded away by the wire brush. Also do not bead-blast the pistons. **Note:** *On V10 engines, do not attempt to clean off the black coating on the piston skirt. This is a factory-applied dry-film lubricant.*

4   On gasoline engines, use a piston ring groove cleaning tool to remove carbon deposits from the ring grooves. If a tool isn't available, a piece broken off the old ring will do the job. Be very careful to remove only the carbon deposits - don't remove any metal and do not nick or scratch the sides of the ring grooves **(see illustrations). Caution:** *On diesel engines, do not use a ring or tool to clean the grooves. Soak the piston overnight in cold parts cleaner (non-acid), then brush any carbon deposits out of the ring grooves with a nylon brush.*

5   Once the deposits have been removed, clean the piston/rod

18.4a On gasoline engines, the piston ring grooves can be cleaned with a special tool, as shown here . . .

18.4b ... or a section of a broken ring - do not use either method on diesel pistons (only solvent)

assemblies with solvent and dry them with compressed air (if available). **Warning:** *Wear eye protection when using compressed air!* Make sure the oil return holes in the back sides of the ring grooves and the oil hole in the lower end of each rod are clear.

6   If the pistons and cylinder walls aren't damaged or worn excessively, and if the engine block is not rebored, new pistons won't be necessary. Normal piston wear appears as even vertical wear on the piston thrust surfaces and slight looseness of the top ring in its groove. New piston rings, however, should always be used when an engine is rebuilt.

7   Carefully inspect each piston for cracks around the skirt, at the pin bosses and at the ring lands.

8   Look for scoring and scuffing on the thrust faces of the skirt, holes in the piston crown and burned areas at the edge of the crown. If the skirt is scored or scuffed, the engine may have been suffering from overheating and/or abnormal combustion, which caused excessively high operating temperatures. The cooling and lubrication systems should be checked thoroughly. A hole in the piston crown is an indication that abnormal combustion (preignition) was occurring. Burned areas at the edge of the piston crown are usually evidence of spark knock (detonation). If any of the above problems exist, the causes must be corrected or the damage will occur again. The causes may include intake air leaks, incorrect fuel/air mixture, incorrect ignition timing and EGR system malfunctions.

9   Corrosion of the piston, in the form of small pits, indicates that coolant is leaking into the combustion chamber and/or the crankcase. Again, the cause must be corrected or the problem may persist in the rebuilt engine.

10   Measure the piston ring side clearance by laying a new piston ring in each ring groove and slipping a feeler gauge in beside it **(see illustration)**. Check the clearance at three or four locations around each groove. Be sure to use the correct ring for each groove - they are different. If the side clearance is greater than specified, new pistons will have to be used.

11   Check the piston-to-bore clearance by measuring the bore (see Section 16) and the piston diameter. Make sure the pistons and bores are correctly matched. Measure the piston across the skirt, at a 90-degree angle to the piston pin, the specified distance down from the top of the piston or the lower edge of the oil ring groove. Subtract the piston diameter from the bore diameter to obtain the clearance. If it's greater than specified, the block will have to be rebored and new pistons and rings installed.

12   Check the piston-to-rod clearance by twisting the piston and rod in opposite directions. Any noticeable play indicates excessive wear, which must be corrected. The piston/connecting rod assemblies should be taken to an automotive machine shop to have the pistons and rods re-sized and new pins installed.

13   If the pistons must be removed from the connecting rods for any reason, they should be taken to an automotive machine shop. While they are there have the connecting rods checked for bend and twist, since automotive machine shops have special equipment for this purpose. **Note:** *Unless new pistons and/or connecting rods must be installed, do not disassemble the pistons and connecting rods.*

14   Check the connecting rods for cracks and other damage. Temporarily remove the rod caps, lift out the old bearing inserts, wipe the rod and cap bearing surfaces clean and inspect them for nicks, gouges and scratches. After checking the rods, replace the old bearings, slip the caps into place and tighten the nuts finger tight. **Note:** *If the engine is being rebuilt because of a connecting rod knock, be sure to check with an automotive machine shop on the possibility of re-sizing either the small or large end of the rod. If this isn't possible, install new rods.*

2C

19 Crankshaft - inspection

Refer to illustrations 19.1, 19.2, 19.5a, 19.5b and 19.7

1   Remove all burrs from the crankshaft oil holes with a stone, file or scraper **(see illustration)**.

2   Clean the crankshaft with solvent and dry it with compressed air (if available). Be sure to clean the oil holes with a stiff brush and flush them with solvent **(see illustration)**.

3   Check the main and connecting rod bearing journals for uneven wear, scoring, pits and cracks.

4   Check the rest of the crankshaft for cracks and other damage. It should be Magnafluxed to reveal hidden cracks - an automotive machine shop will handle the procedure.

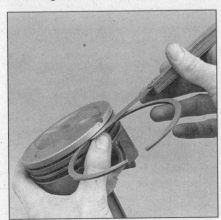

18.10 Check the ring side clearance with a feeler gauge at several points around the groove

19.1 The oil holes should be chamfered so sharp edges don't gouge or scratch the new bearings

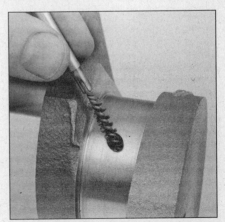

19.2 Use a wire or stiff plastic bristle brush to clean the oil passages in the crankshaft - flush the passages out with solvent

19.5a Measure the diameter of each crankshaft journal at several points to detect taper and out-of-round conditions

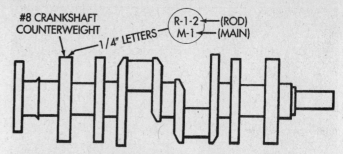

19.5b The engine crankshaft may have a letter/number stamped into one of the counterweights - this marking will reveal the location (journal number) of the undersize rod (R) or (M) main journal - 5.2L V8 shown

19.7 If the seals have worn grooves in the crankshaft journals, or if the seal contact surfaces are nicked or scratched, the new seals will leak

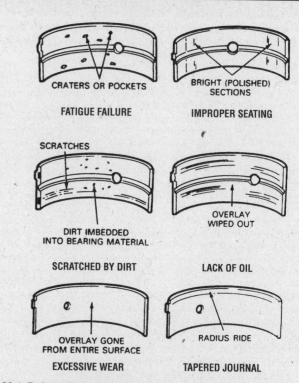

20.1 Before discarding the used bearings, examine them for indications of any possible problems with the crankshaft, noting the bearing location it came from. Here are some typical bearing failures

5   Using a micrometer, measure the diameter of the main and connecting rod journals and compare the results to the Specifications **(see illustration)**. By measuring the diameter at a number of points around each journal's circumference, you'll be able to determine whether or not the journal is out-of-round. Take the measurement at each end of the journal, near the crank throws, to determine if the journal is tapered. Crankshaft runout should be checked also, but large V-blocks and a dial indicator are needed to do it correctly. If you don't have the equipment, have a machine shop check the runout. **Note:** *Factory-undersize journals may be on any crankshaft, indicating by markings* **(see illustration)**. *On the V6 engine, such markings will be on the 6th counterweight (from the front), the 8th on 5.2L V8s and V10s, and the 3rd counterweight on the 5.9L V8.*

6   If the crankshaft journals are damaged, tapered, out-of-round or worn beyond the limits given in the Specifications, have the crankshaft reground by an automotive machine shop. Be sure to use the correct size bearing inserts if the crankshaft is reconditioned.

7   Check the oil seal journals at each end of the crankshaft for wear and damage **(see illustration)**. If the seal has worn a groove in the journal, or if it's nicked or scratched, the new seal may leak when the engine is reassembled. In some cases, an automotive machine shop may be able to repair the journal by pressing on a thin sleeve. If repair isn't feasible, a new or different crankshaft should be installed.

8   Examine the main and rod bearing inserts (see Section 20).

20   Main and connecting rod bearings - inspection and selection

Inspection

Refer to illustration 20.1

1   Even though the main and connecting rod bearings should be replaced with new ones during the engine overhaul, the old bearings should be retained for close examination, as they may reveal valuable information about the condition of the engine **(see illustration)**.

2   Bearing failure occurs because of lack of lubrication, the presence of dirt or other foreign particles, overloading the engine and corrosion. Regardless of the cause of bearing failure, it must be corrected before the engine is reassembled to prevent it from happening again.

3   When examining the bearings, remove them from the engine block, the main bearing caps, the connecting rods and the rod caps and lay them out on a clean surface in the same general position as their location in the engine. This will enable you to match any bearing

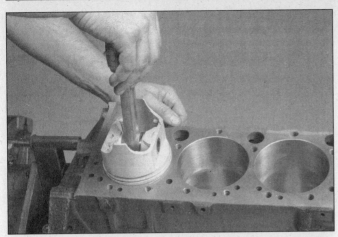

22.3 When checking piston ring end gap, the ring must be square in the cylinder bore (this is done by pushing the ring down with the top of a piston as shown)

problems with the corresponding crankshaft journal.

4   Dirt and other foreign particles get into the engine in a variety of ways. It may be left in the engine during assembly, or it may pass through filters or the PCV system. It may get into the oil, and from there into the bearings. Metal chips from machining operations and normal engine wear are often present. Abrasives are sometimes left in engine components after reconditioning, especially when parts are not thoroughly cleaned using the proper cleaning methods. Whatever the source, these foreign objects often end up embedded in the soft bearing material and are easily recognized. Large particles will not embed in the bearing and will score or gouge the bearing and journal. The best prevention for this cause of bearing failure is to clean all parts thoroughly and keep everything spotlessly clean during engine assembly. Frequent and regular engine oil and filter changes are also recommended.

5   Lack of lubrication (or lubrication breakdown) has a number of interrelated causes. Excessive heat (which thins the oil), overloading (which squeezes the oil from the bearing face) and oil leakage or throw-off (from excessive bearing clearances, worn oil pump or high engine speeds) all contribute to lubrication breakdown. Blocked oil passages, which usually are the result of misaligned oil holes in a bearing shell, will also oil-starve a bearing and destroy it. When lack of lubrication is the cause of bearing failure, the bearing material is wiped or extruded from the steel backing of the bearing. Temperatures may increase to the point where the steel backing turns blue from overheating.

6   Driving habits can have a definite effect on bearing life. Low speed operation in too high a gear (lugging the engine) puts very high loads on bearings, which tends to squeeze out the oil film. These loads cause the bearings to flex, which produces fine cracks in the bearing face (fatigue failure). Eventually the bearing material will loosen in pieces and tear away from the steel backing. Short trip driving leads to corrosion of bearings because insufficient engine heat is produced to drive off the condensed water and corrosive gases. These products collect in the engine oil, forming acid and sludge. As the oil is carried to the engine bearings, the acid attacks and corrodes the bearing material.

7   Incorrect bearing installation during engine assembly will lead to bearing failure as well. Tight fitting bearings leave insufficient bearing oil clearance and will result in oil starvation. Dirt or foreign particles trapped behind a bearing insert result in high spots on the bearing which lead to failure.

8   If you need to use a STANDARD size main bearing, install one that has the same number as the original bearing.

9   If you need to use a STANDARD size rod bearing, install one that has the same number as the number stamped into the connecting rod cap.

10   Remember, the oil clearance is the final judge when selecting new bearing sizes for either main or rod bearings. If you have any questions or are unsure which bearings to use, get help from a dealer parts or service department or other parts supplier.

21 Engine overhaul - reassembly sequence

1   Before beginning engine reassembly, make sure you have all the necessary new parts, gaskets and seals as well as the following items on hand:

> Common hand tools
> A torque wrench
> Piston ring installation tool
> Piston ring compressor
> Short lengths of rubber or plastic hose to fit over connecting rod bolts
> Plastigage
> Feeler gauges
> A fine-tooth file
> New engine oil
> Engine assembly lube or moly-base grease
> Gasket sealant
> Thread-locking compound
> Tappet clamps, trough and tappet "fishing" tool (diesel)

2   In order to save time and avoid problems, engine reassembly must be done in the following general order:

Gasoline engines

> Piston rings
> Main bearings and crankshaft
> Piston/connecting rod assemblies
> Rear main oil seal
> Cylinder head(s) and rocker arms or lifters
> Camshaft
> Timing chain, gears and cover
> Oil pump
> Oil pick-up tube
> Oil pan
> Valve cover(s)
> Intake and exhaust manifolds
> Flywheel/driveplate

Diesel engine

> Crankshaft
> Connecting rods and pistons
> Camshaft and tappets
> Cylinder head
> Gear case
> Timing gears
> Oil pump
> Gearcase front cover
> Water pump
> Fuel injection pump
> Rocker arms, pushrods
> Valve covers
> High pressure fuel lines
> Fuel filter
> Fuel transfer pump
> Fuel heater (after installation in vehicle)
> Turbocharger and exhaust manifold
> Fan drive assembly
> Oil pan

22 Piston rings - installation

Refer to illustrations 22.3, 22.4, 22.5, 22.9a, 22.9b and 22.12

1   Before installing the new piston rings, the ring end gaps must be checked. It's assumed that the piston ring side clearance has been checked and verified correct (see Section 18).

2   Lay out the piston/connecting rod assemblies and the new ring sets so the ring sets will be matched with the same piston and cylinder during the end gap measurement and engine assembly.

3   Insert the top (number one) ring into the first cylinder and square it up with the cylinder walls by pushing it in with the top of the piston **(see illustration)**. The ring should be near the bottom of the cylinder,

2C

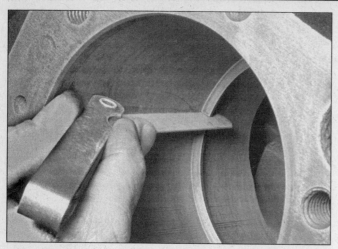

22.4 With the ring square in the cylinder, measure the end gap with a feeler gauge

22.5 If the end gap is too small, clamp a file in a vise and file the ring ends (from the outside in only) to enlarge the gap slightly

at the lower limit of ring travel.

4   To measure the end gap, slip feeler gauges between the ends of the ring until a gauge equal to the gap width is found **(see illustration)**. The feeler gauge should slide between the ring ends with a slight amount of drag. Compare the measurement to the Specifications. If the gap is larger or smaller than specified, double-check to make sure you have the correct rings before proceeding.

5   If the gap is too small, it must be enlarged or the ring ends may come in contact with each other during engine operation, which can cause serious damage to the engine. The end gap can be increased by filing the ring ends very carefully with a fine file. Mount the file in a vise equipped with soft jaws, slip the ring over the file with the ends contacting the file face and slowly move the ring to remove material from the ends **(see illustration)**. **Caution:** *When performing this operation, file only from the outside in.*

6   Excess end gap is not critical unless it is well beyond the limit in the Specifications. Again, double-check to make sure you have the correct rings for your engine. **Note:** *For some engines, special ,"gappable" ring sets are available that are slightly oversize, which gives them a too-tight end gap that can be filed exactly to your gap specifications.*

7   Repeat the procedure for each ring that will be installed in the first cylinder and for each ring in the remaining cylinders. Remember to keep rings, pistons and cylinders matched up.

8   Once the ring end gaps have been checked/corrected, the rings can be installed on the pistons.

9   The oil control ring (lowest one on the piston) is usually installed first. It's composed of three separate components. Slip the

spacer/expander into the groove **(see illustration)**. If an anti-rotation tang is used, make sure it's inserted into the drilled hole in the ring groove. Next, install the lower side rail. Don't use a piston ring installation tool on the oil ring side rails, as they may be damaged. Instead, place one end of the side rail into the groove between the spacer/expander and the ring land, hold it firmly in place and slide a finger around the piston while pushing the rail into the groove **(see illustration)**. Next, install the upper side rail in the same manner. **Note:** *On diesel engines, the oil control (lowest) ring has a different configuration and requires only one rail (expander) spacer, which goes below the oil control ring, with its gap 180-degrees away from the oil control ring gap.*

10   After the three oil ring components have been installed, check to make sure that both the upper and lower side rails can be turned smoothly in the ring groove.

11   The number two (middle) ring is installed next. It's usually stamped with a mark which must face up, toward the top of the piston. **Note:** *Always follow the instructions printed on the ring package or box - different manufacturers may require different approaches. Do not mix up the top and middle rings, as they have different cross-sections.*

12   Use a piston ring installation tool and make sure the identification mark is facing the top of the piston, then slip the ring into the middle groove on the piston. Don't expand the ring any more than necessary to slide it over the piston **(see illustration)**.

13   Install the number one (top) ring in the same manner. Make sure the mark is facing up. Be careful not to confuse the number one and number two rings.

14   Repeat the procedure for the remaining pistons and rings.

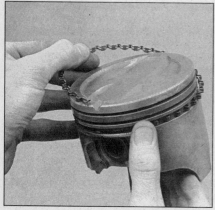

22.9a Installing the spacer/expander in the oil control ring groove . . .

22.9b . . . followed by the side rails - DO NOT use a piston ring installation tool when installing the oil ring side rails

22.12 Installing the compression rings with a ring expander - the mark (arrow) must face up

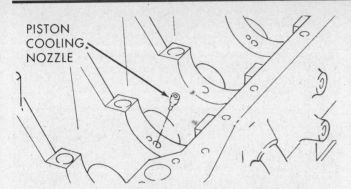

23.5 On diesel engines, make sure the piston cooling nozzles are in place in each main bearing saddle and that their oil passages are clear

23 Crankshaft - installation and main bearing oil clearance check

Refer to illustration 23.5

1 Crankshaft installation is the first major step in engine reassembly. It's assumed at this point that the engine block and crankshaft have been cleaned, inspected and repaired or reconditioned.

2 Position the engine with the bottom facing up.

3 Remove the main bearing cap bolts and lift out the caps. Lay the caps out in the proper order to ensure correct installation.

4 If they're still in place, remove the old bearing inserts from the block and the main bearing caps. Wipe the main bearing surfaces of the block and caps with a clean, lint-free cloth. They must be kept spotlessly clean!

5 On diesel engines, the main bearing saddles in the block have "piston cooling nozzles", which are sized jets to direct oil to the underside of the pistons to cool them **(see illustration)**. Before installing the main bearings or crankshaft, make sure these nozzles are in place, and check that they are clean by poking a wire through them.

Main bearing oil clearance check

Refer to illustration 23.11 and 23.15

6 Clean the back sides of the new main bearing inserts and lay the bearing half with the oil groove and hole in each main bearing saddle in the block (on all engines covered by this manual, the bearings with oil holes go in the block and those without oil holes go in the caps). Lay the other bearing half from each bearing set in the corresponding main bearing cap. Make sure the tab on each bearing insert fits into the

23.15 Compare the width of the crushed Plastigage to the scale on the envelope to determine the main bearing oil clearance (always take the measurement at the widest point of the Plastigage); be sure to use the correct scale - standard and metric ones are included

23.11 Lay the Plastigage strips (arrow) on the main bearing journals, parallel to the crankshaft centerline

recess in the block or cap. Also, the oil holes in the block must line up with the oil holes in the bearing insert. **Caution:** *Do not hammer the bearings into place and don't nick or gouge the bearing faces. No lubrication should be used at this time.*

7 The thrust bearings must be installed in the number three main bearing saddle on V8 and V10 engines. The thrust bearing on V6 engines is the number 2 main, and the number 6 on the diesel engine.

8 Clean the faces of the bearings in the block and the crankshaft main bearing journals with a clean, lint-free cloth. Check or clean the oil holes in the crankshaft, as any dirt here can go only one way - straight through the new bearings.

9 Once you're certain the crankshaft is clean, carefully lay it in position in the main bearings, lowering it straight down, not at any angle. No lubricant should be used at this time. If you're working on a V10 engine, have someone help you lower the crankshaft in. If you're working on a diesel engine, use an engine hoist and cloth sling, since the crankshaft is quite heavy.

10 Before the crankshaft can be permanently installed, the main bearing oil clearance must be checked.

11 Trim several pieces of the appropriate size Plastigage (they must be slightly shorter than the width of the main bearings) and place one piece on each crankshaft main bearing journal, parallel with the journal axis **(see illustration)**.

12 Clean the faces of the bearings in the caps and install the caps in their respective positions (don't mix them up) with the arrows pointing toward the front of the engine. Don't disturb the Plastigage. Apply a light coat of oil to the bolt threads and the undersides of the bolt heads, then install them. **Note:** *On diesel engines, make sure the cap dowels are in place on the caps, and install the caps carefully to avoid cocking the dowels in the block.*

13 Working from the center out, tighten the main bearing cap bolts, in three steps, to the torque listed in this Chapter's Specifications. Don't rotate the crankshaft at any time during this operation!

14 Remove the bolts and carefully lift off the main bearing caps. Keep them in order. Don't disturb the Plastigage or rotate the crankshaft. If any of the main bearing caps are difficult to remove, tap them gently from side-to-side with a soft-face hammer to loosen them.

15 Compare the width of the crushed Plastigage on each journal to the scale printed on the Plastigage envelope to obtain the main bearing oil clearance **(see illustration)**. Check the Specifications to make sure it's correct.

16 If the clearance is not as specified, the bearing inserts may be the wrong size which means different ones will be required (see Section 20). Before deciding that different inserts are needed, make sure that no dirt or oil was between the bearing inserts and the caps or block when the clearance was measured. If the Plastigage is noticeably wider at one end than the other, the journal may be tapered (see Section 19).

17 Carefully scrape all traces of the Plastigage material off the main bearing journals and/or the bearing faces. Don't nick or scratch the bearing faces.

23.19 Install the new upper rear seal in the groove in the block, with the white paint mark facing the rear

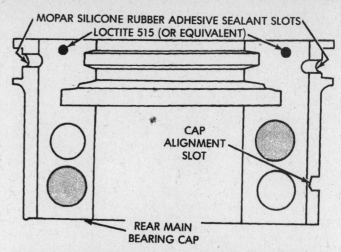

23.21 On V6 and V8 engines, apply a drop of Loctite 515 on either side of the rear cap - apply RTV sealant in the slots between the cap and block after cap installation

Final crankshaft installation

Refer to illustrations 23.19 and 23.21

18   Carefully lift the crankshaft straight up out of the engine. Clean the bearing faces in the block, then apply a thin, uniform layer of clean moly-base grease or engine assembly lube to each of the bearing surfaces. Coat the thrust surfaces as well.

19   Install the rear main oil seal halves into the engine block and rear main bearing cap (V6 and V8 engines) with the white paint facing the rear of the engine. It's not necessary to "shoehorn" the upper seal half into the engine - simply press it into place while the crankshaft is removed **(see illustration)**. Lubricate the crankshaft surfaces that contact the oil seals with moly-base grease, engine assembly lube or clean engine oil. Place the new lower seal half in the rear main cap with the white paint mark facing the rear of the engine. **Note:** *On the V10 and diesel engines, the rear seal is a one-piece unit pressed into a seal retainer plate at the back of the block. Refer to Part A or B of this Chapter for seal/retainer replacement. If your engine is on an engine stand, it may be difficult to replace the rear seal or retainer plate, so install it after the engine is off the stand, just before installation in the vehicle.*

20   Make sure the crankshaft journals are clean, then lay the crankshaft back in place in the block, lowering it straight down. Clean the faces of the bearings in the caps or cap assembly, then apply the same lubricant to them. Install the caps in their respective positions with the arrows pointing toward the front of the engine.

21   Thoroughly clean the area that the rear main cap sits on (V6 and V8 engines), and the mating face of the rear main cap. Apply a drop of Loctite 515 or equivalent on each side of the rear main cap **(see**

illustration). Install the cap quickly and tighten it to the torque listed in this Chapter's Specifications. After tightening, apply RTV sealant to the two slots between the block and rear cap.

22   Apply a light coat of oil to the bolt threads and the undersides of the bolt heads, then install them. Tighten all except the thrust cap bolts to the torque listed in this Chapter's Specifications (work from the center out and approach the final torque in three steps). Tighten the thrust cap bolts to 10-to-12 ft-lbs. Tap the ends of the crankshaft forward and backward with a lead or brass hammer to line up the thrust bearing and crankshaft surfaces. Re-tighten all main bearing cap bolts to the specified torque, following the recommended sequence.

23   Rotate the crankshaft a number of times by hand to check for any obvious binding.

24   Check the crankshaft endplay with a feeler gauge or a dial indicator (see Section 14). The endplay should be correct if the crankshaft thrust faces aren't worn or damaged and new thrust washers have been installed.

24   Pistons/connecting rods - installation and rod bearing oil clearance check

Refer to illustrations 24.3, 24.5a, 24.5b, 24.5c, 24.9, 24.11, 24.13 and 24.17

1   Before installing the piston/connecting rod assemblies, the cylinder walls must be perfectly clean, the top edge of each cylinder must

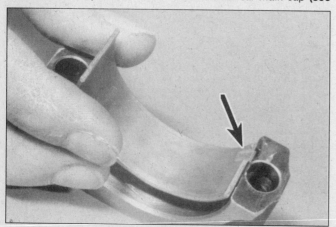

24.3 Make sure the bearing tang fits securely into the notch in the rod cap

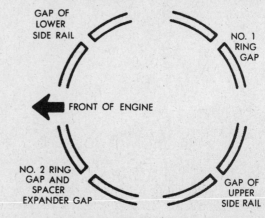

24.5a Position the ring end gaps as shown here before installing the pistons in the block - V6 and V8 engines

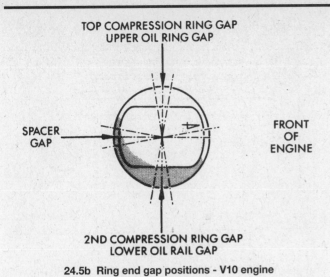

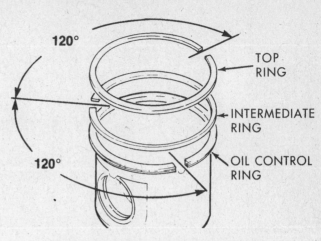

24.5b Ring end gap positions - V10 engine

24.5c Ring end gap positions - diesel engine

be chamfered, and the crankshaft must be in place.
2   Remove the cap from the end of the number one connecting rod (refer to the marks made during removal). Remove the original bearing inserts and wipe the bearing surfaces of the connecting rod and cap with a clean, lint-free cloth. They must be kept spotlessly clean.

Connecting rod bearing oil clearance check

3   Clean the back side of the new upper bearing insert, then lay it in place in the connecting rod. Make sure the tab on the bearing fits into the recess in the rod **(see illustration)** so the oil holes line up. Don't hammer the bearing insert into place and be very careful not to nick or gouge the bearing face. Don't lubricate the bearing at this time.
4   Clean the back side of the other bearing insert and install it in the rod cap. Again, make sure the tab on the bearing fits into the recess in the cap, and don't apply any lubricant. It's critically important that the mating surfaces of the bearing and connecting rod are perfectly clean and oil free when they're assembled.
5   Position the piston ring gaps at staggered intervals around the piston **(see illustrations)**.
6   Slip a section of plastic or rubber hose over each connecting rod cap bolt **(see illustration 13.5)**.
7   Lubricate the piston and rings with clean engine oil and attach a piston ring compressor to the piston. Leave the skirt protruding about 1/4-inch to guide the piston into the cylinder. The rings must be compressed until they're flush with the piston.

8   Rotate the crankshaft until the number one connecting rod journal is at BDC (bottom dead center) and apply a coat of engine oil to the cylinder walls.
9   With the mark on top of the piston **(see illustration)** facing the front (timing chain end) of the engine, gently insert the piston/connecting rod assembly into the number one cylinder bore and rest the bottom edge of the ring compressor on the engine block.
10   Tap the top edge of the ring compressor to make sure it's contacting the block around its entire circumference.
11   Gently tap on the top of the piston with the end of a wooden or plastic hammer handle **(see illustration)** while guiding the end of the connecting rod into place on the crankshaft journal. The piston rings may try to pop out of the ring compressor just before entering the cylinder bore, so keep some pressure on the ring compressor. Work slowly, and if any resistance is felt as the piston enters the cylinder, stop immediately. Find out what's hanging up and fix it before proceeding. Do not, for any reason, force the piston into the cylinder - you might break a ring and/or the piston.
12   Once the piston/connecting rod assembly is installed, the connecting rod bearing oil clearance must be checked before the rod cap is permanently bolted in place.
13   Cut a piece of the appropriate size Plastigage slightly shorter than the width of the connecting rod bearing and lay it in place on the number one connecting rod journal, parallel with the journal axis **(see illustration)**.

24.9 When installed, the mark/notch (arrow) in the piston must face the front of the engine

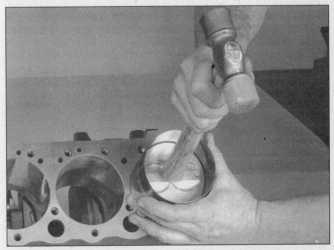

24.11 The piston can be driven gently into the cylinder bore with the end of a wooden or plastic hammer handle

24.13 Lay the Plastigage strips on each rod bearing journal, parallel to the crankshaft centerline

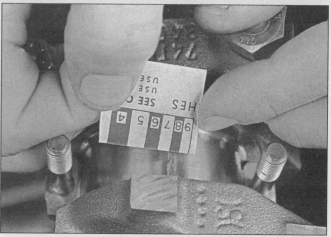

24.17 Measuring the width of the crushed Plastigage to determine the rod bearing oil clearance (be sure to use the correct scale - standard and metric ones are included)

14   Clean the connecting rod cap bearing face, remove the protective hoses from the connecting rod bolts and install the rod cap. Make sure the mating mark on the cap is on the same side as the mark on the connecting rod. Check the cap to make sure the front mark is facing the timing chain end of the engine.

15   Apply a light coat of oil to the undersides of the nuts, then install and tighten them to the torque listed in this Chapter's Specifications. Use a thin-wall socket to avoid erroneous torque readings that can result if the socket is wedged between the rod cap and nut. If the socket tends to wedge itself between the nut and the cap, lift up on it slightly until it no longer contacts the cap. Do not rotate the crankshaft at any time during this operation.

16   Remove the nuts and detach the rod cap, being very careful not to disturb the Plastigage.

17   Compare the width of the crushed Plastigage to the scale printed on the Plastigage envelope to obtain the oil clearance **(see illustration)**. Compare it to the Specifications to make sure the clearance is correct.

18   If the clearance is not as specified, the bearing inserts may be the wrong size (which means different ones will be required). Before deciding that different inserts are needed, make sure that no dirt or oil was between the bearing inserts and the connecting rod or cap when the clearance was measured. Also, recheck the journal diameter. If the Plastigage was wider at one end than the other, the journal may be tapered (see Section 19).

Final connecting rod installation

19   Carefully scrape all traces of the Plastigage material off the rod journal and/or bearing face. Be very careful not to scratch the bearing - use your fingernail or the edge of a credit card.

20   Make sure the bearing faces are perfectly clean, then apply a uniform layer of clean moly-base grease or engine assembly lube to both of them. You'll have to push the piston into the cylinder to expose the face of the bearing insert in the connecting rod - be sure to slip the protective hoses over the rod bolts first.

21   Slide the connecting rod back into place on the journal, remove the protective hoses from the rod cap bolts, install the rod cap and tighten the nuts to the torque listed in this Chapter's Specifications.

22   Repeat the entire procedure for the remaining pistons/connecting rods.

23   The important points to remember are:

a) *Keep the back sides of the bearing inserts and the insides of the connecting rods and caps perfectly clean when assembling them.*

b) *Make sure you have the correct piston/rod assembly for each cylinder.*

c) *The dimple on the piston must face the front (timing chain end) of the engine.*

d) *Lubricate the cylinder walls with clean oil.*

e) *Lubricate the bearing faces when installing the rod caps after the oil clearance has been checked.*

24   After all the piston/connecting rod assemblies have been properly installed, rotate the crankshaft a number of times by hand to check for any obvious binding.

25   As a final step, the connecting rod side clearance (endplay) must be checked (see Section 13).

26   Compare the measured side clearance to the Specifications to make sure it's correct. If it was correct before disassembly and the original crankshaft and rods were reinstalled, it should still be right. If new rods or a new crankshaft were installed, the side clearance may be inadequate. If so, the rods will have to be removed and taken to an automotive machine shop for re-sizing.

27   Adjust the oil pickup tube and screen the correct distance above the bottom of the oil pan (see Chapter 2A or 2B) and reinstall the oil pan.

28   The rest of the assembly procedure is the reverse of the removal procedure.

25   Initial start-up and break-in after overhaul

Warning: *Have a fire extinguisher handy when starting the engine for the first time.*

1   Once the engine has been installed in the vehicle, double-check the engine oil and coolant levels. Add one pint of Chrysler Crankcase Conditioner (part no. 4318002) or equivalent.

2   Start the engine. It may take a few moments for the gasoline to reach the fuel injectors but the engine should start without a great deal of effort.

3   After the engine starts, it should be allowed to warm up to normal operating temperature. While the engine is warming up, make a thorough check for oil and coolant leaks.

4   Shut the engine off and recheck the engine oil and coolant levels.

5   Drive the vehicle to an area with no traffic, accelerate rapidly from 30 to 50 mph, then allow the vehicle to slow to 30 mph with the throttle closed. Repeat the procedure 10 or 12 times. This will load the piston rings and cause them to seat properly against the cylinder walls. Check again for oil and coolant leaks.

6   Drive the vehicle gently for the first 500 miles (no sustained high speeds) and keep a constant check on the oil level. It is not unusual for an engine to use oil during the break-in period.

7   At approximately 500 to 600 miles, change the oil and filter.

8   For the next few hundred miles, drive the vehicle normally. Do not pamper it or abuse it.

9   After 2000 miles, change the oil and filter again and consider the engine fully broken in.

Chapter 3
Cooling, heating and air conditioning systems

Contents

Specifications

General

Coolant capacity	See Chapter 1
Radiator pressure cap rating	14 to 18 psi
Thermostat opening temperature	
Gasoline engines	192 to 199-degrees F
Diesel engine	188-degrees F

Torque specifications

	Ft-lbs (unless otherwise indicated)
Water pump pulley attaching bolts	
V6 and V8	20
V10	192 in-lbs
Fan drive hub pulley bolts (diesel)	200 in-lbs
Fan clutch-to-fan blade bolts	17
Fan assembly-to-drive hub nut	42
Thermostat housing bolts	
V6 and V8	200 in-lbs
V10	220 in-lbs
Diesel	216 in-lbs
Water pump attaching bolts	
Gasoline engines	30
Diesel engine	216 in-lbs

1   General information

The cooling system consists of a radiator and coolant reserve system, a radiator pressure cap, a thermostat (of varying temperatures depending on year and model), a four, five or seven blade fan, and a belt-driven water pump.

The radiator cooling fan is mounted on the front of the water pump on gasoline models, and on its own bearing/mount on the diesel engine, separate from the water pump, which has its own pulley. The cooling fan incorporates a fluid drive fan clutch (viscous fan clutch) which saves horsepower and reduces noise. A fan shroud is mounted on the rear of the radiator to direct air flow through the radiator.

The system is pressurized by a spring-loaded radiator cap, which, by maintaining pressure, increases the boiling point of the coolant. If the coolant temperature goes above this increased boiling point, the extra pressure in the system forces the radiator cap valve off its seat and exposes the overflow pipe or hose. The overflow pipe/hose leads to a coolant recovery system. This consists of a plastic reservoir into which the coolant that normally escapes due to expansion is retained. When the engine cools, the excess coolant is drawn back into the radiator by the vacuum created as the system cools, maintaining the system at full capacity. This is a continuous process and provided the level in the reservoir is correctly maintained, it is not necessary to add coolant to the radiator.

Coolant is drawn from the radiator up the lower radiator hose to the water pump, where it is forced through the water passages in the cylinder block. The coolant then travels up into the cylinder head, circulates around the combustion chambers and valve seats, travels out of the cylinder head past the open thermostat into the upper radiator hose and back into the radiator. The radiator in all models is of cross-flow design, with tanks on either side. On V6 and V8 models, the core is aluminum and the tanks are plastic, while the V10 and Cummins diesel engines use a brass-and-copper radiator.

When the engine is cold, the thermostat restricts the circulation of coolant to the engine. When the minimum operating temperature is reached, the thermostat begins to open, allowing coolant to return to the radiator.

Automatic transmission-equipped models with gasoline engines have a cooler element incorporated into the radiator to cool the transmission fluid. On diesel models with automatic transmissions, a separate transmission oil cooler is mounted on the right rear side of the engine block, that receives water circulation through pipes from the front of the engine.

The heating system works by directing air through the heater core mounted in the instrument panel and then to the interior of the vehicle by a system of ducts. Temperature is controlled by mixing heated air with fresh air, using a system of flapper doors in the ducts, and a blower motor.

Air conditioning is an optional accessory, consisting of an evaporator core located under the instrument panel, a condenser in front of the radiator, an accumulator in the engine compartment and a belt-driven compressor mounted at the front of the engine.

2   Antifreeze/coolant - general information

Refer to illustration 2.6

Warning: *Do not allow antifreeze to come in contact with your skin or painted surfaces of the vehicle. Rinse off spills immediately with plenty of water. Antifreeze is highly toxic if ingested. Never leave antifreeze lying around in an open container or in puddles on the floor; children and pets are attracted by it's sweet smell and may drink it. Check with local authorities about disposing of used antifreeze. Many communities have collection centers which will see that antifreeze is disposed of safely. Never dump used antifreeze on the ground or pour it into drains.*
Note: *Non-toxic antifreeze is now manufactured and available at local auto parts stores, but even these types should be disposed of properly.*

The cooling system should be filled with a water/ethylene glycol based antifreeze solution which will prevent freezing down to at least -

2.6 An inexpensive hydrometer can be used to test the condition of your coolant

20 degrees F (even lower in cold climates). It also provides protection against corrosion and increases the coolant boiling point.

The cooling system should be drained, flushed and refilled at least every other year (see Chapter 1). The use of antifreeze solutions for periods of longer than two years is likely to cause damage and encourage the formation of rust and scale in the system.

Before adding antifreeze to the system, check all hose connections. Antifreeze can leak through very minute openings.

The exact mixture of antifreeze to water which you should use depends on the relative weather conditions. The mixture should contain at least 50-percent antifreeze, but should never contain more than 70-percent antifreeze. Consult the mixture ratio chart on the antifreeze container before adding coolant. Hydrometers are available at most auto parts stores to test the coolant **(see illustration)**. Use antifreeze which meets the vehicle manufacturer's specifications, and look on the antifreeze container for specific mention of ingredients for maximum protection of aluminum cooling system components.

3   Thermostat - check and replacement

Warning: *The engine must be completely cool when this procedure is performed.*
Note: *Don't drive the vehicle without a thermostat! The computer (if so equipped) may stay in open loop and emissions and fuel economy will suffer. Diesel engines will overheat without a thermostat.*

Check

1   Before condemning the thermostat, check the coolant level, drivebelt tension and temperature gauge (or light) operation.
2   If the engine takes a long time to warm up, the thermostat is probably stuck open. Replace the thermostat.
3   If the engine runs hot, check the temperature of the upper radiator hose. If the hose isn't hot, the thermostat is probably stuck shut. Replace the thermostat.
4   If the upper radiator hose is hot, it means the coolant is circulating and the thermostat is open. Refer to the *Troubleshooting* Section for the cause of overheating.
5   If an engine has been overheated, you may find damage such as leaking head gaskets, scuffed pistons and warped or cracked cylinder heads.

Replacement

Refer to illustrations 3.8, 3.9a, 3.9b, 3.9c, 3.10a, 3.10b and 3.13

6   Disconnect the battery cable at the negative battery terminal. On diesel models, disconnect the negative cables from both batteries.

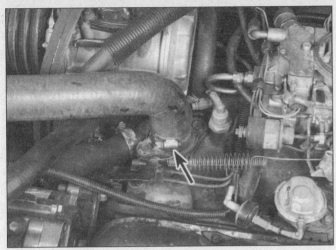

3.8 Loosen the clamp (arrow) and disconnect the upper radiator hose from the thermostat cover (V8 shown)

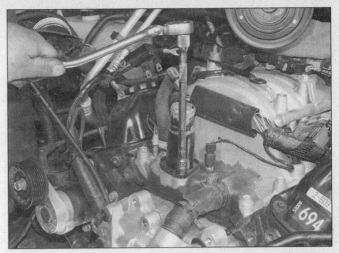

3.9a Remove the bolts and lift the thermostat cover off (V8 shown)

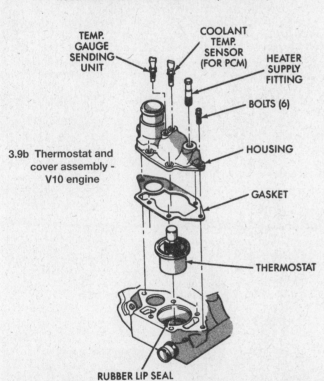

3.9b Thermostat and cover assembly - V10 engine

TEMP. GAUGE SENDING UNIT

COOLANT TEMP. SENSOR (FOR PCM)

HEATER SUPPLY FITTING

BOLTS (6)

HOUSING

GASKET

THERMOSTAT

RUBBER LIP SEAL

3.9c On the diesel engine, the alternator bracket (large arrow) must be removed, then remove the bolts (three small arrows) and lift the thermostat cover off

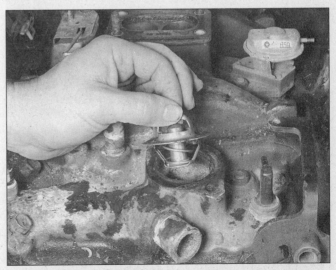

3.10a Note how its installed, then remove the thermostat

Drain coolant (about 1 gallon) from the radiator, until the coolant level is below the thermostat housing. Remove the drivebelt from V6, V8 and diesel models.

7   On V6, V8 and diesel models, unbolt the alternator (see Chapter 5) and set it aside for access to the thermostat. On diesel models, remove the alternator mounting bracket. On gasoline models, remove the alternator support brace.

8   Disconnect the upper radiator hose from the thermostat cover **(see illustration)**.

9   Remove the bolts and lift the cover off **(see illustrations)**. It may be necessary to tap the cover with a soft-face hammer to break the gasket seal. **Note:** *On V10 and diesel models, a smaller hose must also be disconnected from the thermostat cover, and on the V10 only, two temperature sensors must be disconnected.*

10   Note how it's installed, then remove the thermostat **(see illustration)**. Be sure to use a replacement thermostat with the correct opening temperature (see this Chapter's Specifications). On diesel models,

3.10b On the diesel engine, the thermostat seal is a rubber gasket (arrow) that seals against the engine lift bracket

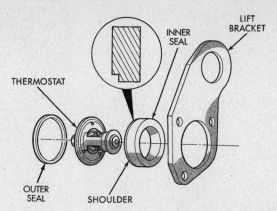

3.13 Thermostat and seals installation details - diesel engine

remove the thermostat, inner thermostat seal and engine lift bracket **(see illustration)**.

11   On gasoline models, use a scraper or putty knife to remove all traces of old gasket material and sealant from the gasket mating surfaces. **Caution:** *Be careful not to gouge or damage the gasket surfaces, or a leak could develop after assembly.* Make sure no gasket material falls into the coolant passages; it is a good idea to stuff a rag in the passage. Wipe the mating surfaces with a rag saturated with lacquer thinner or acetone.

12   On gasoline models, install the thermostat with the spring end directed in, toward the engine **(see illustration 3.10a)**. Apply a thin coat of RTV sealant to both sides of the new gasket and position it over the thermostat. Make sure the holes in the gasket align with the bolt holes in the housing. On V10 models, the thermostat sits in a special seal (rubber seal with a metal shoulder) that fits down low in the intake manifold. If the seal is worn or damaged, replace it, using RTV sealant around the metal edge.

13   On diesel models, install a new outer O-ring seal into the thermostat cover. Place the thermostat and a new inner seal, with the cut-out shoulder towards the thermostat, into the cover **(see illustration)**. Install the thermostat housing, seals and lift bracket onto the engine as an assembly. Tighten the bolts to the torque listed in this Chapter's Specifications.

14   On gasoline models, carefully position the cover over the thermostat and install the bolts. **Note:** *On V6 and V8 models, the thermostat cover is stamped with "Front", this must face the front of the engine during installation for adequate clearance for hose installation.* Tighten the bolts to the torque listed in this Chapter's Specifications - do not over-tighten the bolts or the cover may crack or become distorted, be especially careful with the V10 cover, which is plastic.

15   Reattach the radiator hose and heater hose or check valve hose (if equipped), to the cover and tighten the clamps - now may be a good time to check and replace the hoses and clamps (see Chapter 1).

16   Install the alternator, brackets and drivebelt. Refer to Chapter 1 and refill the cooling system, then run the engine and check carefully for leaks.

17   Repeat steps 1 through 5 to be sure the repairs corrected the previous problem(s).

4   Engine cooling fan and fan clutch - check, removal and installation

Warning: *Keep hands, tools and clothing away from the fan when the engine is running. To avoid injury or damage DO NOT operate the engine with a damaged fan. Do not attempt to repair fan blades - replace a damaged fan with a new one.*

Check

Warning: *In order to check the fan clutch, the engine will need to be at operating temperature, so while going through checks prior to Step 5 be careful that the engine is NOT started while the checks are being completed. Severe personal injury can result!*

1   Symptoms of failure of the fan clutch are continuous noisy operation, looseness, vibration and evidence of silicone fluid leaks.

2   Rock the fan back and forth by hand to check for excessive bearing play.

3   With the engine cold, turn the blades by hand. The fan should turn freely.

4   Visually inspect for substantial fluid leakage from the fan clutch assembly, a deformed bi-metal spring or grease leakage from the cooling fan bearing. If any of these conditions exist, replace the fan clutch.

5   When the engine is warmed up, turn off the ignition switch and disconnect the cable from the negative battery terminal. Turn the fan by hand. Some resistance should be felt. If the fan turns easily, replace the fan clutch.

Removal and installation

Refer to illustrations 4.9, 4.10, 4.11 and 4.13

6   Disconnect the battery cable at the negative battery terminal. On diesel models, disconnect the negative cables from both batteries.

7   Remove the serpentine drivebelt (see Chapter 1).

8   On all except V10 models, remove the coolant reservoir from the fan shroud and set it aside without draining the tank or disconnecting the hose (see Section 5).

9   Disconnect the electrical connectors at the windshield washer

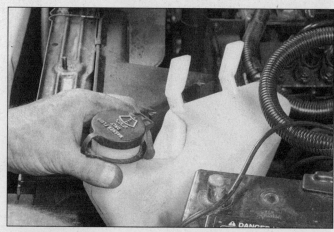

4.9 From below the fan shroud, disconnect and plug the hose from the washer tank, disconnect the two electrical connectors, and pull straight up to disengage the tank from the left side of the fan shroud

4.10 Remove the fan shroud bolts (small arrows indicate the right-hand bolts) - there are two on either side of the radiator - larger arrow indicates where coolant reservoir had been

4.11 A 36mm fan wrench (arrow) must be used to turn the large nut while the fan pulley is held stationary with a large screwdriver or pliers (diesel shown)

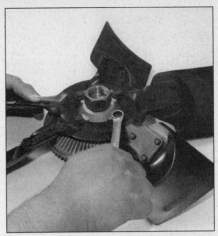

4.13 Remove the fan blade-to- fan clutch mounting bolts

reservoir and remove the reservoir from the fan shroud (see illustration).

10   Remove the fan shroud mounting bolts (see illustration).

11   A special 36mm fan wrench, obtainable at most auto parts stores, is required to remove the cooling fan. The fan attaches to the drive hub with a large nut that is part of the fan clutch. Hold pulley with a large screwdriver wedged between the pulley bolts, or a large pair of adjustable pliers and loosen the drive nut with the special tool (see illustration). The threads on the nut are RIGHT-HAND threads on all gasoline models (turn counterclockwise to remove) and LEFT-HAND threads on diesel models (turn clockwise to remove).

12   Lift the cooling fan assembly and the fan shroud up and out of the engine compartment together.

13   The fan clutch can be unbolted from the fan blade assembly for replacement (see illustration). Caution: To prevent silicone fluid from draining from the clutch assembly into the fan drive bearing and ruining the lubricant, DON'T place the drive unit in a position with the rear of the shaft pointing down. Store the fan in its upright position if possible.

14   Installation is the reverse of removal. Tighten the fan clutch-to-fan blade bolts and the fan assembly-to-drive hub nut to the torque listed in this Chapter's Specifications.

5   Radiator and coolant reservoir tank - removal and installation

Warning: *The engine must be completely cool when this procedure is performed.*

Removal

Refer to illustrations 5.2a, 5.2b, 5.3a, 5.3b, 5.5 and 5.6

1   Disconnect the battery cable at the negative battery terminal. On diesel models, disconnect both negative battery cables and remove the nuts holding the positive cable to the fan shroud.

2   Refer to Section 4 and remove the cooling fan and fan shroud. **Note:** *On all models except the V10, pull straight up on the coolant recovery tank to remove it from the top of the fan shroud (see illustration).* On V10 models, the coolant tank is bolted to the right inner fender panel (see illustration).

3   Drain the cooling system as described in Chapter 1, then disconnect the overflow hose and the upper and lower radiator hoses from the radiator (see illustrations). Refer to the coolant **Warning** in Section 2.

5.2a Pull straight up on the coolant reservoir tank to separate it from the fan shroud

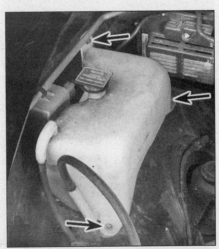

5.2b The coolant reservoir tank on V10 models is attached to the inner fender panel with screws (arrows)

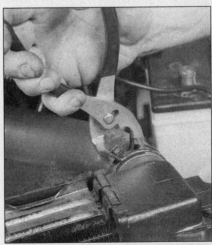

5.3a Squeeze the ends of the hose clamp together with large pliers, slide the clamp back over the hose and disconnect the upper radiator hose from the radiator

3

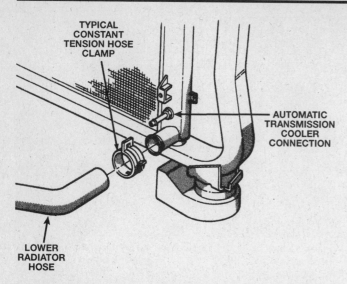

5.3b Slide the lower clamp back over the lower radiator hose and separate the hose from the radiator - disconnect the two transmission cooler lines if equipped

4   If equipped with an automatic transmission cooler, remove the cooler lines from the radiator **(see illustration 5.3b)** - be careful not to damage the lines or fittings. Plug the ends of the disconnected lines to prevent leakage and stop dirt from entering the system. Have a drip pan ready to catch any spills. **Note:** *This is not necessary on diesel models, on which an oil-to-water transmission cooler is mounted on the right rear of the engine, not the radiator. The diesel transmission fluid is further cooled by a separate oil-to-air cooler mounted ahead of the radiator on the left side, which is not connected to the radiator.*
5   The radiator is supported by two lower rubber mounts and secured at the top of the radiator with two bolts. Remove these two bolts **(see illustration)**.
6   Pry up at the bottom of the radiator mounts until the alignment dowels clear the rubber insulators. They may stick. Lift the radiator from the engine compartment **(see illustration)**.

Installation

7   Replace any damaged hose clamps and radiator hoses.
8   Radiator installation is the reverse of removal, but make sure the rubber insulators are in place on the projections at the bottom of the radiator.
9   Make sure the coolant reservoir is clean and free of debris which

5.5 Remove the two upper radiator mounting bolts

could be drawn into the radiator (wash it with soapy water and a brush if necessary, then rinse thoroughly).
10   After installation, fill the system with the proper mixture of antifreeze, and also check the automatic transmission fluid level, where applicable (see Chapter 1).

6   Water pump - check

Refer to illustrations 6.2 and 6.4
1   Water pump failure can cause overheating and serious damage to the engine. There are three ways to check the operation of the water pump while it is installed on the engine. If any one of the following quick-checks indicates water pump problems, it should be replaced immediately.
2   A seal protects the water pump impeller shaft bearing from contamination by engine coolant. If this seal fails, a weep hole in the water pump snout will leak coolant **(see illustration)** (an inspection mirror can be used to look at the underside of the pump if the hole isn't on top). If the weep hole is leaking, shaft bearing failure will follow. Replace the water pump immediately.
3   Besides contamination by coolant after a seal failure, the water pump impeller shaft bearing can also be prematurely worn out by an improperly-tensioned drivebelt. When the bearing wears out, it emits a high pitched squealing sound. If such a noise is coming from the water pump during engine operation, the shaft bearing has failed - replace

5.6 After prying the bottom of the radiator loose from the rubber insulators, pull the radiator straight up and out

6.2 Check the water pump weep hole (arrow) for leakage

6.4 Check the pump for loose or rough bearings (this can be done with the fan and pulley in place)

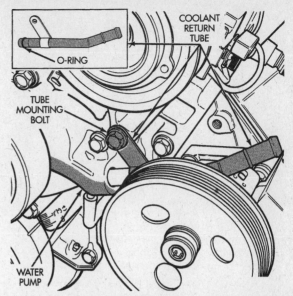

7.5 On V6 and V8 models, the coolant return tube must be unbolted and twisted out of the pump

the water pump immediately. **Note:** *Don't mistake drivebelt slippage, which causes a squealing sound, for water pump bearing failure.*

4   To identify excessive bearing wear before the bearing actually fails, grasp the water pump pulley and try to force it up-and-down or from side-to-side **(see illustration)**. If the pulley can be moved either horizontally or vertically, the bearing is nearing the end of its service life. Replace the water pump.

5   It is possible for a water pump to be bad, even if it doesn't howl or leak water. Sometimes the fins on the back of the impeller can corrode away until the pump is no longer effective. The only way to check for this is to remove the pump for examination.

7   Water pump - removal and installation

Removal

Refer to illustrations 7.5, 7.6a, 7.6b and 7.6c

1   Disconnect the battery cable at the negative battery terminal. On diesel models, disconnect the negative cables from both batteries.

2   Drain the coolant (see Chapter 1).

3   Remove the drivebelt (see Chapter 1). **Note:** *Take note of the serpentine belt routing (see Chapter 1). Improper belt reinstallation could cause the water pump to turn the wrong way and cause overheating.*

4   Remove the cooling fan and fan shroud assembly (see Section 4). On gasoline models, remove water pump pulley.

5   Detach the coolant hoses from the water pump on gasoline models. **Note:** *The coolant return hose on V6 and V8 models is attached to a tube in the water pump. The tube is O-ring sealed and is held in by a tab and bolt. Remove the bolt and pull the tube from the pump* **(see illustration)**.

6   Remove the water pump mounting bolts and detach the pump **(see illustrations)**. It may be necessary to tap the pump with a soft-face hammer to break the gasket seal.

7   Inspect the pump's impeller blades on the backside for corrosion. If any fins are missing or badly corroded, replace the pump with a new one.

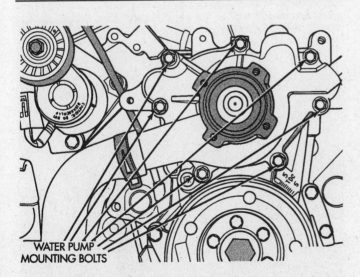

7.6a Remove the water pump mounting bolts (arrows) and detach the pump - V6 and V8 models

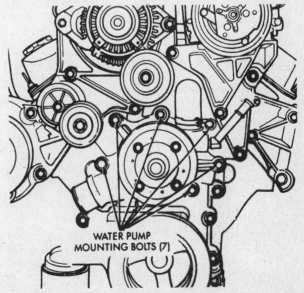

7.6b Water pump mounting bolt locations (arrows) - V10 models

7.6c   Remove two bolts to remove the water pump from the diesel engine - no hoses are connected to it, and the pulley is part of the pump

7.8   Remove all traces of sealant or gasket material - use care to avoid gouging the soft aluminum

7.10   On diesel and V10 model water pumps, replace the O-ring (arrow) - apply a small amount petroleum jelly to hold it in place (diesel pump shown)

Installation

Refer to illustrations 7.8 and 7.10

8   Clean the sealing surfaces of all gasket material on both the water pump and block **(see illustration)**. Wipe the mating surfaces with a rag saturated with lacquer thinner or acetone.

9   On V6 and V8 models, apply a thin layer of RTV sealant to both sides of the new gasket.

10   Install the gasket on the water pump. Both V10 and diesel models use an O-ring on the water pump instead of a traditional gasket. Apply petroleum jelly to the new O-ring to hold it in place during installation **(see illustration)**.

11   Place the water pump in position and install the bolts finger tight. Use caution to ensure that the gasket doesn't slip out of position, and that you have the right-length bolts in the right holes. Tighten the bolts to the torque listed in this Chapter's Specifications.

12   On gasoline models, install the water pump pulley and tighten the bolts to the torque listed in this Chapter's Specifications.

13   Install the coolant hoses and hose clamps. Tighten the hose clamps securely.

14   Install the drivebelt (see Chapter 1).

15   Install the cooling fan and fan shroud (see Section 4).

16   Add coolant to the specified level (see Chapter 1).

17   Reconnect the battery cable to the negative battery terminal.

18   Start the engine and check for the proper coolant level and the water pump and hoses for leaks.

8   Coolant temperature sending unit - check and replacement

Warning: *Wait until the engine is completely cool before beginning this procedure.*

Check

Refer to illustration 8.1a, 8.1b and 8.1c

1   The coolant temperature indicator system is composed of a light or temperature gauge mounted in the instrument panel and a coolant temperature sending unit mounted on the engine **(see illustrations)**. Some vehicles have more than one sending unit, but only one is used for the indicator system. The other is used to send temperature information to the computer.

2   If an overheating indication occurs, check the coolant level in the system and then make sure the wiring between the light or gauge and the sending unit is secure and all fuses are intact.

3   With the ignition switch turned On, disconnect the sender. The gauge should read at the low end of its scale.

4   If the gauge doesn't move, the gauge or ignition switch may be faulty or the circuit may be open. Test the circuit by grounding the wire to the sending unit while the ignition is On (engine NOT running). If the gauge deflects full scale or the light comes on, it means the gauge is working, so replace the sending unit.

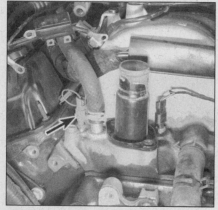

8.1a   The coolant-temperature sending unit (arrow) is located near the front of the intake manifold on V6 and V8 models - the other sender to the right is for the computer

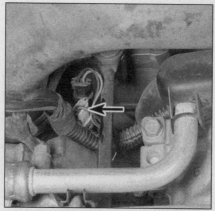

8.1b   Coolant temperature sender (arrow) location - V10 models (the other temperature sensor is for the computer)

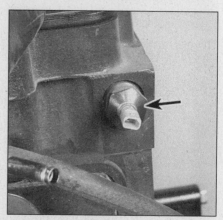

8.1c   The coolant temperature sender is located at the left rear corner of the cylinder head on diesel models

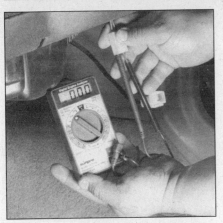

9.2 Connect a voltmeter to the blower motor connector and check for battery voltage

9.5 The blower motor (1) and blower motor resistor (2) locations, under the right side of the instrument panel

9.7 Check for continuity through the blower motor resistor - if there's no continuity through any combination of the four terminals, replace it

Replacement

5   Make sure the engine is cool before removing the defective sending unit. There will be some coolant loss as the unit is removed, so be prepared to catch it. Refer to the coolant **Warning** in Section 2.

6   Prepare the new sending unit by coating the threads with Teflon pipe sealant or wrapping them with Teflon tape. Disconnect the electrical connector, unscrew the sensor from the engine and install the replacement. **Note:** *When reconnecting the sender in the thermostat housing on V10 models, make sure the ground wire is intact. The housing is plastic, so check for continuity to ground between the sender body and a good engine ground. If there is no continuity, repair the ground wire circuit to the sender.*

7   Check the coolant level after the replacement unit has been installed and add coolant, if necessary (see Chapter 1). Check now for proper operation of the gauge and sending unit.

9   Blower motor and circuit - check

Check

Refer to illustrations 9.2, 9.5 and 9.7

1   Check the fuse and all connections in the circuit for looseness and corrosion. Make sure the battery is fully charged.

2   If the blower motor does not operate, disconnect the electrical connector at the blower motor, turn the ignition key On (engine not running) and check for battery voltage on the dark green wire terminal **(see illustration)**. If battery voltage is not present, there is a problem in

the ignition feed circuit.

3   If battery voltage is present, reconnect the terminal to the blower motor and backprobe the black/tan wire terminal with a jumper wire connected to ground. If the motor still does not operate, the motor is faulty.

4   If the motor is good, but doesn't operate at any speed, the heater/air conditioning control switch is probably faulty. Remove the control assembly (see Section 12) and check for continuity through the switch in each position.

5   If the blower motor operates at High speed, but not at one or more of the lower speeds, check the blower motor resistor, located under the instrument panel on the passenger side **(see illustration)**.

6   Disconnect the electrical connector from the blower motor resistor. Remove the screws and withdraw the resistor from the housing.

7   Using a continuity tester on the blower motor resistor, check between each input terminal (from the blower speed switch side) to the output terminal (to the blower). There should be continuity. If not, replace the resistor **(see illustration)**.

10   Blower motor - removal and installation

Refer to illustrations 10.1, 10.2 and 10.3

1   Disconnect the electrical connector to the blower motor and remove the three screws retaining the blower to the housing **(see illustration)**.

2   Pull the blower motor and fan straight out **(see illustration)**, being careful not to bend the fan assembly.

3   To remove the fan from the blower motor, squeeze the spring clip

10.1 Remove the three screws (arrows) retaining the blower motor to the housing

10.2 Pull the blower motor and fan straight out of the housing

3

10.3 Remove the fan by squeezing the spring clip together and slipping the fan off the shaft

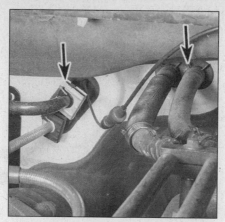

11.3 Loosen the hose clamps and disconnect the heater hoses from the heater core tubes at the firewall (right arrow), then disconnect the two refrigerant lines (left arrow)

11.6 Remove the nuts from the studs on the engine compartment side of the firewall - one more (not seen here) is at the center of the firewall above the engine

together and slip the fan off the shaft **(see illustration)**.
4   Installation of the fan onto the motor and reassembly of blower motor to the heater housing is the reverse of removal.

11   Heater core - removal and installation

Warning 1: *These models are equipped with an airbag. The airbag is armed and can deploy (inflate) anytime the battery is connected. To prevent accidental deployment (and possible injury), disconnect the negative battery cable whenever working near airbag components. After the battery is disconnected, wait at least 2 minutes before beginning work (the system has a back-up capacitor that must fully discharge). For more information see Chapter 12.*

Warning 2: *The air conditioning system is under high pressure. DO NOT loosen any fittings or remove any components until after the system has been discharged. Air conditioning refrigerant should be properly discharged into an EPA-approved container at a dealer service department or an automotive air conditioning facility. Always wear eye protection when disconnecting air conditioning system fittings.*

Removal

Refer to illustrations 11.3, 11.6, 11.8a, 11.8b, 11.9 and 11.10

1   If equipped with air conditioning, have the system discharged at a dealer service department or automotive air conditioning facility. Disconnect the battery cable at the negative battery terminal. On diesel

models, disconnect the negative cables from both batteries.
2   Drain the cooling system (see Chapter 1).
3   Disconnect the heater hoses at the heater core inlet and outlet on the engine side of the firewall **(see illustration)**. Cap the open fittings.
4   Using spring-lock coupling tools (see Section 16), disconnect the refrigerant lines at the firewall **(see illustration 11.3)**. Cap the open lines to prevent entry of contaminants.
5   On V10 models, refer to Section 5 and remove the coolant reservoir tank. Refer to Chapter 6 and remove the PCM without disconnecting its wires. On diesel models, remove the air cleaner housing for access to the PCM (see Chapter 4B).
6   Remove the four nuts from the heater/air conditioning unit studs on the engine compartment side of the firewall **(see illustration)**. Refer to Section 15 for removal of the accumulator. After it is removed, remove the nut from the mounting stud that held the accumulator to the firewall. One stud/nut is at the center of the firewall, to the right of the heater hose connections.
7   Refer to Chapter 11 for removal of the instrument panel, and Section 11 of this Chapter for removal and disconnection of the heater/air conditioning controls.
8   Remove the bolts retaining the heater/air conditioning unit to the cowl **(see illustrations)**.
9   Move the heater housing to the rear until it clears the studs and remove the unit from the vehicle **(see illustration)**. Make sure the heater core inlet and outlet pipes are securely plugged to prevent coolant from spilling into the passenger compartment. **Note:** *The*

11.8a Remove the right-side kick panel and remove the bolt (arrow) holding the heater/air conditioning unit to the cowl . . .

11.8b . . . then remove the nut from this stud - remove the ground strap from the stud, then the final nut (on the same stud) holding the unit to the firewall

11.9 With everything disconnected, the entire heater/air conditioner unit can be removed from the vehicle

11.10 Remove these three screws (arrows) and the clamps and slide the heater core straight out of the housing

12.3 Remove the four screws (arrows) retaining the heater/air conditioning control assembly to the instrument panel

heater blend door cable must be disconnected, either at the controls (see Section 12) or at the heater/air conditioning housing assembly.

10   The heater core itself is retained by three screws in the housing, one that clamps the tubes near the firewall, and two on a clamp near the core **(see illustration)**. remove the three screws and clamps, then pull the heater core straight out of the housing.

11   Remove and save any sealing material around the core or tubes.

Installation

12   Installation is the reverse of removal. Be sure to reinstall any sealing materials around the heater core, doors, or ducting.

13   Refill the cooling system (see Chapter 1).

14   Start the engine and check for proper operation. If equipped with air conditioning, have the air conditioning system evacuated and recharged at a dealership service facility or air conditioning shop.

12 Heater and air conditioning control assembly - removal, installation and vacuum check

Warning: *These models are equipped with an airbag. The airbag is armed and can deploy (inflate) anytime the battery is connected. To prevent accidental deployment (and possible injury), disconnect the negative battery cable whenever working near airbag components. After the battery is disconnected, wait at least 2 minutes before beginning work (the system has a back-up capacitor that must fully discharge). For more information see Chapter 12.*

Removal and installation

Refer to illustrations 12.3, 12.4a and 12.4b

1   Disconnect the battery cable from the negative battery terminal. On diesel models, disconnect the negative cables from both batteries.

2   Remove the trim bezel that surrounds the heater/air conditioning control assembly (see Chapter 11).

3   Remove the four control assembly retaining screws **(see illustration)**.

4   Remove the heater/air conditioning control assembly from the instrument panel and disconnect the blend-air control cable, electrical connector and vacuum lines from the control assembly **(see illustrations)**. **Caution:** *Be careful when removing the vacuum lines to avoid cracking the plastic connectors and causing a vacuum leak (possibly internal within the control assembly).*

5   To install the control assembly, reverse the removal procedure. **Caution:** *When reconnecting vacuum lines to the control assembly, do not use any lubricant to make them slip on easier, it can affect vacuum operation. If necessary, use a very small amount of plain water to make reconnection easier.*

Control assembly vacuum check

Refer to illustrations 12.10 and 12.11

6   Vacuum is supplied to the heater/air conditioning control assembly by tubing attached to the intake manifold. A check valve is used in the line. Inspect the supply line, from the intake manifold to the control assembly, for damage or leaks.

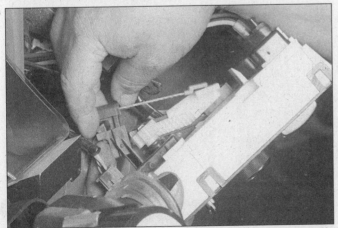

12.4a Pull the control assembly away from the instrument panel, disconnect the blend cable by depressing the red "flag" tab, then disconnect the cable housing from the control assembly

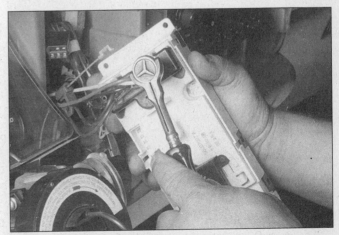

12.4b Disconnect the vacuum connector by removing the two plastic nuts

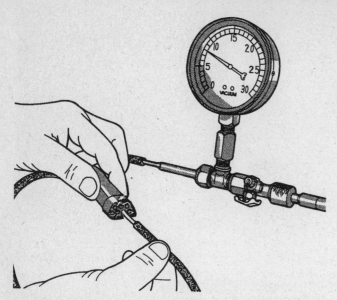

12.10 Apply 8 inches of vacuum to each of the seven ports of the heater/air conditioning control assembly vacuum harness connector

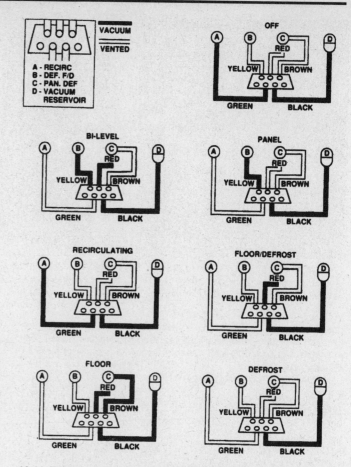

12.11 The vacuum circuit chart indicates the destination of each line in the vacuum harness and in which mode they are supplied vacuum

7   With the engine OFF, remove the check valve from the black vacuum supply line connected to the intake manifold (be sure to note the installed direction of the valve in the line). Apply 8 inches of vacuum, with a hand-held vacuum pump, to the engine side of the check valve. You should be able to pull air through the check valve.

8   Apply vacuum to the heater/air conditioning control side of the valve. The valve should hold vacuum. If not, replace the check valve.

9   Reconnect the check valve in the vacuum line, in the proper direction and connect the hose onto the intake manifold.

10   Pull the heater/air conditioning control panel away from the instrument panel and disconnect the vacuum harness from the control assembly **(see illustration 12.4b)**. Apply 8 inches of vacuum to each of the seven ports on the harness connector **(see illustration)**.

11   If any of the circuits don't hold vacuum, follow the lines to their destination **(see illustration)**, isolate the source of the leak and repair it.

13   Air conditioning and heating system - check and maintenance

Refer to illustration 13.5

Warning: *The air conditioning system is under high pressure. DO NOT loosen any fittings or remove any components until after the system has been discharged. Air conditioning refrigerant should be properly discharged into an EPA-approved recovery container at a dealer service department or an automotive air conditioning facility. Always wear eye protection when disconnecting air conditioning system fittings.*

1   The following maintenance steps should be performed on a regular basis to ensure that the air conditioner continues to operate at peak efficiency.

a) *Check the tension of the drivebelt and adjust if necessary (see Chapter 1).*

b) *Check the condition of the hoses. Look for cracks, hardening and deterioration. Look at potential leak areas for signs of refrigerant oil leaking.* **Warning:** *Do not replace air conditioning hoses until the system has been properly discharged (see* **Warning** *above).*

c) *Check the fins of the condenser for leaves, bugs and other foreign material. A soft brush and compressed air can be used to remove them.*

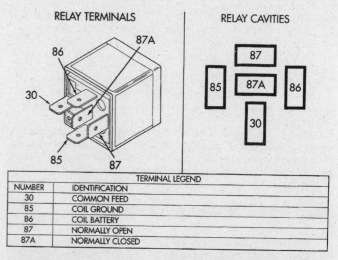

TERMINAL LEGEND	
NUMBER	IDENTIFICATION
30	COMMON FEED
85	COIL GROUND
86	COIL BATTERY
87	NORMALLY OPEN
87A	NORMALLY CLOSED

13.5 Air conditioning clutch relay terminal identification - when not energized, there should be continuity through the relay between terminals 87A and 30, and no continuity between terminals 87 and 30. There should be 75 ohms resistance between terminals 85 and 86. With the relay energized (attach a ground wire to terminal 85 and 12-volts to terminal 86), there should be continuity between terminals 30 and 87, and no continuity between terminals 87A and 30

13.9 Feel the two refrigerant pipes leading to the evaporator - the inlet line (lower pipe) should be cold and the outlet slightly cooler

13.12 A basic charging kit for 134a systems is available at most auto parts stores - it must say 134a (not R-12) and so should the 12-ounce can of refrigerant

13.15 Add refrigerant to the system at the low-pressure port

d) *Check the wire harness for correct routing, broken wires, damaged insulation, etc. Make sure the electrical connectors are clean and tight.*

e) *Maintain the correct refrigerant charge.*

2   The system should be run for about 10 minutes at least once a month. This is particularly important during the winter months because long-term non-use can cause hardening of the internal seals.

3   Leaks in the air conditioning system are best spotted when the system is brought up to operating temperature and pressure, by running the engine with the air conditioning ON for five minutes. Shut the engine off and inspect the air conditioning hoses and connections. Traces of oil usually indicate refrigerant leaks.

4   Because of the complexity of the air conditioning system and the special equipment required to effectively work on it, accurate troubleshooting of the system should be left to a professional technician.

5   If the air conditioning system doesn't operate at all, check the fuse panel and the air conditioning relay, located in the Power Distribution Center (PDC) in the engine compartment. Refer to Chapter 1 for the location of the air conditioning clutch relay in the Power Distribution Center. Remove the relay and check it for continuity **(see illustration)**. Check for battery voltage at the number 30 cavity in the PDC. There should be battery voltage present at all times. Check for continuity between cavity 87 and the relay side of the air conditioning compressor connector. There should be battery voltage at cavity 86 only when the key is ON.

6   The most common cause of poor cooling is simply a low system refrigerant charge. If a noticeable drop in cool air output occurs, the following quick check will help you determine if the refrigerant level is low. For more complete information on the air conditioning system, refer to the *Haynes Automotive Heating and Air Conditioning Manual*.

Checking the refrigerant charge

Refer to illustration 13.9

7   Warm the engine up to normal operating temperature.

8   Place the air conditioning temperature selector at the coldest setting and put the blower at the highest setting. Open the doors (to make sure the air conditioning system doesn't cycle off as soon as it cools the passenger compartment).

9   With the compressor engaged - the clutch will make an audible click and the center of the clutch will rotate. After the system reaches operating temperature, feel the two pipes connected to the evaporator at the firewall **(see illustration)**.

10   The pipe leading from the fixed-orifice (located in the condenser outlet line) to the evaporator should be cold, and the evaporator out-

let line should be slightly colder (3 to 10-degrees F). If the outlet is considerably warmer than the inlet, the system needs a charge. Insert a thermometer in the center air distribution duct while operating the air conditioning system - the temperature of the output air should be 35-40 degrees F below the ambient air temperature (down to approximately 40-degrees F). If the air isn't as cold as it used to be, the system probably needs a charge. Further inspection or testing of the system is beyond the scope of the home mechanic and should be left to a professional.

11   If the accumulator inlet pipe has frost accumulation or feels cooler than the accumulator surface, the refrigerant charge is low. Add refrigerant.

Adding refrigerant

Refer to illustrations 13.12, 13.15 and 13.16

12   Buy an automotive charging kit at an auto parts store. A charging kit includes a 14-ounce can of refrigerant, a tap valve and a short section of hose that can be attached between the tap valve and the system low side service valve **(see illustration)**. Because one can of refrigerant may not be sufficient to bring the system charge up to the proper level, it's a good idea to buy a couple of additional cans. Try to find at least one can that contains red refrigerant dye. If the system is leaking, the red dye will leak out with the refrigerant and help you pinpoint the location of the leak.

Caution: *There are two types of refrigerant, R-12, used on older vehicles, and the more environmentally-friendly R-134a used in all the models covered by this manual. The two refrigerants (and their appropriate refrigerant oils) are not compatible and must never be mixed or components will be damaged. Use only R-134a refrigerant in the models covered by this manual.*

13   Connect the charging kit by following the manufacturer's instructions. **Warning:** *DO NOT hook the charging kit hose to the system high side!* The fittings on the charging kit are designed to fit **only** on the low side of the system.

14   Back off the valve handle on the charging kit and screw the kit onto the refrigerant can, making sure first that the O-ring or rubber seal inside the threaded portion of the kit is in place. **Warning:** *Wear protective eyewear when dealing with pressurized refrigerant cans.*

15   Remove the dust cap from the low-side charging port and attach the quick-connect fitting on the kit hose **(see illustration)**.

16   Warm the engine to normal operating temperature and turn on the air conditioner. Keep the charging kit hose away from the fan and other moving parts. **Note:** *The charging process requires the compressor to be running. If the clutch cycles off, disconnect the cycling switch electrical connector from the accumulator and attach a jumper wire (see*

13.16 Disconnect the cycling switch electrical connector from the accumulator and connect the two terminal connectors with a jumper wire to keep the compressor clutch engaged

14.3 Disconnect the electrical connector (small arrow) from the air conditioning compressor and remove the refrigerant line fitting bolt (larger arrow) from the top of the compressor

14.5 On diesel models, the compressor is mounted low on the right side of the engine - three of the four bolts (arrows) are shown, one is further back and accessible from underneath

illustration). *This will keep the compressor ON.*

17 Turn the valve handle on the kit until the stem pierces the can, then back the handle out to release the refrigerant. You should be able to hear the rush of gas. Add refrigerant to the low side of the system until both the accumulator surface and the evaporator inlet pipe feel about the same temperature . Allow stabilization time between each addition. **Warning:** *Never add more than two cans of refrigerant to the system. The can may tend to frost up, slowing the procedure. Wrap a shop towel wet with hot water around the bottom of the can to keep it from frosting.*

18 If you have an accurate thermometer, place it in the center air conditioning duct inside the vehicle to monitor the air temperature. A charged system that is working properly, should output air down to approximately 40-degrees F. If the ambient (outside) air temperature is very high, say 110-degrees F, the duct air temperature may be as high as 60-degrees F, but generally the air conditioning is 30-50 degrees F cooler than the ambient air.

19 When the can is empty, turn the valve handle to the closed position and release the connection from the low-side port. Replace the dust cap.

20 Remove the charging kit from the can and store the kit for future use with the piercing valve in the UP position, to prevent inadvertently piercing the can on the next use.

Heating systems

21 If the carpet under the heater core is damp, or if antifreeze vapor or steam is coming through the vents, the heater core is leaking. Remove it (see Section 12) and install a new unit (most radiator shops will no longer repair a leaking heater core).

22 If the air coming out of the heater vents isn't hot, the problem could stem from any of the following causes:

a) *The thermostat is stuck open, preventing the engine coolant from warming enough to carry heat to the heater core. Replace the thermostat (see Section 3).*

b) *A heater hose is blocked, preventing the flow of coolant through the heater core. Feel both heater hoses at the firewall. They should be hot. If one of them is cold, there is an obstruction in one of the hoses or in the heater core. Detach the hoses and back flush the heater core with a water hose. If the heater core is clear but circulation is impeded, remove the two hoses and flush them out with a water hose.*

c) *If flushing fails to remove the blockage from the heater core, the core must be replaced (see Section 11).*

23 It is also possible that the water pump could be bad, failing to circulate enough hot water to the heater core. Refer to Sections 6 and 7.

14 Air conditioning compressor - removal and installation

Warning: *The air conditioning system is under high pressure. DO NOT loosen any fittings or remove any components until after the system has been discharged. Air conditioning refrigerant should be properly discharged into an EPA-approved container at a dealer service department or an automotive air conditioning facility. Always wear eye protection when disconnecting air conditioning system fittings.*

Removal

Refer to illustrations 14.3 and 14.5

1 Have the system discharged at a dealer service department or automotive air conditioning facility. Disconnect the battery cable at the negative battery terminal. On diesel models, disconnect the negative cables from both batteries.

2 Clean the top of the compressor thoroughly around the refrigerant line fittings.

3 Disconnect the electrical connector from the air conditioning compressor and disconnect the suction and discharge lines from the top of the compressor **(see illustration)**. Plug the open fittings to prevent the entry of dirt and moisture.

4 Remove the drivebelt (refer to Chapter 1).

5 Remove the compressor-to-bracket bolts and nuts and lift the compressor from the engine compartment **(see illustration)**.

Installation

6 If a new compressor is being installed, pour the oil from the old compressor into a graduated container and add that exact amount of new refrigerant oil to the new compressor. **Caution:** *The oil used during servicing the system* **must** *be compatible with refrigerant R-134a.* Also follow any directions included with the new compressor, some replacement compressors come with new refrigerant oil in them.

7 Place the compressor in position on the bracket and install the nuts and bolts finger tight. Once all the compressor mounting nuts and bolts are installed, tighten them securely.

8 Install the drivebelt (see Chapter 1).

9 Reconnect the electrical connector to the compressor. Install the line fitting bolt(s) to the compressor, using new O-rings lubricated with clean refrigerant oil, and tighten them securely.

10 Reconnect the battery cable to the negative battery terminal.

11 Take the vehicle to a dealer service department or an air conditioning shop and have the system evacuated, recharged and leak tested.

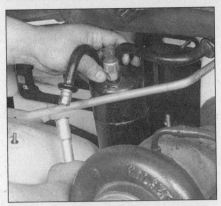

15.2 Disconnect the refrigerant line fittings by using a spring lock coupling tool - clamp the tool around the fitting, then pull the line connection apart

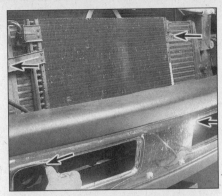

16.2a The air conditioning condenser is located in front of the radiator (or intercooler on diesel models) - arrows indicate mounting bolts, two of which are accessible through holes in the front bumper

16.2b On V10 models, and as optional equipment on other models, the left condenser mount is slightly different, to make room for the auxiliary transmission oil cooler (arrow)

15 Air conditioning accumulator - removal and installation

Warning: *The air conditioning system is under high pressure. DO NOT loosen any fittings or remove any components until after the system has been discharged. Air conditioning refrigerant should be properly discharged into an EPA-approved container at a dealer service department or an automotive air conditioning facility. Always wear eye protection when disconnecting air conditioning system fittings.*

Removal

Refer to illustration 15.2

1   Have the system discharged at a dealer service department or automotive air conditioning facility. Disconnect the battery cable at the negative battery terminal. On diesel models, disconnect the negative cables from both batteries. Disconnect the cycling switch plug **(see illustration 13.16)**.
2   Using spring-lock coupling tools (see Section 16), disconnect the refrigerant inlet and outlet lines **(see illustration)**. Cap or plug the open lines immediately to prevent the entry of dirt or moisture.
3   Loosen the mounting bolt and slide the accumulator assembly forward out of the mounting bracket.

Installation

4   If you are replacing the accumulator with a new one, add one ounce of fresh refrigerant oil to the new unit. **Caution:** *The oil used during servicing the system* ***must*** *be compatible with refrigerant R-134a.*
5   Place the new accumulator into position and start the mounting bolt into the bracket.
6   Connect the inlet and outlet lines, using clean refrigerant oil on the new O-rings. Tighten the mounting bolt after the lines are secured. **Caution:** *The oil and O-rings used during servicing the system* ***must*** *be compatible with refrigerant R-134a.*
7   Connect the cable to the negative terminal of the battery(s) and reconnect the cycling switch plug.
8   Have the system evacuated, recharged and leak tested by a dealer service department or an air conditioning shop.

16 Air conditioning condenser and fixed-orifice tube - removal and installation

Warning: *The air conditioning system is under high pressure. DO NOT loosen any fittings or remove any components until after the system has been discharged. Air conditioning refrigerant should be properly discharged into an EPA-approved container at a dealer service department or an automotive air conditioning facility. Always wear eye protection when disconnecting air conditioning system fittings.*

16.3a To disconnect any of the air conditioning lines, first pull off the factory clip . . .

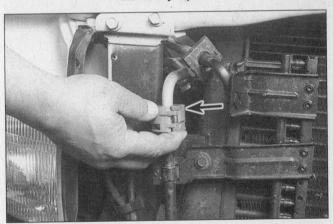

16.3b . . . then install the spring-lock coupling tool, push the two connected lines together . . .

Removal

Refer to illustrations 16.2a, 16.2b, 16.3a, 16.3b, 16.3c and 16.3d

1   Have the system discharged at a dealer service department or automotive air conditioning facility. Disconnect the battery cable at the negative battery terminal. On diesel models, disconnect the negative cables from both batteries.
2   The condenser is mounted in front of the radiator, and is easily accessed for removal after opening the hood **(see illustrations)**.
3   Using a spring-lock coupling tool, disconnect the refrigerant line

16.3c . . . then remove the tool and pull the lines apart

16.3d The fixed-orifice tube is located in the condenser outlet line

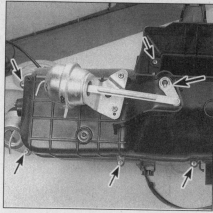

17.4 Remove the vacuum motor arm from the shaft (large arrow), then remove the screws retaining the two halves together (arrows) - one screw is located inside the duct

fittings. Use needle-nose pliers to withdraw the fixed-orifice tube from the condenser outlet line. Cap the open fittings to prevent the entry of dirt and moisture **(see illustrations)**.

4   Unbolt the condenser. On gasoline-engine models, the condenser is bolted at the top to the core support, while on diesel models, the condenser is bolted top and bottom to the intercooler **(see illustrations 16.2a and 16.2b)**.

5   Lift the condenser from the vehicle. **Caution:** *The condenser is made of aluminum - be careful not to damage it during removal.*

Installation

6   Installation is the reverse of removal. Be sure to use new O-rings on the refrigerant line fittings (lubricate the O-rings with clean refrigerant oil). **Caution:** *The oil and O-rings used during servicing the system must be compatible with refrigerant R-134a.*

7   Have the system evacuated, recharged and leak tested by the shop that discharged it. If a new condenser is installed, add 1 oz of new refrigerant oil to the system.

---

17   Air conditioning evaporator - removal and installation

Warning 1: *These models are equipped with an airbag. The airbag is armed and can deploy (inflate) anytime the battery is connected. To prevent accidental deployment (and possible injury), disconnect the negative battery cable whenever working near airbag components. After the battery is disconnected, wait at least 2 minutes before beginning work (the system has a back-up capacitor that must fully discharge). For more information see Chapter 12.*

Warning 2: *The air conditioning system is under high pressure. DO NOT loosen any fittings or remove any components until after the system has been discharged. Air conditioning refrigerant should be properly discharged into an EPA-approved container at a dealer service department or an automotive air conditioning facility. Always wear eye protection when disconnecting air conditioning system fittings.*

Removal

Refer to illustrations 17.4 and 17.6

Note: *All models require complete removal of the heater/evaporator case for evaporator core removal.*

1   Have the system discharged at a dealer service department or automotive air conditioning facility.

2   Disconnect the battery cable at the negative battery terminal. On diesel models, disconnect the negative cables from both batteries. Drain the cooling system (see Chapter 1).

3   Follow the procedures in Section 11 for removing the heater/evaporator case from the vehicle.

4   The heater/air conditioning case consists of two halves. Carefully place the unit upside down and remove the screws retaining the two halves together **(see illustration)**.

5   Remove the lower half of the case.

6   Remove the heating duct and screw, then pull the evaporator out of the case **(see illustration)**.

Installation

7   Installation is the reverse of the removal procedure. Use new O-rings on all connections, lubricated by refrigerant oil. **Caution:** *The oil and O-rings used during servicing the system **must** be compatible with refrigerant R-134a.*

8   If a new evaporator has been installed, add 1 ounce of refrigerant oil.

9   Have the air conditioning system evacuated, recharged and leak-tested by the shop that discharged it.

17.6 Remove the evaporator from the bottom of the case - keep the sealing materials intact for reassembly

Chapter 4 Part A
Fuel and exhaust systems - gasoline engines

Contents

Specifications

General

Fuel pressure	35 to 45 psi
Fuel injector resistance	12.4 ohms

Torque specifications

Ft-lbs (unless otherwise indicated)

Throttle body mounting nuts	19
Fuel rail mounting bolts	
V6 and V8 engines	108 in-lbs
V10 engine	136 in-lbs

2.3a Connect a fuel pressure gauge to the fuel rail at the test port and use the valve to bleed off the excess fuel into an approved fuel container

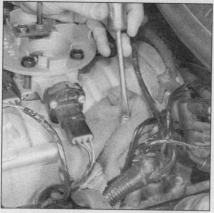

2.3b Use a small screwdriver or punch to depress the Schrader valve within the fuel pump test port. Be sure to catch any residual fuel using a rag (cover the screwdriver tip and valve with a rag to prevent fuel spray)

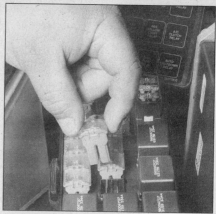

3.2 Check to make sure the fuel pump fuse is not blown

1   General information

The gasoline-powered vehicles covered by this manual are equipped with a sequential Multi Port Fuel Injection (MPFI) system. This system uses timed impulses to sequentially inject the fuel directly into the intake ports of each cylinder. The injectors are controlled by the Powertrain Control Module (PCM). The PCM monitors various engine parameters and delivers the exact amount of fuel, in the correct sequence, into the intake ports.

All models are equipped with an electric fuel pump, mounted in the fuel tank. It is necessary to remove the fuel tank for access to the fuel pump. The fuel level sending unit is an integral component of the fuel pump and it must be removed from the fuel tank in the same manner. These systems are equipped with a "returnless" fuel system. The fuel pressure regulator is mounted on top of the fuel pump/fuel level sending unit module. Regulated fuel is sent to the fuel rail and excess fuel is bled off into the tank.

The exhaust system consists of exhaust manifolds, a catalytic converter, an exhaust pipe and a muffler. Each of these components is replaceable. For further information regarding the catalytic converter, refer to Chapter 6.

2   Fuel pressure relief procedure

Refer to illustrations 2.3a and 2.3b

Warning: *Gasoline is extremely flammable, so take extra precautions when you work on any part of the fuel system. Don't smoke or allow open flames or bare light bulbs near the work area, and don't work in a garage where a natural gas-type appliance (such as a water heater or a clothes dryer) with a pilot light is present. Since gasoline is carcinogenic, wear latex gloves when there's a possibility of being exposed to fuel, and, if you spill any fuel on your skin, rinse it off immediately with soap and water. Mop up any spills immediately and do not store fuel-soaked rags where they could ignite. The fuel system is under constant pressure, so, if any fuel lines are to be disconnected, the fuel pressure in the system must be relieved first. When you perform any kind of work on the fuel system, wear safety glasses and have a Class B type fire extinguisher on hand.*

Models with a test port on the fuel rail

1   Detach the cable from the negative battery terminal. Unscrew the fuel filler cap to relieve pressure built up in the fuel tank.
2   Remove the cap from the fuel pressure test port located on the fuel rail.

3.4a Connect the fuel pressure gauge to the fuel rail and observe the fuel pressure with the engine idling (5.2L engine shown)

3   Use one of the two following methods:
  a) *Attach a fuel pressure gauge equipped with a bleeder hose (commonly available at auto parts stores) to the test port Schrader valve on the fuel rail* **(see illustration)**. *Place the gauge bleeder hose in an approved fuel container. Open the valve on the gauge to relieve pressure.*
  b) *Locate the fuel pressure test port and carefully place several shop towels around the test port and the fuel rail. Remove the cap and, using the tip of a screwdriver, depress the Schrader valve and let the fuel drain into the shop towels* **(see illustration)**. *Be careful to catch any fuel that might spray up by using another shop towel.*
4   Unless this procedure is followed before servicing fuel lines or connections, fuel spray (and possible injury) may occur.
5   Install the cap onto the fuel pressure test port.

Models without a test port on the fuel rail

6   Remove the fuel pump relay from the Power Distribution Center in the engine compartment (you can identify the relays by looking at the underside of the Power Distribution Center cover).
7   Start the engine and let it run until it dies. Turn the ignition key to the Off position.
8   Disconnect the electrical connector from the most easily accessible injector. Using a jumper wire, connect one of the injector terminals to ground. Use another jumper wire connected to the positive terminal

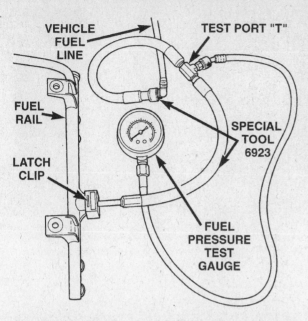

3.4b A special adapter hose will be required to attach a fuel pressure gauge if the fuel rail isn't equipped with a test port

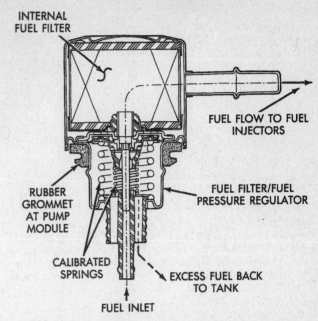

3.6 Details of the fuel pressure regulator/fuel filter on the returnless fuel system

of the battery and energize the injector to bleed off the remaining pressure in the fuel rail. **Caution:** *Don't energize the injector for more than four seconds at a time, or it will be damaged.*

9   Disconnect the cable from the negative terminal of the battery before beginning work on the fuel system.

10   Removing the fuel pump relay and running the engine may have set a trouble code in the PCM. See Chapter 6 for more information on trouble codes.

3   Fuel pump/fuel pressure - check

Warning: *Gasoline is extremely flammable, so take extra precautions when you work on any part of the fuel system. Don't smoke or allow open flames or bare light bulbs near the work area, and don't work in a garage where a natural gas-type appliance (such as a water heater or a clothes dryer) with a pilot light is present. Since gasoline is carcinogenic, wear latex gloves when there's a possibility of being exposed to fuel, and, if you spill any fuel on your skin, rinse it off immediately with soap and water. Mop up any spills immediately and do not store fuel-soaked rags where they could ignite. The fuel system is under constant pressure, so, if any fuel lines are to be disconnected, the fuel pressure in the system must be relieved first (see Section 2 for more information). When you perform any kind of work on the fuel system, wear safety glasses and have a Class B type fire extinguisher on hand.* **Note:** *These systems are equipped with a "returnless" fuel system. The fuel pressure regulator is mounted on top of the fuel pump/fuel level sending unit module.*

Preliminary check

Refer to illustration 3.2

Note: *On all models, the fuel pump is located inside the fuel tank (see Section 7).*

1   If you suspect insufficient fuel delivery, first inspect all fuel lines to ensure that the problem is not simply a leak in a line.

2   Set the parking brake and have an assistant turn the ignition switch to the ON position while you listen to the fuel pump (inside the fuel tank). You should hear a "whirring" sound, lasting for a couple of seconds. Start the engine. The whirring sound should now be continuous (although harder to hear with the engine running). If there is no

sound, either the fuel pump fuse **(see illustration)**, fuel pump, fuel pump relay, ASD relay or related circuits are defective (proceed to Step 10).

Pressure check

Refer to illustrations 3.4a, 3.4b and 3.6

3   Relieve the fuel pressure (see Section 2).

4   Remove the cap from the fuel pressure test port (if equipped) on the fuel rail and attach a fuel pressure gauge **(see illustration)**. If the fuel rail is not equipped with a test port, disconnect the fuel line from the fuel rail and connect a fuel pressure gauge using adapter tool no. 6923, or equivalent **(see illustration)**.

5   Start the engine and check the pressure on the gauge, comparing your reading with the pressure listed in this Chapter's Specifications.

6   If the pressure is higher or lower than specified, inspect the fuel filter - make sure it isn't clogged (see Chapter 1). **Note:** *Because the fuel pressure regulator/fuel filter is mounted on top of the fuel pump/sending unit assembly, access makes testing very difficult* **(see illustration)**. *The fuel pump and fuel pressure regulator/fuel filter work together to deliver the proper amount of fuel pressure to the fuel injection system. If fuel pressure is high, the fuel pressure regulator/fuel filter is the cause. However, if the fuel pressure is low, the problem could be the fuel pump and/or fuel pressure regulator/fuel filter. It is recommended that the home mechanic replace both the fuel pump and fuel pressure regulator/fuel filter in the event of low fuel pressure. The fuel pump replacement procedure is located in Section 7 and the fuel pressure regulator/fuel filter replacement procedure is located in Section 14.*

7   If there is no fuel pressure, check the fuel pump (see below).

Component checks

Fuel pump

8   If you suspect a problem with the fuel pump, verify the pump actually runs. Have an assistant turn the ignition switch to ON - you should hear a brief "whirring" noise as the pump comes on and pressurizes the system. Have the assistant start the engine. This time you should hear a constant whirring sound from the pump (but it's more difficult to hear with the engine running).

9   If the pump does not come on (makes no sound), proceed to the next step and check the fuel pump circuit and relays for proper operation.

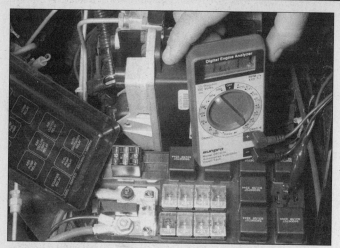

3.11a Locate the fuel pump relay in the Power Distribution Center and check for battery voltage to the relay

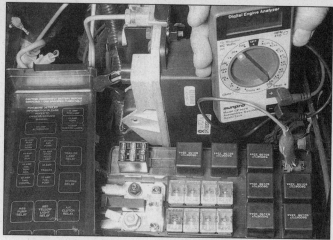

3.11b Check for battery voltage to the ASD relay also

Main relays

Refer to illustrations 3.11a, 3.11b, 3.13 and 3.14

Note: *The Automatic Shutdown (ASD) relay and the fuel pump relay must both be tested to insure proper fuel pump operation. Testing procedures for the ASD relay and the fuel pump relay are identical.*

10   To test a relay, first remove it from its location in the engine compartment Power Distribution Center. Turn the relay over and note the terminal numbers on the bottom.

11   Verify that there is battery voltage at the terminal on the panel that corresponds with terminal 30 of the relay **(see illustrations)**. This terminal should have voltage present with or without the ignition key turned On. Now check the terminal on the panel that corresponds with terminal 86 on the relay - it should have voltage present only with the ignition key turned On.

12   If there is no voltage, check the fuel pump fuse. If voltage is not present at the fuse, check the wiring and connectors to the fuse panel.

13   Connect the probes of an ohmmeter to terminals 86 and 85 and check the resistance. There should be approximately 75 ohms resistance **(see illustration)**.

14   Now connect the ohmmeter probes to terminals 30 and 87A and check for continuity. Continuity should be present **(see illustration)**.

15   Check for continuity between terminals 30 and 87. There should be no continuity.

16   Using jumper wires, connect battery voltage to the no. 86 terminal, ground the number 85 terminal and verify that there's continuity between the terminals 87 and 30. If there isn't, replace the relay.

4   Fuel lines and fittings - repair and replacement

Warning: *Gasoline is extremely flammable, so take extra precautions when you work on any part of the fuel system. Don't smoke or allow open flames or bare light bulbs near the work area, and don't work in a garage where a natural gas-type appliance (such as a water heater or a clothes dryer) with a pilot light is present. Since gasoline is carcinogenic, wear latex gloves when there's a possibility of being exposed to fuel, and, if you spill any fuel on your skin, rinse it off immediately with soap and water. Mop up any spills immediately and do not store fuel-soaked rags where they could ignite. The fuel system is under constant pressure, so, if any fuel lines are to be disconnected, the fuel pressure in the system must be relieved first (see Section 2). When you perform any kind of work on the fuel system, wear safety glasses and have a Class B type fire extinguisher on hand.*

1   Always relieve the fuel pressure before servicing fuel lines or fittings (see Section 2).

2   The fuel feed and vapor lines extend from the fuel tank to the engine compartment. The lines are secured to the underbody with clip and screw assemblies. These lines must be occasionally inspected for leaks, kinks and dents.

3   If evidence of dirt is found in the system or fuel filter during disassembly, the line should be disconnected and blown out. Check the fuel strainer on the fuel gauge sending unit (see Section 6) for damage and deterioration.

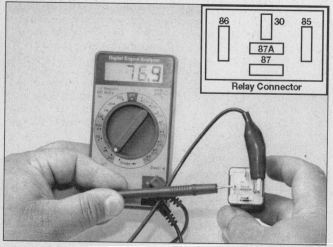

3.13 Check the resistance between terminals number 86 and number 85 - it should be approximately 75 ohms

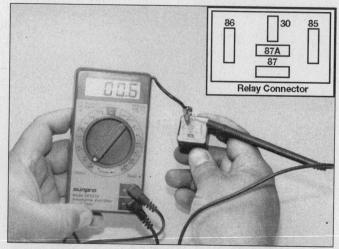

3.14 Also check the resistance between terminals number 87A and 30 - continuity should exist

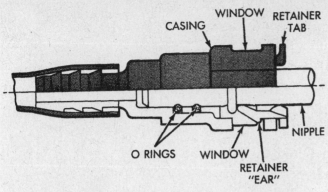

4.11a Cross-sectional view of a two-tab quick-connect fuel line fitting

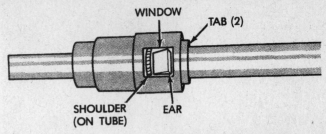

4.11b Plastic tab type quick-connect fitting with a window style body

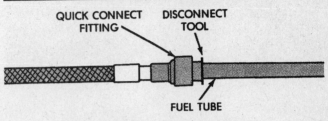

4.11c Metal quick-connect fittings

Steel tubing

4   If replacement of a fuel line or emission line is called for, use tubes/hoses meeting Chrysler specification or its equivalent.

5   Don't use copper or aluminum tubing to replace steel tubing. These materials cannot withstand normal vehicle vibration.

6   Because fuel lines used on fuel-injected vehicles are under high pressure, they require special consideration.

7   Some fuel lines have threaded fittings with O-rings. Any time the fittings are loosened to service or replace components:
  a) *Use a backup wrench while loosening and tightening the fittings.*
  b) *Check all O-rings for cuts, cracks and deterioration. Replace any that appear hardened, worn or damaged.*
  c) *If the lines are replaced, always use original equipment parts, or parts that meet the original equipment standards specified in this Section.*

Flexible hose

Warning: *Use only original equipment replacement hoses or their equivalent. Others may fail from the high pressures of this system.*

8   Don't route fuel hose within four inches of any part of the exhaust system or within ten inches of the catalytic converter. Metal lines and rubber hoses must never be allowed to chafe against the frame. A minimum of 1/4-inch clearance must be maintained around a line or hose to prevent contact with the frame.

Removal and installation

Refer to illustrations 4.11a, 4.11b and 4.11c

9   Relieve the fuel pressure.

10   Remove all fasteners attaching the lines to the vehicle body.

11   There are various methods depending upon the type of quick-disconnect fitting on the fuel line **(see illustrations)**. Carefully remove the

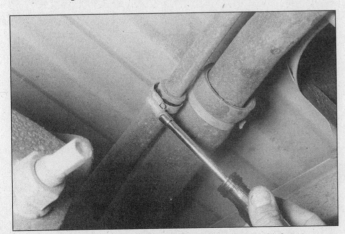

5.5 Remove the clamps that retain the fuel inlet and fuel vapor hoses

fuel lines from the chassis. **Caution:** *The plastic ring type fittings are not serviced separately. Do not attempt to service these types of fuel lines in the event the clip or line becomes damaged. Replace the entire fuel line as an assembly.*

12   Installation is the reverse of removal. Be sure to use new O-rings at the threaded fittings (if equipped).

Repair

13   In the event of any fuel line damage (metal or flexible lines) it is necessary to replace the damaged lines with factory replacement parts. Others may fail from the high pressures of this system.

5   Fuel tank - removal and installation

Refer to illustrations 5.5, 5.6a, 5.6b, 5.10 and 5.11

Warning: *Gasoline is extremely flammable, so take extra precautions when you work on any part of the fuel system. Don't smoke or allow open flames or bare light bulbs near the work area, and don't work in a garage where a natural gas-type appliance (such as a water heater or a clothes dryer) with a pilot light is present. Since gasoline is carcinogenic, wear latex gloves when there's a possibility of being exposed to fuel, and, if you spill any fuel on your skin, rinse it off immediately with soap and water. Mop up any spills immediately and do not store fuel-soaked rags where they could ignite. The fuel system is under constant pressure, so, if any fuel lines are to be disconnected, the fuel pressure in the system must be relieved first (see Section 2 for more information). When you perform any kind of work on the fuel system, wear safety glasses and have a Class B type fire extinguisher on hand.*

Note: *The following procedure is much easier to perform if the fuel tank is empty. Some tanks have a drain plug for this purpose. If the tank does not have a drain plug, the fuel can be siphoned from the tank using a siphoning kit, available at most auto parts stores. NEVER start the siphoning action with your mouth!*

1   Remove the fuel tank filler cap to relieve fuel tank pressure.

2   Relieve the fuel system pressure (see Section 2).

3   Detach the cable from the negative terminal of the battery.

4   Siphon the fuel into an approved gasoline container, using a siphoning kit (available at most auto parts stores).

5   Remove the fuel inlet and vent hose clamps and detach the hoses from the filler and vent pipes **(see illustration)**. It may be necessary to remove the left rear wheel on some models to ease accessibility. If so, first loosen the wheel lug nuts, raise the rear of the vehicle and support it securely on jackstands, then remove the wheel. Block the front wheels to prevent the vehicle from rolling.

4A

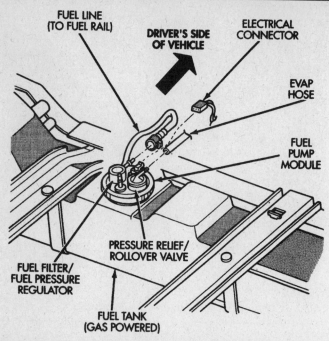

5.6 Fuel tank connections - models with gasoline engines (diesel-powered models don't have an EVAP hose, but have a fuel return line)

5.10 Remove the fuel tank strap bolts and detach the straps from the chassis

6　Disconnect the hoses from the fuel pump module **(see illustration)**.

7　Reach up and over the top of the fuel tank and disconnect the electrical connector from the fuel pump module. It may be necessary to remove the fuel tank straps and slightly lower the tank to be able to access the fuel pump module.

8　On gasoline fuel tanks, disconnect the EVAP hose from the pressure relief/rollover valve.

9　Support the fuel tank with a floor jack. Place a piece of wood between the jack head and the fuel tank to protect the tank.

10　Remove the fuel tank strap bolts and the fuel tank strap **(see illustration)**.

11　If equipped, remove the bolts that retain the heat shield to the frame **(see illustration)**. Remove the heat shield.

12　Remove the tank from the vehicle.

13　Installation is the reverse of removal.

6　Fuel tank cleaning and repair - general information

1　The fuel tanks installed in the vehicles covered by this manual are made of plastic and are not repairable.

2　If the fuel tank is removed from the vehicle, it should not be placed in an area where sparks or open flames could ignite the fumes coming out of the tank. Be especially careful inside a garage where a natural gas-type appliance is located, because the pilot light could cause an explosion.

7　Fuel pump - removal and installation

Refer to illustrations 7.4, 7.5 and 7.6

Warning: *Gasoline is extremely flammable, so take extra precautions when you work on any part of the fuel system. Don't smoke or allow open flames or bare light bulbs near the work area, and don't work in a garage where a natural gas-type appliance (such as a water heater or a clothes dryer) with a pilot light is present. Since gasoline is carcinogenic, wear latex gloves when there's a possibility of being exposed to fuel, and, if you spill any fuel on your skin, rinse it off immediately with soap and water. Mop up any spills immediately and do not store fuel-soaked rags where they could ignite. The fuel system is under constant*

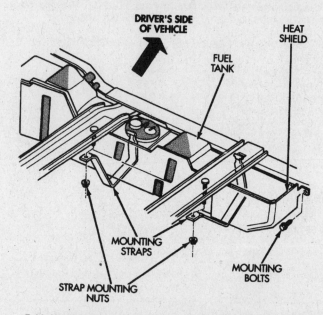

5.11 If the vehicle is equipped with a fuel tank heat shield, remove the bolts and separate it from the tank

pressure, so, if any fuel lines are to be disconnected, the fuel pressure in the system must be relieved first (see Section 2) for more information). When you perform any kind of work on the fuel system, wear safety glasses and have a Class B type fire extinguisher on hand.

Caution: *Be sure to change the fuel pump module gasket and locknut whenever the fuel pump/sending unit assembly is removed for servicing.*

1　Relieve the fuel system pressure (see Section 2).

2　Detach the cable from the negative battery terminal.

3　Remove the fuel tank from the vehicle (see Section 5).

4　Note the direction of the fuel filter/pressure regulator, pressure relief rollover valve and fuel pump electrical connector. They should be pointed toward the driver's side of the vehicle **(see illustration)**.

5　The fuel pump assembly locknut is threaded onto the fuel tank. Turn the locknut counterclockwise to remove it **(see illustration)**. If the assembly is difficult to turn, use a large pair of pliers or a chain wrench to loosen it.

6　Remove the fuel pump/fuel level sending unit from the tank **(see illustration)**. Angle the assembly slightly to avoid damaging the fuel level sending unit float.

7　The electric fuel pump is not serviceable. In the event of failure, the complete assembly must be replaced.

8　Installation is the reverse of removal.

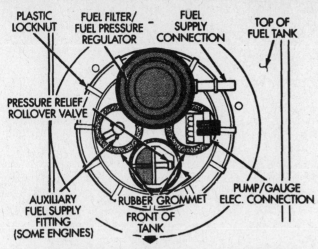

7.4 Note that all the fuel supply fittings and electrical connectors must point to the driver's side of the vehicle

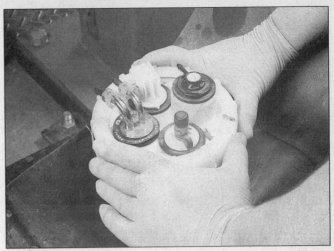

7.5 Remove the fuel pump/fuel level sending unit by turning the locknut counterclockwise

7.6 Lift the fuel pump/fuel level sending unit from the tank

8 Fuel level sending unit - check and replacement

Warning: *Gasoline is extremely flammable, so take extra precautions when you work on any part of the fuel system. Don't smoke or allow open flames or bare light bulbs near the work area, and don't work in a garage where a natural gas-type appliance (such as a water heater or a clothes dryer) with a pilot light is present. Since gasoline is carcinogenic, wear latex gloves when there's a possibility of being exposed to fuel, and, if you spill any fuel on your skin, rinse it off immediately with soap and water. Mop up any spills immediately and do not store fuel-soaked rags where they could ignite. The fuel system is under constant pressure, so, if any fuel lines are to be disconnected, the fuel pressure in the system must be relieved first (see Section 2). When you perform any kind of work on the fuel system, wear safety glasses and have a Class B type fire extinguisher on hand.*

Check

Refer to illustrations 8.3, 8.4 and 8.7

1   Remove the fuel pump/fuel level sending unit assembly (see Section 7).
2   Connect the probes of an ohmmeter to the two center terminals of the fuel level sending unit electrical and check for resistance **(see illustration 8.3)**.
3   First, check the resistance of the sending unit with the fuel tank completely full. Move the float to the up position. The resistance of the sending unit should be about 10 ohms **(see illustration)**.
4   Position the float in the down (empty) position. The resistance should be approximately 112 ohms **(see illustration)**.
5   If the readings are incorrect or there is very little change in resistance as the float travels from full to empty, replace the fuel level sending unit assembly.

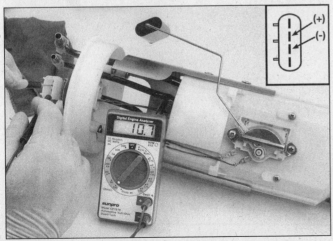

8.3 Measure the resistance of the fuel level sending unit with the float raised (full tank) . . .

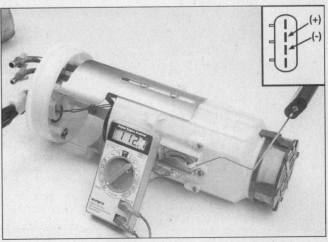

8.4 . . . and then with the float lowered (empty tank)

4A

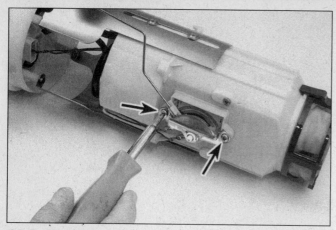

8.7 Remove the fuel level sending unit mounting screws (arrows)

Replacement

6   Separate the fuel level sending unit wire terminals from the module connector.

7   Remove the screws that retain the fuel level sending unit to the assembly **(see illustration)**.

8   Lift the fuel level sending unit from the assembly.

9   Installation is the reverse of removal.

9   Air cleaner assembly - removal and installation

Refer to illustrations 9.2a, 9.2b and 9.3

1   Detach the cable from the negative battery terminal.

2   Remove the air cleaner cover and filter element **(see illustrations)**.

3   Remove the nuts that hold the air cleaner housing to the mounting studs **(see illustration)**.

4   Lift the assembly up and detach it from the fresh air intake duct, then remove it from the engine compartment.

5   Installation is the reverse of removal.

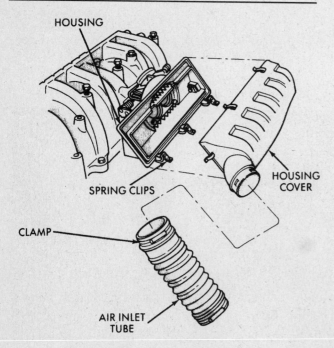

9.2b Air cleaner details on the V10 engine

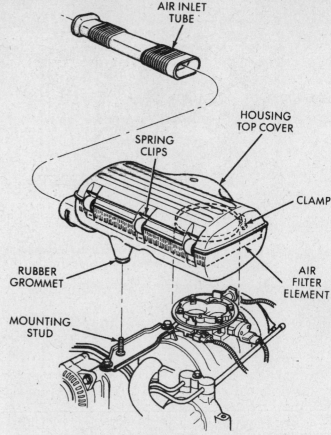

9.2a Air cleaner installation details on the V6 and V8 engines

10   Accelerator cable - replacement

Refer to illustrations 10.2, 10.3 and 10.4

1   Detach the cable from the negative battery terminal.

2   Rotate the throttle lever and separate the cable end from the slotted portion of the throttle lever **(see illustration)**.

3   Push in on the tab and release the accelerator cable retainer from the bracket **(see illustration)**.

4   Working underneath the dash, detach the cable from the accelerator pedal **(see illustration)**.

9.3 Remove the nuts (arrows) and lift the air cleaner housing from the vehicle (V10 engine shown)

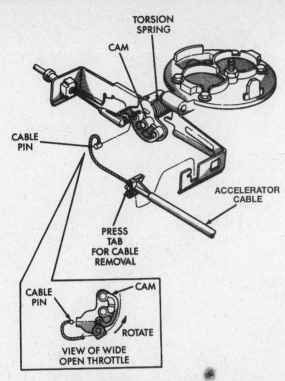

10.2 Rotate the throttle lever and slide the cable end
out of the recess

5   Press in on the tabs of the cable retainer and push the cable
through the firewall and into the engine compartment.
6   Installation is the reverse of removal.

11 Fuel injection system - general information

Refer to illustration 11.1

The sequential Multi Port Fuel Injection (MPFI) system consists of
three sub-systems: air intake, electronic control and fuel delivery. The
system uses a Powertrain Control Module (PCM) along with the sensors (coolant temperature sensor, Throttle Position Sensor (TPS), Manifold Absolute Pressure (MAP) sensor, oxygen sensor, etc.) to determine the proper air/fuel ratio under all operating conditions **(see illustration)**.

The fuel injection system and the emissions and engine control
system are closely linked in function and design. For additional information, refer to Chapter 6.

Air intake system

The air intake system consists of the air cleaner, the air intake
ducts, the throttle body, the idle control system, the air intake plenum
and the intake manifold.

A throttle position sensor is attached to the throttle shaft to monitor changes in the throttle opening. The MAP sensor is attached to
throttle body.

When the engine is idling, the air/fuel ratio is controlled by the idle
air control system, which consists of the Powertrain Control Module
(PCM) and the Idle Air Control (IAC) valve. The IAC valve is controlled
by the PCM and is opened and closed depending upon the running
conditions of the engine (air conditioning system, power steering, cold
and warm running etc.). This valve regulates the amount of airflow past
the throttle plate and into the intake manifold, thus increasing or
decreasing the engine idle speed. The PCM receives information from
the sensors (vehicle speed, coolant temperature, air conditioning,
power steering mode etc.) and adjusts the idle according to the
demands of the engine and driver.

Electronic emissions and engine control system

The electronic emissions and engine control system is explained
in detail in Chapter 6.

Fuel delivery system

The fuel delivery system consists of these components: The fuel
pump, the pressure regulator, the fuel rail and the fuel injectors.

The fuel pump is an in-line, direct drive type. Fuel is drawn
through a filter into the pump, flows past the armature through the
one-way valve, passes through another filter and is delivered to the
injectors. A relief valve prevents excessive pressure build-up by opening in the event of a blockage in the discharge side and allowing fuel to
flow from the high to the low pressure side.

The pressure regulator maintains a constant fuel pressure to the
injectors. Excess fuel is routed back to the fuel tank through the fuel
pressure regulator. **Note:** *These systems are equipped with a returnless fuel system. The fuel pressure regulator is mounted on top of the
fuel pump/fuel level sending unit module.*

The injectors are solenoid-actuated pintle types consisting of a
solenoid, plunger, needle valve and housing. When current is applied
to the solenoid coil, the needle valve raises and pressurized fuel squirts
out the nozzle. The injection quantity is determined by the length of
time the valve is open (the length of time during which current is supplied to the solenoid coils).

Because it determines opening and closing intervals, which in

4A

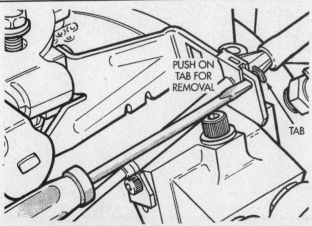

10.3 Use a flat bladed screwdriver to depress the tabs,
disconnecting the cable from the bracket

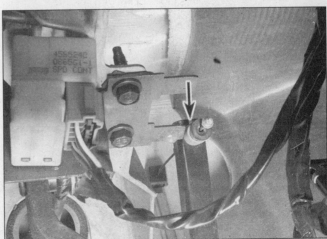

10.4 Pull the accelerator cable out of the grommet and slide the
cable through the slot (arrow) in the end of the pedal assembly

11.1 Fuel injection component locations on the V10 engine

1	Manifold Absolute Pressure (MAP) sensor	4	Air intake duct	7	Coolant temperature sensor
2	Throttle body	5	Power distribution center	8	Powertrain Control Module (PCM)
3	Idle Air Control (IAC) valve	6	Air intake temperature sensor (on intake manifold near air intake plenum)		

turn, determines the air-fuel mixture ratio - injector timing must be quite accurate. To attain the best possible injector response, the current rise time, when voltage is being applied to each injector coil, must be as short as possible. The number of windings in the coil has therefore been reduced to lower the inductance in the coil. However, this creates low coil resistance, which could compromise the durability of the coil. The flow of current in the coil is therefore restricted by a resistor installed in the injector wire harness.

The Automatic Shutdown (ASD) relay and the fuel pump relay are contained within Power Distribution Center, which is located in the left side of the engine compartment. The ASD relay connects battery voltage to the fuel injectors and the ignition coil while the fuel pump relay connects battery voltage only to the fuel pump. If the PCM senses there is NO signal from the camshaft or crankshaft sensors while the ignition key is RUN or cranking, the PCM will de-energize both relays.

12   Fuel injection system - check

Refer to illustrations 12.7, 12.8 and 12.9
Note: *The following procedure is based on the assumption that the fuel pressure is adequate (see Section 3).*

1   Check all electrical connectors that are related to the system. Check the ground wire connections on the intake manifold for tightness. Loose connectors and poor grounds can cause many problems that resemble more serious malfunctions.

2   Check to see that the battery is fully charged, as the control unit and sensors depend on an accurate supply voltage in order to properly meter the fuel.

3   Check the air filter element - a dirty or partially blocked filter will severely impede performance and economy (see Chapter 1).

4   If a blown fuse is found, replace it and see if it blows again. If it does, search for a grounded wire in the harness to the fuel pump.

5   Check the air intake duct to the intake manifold for leaks, which will result in an excessively lean mixture. Also check the condition of all vacuum hoses connected to the intake manifold.

6   Remove the air intake duct from the throttle body and check for dirt, carbon or other residue build-up. If it's dirty, clean it with carburetor cleaner spray and a toothbrush.

7   With the engine running, place an automotive stethoscope against each injector, one at a time, and listen for a clicking sound, indicating operation **(see illustration)**. If you don't have a stethoscope, place the tip of a screwdriver against the injector and listen through the handle.

8   Unplug the injector electrical connectors and test the resistance of each injector **(see illustration)**. Compare the values to the Specifi-

12.7 Use a stethoscope to determine if the injectors are working properly - they should make a steady clicking sound that rises and falls with engine speed changes

12.8 Measure the resistance of each injector. It should be approximately 12 to 15 ohms

12.9 Install the "noid" light (available at most auto parts stores) into each injector electrical connector and confirm that it blinks when the engine is cranking or running

13.13a Remove the four nuts (arrows) and separate the throttle body from the intake manifold (5.2L V8 engine shown)

cations listed in this Chapter.

9   Install an injector test light ("noid" light) into each injector electrical connector, one at a time **(see illustration)**. Crank the engine over. Confirm that the light flashes evenly on each connector. This will test for voltage to the injector.

10   The remainder of the system checks can be found in the following Sections.

13 Throttle body - check, removal and installation

Check

1   On top of the throttle body, locate the vacuum hose that goes to the canister purge control solenoid. Detach it from the throttle body and attach a vacuum gauge in its place.

2   Start the engine and warm it to its normal operating temperature. Verify the gauge indicates no vacuum.

3   Open the throttle slightly from idle and verify that the gauge indicates vacuum. If the gauge indicates no vacuum, check the port to make sure it is not clogged. Clean it with carburetor cleaner spray if necessary.

4   Stop the engine and verify the accelerator cable and throttle valve operate smoothly without binding or sticking.

5   If the accelerator cable or throttle valve binds or sticks, check for a build-up of sludge on the cable or throttle shaft.

6   If a build-up of sludge is evident, try removing it with carburetor cleaner or a similar solvent.

7   If cleaning fails to remedy the problem, replace the throttle body.

Removal and installation

Refer to illustrations 13.13a and 13.13b

Warning: *Wait until the engine is completely cool before beginning this procedure.*

8   Detach the cable from the negative battery terminal.

9   Remove the air cleaner assembly (see Section 9).

10   Unplug the TPS, IAC and MAP sensor connectors from the throttle body.

11   Label and detach all vacuum hoses from the throttle body.

12   Detach the accelerator cable (see Section 10) and, if equipped, the transmission throttle valve cable (see Chapter 7B).

13   Unscrew the mounting bolts/nuts and remove the throttle body and gasket **(see illustrations)**. Remove all traces of old gasket material from the throttle body and intake manifold.

14   Installation is the reverse of removal. Be sure to use a new gasket. Adjust the accelerator cable (see Section 10) and, if equipped, the throttle valve cable (see Chapter 7B).

14 Fuel pressure regulator/fuel filter - replacement

Refer to illustrations 14.5 and 14.6

Warning: *Gasoline is extremely flammable, so take extra precautions when you work on any part of the fuel system. Don't smoke or allow open flames or bare light bulbs near the work area, and don't work in a garage where a natural gas-type appliance (such as a water heater or a clothes dryer) with a pilot light is present. Since gasoline is carcinogenic, wear latex gloves when there's a possibility of being exposed to fuel, and, if you spill any fuel on your skin, rinse it off immediately with soap and water. Mop up any spills immediately and do not store fuel-soaked rags where they could ignite. The fuel system is under constant pressure, so, if any fuel lines are to be disconnected, the fuel pressure in the system must be relieved first (see Section 2). When you perform any kind of work on the fuel system, wear safety glasses and have a Class B type fire extinguisher on hand.*

Note1: *These engines are equipped with a "returnless" fuel system. The fuel pressure regulator is mounted on top of the fuel pump/fuel level sending unit assembly.*

Note 2: *The fuel filter requires service only when a fuel contamination problem is suspected.*

1   Relieve the fuel system pressure (see Section 2).

2   Detach the cable from the negative battery terminal.

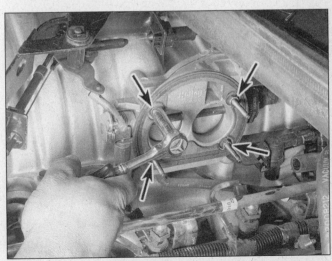

13.13b Throttle body mounting nuts (arrows) on the V10 engine

4A

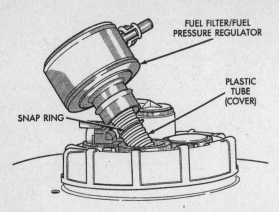

14.5 Remove the fuel pressure regulator/fuel filter by carefully twisting and prying the assembly out of the rubber grommet

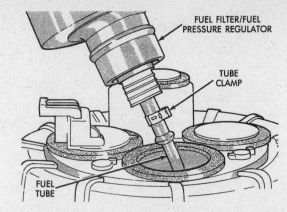

14.6 Disconnect the tube clamp from the fuel tube using a pair of cutting pliers

3   Remove the fuel tank (see Section 5).
4   Remove the fuel pressure regulator/fuel filter by gently prying the unit from the rubber grommet. **Caution:** *Do not pull the fuel pressure regulator/fuel filter unit out more than three inches or damage to the coiled tube may result.*
5   Remove the snap-ring that retains the convoluted tube cover to the regulator/filter. Slide the plastic tube down the fuel line to expose the fuel tube clamp **(see illustration)**.
6   Disconnect the tube clamp from the fuel tube and separate the fuel pressure regulator/fuel filter from the fuel pump assembly **(see illustration)**. **Note:** *It will be necessary to cut the clamp using cutting pliers.*
7   Installation is the reverse of removal.

15   Fuel injectors - check, removal and installation

Warning: *Gasoline is extremely flammable, so take extra precautions when you work on any part of the fuel system. Don't smoke or allow open flames or bare light bulbs near the work area, and don't work in a garage where a natural gas-type appliance (such as a water heater or a clothes dryer) with a pilot light is present. Since gasoline is carcinogenic, wear latex gloves when there's a possibility of being exposed to fuel, and, if you spill any fuel on your skin, rinse it off immediately with soap and water. Mop up any spills immediately and do not store fuel-soaked rags where they could ignite. The fuel system is under constant pressure, so, if any fuel lines are to be disconnected, the fuel pressure in the system must be relieved first (see Section 2). When you perform any kind of work on the fuel system, wear safety glasses and have a Class B type fire extinguisher on hand.*

Check

1   Start the engine and warm it to its normal operating temperature.
2   With the engine idling, unplug each injector one-at-a-time, note the change in idle speed then reconnect the injector. If the idle speed drop is almost the same for each cylinder, the injectors are operating correctly. If unplugging a particular injector fails to change the idle speed, proceed to the next step.
3   Turn the engine off. Remove the connector from the injector, and measure the resistance between the two terminals of the injector **(see illustration 12.8)**.
4   The resistance should be approximately 12 to 15 ohms. If not, replace it with a new one.
5   If the resistance is as specified, connect a high-impedance voltmeter or a special injector harness test light (noid light), (available at most auto parts stores) to the electrical connector **(see illustration 12.9)**.

   a) *If the voltage fluctuates between zero and two volts (or the light flashes), the injector is receiving proper voltage.*
   b) *If there is no voltage, check the wiring harness (see Chapter 12).*
   c) *If the wiring harness is not damaged or shorted, check the wiring between the PCM and the injector(s) for a short circuit, or a break in the wire or bad connection.*

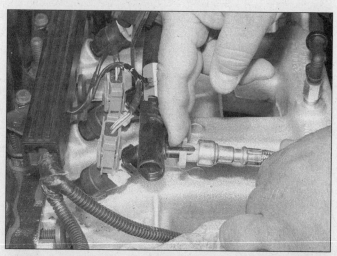

15.12a To disconnect the fuel line from the fuel rail, remove the safety clip from the connector (5.2L V8 engine shown) . . .

15.12b . . . then slide a plastic disconnect tool onto the fuel line and push the tool into the connector to force it off the fuel line lip

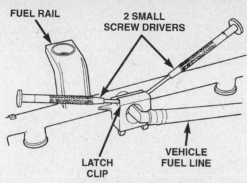

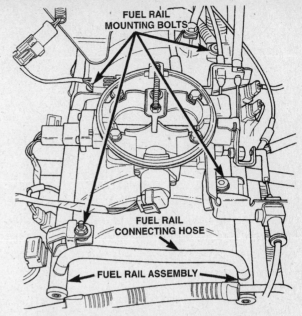

15.12c On later models the fuel line is secured to the fuel rail by a clip that must be pried off

Removal

Refer to illustrations 15.12a, 15.12b, 15.12c, 15.13, 15.14a and 15.14b

6   Detach the cable from the negative battery terminal.

7   Relieve the fuel pressure (see Section 2).

8   On V10 engines, remove the air intake plenum (see Chapter 2A).

9   On V6 and V8 engines, remove the throttle body, if necessary for clearance (see Section 13). Also remove the canister purge solenoid.

10   Unplug the injector connectors. Clearly label and remove any vacuum hoses or electrical wiring that will interfere with the fuel rail removal.

11   Detach any ground cables from the fuel rail. Remove the air conditioning compressor-to-intake manifold bracket, if so equipped.

12   Detach the fuel line from the fuel rail **(see illustrations)**.

13   Remove the mounting nuts **(see illustration)** and lift the fuel rail assembly along with the fuel injectors from the engine compartment.

14   Remove the injector(s) from the fuel rail assembly remove and discard the O-rings **(see illustrations)**. **Note:** *Whether you're replacing an injector or a leaking O-ring, it's a good idea to remove all the injectors from the fuel rail and replace all the O-rings.*

Installation

Refer to illustration 15.18

15   Coat the new seal rings with clean engine oil and slide them onto the injectors.

16   Coat the new O-rings with clean engine oil and install them on the injector(s), then insert each injector into its corresponding bore in the fuel rail.

17   Install the injector and fuel rail assembly on the intake manifold. Make sure the injectors are fully seated, then tighten the fuel rail mounting nuts to the torque listed in this Chapter's Specifications.

18   The remainder of installation is the reverse of removal. **Note:** *On later models that use a clip to secure the fuel line to the fuel rail, be sure*

15.13 Remove the bolts that secure the fuel rail to the intake manifold

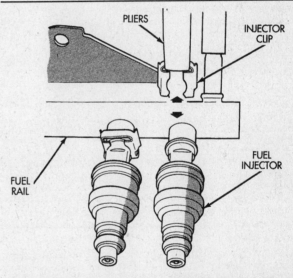

15.14a Pull the injector retaining clips from the fuel rail assembly

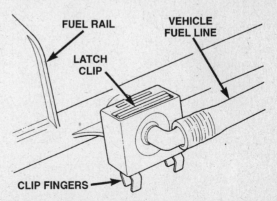

15.18 Make sure the fuel line is completely seated in the fuel rail and latch clip is properly secured

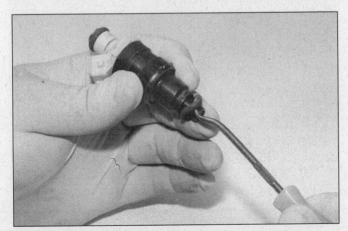

15.14b Carefully remove the O-rings from the injector

4A

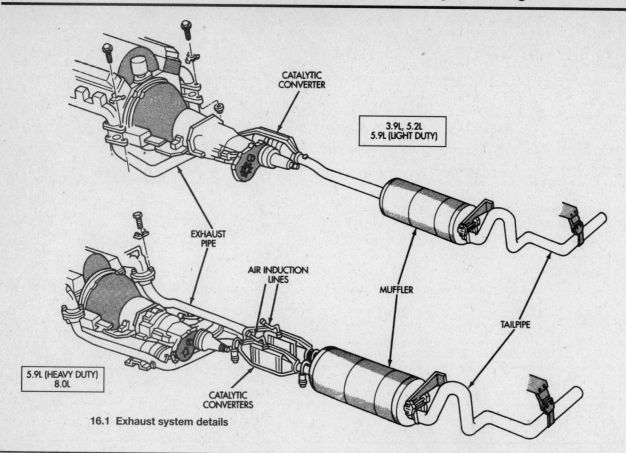

CATALYTIC CONVERTER

3.9L, 5.2L 5.9L (LIGHT DUTY)

EXHAUST PIPE

AIR INDUCTION LINES

MUFFLER

TAILPIPE

5.9L (HEAVY DUTY) 8.0L

CATALYTIC CONVERTERS

16.1 Exhaust system details

the fuel line is completely inserted and the clip is properly seated **(see illustration)**.
19   After the injector/fuel rail assembly installation is complete, turn the ignition switch to ON, but don't operate the starter (this activates the fuel pump for about two seconds, which builds up fuel pressure in the fuel lines and the fuel rail). Repeat this about two or three times, then check the fuel lines, rail and injectors for fuel leakage.

16   Exhaust system servicing - general information

Refer to illustration 16.1
Warning: *Inspection and repair of exhaust system components should be done only after enough time has elapsed after driving the vehicle to allow the system components to cool completely. Also, when working under the vehicle, make sure it is securely supported on jackstands.*
1   The exhaust system consists of the exhaust manifold(s), the catalytic converter, the muffler, the tailpipe and all connecting pipes, brackets, hangers and clamps. The exhaust system is attached to the body with mounting brackets and rubber hangers **(see illustration)**. If any of the parts are improperly installed, excessive noise and vibration will be transmitted to the body.

Muffler and pipes

2   Conduct regular inspections of the exhaust system to keep it safe and quiet. Look for any damaged or bent parts, open seams, holes, loose connections, excessive corrosion or other defects which could allow exhaust fumes to enter the vehicle. Also check the catalytic converter when you inspect the exhaust system (see below). Deteriorated exhaust system components should not be repaired; they should be replaced with new parts.
3   If the exhaust system components are extremely corroded or rusted together, welding equipment will probably be required to remove them. The convenient way to accomplish this is to have a muffler repair shop remove the corroded sections with a cutting torch. If,

however, you want to save money by doing it yourself (and you don't have a welding outfit with a cutting torch), simply cut off the old components with a hacksaw. If you have compressed air, special pneumatic cutting chisels can also be used. If you do decide to tackle the job at home, be sure to wear safety goggles to protect your eyes from metal chips and work gloves to protect your hands.
4   Here are some simple guidelines to follow when repairing the exhaust system:
   a) *Work from the back to the front when removing exhaust system components.*
   b) *Apply penetrating oil to the exhaust system component fasteners to make them easier to remove.*
   c) *Use new gaskets, hangers and clamps when installing exhaust systems components.*
   d) *Apply anti-seize compound to the threads of all exhaust system fasteners during reassembly.*
   e) *Be sure to allow sufficient clearance between newly installed parts and all points on the underbody to avoid overheating the floor pan and possibly damaging the interior carpet and insulation. Pay particularly close attention to the catalytic converter and heat shield.*

Catalytic converter

Warning: *The converter gets very hot during operation. Make sure it has cooled down before you touch it.*
Note: *See Chapter 6 for more information on the catalytic converter.*
5   Periodically inspect the heat shield for cracks, dents and loose or missing fasteners.
6   Remove the heat shield and inspect the converter for cracks or other damage.
7   If the converter must be replaced, remove the mounting nuts from the flanges at each end, detach the rubber mounts and separate the converter from the exhaust system (you should be able to push the exhaust pipes at each end out of the way to clear the converter studs.
8   Installation is the reverse of removal. Be sure to use new gaskets.

Chapter 4 Part B
Fuel and exhaust systems - diesel engine

Contents

1   General Information

General information

Refer to illustrations 1.4a through 1.4d

The fuel system is what most sets apart diesel engines from their gasoline powered cousins. Simply stated, fuel is injected directly into the combustion chambers; the more fuel injected, the more power the engine produces. Unlike gasoline engines, diesels have no throttle plate to limit the entry of air into the intake manifold. The only control is the amount of fuel injected; an unrestricted supply of air is always available through the intake.

There are two major sub-systems in the fuel injection system; the

low pressure (also known as the supply or transfer) portion and the high-pressure injection (delivery) portion.

The low pressure system "transfers" fuel from the tank to the engine for use by the injection pump. Fuel is drawn by the low pressure pump through a series of screens and filter/water separators via fuel lines to the high-pressure injection pump. A bypass system allows excess fuel to return to the tank.

A high-pressure fuel injection pump **(see illustrations)** meters fuel to the cylinders in minute high-pressure squirts. These fuel pulses are directed to the fuel injectors of each cylinder in the firing order of the engine. When more power and speed is desired, the fuel injection system simply sprays more fuel into the cylinders. When a preset maximum engine speed is reached, a governor limits the delivery of fuel, thereby limiting speed.

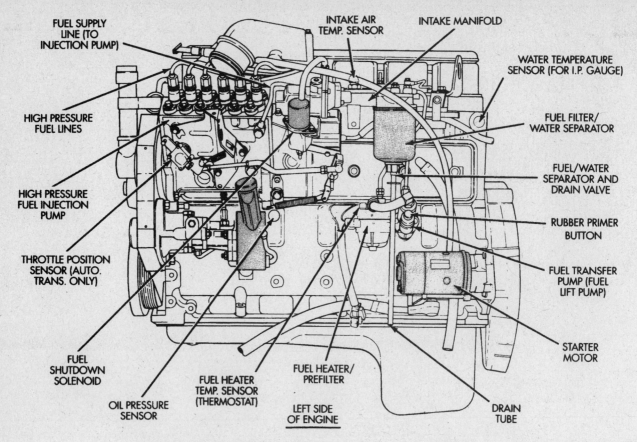

FUEL SUPPLY
LINE (TO
INJECTION PUMP)

INTAKE AIR
TEMP. SENSOR

INTAKE MANIFOLD

HIGH PRESSURE
FUEL LINES

WATER TEMPERATURE
SENSOR (FOR I.P. GAUGE)

FUEL FILTER/
WATER SEPARATOR

HIGH PRESSURE
FUEL INJECTION
PUMP

FUEL/WATER
SEPARATOR AND
DRAIN VALVE

RUBBER PRIMER
BUTTON

THROTTLE POSITION
SENSOR (AUTO.
TRANS. ONLY)

FUEL TRANSFER
PUMP (FUEL
LIFT PUMP)

FUEL
SHUTDOWN
SOLENOID

FUEL HEATER
TEMP. SENSOR
(THERMOSTAT)

FUEL HEATER/
PREFILTER

STARTER
MOTOR

OIL PRESSURE
SENSOR

LEFT SIDE
OF ENGINE

DRAIN
TUBE

1.4a Location of the fuel system components on the diesel engine

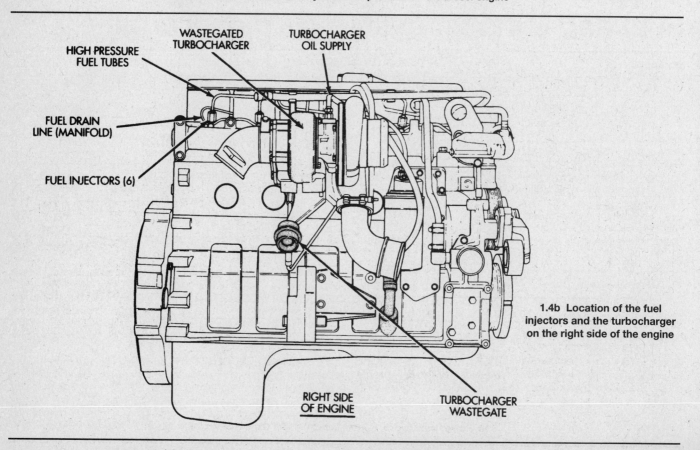

HIGH PRESSURE
FUEL TUBES

WASTEGATED
TURBOCHARGER

TURBOCHARGER
OIL SUPPLY

FUEL DRAIN
LINE (MANIFOLD)

FUEL INJECTORS (6)

1.4b Location of the fuel
injectors and the turbocharger
on the right side of the engine

RIGHT SIDE
OF ENGINE

TURBOCHARGER
WASTEGATE

1.4c Underhood locations of diesel fuel injection system components

1   Turbocharger
2   Fuel injector

3   Air intake heater
4   Fuel injection pump

5   Intake manifold
6   Exhaust manifold

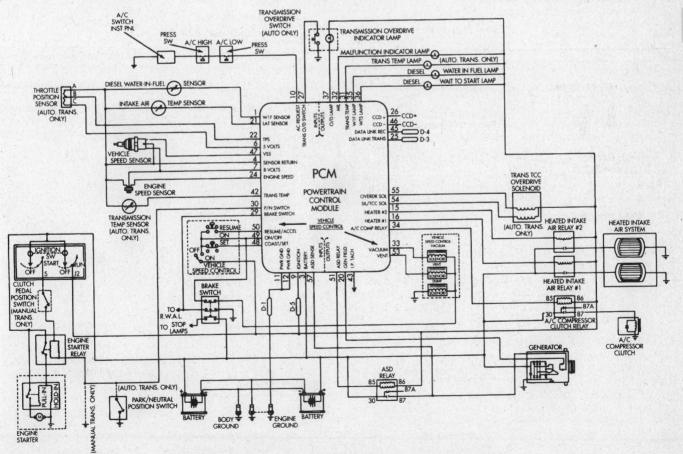

1.4d Powertrain control system schematic for the diesel engine

The injection of fuel also determines the timing of combustion, similar to spark timing in a gasoline engine. As engine speed increases, timing must be advanced.

Fuel system problems are by far the most frequent cause of breakdowns and loss of power in diesel-powered vehicles. Whenever a diesel engine quits running or loses power for no apparent reason, check the fuel system first. Begin with the most obvious items, such as the fuel filter and damaged fuel lines. If the vehicle has multiple fuel tanks, suspect a faulty tank switchover valve.

The fuel system on diesel engines is extremely sensitive to contamination. Fuel contamination can be a serious problem due to the very small clearances in the injection pump and the minute orifices in the injection nozzles. The injection pump and the injectors can be damaged or ruined.

Water-contaminated diesel fuel is a major problem. If it remains in the fuel system too long, water will cause serious and expensive damage. The fuel lines and the fuel filter can also become plugged with rust particles, or clogged with ice in cold weather.

Diesel fuel contamination

Before you replace an injection pump or some other expensive component, find out what caused the failure. If water contamination is present, buying a new or rebuilt pump or other component won't do much good. The following procedure will help you determine if water contamination is present:

a) Remove the engine fuel filter and inspect the contents for the presence of water or gasoline (see Chapter 1).
b) If the vehicle has been stalling, performance has been poor or the engine has been knocking loudly, suspect fuel contamination. Gasoline or water must be removed by flushing (see below).
c) If you find a lot of water in the fuel filter, remove the injection pump fuel return line and check for water there. If the pump has water in it, flush the system.
d) Small quantities of surface rust won't create a problem. If contamination is excessive, the vehicle will probably stall.
e) Sometimes contamination in the system becomes severe enough to cause damage to the internal parts of the pump. If the damage reaches this stage, have the damaged parts replaced and the pump rebuilt by an authorized fuel injection shop, or buy a rebuilt pump.

Storage

Good quality diesel fuel contains inhibitors to stop the formation of rust in the fuel lines and the injectors, so as long as there are no leaks in the fuel system, it's generally safe from water contamination. Diesel fuel is usually contaminated by water as a result of careless storage. There's not much you can do about the storage practices of service stations where you buy diesel fuel, but if you keep a small supply of diesel fuel on hand at home, as many diesel owners do, follow these simple rules:

a) Diesel fuel "ages" and goes stale. Don't store containers of diesel fuel for long periods of time. Use it up regularly and replace it with fresh fuel.
b) Keep fuel storage containers out of direct sunlight. Variations in heat and humidity promote condensation inside fuel containers.
c) Don't store diesel fuel in galvanized containers. It may cause the galvanizing to flake off, contaminating the fuel and clogging filters when the fuel is used.
d) Label containers properly, as containing diesel fuel.

Fighting fungi and bacteria with biocides

If there's water in the fuel, fungi and/or bacteria can form in warm or humid weather. Fungi and bacteria plug fuel lines, fuel filters and injection nozzles; they can also cause corrosion in the fuel system.

If you've had problems with water in the fuel system and you live in a warm or humid climate, have your dealer correct the problem. Then, use a diesel fuel biocide to sterilize the fuel system in accordance with the manufacturer's instructions. Biocides are available from your dealer, service stations and auto parts stores. Consult your dealer for advice on using biocides in your area and for recommendations on which ones to use.

Cleaning the low-pressure fuel system

Warning: Diesel fuel is flammable, so take extra precautions when you work on any part of the fuel system. Don't smoke or allow open flames or bare light bulbs near the work area, and don't work in a garage where a natural gas-type appliance (such as a water heater or a clothes dryer) with a pilot light is present. Since diesel fuel is carcinogenic, wear latex gloves when there's a possibility of being exposed to fuel, and, if you spill any fuel on your skin, rinse it off immediately with soap and water. Mop up any spills immediately and do not store diesel fuel-soaked rags where they could ignite. When you perform any kind of work on the fuel system, wear safety glasses and have a Class B type fire extinguisher on hand.

Water in fuel system

1   Disconnect the ground cables from the negative terminals of the batteries.
2   Drain the fuel tank into an approved container and dispose of it properly.
3   Remove the tank gauge sending unit (see Chapter 4A).
4   Thoroughly clean the fuel tank. If it's rusted inside, send it to a repair shop or replace it. Clean or replace the fuel pick-up filter.
5   Reinstall the fuel tank but don't connect the fuel lines to the fuel tank yet.
6   Disconnect the main fuel line from the low-pressure fuel pump. Remove the fuel filter (see Chapter 1). Using low air pressure, blow out the line toward the rear of the vehicle. **Warning:** Wear eye protection when using compressed air.
7   Temporarily disconnect the fuel return fuel line at the injection pump and again, using low air pressure, blow out the line toward the rear of the vehicle.
8   Reconnect the main fuel and return lines at the tank. Fill the tank to a fourth of its capacity with clean diesel fuel. Install the cap on the fuel filler neck.
9   Discard the fuel filter.
10   Connect the fuel line to the fuel pump.
11   Reconnect the battery cables.
12   Purge the fuel pump and pump-to-filter line by cranking the engine until clean fuel is pumped out. Catch the fuel in a closed metal container.
13   Install a new fuel filter.
14   Install a hose from the fuel return line (from the injection pump) to a closed metal container with a capacity of at least two gallons.
15   Crank the engine until clean fuel appears at the return line. Don't crank the engine for more than 30 seconds at a time. If it's necessary to crank it again, allow a three-minute interval before resuming.
16   Loosen each high-pressure line fitting at the injector nozzles. Loosen the fittings only enough to allow fuel to seep out.
17   Crank the engine until clean fuel appears at each nozzle. Don't crank the engine for more than 30 seconds at a time. If it's necessary to crank it again, allow a three-minute interval before resuming.

Gasoline in the fuel system

Warning: Diesel fuel is flammable, so take extra precautions when you work on any part of the fuel system. Don't smoke or allow open flames or bare light bulbs near the work area, and don't work in a garage where a natural gas-type appliance (such as a water heater or a clothes dryer) with a pilot light is present. Since diesel fuel is carcinogenic, wear latex gloves when there's a possibility of being exposed to fuel, and, if you spill any fuel on your skin, rinse it off immediately with soap and water. Mop up any spills immediately and do not store diesel fuel-soaked rags where they could ignite. When you perform any kind of work on the fuel system, wear safety glasses and have a Class B type fire extinguisher on hand.

If gasoline has been accidentally pumped into the fuel tank, it should be drained immediately. Gasoline in the fuel in small amounts - up to 30 percent - isn't usually noticeable. At higher ratios, the engine may make a knocking noise, which will get louder as the ratio of gasoline increases. Here's how to rid the fuel system of gasoline:
18   Drain the fuel tank into an approved container and fill the tank with clean, fresh diesel fuel (see Chapter 4A).

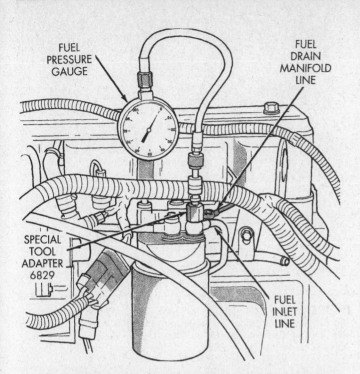

2.6   Remove the fuel drain manifold line from the right side fitting on the fuel filter/water separator, install the special adapter and connect the fuel pressure gauge to the adapter.

19   Remove the fuel line between the fuel filter and the injection pump.

20   Connect a short pipe and hose to the fuel filter outlet and run it to a closed metal container.

21   Crank the engine to purge gasoline out of the fuel pump and fuel filter. Don't crank the engine more than 30 seconds. Allow two or three minutes between cranking intervals for the starter to cool.

22   Remove the short pipe and hose and install the fuel line between the fuel filter and the injection pump.

23   Try to start the engine. If it doesn't start, purge the injection pump and lines: Loosen the fuel line fittings a little, just enough for fuel to leak out. Depress the accelerator pedal to the floor and, holding it there, crank the engine until all gasoline is removed, i.e. diesel fuel leaks out of the fittings. Tighten the fittings. Limit cranking to 30 seconds with two or three minute intervals between cranking. **Warning:** *Avoid sources of ignition and have a fire extinguisher handy.*

24   Start the engine and run it at idle for 15 minutes.

"Water-In-Fuel" (WIF) warning system

25   The system detects the presence of water in the fuel filter when it reaches excessive amounts. Water is detected by a probe located in the fuel filter that completes a circuit through a wire to a light in the instrument cluster that reads "Water In Fuel."

26   This system includes a bulb-check feature - when the ignition is turned on, the bulb glows momentarily, then fades away.

27   If the light comes on immediately after you've filled the tank or let the vehicle sit for an extended period of time, drain the water from the system immediately. Do not start the engine. There might be enough water in the system to shut the engine down before you've driven even a short distance. If, however, the light comes on during a cornering or braking maneuver, there's less water in the system; the engine probably won't shut down immediately, but you still should drain the water soon.

28   Water is heavier than diesel fuel, so it sinks to the bottom of the fuel tank. An extended return pipe on the fuel tank sending unit, which reaches down into the bottom of the tank, enables you to siphon most of the water from the tank without having to remove the tank. But siphoning won't remove all of the water; you'll still need to remove the

tank and thoroughly clean it. **Warning:** *Do not start a siphon by mouth - use a siphoning kit (available at most auto parts stores).*

2   Transfer pump/fuel pressure check and replacement

Warning: *Diesel fuel is flammable, so take extra precautions when you work on any part of the fuel system. Don't smoke or allow open flames or bare light bulbs near the work area, and don't work in a garage where a natural gas-type appliance (such as a water heater or a clothes dryer) with a pilot light is present. Since diesel fuel is carcinogenic, wear latex gloves when there's a possibility of being exposed to fuel, and, if you spill any fuel on your skin, rinse it off immediately with soap and water. Mop up any spills immediately and do not store diesel fuel-soaked rags where they could ignite. When you perform any kind of work on the fuel system, wear safety glasses and have a Class B type fire extinguisher on hand.*

1   There are some simple tests you can perform to determine whether the in-tank fuel pump is operating satisfactorily. But first, do the following preliminary inspection:

Preliminary inspection

2   Check the fuel line fittings and connections - make sure they're tight. If a fitting is loose, air and/or fuel leaks may occur.

3   Check for bends or kinks in the fuel lines.

4   Start the engine and let it warm up. With the engine idling, conduct the following preliminary inspection before proceeding to the actual fuel pump tests:

a)   *Look for leaks at the pressure (outlet) side of the pump.*

b)   *Look for leaks on the suction (inlet) side of the pump. A leak on the suction side will let air into the pump and reduce the volume of fuel on the pressure (outlet) side of the pump.*

c)   *Inspect the fittings on the transfer pump for leaks. Tighten or replace the fittings as necessary.*

d)   *Look for leaks around the diaphragm, the flange and the breather holes in the pump housing. If any of them are leaking, replace the pump.*

Transfer pump pressure check

Refer to illustrations 2.6, 2.13, 2.14a and 2.14b

Note: *Fuel system pressure drop check can be performed with a fuel pressure gauge connected to, the inlet and then the outlet side of the fuel filter/water separator. The difference between these two pressure readings will indicate a fuel pressure drop. The maximum amount of fuel pressure drop across the fuel/filter water separator is 5 psi. It is best if the fuel filter/water separator is replaced with a new filter before conducting any fuel pressure checks.*

5   The maximum amount of fuel pressure drop across the fuel filter/water separator is 5 psi. This fuel system pressure check can be performed with a fuel pressure gauge connected to first, the inlet side and then the outlet side of the fuel filter/water separator. Remove the clamp bolt on the fuel drain manifold line to allow movement.

6   Remove the banjo fitting on the inlet side of the fuel filter/water separator (from the transfer pump) **(see illustration)** and move the outlet line out of the way.

7   Install a fuel pressure gauge, with a special adapter (Chrysler tool no. 6829 or equivalent), to the fitting. The gauge should span 0 to 100 psi.

8   Start the engine and observe the fuel pressure readings. Minimum fuel pressure should be 25 psi. If not, proceed to Steps 12 through 16.

9   If the pressure is correct, remove the fuel pressure gauge and install the banjo fittings and fuel lines to the inlet fitting.

10   Remove the OUTLET banjo fitting, install the fuel pressure gauge and start the engine. Observe the fuel pressure readings. The pressure should not exceed 5 psi.

11   If the fuel pressure has exceeded the specified amount, change the filter in the fuel filter/water separator (see Chapter 1) and check the fuel line for restrictions. If the **WATER IN FUEL** warning light on the dash remains on, drain all the water out of the fuel filter/water separator. If water collects very quickly in the separator, remove the fuel tank

4B

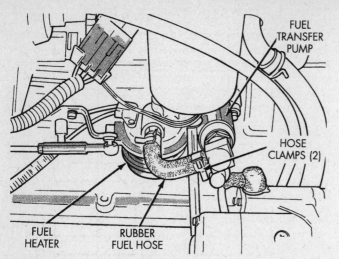

2.13 Remove the rubber fuel hose from the fuel heater and the transfer pump

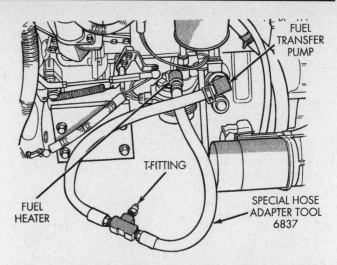

2.14a Install the special fuel hose with the adapter between the fuel heater and the transfer pump

and flush the lines (see Section 1).

12   An improperly operating fuel transfer pump can cause low engine power and/or hard engine starting. Fuel leaking from the weep hole indicates that the transfer pump must be replaced. Also, low transfer pump pressure output can be caused by a worn or damaged eccentric on the engine camshaft.

13   Remove the rubber fuel hose between the fuel heater and the transfer pump **(see illustration)**.

14   Install a special hose adapter (Chrysler tool no. 6837 or equivalent) between the disconnected fittings and tighten them with clamps. Install a vacuum gauge to the T-fitting **(see illustrations)**.

15   Start the engine and observe the vacuum gauge. The vacuum gauge will not read vacuum until the transfer pump begins to operate at full capacity. Vacuum should not exceed 4 in-Hg.

16   If the vacuum (restriction) is higher than the specified amount, check for a kinked fuel line or a plugged fuel tank vent (see Section 3). A partially clogged in-tank fuel filter can cause excess vacuum.

17   Remove the vacuum gauge and the fuel line adapter tool and install the rubber hose onto the fittings.

Fuel volume test

Refer to illustrations 2.18, 2.20 and 2.21

18   Connect a hand-held tachometer specifically designed for diesel fuel injection systems (Cummins tool no. 3377462, Snap-On tool no.

MT139, or equivalent). **Caution:** *To prevent the engine from starting, disconnect the electrical connector at the fuel shutdown solenoid* **(see illustration)**. *Crank the engine and allow the engine to run the remaining fuel out of the injection pump and lines before proceeding with the fuel volume test.*

19   Remove the clamp bolt retaining the fuel drain manifold line from the cylinder head **(see illustration 2.6)**.

20   Remove the banjo bolt from the fuel INLET line and install a drain hose **(see illustration)**. **Note:** *It will be necessary to install a special fitting (Chrysler tool no. 6836 or equivalent) onto the fuel filter/water separator INLET to be able to install the fuel drain line.*

21   With the end of the drain in a graduated container, crank the engine for exactly 30 seconds and measure the amount of fuel **(see illustration)**. **Note:** *Be sure to monitor the rpm carefully while the engine is cranking to obtain accurate test results.*

22   Inject the two parameters onto the graph and if the intersection point is below the flow line, then the transfer pump is defective.

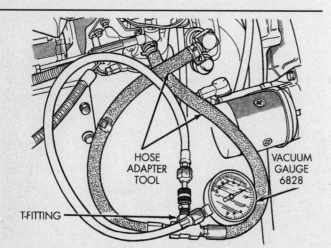

2.14b Install the vacuum gauge and check for excessive amounts of fuel system vacuum

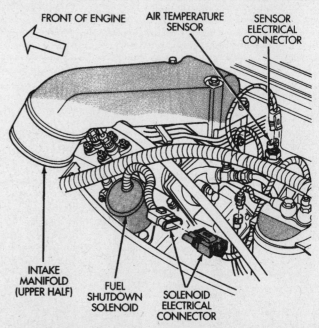

2.18 Before checking the fuel volume, disconnect the fuel shutdown solenoid electrical connector

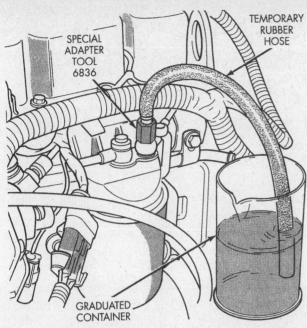

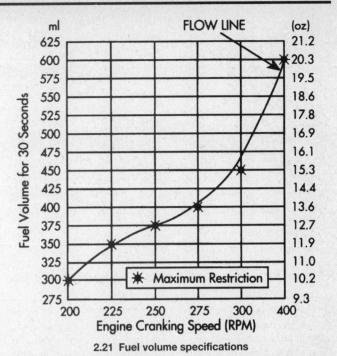

2.20 Allow the fuel to flow into a graduated container

2.21 Fuel volume specifications

Transfer pump replacement

Refer to illustrations 2.27 and 2.28

23   Disconnect the metal fuel lines and fuel hoses from the transfer pump.
24   Remove the starter from the engine (see Chapter 5).
25   Place a drain pan below the transfer pump.
26   Remove the fuel lines from the transfer pump and the fuel heater housing.
27   Remove the nuts that retain the transfer pump to the side of the engine block **(see illustration)**.
28   Lift the transfer pump and fuel heater from the block and remove the drive rod from the assembly **(see illustration)**.
29   Installation is the reverse of removal. Be sure to use new gaskets and lubricate the ends of the drive rod with engine assembly lube.

3   Fuel lines and fittings - repair and replacement

Warning 1: *Diesel fuel is flammable, so take extra precautions when you work on any part of the fuel system. Don't smoke or allow open flames or bare light bulbs near the work area, and don't work in a garage where a natural gas-type appliance (such as a water heater or a clothes dryer)*

with a pilot light is present. Since diesel fuel is carcinogenic, wear latex gloves when there's a possibility of being exposed to fuel, and, if you spill any fuel on your skin, rinse it off immediately with soap and water. Mop up any spills immediately and do not store diesel fuel-soaked rags where they could ignite. When you perform any kind of work on the fuel system, wear safety glasses and have a Class B type fire extinguisher on hand.
Warning 2: *The pressure in the high-pressure fuel lines can reach up to 17,400 psi, therefore, use extreme caution when inspecting for high-pressure fuel leaks. Do not move your hand near a suspect leak - instead, use a piece of cardboard. high-pressure fuel leaks can injure your skin.*
Caution: *Do not attempt to weld high-pressure fuel lines or to repair lines that are damaged. Use only factory replacement fuel lines.*

High-pressure fuel line leak test

1   Start the engine and move a piece of clean cardboard over and around the high-pressure fuel lines and check for fuel spray onto the cardboard. If a high-pressure line connection is leaking, first, bleed the system (see Chapter 1, *Fuel filter/water separator check and replacement*). Next, tighten the fuel line.
2   Clamp the high-pressure fuel lines in place in their holders. Do not allow any fuel lines to contact each other or other components.

4B

2.27 Remove the transfer pump mounting bolts (arrows)

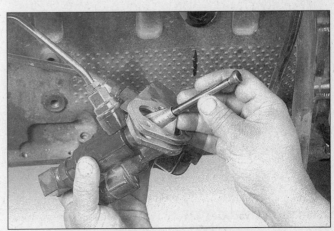

2.28 Remove the drive rod from the transfer pump

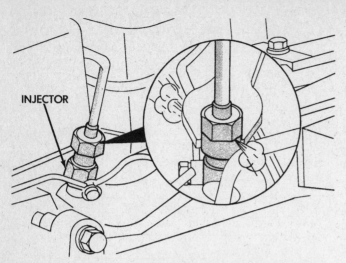

3.4 Carefully crack open the injector line fitting at the injector(s) to bleed out any last remnants of trapped air

3.9 Remove the high-pressure fuel line clamp

Bleeding high-pressure fuel lines

Refer to illustration 3.4

Warning: *Do not bleed fuel from the fuel system on a HOT engine. Do not allow fuel to spray onto the exhaust manifold at any time during the bleeding procedure. Exercise caution when working on the engine while it's running.*

3   First, perform the manual bleeding procedure as detailed in Chapter 1, *Fuel filter/water separator check and replacement.*

4   Working on one injector at a time, loosen the high-pressure fuel line fitting at the injector **(see illustration)**.

5   Disconnect the electrical connector at the fuel shutdown solenoid **(see illustration 2.18)**. Have an assistant crank the engine over while observing that all the air is bled from the line. **Caution:** *Do not operate the starter for more than 30 seconds at a time. Wait two minutes to allow cooling the starter assembly before cranking the engine again.*

6   Plug-in the electrical connector to the fuel shutdown solenoid. Start the engine and bleed one injector at a time until the engine runs smoothly.

Replacing high-pressure fuel lines

Refer to illustrations 3.9 and 3.10

Warning: *Allow the engine to rest for approximately three minutes before disconnecting the high-pressure fuel lines. The extremely high-fuel pressure in the lines may cause skin damage or leak excessive amounts of fuel over the engine area. Fuel pressure will dissipate after a three minute period.*

7   Disconnect the fuel lines from the fuel injection pump. **Note:** *Place shop towels around the injector lines to soak up any residual fuel.*

8   Disconnect the fuel lines from the injectors.

9   Remove the bolts that retain the fuel line clamps **(see illustration)**.

10   Lift the fuel rail assembly from the engine compartment **(see illustration)**.

11   Installation is the reverse of removal. Be sure to bleed the high-pressure system after all the lines are in place.

---

4   Fuel injection pump - replacement and timing adjustment

Warning: *Diesel fuel is flammable, so take extra precautions when you work on any part of the fuel system. Don't smoke or allow open flames or bare light bulbs near the work area, and don't work in a garage where a natural gas-type appliance (such as a water heater or a clothes dryer) with a pilot light is present. Since diesel fuel is carcinogenic,*

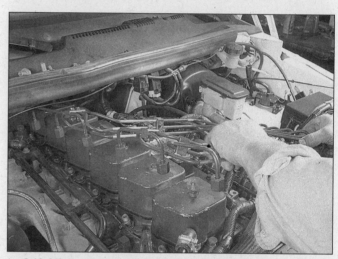

3.10 Lift the high-pressure fuel line assembly off the engine

wear latex gloves when there's a possibility of being exposed to fuel, and, if you spill any fuel on your skin, rinse it off immediately with soap and water. Mop up any spills immediately and do not store diesel fuel-soaked rags where they could ignite. When you perform any kind of work on the fuel system, wear safety glasses and have a Class B type fire extinguisher on hand.

Note: *It is necessary to check the fuel injection pump timing any time the original pump is removed or a rebuilt pump is installed in place of the original. The adjustment procedure is difficult, requires special tools and must be set exactly to the manufacturer's specifications. It is recommended that the pump timing be performed by a dealer service department or other qualified diesel technician.*

Removal

Refer to illustrations 4.5, 4.10a, 4.10b, 4.11, 4.12, 4.13, 4.14, 4.15a, 4.15b, 4.15c, 4.15d, 4.15e, 4.16, 4.17, 4.18 and 4.19

1   Disconnect the negative battery cable from both batteries.

2   If equipped with an automatic transmission, disconnect the electrical connector from the TPS sensor located on the side of the fuel injection pump (see Chapter 6).

3   Disconnect the electrical connector at the fuel shutdown solenoid (see Section 7).

4   Disconnect the main engine wiring harness at the top of the fuel injection pump and move it to the side.

5   Remove the intake manifold-to-intercooler air duct assembly **(see illustration)**.

4.5 Remove the intercooler-to-intake manifold air duct assembly

4.10a Disconnect the oil feed line from the injection pump

4.10b Disconnect the fuel line from the back of the fuel injection pump

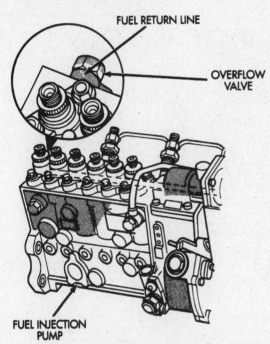

4.11 Location of the injection pump overflow valve

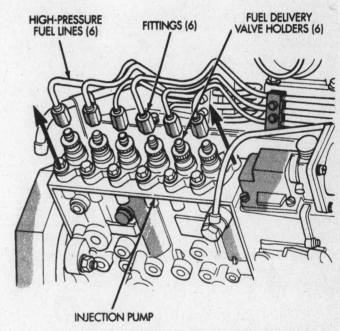

4.12 Remove the high-pressure fuel lines from the fuel injection pump

4B

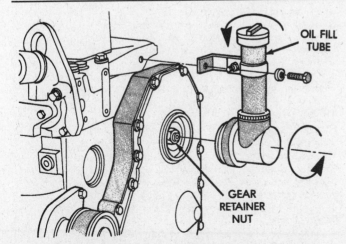

4.13 Remove the oil fill tube mounting bolt and rotate the assembly counterclockwise to remove it from the front cover

6   Remove the engine oil dipstick tube from the engine (see Chapter 2B).

7   Disconnect the air heater wires and remove the intake air heater assembly from the intake manifold (see Section 8).

8   Remove the accelerator cable, bracket and linkage assembly from the side of the fuel injection pump.

9   Disconnect the turbocharger wastegate oil line and pressure line from the air flow control valve at the rear of the fuel injection pump.

10   Disconnect the lines from the pump **(see illustrations)** and the fuel filter/water separator (see Section 3). Place a shop rag or towel beneath the fuel lines to catch any residual fuel.

11   Remove the fuel overflow valve and the fuel return line from the fuel injection pump **(see illustration)**.

12   Disconnect the six high-pressure fuel lines from the fuel delivery valve holders **(see illustration)** at the top of the injection pump. Place shop rags beneath to catch any residual fuel. Cap the fuel lines, the high-pressure fittings on the fuel injection pump and the fuel injectors to prevent the entry of dirt or contamination.

13   Remove the oil fill tube bracket mounting bolt **(see illustration)** and twist the assembly counterclockwise to remove it from the gear housing cover.

4.14 Paint an alignment mark on the front pulley directly in front of the cover and bolt assembly

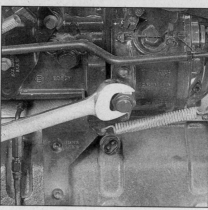

4.15a Remove the fuel injection pump alignment pin access cover

4.15b Be prepared to catch the oil as the cover is removed

4.15c Reverse the alignment pin and install it with the notched end facing into the fuel injection pump

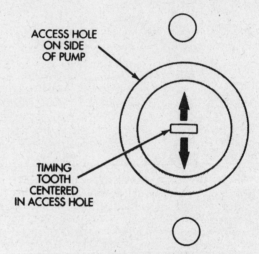

4.15d Make sure the timing tooth is centered inside the access hole

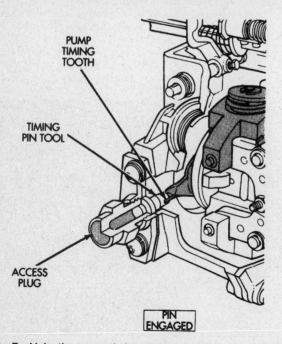

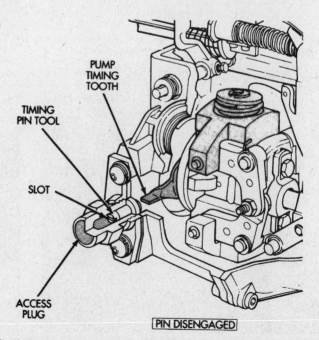

4.15e Fuel injection pump timing pin installation details - with the timing pin engaged the fuel injection pump is locked at number one TDC

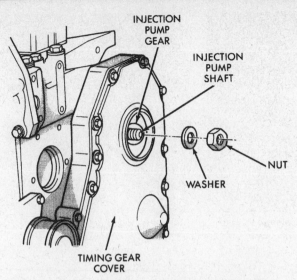

4.16 Remove the injection pump gear nut and washer

4.17 Pull the gear loose from the fuel injection pump - cover removed for clarity

14   Locate the camshaft gear timing pin and set the engine on TDC for cylinder number 1 by following the procedure in Chapter 2B, Section 3. **Caution:** *The engine and the fuel injection pump must be set on number 1 TDC before removing or installing the fuel injection pump to maintain proper fuel injection pump timing. After locating TDC for number one cylinder, remove the timing pin to prevent accidental shearing of the pin.* Apply a paint mark on the front pulley indicating the position of the engine at TDC **(see illustration)**.

15   The fuel injection pump is equipped with another alignment pin designed specifically to lock the pump shaft on number one TDC while the pump remains off the engine **(see illustrations)**. This alignment pin must be locked into place before the fuel injection pump is removed from the engine to maintain the pump timing. Before removing the pump, remove the access cover and reverse the timing pin, installing it with the slotted end engaging the timing tooth and reinstall the access cover **(see illustrations)**. The timing pin must be reversed (unlocked) once the fuel injection pump is installed back onto the engine and ready to start. If a new or rebuilt pump will be installed, the pump should come from the factory with the slotted end of the pin engaged with the timing tooth.

16   Remove the nut and washer retaining the gear to the fuel injection pump shaft **(see illustration)**. **Note:** *Position a shop rag or towel into the housing cover opening to prevent the nut or washer from falling into the gear housing. If the gear nut or washer is accidentally dropped into*

the housing, the cover must be completely removed to retrieve them.

17   Using a gear puller (Chrysler tool no. L-4407A or equivalent) and two metric bolts (M8 X 1.24 mm), pull the fuel injection pump gear forward until it loosens from the injection pump shaft. **Caution:** *Pull the gear out until it's just loose from the fuel injection pump shaft. Do not continue pulling or damage to the cover may occur.*

18   Remove the two fuel injection pump bracket mounting bolts **(see illustration)**.

19   Remove the four fuel injection pump-to-gear housing mounting nuts **(see illustration)**.

20   Remove the pump from the gear housing. **Caution:** *The pump is very heavy - you may require the help of an assistant.* Be careful not to damage the injection pump shaft when removing the fuel injection pump.

21   Clean the injection pump O-ring mounting surfaces on both the gear housing and the fuel injection pump.

Installation

Refer to illustrations 4.24 and 4.40

Caution: *The engine must be positioned on TDC for number one cylinder before the fuel injection pump is installed to maintain proper fuel injection pump timing. Engage the camshaft gear timing pin before proceeding with installation (see Chapter 2B).*

22   In the event the original pump or new pump is not locked in place at TDC with the fuel injection pump timing pin, it will be necessary to rotate the pump shaft until the timing tooth is visible in the plug open-

4B

4.18 Remove the two fuel injection pump bracket mounting bolts (arrows)

4.19 Remove the four fuel injection pump mounting nuts (arrows) - two of the nuts are not visible in this photo

ing **(see illustration 4.15e)**. Install the slotted end of the timing pin tool over the timing tooth and lock it into place. Do not force the slots in the tool over the timing tooth. **Note:** *New or rebuilt pumps should have the pin locked in place. Be sure to verify this before proceeding with the installation.*

23 Check the condition of the rubber O-ring at the fuel injection pump mounting area. If the seal is worn or damaged, replace it with a new part.

24 Apply clean engine oil to the injection pump mounting flange opening in the gear cover housing to allow easier fuel injection pump installation **(see illustration)**. **Note:** *Make sure that there is no oil residue on the fuel injection pump shaft or camshaft gear. This is crucial when obtaining the correct camshaft-to-injection pump torque specifications.*

25 Install the fuel injection pump onto the mounting flange while inserting the pump shaft through the gear.

26 Install the four pump mounting nuts finger tight. Do not attempt to "pull-in" the pump by tightening the mounting nuts. This will damage the gear and shaft assembly. Make sure the pump is seated onto the gear housing before the nuts are tightened.

27 Install the two vertical fuel injection pump mounting bracket bolts.

28 Tighten the four pump mounting nuts to 18 ft-lbs, then tighten the bracket bolts.

29 Install the injection pump drive shaft washer and nut and tighten the nut in two stages. First, tighten it to approximately 7 to 11 ft-lbs. This will keep it from moving while you remove the timing pins.

30 Disengage the camshaft gear timing pin from the camshaft gear.

31 Unscrew the access plug on the side of the pump and remove the injection pump tooth alignment pin.

32 Tighten the injection pump drive shaft nut to the final torque. Use the barring tool (see Chapter 2B, Section 3) to hold the engine while tightening the pump shaft nut to 144 ft-lbs.

33 Retighten the fuel injection pump mounting nuts to 18 ft-lbs.

34 Verify that the fuel injection pump is timed correctly as follows:

Step 1) Rotate the engine clockwise (as viewed from the front of the engine compartment) with the barring tool. Continue rotating the engine until the camshaft gear timing pin engages the hole in the camshaft gear. The engine is now at TDC (see Chapter 2B).

Step 2) Remove the access cover and check the position of the fuel injection pump timing tooth. Install the alignment pin to check the position. If the timing pin will not engage the timing tooth, remove the pump gear nut and loosen the pump gear from the pump shaft with the puller. With the gear loose, rotate the injection pump shaft until the timing tooth is centered in the access hole. Remove the timing pins, tighten the fuel injection pump gear and remove the barring tool.

This step is simply to get the pump timing close to the correct setting. The fuel injection pump still must be timed properly in order to insure proper operation of the fuel system. Follow the adjustment procedure beginning with Step 55.

35 Remove the timing pin from the fuel injection pump. Reverse the position of the pin and install it into the pump. The slotted end should be facing OUT. Install the access cover, with the sealing washer, and tighten it to 11 ft-lbs.

36 Install the engine oil supply line and fuel return line/overflow valve to the fuel injection pump.

37 Install the six high-pressure fuel lines to the top of the fuel injection pump. Tighten the line fittings to 22 ft-lbs.

38 Install the low-pressure fuel supply line to the fuel injection pump.

39 Install the wastegate line to the turbocharger and AFC sensing line to the fuel injection pump.

40 Pre-lubricate the fuel injection pump before operation. All new and rebuilt units must be lubricated to ensure safe operation initially. Failure to lubricate the pump may result in premature governor wear. Remove the 10 mm hex fill plug on the top of the fuel injection pump governor **(see illustration)**. Add 25 ounces of clean engine oil through this opening. Install the oil fill plug and tighten it to 21 ft-lbs.

41 Connect the throttle linkage to the fuel injection pump.

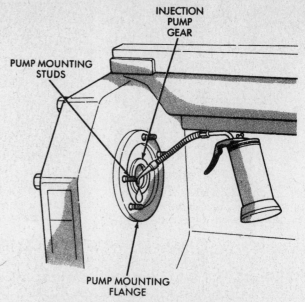

4.24 Apply a light film of oil to the gear cover

42 Connect the electrical connector to the fuel shutdown solenoid.

43 Connect the main engine wiring harness to the top of the fuel injection pump.

44 Install the engine oil dipstick tube mounting clamp at the opening to the intake manifold.

45 Install the oil fill tube and tube adapter.

46 Install the oil fill tube bracket and mounting bolt.

47 Plug in the TPS electrical connector.

48 Install the air cleaner housing-to-turbocharger tube at the air cleaner housing.

49 Install the intake manifold air heater assembly (see Section 8). Be sure to use a new gasket.

50 Install the intake manifold intercooler tube.

51 Check and adjust throttle linkage.

52 Bleed the air from the fuel injection pump and system (refer to Chapter 1).

53 Adjust the low idle speed if necessary (refer to Section 9).

54 Be sure to check the engine oil level (see Chapter 1).

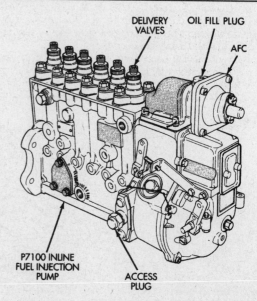

4.40 Location of the oil fill plug on top of the injection pump

4.56 Remove the number one cylinder high-pressure line from the pump

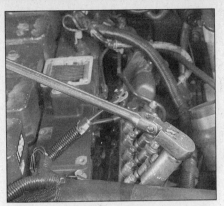

4.57 Use a special socket to loosen the delivery valve holder

4.58 Remove the delivery valve holder, spring, fill piece and shims

4.59 Use a magnet to lift out the two-piece delivery valve assembly

Timing adjustment

Refer to illustrations 4.56, 4.57, 4.58, 4.59, 4.60, 4.62, 4.63, 4.64a, 4.64b, 4.67 and 4.84

Note: *It is necessary to check the fuel injection pump timing when the original pump is removed or a rebuilt pump is installed in place of the original. The following procedure is difficult, requires special tools; and must be set exactly to the manufacturer's specifications. It is recommended that the pump timing be performed by a dealer service department or other qualified diesel technician.*

55   Locate the camshaft gear timing pin and position the engine on TDC for cylinder number 1 by following the procedure in Chapter 2B, Section 3. **Note:** *After locating TDC for number one cylinder, remove*

the timing pin to prevent accidental shearing of the pin. Apply a paint mark on the front pulley to indicate the position of TDC **(see illustration 4.14)**. It is a good idea to remove the star-shaped clip on the locating tool to allow free movement through the housing into the camshaft gear. This will give the hand an easy touch when the hole approaches the tip of the locating pin, allowing the pin to drop easily into place.

56   Remove the number 1 cylinder high-pressure line from the fuel injection pump **(see illustration)**.

57   Loosen (but don't remove) the delivery valve holder using a special socket (Chrysler tool no. 6804 or equivalent) **(see illustration)**. There is an external O-ring on the holder to help prevent debris from dropping down into the fuel injection pump.

58   Remove the delivery valve holder by carefully tipping the holder outward with one hand while using the other hand to hold the spring, fill piece and shims from falling out of the holder **(see illustration)**. Carefully place these parts as an assembly onto a clean work area.

59   If equipped, use a magnet and remove the two-piece delivery valve assembly from the pump **(see illustration)**.

60   Using a pick, remove the copper delivery valve washer from the top of the pumping element **(see illustration)**. Be careful not to scratch the top of the plunger (barrel assembly) during this process. Discard the used delivery valve washer. A new washer will be used for reassembly.

61   Install the dial indicator adapter (Chrysler tool no. 6842 or equivalent) in place of the number 1 delivery valve holder and tighten the set screw lightly.

62   Install the dial indicator and tip (Chrysler tool no. 6859 and 6843 or equivalent) into the adapter. Loosen the set screw, position the dial indicator to read between 7.0 and 9.0 mm and tighten the set screw **(see illustration)**. **Note:** *The dial indicator is capable of measuring from*

4B

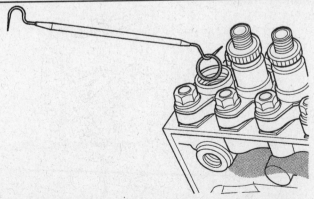

4.60 If equipped, remove the copper delivery valve washer

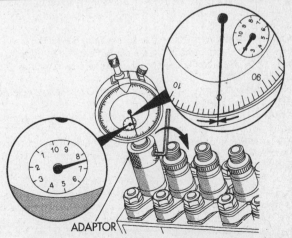

4.62 Set the dial indicator between 7 and 9 mm and tighten the set screw

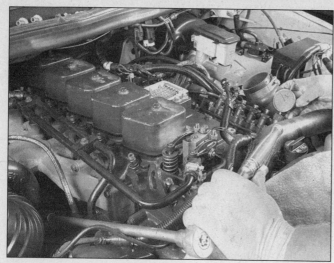

4.63 Observe the paint mark as the engine is rotated counterclockwise (as viewed from the front) then zero the dial indicator on the bottom of its stroke

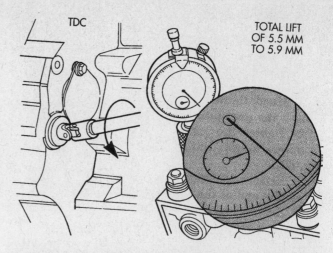

4.64a Count the complete rotations of the dial (first digit) then the decimal reading (second and third digit) as the plunger reaches the top of its travel

0 to 20.00 mm lift. The small inner dial is marked in increments of 1 mm. The large outer dial is marked in increments of 0.01mm. One revolution of the outer dial is equal to 1 mm. The inner dial indicates 0 to 10 mm but will rotate twice as the indicator goes through the full range.

63   Using the engine barring tool, rotate the engine opposite of normal engine rotation (counterclockwise as viewed from the front) until you see the dial indicator reading stop dropping **(see illustration)**. This is the inner base circle (bottom travel) of the fuel injection pump cam. Zero the dial indicator and note the reading on the small inner dial. This action will drop the plunger to the lowest point of travel within the fuel injection pump. **Note:** *Do not be confused by the direction of rotation. Follow the directions carefully, rotating the front pulley in the correct direction by turning the barring tool opposite to the direction specified.*

64   Rotate the engine slowly clockwise, until the paint marks you made on the pulley align (TDC). Note the fuel injection pump lift setting on the dial indicator **(see illustration)**. This will give the total travel of the plunger from top to bottom. Locate the engine data plate on the left side of the timing gear cover **(see illustration)**. Record the "Timing - TDC" specification listed in degrees. Compare these specifications to the chart for your specific model. Use the CPL number stamped onto the engine plate to cross-reference the pump plunger lift specification.

49 STATE MODELS
CPL 1549, 1550, 1815, 1816, 1959

Static timing (degrees BTDC)	Plunger lift (mm) at TDC
11.5	5.5
12.0	5.6
12.5	5.7
13.0	5.8
13.5	5.9

49 STATE, AUTOMATIC TRANSMISSION
CPL 2022

Static timing (degrees BTDC)	Plunger lift (mm) at TDC
12.0	4.1
12.5	4.2
13.0	4.3
13.5	4.4
14.0	4.5

49 STATE, MANUAL TRANSMISSION
CPL 2023

Static timing (degrees BTDC)	Plunger lift (mm) at TDC
11.5	4.7
12.0	4.8
12.5	4.9
13.0	5.0
13.5	5.1

CALIFORNIA, AUTOMATIC TRANSMISSION, FROM JANUARY 1995
CPL 1968

Static timing (degrees BTDC)	Plunger lift (mm) at TDC
12.5	4.20
13.0	4.28
13.5	4.36
14.0	4.44
14.5	4.52

CALIFORNIA with EGR system
CPL 1863

Static timing (degrees BTDC)	Plunger lift (mm) at TDC
11.5	4.0
12.0	4.1
12.5	4.2
13.0	4.3
13.5	4.4

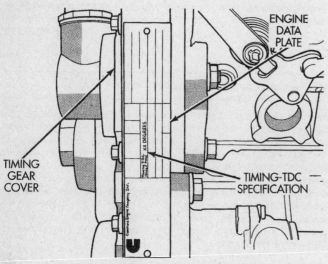

4.64b Location of the engine data plate

4.67 Remove the nut from the fuel injection pump gear

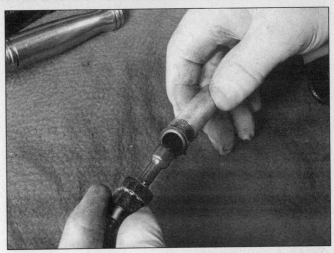

4.84 Use a small pipe to install the retaining clip over the locating pin after it is installed in the housing

65   If the specifications do not match, it will be necessary to adjust the pump timing. The fuel injection pump must be released from the gear and adjusted until the exact lift measurement is attained as follows:

66   Remove the oil filler tube and adapter elbow from the front of the gear housing **(see illustration 4.13)**.

67   Loosen the fuel injection pump gear nut **(see illustration)** and using a magnet, remove the nut and washers. Use the barring tool and a breaker bar to prevent the engine from rotating when loosening the nut. **Caution:** *Be very careful not to drop the nut and washer into the gear housing.*

68   Chrysler recommends using a special washer and bearing kit to prevent from losing the timing setting. It is possible to time the pump without them but it will require a steady hand to prevent the pump from rotating when the gear is loosened. The barring tool, extension and breaker bar must be held firmly when loosening or tightening the gear nut. If the home mechanic chooses to use this procedure, using a magnet, install the special bearing and thrust washer kit (Chrysler tool no. 6862 or equivalent) onto the shaft. Position the parts in this order:

a) *thrust washer*
b) *bearing*
c) *thrust washer*

Do not tighten the nut at this time

69   Slowly rotate the engine clockwise until reaching the required lift setting on the dial indicator. **Note:** *The injection pump shaft should rotate with the engine since the injection pump gear is still locked to the fuel injection pump shaft.*

70   With the fuel injection pump at the correct plunger lift setting, use a gear puller (Chrysler tool no. L-4407A or equivalent) to pull the injection pump gear off the taper of the fuel injection pump input shaft **(see illustration 4.17)**. With the gear loose, double-check to make sure that the lift setting has not changed. Leave the gear puller installed.

71   Rotate the engine 20 to 30-degrees counterclockwise, then clockwise back to TDC (paint mark). This will remove any backlash from the gears. The setting on the dial indicator should not move at this time because the pump shaft has been disconnected from the gear.

72   Loosen but do not remove the gear puller bolts. Using the gear puller, rotate the pump gear (by hand) counterclockwise while pushing the gear onto the shaft. This will remove backlash between the injection pump and the camshaft gears.

73   Install the pump gear nut and washer.

74   Hand-tighten the pump gear nut and remove the gear puller.

75   Tighten the pump gear nut to 11 ft-lbs to seat the gear to the pump shaft taper.

76   If the special washers and bearing tools were used, remove them from the pump shaft using a magnet on the end of the shaft to prevent

the parts from dropping down into the gear housing.

77   Prevent the engine from turning using the barring tool and torque the fuel injection pump gear nut to 144 ft-lbs.

78   Repeat Steps 63 and 64 to verify the final timing adjustment. If the Specifications are not correct, repeat the timing adjustment procedure.

79   Remove the dial indicator and adapter from the fuel injection pump.

80   If equipped, install a new copper delivery valve washer onto the fuel injection pump. Install the delivery valve assembly on top of the sealing washer **(see illustration 4.60)**. **Caution:** *Follow the installation procedure exactly. Incorrect installation and tightening of the delivery valve will result in damage and fuel leaks.*

81   Lubricate the threads and clamping surface of the delivery valve holder using a few drops of the SAE 90 hypoid gear oil. Install the delivery valve holder assembly taking care not to displace the delivery valve spring, fill piece or any shims.

82   Pre-tighten the delivery valve holder to 29 ft-lbs. Using a single motion, tighten the holder to 85 ft-lbs.

83   Install the other engine components removed during the adjustment procedure. Leave the number 1 injector line loose to facilitate bleeding the air out of the system. Refer to Section 3 for the correct high-pressure bleeding procedure.

84   The remainder of installation is the reverse of removal. **Note:** *An easy way to install the star-shaped clip back onto the TDC locating pin is to use a small diameter pipe* **(see illustration)**. *Install the pin into the housing, place the clip on the end of the pin and slide it over the handle into the housing. The clip will snap once its in place. This clip retains the pin inside the housing, preventing it from falling out when the engine is running.*

---

5   Fuel injectors - check and replacement

Warning: *Diesel fuel is flammable, so take extra precautions when you work on any part of the fuel system. Don't smoke or allow open flames or bare light bulbs near the work area, and don't work in a garage where a natural gas-type appliance (such as a water heater or a clothes dryer) with a pilot light is present. Since diesel fuel is carcinogenic, wear latex gloves when there's a possibility of being exposed to fuel, and, if you spill any fuel on your skin, rinse it off immediately with soap and water. Mop up any spills immediately and do not store diesel fuel-soaked rags where they could ignite. When you perform any kind of work on the fuel system, wear safety glasses and have a Class B type fire extinguisher on hand.*

Check

1   A leaking fuel injector could cause several symptoms depending

4B

5.4a Remove the fuel drain manifold fitting from each injector and from the top fitting on the fuel filter/water separator

5.4b Lift the fuel drain manifold from the engine

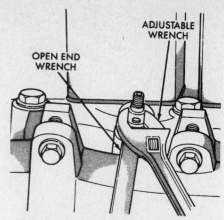

5.7a Use two wrenches to remove early style injectors

on the severity of the leak. Fuel knock, poor acceleration and performance, low fuel economy and rough engine idle can be caused by pintle leaks. Defective needle valve operation may cause engine misfire. **Note:** *A leak in the high-pressure fuel line(s) can cause many of the same problems and symptoms. Check for fuel line leaks before proceeding (see Section 3).* The injector opening or "pop-off" pressure is approximately 3,820 psi. Any checks on diesel fuel injectors should be performed by the dealer service department or other qualified diesel repair facility. Injectors require special adapters and special high-pressure testing equipment for accurate results.

Removal

Refer to illustrations 5.4a, 5.4b, 5.7a, 5.7b and 5.8

2   Disconnect the negative battery cable from each battery.
3   Remove the high-pressure fuel lines from the fuel injection pump (see Section 3). **Warning:** *Allow the engine to rest for approximately three minutes before disconnecting the high-pressure fuel lines. The extremely high fuel pressure in the lines may cause skin damage and leak excess amounts of fuel over the engine area. Fuel pressure will dissipate after a three minute period. The pressure in the high-pressure fuel lines can reach up to 17,400 psi, therefore, use extreme caution when inspecting for fuel leaks. Do not move your hand near a suspect leak - instead, use a piece of cardboard. high-pressure fuel leaks can injure your skin upon contact.*
4   Remove the fuel drain manifold **(see illustrations)**.
5   Clean the area around the injector. Make sure there is no grease, oil or rust around the injector hold-down nut. **Note:** *It is a good idea to spray penetrating lubricant around the hold-down nuts at the top of the injector to loosen the rust from the threads.*

6   Strike the injector using a brass drift to break the rust loose, if necessary.
7   Remove the injector **(see illustrations)**.
8   If the injector is difficult to remove, use a special injector puller (Cummins tool no. 3823276 or equivalent) **(see illustration)**.

Installation

Refer to illustrations 5.9, 5.10a, 5.10b, 5.11 and 5.12

9   Clean the cylinder head bore for each injector with a wire brush that is capable of reaching the injector threads **(see illustration)**.
10   Install a new copper washer onto the tip of the injector. **Note:** *Chrysler requires that the injector washer be a specified thickness. The thickness varies, depending upon the diameter of the injector tip* **(see illustration)**, *CPL number and part number stamped onto the injector body. If an original washer is available, measure the thickness and replace it with one of the same* **(see illustration)**. *If the old washer is not available, consult a dealer parts department for the necessary information.*
11   Apply a coating of anti-seize to the threads of the injector hold-down nut and between the top of the nut and injector body **(see illustration)**.
12   Install the injector into the cylinder head. Align the tab on the injector body with the notch in the cylinder bore **(see illustration)**. **Note:** *Install the O-ring onto the injector if equipped.*
13   Tighten the injector hold-down nut to 44 ft-lbs.
14   Connect the fuel drain manifold to the injectors.
15   Connect the high-pressure fuel lines and bleed the system (see Section 3).
16   Connect the negative battery cable to each battery.

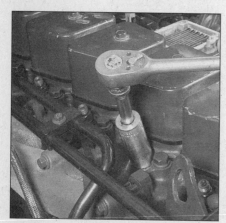

5.7b Use a deep socket to remove the later style injectors

5.8 Use a special slide hammer to remove the fuel injectors

5.9 Clean the injector bore and threads with a small wire brush

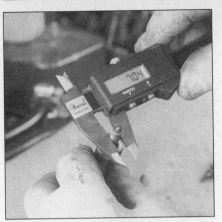

5.10a Measure the diameter of the injector tip to determine correct washer size . . .

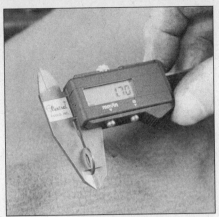

5.10b . . . or measure the thickness of an original copper washer

5.11 Apply a small amount of anti-seize compound to the threads of the injector

6 Fuel heater - check and replacement

Check

Refer to illustrations 6.5, 6.7 and 6.8

1   The fuel heater is used to prevent diesel fuel from waxing during cold weather operation. The fuel heater is located on the left side of the engine block above the starter **(see illustration 1.4a)**. A fuel heater system problem can cause wax build-up in the fuel filter/water separator. This clogging effect causes hard starting and engine revving problems. This condition can also cause blue or white fog-like exhaust.

2   The heater assembly consists of a built in thermosensor that detects the fuel temperature. When the temperature is below 40-degrees F, the built-in sensor allows current to flow to the heater element during the warming period. The thermosensor shuts off the flow of current when the fuel temperature reaches 80-degrees F.

3   Voltage to operate the fuel heater is supplied from the ignition switch and through the fuel heater relay. The fuel heater relay is located near the brake master cylinder. The fuel heater relay, sensor and fuel heater are not controlled by the PCM.

4   The fuel heater assembly is equipped with a pre-filter to prevent contaminants from entering the fuel system.

5   Disconnect the fuel heater electrical connector and, using an ohmmeter, check the resistance across the two terminals at the fuel heater **(see illustration)**. Resistance should be approximately 1 ohm cold (40-degrees F) to 1,000 ohms warm (80-degrees F).

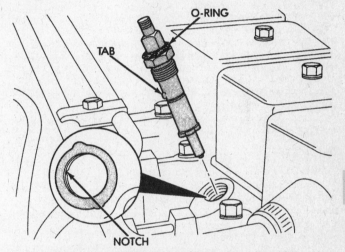

O-RING
TAB
NOTCH

5.12 Align the tab on the injector with the notch in the injector bore

6   Working on the fuel temperature sensor side of the same electrical connector, check the fuel temperature sensor for continuity. The sensor circuit should be open (no current) when the fuel temperature is above 40-degrees F and closed if the fuel temperature is below 40-degrees F.

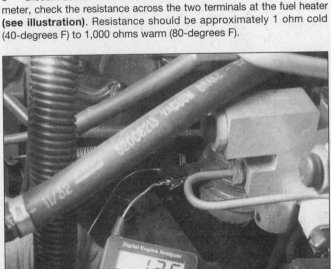

6.5 Measure the resistance of the fuel heater

6.6 Check for battery voltage at the fuel heater electrical connector

4B

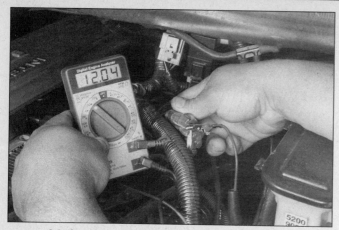

6.8 Check the fuel heater relay for battery voltage

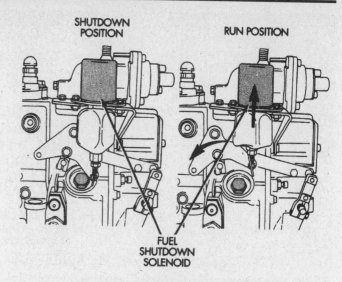

7.3 Fuel solenoid shutdown positions

7   Working on the relay side of the electrical connector, check for 12 volts with the ignition key ON (engine not running) **(see illustration)**. There should be battery voltage available.

8   With the ignition key ON (engine not running), check for battery voltage to the fuel heater relay **(see illustration)**. If battery voltage exists, check the condition of the relay (see Chapter 4A, Section 3).

Replacement

9   Disconnect the negative battery cable.

10   Remove the electrical connector from the fuel heater relay.

11   Remove the mounting bolts and separate the fuel heater from the engine block.

12   Installation is the reverse of removal.

7   Fuel shutdown solenoid - check and replacement

Warning: *Diesel fuel is flammable, so take extra precautions when you work on any part of the fuel system. Don't smoke or allow open flames or bare light bulbs near the work area, and don't work in a garage where a natural gas-type appliance (such as a water heater or a clothes dryer) with a pilot light is present. Since diesel fuel is carcinogenic, wear latex gloves when there's a possibility of being exposed to fuel, and, if you spill any fuel on your skin, rinse it off immediately with soap and water. Mop up any spills immediately and do not store diesel fuel-soaked rags where they could ignite. When you perform any kind of work on the fuel system, wear safety glasses and have a Class B type fire extinguisher on hand.*

Check

Refer to illustrations 7.3, 7.5 and 7.6

1   The fuel shutdown solenoid is used to electrically shut off the flow of diesel fuel to the high pressure fuel injection pump. It is mounted on the side of the fuel injection pump and is connected to the pump with a lever **(see illustration 1.4a)**. The fuel shutdown solenoid and relay are not controlled by the PCM. The solenoid controls the stopping and starting of the engine regardless of the position of the accelerator pedal. With the ignition key in the OFF position, the solenoid plunger is spring loaded in the down position. When the ignition is turned to START (engine cranking), current is supplied to the shutdown solenoid through the fuel shutdown solenoid relay. This high-amperage current supply allows the solenoid shaft to pull-up on the injection pump lever. When the ignition key is released back in the ON position (engine running), low-amperage current is supplied to the other coil in the solenoid, thereby holding the solenoid shaft in the UP position. Voltage to the fuel shutdown solenoid relay is supplied from the ignition key.

2   Turn the ignition key OFF and confirm that the solenoid shaft is down and the injection pump lever is in the down or SHUT DOWN position.

3   Turn the ignition switch to the START (engine cranking) position and see if the solenoid shaft and injection pump lever move to the RUN position **(see illustration)**.

4   Release the ignition key to ON (engine running position) and see if the pump lever is in the RUN position.

5   If the pump lever does not move or partially moves, disconnect the three-wire electrical connector to the fuel shutdown solenoid and check for battery voltage with an assistant cranking the engine **(see illustration)**.

6   If no voltage is present, check the fuel shutdown solenoid relay. Backprobe the relay electrical connector and with the ignition key ON (engine not running), battery voltage should exist **(see illustration)**.

7   If voltage is present to the relay, check the relay itself for correct operation. Refer to the relay checks in Chapter 4A, Section 3).

8   If voltage is present, check for battery voltage at the three-wire electrical connector when the ignition key is in the ON (engine running position). Refer to the wiring diagrams at the end of Chapter 12 for a circuit schematic. **Note:** *In the event that the fuel shutdown solenoid is defective, it will be necessary to adjust the shaft (see Steps 9 through 17).*

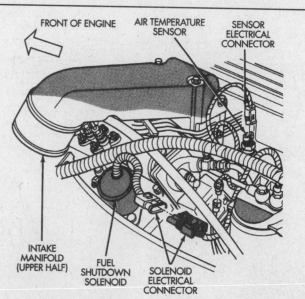

7.5 Disconnect the fuel shutdown solenoid electrical connector

7.6 Check for battery voltage at the fuel shutdown solenoid relay

Solenoid replacement and shaft adjustment

Refer to illustrations 7.16 and 7.17

9   Disconnect the negative battery cables from both batteries
10   Disconnect the solenoid electrical connector.
11   Disconnect the clip at the injection pump shutdown lever.
12   Remove the fuel shutdown solenoid mounting bolts and remove the solenoid from the fuel injection pump.
13   Installation is the reverse of removal. Check and adjust the length of the shaft on the solenoid.
14   Turn the ignition key ON (engine not running).
15   Pull up on the lever using your hand and hold the solenoid lever in place. If the shutdown solenoid is working properly, the lever should remain in the UP position.
16   Measure from the bottom of the solenoid bracket to the top of the injection pump shutdown lever pin. **(see illustration)**. It should be 2.64 (2-41/64) inches.
17   If necessary, loosen the shaft locknut and rotate the adjuster to the correct length **(see illustration)**. Tighten the adjustment nut.

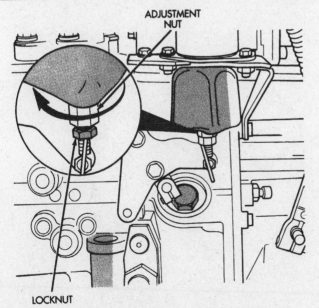

7.17 Loosen the locknut and turn the adjustment nut

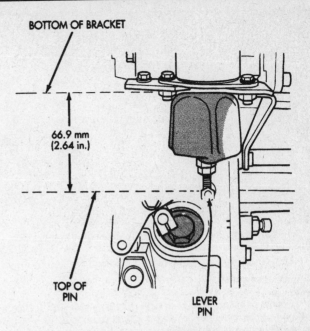

7.16 Measure the distance from the top of the lever pin to the bottom of the bracket

8   Intake manifold heater - check and replacement

Check

Refer to illustrations 8.6a and 8.6b

1   The intake manifold air heater takes the place of the glow plug systems installed on many other diesel engines. This system consists of two heaters mounted inside the intake manifold controlled by two separate relays. Depending upon the condition of the engine, the relays may be energized by the PCM before and after cranking the engine. The heaters provide heated air to the combustion chambers to enhance cold starting.
2   The PCM operates the two heating elements within the air heater assembly through the two intake manifold air heater relays. The air heater relays and the air heater elements may be activated for a maximum time of 3-1/2 minutes. Chrysler suggests in the owner's manual that for quick starting in cold weather, the ignition key be kept in the ON position for approximately 10 to 30 seconds before cranking to allow sufficient warming time. Consult the owner's manual for the temperatures and time tables. Make sure the "Wait-to-Start" light on the dash has canceled before starting the engine.
3   The Post Heat Cycle is the time allowed by the PCM to continue heating the air in the intake manifold after the engine has started. The air temperature in the intake manifold must be below 59-degrees F and the engine speed above 475 rpm for the PCM to allow continued air heating. Depending on how cold the air is, one or both of the relays may be activated. This condition can be observed on the voltmeter on the dash as the high amperage draw from the heating elements causes the voltmeter needle to deflect. This voltmeter movement is a normal function of the heating process.
4   The PCM also contains a shut-off device that will discontinue power to the air heating elements if the engine stalls, if the starter is engaged during the pre-heat cycle, if the starter is operated for more than 10 seconds or if the vehicle speed exceeds 10 mph during the Post Heat Cycle.
5   The preheat cycle can be tested with a voltmeter or test light. If the intake manifold temperature is below 59-degrees F, turn the ignition key to ON (engine not running), observe the "Wait-to-Start" light on the dash and listen for the air heater relays to click ON. **Note:** *If the starter is engaged before the light goes out, the PCM will automatically stop the remaining preheat cycle.*

4B

8.6a Check for battery voltage to the heater relays (arrow)

INTAKE MANIFOLD TEMPERATURE- KEY ON POSITION	PRE-HEAT CYCLE TIME- IGNITION ON, ENGINE NOT RUNNING	POST-HEAT CYCLE - IGNITION ON, ENGINE RUNNING
Above 15° C (59° F)	0 seconds	No
-10° C to 15° C (15° F to 59° F)	10 seconds	Yes
-18° C to -10° F (0° F to 15° F)	15 seconds	Yes
Below -18° C (0° F)	30 seconds	Yes

8.6b The air heater cycling time varies with the temperature of the intake manifold air

6   Check for battery voltage at both relay terminals. The heaters will only be energized for approximately 10 to 30 seconds depending upon the conditions **(see illustrations)**.

Air heater check

Refer to illustrations 8.7 and 8.11

7   Disconnect both negative battery cables. Lift the rubber shields from each of the cable connectors at the intake manifold air heater to expose the cable terminals **(see illustration)**. DO NOT disconnect the cable nuts.
8   Using an ohmmeter, check the resistance of the cable terminals to ground. It should be zero. **Note:** *Check the resistance to ground on the studs also. The readings should be slightly higher but not excessive otherwise corrosion exists on the threads or in the stud-to-ground connection.*
9   If the resistance is more than zero, check for corroded or dirty cable connections and retest before replacing the heater. Also, check both ends of the ground cable at the rear of the heater. It should be zero also.
10   Disconnect both ends of the heater cables and measure the resistance of the heater terminal studs to ground. The resistance should be zero. If all the readings are incorrect, replace the air intake heater with a new part.
11   Check for battery voltage to the heater with the ignition key ON (engine not running) **(see illustration)**. Remember, the voltage reading will only be present for a few seconds.

Air temperature sensor check

12   Refer to Chapter 6, Section 6 for the check and replacement procedures for the air temperature sensor.

Air heater relay test

Refer to illustration 8.14

13   Disconnect the negative battery cable from both batteries.
14   Disconnect the four small relay trigger wires at both relays **(see illustration)**.
15   Disconnect the four large cable terminals on the relay and separate the cables.
16   Attach an ohmmeter across two of the large studs on one of the relays.
17   Attach a jumper wire to the small terminals on the relay (positive and negative). The polarity of the jumper wires is not important.
18   Use the jumper wires to touch the battery positive and negative terminals and listen for a clicking sound from the relay. Also, the ohmmeter should indicate a closed circuit. Test one relay at a time.
19   If the test results are incorrect, replace the relays.

Replacement

Air heater

Refer to illustration 8.22

20   Disconnect the cables from both negative battery terminals.
21   Remove the engine oil dipstick assembly (see Chapter 2B).
22   Remove the two cable nuts at the air heater **(see illustration)**.

8.7 Check the resistance of the ground circuit at the cable nuts

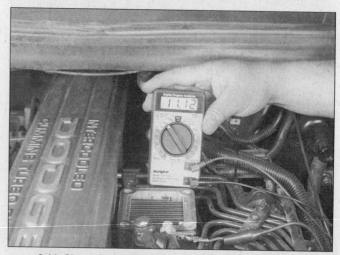

8.11 Check for battery voltage to the air intake heater

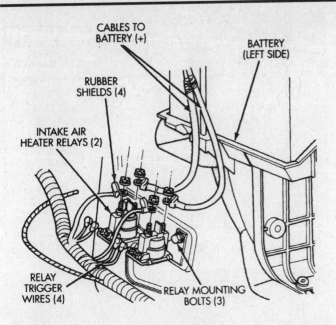

8.14 Remove the trigger wires and the large wires from the relays

23   Remove the intake manifold-to-intercooler air duct assembly **(see illustration 4.5)**.
24   Remove the air heater from the intake manifold.
25   Installation is the reverse of removal. Be sure to use new gaskets on the lower and upper side of the air intake heater.

Relays

26   Disconnect both negative battery terminals.
27   Disconnect the wires from the relay.
28   Unscrew the bolt and remove the relay.
29   Installation is the reverse of removal.

---

9   Idle speed - check and adjustment

Note: *The high idle speed screw is factory sealed and cannot be adjusted. The low idle speed screw is adjustable.*

Idle speed

Refer to illustrations 9.2a and 9.2b

1   Connect a tachometer (Snap-On tool no. MT139, Cummins tool

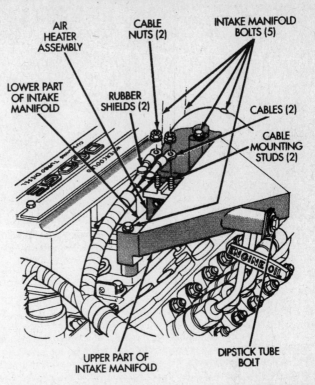

8.22 Remove the cable nuts from the heater cable ends

---

no. MTE 3377462 or equivalent) in accordance with the tool manufacturer's instructions.
2   Bring the engine to normal operating temperature. Adjust the low idle speed screw to obtain the correct idle speed **(see illustrations)**.
3   Tighten the locknut after the correct idle is obtained.

TPS check

4   Refer to Chapter 6 for the TPS check and adjustment procedures.

4B

LOW IDLE SPEED	HIGH IDLE SPEED
With automatic transmission... • 750-800 RPM with transmission in drive and air conditioning on. With manual transmission... • 780 RPM with transmission in neutral and air conditioning on.	Do not attempt to adjust high idle speed. High idle speed adjustment screw is factory sealed. Breaking seal will void injection pump warranty.
• With engine at normal operating temperature. Refer to text for idle adjustment procedures.	

9.2a Idle speed specifications

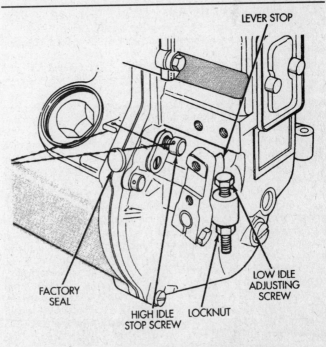

9.2b Low idle speed adjusting screw location

11.11 Apply pressure to the solenoid actuator using a hand-held pressure pump and see if the control rod moves slightly

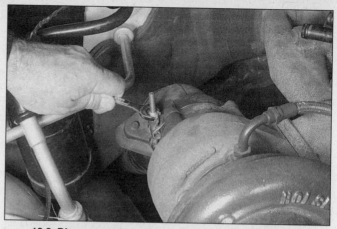

12.3 Disconnect the exhaust downpipe from the flange

10   Turbocharger - general information

The turbocharger increases power by using an exhaust gas-driven turbine to pressurize the air entering the combustion chambers. The amount of boost (intake manifold pressure) is controlled by the wastegate (exhaust bypass valve). The wastegate is operated by a spring-loaded actuator assembly which controls the maximum boost level by allowing some of the exhaust gas to bypass the turbine. The wastegate is controlled by the computer.

All models are equipped with an intercooler. The intercooler reroutes the compressed air intake charge through a series of cooling vents to lower the temperature of the intake charge. The lower air temperature (cooler air is denser) promotes combustion efficiency, increasing power and reducing emissions.

11   Turbocharger - check

Turbocharger check

1   While it is a relatively simple device, the turbocharger is also a precision component which can be severely damaged by an interrupted oil or coolant supply or loose or damaged ducts.
2   Due to the special techniques and equipment required, checking and diagnosis of suspected problems dealing with the turbocharger should be left to a dealer service department. The home mechanic can, however, check the connections and linkages for security, damage and other obvious problems. Also, the home mechanic can check components that govern the turbocharger such as the wastegate solenoid, bypass valve and wastegate actuator. Refer to the checks later in this section.
3   Because each turbocharger has its own distinctive sound, a change in the noise level can be a sign of potential problems.
4   A high-pitched or whistling sound is a symptom of an inlet air or exhaust gas leak.
5   If an unusual sound comes from the vicinity of the turbine, the turbocharger can be removed and the turbine wheel inspected. **Caution:** *All checks must be made with the engine off and cool to the touch and the turbocharger stopped or personal injury could result. Operating the engine without all the turbocharger ducts and filters installed is also dangerous and can result in damage to the turbine wheel blades.*
6   With the engine OFF, reach inside the housing and turn the turbine wheel to make sure it spins freely. If it doesn't, it's possible the cooling oil has sludged or coked from overheating. Push in on the turbine wheel and check for binding. The turbine should rotate freely with no binding or rubbing on the housing. If it does the turbine bearing is worn out.
7   Check the exhaust manifold for cracks and loose connections.
8   Because the turbine wheel rotates at speeds up to 140,000 rpm,

12.4 Disconnect the oil supply line from the turbocharger

severe damage can result from the interruption of coolant or contamination of the oil supply to the turbine bearings. Check for leaks in the coolant and oil inlet lines and obstructions in the oil drain-back line, as this can cause severe oil loss through the turbocharger seals. Burned oil on the turbine housing is a sign of this. **Caution:** *Whenever a major engine bearing such as a main, connecting rod or camshaft bearing is replaced, the turbocharger should be flushed with clean oil.*

Wastegate solenoid check

Refer to illustration 11.11

9   The turbocharger wastegate provides additional low speed boost without over-boost at high speeds. This increases low speed torque and better driveability. It is important that the wastegate assembly is properly adjusted. The wastegate actuator (solenoid) is controlled by the pressure signal produced by the release of warm, compressed air from the turbocharger.
10   Remove the pressure hose from the wastegate actuator (solenoid).
11   Connect a hand-held pressure pump to the hose and apply approximately 19.3 psi pressure to the actuator **(see illustration)**.
12   The control rod should move slightly and hold its position.
13   If the test results are incorrect, replace the wastegate solenoid.

12   Turbocharger replacement and wastegate adjustment

Caution: *The turbocharger is a high-speed component, assembled and balanced to very fine tolerances. Do not disassemble it or try to repair it. Turbochargers should only be overhauled or repaired by authorized turbocharger repair shops or damage could result to the turbocharger and/or the engine.*

12.6a Spray a small amount of penetrating oil onto the exhaust nuts before removing them

12.6b Carefully lift the turbocharger from the engine compartment

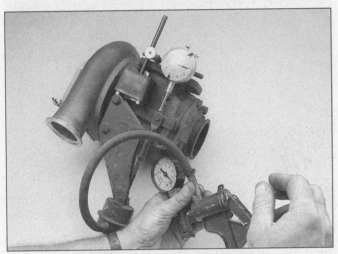

12.12 Apply 15 to 20 psi to actuator

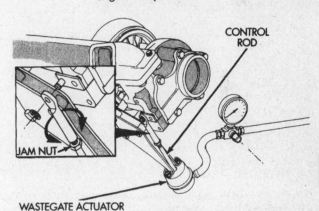

12.15 Loosen the jam nut and turn the clevis to adjust the control rod travel

Removal

Refer to illustrations 12.3, 12.4, 12.6a and 12.6b

1   Disconnect the negative battery cables from both batteries.

2   Disconnect the air intake hose from the turbocharger.

3   Disconnect the exhaust downpipe from the rear of the turbocharger **(see illustration)**.

4   Disconnect the oil supply line and the oil return line **(see illustration)**. The oil return line is bolted to the bottom of the turbocharger. Be ready with a rag to catch any oil from the lines as they are disconnected.

5   Unbolt the clamp and pull off the intercooler duct from the bottom of the compressor.

6   Remove the four nuts holding the turbocharger to the exhaust manifold and remove the turbocharger, being careful not to damage the wastegate actuator rod, line or bracket **(see illustrations)**. Note: *The wastegate actuator is precisely adjusted. Be careful when laying the complete turbocharger unit on the bench, so as not to disturb wastegate actuator alignment.*

Installation

7   Use a die to clean the studs in the turbocharger mounting portion of the exhaust manifold and coat them with anti-seize compound. Bolt the turbocharger onto the exhaust manifold, using a new gasket.

8   Reinstall the oil drain line fitting and line with a new gasket.

9   Prime the center bearing of the turbocharger with oil by squirting some clean engine oil into the oil supply hole on top, while turning the compressor wheel, then install the supply line. **Warning:** *The turbine or compressor wheels have very sharp blades; do not turn the blades with your fingers. Use a plastic pen.*

10   The remainder of installation is the reverse of removal.

Wastegate adjustment

Refer to illustrations 12.12 and 12.15

11   The turbocharger wastegate controls over-boosting and is precisely adjusted at the factory. It need not be readjusted unless it is damaged or the components have been replaced. **Caution:** *Do not adjust the wastegate to increase the operating pressure (boost) or damage to the turbocharger may result.*

12   Install a dial indicator to check the movement of the actuator rod at the turbocharger. Pull the hose from the actuator and apply 15 to 20 psi of air pressure to the actuator **(see illustration)**. This will seat the components.

13   Release the air pressure and zero the dial indicator. Apply 19.3 psi of air pressure to the actuator with a hand pump while watching the dial indicator. The rod should move a total of 0.013 to 0.050 (1/64 to 3/64) inch.

14   If adjustment is necessary, apply air pressure again to allow the rod to remove the pressure from the wastegate lever. Remove the nut and pull the clevis off the lever.

15   Loosen the jam nut and turn the clevis either in or out as necessary **(see illustration)**, then replace the clevis on the lever. Try the test again to check the actuator rod travel (refer to Steps 12 and 13).

16   Once the adjustment is correct, tighten the jam nut on the clevis.

13.6a Remove the clamps and lift the wiring harness from the radiator support

13.6b Remove the bolts that retain the radiator support to the fender

13 Intercooler - removal and installation

Refer to illustrations 13.6a, 13.6b and 13.7

1   All diesel models covered by this manual are equipped with an intercooler.
2   Raise the vehicle and support it securely with jackstands.
3   If the engine is equipped with air conditioning, remove the condenser (see Chapter 3).
4   Remove the front bumper (see Chapter 11).
5   Loosen the hose clamps, then disconnect the air hoses from the intercooler.
6   Remove the wiring harness and the radiator support **(see illustrations)**.
7   Remove the mounting bolts **(see illustration)**, lift the bottom of the intercooler from the rubber mounts and pull the intercooler straight out from the engine compartment.
8   Inspect the intercooler for cracks and damage to the flanges, tubes and fins. Replace it or have it repaired if necessary.
9   Installation is the reverse of removal.

14 Accelerator cable - replacement

Refer to illustrations 14.1

1   Use a screwdriver to pry the cable end off of the throttle lever **(see illustration)**.

13.7 Remove the intercooler nuts

2   Separate the accelerator cable casing from its bracket by lubricating both sides of the grommet and working the grommet through the bracket with a screwdriver **(see illustration)**.
3   Working underneath the dash, detach the cable from the accelerator pedal **(see illustration 10.4 in Chapter 4, Part A)**.
4   Pinch the tabs on the cable housing retainer and push the cable through the firewall and into the engine compartment.
5   Installation is the reverse of removal.

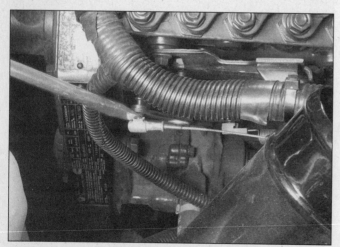

14.1 Use a blunt screwdriver to . . .

14.2 . . . hold the cable nut while turning

Chapter 5
Engine electrical systems

Contents

Specifications

Ignition system

Coil
  V6 and V8 engines
    Diamond

Primary resistance	0.97 to 1.18 ohms
Secondary resistance	11,300 to 15,300 ohms

    Toyodenso

Primary resistance	0.95 to 1.20 ohms
Secondary resistance	11,300 to 13,300 ohms

  V10 engine

Primary resistance	0.53 to 0.65 ohms
Secondary resistance	10,900 to 14,700 ohms

1   General information

The engine electrical systems include all ignition, charging and starting components. Because of their engine-related functions, these components are discussed separately from chassis electrical devices such as the lights, the instruments, etc. (which are included in Chapter 12).

Always observe the following precautions when working on the electrical systems:

a) *Be extremely careful, when servicing engine electrical components. They are easily damaged if checked. connected or handled improperly.*

b) *Never leave the ignition switch on for long periods of time with the engine off.*

c) *Don't disconnect the battery cables while the engine is running.*

d) *Maintain correct polarity when connecting a battery cable from another vehicle during jump starting.*

e) *Always disconnect the negative cable first and hook it up last or the battery may be shorted by the tool being used to loosen the cable clamps.*

It's also a good idea to review the safety-related information regarding the engine electrical systems located in the *Safety First* section near the front of this manual before beginning any operation included in this Chapter.

2   Battery - emergency jump starting

Refer to the *Booster battery (jump) starting* procedure at the front of this manual.

3   Battery cables - check and replacement

1   Periodically inspect the entire length of each battery cable for damage, cracked or burned insulation and corrosion. Poor battery cable connections can cause starting problems and decreased engine performance.

2   Check the cable-to-terminal connections at the ends of the cables for cracks, loose wire strands and corrosion. The presence of white, fluffy deposits under the insulation at the cable terminal connection is a sign that the cable is corroded and should be replaced. Check the terminals for distortion, missing mounting bolts and corrosion.

3   When removing the cables, always disconnect the negative cable first and hook it up last or the battery may be shorted by the tool used to loosen the cable clamps. Even if only the positive cable is being replaced, be sure to disconnect the negative cable from the battery first (see Chapter 1 for further information regarding battery cable removal).

4   Disconnect the old cables from the battery, then trace each of them to their opposite ends and detach them from the starter solenoid and ground terminals. Note the routing of each cable to ensure correct installation.

5   If you are replacing either or both of the old cables, take them with you when buying new cables. It is vitally important that you replace the cables with identical parts. Cables have characteristics that make them easy to identify: positive cables are usually red and larger in cross-section; ground cables are usually black and smaller in cross-section.

6   Clean the threads of the solenoid or ground connection with a wire brush to remove rust and corrosion. Apply a light coat of battery terminal corrosion inhibitor or petroleum jelly to the threads to prevent future corrosion.

7   Attach the cable to the solenoid or ground connection and tighten the mounting nut/bolt securely.

8   Before connecting a new cable to the battery, make sure that it reaches the battery post without having to be stretched.

9   Connect the positive cable first, followed by the negative cable.

4   Battery - removal and Installation

Refer to illustrations 4.2, 4.4a and 4.4b

Note: *If the vehicle will be stored (no starting) for more than 20 days, it will be necessary to remove the IOD fuse in the Power Distribution Center to avoid excessive battery discharging.*

1   Disconnect both cables from the battery terminals. **Caution:** *Always disconnect the negative cable first and hook it up last or the battery may be shorted by the tool being used to loosen the cable clamps.*

2   Remove the battery hold-down clamp **(see Illustration)**.

3   Lift out the battery. Be careful - it's heavy. **Note:** *Battery straps and*

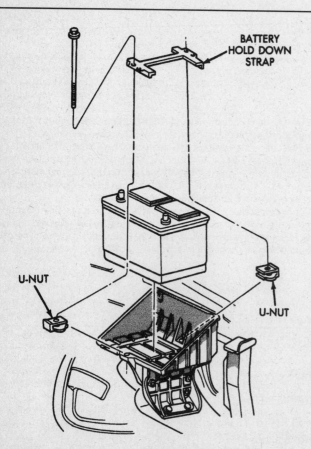

4.2   **Remove the bolts and detach the hold-down clamp from the battery tray**

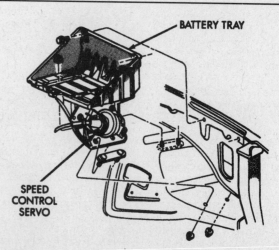

4.4a   **Battery tray and hold-down assembly (gasoline engine with speed control)**

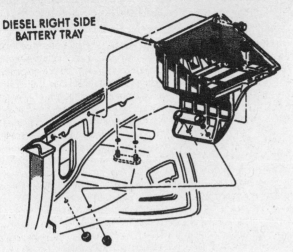

4.4b Battery tray and hold-down assembly (diesel engine auxiliary battery)

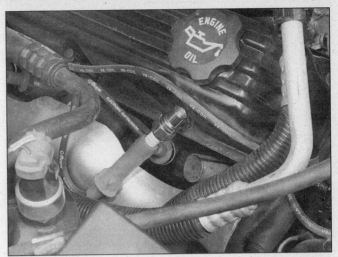

6.3 To use a calibrated ignition tester, simply disconnect a spark plug wire, connect it to the tester, clip the tester to a convenient ground and crank the engine over - if there's enough power to fire the plug, sparks will be visible between the electrode tip and the tester body

handlers are available at most auto parts stores for a reasonable price. They make it easier to remove and carry the battery.

4   While the battery is out, inspect the area underneath the tray for corrosion **(see illustrations)**.

5   If corrosion has leaked down past the battery tray, remove the bolts and lift the tray out. Use baking soda to clean the deposits from the metal to prevent further oxidation, then spray the area with a rust-inhibiting paint.

6   If you are replacing the battery, make sure you get one that's identical, with the same dimensions, amperage rating, cold cranking rating, etc.

7   Installation is the reverse of removal.

5   Ignition system - general information

The V6 and V8 engines covered by this manual are equipped with the **Camshaft Position Sensor Electronic Ignition** system. This system is equipped with a camshaft position sensor that is located in the distributor at the rear of the engine. The entire ignition system consists of the ignition coil, the camshaft position sensor (distributor), the crankshaft position sensor and the Powertrain Control Module (PCM). The PCM controls the ignition timing, spark and advance characteristics for the engine. The ignition timing is not adjustable, therefore, changing the position of the distributor will not change the timing in any way.

The distributor is driven by the camshaft (gear driven) including the distributor rotor. The camshaft position sensor is located inside the distributor and its purpose is to signal the computer concerning fuel and cylinder synchronization. **Note:** *The camshaft position sensor is formerly referred to as the* **switch plate assembly** *within Chrysler parts departments.*

The computerized ignition system provides complete control of the ignition timing by determining the optimum timing using a micro computer in response to engine speed, coolant temperature, throttle position and vacuum pressure in the intake manifold. These parameters are relayed to the PCM by the camshaft position sensor, throttle position sensor (TPS), coolant temperature sensor and MAP Sensor. Ignition timing is altered during warm-up, idling and warm running conditions by the PCM. This electronic ignition system also consists of the ignition switch, battery, coil, distributor, spark plug wires and spark plugs. These ignition systems are equipped with the Multi Port Fuel Injection (MPFI) system.

Refer to a dealer parts department or auto parts store for any questions concerning the availability of the distributor parts and assemblies. Testing the crankshaft position sensor is covered in Chapter 6.

The V10 engine is equipped with a **Distributorless Ignition System (DIS)**. The entire ignition system consists of the ignition switch, the battery, the coil packs, the primary (low voltage) and secondary (high voltage) wiring, the spark plugs, the camshaft position sensor, the crankshaft position sensor and the Powertrain Control Module (PCM). The PCM controls

the ignition timing, spark and advance characteristics for the engine. The ignition timing is not adjustable. The crankshaft and camshaft sensors are both Hall Effect timing devices. Refer to Chapter 6 for testing and replacement procedures for the crankshaft sensor and camshaft sensor.

The crankshaft sensor and camshaft sensor generate pulses that are input to the Powertrain Control Module. The PCM determines crankshaft position from these two sensors. The PCM calculates injector sequence and ignition timing from the crankshaft position.

The PCM regulates the ignition system. The PCM supplies battery voltage to the ignition coil packs through the Automatic Shutdown Relay (ASD). The PCM also controls the ground circuit for the ignition coil.

The computerized ignition system provides complete control of the ignition timing by determining the optimum timing using a micro computer in response to engine speed, coolant temperature, throttle position and vacuum pressure in the intake manifold. These parameters are relayed to the PCM by the camshaft position sensor, crankshaft position sensor, the throttle position sensor (TPS), coolant temperature sensor and MAP Sensor. Ignition timing is altered during warm-up, idling and warm running conditions by the PCM. This electronic ignition system also consists of the ignition switch, battery, spark plug wires and spark plugs.

Refer to a dealer parts department or auto parts store for any questions concerning the availability of the distributor parts and assemblies. Testing the camshaft position sensor and the crankshaft position sensor for the V10 engine is covered in Chapter 6.

6   Ignition system - check

Refer to illustration 6.3, 6.4, 6.9a and 6.9b

Warning: *Because of the very high voltage generated by the ignition system, extreme care should be taken whenever an operation is performed involving ignition components. This not only includes the coil, camshaft position sensor and spark plug wires, but related items connected to the system as well, such as the plug connections, tachometer and any test equipment.*

1   With the ignition switch turned to the "ON" position, a "Battery" light or an "Oil Pressure" light is a basic check for ignition and battery supply to the PCM.

2   Check all ignition wiring connections for tightness, cuts, corrosion or any other signs of a bad connection.

3   Use a calibrated ignition tester to verify adequate secondary voltage (25,000 volts) at each spark plug **(see illustration)**. A faulty or poor connection at that plug could also result in a misfire. Also, check for carbon

5

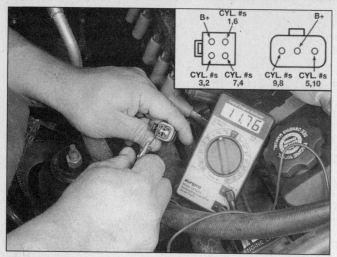

6.4   Check for battery voltage on the B+ terminal of the coil pack (V10 engine shown)

6.9a   Backprobe the coil positive terminal with a pin or clip and see if the test light flashes as the engine is cranked over (5.2L V8 engine shown)

deposits inside the spark plug boot.

4   If NO spark or INTERMITTENT sparks occur check for battery voltage to the ignition coil **(see illustration)**.

5   Using an ohmmeter, check the resistance between the coil terminals. If an opening is found (verified by an infinite reading), replace the coil (see Section 7).

6   Using an ohmmeter, check the resistance of the spark plug wires. Each wire should measure less than 25,000 ohms.

7   Check the operation of the Automatic Shutdown (ASD) relay (see Chapter 4A).

8   Check the operation of the camshaft position sensor (see Section 8) and the crankshaft position sensor (see Chapter 6). **Note:** *The camshaft position sensor checks for the V10 engine are in Chapter 6.*

9   If all the checks are correct, check the voltage signal from the computer as follows:

   a) *On V6 and V8 engines, using an LED-type test light, backprobe the coil positive terminal with a pin and check for a flashing test light while an assistant cranks over the engine* **(see illustration)**.

   b) *On the V10 engine, disconnect the coil pack electrical connector and check for a flashing light on each of the five coil pack terminals* **(see illustration)**.

10   While an assistant is cranking the engine, observe the LED light pulse on and off. If there is no flashing from the test light, most likely the computer is damaged. Have the PCM diagnosed by a dealer service department or other automotive repair shop.

---

7   Ignition coil - check and replacement

V10 engine

Check

Refer to illustrations 7.3a, 7.3b and 7.4

1   Clearly label the spark plug wires, then detach them from the coil pack. Measure the resistance of each cable. It should be 3 to 12 k-ohms per foot of cable. Replace any cable not within this range.

2 .   Unplug the electrical connector on the coil pack.

3   Measure the resistance on the primary side of each coil with a digital ohmmeter **(see illustrations)**. At the coil, connect an ohmmeter between the B+ pin and the pin corresponding to the particular cylinder. Compare your readings with the resistance values listed in this Chapter's Specifications.

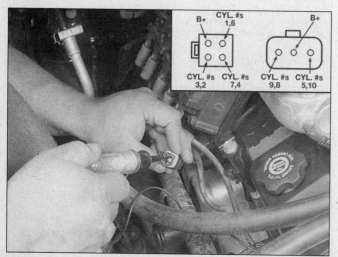

6.9b   Touch the probe of an LED test light to each cylinder coil pack terminal (except B+) and confirm that the test light flashes when the engine is cranked over (V10 engine shown)

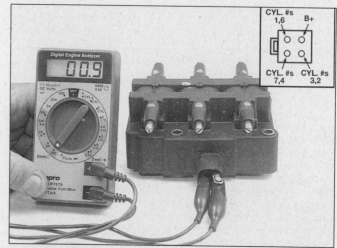

7.3a   Install the positive probe of the ohmmeter onto the B+ terminal and with the negative probe, test each cylinder terminal for the primary circuit resistance value. They all should be the same value

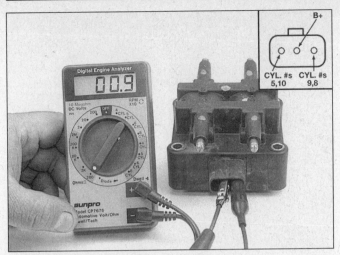

7.3b Perform the same tests to the other coil pack and check primary resistance

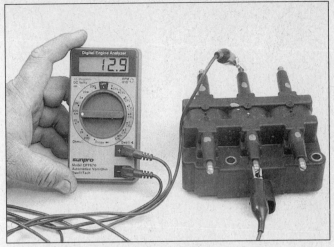

7.4 Install the ohmmeter probes onto the secondary tower for each coil pack pair. Each coil pair should have the same secondary resistance value

4   Measure the secondary resistance of the coil between the paired high tension towers of each group of cylinders **(see illustration)**. Compare your readings with the resistance values listed in this Chapter's Specifications.

5   If any coil in the coil pack fails either of the above tests, replace the coil pack.

6   Installation is the reverse of removal.

Replacement

Refer to illustration 7.9

7   Clearly label the spark plug wires, then detach them from the coil pack.

8   Unplug the electrical connector on the coil pack.

9   Remove the coil pack mounting bolts **(see illustration)** and detach it from the engine.

V6 and V8 engines

Refer to illustrations 7.13 and 7.14

10   Mark the wires and terminals with pieces of numbered tape, then remove the primary wires and the high-tension lead from the coil.

11   Clean the outer case and check it for cracks and other damage.

12   Clean the coil primary terminals and check the coil tower terminal for corrosion. Clean it with a wire brush if any corrosion is found.

13   Check the coil primary resistance by attaching the leads of an ohmmeter to the positive and negative terminals. Compare the measured resistance to the value listed in this Chapter's Specifications

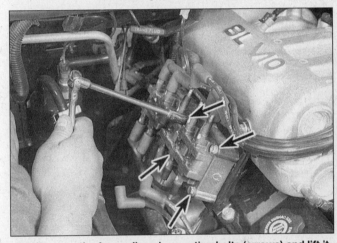

7.9 Remove the four coil pack mounting bolts (arrows) and lift it from the engine compartment (V10 engine shown)

(see illustration).

14   Check the coil secondary resistance by hooking one of the ohmmeter leads to one of the primary terminals and the other ohmmeter lead to the large center terminal **(see illustration)**. Compare the mea-

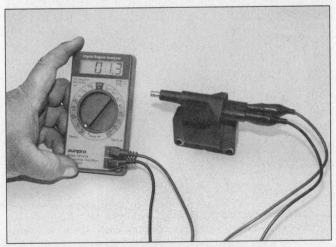

7.13 Checking the coil primary resistance

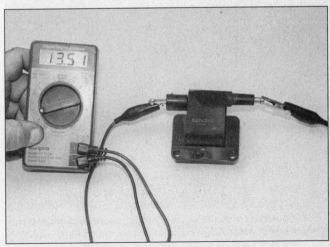

7.14 Checking the coil secondary resistance

5

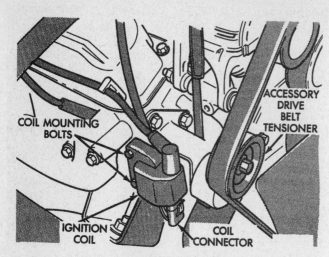

7.17a Location of the ignition coil on V6 and V8 engines (except 5.9L HDC models)

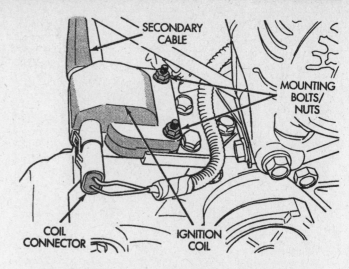

7.17b Location of the ignition coil on the 5.9L HDC engine

sured resistance to the value listed in this Chapter's Specifications.

15   If the measured resistances are not as specified, the coil is defective and should be replaced with a new one.

16   It is essential for proper operation of the ignition system that all coil terminals and wires be kept clean and dry.

Removal and installation

Refer to illustrations 7.17a and 7.17b

17   To remove the coil, remove the mounting bolts **(see illustrations)**. **Warning:** *Do not remove the coil mounting bracket-to-cylinder head mounting bolts. The coil mounting bracket is under tension from the accessory drivebelt tensioner. If the bracket must be removed, be sure to remove the drivebelt first (see Chapter 1).*

18   Installation is the reverse of removal.

8   Camshaft Position Sensor (V6 and V8 engines) - check and replacement

Note: *The camshaft position sensor check and replacement for the V10 engine is covered in Chapter 6, Section 6.*

Check

Refer to illustration 8.7

1   Remove the distributor cap (see Chapter 1).

2   Install paper clips or pins into the back side of the distributor wire harness connector to make contact with the terminals. Be sure not to damage the wire harness when installing the clips.

3   Connect the positive (+) lead of the voltmeter onto the sensor output wire. Refer to the wiring diagrams in Chapter 12 for additional information on the harness schematic.

4   With the voltmeter installed. Rotate the engine with the starter until the rotor is pointed toward the rear of the vehicle. The moveable pulse ring will be contained within the magnetic pick-up.

5   With the ignition key turned ON (engine not running), the voltmeter should read approximately 5 volts.

6   If there is no voltage, check for voltage on the supply wire (refer to the wiring diagrams at the end of Chapter 12). There should be approximately 8.0 volts with the ignition key ON (engine not running).

7   If voltage is present, install the probes of the voltmeter onto the signal wire (tan/yellow wire) and crank the engine over and observe the voltage reading. The meter should fluctuate between zero and 5.0 volts indicating that the ignition signal is pulsing properly **(see illustration)**.

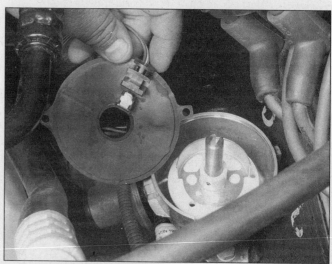

8.7 Connect the positive probe of the voltmeter onto the tan/yellow wire on the camshaft position sensor electrical connector and see if the voltage fluctuates between 0 and 5.0 volts

8.12 Carefully lift the camshaft position sensor from the distributor

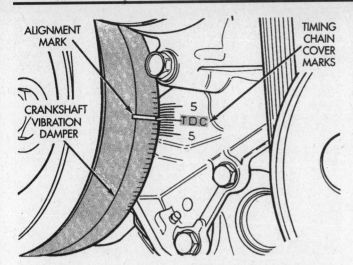

9.4 Be sure the alignment mark on the crankshaft vibration damper aligns with the TDC mark on the timing chain cover while the distributor rotor points to the distributor cap terminal that fires the number 1 cylinder on the engine

8   If the camshaft position sensor fails either of the above checks, replace it.

Replacement

Refer to illustration 8.12

9   Disconnect the negative battery cable from the battery terminal.
10   Remove the distributor cap from the distributor (see Chapter 1).
11   Remove all the electrical connectors from the camshaft position sensor.
12   Remove the camshaft position sensor from the distributor **(see illustration)**.
13   Installation is the reverse of removal.

9   Distributor (V6 and V8 engines) - removal and installation

Removal

Refer to illustrations 9.4, 9.5 and 9.7

1   Detach the cable from the negative battery terminal.

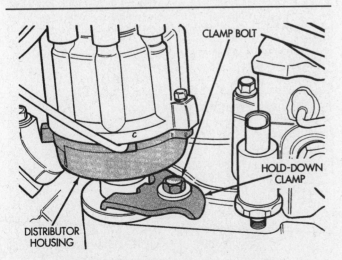

9.7 Location of the hold-down clamp bolt

9.5 Mark the position of the distributor body to the engine (arrows) (5.2L V8 engine with the intake manifold removed for clarity)

2   Detach any clamps and electrical connectors on the distributor. Mark the wires and hoses so they can be returned to their original locations.
3   Look for a raised number or letter on the distributor cap. This marks the location for the number one cylinder spark plug wire terminal. If the cap does not have a mark for the number one terminal, locate the number one spark plug and trace the wire back to the terminal on the cap.
4   Remove the distributor cap (see Chapter 1) and rotate the engine until the rotor is pointing toward the number one spark plug terminal (see the TDC locating procedure in Chapter 2A) **(see illustration)**.
5   Make a mark on the edge of the distributor body directly below the rotor tip and in line with it (if the rotor on your engine has more than one tip, use the center one for reference). Also, mark the distributor base to the engine to ensure the distributor is installed correctly **(see illustration)**.
6   If not already done, unplug the ignition wires.
7   Remove the distributor hold-down bolt and pull out the distributor **(see illustration)**. **Caution:** *Do not turn the crankshaft while the distributor is out of the engine, or the alignment marks will be useless.*

Installation

Note: *If the crankshaft has been moved while the distributor is out, the number one piston must be repositioned at TDC. This can be done by feeling for compression pressure at the number one spark plug hole as the crankshaft is turned. Once compression is felt, align the ignition timing zero mark with the pointer.*

8   Install a new O-ring on the distributor housing.
9   Insert the distributor into the engine block in exactly the same relationship to the engine block that it was in when removed. Turn the rotor until it aligns with the mark on the distributor housing (that you made in Step 5) before installing it into the engine.
10   Recheck the alignment marks between the distributor base and the engine block to verify the distributor is in the same position it was in before removal. Also check the rotor to see if it's aligned with the mark you made on the distributor.
11   Loosely install the hold-down bolt(s).
12   The remainder of installation is the reverse of removal. Check the ignition timing (see Chapter 1) and tighten the distributor hold-down bolt(s) securely.

10   Charging system - general information and precautions

The charging system includes the alternator, a charge indicator

5

light, the battery, the Powertrain Control Module (PCM), the ASD relay, a fusible link and the wiring between all the components. The charging system supplies electrical power for the ignition system, the lights, the radio, etc. The alternator is driven by a serpentine drivebelt at the front of the engine.

The alternator control system within the PCM regulates the voltage generated at the alternator in accordance with driving conditions. Depending upon electric load, vehicle speed, engine coolant temperature, accessories (air conditioning system, radio, cruise control etc.) and the intake air temperature, the system will adjust the amount of voltage generated, creating less load on the engine.

The purpose of the voltage regulator is to limit the alternator's voltage to a preset value. This prevents power surges, circuit overloads, etc., during peak voltage output. The voltage regulator is contained within the PCM and in the event of failure, the PCM must replaced as a single unit.

The gasoline engines are equipped with either a Nippondenso 75, 90 or 120 amp alternator. The diesel engines are equipped with a Nippondenso 120 amp alternator. The alternator must be replaced as a single unit in the event of failure.

The charging system doesn't ordinarily require periodic maintenance. However, the drivebelt, battery, harness wires and connections should be inspected at the intervals outlined in Chapter 1.

The dashboard warning light should come ON when the ignition key is turned to ON, but it should go off immediately after the engine is started. If it remains on, there is a malfunction in the charging system (see Section 11). Some vehicles are also equipped with a voltmeter. If the voltmeter indicates abnormally high or low voltage, check the charging system (see Section 11).

Be very careful when making electrical circuit connections to a vehicle equipped with an alternator and note the following:

a) *When reconnecting wires to the alternator from the battery, be sure to note the polarity.*

b) *Before using arc welding equipment to repair any part of the vehicle, disconnect the wires from the alternator and the battery terminals.*

c) *Never start the engine with a battery charger connected.*

d) *Always disconnect both battery cables before using a battery charger.*

e) *The alternator is turned by an engine drivebelt which could cause serious injury if your hands, hair or clothes become entangled in it with the engine running.*

f) *Because the alternator is connected directly to the battery, it could arc or cause a fire if overloaded or shorted out.*

g) *Wrap a plastic bag over the alternator and secure it with rubber bands before steam cleaning the engine.*

11   Charging system - check

Refer to illustration 11.3

Note: *These vehicles are equipped with an On-Board Diagnostic (OBD) system that is useful for detecting charging system problems. Refer to Chapter 6 for the list of diagnostic codes and the code extracting procedures for the charging system.*

1   If a malfunction occurs in the charging circuit, do not immediately assume that the alternator is causing the problem. First check the following items:

a) *The battery cables where they connect to the battery. Make sure the connections are clean and tight.*

b) *The battery electrolyte specific gravity. If it is low, charge the battery.*

c) *Check the external alternator wiring and connections.*

d) *Check the drivebelt condition and tension (see Chapter 1).*

e) *Check the alternator mounting bolts for tightness.*

f) *Run the engine and check the alternator for abnormal noise.*

2   Using a voltmeter, check the battery voltage with the engine off. It should be approximately 12 volts.

11.3 To measure battery voltage, attach the voltmeter leads to the battery terminals (engine OFF) - to measure charging voltage, start the engine

3   Start the engine and check the battery voltage again. It should now be approximately 14 to 15-volts **(see illustration)**.

4   If the indicated voltage reading is less or more than the specified charging voltage, have the PCM checked at a dealer service department. The voltage regulator on these models is contained within the PCM and it cannot be adjusted, removed or tampered with in any way.

5   Due to the special equipment necessary to test or service the alternator, it is recommended that if a fault is suspected, the vehicle be taken to a dealer or a shop with the proper equipment. Because of this, the home mechanic should limit maintenance to checking connections and the inspection and replacement of the alternator.

6   Some models are equipped with an ammeter on the instrument panel that indicates charge or discharge - current passing in or out of the battery. With the electrical equipment switched ON, and the engine idling, the gauge needle may show a discharge condition. At fast idle or normal driving speeds the needle should stay on the charge side of the gauge, with the charged state of the battery determining just how far over (the lower the battery state of charge, the farther the needle should swing toward the charge side).

7   Some models are equipped with a voltmeter on the instrument panel that indicates battery voltage with the key on and engine off, and alternator output when the engine is running.

8   The charge light on the instrument panel illuminates with the key on and engine not running, and should go out when the engine runs.

9   If the gauge does not show a charge when it should or the alternator light (if equipped) remains on, there is a fault in the system. Before inspecting the brushes or replacing the alternator, the battery condition, alternator belt tension and electrical cable connections should be checked.

12   Alternator - removal and installation

Refer to illustrations 12.2, 12.4a and 12.4b

1   Detach the cable from the negative terminal of the battery.

2   Mark and detach the electrical connector and any ground straps from the alternator **(see illustration)**.

3   Loosen the tensioner pulley, then detach the serpentine drivebelt (see Chapter 1).

4   Remove the mounting bolts and separate the alternator from the engine **(see illustrations)**.

5   If you are replacing the alternator, take the old one with you when purchasing a replacement unit. Make sure the new/rebuilt unit looks identical to the old alternator. Look at the terminals - they should be the same in number, size and location as the terminals on the old alter-

12.2 Disconnect the alternator electrical connections (diesel engine shown)

12.4a Remove the upper alternator mounting bolt

12.4b Remove the lower alternator mounting bolt

nator. Finally, look at the identification numbers - they will be stamped into the housing or printed on a tag attached to the housing. Make sure the numbers are the same on both alternators.

6   Many new/rebuilt alternators do not have a pulley installed, so you may have to switch the pulley from the old unit to the new/rebuilt one. When buying an alternator, find out the shop's policy regarding pulleys; some shops will perform this service free of charge.

7   Installation is the reverse of removal.

8   After the alternator is installed, install the drivebelt (see Chapter 1).

9   Check the charging voltage to verify proper operation of the alternator (see Section 9).

13   Starting system - general information and precautions

The starter motor assembly installed on these engines uses a planetary gear reduction drive. This starter/solenoid assembly is made by Nippondenso and provides higher rotational speeds for starting. These starter/solenoid assemblies are serviced as a complete unit. If either component fails, then the entire assembly must be replaced. This unit is sold strictly as a complete assembly. Check with your local dealer parts department before disassembly.

The sole function of the starting system is to turn over the engine quickly enough to allow it to start.

The starting system consists of the battery, the starter motor, the starter solenoid and the wires connecting them. The solenoid is mounted directly on the starter motor.

The solenoid/starter motor assembly is installed on the lower part of the engine, next to the transmission bellhousing.

When the ignition key is turned to the START position, the starter solenoid is actuated through the starter control circuit which includes a starter relay located in the Power Distribution Center. The starter solenoid then connects the battery to the starter. The battery supplies the electrical energy to the starter motor, which does the actual work of cranking the engine.

Always observe the following precautions when working on the starting system:

a) *Excessive cranking of the starter motor can overheat it and cause serious damage. Never operate the starter motor for more than 15 seconds at a time without pausing to allow it to cool for at least two minutes.*

b) *The starter is connected directly to the battery and could arc or cause a fire if mishandled, overloaded or shorted out.*

c) *Always detach the cable from the negative terminal of the battery before working on the starting system.*

14   Starter motor - in-vehicle check

Note: *Before diagnosing starter problems, make sure the battery is fully charged.*

1   If the starter motor does not turn at all when the switch is operated, make sure the shift lever is in Neutral or Park (automatic transmission) or the clutch pedal is depressed (manual transmission).

2   Make sure the battery is charged and all cables, both at the battery and starter solenoid terminals, are clean and secure.

3   If the starter motor spins but the engine is not cranking, the overrunning clutch in the starter motor is slipping and the starter motor must be replaced. Also, the ring gear on the flywheel or driveplate may be worn.

4   If, when the switch is actuated, the starter motor does not operate at all but the solenoid clicks, the problem lies with either the battery, the main solenoid contacts or the starter motor itself (or the engine is seized).

5   If the solenoid plunger cannot be heard when the switch is actuated, the battery is bad, the fusible link is burned (the circuit is open) or the solenoid itself is defective.

6   To check the solenoid, connect a jumper lead between the battery and the ignition switch wire terminal (the small terminal) on the solenoid. If the starter motor now operates, the solenoid is OK and the problem is in the ignition switch, neutral start switch, starter relay or the wiring.

5

15.2 Remove the electrical connectors from the starter solenoid (diesel engine shown)

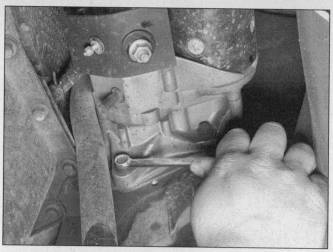

15.3 Starter motor installation details on the V10 engine

7   Locate the starter relay in the power distribution center under the hood. Remove the relay and perform the identical tests as for the Automatic Shutdown Relay (ASD) and the fuel pump relay in Chapter 4A, Section 3.

8   If the starter motor still does not operate, remove the starter/solenoid assembly for exchange at a dealer parts department or other qualified parts store.

9   If the starter motor cranks the engine at an abnormally slow speed, first make sure that the battery is charged and that all terminal connections are tight. If the engine is partially seized or has the wrong viscosity oil in it, it will crank slowly.

10   Run the engine until normal operating temperature is reached, then disconnect the coil wire from the distributor cap and ground it on the engine (V8), disconnect the ignition coil packs (V10) or disconnect the fuel shutdown solenoid (diesel).

11   Connect a voltmeter positive lead to the positive battery post and connect the negative lead to the negative post.

12   Crank the engine and take the voltmeter readings as soon as a steady figure is indicated. Do not allow the starter motor to turn for more than l5 seconds at a time. A reading of nine volts or more, with the starter motor turning at normal cranking speed, is normal. If the reading is nine volts or more but the cranking speed is slow, the motor, solenoid contacts or circuit connections are faulty. If the reading is less than nine volts and the cranking speed is slow, the starter motor is probably bad.

15   Starter motor - removal and installation

Refer to illustration 15.2 and 15.3

1   Detach the cable from the negative terminal of the battery.

2   Clearly label, then disconnect the wires from the terminals on the starter motor solenoid **(see illustration)**. Disconnect any clips securing the wiring to the starter.

3   Remove the mounting bolts **(see illustration)** and detach the starter.

4   Installation is the reverse of removal.

Chapter 6
Emissions and engine control systems

Contents

Specifications

Torque specifications

Crankshaft sensor retaining bolt	70 in-lb
Camshaft sensor retaining bolt (V10)	50 in-lb
EGR tube mounting nuts	204 in-lb
EGR valve bolts	200 in-lb
Speedometer adapter clamp screw	100 in-lb

6

1   General information

Refer to illustrations 1.3a, 1.3b, 1.3c, 1.6a and 1.6b

To prevent pollution of the atmosphere from incompletely burned and evaporating gases, and to maintain good driveability and fuel economy, a number of emission control systems are incorporated. The principal systems are:

Gasoline engines

Positive Crankcase Ventilation (PCV) system
Evaporative Emission Control (EVAP) system
Exhaust Gas Recirculation (EGR) system
Catalytic converter
Powertrain Control Module (PCM) (computer)
Information sensors and output actuators

Diesel engines

Exhaust Gas Recirculation (EGR) system (some models)
Air intake heater system
Catalytic converter
Powertrain Control Module (PCM) (computer)
Information sensors and output actuators

The Sections in this Chapter include general descriptions, checking procedures within the scope of the home mechanic and component replacement procedures (when possible) for each of the systems listed above.

Before assuming an emissions control system is malfunctioning, check the fuel and ignition systems carefully. The diagnosis of some emission control devices requires specialized tools, equipment and training. If checking and servicing become too difficult or if a procedure is beyond your ability, consult a dealer service department. Remember, the most frequent cause of emissions problems is simply a loose or broken vacuum hose or wire, so always check the hose and electrical connections first **(see illustrations)**.

This doesn't mean, however, that emission control systems are particularly difficult to maintain and repair. You can quickly and easily perform many checks and do most of the regular maintenance at home with common tune-up and hand tools. **Note:** *Because of a Federally mandated extended warranty which covers the emission control system components, check with your dealer about warranty coverage before working on any emissions-related systems. Once the warranty has expired, you may wish to perform some of the component checks and/or replacement procedures in this Chapter to save money.*

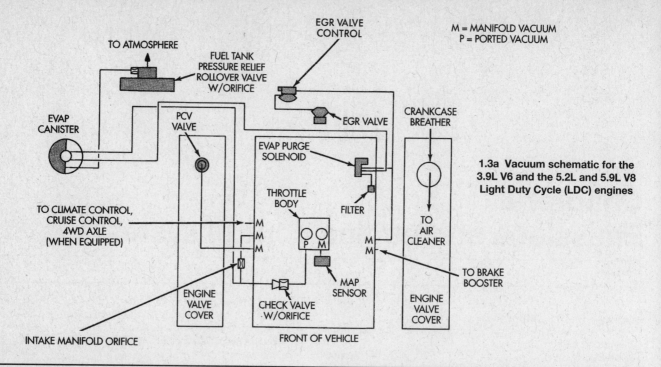

1.3a Vacuum schematic for the 3.9L V6 and the 5.2L and 5.9L V8 Light Duty Cycle (LDC) engines

Pay close attention to any special precautions outlined in this Chapter. It should be noted that the illustration of the various systems may not exactly match the system installed on your vehicle because of changes made by the manufacturer during production or from year-to-year.

A Vehicle Emissions Control Information (VECI) label is located in the engine compartment **(see illustrations)**. This label contains important emissions specifications and adjustment information. When servicing the engine or emissions systems, the VECI label in your particular vehicle should always be checked for up-to-date information.

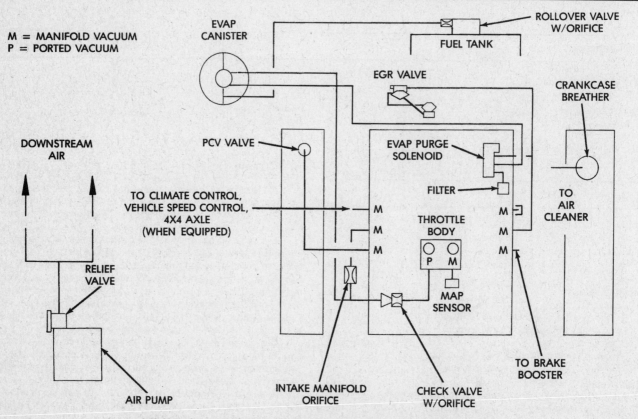

1.3b Vacuum schematic for the 5.9L V8 Heavy Duty Cycle (HDC) engine

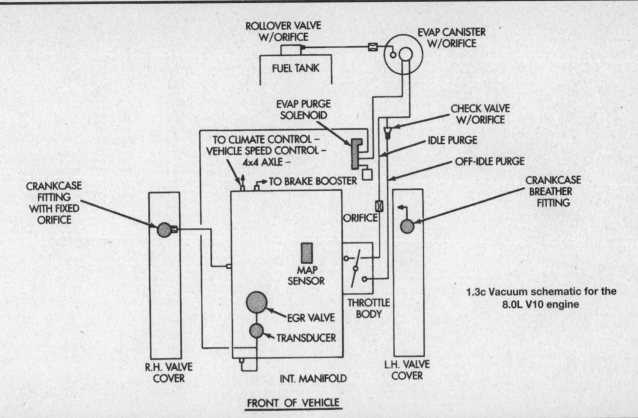

1.3c Vacuum schematic for the 8.0L V10 engine

1.6a The Vehicle Emission Control Information (VECI) label on V10 models is located on the front bracket assembly and contains information on idle speed adjustment, ignition timing, location of the emissions control devices on the vehicle, etc.

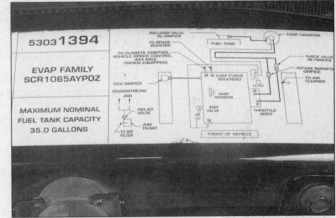

1.6b Location of the vacuum schematic on V10 models

2   Engine control system, information sensors and output actuators for gasoline engines - description

Refer to illustrations 2.2, 2.3a and 2.3b

1   The gasoline engines are equipped with "sequentially" operated fuel injectors. A fuel injector is located in each intake port. The system fires each injector in sequence, timed with the opening of each intake valve. The Sequential Electronic Fuel Injection (SEFI) system provides the correct air-fuel ratio under all driving conditions.

2   The "brain" of all SEFI systems is a computer known as a Powertrain Control Module (PCM). The PCM is located at the front corner of the engine compartment **(see illustration)**.

3   The PCM receives variable voltage inputs from a variety of sensors, switches and relays **(see illustrations)**. All inputs are converted

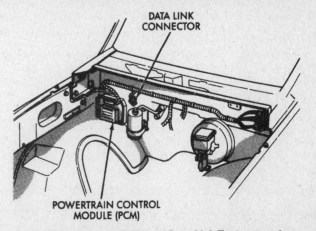

2.2 Location of the PCM and Data Link Test connector

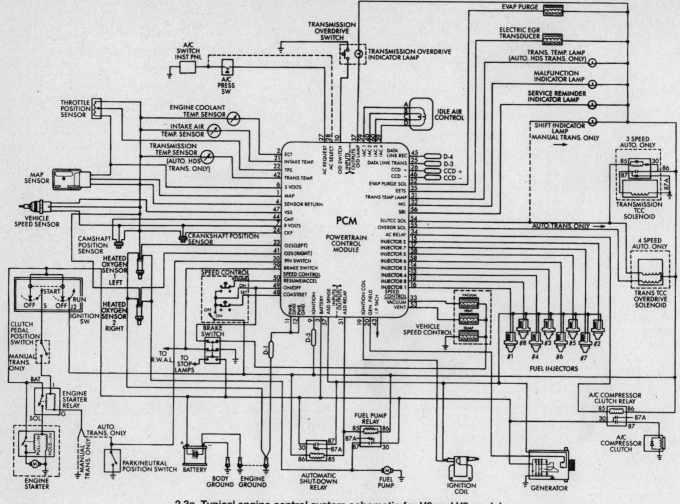

2.3a Typical engine control system schematic for V6 and V8 models

into digital signals which are "read" by the PCM, which constantly fine-tunes such variables as ignition timing, spark advance, ignition coil dwell, fuel injector pulse width and idle speed to minimize exhaust emissions and enhance driveability. It also controls the operation of the radiator cooling fan, the alternator charging rate and such emissions-related components as the EGR solenoids and the purge solenoid for the EVAP canister. The PCM even updates and revises its own programming in response to changing operating conditions.

4   The PCM also constantly monitors many of its own input and output circuits. If a fault is found in the SEFI system, the information is stored in the PCM memory. You really can't check or test the components of the SEFI system without an expensive factory tool, the Diagnostic Readout Box DRB II (Chrysler tool no. C-4805) or its equivalent, but you can often determine where a problem is coming from, or at least which circuit it's in. This process always begins with reading any stored fault codes to identify the general location of a problem, followed by a thorough visual inspection of the system components to ensure that everything is properly connected and/or plugged in. The most common cause of a problem in any SEFI system is a loose or corroded electrical connector or a loose vacuum line. To learn how to output this information and display it on the CHECK ENGINE light on the dash, refer to Section 5.

Information sensors and output actuators

5   Various components either provide basic information to the PCM (sensors) or are controlled by the PCM (actuators); they include:

Air conditioning clutch relay
Auto shutdown (ASD) relay

Brake switch
Camshaft position sensor
Air temperature sensor
Coolant temperature sensor
Crankshaft position sensor
Manifold Absolute Pressure (MAP) sensor
Oxygen sensor
Throttle Position Sensor (TPS)
Idle Air Control (IAC) valve
Transmission neutral-safety switch
Vehicle Speed Sensor (VSS)

Air conditioning clutch relay

Refer to illustration 2.6

6   The air conditioning clutch relay is controlled by the PCM. The air conditioning clutch relay is operated by switching the ground circuit for the air conditioning clutch relay on and off. When the PCM receives a request from the air conditioning (climate control system) it will adjust the idle air control motor position. The air conditioning clutch control relay is located in the Power Distribution Center next to the battery **(see illustration)**.

Automatic shutdown (ASD) relay

7   If there's no ignition (distributor) signal, or cam or crank reference sensor signal, present when the ignition key is turned to the RUN position, the auto shutdown relay interrupts power to the electric fuel pump, the fuel injectors, the ignition coil and the heated oxygen

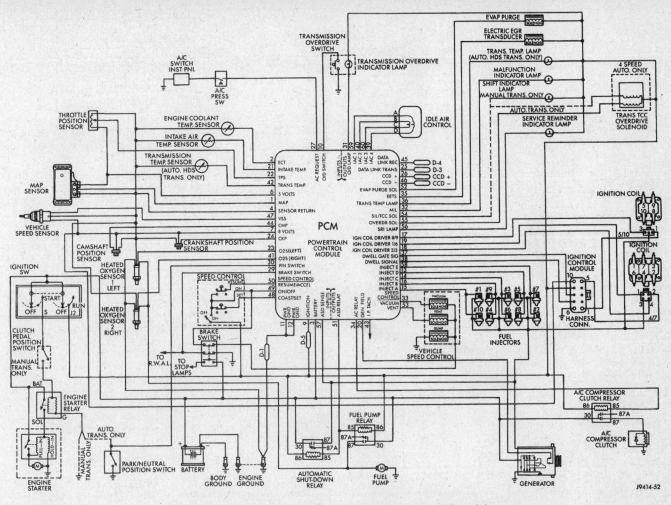

2.3b Typical engine control system schematic for V10 models

sensor. The cut-out relay is located in the Power Distribution Center next to the battery. For ASD relay and fuel pump relay locations and testing procedures, refer to Chapter 5.

Camshaft position sensor

Refer to illustrations 2.8a, 2.8b and 2.8c

8   The camshaft position sensor provides cylinder identification to the PCM to synchronize the fuel system with the ignition system. There are two types of camshaft positions sensors; one for the Distributor-less Ignition Systems (DIS) on the V10 engine **(see illustration)** and the other for the distributor-type ignition system on the V6 and V8 engines **(see illustration)**. On V10 models, the camshaft sensor is located in the timing chain case cover on the left front side of the engine. The camshaft sensor detects notches in the camshaft sprocket **(see illus-**

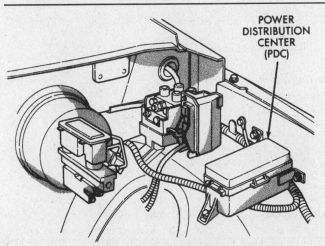

2.6 Location of the Power Distribution Center

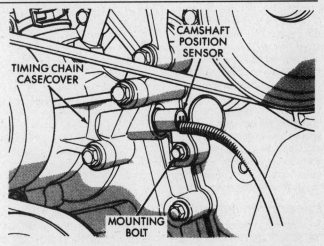

2.8a Camshaft position sensor location on the V10 engine

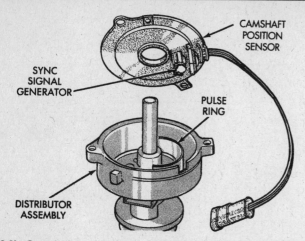

2.8b Camshaft position sensor location on the V6 and V8 engines

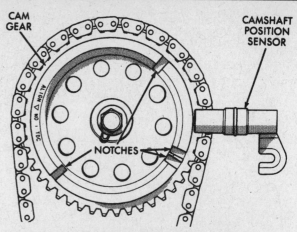

2.8c The Camshaft Position Sensor detects notches in the camshaft sprocket on the V10 engine

tration). The face of the sensor is positioned next to this gear with a small space between called the air gap. The sensor generates pulses as groups of notches on the camshaft sprocket pass underneath it. When metal aligns with the sensor, the voltage pulses low (approximately 0.3 volts) and when the notch aligns with the sensor, voltage increases suddenly to about 5.0 volts. These voltage pulses are in turn processed by the PCM which in turn determines ignition timing. On distributor-type ignition systems, the synchronizing signal is generated from a Hall Effect device, called the sync signal generator, located within the Camshaft Position Sensor. The sync signal generator detects a rotating pulse ring on the distributor shaft. The pulse ring rotates 180 degrees through the sync signal generator. Its signal is used in conjunction with the crankshaft position sensor to determine between the fuel injection and the ignition spark functions.

Air temperature sensor

Refer to illustrations 2.9a, 2.9b and 2.9c

9   The air temperature sensor **(see illustrations)**, mounted in the

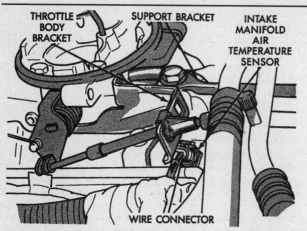

2.9a Location of the air temperature sensor on the V6 engine

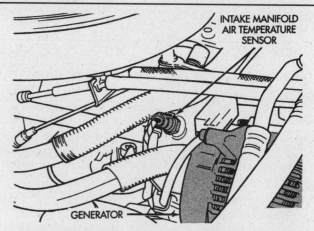

2.9b Location of the air temperature sensor on V8 engines

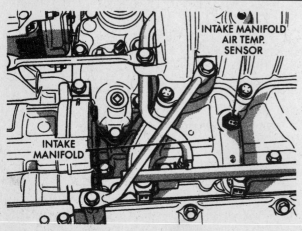

2.9c Location of the air temperature sensor on the V10 engine

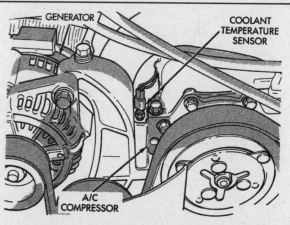

2.10a Location of the coolant temperature sensor on V6 and V8 engines

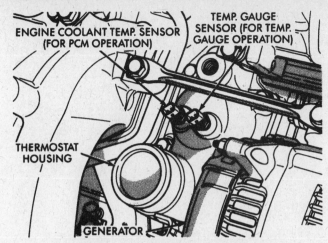

2.10b Location of the coolant temperature sensor
on the V10 engine

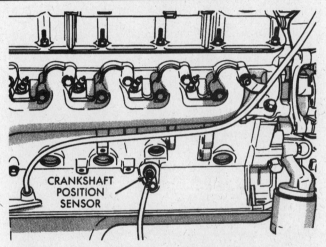

2.11b Location of the crankshaft sensor on the V10 engine

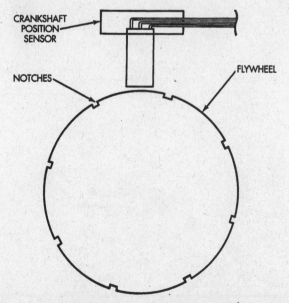

2.11c The crankshaft position sensor detects notches in the
flywheel/driveplate on V6 and V8 models

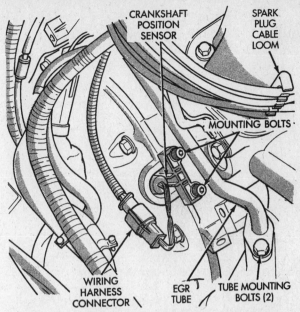

2.11a Location of the crankshaft position sensor
on V6 and V8 engines

intake manifold, measures the temperature of the incoming air and sends this information to the PCM. This data is used by the PCM to modify the air/fuel mixture.

Coolant temperature sensor

Refer to illustrations 2.10a and 2.10b

10   The coolant temperature sensor **(see illustrations)**, which is threaded into the thermostat housing, monitors coolant temperature and sends this information to the PCM. This data, along with the information from the air temperature sensor, is used by the PCM to determine the correct air/fuel mixture and idle speed while the engine is warming up. The sensor is also used to activate the radiator fan.

Crankshaft position sensor

Refer to illustrations 2.11a, 2.11b, 2.11c, and 2.11d

11   The crankshaft position sensor is mounted on the passenger side of the transmission bellhousing on V6 and V8 models and on the lower right side of the engine block on V10 models **(see illustrations)**. This sensor sends information to the PCM regarding engine crankshaft position. The sensor "reads" the notches in the flywheel/driveplate (V6 and V8) or crankshaft (V10) **(see illustrations)**.

6

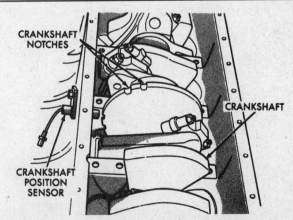

2.11d On V10 models, the crankshaft position sensor detects
notches in the crankshaft timing ring, which is part
of the crankshaft

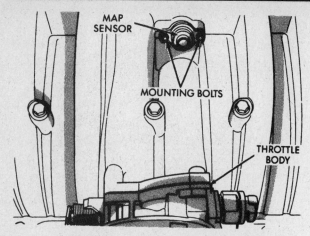

2.12 The MAP sensor on the V10 is located on the air intake plenum

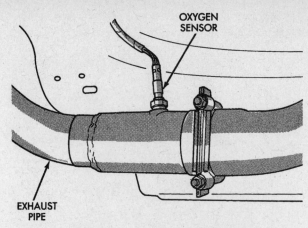

2.14a Location of the oxygen sensor on V6 and V8 Light Duty Cycle (LDC) engines

Manifold Absolute Pressure (MAP) sensor

Refer to illustration 2.12

12   The MAP sensor is located on the throttle body on V6 and V8 models **(see illustration 2.15a)** or on the air intake plenum on V10 models **(see illustration)**. It monitors intake manifold directly through a port in the throttle body. The MAP sensor transmits this data, along with data on barometric pressure, in the form of a variable voltage output to the PCM. When combined with data from other sensors, this information helps the PCM determine the correct air-fuel mixture ratio.

Miscellaneous switches

13   Various switches (such as the transmission neutral safety switch, the air conditioning switch, the speed control switch and the brake light switch) provide information to the PCM, which adjusts engine operation in accordance with what switch states are present at these inputs. The state of these switch inputs (high/low) is difficult to determine without the Chrysler DRB II (or equivalent) diagnostic tool.

Oxygen sensor

Refer to illustrations 2.14a and 2.14b

14   The oxygen sensor, which is mounted in the exhaust down-pipe **(see illustrations)**, produces a voltage signal when exposed to the oxygen present in the exhaust gases. The sensor is electrically heated

internally for faster warm-up. When there's a lot of oxygen present (lean mixture), the sensor produces a low voltage signal; when there's little oxygen present (rich mixture), it produces a signal of higher voltage. By monitoring the oxygen content and converting it to electrical voltage, the sensor acts as a lean-rich switch. The voltage signal to the PCM alters the pulse width of the injectors.

Throttle Position Sensor (TPS)

Refer to illustrations 2.15a and 2.15b

15   The TPS, located on the throttle body **(see illustrations)**,

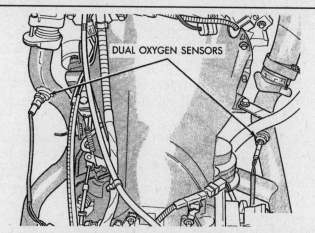

2.14b Location of the oxygen sensors on the V10 and V8 Heavy Duty Cycle (HDC) engines

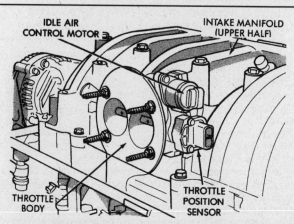

2.15a TPS and IAC location on V6 and V8 engines

2.15b TPS and IAC location on the V10 engine

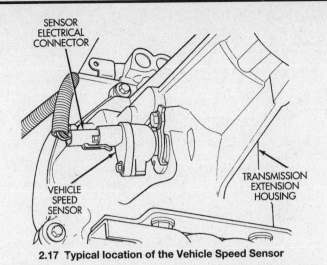

2.17 Typical location of the Vehicle Speed Sensor

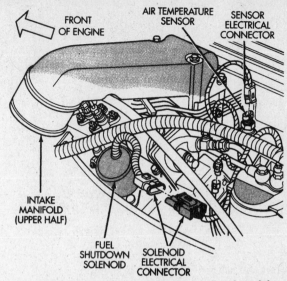

3.8 Air temperature sensor location - diesel models

monitors the angle of the throttle plate. The voltage signal increases or decreases in accordance with the opening angle of the throttle plate. This data, when relayed to the PCM, along with data from several other sensors, enables the computer to adjust the air/fuel ratio in accordance with the operating conditions, such as acceleration, deceleration, idle and wide open throttle.

Idle Air Control (IAC) valve

16   The IAC valve is mounted on the throttle body **(see illustrations 2.15a and 2.15b)**. The PCM controls the engine idle speed with the IAC valve, opening and closing the valve slightly to compensate for various engine loads in an attempt to maintain a steady idle speed. A set screw, adjusted at the factory, limits the throttle plate travel, since the PCM controls the idle speed, DO NOT attempt to adjust the idle speed with this set screw.

Vehicle Speed Sensor (VSS)

Refer to illustration 2.17

17   The Vehicle Speed Sensor, located in the transmission/transfer case extension housing **(see illustration)**, senses vehicle motion. The sensor generates pulses for every revolution of the driveshaft and transmits them as voltage signals to the PCM. These signals are compared by the PCM with the throttle signal from the throttle position sensor so it can distinguish between a closed throttle deceleration and normal idle (vehicle stopped) condition. Under deceleration conditions, the PCM controls the IAC valve to maintain the desired MAP value; under idle conditions, the PCM adjusts the IAC valve to maintain the desired engine speed.

3   Engine control system, information sensors and output actuators for diesel engines - description

1   The diesel engine is equipped with a high pressure fuel injection pump and six fuel injectors. The injectors are located on the left side of the cylinder head. This mechanical system fires each injector in sequence, timed with TDC on the compression stroke of each cylinder. The high pressure fuel injection pump is driven by a gear connected to the camshaft.

2   The diesel fuel injection system is not electronic, although the Powertrain control Module is involved with some (limited) drivetrain functions, it does not control the fuel delivery system.

3   The PCM receives variable voltage inputs from a variety of sensors, switches and relays. All inputs are converted into digital signals which are "read" by the PCM. The PCM controls certain functions such as air conditioning controls, TCC activation, the transmission overdrive solenoid and cruise control to minimize exhaust emissions and enhance driveability. The PCM also controls the intake manifold air heater, the ASD

relay and the alternator charging rate. The PCM is located at the front corner of the engine compartment **(see illustration 2.2)**.

4   The PCM constantly monitors many of its own input and output circuits. If a fault is found in the diesel fuel injection system, the information is stored in the PCM memory. You really can't check or test the components without an expensive factory tool, the Diagnostic Readout Box DRB II (Chrysler tool no. C-4805) or its equivalent, but you can often determine where a problem is coming from, or at least which circuit it's in. This process always begins with reading any stored trouble codes to identify the general location of a problem, followed by a thorough visual inspection of the system components to ensure that everything is properly connected and/or plugged in. To learn how to output this information and display it on the CHECK ENGINE light on the dash, refer to Section 5.

Information sensors and output actuators

5   Various components either provide basic information to the PCM (sensors) or are controlled by the PCM (actuators); they include:

Air conditioning clutch relay
Auto shutdown (ASD) relay
Brake switch
Air temperature sensor
Throttle Position Sensor (TPS)
Transmission neutral-safety switch
Vehicle Speed Sensor (VSS)
Engine speed sensor

Air conditioning clutch relay

6   The air conditioning clutch relay is controlled by the PCM. The air conditioning clutch relay is operated by switching the ground circuit for the air conditioning clutch relay on and off. When the PCM receives a request from the air conditioning (climate control system) it will activate the air conditioning clutch relay. The air conditioning clutch control relay is located in the Power Distribution Center next to the battery **(see illustration 2.6)**.

Automatic shutdown (ASD) relay

7   The PCM controls the operation of the ASD relay. The ASD relay provides power to the alternator field for charging system operation.

Air temperature sensor

Refer to illustration 3.8

8   The air temperature sensor **(see illustration)**, which is mounted in the intake manifold, measures the temperature of the incoming air and sends this information to the PCM. This data is used by the PCM to control the cycling time of the air heater.

6

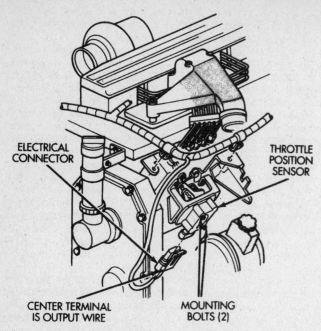

3.10 TPS location - diesel models

Miscellaneous switches

9   Various switches (such as the transmission neutral safety switch, the air conditioning switch, the speed control switch and the brake light switch) provide information to the PCM, which adjusts automatic transmission, air conditioning and cruise control operation in accordance with switch states present at these inputs. The state of these switch inputs (high/low) is difficult to determine without the DRB II diagnostic meter.

Throttle Position Sensor (TPS)

Refer to illustration 3.10

10   The TPS is used only on models equipped with an automatic transmission. It is located on the side of the fuel injection pump (see

illustration). The voltage signal from the TPS increases or decreases in accordance with the opening or closing of the throttle lever. This data, when relayed to the PCM, along with data from several other sensors, enables the computer to determine 3-4 upshifts and 4-3 downshifts for transmission operation. It is also used to determine the correct operation of the TCC system.

Vehicle Speed Sensor (VSS)

11   The Vehicle Speed Sensor, located in the transmission extension housing (see illustration 2.16), senses vehicle motion. The sensor generates pulses for every revolution of the driveshaft and transmits them as voltage signals to the PCM. These signals are used to determine vehicle speed and distance traveled. The PCM used the VSS signal to control operation of the cruise control system, the transmission overdrive solenoid and the torque converter clutch.

Engine speed sensor

Refer to illustration 3.12

12   The engine speed sensor is mounted to the front of the engine (see illustration). It generates an rpm signal to the PCM for the purpose of controlling the proper shift times for the overdrive transmission. The speed sensor acts in conjunction with the VSS and the TPS. The engine speed sensor also works as an input for the PCM to control the generator field, vehicle cruise control, TCC system and tachometer.

4   Powertrain Control Module (PCM) - removal and installation

Refer to illustration 4.4

Note: *Avoid static electricity damage to the PCM by grounding yourself to the body of the vehicle before touching the PCM and using a special anti-static pad to store the PCM on, once it is removed.*

1   Disconnect the cable from the negative battery terminal.
2   Remove the air cleaner assembly (see Chapter 4).
3   Remove the bolts that retain the PCM to the engine compartment and lift the assembly from the vehicle.
4   Remove the harness retaining bolt for the PCM electrical connector (see illustration).
5   Installation is the reverse of removal.

5   On-Board Diagnosis (OBD) system - description and code access

Note: *The OBD system on gasoline engines and diesel engines are identical in operation. Because the fuel injection system is a mechanical system on diesel engines, the number and type of codes differ. Follow the same code extracting procedure but refer to the correct*

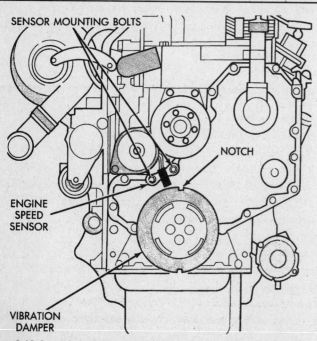

3.12 Location of the engine speed sensor - diesel models

4.4 Remove the PCM electrical connector retaining bolt

code chart for gasoline or diesel models.

1   The CHECK ENGINE light or MIL light, located in the instrument panel, flashes on for three seconds as a bulb test when the engine is started. If a problem is detected in the engine control system, the light comes on and stays on and a code is stored in the PCM memory. The self-diagnosis information contained in the PCM (computer) can be accessed either by the ignition key or by using a special SCAN tool, such as the Diagnostic Readout Box (DRB II) or equivalent. The SCAN tool is attached to the diagnostic connector in the engine compartment and reads the codes and parameters on the digital display screen. SCAN tools are expensive and most home mechanics prefer to use the alternate method. The drawback with the ignition key method is that it does not access all the available codes for display. Most problems can be solved or diagnosed quite easily and if the information cannot be obtained readily, have the vehicle's self-diagnosis system analyzed by a dealer service department or other properly-equipped repair shop.

2   To obtain the codes using the ignition key method, first set the parking brake and place the shift lever in neutral (manual) or Park (automatic). Start the engine and raise the engine speed to approximately 2,500 rpm; slowly allow the engine speed to return to idle. Also cycle the air conditioning system (on briefly, then off). If equipped with an automatic transmission, place your foot on the brake and select each position on the transmission (Reverse, Drive, Low etc.), finally bringing the shifter back to Park and turn off the engine. This will allow the computer to obtain any fault codes that might be linked to any of the sensors controlled by the transmission, engine speed or air conditioning system.

3   To display the codes on the dashboard CHECK ENGINE light (or MIL Malfunction Indicator light), turn the engine off, then turn the ignition key ON, OFF, ON, OFF and finally ON, without starting the engine. The codes will begin to flash. The light will blink the number of the first digit then pause and blink the number of the second digit. For example: Code 23, air temperature sensor circuit, would be indicated by two flashes, then a pause followed by three flashes.

4   Certain criteria must be met for a fault code to be entered into the PCM memory. The criteria might be a specific range of engine rpm, engine temperature or input voltage. It's possible that a fault code for a particular monitored circuit may not be entered into the memory despite a malfunction. This may happen because one of the fault code criteria has not been met. For example; The engine must be operating between 750 and 2,000 rpm in order to monitor the MAP sensor circuit correctly. If the engine speed is raised above 2,400 rpm, the MAP sensor output circuit shorts to ground and will not allow a fault code to be entered into the memory. Then again, the exact opposite could occur: A code is entered into the memory that suggests a malfunction within another component that is not monitored by the computer. For example; a fuel pressure problem cannot register a fault directly but instead, it will cause a rich or lean fuel mixture problem. Consequently, this will cause an oxygen sensor malfunction resulting in a stored code in the computer for the oxygen sensor. Be aware of the interrelationship of the sensors and circuits and the overall relationship of the emissions control and fuel injection systems.

5   The accompanying table is a list of the typical trouble codes which may be encountered while diagnosing the system. Also included are simplified troubleshooting procedures. Before outputting the trouble codes, thoroughly inspect ALL electrical connectors and hoses. Make sure all electrical connections are tight, clean and free of corrosion; make sure all hoses are properly connected, fit tightly and are in good condition (no cracks or tears).

If the problem persists after these checks have been made, more detailed service procedures will have to be performed by a dealer service department or other qualified repair shop.

Trouble codes for models equipped with a gasoline engine

Note: *Not all trouble codes apply to all models.*

Code 11	No distributor reference signal detected during engine cranking. Check the circuit between the distributor and the PCM.
Code 12	Problem with the battery connection. Direct battery input to PCM disconnected within the last 50 ignition key-on cycles.
Code 13**	Indicates a problem with the MAP sensor vacuum system.
Code 14**	MAP sensor voltage too low or too high.
Code 15**	A problem with the vehicle distance/speed signal. No distance/speed sensor signal detected during road load conditions.
Code 17	Engine is cold too long. Engine coolant temperature remains below normal operating temperatures during operation (check the thermostat).
Code 21**	Problem with oxygen sensor signal circuit. Sensor voltage to computer not fluctuating.
Code 22**	Coolant sensor voltage too high or too low. Test coolant temperature sensor.
Code 23**	Indicates that the air temperature sensor input is below the minimum acceptable voltage or sensor input is above the maximum acceptable voltage.
Code 24**	Throttle position sensor voltage high or low. Test the throttle position sensor.
Code 25**	Idle Air Control (IAC) valve circuits. A shorted condition is detected in one or more of the IAC valve circuits.
Code 27	One of the injector control circuit output drivers does not respond properly to the control signal. Check the circuits.
Code 31**	Problem with the canister purge solenoid circuit.
Code 32**	An open or shorted condition detected in the EGR solenoid circuit. Possible air/fuel ratio imbalance not detected during diagnosis.
Code 33	Air conditioner clutch relay circuit. An open or shorted condition detected in the air conditioning clutch relay circuit.
Code 34	Open or shorted condition detected in the speed control vacuum or vent solenoid circuits.
Code 35	Open or shorted condition detected in the radiator fan low speed relay circuit.
Code 41**	Problem with the charging system. Occurs when battery voltage from the ASD relay is below 11.75 volts.
Code 42	Auto shutdown relay (ASD) control circuit indicates an open or shorted circuit condition.
Code 43**	Peak primary circuit current not achieved with the maximum dwell time.
Code 44	Battery temperature sensor volts malfunction. Problem with the battery temperature voltage circuit in the PCM.
Code 45	Transmission overdrive solenoid circuit malfunction. An open or short circuit problem exists in the transmission overdrive solenoid circuit.
Code 46**	Charging system voltage too high. Computer indicates that the battery voltage is not properly regulated.

6

Trouble codes for models equipped with a gasoline engine (continued)

Code 47**	Charging system voltage too low. Battery voltage sense input below target charging voltage during engine operation and no significant change in voltage detected during active test of alternator output.
Code 51	Oxygen sensor signal input indicates lean fuel/air ratio condition during engine operation.
Code 52**	Oxygen sensor signal input indicates rich fuel/air ratio condition during engine operation.
Code 53	Internal PCM failure detected.
Code 54	No camshaft position sensor signal from distributor. Problem with the distributor synchronization circuit.
Code 55	Completion of fault code display on CHECK ENGINE lamp. This is an end of message code.
Code 62	PCM failure to update the SRI (service reminder indicator) mileage setting in the EEPROM.
Code 63	Controller failure. EEPROM write denied. Check the PCM.
Code 71**	Auxiliary 5 volt supply output voltage signal is low. The 5 volt output signal from the regulator is not reaching the required voltage amount.
Code 72**	Catalytic converter efficiency failure. The catalytic converter is not converting emissions in the proper ratio.

Trouble codes for models equipped with a diesel engine

Note: *Not all trouble codes apply to all models*

Code 11	No crank reference signal detected during engine cranking
Code 12	No codes. Problem with the battery connection. Direct battery input to the PCM disconnected within the last 50 ignition key-on cycles.
Code 15**	No vehicle speed sensor signal. No VSS signal detected by the PCM during driving conditions.
Code 23**	Intake air temperature sensor voltage high or low. Intake manifold air temperature sensor circuit signals above or below the acceptable voltage.
Code 24**	Throttle position sensor (TPS) voltage high or low. Test the throttle position sensor.
Code 33	Air conditioner clutch relay circuit. An open or shorted condition detected in the air conditioning clutch relay circuit.
Code 34	Open or shorted condition detected in the speed control vacuum or vent solenoid circuits.
Code 37**	Torque Converter Clutch (TCC) solenoid circuit open or shorted.
Code 37**	Transmission temperature sensor voltage signal above or below acceptable voltage values.
Code 41**	Problem with the charging system. Occurs when battery voltage from the ASD relay is below 11.75-volts.
Code 42	Auto shutdown relay (ASD) control circuit indicates an open or shorted circuit condition.
Code 44	Battery temperature sensor volts malfunction. Problem with the battery temperature voltage circuit in the PCM.
Code 45	Transmission overdrive solenoid circuit malfunction. An open or short circuit problem exists in the transmission overdrive solenoid circuit.
Code 46**	Charging system voltage too high. Computer indicates that the battery voltage is not properly regulated.
Code 47**	Charging system voltage too low. Battery voltage sense input below target charging voltage during engine operation and no significant change in voltage detected during active test of alternator output.
Code 53	Internal PCM failure detected.
Code 55	Completion of fault code display on CHECK ENGINE lamp. This is an end of message code.
Code 63	Controller failure. EEPROM write denied. Check the PCM.

*****These codes light up the CHECK ENGINE light on the instrument panel during engine operation once the trouble code has been recorded.*

---

6   Information sensors and output actuators - check and replacement

Note: *After performing checking procedure to any of the sensors or actuators, be sure to clear the PCM of all trouble codes by disconnecting the cable from the negative terminal of the battery for at least ten seconds.*

Oxygen sensor

General description

Refer to illustration 6.1

1   The oxygen sensor, which is located in the exhaust manifold **(see illustrations 2.14a and 2.14b)**, monitors the oxygen content of the exhaust gas stream. The oxygen content in the exhaust reacts with the oxygen sensor to produce a voltage output which varies from 0.1-volt (high oxygen, lean mixture) to 0.9-volts (low oxygen, rich mixture). The PCM constantly monitors this variable voltage output to determine the ratio of oxygen to fuel in the mixture. The PCM alters the air/fuel mix-ture ratio by controlling the pulse width (open time) of the fuel injectors. A mixture ratio of 14.7 parts air to 1 part fuel is the ideal mixture ratio for minimizing exhaust emissions, thus allowing the catalytic converter to operate at maximum efficiency. It is this ratio of 14.7 to 1 which the PCM and the oxygen sensor attempt to maintain at all times. **Note:** Some *1996 models use a pre-catalyst oxygen sensor and a post-catalyst oxygen sensor* **(see illustration)**.

2   The oxygen sensor produces no voltage when it is below its normal operating temperature of about 600-degrees F. During this initial period before warm-up, the PCM operates in OPEN LOOP mode.

3   If the engine reaches normal operating temperature and/or has been running for two or more minutes, and if the oxygen sensor is producing a steady signal voltage below 0.45-volts at 1,500 rpm or greater, the PCM will set a Code 51 or 52. The PCM will also set a code 21 if it detects any problem with the oxygen sensor circuit.

4   When there is a problem with the oxygen sensor or its circuit, the PCM operates in the open loop mode - that is, it controls fuel delivery in accordance with a programmed default value instead of feedback information from the oxygen sensor.

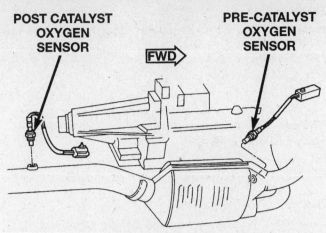

6.1 1996 models are equipped with a pre-catalyst and post-catalyst oxygen sensor

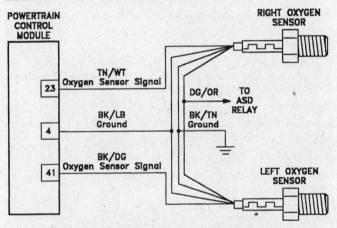

6.7b Typical oxygen sensor wiring schematic

6.7a Install a pin into the electrical connector and backprobe the oxygen sensor electrical connector SIGNAL wire terminal to monitor the sensor output signal voltage

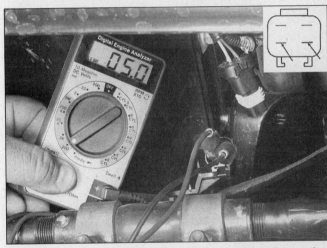

6.11 Measure the resistance of the oxygen sensor heater on the white wires. It should be 5 to 7 ohms

6

5   The proper operation of the oxygen sensor depends on four conditions:

a) *Electrical - The low voltages generated by the sensor depend upon good, clean connections which should be checked whenever a malfunction of the sensor is suspected or indicated.*

b) *Outside air supply - The sensor is designed to allow air circulation to the internal portion of the sensor. Whenever the sensor is removed and installed or replaced, make sure the air passages are not restricted.*

c) *Proper operating temperature - The PCM will not react to the sensor signal until the sensor reaches approximately 600-degrees F. This factor must be taken into consideration when evaluating the performance of the sensor.*

d) *Unleaded fuel - The use of unleaded fuel is essential for proper operation of the sensor. Make sure the fuel you are using is of this type.*

6   In addition to observing the above conditions, special care must be taken whenever the sensor is serviced.

a) *The oxygen sensor has a permanently attached pigtail and electrical connector which should not be removed from the sensor. Damage or removal of the pigtail or electrical connector can adversely affect operation of the sensor.*

b) *Grease, dirt and other contaminants should be kept away from the electrical connector and the louvered end of the sensor.*

c) *Do not use cleaning solvents of any kind on the oxygen sensor.*

d) *Do not drop or roughly handle the sensor.*

e) *The silicone boot must be installed in the correct position to prevent the boot from being melted and to allow the sensor to operate properly.*

Check

Refer to illustrations 6.7a, 6.7b, 6.11, 6.12 and 6.14

7   Locate the oxygen sensor electrical connector and insert a long pin into the oxygen sensor connector black/dark green (left oxygen sensor) or tan/white (right oxygen sensor) signal voltage wire **(see illustrations)**. **Note:** *On models equipped with pre-and post-catalyst sensors, the SIGNAL wire on the pre-catalyst oxygen sensor is tan/white or tan/red and the SIGNAL wire on the post-catalyst oxygen sensor is orange/black.*

8   Install the positive probe of a voltmeter onto the correct pin and the negative probe to ground. **Note:** *Consult the wiring diagrams at the end of Chapter 12 for additional information on the oxygen sensor electrical connector wire color designations.*

9   Start the engine and monitor the voltage signal (millivolts) as the engine goes from cold to warm.

10   The oxygen sensor will produce a steady voltage signal at first (open loop) of approximately 0.1 to 0.2 volts with the engine cold. After a period of approximately two minutes, the engine will reach operating temperature and the oxygen sensor will start to fluctuate between 0.1 to 0.9 volts (closed loop). If the oxygen sensor fails to reach the closed loop mode or there is a very long period of time until it does switch into closed loop mode, replace the oxygen sensor with a new part.

11   Also inspect the oxygen sensor heater. Disconnect the oxygen sensor electrical connector and connect an ohmmeter between the two white wires. It should measure approximately 5 to 7 ohms **(see illustration)**.

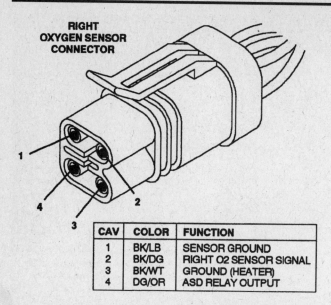

CAV	COLOR	FUNCTION
1	BK/LB	SENSOR GROUND
2	BK/DG	RIGHT O2 SENSOR SIGNAL
3	BK/WT	GROUND (HEATER)
4	DG/OR	ASD RELAY OUTPUT

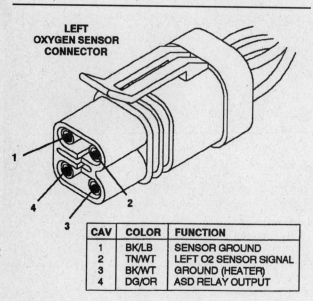

CAV	COLOR	FUNCTION
1	BK/LB	SENSOR GROUND
2	TN/WT	LEFT O2 SENSOR SIGNAL
3	BK/WT	GROUND (HEATER)
4	DG/OR	ASD RELAY OUTPUT

6.12 Check for battery voltage to the heater on the ASD relay output terminal

12   Check for proper supply voltage to the heater. Measure the voltage on the oxygen sensor electrical connector between the dark green/orange wire terminal (+) and the black/white wire terminal (-) **(see illustration)**. There should be battery voltage with the ignition key ON (engine not running). If there is no voltage, check the circuit between the ASD relay, the PCM and the sensor. **Note:** *It is important to remember that supply voltage will only last approximately 2 seconds because the PCM will turn the system off if the engine is not started.*
13   If the oxygen sensor fails any of these tests, replace it with a new part.
14   Access to the oxygen sensors electrical connectors can make monitoring the SIGNAL voltage changes difficult without removing several components to allow room for connecting the volt/ohmmeter electrical leads. A SCAN tool is available from some automotive parts stores and specialty tool companies that can be plugged into the test connector for the purpose of monitoring the computer and the sensors **(see illustration)**. Install the SCAN tool and switch to the oxygen sensor mode and monitor the oxygen sensor varying millivolt signals. The SCAN tool should indicate approximately 100 to 200 millivolts when cold and then fluctuate from 300 to 800 millivolts warm (closed loop).

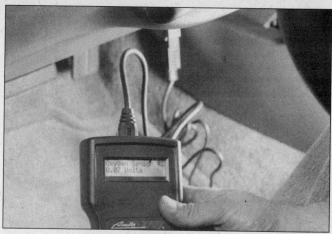

6.14 Install the SCAN tool into the test connector under the dash (arrow) and monitor the oxygen sensor crosscounts (millivolt signal)

6.17 Use a special slotted socket to remove the oxygen sensor from the exhaust pipe

Replacement

Refer to illustration 6.17

Note: *Because it is installed in the exhaust manifold or pipe, which contracts when cool, the oxygen sensor may be very difficult to loosen when the engine is cold. Rather than risk damage to the sensor (assuming you are planning to re-use it in another manifold or pipe), start and run the engine for a minute or two, then shut it off. Be careful not to burn yourself during the following procedure.*
15   Disconnect the cable from the negative battery terminal.
16   Raise the vehicle and place it securely on jackstands.
17   Carefully disconnect the electrical connector from the sensor and unscrew the sensor from the exhaust pipe **(see illustration)**.
18   Anti-seize compound must be used on the threads of the sensor to facilitate future removal. The threads of new sensors will already be coated with this compound, but if an old sensor is removed and reinstalled, recoat the threads.
19   Install the sensor and tighten it securely.
20   Reconnect the electrical connector of the pigtail lead to the main engine wiring harness.
21   Lower the vehicle, take it on a test drive.

Manifold Absolute Pressure (MAP) sensor

General description

22   The Manifold Absolute Pressure (MAP) sensor monitors the intake manifold pressure changes resulting from changes in engine load and speed and converts the information into a voltage output. The PCM

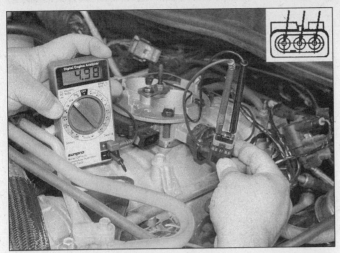

6.25 Using a voltmeter, check for reference voltage to the MAP sensor on the purple/white (+) wire terminal and black/light blue (-) wire terminal. It should be approximately 5.0 volts (V8 engine shown)

6.26 With the ignition key ON (engine not running), check the signal voltage on the dark green/red wire terminal (+) and the black/light blue wire terminal (-). It should be approximately 4.5 volts

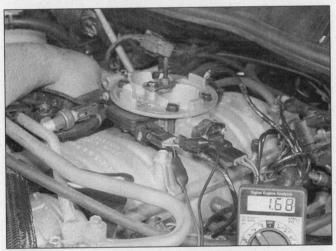

6.27 Next, start the engine and check the MAP sensor voltage with the engine idling - it should be between 0.5 and 2.0 volts

6.30 Remove the bolts (arrows) that retain the MAP sensor to the throttle body (V8 engine shown)

uses the MAP sensor to control fuel delivery and ignition timing. The PCM will receive information as a voltage signal that will vary from 1.0 to 1.5 volts at closed throttle (high vacuum) and 4.0 to 4.5 volts at wide open throttle (low vacuum). The MAP sensor is located on the air intake plenum (V10) or on the throttle body (V6 and V8) (see illustrations 2.12 and 2.15a).

23   A failure in the MAP sensor circuit should set a Code 13 or a Code 14.

Check

Refer to illustrations 6.25, 6.26 and 6.27

24   Check the electrical connector at the sensor for a snug fit. Check the terminals in the connector and the wires leading to it for looseness and breaks. Repair as required.

25   Disconnect the MAP sensor connector, turn the ignition key ON (engine not running) and check for voltage on the reference wire (purple/white wire) (+) and ground wire (black/light blue) (-) (see illustration). There should be approximately 5 volts.

26   Connect the electrical connector to the MAP sensor, backprobe the MAP sensor electrical connector using a pin and check for voltage on the signal wire (dark green/red wire) (+) with the ignition key on (engine not running). There should be approximately 4.5 volts (see illustration).

27   Start the engine with the positive probe of the voltmeter on the signal wire (dark green/red wire terminal) and allow it to idle (see illustration). Note the voltage reading, it should be between 0.5 and 2.0 volts. Slowly raise the rpm and observe the voltage increase as vacuum decreases. If the readings are incorrect, replace the MAP sensor with a new part.

28   An alternate method of diagnosing the MAP sensor is by the use of an electronic SCAN tool. The SCAN tool can be plugged into the test connector for the purpose of monitoring the computer and the sensors and are available from some automotive parts stores and specialty tool companies. Install the SCAN tool and switch to the MAP mode and monitor the voltage signal with the engine at idle and high rpm (see illustration 6.14). Raise the engine rpm and observe that as engine rpm increases (decreasing vacuum) the MAP signal voltage increases. If the MAP sensor voltage readings are incorrect, replace the MAP sensor.

Replacement

Refer to illustration 6.30

29   Disconnect the electrical connector from the MAP sensor.

30   Remove the bolts that retain the MAP sensor to the throttle body and remove the MAP sensor (see illustration).

31   Installation is the reverse of removal.

6

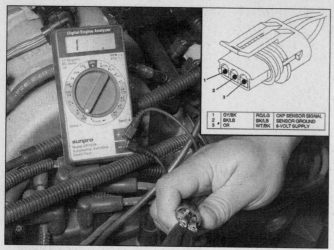

6.33 Working on the computer side of the electrical connector, check the reference voltage on the orange wire terminal. It should be approximately 8.0 volts (1994 and 1995 models)

6.40a Disconnect the electrical connector to the coolant temperature sensor and measure the resistance across the sensor terminals

Crankshaft position sensor

General description

32   The crankshaft position sensor determines the timing for the fuel injection and ignition on each cylinder. It also detects engine RPM. The crankshaft position sensor is a Hall-Effect device. On V6 and V8 engines, the crankshaft sensor is mounted on the bellhousing and detects notches in the driveplate (see illustration 2.11c). On the V10 engine, it is mounted on the side of the engine block and detects notches in the crankshaft (see illustration 2.11d). The engine will not operate if the PCM does not receive a crankshaft position sensor input.

Check

Refer to illustrations 6.33

33   Check the reference voltage to the crankshaft sensor from the PCM. Locate the crankshaft sensor electrical connector (see illustration). Disconnect the connector and turn the ignition key ON (engine not running). On 1994 and 1995 models, install the positive probe (+) of the voltmeter to the orange wire terminal and the negative probe (-) to the black/light blue wire terminal. There should be approximately 8.0 volts present. On 1996 models, install the positive probe (+) of the voltmeter to the purple/white wire terminal and the negative probe (-) to the black/light blue wire terminal. There should be approximately 5.0 volts present.

34   If reference voltage is present, check for the crank sensor signal. Reconnect the electrical connector to the sensor. Backprobe the gray/black wire terminal (+) and the light blue/black wire terminal (-) using a pins or paper clips and monitor the voltage changes as you turn the engine over slowly using a socket and wrench on the crankshaft pulley or by tapping the ignition key without starting the engine. The voltage will fluctuate from 0.3 (metal under sensor) to 5.0 volts (slots under sensor). This can be a difficult test to perform, the engine must be rotated slowly and the voltage will fluctuate very fast. So watch the meter closely, you're not so concerned with obtaining the exact voltage readings, but you want to see the fluctuation, indicating the sensor is operating properly.

35   Because the crankshaft sensor is very difficult to reach, it may be easier to use a SCAN tool or have the system checked at a dealer service department. The SCAN tool can be plugged into the test connector for the purpose of monitoring the computer and the sensors. This special tool is available from some automotive parts stores and specialty tool companies.

Replacement

36   Disconnect the crankshaft sensor wiring harness connector.
37   Remove the crankshaft sensor mounting bolts. Use only the original bolts to mount the sensor, they are machined to correctly space the sensor to the flywheel.
38   Installation is the reverse of removal. Tighten the bolt(s) to the torque listed in this Chapter's Specifications.

Engine Coolant Temperature (ECT) sensor

General description

39   The coolant temperature sensor is a thermistor (a resistor which varies the value of its resistance in accordance with temperature changes) (see illustrations 2.10a and 2.10b). The change in the resistance values will directly affect the voltage signal from the coolant sensor to the PCM. As the sensor temperature INCREASES, the resistance values will DECREASE. As the sensor temperature DECREASES, the resistance values will INCREASE. A failure in the coolant sensor circuit should set a Code 22. These codes indicate a failure in the coolant temperature circuit, so the appropriate solution to the problem will be either repair of a wire or replacement of the sensor.

TEMPERATURE		RESISTANCE (OHMS)	
C	**F**	**MIN**	**MAX**
−40	−40	291,490	381,710
−20	−4	85,850	108,390
−10	14	49,250	61,430
0	32	29,330	35,990
10	50	17,990	21,810
20	68	11,370	13,610
25	77	9,120	10,880
30	86	7,370	8,750
40	104	4,900	5,750
50	122	3,330	3,880
60	140	2,310	2,670
70	158	1,630	1,870
80	176	1,170	1,340
90	194	860	970
100	212	640	720
110	230	480	540
120	248	370	410

6.40b Engine Coolant Temperature sensor resistance chart (can also be used for the Air Temperature sensor)

6.41 Check the reference voltage from the PCM to the ECT with the ignition key ON (engine not running). It should be approximately 5.0 volts

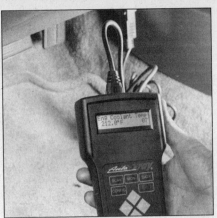

6.42 Using a SCAN tool to monitor the engine coolant temperature

6.43 Use an end-wrench to remove the Engine Coolant Temperature sensor from the intake manifold (V8 engine shown)

Check

Refer to illustrations 6.40a, 6.40b 6.41 and 6.42

40   To check the sensor, disconnect the electrical connector and measure the resistance of the coolant temperature sensor with the engine cold (50 to 80-degrees F) **(see illustration)**. Next, start the engine and warm it up until it reaches operating temperature (170 to 200-degrees F). Compare the sensor resistance with the resistance chart **(see illustration)**. If the resistance is not within specifications, replace the sensor.

41   Check the reference voltage from the PCM to the sensor. With the ignition key ON (engine not running), place the positive probe (+) of the voltmeter on the tan/black wire terminal and the negative probe (-) on the black/blue wire terminal **(see illustration)**. It should be approximately 5.0 volts.

42   Access to the coolant temperature sensor may be difficult on some models. A SCAN tool is available from some automotive parts stores and specialty tool companies that can be plugged into the diagnostic connector for the purpose of monitoring the computer and the sensors. Install the SCAN tool, switch to the ECT mode and monitor the temperature of engine **(see illustration)**. The SCAN tool should indicate between 75 to 90-degrees F (cold engine). Allow the engine to idle for several minutes and observe the coolant temperature increase as the engine progressively warms-up. The temperature should indicate between 180 to 210-degrees F when fully warmed-up. **Note:** *If*

there is not a definite change in temperature, remove the coolant temperature sensor and check the resistance in a pan of heated water to simulate warm-up conditions. If the sensor tests are good, check the wiring harness from the sensor to the computer.

Replacement

Refer to illustration 6.43

Warning: *Wait until the engine is completely cool before beginning this procedure.*

43   Partially drain the cooling system (see Chapter 1). Release the locking tab, unplug the electrical connector, then carefully unscrew the sensor **(see illustration)**. **Caution:** *Handle the coolant sensor with care. Damage to this sensor will affect the operation of the entire fuel injection system.*

44   Before installing the new sensor, wrap the threads with Teflon sealing tape to prevent leakage and thread corrosion.

45   Installation is the reverse of removal.

Throttle Position Sensor (TPS)

General description

Gasoline models

46   The Throttle Position Sensor (TPS) is located on the end of the throttle shaft on the throttle body **(see illustrations 2.15a and 2.15b)**. By monitoring the output voltage from the TPS, the PCM can determine fuel delivery based on throttle valve angle (driver demand). A broken or loose TPS can cause intermittent bursts of fuel from the injector and an unstable idle because the PCM thinks the throttle is moving. A problem with the TPS circuit will set a code 24.

Diesel models

47   The Throttle Position Sensor (TPS) is located on the side of the fuel injection pump **(see illustration 3.10)**. It is used only on models equipped with an automatic transmission. The variable voltage signal, sent to the PCM, is used to determine transmission shift solenoid and torque converter clutch operation. The check and replacement procedures are identical to gasoline equipped models.

Check

Refer to illustrations 6.48, 6.49a, 6.49b, 6.50a and 6.50b

48   Locate the Throttle Position Sensor (TPS) on the throttle body or fuel injection pump. Disconnect the TPS electrical connector and using a voltmeter, check the reference voltage from the PCM. Install the positive probe (+) onto the purple/white wire terminal and the negative probe (-) onto the black/light blue wire terminal **(see illustration)**. The voltage should read approximately 5.0 volts.

49   Next, install the electrical connector onto the TPS and check the TPS signal voltage by backprobing the electrical connector with

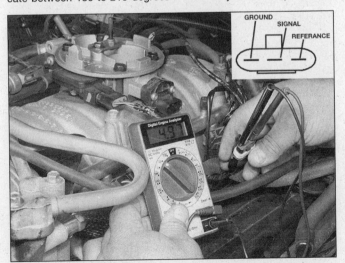

6.48 Check for reference voltage to the TPS sensor on the purple/white wire terminal (+) and the black/light blue wire terminal (-) (ground). It should be approximately 5.0 volts

6

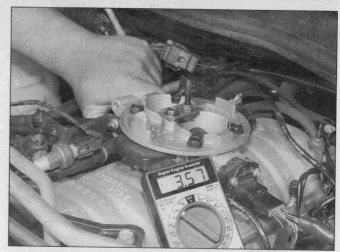

6.49a   **Check the SIGNAL voltage from the orange/dark blue wire terminal (+) and the black/light blue wire terminal (-). First, check the voltage with the throttle completely closed. It should be approximately 0.5 to 1.5 volts**

6.49b   **Next, using your hand, rotate the throttle linkage to wide open throttle and check the voltage signal. It should be 3.5 to 4.5 volts**

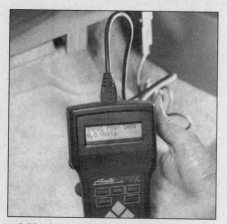

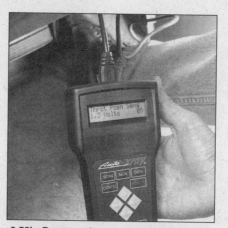

6.50a   **Monitor the TPS voltage using a SCAN tool with the throttle closed**

6.50b   **Depress the accelerator pedal and observe the voltage values increase**

6.53   **Remove the Torx bolts (arrows) from the TPS (V8 model shown)**

straight pins. With the throttle fully closed, connect the positive probe (+) of the voltmeter onto the orange/dark blue wire terminal and the negative probe (-) to the black/light blue wire terminal **(see illustrations)**. Gradually open the throttle valve and observe the TPS sensor voltage. With the throttle valve fully closed, the voltage should read approximately 0.5 to 1.5 volt. Slowly move the throttle valve and observe a change in voltage as the sensor travels from idle to full throttle. The voltage should increase to approximately 3.5 to 4.5 volts. If the readings are incorrect, replace the TPS sensor.

50   An alternate method of diagnosing the TPS sensor is by the use of an electronic SCAN tool. SCAN tools can be plugged into the test connector for the purpose of monitoring the computer and the sensors and are available from some automotive parts stores and specialty tool companies **(see illustrations)**. Install the SCAN tool, switch to the TPS mode and monitor the voltage signal.

51   A problem in any of the TPS circuits will set a Code 24. Once a trouble code is set, the PCM will use an artificial default value for throttle position and some vehicle performance will return.

Replacement

Refer to illustrations 6.53 and 6.54

52   Disconnect the electrical connector from the TPS.

53   Remove the mounting screws from the TPS and remove the TPS from the throttle body or fuel injection pump **(see illustration)**.

54   When installing the TPS, be sure to align the socket locating tangs on the TPS with the throttle shaft in the throttle body or fuel

injection pump **(see illustration)**.

55   Installation is the reverse of removal. Be sure the throttle valve is fully closed once the TPS is mounted. If it isn't, rotate the TPS to allow complete closure before tightening the mounting screws.

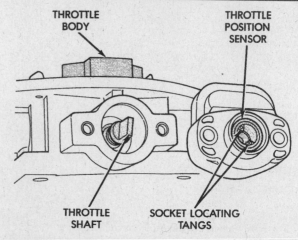

6.54   **Align the socket locating tangs on the throttle shaft (V8 model shown)**

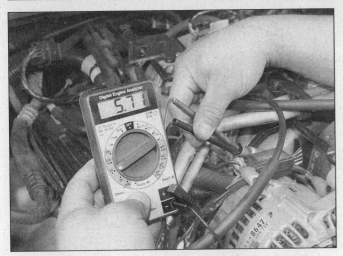

6.57 Check the resistance of the air temperature sensor
(V8 model shown)

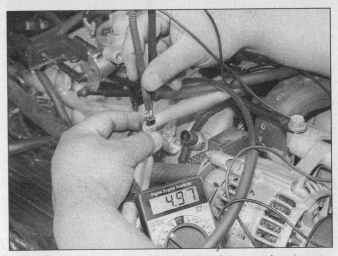

6.58 Check the reference voltage to the air temperature sensor
(V8 model shown)

Air Temperature sensor

General information

56   The air temperature sensor is located in the intake manifold (see Section 2 or Section 3). This sensor is also referred to as the Intake Air Temperature (IAT) sensor. This sensor operates as a negative temperature coefficient (NTC) device. As the sensor temperature INCREASES, the resistance values will DECREASE. As the sensor temperature DECREASES, the resistance values will INCREASE. Most cases, the appropriate solution to the problem will be either repair of a wire or replacement of the sensor.

Check

Refer to illustrations 6.57 and 6.58

57   With the ignition switch OFF, disconnect the electrical connector from the air temperature sensor. Using an ohmmeter, measure the resistance between the two terminals on the sensor while it is completely cold (50 to 80-degrees F) **(see illustration)**. Next, start the engine and warm it up until it reaches operating temperature (180 to 200-degrees F) and check the resistance again. Compare your measurements to the resistance chart **(see illustration 6.40b)**.

58   With the ignition key ON (engine not running), check for a reference voltage from the PCM on the harness connector to the sensor **(see illustration)**. Connect the positive probe (+) of the voltmeter to the black/red wire terminal and the negative (-) probe to the black/light blue wire terminal. Reference voltage should be approximately 5.0 volts.

59   If the sensor resistance test results are incorrect, replace the air temperature sensor.

60   If the sensor checks out okay but there is still a problem, have the vehicle checked at a dealer service department or other qualified repair shop, as the PCM may be malfunctioning.

Replacement

61   Unplug the electrical connector from the air temperature sensor.

62   Unscrew the sensor from the intake manifold and remove the air temperature sensor.

63   Installation is the reverse of removal.

Vehicle Speed Sensor

General description

64   The Vehicle Speed Sensor (VSS) is located on the transmission (2WD models) or transfer case (4WD models) extension housing. This sensor is a permanent magnetic variable reluctance sensor that produces a pulsing voltage whenever vehicle speed is over 3 mph. These pulses are translated by the PCM and provided to other systems for fuel and transmission shift control.

6.67 Remove the VSS mounting bolt (arrow)
(NV 4500 transmission shown)

Check

65   To check the vehicle speed sensor, disconnect the electrical connector to the sensor. Using a voltmeter, check for reference voltage to the sensor. Connect the positive probe (+) to the orange wire terminal and the negative probe (-) to the black/light blue wire terminal. The reference voltage should be approximately 8.0 volts. Next, check the signal voltage from the PCM. Connect the positive probe (+) to the white/orange wire terminal and the negative probe (-) to the black/light blue wire terminal. The signal voltage should be approximately 5 volts. If there is no reference or signal voltage available, have the PCM diagnosed by a dealership service department.

66   If the reference and signal voltages are available, remove the speedometer adapter (see below) and check the speedometer pinion for damaged or stripped teeth. If the speedometer pinion is good, have the VSS checked at a dealer service department or other qualified repair facility.

Replacement

Refer to illustrations 6.67, 6.69 and 6.70

67   To replace the VSS, disconnect the electrical connector from the VSS. Remove the retaining bolt and withdraw the VSS from the speedometer adapter **(see illustration)**.

68   Thoroughly clean the adapter flange and mounting area in the transmission and note the relationship of the adapter-to-transmission for proper alignment.

6

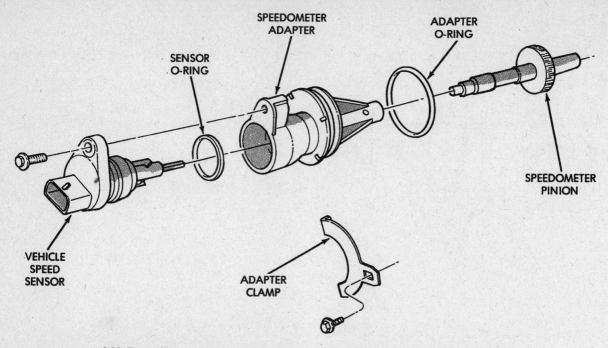

6.69 Typical Vehicle Speed Sensor, adapter and speedometer pinion installation details

69   Remove the adapter clamp bolt and clamp and withdraw the adapter and speedometer pinion from the transmission **(see illustration)**.

70   Remove the speedometer pinion from the adapter and check the gear teeth for damage. Count the number of teeth on the speedometer pinion and note the corresponding index number on the speedometer adapter **(see illustration)**.

71   Install VSS into speedometer adapter and tighten the mounting screw. Install the speedometer pinion into the adapter.

72   Install new O-rings on the adapter and lubricate the O-rings and the speedometer pinion with automatic transmission fluid.

73   Install the assembly into the transmission or transfer case.

74   Turn the VSS assembly until the correct index numbers on the speedometer adapter are positioned at 6 o'clock. For example: if the speedometer pinion has 35 teeth, position the 32-38 index number straight down (6 o'clock).

75   Install the speedometer adapter clamp and retaining screw. Tighten the screw to the torque listed in this Chapter's Specifications.

76   Installation is the reverse of removal.

Lock-up control solenoid

77   The lock-up control solenoid is a computer controlled output actuator contained in the automatic transmission that is used to activate the lock-up torque converter. If a problem is suspected with the lock-up control solenoid or transmission torque converter clutch, take the vehicle to a dealer service department or automatic transmission repair specialist for diagnosis and repair.

Camshaft position sensor (V10 models)

Note: *The camshaft position sensor check and replacement for V6 and V8 models is covered in Chapter 5, Section 8.*

General description

78   The camshaft position sensor used on the V10 engine provides cylinder identification to the PCM to synchronize the fuel system with the ignition system (see Section 2). The synchronizing signal is generated from notches located in the camshaft sprocket. When metal aligns with the sensor the voltage pulses low (approximately 0.3 volts) and when the notch aligns with the sensor, voltage increases suddenly to about 5.0 volts. These voltage pulses are in turn processed by the PCM which in turn determines ignition timing.

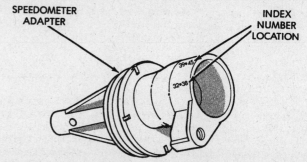

6.70 The number of teeth on the speedometer pinion should fall within one of the groups of numbers on the speedometer adapter

Check

79   To check the camshaft position sensor circuit, disconnect the sensor electrical connector. Turn the ignition key to ON but do not start the engine.

80   Check the reference voltage from the PCM. Working on the engine harness connector, measure the voltage between the orange wire terminal (+) on 1994 and 1995 models or the purple/white wire terminal (+) on 1996 models and the black/light blue wire terminal (-). Reference voltage should be 8 volts for 1994 and 1995 models and 5.0 volts for 1996 models.

81   If reference voltage is present, check for the cranking signal. Install the electrical connector onto the camshaft sensor, backprobe the tan/yellow wire terminal (+) and the black/light blue wire terminal (-) using a pin or paper clip and monitor the voltage changes as you turn the engine over slowly using a socket and wrench on the crankshaft pulley or by tapping the ignition key without starting the engine. The voltage will fluctuate from 0.3 (metal under sensor) to 5.0 volts (slots under sensor). This can be a difficult test to perform, the engine must be rotated slowly and the voltage will fluctuate very fast. So watch the meter closely, you're not so concerned with obtaining the exact voltage readings, but you want to see the fluctuation, indicating the sensor is operating properly.

82   If the voltage readings are both correct, have the camshaft position sensor diagnosed by a dealer service department or other qualified repair shop.

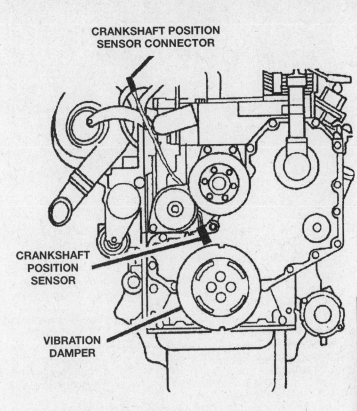

CRANKSHAFT POSITION
SENSOR CONNECTOR

CRANKSHAFT
POSITION
SENSOR

VIBRATION
DAMPER

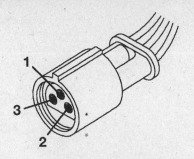

CAV	COLOR	FUNCTION
1	OR	8-VOLT SUPPLY
2	BK/LB	SENSOR GROUND
3	GY/*	CKP SENSOR SIGNAL

6.90 Engine speed sensor details for the diesel engine

83   It may be necessary to observe the actual camshaft sensor signal while the engine is running. A SCAN tool is available from some automotive parts stores and specialty tool companies that can be plugged into the test connector for the purpose of monitoring the computer and the sensors. Install the SCAN tool and switch to the camshaft sensor mode and monitor the voltage signal from the camshaft position sensor.

Replacement

84   Disconnect the negative terminal from the battery.
85   Disconnect the electrical connector from the sensor.
86   Remove the bolt from the camshaft sensor and lift the sensor from the timing cover.
87   Installation is the reverse of removal. Be sure to install the paper spacer onto the camshaft sensor and tighten the camshaft sensor bolt to the torque listed in this Chapter's Specifications.

Park/neutral position switch

88   Refer to Chapter 7, Part B for the check and replacement procedures for the park/neutral position switch (neutral start switch).

Engine speed sensor (diesel models)

General description

89   The engine speed sensor is a Hall Effect type sensor used to detect crankshaft speed and crankshaft position. The PCM supplies 8 volts reference signal to the speed sensor. The PCM also supplies a 5 volt "pull-up" signal to the sensor. The sensor signal is created when the slots cut in the vibration damper pass under the sensor. When the slot is under the engine speed sensor, the signal voltage is high, approximately 5.0 volts. When the smooth edge of the damper is under the sensor, the signal is low, approximately 0.3 volts. The speed sensor uses slotted holes on the sensor body to adjust the depth. A brass, non-magnetic feeler gauge is used to measure the clearance.

6.93 Location of the speed sensor mounting nuts (arrows)

Check

Refer to illustration 6.90

90   Disconnect the speed sensor harness connector **(see illustration)**. Working on the harness connector, measure the reference voltage with the ignition key ON (engine not running) between the orange wire terminal (+) on 1994 and 1995 models or the purple/white wire terminal (+) and the black/light blue wire terminal (-). Reference voltage should be approximately 8.0 volts on 1994 and 1995 models and 5 volts on 1996 models.

91   If the reference voltage is correct, the cranking signal can be checked in the same manner as the gasoline engine crankshaft or camshaft position sensors. The engine speed sensor system can also be checked with a SCAN tool.

Replacement

Refer to illustrations 6.93 and 6.96

92   The engine speed sensor is located on the front of the engine. Disconnect the speed sensor electrical connector.

93   Remove the nuts that retain the speed sensor to the timing cover bracket **(see illustration)**.

94   Install the new speed sensor. Install the mounting spacers from the original speed sensor and tighten the nuts finger tight.

95   Route the speed sensor wiring harness behind the pulleys and tighten the harness clips to the engine.

6

6.96 Checking the speed sensor clearance using a brass feeler gauge

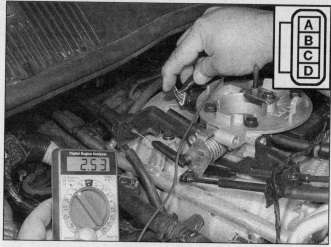

6.102 Check for battery voltage on the IAC connector Terminal A (purple/black wire) and then again on Terminal B (brown/white wire)

96   Adjust the sensor-to-damper clearance with a 0.050-inch brass feeler gauge positioned between the sensor and the vibration damper **(see illustration)**. Gently position the sensor until you can slide the feeler gauge between the sensor and vibration damper with a slight amount of drag.

97   Tighten the sensor mounting nuts to the torque listed in this Chapter's Specifications.

98   Remove the feeler gauge and connect the speed sensor electrical connector.

Idle Air Control (IAC) valve

General description

99   The idle speed is controlled by the IAC valve **(see illustrations 2.15a and 2.15b)**. This valve changes the amount of air that will bypass into the intake manifold. The IAC valve is controlled by the PCM and is opened and closed depending upon the running conditions of the engine (air conditioning system, power steering, cold and warm running etc.).

Check

Refer to illustrations 6.102, 6.104 and 6.105

100   Chrysler recommends the use of a special IAC "exerciser" tool installed in series between the IAC valve and the harness electrical connector for testing purposes. There are several tests the home

mechanic can perform on the IAC system to verify operation but they are limited and are useful only in the case of definite problems rather than intermittent failure.

101   Disconnect the electrical connector from the IAC valve and listen carefully for a change in the idle. Connect the IAC valve electrical connector and turn the air conditioning on and listen for a change in idle rpm. When the engine is cold, the IAC valve should vary the idle as the engine begins to warm-up and also when the air conditioning compressor is turned ON. If there are no obvious signs that the IAC valve is working, continue testing.

102   Use a voltmeter and test for voltage to the IAC valve with the ignition key ON (engine not running). Backprobe the IAC valve electrical connector and check for battery voltage on the purple/black wire (+) and the brown/white wire (-) **(see illustration)**. **Note:** *Voltage should also be present when the engine is running but monitoring the voltage changes as the engine rpm fluctuates is difficult without a factory designed SCAN tool.*

103   If there is no voltage present, have the electrical circuit for the IAC valve diagnosed by a dealer service department or other qualified repair shop.

104   If the computer is delivering voltage to the IAC valve, check that the IAC valve is not frozen or defective. Remove the IAC valve and leaving the IAC valve connected, turn the ignition key ON (engine not running). The pintle should retract (pull in) **(see illustration)**.

6.104 Remove the IAC valve from the throttle body but do not disconnect the electrical connector. Confirm that the pintle moves with the ignition key ON

6.105 Plug the SCAN tool into the diagnostic test connector (arrow) under the driver's dash

6.107 Remove the screws from the IAC valve (V8 engine shown)

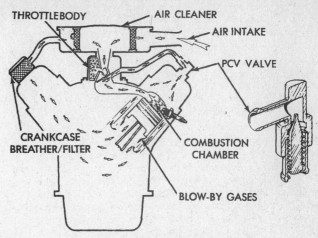

7.1a Schematic of a typical PCV system

105 There is an alternate method for testing the IAC valve. A SCAN tool is available from some automotive parts stores and specialty tool companies that can be plugged into the ALDL for the purpose of monitoring the computer and the sensors. Install the SCAN tool and switch to the IAC position mode and monitor the steps (valve winding position) **(see illustration)**. The SCAN tool should indicate between 10 to 200 steps depending upon the rpm range. Allow the engine to idle for several minutes and while observing the count reading, snap the throttle to achieve high rpm (under 3,500). Repeat the procedure several times and observe the SCAN tool steps when the engine returns to idle. The readings should be within 5 to 10 steps each time. If the readings fluctuate greatly, replace the IAC valve. **Note:** *When the IAC valve electrical connector is disconnected for testing, the PCM will have to "relearn" its idle mode. In other words, it will take a certain amount of time before the idle valve resets for the correct idle speed. Make sure the idle is smooth before plugging in the SCAN tool.*

Replacement

Refer to illustration 6.107

106 Disconnect the electrical connector from the IAC valve.
107 Remove the two mounting screws from the valve **(see illustration)** and lift it from the throttle body.
108 Installation is the reverse of removal. Be sure to install a new O-ring.

7 Positive Crankcase Ventilation (PCV) system

Refer to illustrations 7.1a, 7.1b and 7.1c
Note: *The V10 engine is equipped with a Crankcase Ventilation (CCV) system. This system operates the same as the conventional PCV system but it does not use the vacuum control valve. Instead, a molded vacuum tube connects manifold vacuum to the top of the right cylinder head valve cover. The vacuum tube contains a fixed orifice of a calibrated size. It meters the amount of crankcase vapors drawn out of the engine. A fresh air supply hose from the air cleaner is connected to the front of the cylinder head at the valve cover. When the engine is running, fresh air enters the engine and mixes with the crankcase vapors. Manifold vacuum draws the vapor/air mixture through the fixed orifice and into the intake manifold and consumes them during combustion.*

1 The Positive Crankcase Ventilation (PCV) system **(see illustrations)** reduces hydrocarbon emissions by scavenging crankcase vapors. It does this by circulating fresh air from the air cleaner through the crankcase, where it mixes with blow-by gases and is then rerouted through a PCV valve to the intake manifold.
2 The main components of the PCV system are the PCV valve, a blow-by filter and the vacuum hoses connecting these two components with the engine.

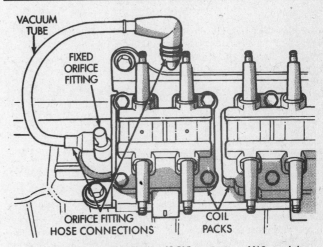

7.1b Crankcase Ventilation (CCV) system on V10 models

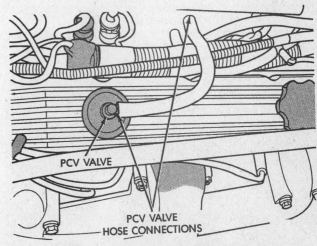

7.1c PCV valve location on the V6 and V8 engines

3 To maintain idle quality, the PCV valve restricts the flow when the intake manifold vacuum is high. If abnormal operating conditions (such as piston ring problems) arise, the system is designed to allow excessive amounts of blow-by gases to flow back through the crankcase vent tube into the air cleaner to be consumed by normal combustion.
4 Checking and replacement of the PCV valve is covered in Chapter 1.

8 Exhaust Gas Recirculation (EGR) system

Note: *If the EGR valve control solenoid becomes disconnected or damaged, the electrical signal will be lost and the EGR valve will be open at all times during warm-up and driving conditions. The associated symptoms will be rough idle and poor performance.*

General description

Refer to illustration 8.1

1   The EGR system reduces tailpipe emissions by recirculating exhaust gas through the EGR valve and intake manifold into the combustion chambers **(see illustration)**.

2   The EGR system consists of the EGR valve, EGR backpressure transducer and the EGR control solenoid valve, the Powertrain Control Module (PCM) and various sensors. The PCM memory is programmed to produce the ideal EGR valve lift for each operating condition. An EGR valve lift sensor detects the amount of EGR valve lift and sends this information to the PCM. The PCM then compares it with the ideal EGR valve lift, which is determined by data received from the other sensors. If there's any difference between the two, the PCM triggers the EGR control solenoid valve to reduce the amount of vacuum applied to the EGR valve.

Check

Refer to illustrations 8.6, 8.10 and 8.11

3   Start the engine and warm it up to normal operating temperature.

4   Check the condition of all the EGR system hoses and tubes for leaks, cracks, kinks or hardening of the rubber hoses. Make sure all the hoses are intact before proceeding with the EGR check.

5   Check the vacuum schematics in Section 1 for the correct EGR system hose routing. Reroute the hoses if necessary.

6   Detach the vacuum hose from the EGR valve and attach a hand-held vacuum pump to the valve **(see illustration)**.

7   Start the engine and apply 5 in-Hg of vacuum to the EGR valve. The idle speed should drop considerably or even stall as vacuum is applied. This indicates that the EGR valve is operating properly.

8   If the engine speed does not change, this indicates a possible faulty EGR valve, blocked or plugged EGR tube or passages in the intake and exhaust manifolds that may be plugged with carbon.

9   Apply vacuum to the EGR valve and observe the stem on the EGR valve for movement. If the valve opens and closes correctly and the engine does not stall, check the passages.

10   Install a vacuum gauge into the EGR control solenoid vacuum line, start the engine and verify that the system is receiving the proper amount of vacuum **(see illustration)**.

11   Also, disconnect the EGR control solenoid electrical connector

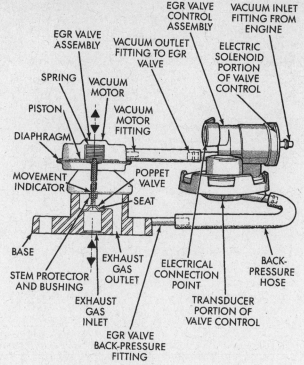

8.1 Typical EGR valve and related components

and check for battery voltage with the ignition key ON (engine not running) **(see illustration)**.

12   Remove the EGR tube and check for plugged ports in the manifolds, bent tubes or other problems. If necessary replace the EGR tube with a new part. **Note:** *If the EGR valve is severely plugged with carbon deposits, do not attempt to scrape them out. Replace the unit.*

Replacement

Refer to illustrations 8.14a, 8.14b, 8.15a and 8.15b

13   Unplug the electrical connector and disconnect the vacuum hose to the EGR control solenoid.

14   Remove the EGR tube mounting bolts **(see illustrations)** and separate the tube from the engine.

15   Remove the nuts that secure the EGR valve and lift the EGR valve, control solenoid and transducer assembly from the engine as a single unit **(see illustrations)**.

8.6 Install a hand-held vacuum pump onto the EGR valve and observe that the valve diaphragm moves up and down freely without any binding - the engine should stall with vacuum applied

8.10 Check for vacuum to the EGR control solenoid with the engine running

8.11 With the ignition key ON (engine not running) there should be battery voltage present at the EGR control solenoid electrical connector

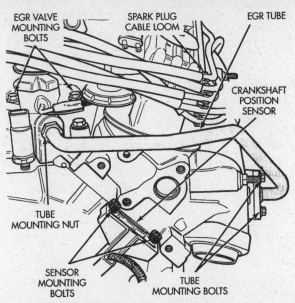

8.14a Remove the EGR tube and check for blockage or damage (V6 and V8 engines shown)

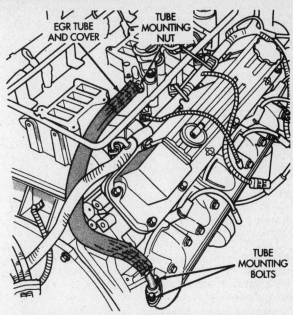

8.14b EGR tube mounting details for the V10 model

16 Clean the mating surfaces of the EGR valve and adapter.
17 Install the EGR valve assembly, using a new gasket. Tighten the nuts securely.
18 Connect the electrical connector and the vacuum hose to the EGR valve control solenoid.

9 Evaporative emissions control (EVAP) system

General description

Refer to illustrations 9.5, 9.6a and 9.6b

1 The fuel evaporative emissions control system absorbs fuel vapors from the fuel tank and, during engine operation, releases them into the engine intake system where they mix with the incoming air-fuel mixture.
2 Every evaporative system employs a canister filled with activated charcoal to absorb fuel vapors.
3 The fuel tank filler cap is fitted with a two-way valve as a safety device. The valve vents fuel vapors to the atmosphere if the evaporative control system fails.
4 Another fuel cut-off valve (fuel tank rollover valve), mounted on the fuel tank, regulates fuel vapor flow from the fuel tank to the charcoal canister, based on the pressure or vacuum caused by temperature changes.
5 After passing through the two-way valve, fuel vapor is carried by vent hoses to the charcoal canister **(see illustration)**. The activated charcoal in the canister absorbs and stores these vapors.

6

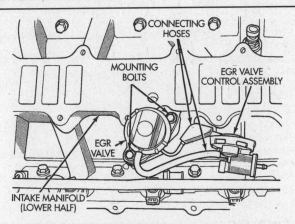

8.15a Location of the EGR system components on the V10 engine

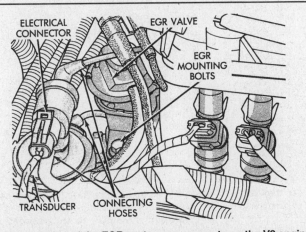

8.15b Location of the EGR system components on the V8 engine

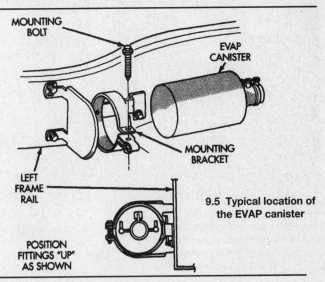

9.5 Typical location of the EVAP canister

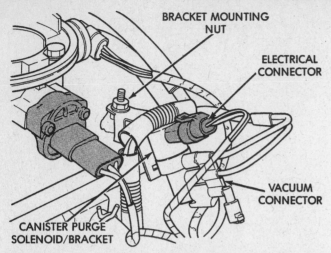

9.6a The canister purge control solenoid is located in the right corner of the engine compartment near the throttle body (V6 and V8 engines shown)

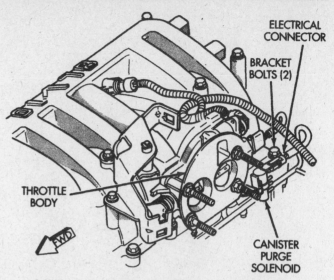

9.6b Location of the canister purge control solenoid on V10 models

6   When the engine is running and warmed to a pre-set temperature, a purge control solenoid **(see illustrations)**, allows a purge control diaphragm valve in the charcoal canister to be opened by intake manifold vacuum. Fuel vapors from the canister are then drawn through the purge control diaphragm valve by intake manifold vacuum. The duty cycle of the EVAP purge control solenoid regulates the rate of flow of the fuel vapors from the canister to the throttle body. The PCM controls the purge control solenoid. During cold running conditions and hot start time delay, the PCM does not energize the solenoid. After the engine has warmed up to the correct operating temperatures the PCM purges the vapors into the throttle body according to the running conditions of the engine. The PCM will cycle (ON then OFF) the purge control solenoid about 5 to 10 times per second. The flow rate will be controlled by the pulse width or length of time the solenoid is allowed to be energized.

Check

Refer to illustrations 9.8, 9.10 and 9.17

Note: *The evaporative control system, like all emission control systems, is protected by a Federally-mandated extended warranty (5 years or 50,000 miles at the time this manual was written). The EVAP system probably won't fail during the service life of the vehicle; however, if it does, the hoses or charcoal canister are usually to blame.*

7   Always check the hoses first. A disconnected, damaged or

9.8 With the engine warmed up, observe the vacuum gauge. There should be no vacuum present to the purge control solenoid when the engine is cold

9.10 Check for battery voltage at the purge control solenoid electrical connector

9.17 Monitor the purge control solenoid duty cycle (ON time) as the engine goes from cold to warm running conditions

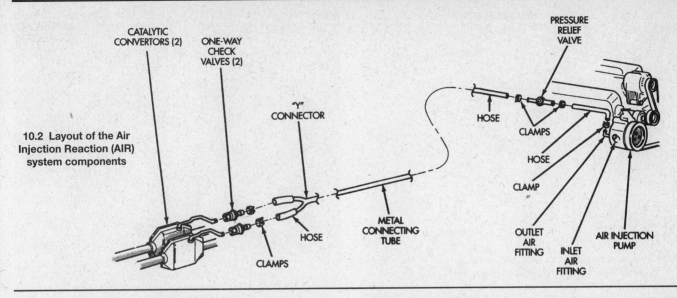

10.2 Layout of the Air Injection Reaction (AIR) system components

missing hose is the most likely cause of a malfunctioning EVAP system. Refer to the Vacuum Hose Routing Diagram (attached to the radiator support) to determine whether the hoses are correctly routed and attached. Repair any damaged hoses or replace any missing hoses as necessary.

8   Disconnect the vacuum hose from the purge control diaphragm valve (located on the intake manifold) and connect a vacuum gauge to the hose **(see illustration)**. Start the engine and allow it to idle. There should be NO vacuum present with the engine temperature below 167-degrees F.

9   If there is no vacuum present, proceed to Step 13.

10   If there is vacuum present, disconnect the electrical connector on the purge control solenoid and check for battery voltage **(see illustration)**.

11   If battery voltage is present, replace the purge cut-off solenoid valve.

12   If there is no battery voltage, repair the wiring harness to the PCM.

13   Warm the engine up to normal operating temperature. If there

originally was no vacuum on the purge control diaphragm valve, check the vacuum source.

14   If there is vacuum present, proceed to Step 16.

15   If there is no vacuum present, trace the vacuum line to the manifold and check for damaged hoses or blocked ports.

16   If vacuum was originally present, have the fuel tank rollover valve tested by a dealer service department.

17   An alternate method of diagnosing the purge control solenoid sensor is by the use of an electronic SCAN tool. SCAN tools can be plugged into the test connector for the purpose of monitoring the computer, sensors and output actuators and are available from some automotive parts stores and specialty tool companies. Install the SCAN tool and switch to the purge control solenoid mode and monitor the voltage signal (duty cycle) **(see illustration)**. The SCAN tool should indicate a percentage of dwell time (ON time). Allow the engine to warm up and observe the purge control solenoid open to circulate the crankcase vapors.

Fuel tank rollover valve

18   Remove fuel tank (see Chapter 4A).

19   The valve is seated in the fuel pump assembly **(see illustration 7.4 in Chapter 4A)**. Remove the valve by prying one side up and rolling the grommet out of the tank along with the valve.

20   Installation is the reverse of removal.

10   Air Injection Reaction (AIR) system (HDC V8 and V10 engines)

General information

Refer to illustrations 10.2, 10.3a and 10.3b

1   The air injection exhaust emission control system reduces carbon monoxide and hydrocarbon content in the exhaust gases by injecting fresh air into the hot exhaust gases leaving the exhaust ports. When fresh air is mixed with the hot exhaust gases, oxidation is increased, reducing the concentration of hydrocarbons and carbon monoxide and converting them into harmless carbon dioxide and water. The system does not interfere with the NOx emission controls of the engine.

2   The air injection system is used on Heavy Duty Cycle (HDC) V8 and V10 engines. The AIR system consists of the belt driven AIR pump, an air pressure relief valve, rubber connecting hoses with clamps, metal connecting air tubes, two-way check valves and an air pump filter **(see illustration)**.

3   On V8 models, the air is drawn into the pump through a rubber tube that is connected to a fitting on the air cleaner **(see illustration)**. On V10 models, air is drawn into the pump through a rubber tube that

10.3a Air inlet tube location for the air pump - V8 model

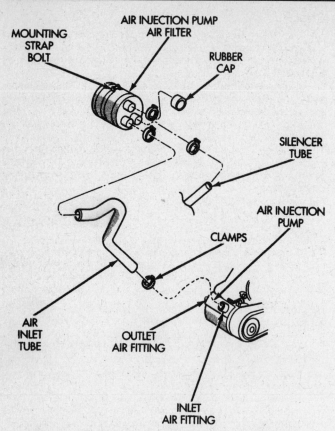

10.3b Air inlet tube location for the air pump - V10 model

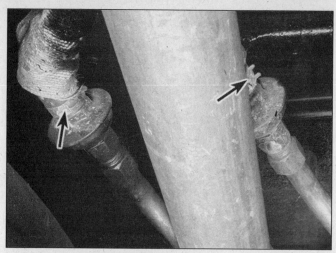

10.10 Remove the clamps from the one-way check valves and with the engine idling, observe that no exhaust leaks into the atmosphere

is connected to a fitting on the air injection pump filter housing **(see illustration)**.

4   Air is compressed by the air injector pump. It is expelled from the pump and routed into a rubber tube where it reaches the air pressure relief valve. Pressure relief holes in the relief valve will prevent excess downstream pressure. If excess pressure occurs at the relief valve, it will be vented into the atmosphere. Air is routed from there to a "Y" connector through two one-way check valves and injected at both of the catalytic converters. The two-way valves protect the hoses, air pump and injection tubes from hot exhaust gases backing up into the system. Air is allowed to flow through these valves in ONE direction only.

5   The air pump is mounted on the front of the engine and driven by a belt connected to the front pulley. Under normal operating conditions, noise from the pump rises in pitch as engine speed increases. Do not attempt to lubricate the AIR pump using oil or any spray penetrant. Oil in the pump will cause damage.

Check

Refer to illustrations 10.10 and 10.13

Air supply pump

6   Check the drivebelt tension (see Chapter 1).
7   Disconnect the air supply hose from the pressure relief valve.
8   The pump is operating satisfactorily if airflow is felt at the pump outlet with the engine running at idle, increasing as the engine speed increases.
9   If little or no air flow is felt, replace the pump with a rebuilt or new unit.

One-way check valves

10   Disconnect the rubber air tube from the intake side of the check valves **(see illustration)**.
11   Start the engine and observe that no exhaust fumes escape through the valve. If there are signs of leakage, replace the check valves with new parts.

Replacement

12   To replace the one-way check valves, the pressure relief valve or any of the hoses and clamps, clearly label, then disconnect the hoses leading to them. Replace the faulty component and reattach the hoses to the proper ports. Make sure the hoses are in good condition. If not, replace them with new ones.
13   To replace the air supply pump, first remove the engine drivebelt (see Chapter 1), then remove the pump mounting bolts **(see illustration)** from the mounting bracket. Label all hoses and wire connections.
14   After the new pump is installed, check the drivebelts (see Chapter 1).

11   Catalytic converter

Note: *Because of a Federally mandated extended warranty which covers emissions-related components such as the catalytic converter, check with a dealer service department before replacing the converter at your own expense.*

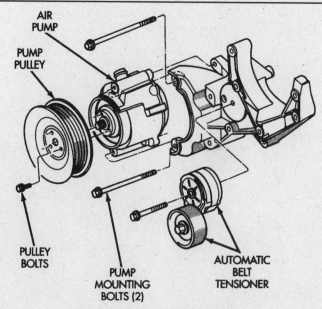

10.13 AIR pump mounting details

11.1 Dual catalytic converters on the V10 engine

General description

Refer to illustration 11.1

1   The catalytic converter **(see illustration)** is an emission control device added to the exhaust system to reduce pollutants from the exhaust gas stream. There are two types of converters. The conventional oxidation catalyst reduces the levels of hydrocarbon (HC) and carbon monoxide (CO). The three-way catalyst lowers the levels of oxides of nitrogen (NOx) as well as hydrocarbons (HC) and carbon monoxide (CO).

Check

2   The test equipment for a catalytic converter is expensive and highly sophisticated. If you suspect that the converter on your vehicle is malfunctioning, take it to a dealer or authorized emissions inspection facility for diagnosis and repair.

3   Whenever the vehicle is raised for servicing of underbody components, check the converter for leaks, corrosion, dents and other damage. Check the welds/flange bolts that attach the front and rear ends of the converter to the exhaust system. If damage is discovered, the converter should be replaced.

4   Although catalytic converters don't break too often, they can become plugged. The easiest way to check for a restricted converter is to use a vacuum gauge to diagnose the effect of a blocked exhaust on intake vacuum.

 a) *Open the throttle until the engine speed is about 2000 rpm.*
 b) *Release the throttle quickly.*
 c) *If there is no restriction, the gauge will quickly drop to not more than 2 in-Hg or more above its normal reading.*
 d) *If the gauge does not show 5 in-Hg or more above its normal reading, or seems to momentarily hover around its highest reading for a moment before it returns, the exhaust system, or the converter, is plugged (or an exhaust pipe is bent or dented, or the core inside the muffler has shifted).*

Replacement

5   Refer to the exhaust system removal and installation Section in Chapter 4, Part A.

6

Notes

Chapter 7 Part A
Manual transmission

Contents

Specifications

General

Transmission lubricant type.. See Chapter 1

Torque specifications   Ft-lbs (unless otherwise indicated)

Crossmember-to-frame rail bolts 50
Shift tower-to-transmission bolts (NV3500) .... 60 to 84 in-lbs
Transmission-to-engine bolts (NV3500) 33
Engine-to-transmission nuts (NV3500)... 110 in-lbs
Transmission-to-clutch housing bolts (NV4500) 50

1   General information

The vehicles covered by this manual are equipped with a manual or an automatic transmission. Information on the manual transmission is included in this Part of Chapter 7. Information on the automatic transmission can be found in Part B of this Chapter.

Vehicles equipped with a manual transmission use either an NV3500 or an NV4500. The NV3500 is used with 3.9L and 5.2L engines; the standard version NV4500 is used with most 5.2L and 5.9L gasoline engines; the heavy-duty version NV4500 is used in V10, Cummins Turbo Diesel and some heavy-duty V8 models. Both units are top-loader five-speeds with internal shift mechanisms.

Depending on the cost of having a transmission overhauled, it might be a better idea to replace it with a used or rebuilt unit. Your local dealer or transmission shop should be able to supply information concerning cost, availability and exchange policy. Regardless of how you decide to remedy a transmission problem, you can still save a lot of money by removing and installing the unit yourself.

2   Extension housing oil seal - replacement

Refer to illustrations 2.4 and 2.6

1   Oil leaks frequently occur due to wear of the extension housing oil seal. Replacement of these seals is relatively easy, since the repairs can usually be performed without removing the transmission from the vehicle.

2   The extension housing oil seal is located at the extreme rear of the transmission, where the driveshaft is attached. If leakage at the seal is suspected, raise the vehicle and support it securely on jackstands. If the seal is leaking, transmission lubricant will be built up on the front of the driveshaft and may be dripping from the rear of the transmission.

2.4 Use a hammer and chisel to dislodge the rear seal

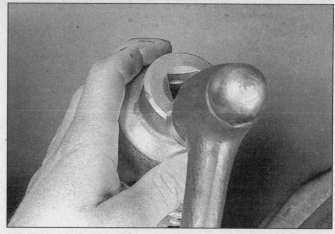

2.6 A large socket can be used to drive the new seal into the bore

3   Remove the driveshaft (see Chapter 8).

4   Using a chisel and hammer, carefully pry the oil seal out of the rear of the transmission **(see illustration)**. Do not damage the splines on the transmission output shaft.

5   If the oil seal cannot be removed with a chisel, a special oil seal removal tool (available at auto parts stores) will be required.

6   Using a large section of pipe or a very large deep socket as a drift, install the new oil seal **(see illustration)**. Drive it into the bore squarely and make sure it's completely seated.

7   Lubricate the splines of the transmission output shaft and the outside of the driveshaft yoke with lightweight grease, then install the driveshaft (see Chapter 8). Be careful not to damage the lip of the new seal.

---

3   Shift lever - removal and installation

NV3500

Refer to illustrations 3.4, 3.5, 3.6 and 3.7

Note: *The shift lever assembly can be disassembled for cleaning, but the only part that can be replaced separately is the boot. The tower, shift lever and and other components are NOT available separately; if the shift lever, tower or any other part is defective or worn out, you must replace the entire shift lever assembly.*

1   Place the shift lever in Neutral.

2   Remove the shift lever boot retainer screws **(see illustra-**

tion 3.10a), slide the boot up the shift lever extension, then unscrew the boot retainer plate **(see illustration 3.10b)**.

3   Remove the bolts attaching the shift tower and shift lever assembly to the transmission.

4   Remove the shift tower and lever as an assembly **(see illustration)**.

5   If (and only if) it's necessary to separate the shift lever extension from the shift lever, you'll need to obtain the special remover/installer tool (6783, or a suitable equivalent).

a) *Scribe or mark the relationship of the shift lever extension to the shift lever.*

b) *Position the notched lower end of the tool just under the square shank of the shift lever (see illustration).*

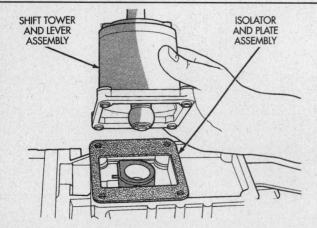

3.4 Remove the shift tower and lever as an assembly; note that the narrow side of the isolator and plate assembly goes on the left (driver's) side

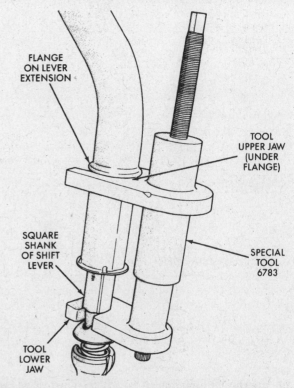

3.5 Position the notched lower end of the remover/installer tool just under the square shank of the shift lever and the upper jaws under the flange on the shift lever extension, then tighten the tool screw to pull the the extension off the shift lever

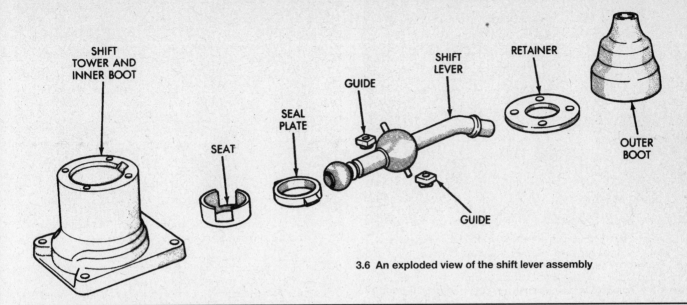

3.6 An exploded view of the shift lever assembly

c) *Position the tool's upper jaws under the flange on the shift lever extension.*

d) *Tighten the tool screw to pull the the extension off the square shank of the shift lever.*

e) *Remove the lever extension and the tool.*

6   Disassemble the shift lever assembly **(see illustration)**, clean the parts in solvent, blow everything dry with compressed air, coat all frictions surfaces with clean multi-purpose grease and reassemble.

7   To install the lever extension on the shift lever:

a) *Reposition the upper jaw of the remover/installer tool (6783, or a suitable equivalent) above the flange on the lever extension* **(see illustration)**.

b) *Tighten the tool screw to press the extension back onto the lever. Make sure the extension is aligned with the scribe mark on the square shank of the shift lever.*

c) *Remove the special tool.*

8   Installation is otherwise the reverse of removal. Be sure to tighten the shift tower bolts to the torque listed in this Chapter's Specifications.

NV4500

Removal

Refer to illustrations 3.10a, 3.10b, 3.13 and 3.14

9   Shift the transmission into Neutral.

10   If the transmission is installed in the vehicle, remove the shift lever boot retainer screws **(see illustration)**, slide the boot up the shift lever

7A

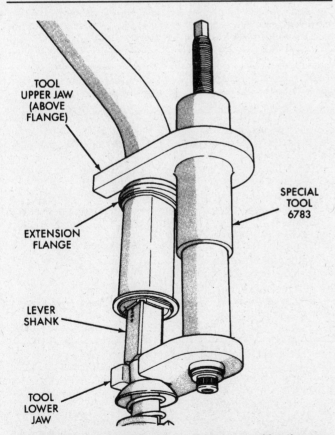

3.7 To install the extension on the shift lever, reposition the upper jaw of the remover/installer tool above the flange on the lever extension and tighten the tool screw to press the extension back onto the lever (make sure the extension is aligned with the scribe mark on the square shank of the shift lever)

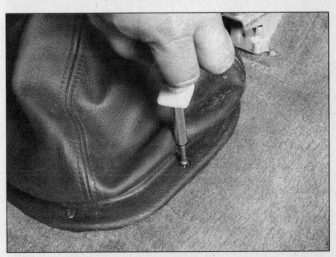

3.10a To detach the extension lever boot from the floor, remove these retainer screws, then slide the boot up the lever so that it's out of the way

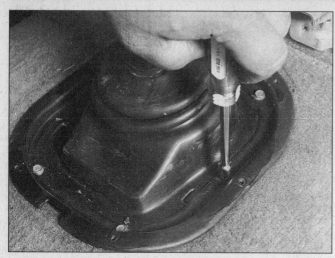

3.10b To detach the boot retainer plate from the floor, remove these screws

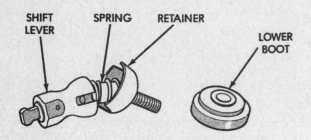

3.14 Lift the shift lever up and remove the lever, retainer and spring as an assembly

extension, then unscrew the boot retainer plate **(see illustration)**.

11   To remove the shift lever extension from the shift lever, you'll need to obtain the special remover/installer tool (6783, or a suitable equivalent):

a) *Scribe or mark the relationship of the shift lever extension to the shift lever.*

b) *Position the notched lower end of the tool just under the square shank of the shift lever* **(see illustration 3.5)**.

c) *Position the tool's upper jaws under the flange on the shift lever extension.*

d) *Tighten the tool screw to pull the the extension off the square shank of the shift lever.*

e) *Remove the lever extension and the tool.*

12   Unseat the shift lever lower boot from the shift tower and slide it off the shift lever.

13   Using two long screwdrivers for leverage, unlock the shift lever retainer. Press the lever retainer down with the screwdrivers, then turn the retainer counterclockwise to release the retainer from the locking pins in the shift tower **(see illustration)**.

14   Lift the shift lever up and remove the lever, retainer and spring as an assembly **(see illustration)**.

Installation

15   Lubricate the shift lever and retainer contact surfaces with petroleum jelly.

16   Install the shift lever as follows:

a) *Note the position information on the square shank of the shift lever. Although the same shift lever is used for all applications, the lever is offset and must be positioned differently in standard and heavy-duty transmissions.*

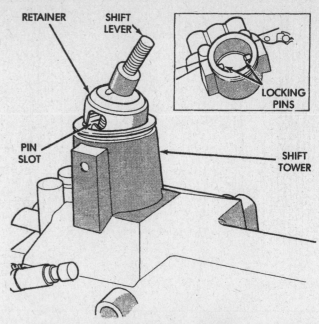

3.13 Using two long screwdrivers for leverage, unlock the shift lever retainer by pressing the lever retainer down with the screwdrivers, then turning the retainer counterclockwise to release the retainer from the locking pins in the shift tower

b) *On heavy-duty transmissions, install the lever so that the "heavy" mark on the lever shank is facing forward.*

c) *On standard-duty transmissions, install the lever so that the "standard" mark on the lever shank is facing forward.*

Caution: *Make sure that the lever has been installed correctly before proceeding. If the shift lever is positioned incorrectly, the lever extension will also be misaligned, causing interference and binding.*

17   Using two long screwdrivers, lock the lever retainer in the shift tower. Push and turn the retainer with the two screwdrivers until it engages both locking pins in the shift tower.

18   Install the lower boot on the shift lever. Seat the boot securely on the shift tower.

19   If the transmission is installed in the vehicle, install the lever extension on the shift lever with Tool 6783 as follows:

a) *Reposition the upper jaw of the remover/installer tool (6783, or a suitable equivalent) above the flange on the lever extension* **(see illustration 3.7)**.

b) *Tighten the tool screw to press the extension back onto the lever. Make sure the extension is aligned with the scribe mark on the square shank of the shift lever.*

c) *Remove the special tool.*

20   If the transmission is installed in the vehicle, slide the boot down the shift lever extension, then install the shift lever boot retainer screws.

---

4   Transmission mount - check and replacement

Check

Refer to illustration 4.2

1   Raise the vehicle and support it securely on jackstands.

2   Insert a large screwdriver or prybar into the space between the transmission extension housing and the crossmember and try to pry the transmission up slightly **(see illustration)**.

3   The transmission should not move much at all and the rubber in the center of the mount should fully insulate the center of the mount from the mount bracket around it.

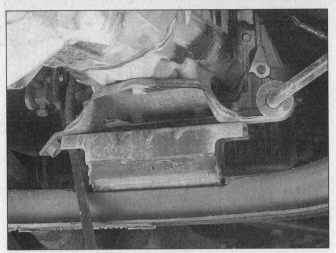

4.2 To check the transmission mount, insert a large screwdriver or prybar between the crossmember and the extension housing and try to lever the transmission up and down and back and forth - it should move very little; if the mount yields easily, it's probably cracked or torn

Replacement

4   To replace the mount, remove the bolts attaching the mount to the crossmember and the bolts attaching the mount to the transmission.

5   Raise the transmission slightly with a jack and remove the mount.

6   Installation is the reverse of the removal procedure. Be sure to tighten all nuts and bolts securely.

---

5   Transmission - removal and installation

Removal

Refer to illustrations 5.17, 5.18a and 5.18b

1   Disconnect the negative cable from the battery.

2   Shift the transmission into Neutral.

3   Detach the shift lever dust boot from the floorpan **(see illustrations 3.10a and 3.10b)**.

4   On models with an NV3500, remove the shift tower and lever assembly and remove the isolator and plate assembly (see Section 3). On models with an NV4500 transmission, remove the extension from the shift lever (see Section 3).

5   Raise the vehicle sufficiently to provide clearance to easily remove the transmission. Support the vehicle securely on jackstands.

6   On models with an NV3500, unplug the electrical connector for the crankshaft position sensor and remove the sensor (see Chapter 6). On all models, unplug the electrical connector for the speed sensor (see Chapter 6) and for the back-up light switch. Disengage the electrical wiring harness from the clips on the transmission.

7   Remove the skid plate, if equipped.

8   If the transmission is going to be torn down, drain the lubricant (see Chapter 1).

9   Remove the driveshaft (see Chapter 8). Use a plastic bag to cover the end of the transmission to prevent fluid loss and contamination.

10   Remove exhaust system components as necessary for clearance (see Chapter 4).

11   Remove the starter motor (see Chapter 5).

12   On 4WD models, remove the transfer case shift linkage and the transfer case (see Chapter 7C).

13   Support the engine from above with an engine hoist, or place a jack (with a block of wood as an insulator) under the engine oil pan. The engine must remain supported at all times while the transmission is out of the vehicle.

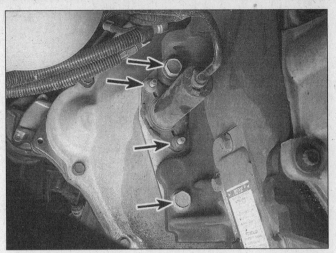

5.17 Remove the two nuts (arrows) which attach the clutch release cylinder to the clutch housing, detach the release cylinder and set it aside for working clearance; to detach the left side of the NV4500 from the clutch housing, remove these two big bolts (arrows)

14   Support the transmission with a jack - preferably a special jack made for this purpose. Safety chains will help steady the transmission on the jack.

15   Raise the engine slightly and disconnect the transmission mount from the extension housing and the center crossmember.

16   Raise the transmission slightly and remove the bolts and nuts attaching the the crossmember to the frame rails.

17   Disconnect the clutch hydraulic release cylinder from the clutch housing **(see illustration)**. Move the cylinder aside for clearance.

18   On NV3500 units, remove the nuts and bolts attaching the transmission to the engine **(see illustration)**. On NV4500 units, remove the

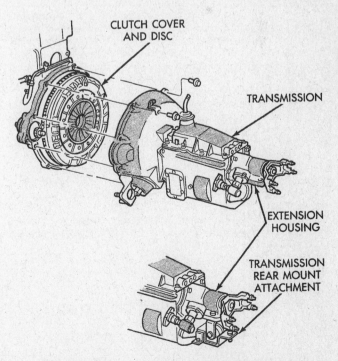

5.18a Transmission-to-engine mounting details (NV3500)

CLUTCH COVER AND DISC

TRANSMISSION

EXTENSION HOUSING

TRANSMISSION REAR MOUNT ATTACHMENT

7A

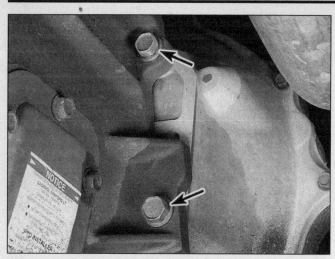

5.18b To detach the right side of the NV4500 transmission from the clutch housing, remove these two big bolts (arrows)

bolts securing the transmission to the clutch housing **(see illustration)**.

19   Make a final check for any wiring or hoses connected to the transmission, then move the transmission and jack toward the rear of the vehicle until the transmission input shaft clears the splined hub in the clutch disc. Keep the transmission level as this is done.

20   Once the input shaft is clear, lower the transmission slightly and remove it from under the vehicle. Before lowering an NV4500 transmission, detach the transmission wiring harness from the clips on the shift cover.

21   While the transmission is removed, be sure to remove and inspect all clutch components (see Chapter 8). (On NV4500 units, you'll have to remove the clutch housing from the engine before you can remove and inspect the clutch assembly.) In most cases, new clutch components should be routinely installed if the transmission is removed.

Installation

22   Insert a small amount of multi-purpose grease into the pilot bearing in the crankshaft and lubricate the inner surface of the bearing. Make sure no grease gets on the input shaft, clutch disc splines or the release lever.

23   Install the clutch components (see Chapter 8).

24   On NV4500 units, attach the clutch housing to the engine and tighten the bolts to the torque listed in the Chapter 8 Specifications.

25   With the transmission secured to the jack as on removal, raise the transmission into position behind the clutch housing and then carefully slide it forward, engaging the input shaft with the clutch plate hub. Do not use excessive force to install the transmission - if the input shaft does not slide into place, readjust the angle of the transmission so it is level and/or turn the input shaft so the splines engage properly with the clutch. On NV4500 units, be sure to attach the transmission wiring harness to the clips on the shift cover before fully raising the transmission into position.

26   On NV3500 units, install the transmission-to-engine bolts and tighten them to the torque listed in this Chapter's Specifications. On

NV4500 units, install the transmission-to-clutch housing bolts and tighten them to the torque listed in this Chapter's Specifications.

27   Install the crossmember and attach it to the frame rails. Install the transmission mount between the extension housing and the crossmember. Carefully lower the transmission extension housing onto the mount and the crossmember. When everything is properly aligned, tighten all nuts and bolts securely.

28   Remove the jacks supporting the transmission and the engine.

29   On 4WD models, install the transfer case and shift linkage (see Chapter 7C).

30   Install the various items removed previously, referring to Chapter 8 for the installation of the driveshaft and clutch release cylinder, Chapter 5 for the starter motor, and Chapter 4 for the exhaust system components.

31   On NV3500 units, install the crankshaft position sensor and plug in the electrical connector for the vehicle speed sensor (see Chapter 6). Plug in the electrical connector for the back-up light switch. Connect any other wiring attached to the transmission.

32   Remove the jackstands and lower the vehicle.

33   On NV3500 units, install the shift tower and extension; on NV4500 units, install the extension (see Chapter 3).

34   Fill the transmission with the specified lubricant to the proper level (see Chapter 1).

35   Connect the negative battery cable.

36   Road test the vehicle for proper operation and check for leakage.

6   Transmission overhaul - general information

Overhauling a manual transmission is a difficult job for the do-it-yourselfer. It involves the disassembly and reassembly of many small parts. Numerous clearances must be precisely measured and, if necessary, changed with select fit spacers and snap-rings. As a result, if transmission problems arise, it can be removed and installed by a competent do-it-yourselfer, but overhaul should be left to a transmission repair shop. Rebuilt transmissions may be available - check with your dealer parts department and auto parts stores. At any rate, the time and money involved in an overhaul is almost sure to exceed the cost of a rebuilt unit.

Nevertheless, it's not impossible for an inexperienced mechanic to rebuild a transmission if the special tools are available and the job is done in a deliberate step-by-step manner so nothing is overlooked.

The tools necessary for an overhaul include internal and external snap-ring pliers, a bearing puller, a slide hammer, a set of pin punches, a dial indicator and possibly a hydraulic press. In addition, a large, sturdy workbench and a vise or transmission stand will be required.

During disassembly of the transmission, make careful notes of how each piece comes off, where it fits in relation to other pieces and what holds it in place. If you note how each part is installed before removing it, getting the transmission back together again will be much easier.

Before taking the transmission apart for repair, it will help if you have some idea what area of the transmission is malfunctioning. Certain problems can be closely tied to specific areas in the transmission, which can make component examination and replacement easier. Refer to the *Troubleshooting* Section at the front of this manual for information regarding possible sources of trouble.

Chapter 7 Part B
Automatic transmission

Contents

Specifications

General

Torque converter bolt length
1994
9.5-inch, 3-lug converter	0.46-inch
9.5-inch, 4-lug converter	0.52-inch
10.0-inch, 4-lug converter	0.52-inch
10.75-inch, 4-lug converter	0.44-inch
1995 and 1996	Specified in parts catalog only

Torque specifications

	Ft-lbs (unless otherwise indicated)
Adjustment swivel lockscrew	90 in-lbs
Neutral start/backup light switch	25
Transmission fluid pan bolts	See Chapter 1

Torque converter-to-driveplate bolts
1994
9.5-inch, 3-lug converter	40
9.5-inch, 4-lug converter	55
10.0-inch, 4-lug converter	55
10.75-inch, 4-lug converter	270 in-lbs

1995 and 1996
10.75-inch converter	270 in-lbs
12.2-inch converter	35

1   General information

All vehicles covered in this manual come equipped with a five-speed manual transmission or a three- or four-speed automatic transmission. Information on the manual transmission is in Part A of this Chapter. You'll also find certain procedures common to both automatic and manual transmissions - such as oil seal replacement - in Part A. Information on the automatic transmission is included in this Part of Chapter 7.

1994 models are equipped with a 32RH, 36RH or 37RH three-speed transmission. The 32RH is used with 3.9L and 5.2L engines; the 36RH is used for heavy-duty 5.2L and 5.9L engine applications; the 37RH is used with the V10 and with the Cummins Turbo Diesel.

1995 models are equipped with a 42RH, 46RH or 47RH four-speed transmission. The 42RH is used with 3.9L engines in 4X2 1500 models; the 46RH is used with 3.9L, 5.2L and 5.9L engines; the 47RH is used with V10 and Cummins Turbo Diesel applications.

1996 models use a 42RE, 46RE or 47RE four-speed transmission with an electronic governor. Their applications are similar to those of 1995 models.

All transmissions are equipped with a torque converter clutch (TCC) that engages in fourth gear, and in third gear when the overdrive switch is turned off. The TCC provides a direct connection between the engine and the drive wheels for improved efficiency and economy. The TCC consists of a solenoid controlled by the Powertrain Control Module (PCM) that locks the converter in third or fourth when the vehicle is cruising on level ground and the engine is fully warmed up.

All four-speed transmissions feature an overdrive unit consisting of an overdrive clutch, direct clutch, planetary gear set and overrunning clutch. The overdrive clutch is applied only in fourth gear. The direct clutch is applied in all ranges except fourth.

Due to the complexity of the automatic transmissions covered in this manual and the need for specialized equipment to perform most service operations, this Chapter contains only general diagnosis, routine maintenance, adjustment and removal and installation procedures.

If the transmission requires major repair work, it should be left to a dealer service department or an automotive or transmission repair shop. You can, however, remove and install the transmission yourself and save the expense, even if the repair work is done by a transmission shop.

2   Diagnosis - general

Note: *Automatic transmission malfunctions may be caused by five general conditions: poor engine performance, improper adjustments, hydraulic malfunctions, mechanical malfunctions or malfunctions in the computer or its signal network (later models). Diagnosis of these problems should always begin with a check of the easily repaired items: fluid level and condition (see Chapter 1), shift linkage adjustment and throttle rod linkage adjustment. Next, perform a road test to determine if the problem has been corrected or if more diagnosis is necessary. If the problem persists after the preliminary tests and corrections are completed, additional diagnosis should be done by a dealer service department or transmission repair shop. Refer to the* Troubleshooting *section at the front of this manual for information on symptoms of transmission problems.*

Preliminary checks

1   Drive the vehicle to warm the transmission to normal operating temperature.
2   Check the fluid level as described in Chapter 1:
   a) *If the fluid level is unusually low, add enough fluid to bring the level within the designated area of the dipstick, then check for external leaks (see below).*
   b) *If the fluid level is abnormally high, drain off the excess, then check the drained fluid for contamination by coolant. The presence of engine coolant in the automatic transmission fluid indi-*

cates that a failure has occurred in the internal radiator walls that separate the coolant from the transmission fluid (see Chapter 3).
   c) *If the fluid is foaming, drain it and refill the transmission, then check for coolant in the fluid or a high fluid level.*
3   Check the engine idle speed. **Note:** *If the engine is malfunctioning, do not proceed with the preliminary checks until it has been repaired and runs normally.*
4   Inspect the shift linkage (see Section 3). Make sure it's properly adjusted and that the linkage operates smoothly.
5   Check the throttle valve cable for freedom of movement. Adjust it if necessary (see Section 4). **Note:** *The throttle valve cable may function properly when the engine is shut off and cold, but it may malfunction once the engine is hot. Check it cold and at normal engine operating temperature.*

Fluid leak diagnosis

6   Most fluid leaks are easy to locate visually. Repair usually consists of replacing a seal or gasket. If a leak is difficult to find, the following procedure may help.
7   Identify the fluid. Make sure it's transmission fluid and not engine oil or brake fluid (automatic transmission fluid is a deep red color).
8   Try to pinpoint the source of the leak. Drive the vehicle several miles, then park it over a large sheet of cardboard. After a minute or two, you should be able to locate the leak by determining the source of the fluid dripping onto the cardboard.
9   Make a careful visual inspection of the suspected component and the area immediately around it. Pay particular attention to gasket mating surfaces. A mirror is often helpful for finding leaks in areas that are hard to see.
10   If the leak still cannot be found, clean the suspected area thoroughly with a degreaser or solvent, then dry it.
11   Drive the vehicle for several miles at normal operating temperature and varying speeds. After driving the vehicle, visually inspect the suspected component again.
12   Once the leak has been located, the cause must be determined before it can be properly repaired. If a gasket is replaced but the sealing flange is bent, the new gasket will not stop the leak. The bent flange must be straightened.
13   Before attempting to repair a leak, check to make sure that the following conditions are corrected or they may cause another leak. **Note:** *Some of the following conditions cannot be fixed without highly specialized tools and expertise. Such problems must be referred to a transmission repair shop or a dealer service department.*

Gasket leaks

14   Check the pan periodically. Make sure the bolts are tight, no bolts are missing, the gasket is in good condition and the pan is flat (dents in the pan may indicate damage to the valve body inside).
15   If the pan gasket is leaking, the fluid level or the fluid pressure may be too high, the vent may be plugged, the pan bolts may be too tight, the pan sealing flange may be warped, the sealing surface of the transmission housing may be damaged, the gasket may be damaged or the transmission casting may be cracked or porous. If sealant instead of gasket material has been used to form a seal between the pan and the transmission housing, it may be the wrong type sealant.

Seal leaks

16   If a transmission seal is leaking, the fluid level or pressure may be too high, the vent may be plugged, the seal bore may be damaged, the seal itself may be damaged or improperly installed, the surface of the shaft protruding through the seal may be damaged or a loose bearing may be causing excessive shaft movement.
17   Make sure the dipstick tube seal is in good condition and the tube is properly seated. Periodically check the area around the speedometer gear or sensor for leakage. If transmission fluid is evident, check the O-ring for damage.

Case leaks

18   If the case itself appears to be leaking, the casting is porous and will have to be repaired or replaced.

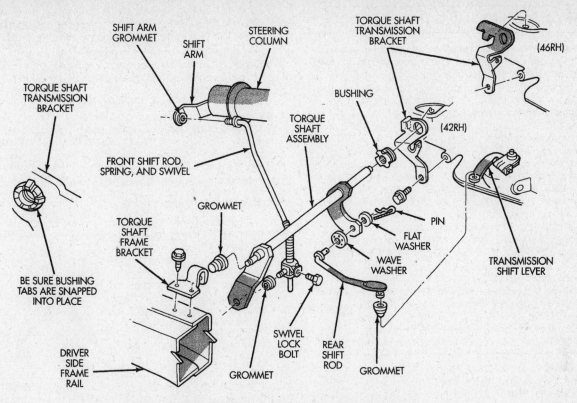

3.4 An exploded view of the shift linkage assembly

19 Make sure the oil cooler hose fittings are tight and in good condition.

Fluid comes out vent pipe or fill tube

20 If this condition occurs, the transmission is overfilled, there is coolant in the fluid, the case is porous, the dipstick is incorrect, the vent is plugged or the drain-back holes are plugged.

3 Shift linkage - check and adjustment

Check

1 To check the adjustment of the shift linkage, verify that the engine starts only in the Park or Neutral position. If the engine starts only in Park or Neutral, the shift linkage is adjusted satisfactorily. If the engine starts in any other gear, or won't start in any gear, either the linkage is out of adjustment or the Neutral start/backup light switch is defective (see Section 5).

Adjustment

Refer to illustrations 3.4 and 3.5

2 Place the shift lever (the one inside the vehicle) in the Park position and lock the steering column with the ignition key.
3 Raise the front of the vehicle and support it securely on jackstands.
4 Before proceeding with the adjustment, inspect the condition of the linkage **(see illustration)**. Note the condition of the shift rod, levers, grommets and torque shaft. Tighten, repair or replace loose, bent, worn or damaged parts as necessary.
5 Loosen the adjustment swivel lock bolt **(see illustration)** and make sure the swivel block is free to turn on the shift rod. If the swivel block binds (even slightly) on the shift rod, clean off any corrosion, dirt or grease with solvent and a wire brush before proceeding.
6 With all linkage assembled and the adjustment swivel lockscrew

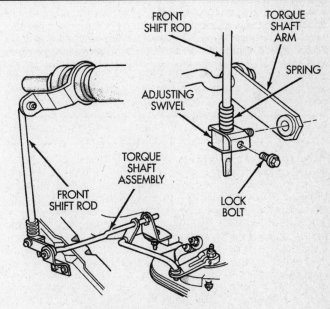

3.5 Shift linkage adjustment details

still loose, move the shift lever on the transmission all the way to its rear detent (the Park position).
7 With the shift lever inside the vehicle and the shift lever on the transmission in their Park positions, tighten the adjustment swivel lockscrew to the torque listed in this Chapter's Specifications.
8 Lower the vehicle and check the shift linkage operation, again making sure the engine starts only in Park or Neutral. The detent position for Neutral and Drive should be within the limits of the shift lever stops.

7B

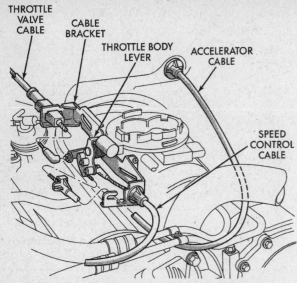

4.1a Throttle valve cable attachment details (V6/V8 engines)

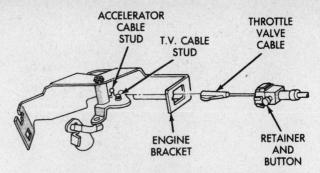

4.1b Throttle valve cable attachment details (V10 engine)

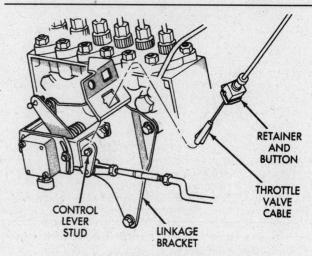

4.1c Throttle valve cable attachment details (Cummins Turbo Diesel engine)

4   Throttle valve cable - check, adjustment and replacement

Check

Refer to illustrations 4.1a, 4.1b and 4.1c

Caution: *This adjustment is critical; it must be correct for the transmission to function correctly. Incorrect adjustment can lead to early transmission failure. When the adjustment is complete, the transmission should shift into third (high) gear at 20 to 30 mph under light throttle pressure. If it does not, take the vehicle to a dealer service department or qualified transmission shop to have the transmission checked.*

1   The throttle lever on the transmission is cable-operated **(see illustrations)**. When the throttle valve cable is correctly adjusted, the throttle lever on the transmission will open and close in accordance with the throttle control lever on the throttle body (gasoline engines) or the injection pump (diesel engines) from idle all the way to wide-open throttle. Correct adjustment ensures simultaneous movement at both throttle levers; the throttle lever on the transmission neither lags behind nor moves ahead of the throttle lever on the throttle body or injection pump.

2   Turn the ignition key to the Off position.

3   On gasoline engines, remove the air cleaner (see Chapter 4).

4   On gasoline engines, verify that the lever on the throttle body is at the curb idle position. Then verify that the throttle lever on the transmission is also at the curb idle position.

5   On diesel engines, verify that the fuel injection pump accelerator linkage is at the curb idle position. Then verify that the throttle lever on the transmission is also at the curb idle position.

6   Detach the cable from the control lever stud on the throttle body or injection pump lever **(see illustration 4.1a, 4.1b or 4.1c)**.

7   Compare the position of the cable end to the attachment stud on the throttle body lever:

   a) *The end of the cable and the attachment stud on the throttle lever should be aligned (or centered on one another) to within 1/32-inch in either direction.*

   b) *If the cable end and the attachment stud are misaligned (off center), the cable must be adjusted as described in the following adjustment procedure.*

8   Reconnect the cable end to the attachment stud.

9   Using an assistant at one end, note the movement of the throttle lever on the transmission and the lever on the throttle body.

   a) *If both levers move simultaneously from idle to half-throttle and back to idle position, the adjustment is correct.*

   b) *If the transmission throttle lever moves ahead of, or lags behind, the throttle body lever, the cable must be adjusted.*

   c) *If the throttle body lever prevents the transmission throttle lever from returning to its closed position, the cable must be adjusted.*

Adjustment

Refer to illustration 4.15

Note: *The adjustment procedure for gas and diesel engines is identical.*

10   Turn the ignition switch to the Off position.

11   On gas engines, remove the air cleaner (see Chapter 4).

12   Detach the end of the cable from the attachment stud on the throttle lever at the throttle body (gas engines) or injection pump (diesels) **(see illustrations 4.1a, 4.1b or 4.1c)**.

13   Verify that the throttle lever on the transmission is in the fully-closed position, then verify that the throttle lever on the throttle body or injection pump is at the curb idle position.

14   Locate the cable lock button (it's part of the cable retainer at the engine-end of the cable). Press the button and release the cable.

15   With the button still pressed in, center the cable end on the attachment stud to within 1/32-inch **(see illustration)**. Release the lock button.

16   Check the cable adjustment (see Steps 1 through 9).

Replacement

Refer to illustration 4.18

17   Raise the vehicle and place it securely on jackstands.

18   Disconnect the cable from the throttle lever on the transmission **(see illustration)**.

19   Rotate the cable out of the transmission bracket.

20   Disengage the cable from the body clips.

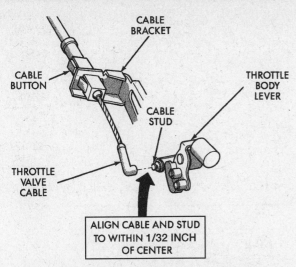

ALIGN CABLE AND STUD
TO WITHIN 1/32 INCH
OF CENTER

4.15 With the lock button pressed in to allow the throttle valve cable to move freely, center the cable end on the attachment stud to within 1/32-inch, then release the lock button

21 Lower the vehicle.
22 Disengage the cable from the engine bracket and from the attachment stud on the lever at the throttle body or injection pump.
23 Note the routing of the old cable, then remove it.
24 Route the new cable exactly as before. Connect it to the engine bracket but don't connect it to the throttle body or injection pump yet.
25 Raise the vehicle and place it securely on jackstands.
26 Attach the cable to the throttle lever on the transmission. Make sure the TV lever return spring is connected. The transmission won't shift properly without this spring.

5 Neutral start/backup light switch - check and replacement

1 The Neutral start/backup switch is threaded into the lower left front edge of the transmission case. The Neutral start and backup light switch functions are combined into one unit, with the center terminal of the switch grounding the starter solenoid circuit when the transmission is in Park or Neutral, allowing the engine to start. The outer terminals make up the backup light switch circuit.

5.3 Unplug the electrical connector from the Neutral start/backup light switch; the center terminal (arrow) is the ground terminal for the starter solenoid circuit when the transmission is in Neutral or Park

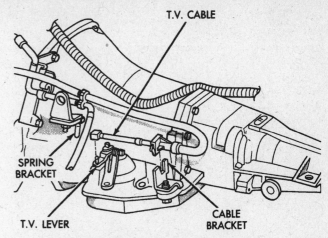

4.18 Throttle valve cable attachment at the throttle lever on the transmission (V6/V8 engines)

Check

Refer to illustration 5.3

2 Prior to checking the switch, make sure the shift linkage is properly adjusted (see Section 3). Raise the vehicle and support it securely on jackstands.
3 Unplug the connector and use an ohmmeter or self-powered test light to check for continuity between the center terminal and the transmission case **(see illustration)**. Continuity should exist only when the transmission is in Park or Neutral.
4 Check for continuity between the two outer terminals. There should be continuity only when the transmission is in Reverse. There should be no continuity between either of the outer terminals and the transmission case.

Replacement

Refer to illustration 5.6

5 Place a container under the transmission to catch the fluid which will be released, then use a six-point socket to remove the switch.
6 Move the shift lever from Park to Neutral. Make sure that the switch operating fingers are centered in the switch opening in the case **(see illustration)**. If they aren't, the shift linkage is incorrectly adjusted or there is an internal problem with the transmission.

7B

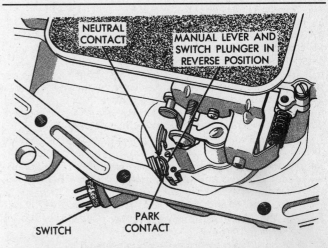

5.6 Make sure that the switch operating fingers are centered in the opening; if they're not, the shift linkage is incorrectly adjusted or there's a problem inside the transmission (transmission oil pan removed for clarity)

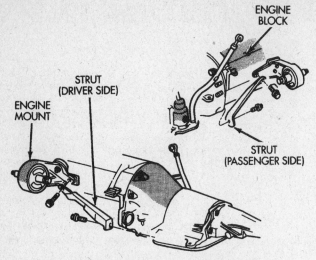

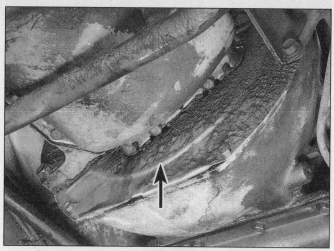

6.5 Engine/transmission strut installation details

6.8 Unbolt and remove the torque converter cover . . .

7   Install the new switch and O-ring (be sure to use a new O-ring, even if installing the original switch), tighten it to the torque listed in this Chapter's Specifications, then recheck the switch before plugging in the connector.

6   Automatic transmission - removal and installation

Removal

Refer to illustrations 6.5, 6.8, 6.10, 6.15 and 6.19

Caution: *The transmission and converter must be removed as a single assembly. If you try to leave the torque converter attached to the driveplate, the converter driveplate, pump bushing and oil seal will be damaged. The driveplate is not designed to support the load, so none of the weight of the transmission should be allowed to rest on the plate during removal.*

1   Disconnect the negative cable from the battery.
2   Raise the vehicle and support it securely on jackstands.
3   If the transmission is being removed for overhaul, remove the oil pan, drain the transmission fluid (see Chapter 1) and reinstall the pan.
4   Remove all exhaust components which interfere with transmission removal (see Chapter 4).

5   Remove the engine-to-transmission struts, if equipped **(see illustration)**.
6   Remove the starter motor (see Chapter 5).
7   Remove the crankshaft position sensor (see Chapter 6).
8   Remove the torque converter cover **(see illustration)**.
9   Mark the relationship of the torque converter to the driveplate so they can be installed in the same position.
10   Remove the torque converter-to-driveplate bolts **(see illustration)**. Turn the crankshaft for access to each bolt. Turn the crankshaft in a clockwise direction only (as viewed from the front).
11   Mark the yokes and remove the driveshaft (see Chapter 8). On 4WD models, remove both driveshafts.
12   Unplug the electrical connectors to the speed sensor (see Chapter 6), the Neutral start/backup light switch (see Section 5) and the transmission solenoid.
13   Disconnect the shift rod and torque shaft from the transmission (see Section 3).
14   Disconnect the throttle cable at the transmission (see Section 4).
15   Remove the fill/dipstick tube bracket bolts and pull the tube out of the transmission **(see illustration)**. Don't lose the tube O-ring (it can be reused if it's still in good shape). On 4WD models, remove the bolt which attaches the transfer case vent tube to the converter housing.
16   On 4WD models, remove the transfer case (see Chapter 7C).

Note: *If you are not planning to replace the transmission, but are removing it in order to gain access to other components such as the torque converter, it isn't really necessary to remove the transfer case.*

6.10 . . . then remove the four torque converter-to-driveplate bolts - be sure to mark the relationship of the torque converter to the driveplate for reassembly reference

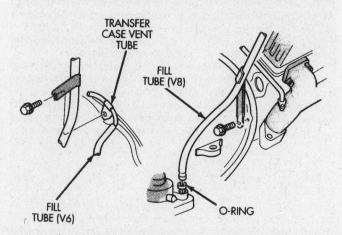

6.15 Fill tube (dipstick tube) installation details

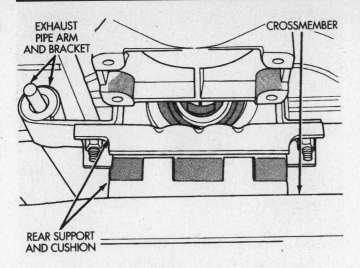

6.19 Rear support (transmission mount) installation details

However, the transmission and transfer case are awkward and heavy when removed and installed as a single assembly; they're much easier to maneuver off and on as separate units. If you decide to leave the transfer case attached, disconnect the shift rod from the transfer case shift lever, or remove the shift lever from the transfer case and tie the rod and lever to the chassis (see Chapter 7C). **Warning:** *If you decide to leave the transfer case attached to the transmission, be sure to use safety chains to help stabilize the transmission and transfer case assembly and to prevent it from falling off the jack head, which could cause serious damage to the transmission and/or transfer case and serious bodily injury to you.*

17   Support the engine with a jack. Use a block of wood under the oil pan to spread the load.

18   Support the transmission with a jack - preferably a jack made for this purpose (available at most tool rental yards). Safety chains will help steady the transmission on the jack.

19   Remove the bolts securing the rear support and cushion to the transmission and crossmember **(see illustration)**, raise the transmission slightly, slide the exhaust hanger arm from the bracket and remove the rear support.

20   Remove the bolts securing the transmission to the engine. **Note:** *The upper bolts are often easier to remove from above, in the engine compartment. Also, on some models, you'll have to remove the oil filter (see Chapter 1) before you can remove the lower right (passenger's side) bolt.*

21   Lower the transmission slightly and disconnect the transmission cooler lines at the transmission, using a flare-nut wrench. **Note:** *You'll need to use a back-up wrench on the transmission cooler line fitting so it doesn't unscrew, causing the line to twist. Plug the ends of the lines to prevent fluid from leaking out after you disconnect them.*

22   Clamp a pair of locking pliers onto the lower portion of the transmission case, just in front of the torque converter (but make sure they're not clamped in front of one of the torque converter-to-driveplate bolt locations, or the driveplate will hang up on the pliers). The pliers will prevent the torque converter from falling out while you're removing the transmission. Move the transmission to the rear to disengage it from the engine block dowel pins and make sure the torque converter is detached from the driveplate. Lower the transmission with the jack.

Installation

23   Prior to installation, make sure the torque converter hub is securely engaged in the pump. If you've removed the converter, spread transmission fluid on the torque converter rear hub, where the transmission front seal rides. With the front of the transmission facing up, rotate the converter back and forth. It should drop down into the transmission front pump in stages. To make sure the converter is fully engaged, lay a straightedge across the transmission-to-engine mating surface and make sure the converter hub is at least 1/2-inch below the straightedge. Reinstall the locking pliers to hold the converter in this position.

24   With the transmission secured to the jack, raise it into position. Connect the transmission fluid cooler lines.

25   Turn the torque converter to line up the holes with the holes in the driveplate. The mark on the torque converter and driveplate made in Step 9 must line up.

26   Move the transmission forward carefully until the dowel pins and the torque converter are engaged. Make sure the transmission mates with the engine with no gap. If there's a gap, make sure there are no wires or other objects pinched between the engine and transmission and also make sure the torque converter is completely engaged in the transmission front pump. Try to rotate the converter - if it doesn't rotate easily, it's probably not fully engaged in the pump. If necessary, lower the transmission and install the converter fully.

27   Install the transmission-to-engine bolts and tighten them securely. As you're tightening the bolts, make *sure* that the engine and transmission mate completely at all points. If not, find out why. Never try to force the engine and transmission together with the bolts or you'll break the transmission case!

28   Install the torque converter-to-driveplate bolts. Tighten them to the torque listed in this Chapter's Specifications. **Caution:** *Using the correct length bolts for bolting the converter to the flywheel is critical. A number of different converters are used on the vehicles covered by this manual. Each uses different length bolts. If the bolts are too long, they will damage the converter. If you're planning to use new bolts, make sure you obtain the bolt length listed in this Chapter's Specifications for the torque converter installed in the vehicle.*

29   Install the transmission mount and crossmember.

30   Remove the jacks supporting the transmission and the engine.

31   Install the fill/dipstick tube assembly and, if applicable, the vent tube for the transfer case.

32   Install the starter motor (see Chapter 5).

33   Connect the shift rod and torque shaft (see Section 3) and the throttle valve cable (see Section 4).

34   Plug in the transmission electrical connectors.

35   Install the torque converter cover and tighten the bolts securely.

36   On 4WD models, install the transfer case, if removed, and the transfer case shift linkage (see Chapter 7C).

37   Install the driveshaft(s) (see Chapter 8).

38   Adjust the shift linkage (see Section 3). Adjust the throttle valve cable (see Section 4).

39   Install any exhaust system components that were removed or disconnected (see Chapter 4).

40   Remove the jackstands and lower the vehicle.

41   Fill the transmission with the specified fluid (see Chapter 1), run the engine and check for fluid leaks.

7B

Notes

Chapter 7 Part C
Transfer case

Contents

Specifications

Torque specifications

	Ft-lbs (unless otherwise indicated)
Shift-rod lock bolt	90 in-lbs
Transfer case-to-transmission nuts	
5/16-inch studs	22 to 30
3/8-inch studs	30 to 35
Companion flange nut	130 to 200

1 General information

The transfer case is a device which transmits power from the transmission to the front and rear driveshafts. The models covered by this manual may be equipped with any one of the following transfer cases, all of them manufactured by New Process (NP) or, as it's known on 1996 models, New Venture (NV):

a) *1994 models are equipped with an NP241 transfer case, which is a part-time unit with a low-range reduction gear system. The NP241 has three operating ranges and a Neutral position. The low-range (4L) position provides a gear reduction ratio of 2.72:1 for increased low speed torque capability. The three operating ranges are 2-high, 4-high and 4-low.*

b) *1995 models are equipped with either an NP231, NP241 or NP241HD (heavy-duty). The NP231 and NP241HD are similar in design and operation to the NP241 described above.*

c) *1996 models are equipped with an NV231, NV241 or NV241HD. Aside from their different designations, these units are identical to the 1994 and 1995 transfer cases.*

2 Shift linkage - adjustment

Refer to illustrations 2.3 and 2.5

1 Move the shift lever into the 2H position.
2 Raise the vehicle and support it securely on jackstands.

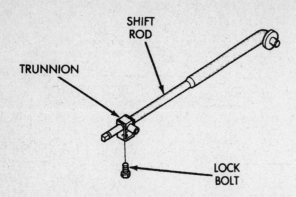

2.3 Transfer case shift linkage adjustment details

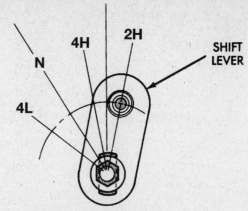

2.5 Make sure the shift lever is in the 2H position before tightening the trunnion lock bolt

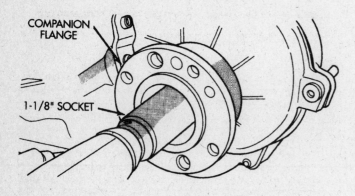

3.6 Remove the companion flange nut and discard the nut; use a new nut when installing the companion flange

3   Loosen the shift-rod lock bolt at the trunnion **(see illustration)**.
4   Check the fit of the shift rod in the trunnion. Make sure it doesn't bind in the trunnion.
5   Verify that the transfer case range lever is in the 2H **(see illustration)** position.
6   Tighten the shift-rod lock bolt to the torque listed in this Chapter's Specifications.
7   Remove the jackstands and lower the vehicle.

3   Oil seal - replacement

1   Disconnect the negative cable from the battery.
2   Raise the vehicle and support it securely on jackstands.
3   Remove the skid plate, if equipped.
4   Drain the transfer case lubricant (see Chapter 1).

Companion flange seal

Refer to illustrations 3.6, 3.7, 3.8, 3.11a and 3.11b
5   Remove the front driveshaft (see Chapter 8).
6   Remove the companion flange nut **(see illustration)**. Discard the nut; it's not reusable.
7   Tap the companion flange off the front output shaft with a brass or plastic dead-blow hammer **(see illustration)**.
8   Remove the companion flange rubber seal from the front output shaft **(see illustration)**.
9   Carefully pry out the old seal with a screwdriver or a seal removal tool. Make sure you don't scratch or gouge the seal bore.
10 Lubricate the lips and the outer diameter of the new seal with multi-purpose grease. Place the seal in position, square to the bore, making sure the garter spring faces toward the inside of the transfer case.
11 Using a factory seal installer **(see illustration)** or a suitable equivalent (a large deep socket with an outside circumference slightly smaller than the circumference of the new seal will work fine), start the seal in the bore with light hammer taps. Continue tapping the seal into

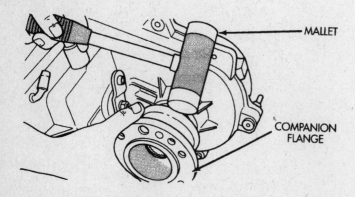

3.7 Tap the companion flange off the front output shaft with a brass or plastic dead-blow hammer

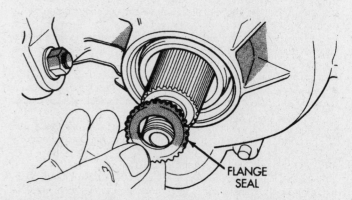

3.8 Remove the companion flange rubber seal from the front output shaft

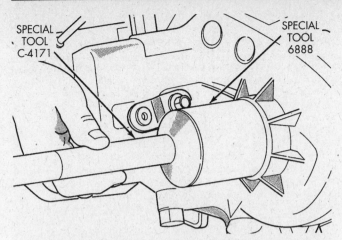

3.11a Using a factory seal installer or a suitable equivalent (a large deep socket with an outside circumference slightly smaller than the circumference of the new seal will work fine), start the seal in the bore with light hammer taps; continue tapping the seal into place until it bottoms against the case

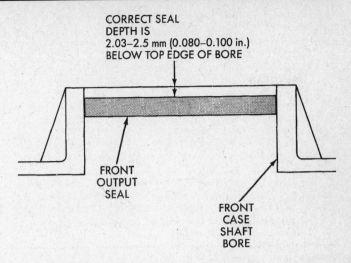

3.11b Verify that the seal is recessed the correct amount

place until it is recessed the correct amount **(see illustration)**.

12 Install a new flange seal on the front output shaft.

13 Install the companion flange on the front output shaft, then install a NEW flange nut and tighten it to the torque listed in this Chapter's Specifications.

14 Install the front driveshaft (see Chapter 8).

15 Remove the jackstands and lower the vehicle.

Extension housing seal

16 This procedure is identical to the extension housing seal replacement procedure for the transmission (see Chapter 7A).

---

4 Transfer case - removal and installation

Removal

Refer to illustration 4.7

1 Disconnect the negative cable from the battery.

2 Raise the vehicle and support it securely on jackstands.

3 Remove the skid plate, if equipped.

4 Drain the transfer case lubricant (see Chapter 1).

5 Unplug the electrical connector from the vehicle speed sensor. Remove the vehicle speed sensor/speedometer adapter assembly (see Chapter 6) to protect it from damage during transfer case removal.

6 Detach all vacuum/vent lines and electrical connectors from the transfer case.

7 Disconnect the shift lever rod from the grommet in the transfer case shift lever **(see illustration)** or from the shift lever arm on the floor, whichever provides easier access. Press the rod out of the grommet with adjustable pliers.

8 Remove the front and rear driveshafts (see Chapter 8).

9 Support the transmission with a transmission jack or a floor jack.

10 Remove the rear crossmember.

11 Support the transfer case with a suitable jack - preferably a special jack made for this purpose. Safety chains will help steady the transfer case on the jack.

12 Remove the transfer case-to-transmission nuts.

13 Make a final check that all wires and hoses have been disconnected from the transfer case, then move the transfer case and jack toward the rear of the vehicle until the transfer case is clear of the transmission. Keep the transfer case level as this is done.

14 Once the input shaft is clear, lower the transfer case and remove it from under the vehicle.

Installation

15 Remove all gasket material from the rear of the transmission overdrive unit or extension housing. Apply Mopar Perfect Seal, silicone sealer or Permatex No. 2 to both sides of the transfer-case-to-transmission gasket and position the gasket on the mating surface of the transmission.

16 With the transfer case secured to the jack as on removal, raise it into position behind the transmission and then carefully slide it forward, engaging the input shaft with the transmission output shaft. Do not use excessive force to install the transfer case - if the input shaft does not slide into place, readjust the angle so it is level and/or turn the input shaft so the splines engage properly with the transmission.

17 Install the transfer case-to-transmission bolts. Tighten the bolts to the torque listed in this Chapter's Specifications.

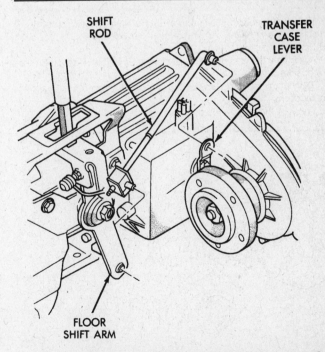

4.7 Disconnect the shift lever rod from the grommet in the transfer case shift lever or from the shift lever arm on the floor (whichever is easier)

7C

18   Remove the safety chains and remove the jack supporting the transfer case.

19   Install the rear crossmember.

20   Remove the jack from under the transmission.

21   Install the driveshafts (see Chapter 8).

22   Reattach all vacuum and/or vent lines. Plug in all electrical connectors.

23   Connect the shift rod to the transfer case shift lever or to the floor-mounted shift lever arm, and adjust the shift linkage (see Section 2).

24   Connect the speedometer cable or install the vehicle speed sensor/speedometer adapter assembly and plug in the electrical connector.

25   Check the lubricant level in the transfer case and top it off as necessary (see Chapter 1). If the vehicle has a manual transmission, this is also a good time to check the lubricant level for the transmission (see Chapter 1).

26   Install the skid plate, if equipped.

27   Remove the jackstands and lower the vehicle.

28   Connect the negative battery cable.

29   Road test the vehicle for proper operation and check for leakage.

5   Transfer case overhaul - general information

Overhauling a transfer case is a difficult job for the do-it-your-selfer. It involves the disassembly and reassembly of many small parts. Numerous clearances must be precisely measured and, if necessary, changed with select fit spacers and snap-rings. As a result, if transfer case problems arise, it can be removed and installed by a competent do-it-yourselfer, but overhaul should be left to a transmission repair shop. Rebuilt transfer cases may be available - check with your dealer parts department and auto parts stores. At any rate, the time and money involved in an overhaul is almost sure to exceed the cost of a rebuilt unit.

Nevertheless, it's not impossible for an inexperienced mechanic to rebuild a transfer case if the special tools are available and the job is done in a deliberate step-by-step manner so nothing is overlooked.

The tools necessary for an overhaul include internal and external snap-ring pliers, a bearing puller, a slide hammer, a set of pin punches, a dial indicator and possibly a hydraulic press. In addition, a large, sturdy workbench and a vise or transmission stand will be required.

During disassembly of the transfer case, make careful notes of how each piece comes off, where it fits in relation to other pieces and what holds it in place. Note how parts are installed when you remove them; this will make it much easier to get the transfer case back together.

Before taking the transfer case apart for repair, it will help if you have some idea what area of the transfer case is malfunctioning. Certain problems can be closely tied to specific areas in the transfer case, which can make component examination and replacement easier. Refer to the *Troubleshooting* section at the front of this manual for information regarding possible sources of trouble.

Chapter 8
Clutch and driveline

Contents

Specifications

General

Clutch disc lining thickness .... 1/16 inch (above rivet)

Torque specifications

Ft-lbs (unless otherwise indicated)

Clutch

Pressure plate-to-flywheel bolts	
5/16-inch bolts	17
3/8-inch bolts	30
Clutch housing-to-engine bolts (NV4500 transmission) **(see illustration 4.22)**	
A bolts	30 to 50 in-lbs
B bolts	20 to 40
C bolts	35 to 65
Slave cylinder mounting nuts	170 to 230 in-lbs

Driveshaft

Center support bearing bolts/nuts	50
Universal joint clamp bolts	
Front driveshaft	
Flange yoke bolts	65
U-joint strap-to-axle yoke bolts	168 in-lbs
Rear driveshaft	
9-1/4 axle	168 in-lbs
Model 60/70/80 axle	22

8

Front and rear axles

Differential cover bolts	See Chapter 1
Front axleshaft hub nut	175
Hub bearing-to-steering knuckle bolts	125
Companion flange-to-differential pinion nut	
Front axle	
Model 44	190 to 290
Model 60	215 to 315
Rear axle	
9-1/4 inch	210 (minimum)
Model 60	215 to 315
Model 70	220 to 280
Model 80	440 to 500
Rear axleshaft (Model 60/70/80)	
Flange bolts	90
Axleshaft locking nut	120 to 140
Pinion shaft lock bolt	96 in-lbs
Shift motor housing bolts	96 in-lbs

1   General information

The information in this Chapter deals with the components from the rear of the engine to the drive wheels, except for the transmission and transfer case, which are dealt with in the previous Chapter. For the purposes of this Chapter, these components are grouped into three categories: clutch, driveshaft and axles. Separate Sections within this Chapter offer general descriptions and checking procedures for components in each of the three groups.

Since nearly all the procedures covered in this Chapter involve working under the vehicle, make sure it's securely supported on sturdy jackstands or on a hoist where the vehicle can be easily raised and lowered.

2   Clutch - description and check

Refer to illustration 2.1

1   All vehicles with a manual transmission use a single dry-plate type clutch and a diaphragm-style pressure plate **(see illustration)**. The transmission input shaft is supported by a pilot bearing in the end of the crankshaft. The clutch disc has a splined hub which allows it to slide along the splines of this input shaft. A sleeve-type release bearing is operated by a release fork in the clutch housing. The fork pivots on a ball stud mounted inside the housing.

2   The clutch disc has damper springs in the disc hub. The disc used with V6 and V8 engines has four damper springs; the disc used with V10s and diesels has five. The two are not interchangeable. The V6/V8 disc has a diameter of 11 inches; the V10/diesel disc has a 12.3-inch diameter. All clutch discs use non-asbestos facing material riveted to the hub.

3   The clutch cover pressure plate is a diaphragm type with a one-piece spring and multiple release fingers.

4   The clutch release system is operated by hydraulic pressure. The hydraulic release system consists of the clutch pedal, a master cylinder and fluid reservoir, the hydraulic line, a slave (release) cylinder, and a release fork mounted inside the clutch housing. When pressure is applied to the clutch pedal to release the clutch, hydraulic pressure is exerted against the release fork by the slave cylinder pushrod. When the release fork is moved, it pushes against the release bearing. The bearing pushes against the fingers of the diaphragm spring of the pressure plate assembly, which in turn releases the clutch plate.

5   The clutch master cylinder, remote reservoir, slave cylinder and lines are serviced as an assembly. They can't be overhauled separately.

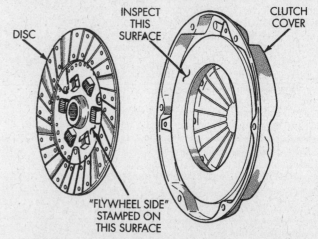

2.1 The clutch disc and clutch cover (pressure plate)

They're filled with fluid during manufacture, then sealed. They must not be disassembled or disconnected. If the system is leaking or has air in it, replace the entire assembly.

6   Terminology can be a problem when discussing the clutch components because common names are in some cases different from those used by the manufacturer. For example, the driven plate is also called the clutch plate or disc, the clutch release bearing is sometimes called a throwout bearing, the release fork is also called a release lever, the release cylinder is called a slave cylinder, and so on.

7   Before replacing any components with obvious damage, some preliminary checks should be performed to diagnose clutch problems.

a) *The first check should be of the fluid level in the clutch master cylinder. If the fluid level is low, add fluid as necessary and inspect the hydraulic system for leaks. If the master cylinder reservoir has run dry, the hydraulic clutch assembly will have to be replaced as a unit. Retest the clutch operation.*

b) *To check "clutch spin down time," run the engine at normal idle speed with the transmission in Neutral (clutch pedal up - engaged). Disengage the clutch (pedal down), wait several seconds and shift the transmission into Reverse. No grinding noise should be heard. A grinding noise would most likely indicate a problem in the pressure plate or the clutch disc (assuming the transmission is in good condition).*

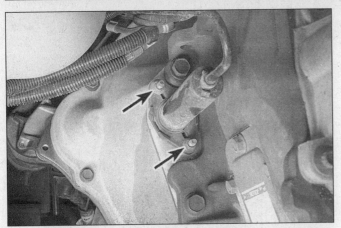

3.3 To detach the clutch slave (release) cylinder from the clutch housing, remove these two nuts (arrows)

c)   To check for complete clutch release, run the engine (with the parking brake applied to prevent movement) and hold the clutch pedal approximately 1/2-inch from the floor. Shift the transmission between 1st gear and Reverse several times. If the shift is rough, component failure is indicated. Check the release cylinder pushrod travel. With the clutch pedal depressed completely, the release cylinder pushrod should extend substantially. If it doesn't, check the fluid level in the clutch master cylinder.

d)   Visually inspect the pivot bushing at the top of the clutch pedal to make sure there is no binding or excessive play.

3   Clutch hydraulic release system - removal and installation

Removal

Refer to illustrations 3.3, 3.4, 3.6a and 3.6b

Note: *The clutch hydraulic release system is serviced as an assembly. The components cannot be serviced separately. They're filled with fluid during manufacture, then sealed. They must not be disassembled or disconnected. If the system is leaking or has air in it, replace the entire assembly.*

1   Raise the vehicle and place it securely on jackstands.
2   On diesel models, remove the slave cylinder shield, if equipped.
3   Remove the nuts attaching the slave cylinder to the clutch housing **(see illustration)** then remove the slave cylinder from the clutch housing.
4   Disengage the clutch hydraulic fluid line from the retaining clip on

3.6a To disconnect the clutch master cylinder pushrod from the pivot pin at the top of the clutch pedal, pry off this retainer clip with a screwdriver

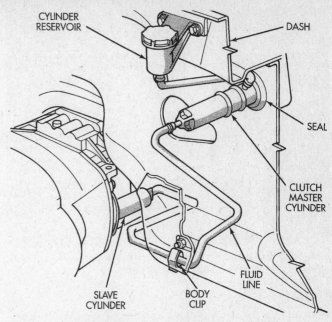

3.4 Clutch hydraulic release system details

the lower edge of the firewall **(see illustration)**.
5   Lower the vehicle.
6   Pry off the retainer clip from the pushrod-to-clutch pedal pin and remove the flat washer and wave washer from the pin **(see illustrations)**.
7   Unplug the electrical connector for the clutch pedal position switch, then slide the master cylinder pushrod off the pin on the clutch pedal. Remove the pin bushing and inspect it. If it's worn, replace it.
8   To avoid spillage, make sure that the cap on the master cylinder's remote reservoir is tight. Remove the reservoir mounting screws.
9   Rotate the clutch master cylinder 45-degrees in a counterclockwise direction to unlock it, then remove it from the firewall. Do not attempt to disconnect the clutch fluid hydraulic line from the master cylinder or the slave cylinder. After removing the master cylinder, remove the rubber seal around the hole in the firewall. Inspect this seal for cracks and tears. If it's damaged or worn, replace it.

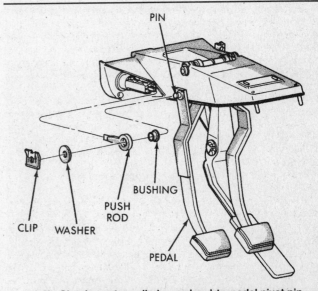

3.6b Clutch master cylinder pushrod-to-pedal pivot pin installation details (some models may be equipped with two washers; one flat, one wave)

8

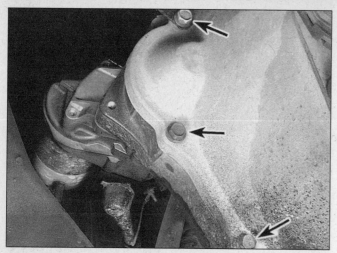

4.5a To detach the clutch housing from the engine, remove these bolts (arrows) from the left side . . .

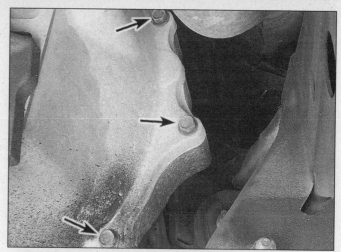

4.5b . . . and these bolts (arrows) from the right side - there are two additional bolts at the top of the bellhousing; a long extension with a flex socket will probably be required to reach them

Installation

Caution: *If you're installing a new clutch hydraulic release system, you'll notice a shipping stop on the master cylinder pushrod. DO NOT remove this shipping stop until after the clutch slave cylinder has been installed but DO remove it BEFORE the clutch is operated.*

10   Carefully maneuver the clutch hydraulic release system assembly into position.

11   Lubricate the firewall seal with liquid dish soap to facilitate installation, then seat the seal in its hole in the firewall.

12   Insert the clutch master cylinder in the firewall. Rotate it 45-degrees in a clockwise direction to lock it into place. If the master cylinder is difficult to lock, the seal may not be fully seated. Pull out the cylinder and make sure that the seal is fully seated.

13   Install the remote reservoir screws and tighten them securely.

14   Install the bushing on the pushrod-to-clutch pedal pivot pin. Be sure to use a new bushing, if necessary.

15   Install the master cylinder pushrod on the pin. Secure the rod with the wave washer, flat washer and retainer clip. Use a new clip if the old one is weak.

16   Plug in the electrical connector for the clutch pedal position switch.

17   Raise the vehicle and place it securely on jackstands.

18   Attach the clutch fluid hydraulic line to the retaining clip near the bottom of the firewall.

19   Install the slave cylinder. Make sure the cap at the end of the cylinder rod is seated properly in the release fork.

20   Install the slave cylinder mounting nuts and tighten them to the torque listed in this Chapter's Specifications.

21   Remove the jackstands and lower the vehicle.

22   If a new clutch hydraulic release system has been installed, remove the plastic shipping stop from the master cylinder pushrod before operating the clutch.

23   Test drive the vehicle and make sure the clutch hydraulic release system is operating properly.

4   Clutch components - removal, inspection and installation

Warning: *Dust produced by clutch wear and deposited on clutch components may contain asbestos, which is hazardous to your health. DO NOT blow it out with compressed air and DO NOT inhale it. DO NOT use gasoline or petroleum-based solvents to remove the dust. Brake system cleaner should be used to flush the dust into a drain pan. After the clutch components are wiped clean with a rag, dispose of the contaminated rags and cleaner in a covered, marked container.*

Removal

Refer to illustrations 4.5a, 4.5b, 4.5c and 4.8

1   Access to the clutch components is normally accomplished by removing the transmission and clutch housing, leaving the engine in the vehicle. If, of course, the engine is being removed for major overhaul, then check the clutch for wear and replace worn components as necessary. However, the relatively low cost of the clutch components compared to the time and trouble spent gaining access to them warrants their replacement anytime the engine or transmission is removed, unless they are new or in near-perfect condition. The following procedures are based on the assumption the engine will stay in place.

2   Detach the clutch slave cylinder from the clutch housing (see Section 3). **Caution:** *Do not disconnect the clutch hydraulic fluid line from the slave cylinder. The hydraulic release system cannot be bled if air is allowed to enter the system.*

3   Remove the transmission (see Chapter 7, Part A). Support the engine while the transmission is out. Preferably, an engine hoist should be used to support it from above. However, if a jack is used underneath the engine, make sure a piece of wood is positioned between the jack and oil pan to spread the load. **Caution:** *The pick-up for the oil pump is very close to the bottom of the oil pan. If the pan is bent or distorted in any way, engine oil starvation could occur.*

4   **Note:** *If the vehicle is equipped with an NV3500 transmission, the following step will not apply, since the clutch housing is an integral part of the transmission case.*

4.5c With the engine removed for clarity, all the clutch housing-to-engine bolt holes are visible, including the two upper ones

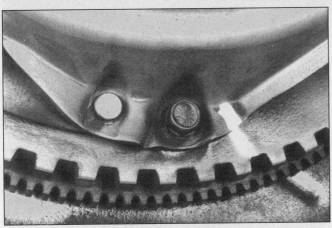

4.8 Be sure to mark the pressure plate and flywheel in order to insure proper alignment during installation (this won't be necessary if a new pressure plate is to be installed)

4.11 Check the flywheel for cracks, hot spots and other obvious defects (slight imperfections can be removed by resurfacing - see an automotive machine shop). This flywheel should be resurfaced

5   Remove the clutch housing-to-engine bolts **(see illustrations)**, then detach the housing. It may have to be gently pried off the alignment dowels with a screwdriver or prybar.

6   The clutch fork and release bearing can remain attached to the clutch housing for the time being.

7   To support the clutch disc during removal, install a clutch alignment tool through the clutch disc hub.

8   Carefully inspect the flywheel and pressure plate for indexing marks. The marks are usually an X, an O or a white letter. If they cannot be found, scribe marks yourself so the pressure plate and the flywheel will be in the same alignment during installation **(see illustration)**.

9   Turning each bolt only 1/4-turn at a time, loosen the pressure plate-to-flywheel bolts. Work in a criss-cross pattern until all spring pressure is relieved. Then hold the pressure plate securely and completely remove the bolts, followed by the pressure plate and clutch disc.

Inspection

Refer to illustrations 4.11, 4.13 and 4.15

10   Ordinarily, when a problem occurs in the clutch, it can be attributed to wear of the clutch driven plate assembly (clutch disc). However, all components should be inspected at this time.

11   Inspect the flywheel for cracks, heat checking, grooves and other obvious defects **(see illustration)**. If the imperfections are slight, a

machine shop can machine the surface flat and smooth, which is highly recommended regardless of the surface appearance. See Chapter 2 for the flywheel removal and installation procedure.

12   Inspect the pilot bearing (see Section 6).

13   Inspect the lining on the clutch disc **(see illustration)**. There should be at least 1/16-inch of lining above the rivet heads. Check for loose rivets, distortion, cracks, broken springs and other obvious damage. As mentioned above, ordinarily the clutch disc is routinely replaced, so if in doubt about the condition, replace it with a new one.

14   The release bearing should also be replaced along with the clutch disc (see Section 5).

15   Check the machined surfaces and the diaphragm spring fingers of the pressure plate **(see illustration)**. If the surface is grooved or otherwise damaged, replace the pressure plate. Also check for obvious damage, distortion, cracking, etc. Light glazing can be removed with sandpaper or emery cloth. If a new pressure plate is required, new and factory-rebuilt units are available.

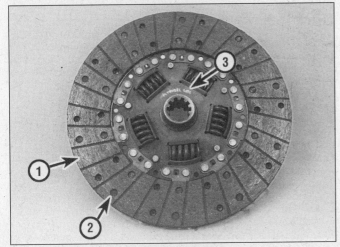

4.13 The clutch plate

1   *Lining* - This will wear down in use
2   *Rivets* - These secure the lining and will damage the flywheel or pressure plate if allowed to contact the surfaces
3   *Markings* - "Flywheel side" or something similar

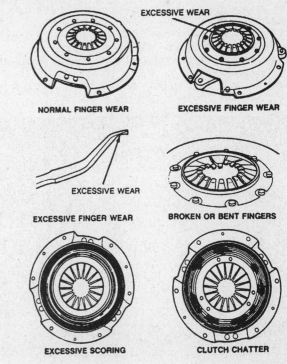

NORMAL FINGER WEAR   EXCESSIVE FINGER WEAR

EXCESSIVE WEAR

EXCESSIVE FINGER WEAR   BROKEN OR BENT FINGERS

EXCESSIVE SCORING   CLUTCH CHATTER

4.15 Replace the pressure plate if excessive wear is noted

8

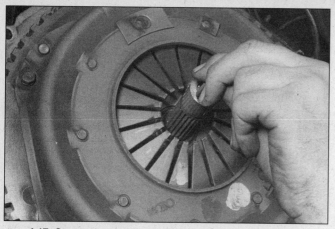

4.17 Center the clutch disc in the pressure plate with an alignment tool before the bolts are tightened

Installation

Refer to illustrations 4.17, 4.19 and 4.22

16 Before installation, clean the flywheel and pressure plate machined surfaces with brake system cleaner, lacquer thinner or acetone. It's important that no oil or grease is on these surfaces or the lining of the clutch disc. Handle the parts only with clean hands.

17 Position the clutch disc and pressure plate against the flywheel with the clutch held in place with an alignment tool (available from auto parts stores) **(see illustration)**. Make sure it's installed properly (the new clutch disc should have *"flywheel side"* stamped on the side that must face toward the flywheel.

18 Tighten the pressure plate-to-flywheel bolts finger tight, working around the pressure plate in a criss-cross pattern.

19 Center the clutch disc by ensuring the alignment tool extends through the splined hub and into the pilot bushing in the crankshaft.

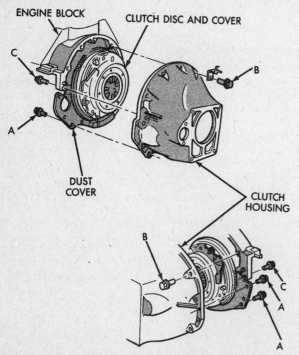

4.22 Bolt torque guide for clutch housing-to-engine bolts and engine-to-clutch housing bolts (NV4500 transmission) (torque specifications for A, B and C bolts are listed in this Chapter's Specifications)

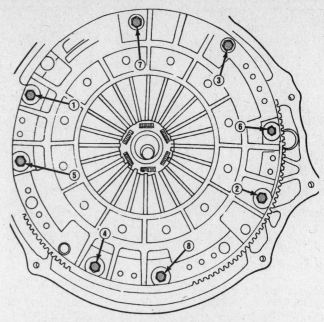

4.19 Clutch pressure plate bolt tightening sequence

Wiggle the tool up, down or side-to-side as needed to bottom the tool in the pilot bearing. Tighten the pressure plate-to-flywheel bolts a little at a time, working in a criss-cross pattern **(see illustration)** to prevent distortion of the cover. After all of the bolts are snug, tighten them to the torque listed in this Chapter's Specifications in this same criss-cross pattern. Remove the alignment tool.

20 Using high-temperature grease, lubricate the fork pivot ball stud, release fork contact areas, the bore of the release bearing, the input shaft pilot hub and splines and the surface of the bearing retainer on which the bearing slides (see Section 5).

21 Install the clutch release bearing and release fork (see Section 5).

22 If equipped with an NV4500 transmission, install the clutch housing and tighten the bolts to the torque listed in this Chapter's Specifications **(see illustration)**.

23 Install the transmission (see Chapter 7, Part A).

5 Clutch release bearing - removal, inspection and installation

Warning: *Dust produced by clutch wear and deposited on clutch components may contain asbestos, which is hazardous to your health. DO NOT blow it out with compressed air and DO NOT inhale it. DO NOT*

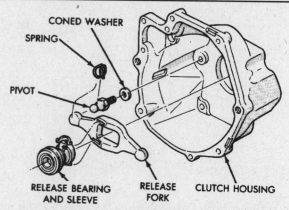

5.4a An exploded view of the clutch release bearing and release fork

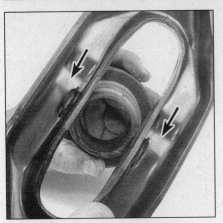

5.4b To detach the release bearing from the release fork, slide the bearing down and disengage the wire retainers from their slots in the fork

5.4c Remove this wire retainer clip for the pivot ball and check it to make sure that it's still a tight fit; if it's loose, replace it

5.5 To check the release bearing, hold the hub in one hand and turn the bearing with the other; if it feels rough or dry, replace it

use gasoline or petroleum-based solvents to remove the dust. Brake system cleaner should be used to flush the dust into a drain pan. After the clutch components are wiped clean with a rag, dispose of the contaminated rags and cleaner in a covered, marked container.

Removal

Refer to illustrations 5.4a, 5.4b and 5.4c

1   Detach the clutch hydraulic release system from the transmission (see Section 3).

2   Remove the transmission (see Chapter 7, Part A).

3   On vehicles equipped with an NV4500 transmission, remove the clutch housing (see Section 4).

4   Disengage the clutch release fork "socket" from the pivot ball, slide the bearing and fork off the input shaft bearing retainer and remove the bearing from the release fork (see illustrations). Remove the spring clip from the release fork (see illustration).

Inspection

Refer to illustration 5.5

5   Hold the center of the bearing and rotate the outer portion while applying pressure (see illustration). If the bearing doesn't turn smoothly or if it's noisy, remove it from the sleeve and replace it with a new one. Wipe the bearing with a clean rag and inspect it for damage, wear and cracks. Don't immerse the bearing in solvent - it's sealed for life and to do so would ruin it. Also check the release fork for cracks and other damage. Note: *In view of the relatively low cost of a release bearing, and the amount of work it takes to remove it, we recommend replacing the bearing whenever it is removed.*

Installation

Refer to illustrations 5.6a, 5.6b, 5.7, 5.8a and 5.8b

6   Apply a light coat of high-temperature grease to the release fork pivot ball, the contact points of the release forks, the bore of the release bearing, the splines of the transmission input shaft and the release bearing sliding surface on the bearing retainer (see illustrations).

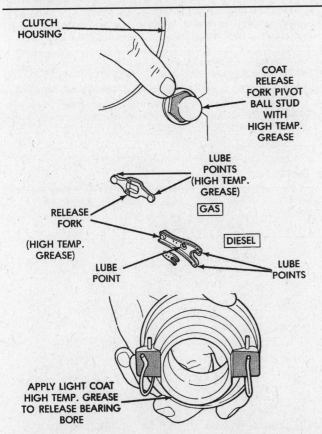

5.6a Be sure to lubricate the release fork pivot ball stud, the contact points of the release fork and the inside of the release bearing with high-temperature grease

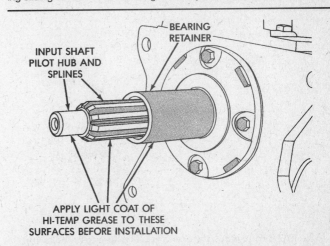

5.6b Be sure to lightly lubricate the bearing retainer surface on which the release bearing slides, the input shaft splines and the "nose" of the input shaft that is supported by the pilot bearing

8

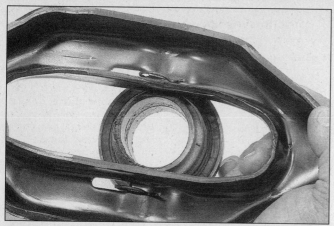

5.7 To attach the release bearing to the release fork, insert the wire retainers through their respective slots in the fork and push the bearing all the way to the right until the clips are fully seated

7   Attach the release bearing to the clutch release fork **(see illustration)**.
8   Lubricate the "socket" in the release fork for the pivot ball and the socket for the slave cylinder pushrod with high-temperature grease **(see illustration)**, slide the release bearing onto the bearing retainer and push the socket of the fork onto the pivot ball until it's firmly seated. Make sure the retaining spring is positioned behind the pivot **(see illustration)**.
9   Apply a light coat of high-temperature grease to the face of the release bearing, where it contacts the pressure plate diaphragm fingers.
10   If equipped with an NV4500 transmission, install the clutch housing and tighten the bolts to the torque listed in this Chapter's Specifications. Install the transmission (See Chapter 7, Part A). Reattach the clutch release linkage (see Section 4).
11   The remainder of installation is the reverse of the removal procedure.

6   Pilot bearing - inspection and replacement

Refer to illustration 6.7

1   A pilot bearing, pressed into the rear of the crankshaft, supports the front of the transmission input shaft. The needle roller bearing is greased at the factory and does not require additional lubrication. The pilot bearing should be inspected whenever the clutch components are removed. Due to its inaccessibility, if you are in doubt as to its condition, replace it with a new one.
2   Remove the transmission (see Chapter 7, Part A).

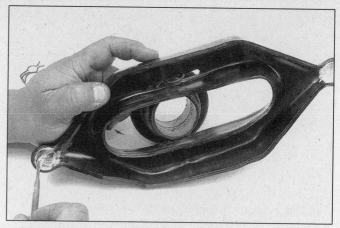

5.8a Lubricate the release fork sockets for the pivot ball and the slave pushrod with high-temperature grease

3   Remove the clutch components (see Section 4).
4   Inspect the bearing for excessive wear, scoring, lack of grease, dryness or obvious damage. If any of these conditions are noted, the bearing should be replaced. A flashlight will be helpful to direct light into the recess.
5   The bearing must be pulled from its hole in the crankshaft, gripping the bearing at the rear. Special tools are available, but you may be able to get by with a an alternative tool or fabricated tool. One method that works well is to use a slide-hammer with a small tip that has two adjustable hooks, 180-degrees apart. Such tips are commonly available for slide-hammers, and are often included with better-quality slide-hammer kits. A slide-hammer is a tool with many uses, such as pulling dents from body parts and removing seals; you'll use it later for more things than just removing bushings. If a slide-hammer with the correct hooked tip is not available, try to find a hooked tool that will fit into the bearing hole and hook behind the bearing, then clamp a large pair of locking pliers to the tool and strike the pliers, near the jaws, to pull the bearing out.
6   To install the new bearing, lightly lubricate the outside surface with multi-purpose grease, then drive it into the recess with a hammer and a bearing driver or a clutch alignment tool **(see illustration)**. Make

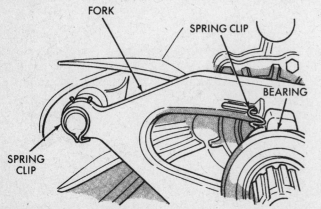

5.8b Make sure the spring clip is engaged with the release fork pivot ball stud and the release fork as shown

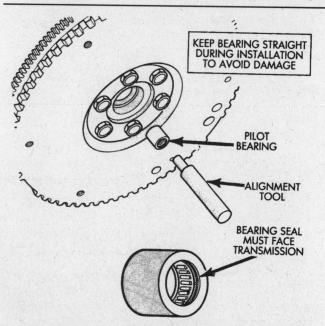

6.7 Use an alignment tool to install the pilot bearing properly; note that the bearing seal must face the transmission

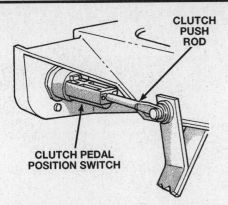

8.1 The clutch pedal position switch is an integral part of the clutch master cylinder pushrod

sure that the bearing seal faces toward the transmission. Don't allow the pilot bearing to become cocked in the bore. Tap it into place until it's flush with the edge of the bearing bore.
7   Lubricate the pilot bearing with high-temperature grease.
8   Install the clutch components (see Section 4).
9   Install the transmission (see Chapter 7, Part A).

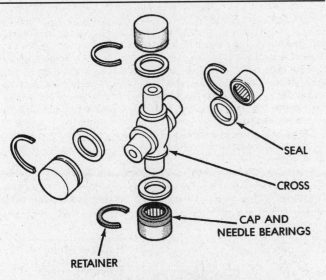

8.2a An exploded view of a typical single-cardan universal joint assembly

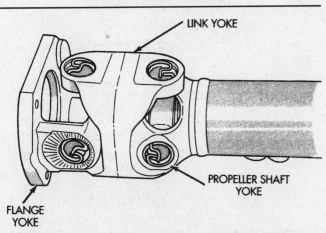

8.2b A typical double-cardan universal joint assembly

7   Clutch pedal position switch - check and replacement

Check

Refer to illustration 7.1
1   The clutch pedal position switch **(see illustration)**, which is part of the starter relay circuit, is mounted on the clutch master cylinder pushrod. The switch closes the starter relay circuit only when the clutch pedal is fully depressed. The switch is an integral part of the clutch master cylinder pushrod and cannot be serviced separately. If the switch must be replaced, so must the clutch hydraulic release system (see Section 3).
2   To test the switch, verify that the engine will not crank over when the clutch pedal is in the released position, and that it does crank over with the pedal depressed.
3   If the engine starts without depressing the clutch pedal, replace the switch.

Replacement

4   Replace the clutch hydraulic release system (see Section 3).

8   Driveshaft and universal joints - general information

Refer to illustrations 8.2a, 8.2b and 8.3
1   A driveshaft is a tube that transmits power between the transmission or transfer case and the differential. Universal joints are located at either end of the driveshaft and allow the driveshaft to operate at different angles as the suspension moves.
2   Two different types of universal joints are used: single-cardan and double-cardan **(see illustrations)**.
3   Some models have a two-piece driveshaft. The two front and rear driveshafts are connected at a center support bearing. There are two types of center bearings: Type 1 is used with the 9-1/4 axle; Type 2 is used with Model 60/70/80 axles **(see illustration)**. Both are mounted in the same location.
4   The rear driveshaft employs a splined yoke at the front, which slips into the extension housing of the transmission. The front driveshaft on 4WD models (and the rear portion of the rear driveshaft on models with a two-piece driveshaft) incorporates a slip yoke as part of the shaft. This arrangement allows the driveshaft to alter its length during vehicle operation. An oil seal prevents fluid from leaking out of the extension housing and keeps dirt from entering the transmission or transfer case. If leakage is evident at the front of the driveshaft, replace the extension housing oil seal (see Chapter 7, Part A).
5   The driveshaft assembly requires very little service. The slip yoke

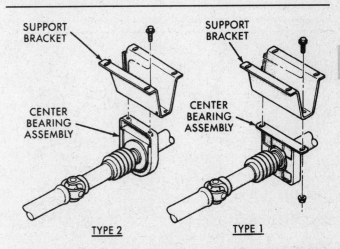

8.3 Type 1 center support bearings are used with the 9-1/4 axle; Type 2s are used with Model 60/70/80 axles

8

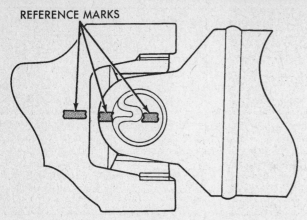

REFERENCE MARKS

10.3 In order to preserve the dynamic balance of the driveshaft when it's reassembled, always make alignment marks on the yokes and on the cross before unbolting the driveshaft

on some Type 1 (9-1/4 axle) driveshafts is equipped with a lubrication fitting and should be lubricated periodically (see Chapter 1). Factory U-joints are lubricated for life and must be replaced if problems develop. The driveshaft must be removed from the vehicle for this procedure. (Some aftermarket universal joints have grease fittings to allow periodic lubrication.)

6   Since the driveshaft is a balanced unit, it's important that no undercoating, mud, etc. be allowed to accumulate on it. When the vehicle is raised for service it's a good idea to clean the driveshaft and inspect it for any obvious damage. Also, make sure the small weights used to originally balance the driveshaft are in place and securely attached. Whenever the driveshaft is removed it must be reinstalled in the same relative position to preserve the balance.

7   Problems with the driveshaft are usually indicated by a noise or vibration while driving the vehicle. A road test should verify if the problem is the driveshaft or another vehicle component. Refer to the *Troubleshooting* section at the front of this manual. If you suspect trouble, inspect the driveline (see the next Section).

9   Driveline inspection

1   Raise the vehicle and support it securely on jackstands.
2   Crawl under the vehicle and visually inspect the driveshaft(s). Look for any dents or cracks in the tubing. If any are found, the driveshaft must be replaced.
3   Check for oil leakage at the front and rear of the driveshaft.

Leakage where the driveshaft enters the transmission extension housing or transfer case indicates a defective extension housing seal (see Chapter 7, Part A). Leakage where the driveshaft enters the differential indicates a defective pinion seal (see Section 19).

4   While under the vehicle, have an assistant rotate a wheel so the driveshaft will rotate. As it does, make sure the universal joints are operating properly without binding, noise or looseness.
5   The universal joints can also be checked with the driveshaft motionless, by gripping your hands on either side of a joint and attempting to twist the joint. Any movement at all in the joint is a sign of considerable wear. Lifting up on the shaft will also indicate movement in the universal joints.
6   Finally, check the driveshaft mounting bolts at the ends to make sure they're tight.

10   Driveshaft - removal and installation

1   Disconnect the negative cable from the battery. Place the transmission in Neutral with the parking brake off. If you're removing the front driveshaft, place the transfer case in Neutral.
2   Raise the vehicle and support it securely on jackstands.

Rear driveshaft assembly

Removal

Refer to illustrations 10.3 and 10.4

3   Make reference marks on the driveshaft and the pinion flange in line with each other **(see illustration)** to ensure that balance is preserved when the driveshaft is reinstalled.
4   Remove the rear universal joint bolts and straps **(see illustration)**. Turn the driveshaft (or wheels) as necessary to bring the bolts into the most accessible position. **Note:** *The manufacturer recommends using new straps and bolts upon installation.*
5   Tape the bearing caps to the cross to prevent the caps from coming off during removal.
6   Lower the rear of the driveshaft. If the driveshaft is a one-piece unit, slide the front end of the driveshaft out of the transmission extension housing; if it's a two-piece driveshaft, unbolt the center support bearing **(see illustration 8.3)** and slide the front end of the front driveshaft out of the extension housing.
7   Wrap a plastic bag over the extension housing and hold it in place with a rubber band. This will prevent loss of fluid and protect against contamination while the driveshaft is out.

Installation

8   Remove the plastic bag from the transmission extension housing and wipe the area clean. Inspect the oil seal carefully. If it's leaking, now is the time to replace it (see Chapter 7, Part A).

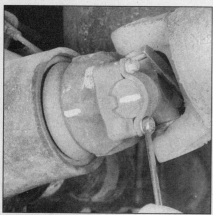

10.4 To hold the U-joint assembly while you break all the strap bolts loose, insert a large screwdriver or prybar through the driveshaft yoke as shown

10.14a Before removing the front driveshaft from a 4WD model, mark the U-joint and pinion yokes . . .

10.14b . . . and mark the transfer case output shaft flange and the driveshaft U-joint flange

11.2a On U-joints with external snap-rings, a pair of needle-nose pliers can be used to remove the snap-rings

11.2b On U-joints with internal snap-rings, remove the inner retainers from the U-joint by tapping them off with a screwdriver and hammer

11.4 To press the universal joint out of the driveshaft yoke, set it up in a vise with the small socket pushing the joint and bearing cap into the large socket

9   Inspect the center support bearing, if equipped. If it's rough or noisy, replace it (see Section 12).

10   Insert the front end of the driveshaft assembly into the transmission extension housing.

11   If the driveshaft is a one-piece unit, raise the rear of the driveshaft into position, checking to be sure the marks are in alignment. If not, turn the pinion flange until the marks line up.

12   If the driveshaft is a two-piece unit, raise the center support bearing and bolt it loosely into place, raise the rear end of the rear shaft into position and make sure the alignment marks are in alignment. If not, turn the pinion flange until they do.

13   Remove the tape securing the bearing caps and install the clamps and bolts. Tighten the strap bolts to the torque listed in this Chapter's Specifications. Lower the vehicle and connect the negative battery cable.

Front driveshaft assembly (4WD models only)

Refer to illustrations 10.14a and 10.14b

14   Be sure to make alignment marks on the driveshaft yokes, the axle pinion yoke and the transfer case output flange **(see illustrations)**.

15   Remove the U-joint strap bolts **(see illustration 10.4)**. **Note:** *The manufacturer recommends using new straps and bolts upon installation.*

11.9 If the snap-ring will not seat in the groove, strike the yoke with a brass hammer - this will relieve the tension that has set up in the yoke, and slightly spring the yoke ears (this should also be done if the joint feels tight when assembled)

16   Remove the bolts from the transfer case yoke flange.

17   Remove the driveshaft.

18   Installation is the reverse of removal. Be sure to tighten the U-joint strap bolts and transfer case output flange bolts to the torque listed in this Chapter's Specifications.

---

11   Universal joints - replacement

Single-cardan U-joints

Refer to illustrations 11.2a, 11.2b, 11.4 and 11.9

Note: *A press or large vise will be required for this procedure. It may be advisable to take the driveshaft to a local dealer service department, service station or machine shop where the universal joints can be replaced for you, normally at a reasonable charge.*

1   Remove the driveshaft as outlined in the previous Section.

2   On U-joints with external snap-rings, use a small pair of pliers to remove the snap-rings from the spider **(see illustration)**. If the U-joint has internal snap-rings, drive the snap-rings out with two screwdrivers **(see illustration)**.

3   Supporting the driveshaft, place it in position on a workbench equipped with a vise.

4   Place a piece of pipe or a large socket, having an inside diameter slightly larger than the outside diameter of the bearing caps, over one of the bearing caps. Position a socket with an outside diameter slightly smaller than that of the opposite bearing cap against the cap **(see illustration)** and use the vise or press to force the bearing cap out (inside the pipe or large socket). Use the vise or large pliers to work the bearing cap the rest of the way out.

5   Transfer the sockets to the other side and press the opposite bearing cap out in the same manner.

6   Pack the new universal joint bearings with grease. Ordinarily, specific instructions for lubrication will be included with the universal joint servicing kit and should be followed carefully.

7   Position the spider in the yoke and partially install one bearing cap in the yoke.

8   Start the spider into the bearing cap and then partially install the other cap. Align the spider and press the bearing caps into position, being careful not to damage the dust seals.

9   Install the snap-rings. If difficulty is encountered in seating the snap-rings, strike the driveshaft yoke sharply with a hammer. This will spring the yoke ears slightly and allow the snap-rings to seat in the groove **(see illustration)**.

10   Install the grease fitting and fill the joint with grease. Be careful not to overfill the joint, as this could blow out the grease seals.

11   Install the driveshaft, tightening the U-joint strap bolts to the torque listed in this Chapter's Specifications.

8

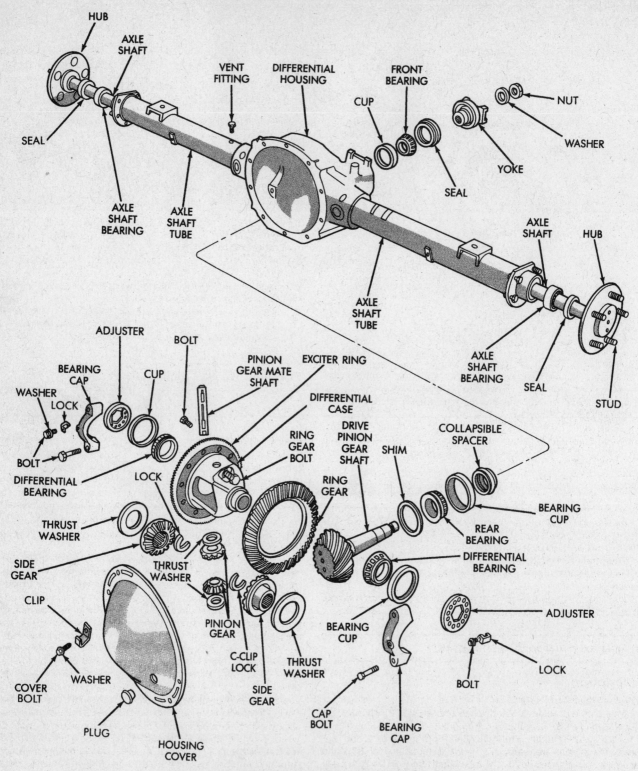

13.1 An exploded view of the 9-1/4 inch rear axle assembly

Double-cardan U-joints

12   Use the above procedure, but note that it will have to be repeated because the double-cardan joint is made up of two single-cardan joints. Also pay attention to how the spring, centering ball and bearing are arranged. **Note:** *Both U-joints in the double-cardan assembly must be replaced at the same time, even if only half of it is worn out.*

12   Driveshaft center bearing - replacement

1   Raise the vehicle and support it securely on jackstands.
2   Remove the driveshaft assembly (see Section 10). Mark the relationship of the front portion of the driveshaft to the rear portion of the driveshaft.

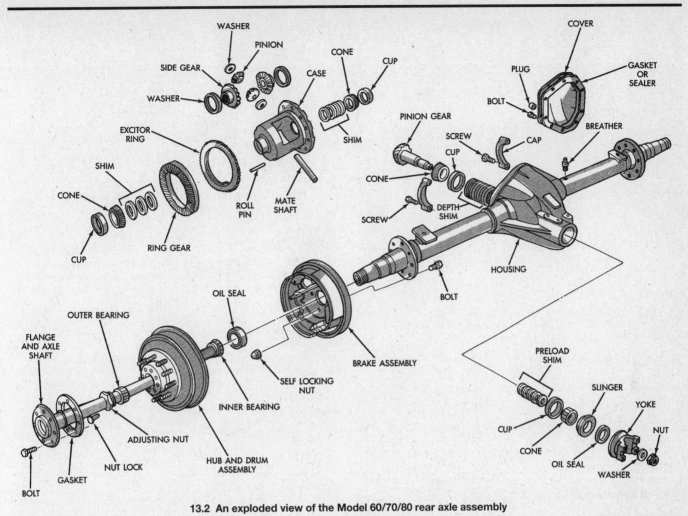

WASHER
PINION
SIDE GEAR
WASHER
EXCITOR RING
SHIM
CONE
CUP
RING GEAR
ROLL PIN
MATE SHAFT
CASE
CONE
CUP
SHIM
PINION GEAR
SCREW
CUP
CONE
SCREW
DEPTH SHIM
COVER
PLUG
BOLT
GASKET OR SEALER
BREATHER
CAP
HOUSING
BOLT
OUTER BEARING
OIL SEAL
FLANGE AND AXLE SHAFT
BRAKE ASSEMBLY
SELF LOCKING NUT
INNER BEARING
ADJUSTING NUT
NUT LOCK
HUB AND DRUM ASSEMBLY
GASKET
BOLT
PRELOAD SHIM
SLINGER
YOKE
NUT
CUP
CONE
OIL SEAL
WASHER

13.2 An exploded view of the Model 60/70/80 rear axle assembly

3   Loosen the slip-joint boot clamp and pull back the boot on the front of the rear driveshaft.
4   Pull the rear driveshaft out of the center bearing.
5   Take the front driveshaft and center bearing to an automotive machine shop and have the old bearing pressed off and a new bearing pressed on.
6   Installation is the reverse of removal. Be sure the match marks line up so the driveshaft is properly "phased."

13   Rear axle - description and check

Description

Refer to illustrations 13.1 and 13.2

1   There are two different rear axle assemblies: 9-1/4 inch axles are a *semi-floating* design, i.e. the axle supports the weight of the vehicle on the axleshaft in addition to transmitting driving forces to the rear wheels. These axles are referred to by the diameter (in inches) of the differential ring gear, hence "9-1/4" **(see illustration)**. 9-1/4 inch axles use "C-washer" locks to secure the axles to the differential. An identification tag specifying the assembly part number and gear ratio is located on the differential cover. The build date identification code is stamped on the rear (cover side) of the axleshaft tube.
2   Heavy duty models use a Model 60, 70 or 80 *full-floating* axle **(see illustration)**. A full floating axleshaft doesn't carry any of the vehicle's weight; this is supported on the axle housing itself by roller bearings. Full-floating axles can be identified by the large hub projecting from the center of the wheel. The axle flange is secured by bolts on the end of the hub. The assembly part number and axle ratio identification tags

for these axles are located on their differential covers. The build date identification code is stamped on the rear (cover side) of the axleshaft tube.
3   All axles also use a *hypoid*-type pinion gear, i.e. the pinion gear teeth are cut in a spiral configuration to allow the centerline of the pinion to be lower than the centerline of the ring gear, so the vehicle floor can be lower. All differential housings are cast iron and the axle tubes are made of steel, pressed and welded into the differential housing. All differentials can be inspected and serviced by removing a pressed-steel access cover from the back side of the differential housing.
4   Most axles use a conventional differential, which allows the driving wheels to rotate at different speeds during cornering (the outside wheel must rotate faster than the inside wheel), while equally dividing the driving torque between the two wheels. In most normal driving situations, this function of the differential is appropriate. However, the total driving torque can't be more than double the torque at the lower-traction wheel. When traction conditions aren't the same for both driving wheels, some of the available traction is lost. So a limited-slip differential is available as an option on all axles. During normal cornering and turning conditions, its controlled internal friction is easily overcome, allowing the driving wheels to turn at different speeds, just like a conventional differential. However, during extremely slippery conditions - mud, ice or snow - a limited-slip differential allows the driving wheel with the better traction condition to develop more driving torque than the other wheel. Thus, the total driving torque can be significantly greater than with a conventional differential. The Model 70 axle uses a Power-Lok limited-slip differential with a two-piece case; Model 60 and 80 axles and 9-1/4 axles use a Trac-Lok limited-slip unit. The Trac-Lok unit is housed inside a one-piece case for the 9-1/4 and Model 60 axles and in a two-piece case for the Model 80.

8

14.3a Remove the pinion shaft lock bolt . . .

14.3b . . . then carefully remove the pinion shaft from the differential carrier (don't turn the wheels or the carrier after the shaft has been removed, or the pinion gears may fall out)

Check

5   Many times, a problem is suspected in an axle area when, in fact, it lies elsewhere. For this reason, a thorough check should be performed before assuming an axle problem.

6   The following noises are those commonly associated with axle diagnosis procedures:

a) *Road noise* is often mistaken for mechanical faults. Driving the vehicle on different surfaces will show whether the road surface is the cause of the noise. Road noise will remain the same if the vehicle is under power or coasting.

b) *Tire noise* is sometimes mistaken for mechanical problems. Tires which are worn or low on pressure are particularly susceptible to emitting vibrations and noises. Tire noise will remain about the same during varying driving situations, where axle noise will change during coasting, acceleration, etc.

c) *Engine and transmission noise* can be deceiving because it will travel along the driveline. To isolate engine and transmission noises, make a note of the engine speed at which the noise is most pronounced. Stop the vehicle and place the transmission in Neutral and run the engine to the same speed. If the noise is the same, the axle is not at fault.

7   Overhaul and general repair of the front or rear axle differential are beyond the scope of the home mechanic due to the many special tools and critical measurements required. Thus, the procedures listed here will involve axleshaft removal and installation, axleshaft oil seal replacement, axleshaft bearing replacement and removal of the entire unit for repair or replacement.

14   Rear axleshaft (9-1/4 inch axle) - removal and installation

Refer to illustrations 14.3a, 14.3b and 14.4

Warning: *The dust created by the brake system may contain asbestos, which is harmful to your health. Never blow it out with compressed air and don't inhale any of it. An approved filtering mask should be worn when working on the brakes. Do not, under any circumstances, use petroleum-based solvents to clean brake parts. Use brake system cleaner only!*

1   The axleshaft is usually removed only when the bearing is worn or the seal is leaking. To check the bearing, raise the vehicle, support it securely on jackstands and remove the wheel and brake drum. Move the axle flange up and down. If the axleshaft moves up and down, bearing wear is excessive. Also check for differential lubricant leaking out from below the axleshaft - this indicates the seal is leaking.

2   Remove the cover from the differential carrier and allow the oil to drain into a suitable container.

3   Remove the lock bolt from the differential pinion shaft and remove the pinion shaft **(see illustrations)**.

4   Push the outer (flanged) end of the axleshaft in and remove the C-lock from the inner end of the shaft **(see illustration)**.

5   Withdraw the axleshaft, taking care not to damage the oil seal in the end of the axle housing as the splined end of the axleshaft passes through it.

6   Installation is the reverse of removal. Apply thread-locking compound to the threads and tighten the pinion shaft lock bolt to the torque listed in this Chapter's Specifications.

7   Always use a new cover gasket and tighten the cover bolts to the torque listed in the Chapter 1 Specifications.

8   Refill the axle with the correct quantity and grade of lubricant (see Chapter 1).

15   Rear axleshaft oil seal (9-1/4 inch axle) - replacement

Refer to illustrations 15.2a, 15.2b and 15.3

1   Remove the axleshaft (see Section 14).

2   Pry the oil seal out of the end of the axle housing with a seal removal tool, a large screwdriver or the inner end of the axleshaft **(see illustrations)**.

3   Apply high-temperature grease to the oil seal recess and tap the new seal evenly into place with a hammer and seal installation tool **(see illustration)**, large socket or piece of pipe so the lips are facing in and the metal face is visible from the end of the axle housing. When correctly installed, the face of the oil seal should be flush with the end of the axle housing.

4   Install the axleshaft (see Section 14).

16   Rear axleshaft bearing (9-1/4 inch axle) - replacement

Refer to illustrations 16.3 and 16.4

1   Remove the axleshaft (see Section 14).

2   Remove the oil seal (see Section 15).

3   Using a slide-hammer-type puller to grip the bearing from behind, extract the bearing from the axle housing **(see illustration)**.

4   Clean out the bearing recess and drive in the new bearing with a bearing installer or a piece of pipe positioned against the bearing outer race **(see illustration)**. Make sure the bearing is tapped in to the full depth of the recess and the numbers on the bearing are visible from the outer end of the axle housing.

5   Install a new oil seal (see Section 15), then install the axleshaft (see Section 14).

14.4 Push the axle flange in, then remove the C-lock from the inner end of the axleshaft

15.2a Use a seal removal tool (shown) or a screwdriver to remove the old seal from the axle housing

15.2b You can even use the end of the axleshaft to pry out the old seal

15.3 Use a seal driver (shown) or a large socket to install the new seal

17 Rear axleshaft (Model 60/70/80 axles) - removal, installation and adjustment

Refer to illustrations 17.2, 17.3, 17.6a and 17.6b

1   Loosen the rear wheel lug nuts. Raise the vehicle and place it securely on jackstands. Remove the rear wheel.

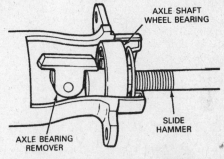

16.3 Use a bearing removal tool attached to a slide hammer to remove the axleshaft bearing

2   Remove the axleshaft flange bolts (see illustration).
3   Pull out the axleshaft (see illustration). Some units may be equipped with tapered dowel pins which can "stick" to the flange and/or the hub and bearing assembly. If the axleshaft is stuck, rap it sharply in the center of the flange with a hammer to knock the dowels loose.
4   While the axleshaft is removed, inspect and, if necessary, replace the hub and bearing seals and bearings (see Section 18). This is also a good time to inspect the rear brake assembly (see Chapter 9).
5   Slip a new gasket over the end of the axleshaft and slide the axleshaft into the axle housing.
6   Before engaging the axleshaft splines with the differential, clean the gasket sealing area, apply silicone sealant to the gasket mating

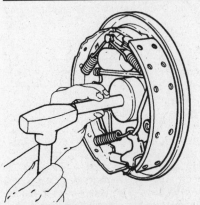

16.4 A correctly sized bearing driver must be used to drive the bearing into the housing

17.2 Remove the axleshaft flange bolts . . .

17.3 . . . and pull out the axleshaft

8

17.6a Before installing the axleshaft, apply a coat of silicone sealant to the mating surface of the hub . . .

17.6b . . . then place the new gasket in position on the hub

18.3a This nut lock must be removed from the keyway . . .

18.3b . . . before loosening the adjusting nut

18.4 Remove the outer bearing

18.5a To remove the hub and bearing assembly, you'll have to pull off the brake drum

surface of the hub **(see illustration)** and place the new gasket in position **(see illustration)**. Push the axleshaft into the axle housing until the axleshaft splines are fully engaged with the differential. If you have difficulty engaging the splines with the differential, have an assistant turn the other wheel slightly while you push on the axleshaft.

7   Install the flange bolts and tighten them to the torque listed in this Chapter's Specifications.

18   Hub and bearing assembly (Model 60/70/80 axles) - removal, installation and adjustment

Warning: *The dust created by the brake system may contain asbestos, which is harmful to your health. Never blow it out with compressed air and don't inhale any of it. An approved filtering mask should be worn when working on the brakes. Do not, under any circumstances, use petroleum-based solvents to clean brake parts. Use brake system cleaner only!*

Removal

Refer to illustrations 18.3a, 18.3b, 18.4, 18.5a, 18.5b, 18.6, 18.7, 18.9a and 18.9b

1   Raise the vehicle, support it securely on jackstands and remove the rear wheels.

2   Remove the axleshaft (see Section 17).

3   Pull out the nut lock **(see illustration)** and remove the adjusting nut **(see illustration)**.

4   Remove the outer wheel bearing **(see illustration)**.

5   Pull the hub and brake drum straight off the axle tube **(see illustration)**. If the hub and drum are stuck, lay them on the floor, tap the studs to knock the hub loose and separate the two **(see illustration)**.

18.5b If the hub and drum are stuck together (which they often are), dropping them on the floor will usually free them; if that doesn't work, tapping on the wheel studs will knock the hub loose from the drum

18.6 To remove the hub inner seal, place the hub assembly in a bench vise and pry the seal out with a seal removal tool (shown) or a screwdriver

18.7 Remove the inner bearing from the hub

18.9a To replace a stud, knock it out with a brass or dead-blow hammer

18.9b To install a stud, insert the stud through the hole in the flange, drop a spacer or a bunch of washers the height of the shoulder over the bolt, install the wheel lug nut and tighten the nut until the stud is pulled up through the flange

6   Place the hub assembly in a bench vise with the inner side facing toward you. Using a large screwdriver, pry bar or seal removal tool to pry out the oil seal (see illustration).

7   Remove the inner wheel bearing from the hub (see illustration).
8   Use solvent to wash the bearings, hub and axle tube. A small brush may prove useful; make sure no bristles from the brush embed themselves between the bearing rollers. Allow the parts to air dry.
9   Carefully inspect the bearings for cracks, wear and damage. Check the axle tube flange, studs, and hub splines for damage and corrosion. Check the bearing cups (races) for pitting or scoring. Worn or damaged components must be replaced with new ones. If necessary, tap the bearing cups from the hub with a hammer and brass drift and install new ones with the appropriate size bearing driver. This is also a good time to replace any damaged or worn wheel studs (see illustrations).
10   Inspect the brake drum for scoring or damage and check the condition of the brake shoes (see Chapter 9).

Installation and adjustment

Refer to illustrations 18.11, 18.12, 18.13a, 18.13b, 18.15a and 18.15b
11   Pack the bearings with wheel bearing grease (see illustration). Work the grease completely into the bearings, forcing it between the rollers, cone and cage. Place the inner bearing into the hub and install the seal (with the seal lip facing into the hub). Using a seal driver or block of wood, drive the seal in until it's flush with the hub. Lubricate the seal with gear oil or grease.
12   Place the hub assembly on the axle tube, taking care not to damage the oil seals. Place the outer bearing into the hub (see illustration).
13   Install a new adjusting nut and tighten it to the torque listed in this Chapter's Specifications (see illustrations).

18.11 Work the grease completely into the rollers

18.12 Slide the hub onto the axle tube and install the outer bearing

18.13a Install a new adjusting nut

8

18.13b Tighten the adjusting nut to the torque listed in this Chapter's Specifications

18.15a Insert a new nut lock into the axle tube keyway . . .

14   Back off the adjusting nut 1/3 of a turn (120-degrees) (this provides 0.001 to 0.010 inch wheel bearing endplay).
15   To lock the adjusting nut in position, install a new locking wedge into the spindle keyway **(see illustrations)** and tap it into the keyway until it stops.
16   Install the axleshaft (see Section 17). Install the brake drum and adjust the shoes if necessary (see Chapter 9).
17   Install the rear wheel, remove the jackstands and lower the vehicle. Tighten the wheel lug nuts to the torque listed in the Chapter 1 Specifications.

19   Pinion oil seal - replacement

1   Disconnect the cable from the negative battery terminal.
2   Loosen the rear wheel lug nuts. Raise the rear of the vehicle and support it securely on jackstands and remove the wheels and brake drums. Block the front wheels to keep the vehicle from rolling off the stands.
3   Mark the relationship of the rear U-joint to the companion flange, disconnect the driveshaft and hang it out of the way with a piece of wire.

9-1/4 inch rear axle and Model 44/60 front and rear axles

Refer to illustrations 19.4, 19.5, 19.7a, 19.7b and 19.11
4   Use an inch-pound torque wrench to determine the torque

18.15b . . . then tap the nut lock into the keyway until it stops (the vertical fingers of the nut lock should be firmly seated against the nylon portion of the adjusting nut)

required to rotate the pinion **(see illustration)**. Record it for use later.
5   Scribe or punch alignment marks on the pinion shaft, nut and flange **(see illustration)**.

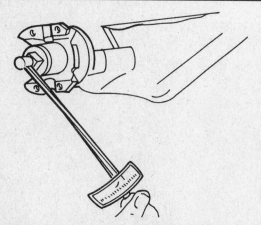

19.4 Use an inch-pound torque wrench to check the torque necessary to turn the pinion

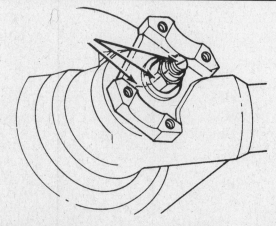

19.5 Mark the relative positions of the pinion, nut and flange (arrows) before removing the nut

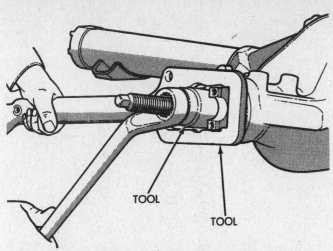

19.7a If you have the factory tool or something similar, it's easy to hold the pinion flange while breaking loose the locknut

19.7b If you don't have the factory tool or one like it, try holding the flange with a prybar or large screwdriver while you loosen the locknut

6   Count the number of threads visible between the end of the nut and the end of the pinion shaft and record it for use later.

7   A special tool (Chrysler tool no. C-3281, or equivalent) can be used to keep the companion flange from moving while the self-locking pinion nut is loosened **(see illustration)**. If the special tool isn't available, try locking the flange with a prybar or a large screwdriver **(see illustration)**.

8   Remove the pinion nut.

9   Withdraw the companion flange. It may be necessary to use a two or three-jaw puller engaged behind the flange to draw it out. Do not attempt to pry behind the flange or hammer on the end of the pinion shaft.

10   Pry out the old seal and discard it.

11   Lubricate the lips of the new seal with high-temperature grease and tap it evenly into position with a seal installation tool or a large socket. Make sure it enters the housing squarely and is tapped in to its full depth **(see illustration)**.

12   Align the mating marks made before disassembly and install the companion flange. If necessary, tighten the pinion nut to draw the flange into place. Do not try to hammer the flange into position.

13   Apply non-hardening sealant to the ends of the splines visible in the center of the flange so oil will be sealed in.

14   Install the washer (if equipped) and pinion nut. Tighten the nut carefully until the original number of threads are exposed and the marks are aligned.

15   Measure the torque required to rotate the pinion and tighten the nut in small increments until it matches the figure recorded in Step 4. In order to compensate for the drag of the new oil seal, the nut should be tightened more until the rotational torque of the pinion exceeds earlier

recording by 10 in-lbs (9-1/4 inch axle) or 5 in-lbs (Model 44/60 axle), with a torque reading of at least 210 ft-lbs on the nut (9-1/4 inch axle), 190 ft-lbs (Model 44 axle) or 215 ft-lbs (Model 60 axle). Be very careful and DO NOT back-off the pinion nut once the tightening procedure is begun.

16   Connect the driveshaft, add the specified lubricant to the differential housing, if necessary (see Chapter 1) and lower the vehicle.

Model 70/80 rear axles

17   Remove the pinion nut. A special tool (Chrysler tool no. C-3281, or equivalent) can be used to keep the companion flange from moving while the self-locking pinion nut is loosened **(see illustration 19.7a)**.

18   Mark the relationship of the companion flange to the pinion shaft and withdraw the companion flange. It may be necessary to use a two or three-jaw puller engaged behind the flange to draw it out. Do not attempt to pry behind the flange or hammer on the end of the pinion shaft.

19   Pry out the old seal and discard it.

20   Lubricate the lips of the new seal with high-temperature grease and tap it evenly into position with a seal installation tool or a large socket. Make sure it enters the housing squarely and is tapped in to its full depth **(see illustration 19.11)**.

21   Align the mating marks made before disassembly and install the companion flange. If necessary, tighten the pinion nut to draw the flange into place. Do not try to hammer the flange into position.

22   Install the washer (if equipped) and pinion nut. Tighten the nut to the torque listed in this Chapter's Specifications.

23   Connect the driveshaft, add gear oil to the differential housing, if necessary (see Chapter 1) and lower the vehicle.

20   Rear axle assembly - removal and installation

Removal

1   Loosen the rear wheel lug nuts, raise the rear of the vehicle and support it securely on jackstands. Block the front wheels to keep the vehicle from rolling off the stands. Remove the rear wheels.

2   Position a jack under the rear axle differential case.

3   Disconnect the driveshaft from the rear axle companion flange. Fasten the driveshaft out of the way with a piece of wire to the underbody.

4   Disconnect the shock absorbers at the lower mounts, then compress them to get them out of the way.

5   If equipped, disconnect the vent hose from the fitting on the axle housing and fasten it out of the way.

6   Disconnect the brake hose from the junction block on the axle

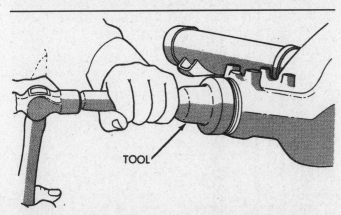

19.11 Use the correct size driver to install the pinion seal

8

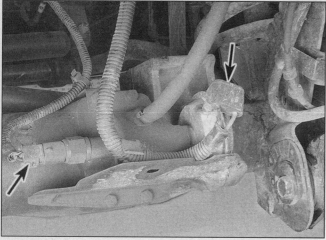

23.2 Unplug the electrical connector (left arrow) from the indicator light switch (right arrow), then unscrew and remove the switch; detach the vent hose and the two vacuum lines from the vacuum shift motor

housing, then plug the hose to prevent fluid leakage. Disconnect the RWAL or ABS wiring (see Chapter 9).

7   Remove the brake drums (see Chapter 9).
8   Disconnect the parking brake cables from the actuating levers and the backing plate (see Chapter 9).
9   Disconnect the spring U-bolts (see Chapter 10). Remove the spacers and clamp plates.
10   Disconnect any wiring interfering with removal.
11   Lower the jack slowly, then remove the rear axle assembly from under the vehicle.

Installation

12   Installation is the reverse of removal. Lower the vehicle weight onto the wheels before tightening the U-bolt nuts completely.
13   Bleed the brakes (see Chapter 9).

21   Front axle assembly - general information

Two types of front driveaxles are used on 4WD vehicles: Model 44 and Model 60 axles. These axles can be distinguished by an identification tag on these covers. The tag contains the assembly part number and gear ratio. The build date identification code is stamped on the front (cover side) of the axleshaft tube.

Some heavy-duty 2WD models use a tube axle instead of independent front suspension. This axle bolts to the suspension arms in the same manner as the Model 44 and Model 60 axles described above.

22   Front axle assembly - removal and installation

1   Loosen the front wheel lug nuts. Raise the vehicle and support it securely with jackstands positioned under the frame rails. Remove the front wheels.
2   Remove the brake calipers and discs (see Chapter 9) and ABS wheel speed sensors, if equipped.
3   On 4WD models, disconnect the vent hose.
4   On 4WD models, remove the front driveshaft (see Section 10). Disconnect the front driveshaft at the drive pinion yoke.
5   Disconnect the stabilizer bar link from the axle bracket (see Chapter 10).
6   Disconnect the shock absorbers from the axle brackets (see Chapter 10).
7   Disconnect the track bar from the axle bracket (see Chapter 10).
8   Disconnect the tie rod and drag link from the steering knuckle (see Chapter 10). Support the axle assembly with a floor jack under

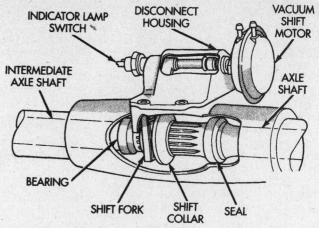

23.5 Vacuum shift motor assembly

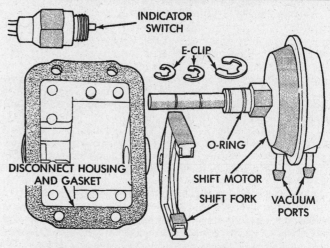

23.6 An exploded view of the shift motor components

the differential. Be sure to use a block of wood to protect the differential housing and cover.
9   Remove the coil springs (see Chapter 10).
10   Disconnect the lower suspension arms from the axle bracket (see Chapter 10). Be sure to mark the cams to ensure proper reassembly.
11   Lower the jack enough to remove the axle.
12   Installation is the reverse of removal. Tighten all bolts to the torque listed in this Chapter's Specifications and in the Specifications in Chapters 9 and 10.

23   Vacuum shift motor - removal and installation

Removal

Refer to illustrations 23.2, 23.5 and 23.6
1   Raise the vehicle and support it securely on jackstands.
2   Unplug the electrical connector for the indicator light switch **(see illustration)**.
3   Unscrew the indicator switch.
4   Detach the two vacuum lines from the vacuum shift motor. Detach the vent hose from the motor.
5   Remove the shift motor housing cover, gasket and shield from the housing **(see illustration)**.
6   Remove the E-clips from the shift motor housing and shaft. Remove the shift motor and shift fork from the housing **(see illustration)**.
7   Remove the O-ring seal from the shift motor shaft.
8   Clean and inspect all parts. If any part is worn or damaged, replace it.

Installation

9   Install a new O-ring on the shift motor shaft.

10   Insert the shift motor shaft through the hole in the housing and shift fork. The offset portion of the shift fork must face toward the differential.

11   Install the E-clips on the shift motor shaft and housing.

12   Install the shift motor housing gasket and cover. Make sure the shift fork is correctly guided into the shift collar groove.

13   Install the shift motor housing shield and bolts. Tighten the bolts to the torque listed in this Chapter's Specifications.

14   Add five ounces of API grade GL 5 hypoid gear lubricant to the shift motor housing. Add lubricant through the indicator switch mounting hole.

15   Install the indicator switch.

16   Attach the vacuum line.

17   Plug in the electrical connector.

24 Hub bearing and front axleshaft (4WD models) - removal and installation

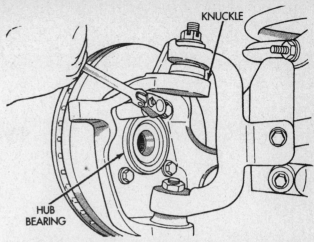

24.4 Remove the hub-to-knuckle bolts from the back of the steering knuckle, then remove the hub bearing assembly from the steering knuckle and axleshaft (axleshaft already removed for clarity)

Removal

Refer to illustration 24.4

Note: *If you're removing the axleshaft in order to replace the axleshaft seal or bearing, we recommend having the job done by a dealer service department or a qualified independent garage. Replacing either the seal or the bearing requires special tools.*

1   Loosen the wheel lug nuts. Raise the vehicle and support it securely on jackstands. Remove the wheel.

2   Remove the brake caliper and support it out of the way with wire (see Chapter 9). Remove the brake disc.

3   Remove the cotter pin and axle hub nut.

4   Remove the hub-to-knuckle bolts **(see illustration)**.

5   Remove the hub bearing from the steering knuckle and axleshaft.

6   Remove the brake dust shield from the steering knuckle.

7   Carefully pull the axleshaft from the axle housing. If the U-joint is worn out, it can be replaced uusing the procedure described in Section 11.

Installation

8   Clean the axleshaft and apply a thin film of wheel bearing grease to the shaft splines, seal contact surface and hub bore. Install the axleshaft, engaging the splines with the differential side gears. Be very careful not to damage the axleshaft oil seals.

9   Install the dust shield.

10   Install the hub bearing. Install the hub bearing-to-steering knuckle bolts and tighten them to the torque listed in this Chapter's Specifications.

11   Install the axleshaft washer and nut, tighten the nut to the torque listed in this Chapter's Specifications. Loosen or tighten the nut to nearest cotter pin hole and install a new cotter pin.

12   Install the brake disc and caliper (see Chapter 9).

13   Install the wheel and hand tighten the wheel lug nuts.

14   Remove the jackstands, lower the vehicle and tighten the wheel lug nuts to the torque listed in the Chapter 1 Specifications.

8

Notes

Chapter 9   Brakes

Contents

Specifications

General
Brake fluid type	See Chapter 1
Brake pedal specifications	See Chapter 1

Disc brakes
Brake pad minimum thickness	See Chapter 1
Disc lateral runout limit	0.004 inch
Disc minimum thickness	Cast into disc

Drum brakes
Minimum brake lining thickness	See Chapter 1
Maximum drum diameter	Cast into drum

Torque specifications
Ft-lbs (unless otherwise indicated)
Caliper mounting bolts	38
Master cylinder mounting nuts	200 to 300 in-lbs
Brake booster mounting nuts	200 to 300 in-lbs

9

1 General information

General

All models covered by this manual are equipped with front disc brakes and rear drums. All front disc brakes use single-piston, sliding type calipers with semi-metallic pads. Two different caliper styles and three caliper piston bore sizes are used on various models. The caliper styles are similar in appearance. The main difference between them is their physical size and the type of caliper mounting bolt bushing used. The calipers on 1500 (1/2-ton) models use 2.95-inch pistons; the calipers on 2500 (3/4-ton) models use 3.1-inch pistons; the calipers on 3500 (1-ton) and 2500 4 X 4 models with a Dana 60 front axle have 3.385-inch pistons. All brake discs are vented.

The rear drum brakes are semi-floating, self-energizing, servo action design. The brake shoes are not fixed on the support plate. This type of brake allows the shoes to pivot and move vertically to a certain extent. Three different size drum brake assemblies are used: 1/2-ton models used 11 X 2 inch units; 3/4-ton models use 13 X 2.5 inch units; 1-ton models use 13 X 3.5 inch units. Two wheel cylinders are used: the cylinders used on 1/2- and 3/4-ton models have a bore diameter of 0.937 (15/16) inch; the cylinders used on 1-ton models have a bore diameter of 1.06 (1-1/16) inch.

All brakes are self-adjusting. The front disc brakes automatically compensate for pad wear, while the rear drum brakes incorporate an adjustment mechanism which is activated as the brakes are applied.

The hydraulic system has separate circuits for the front and rear brakes. If one circuit fails, the other circuit will remain functional and a warning indicator will light up on the dashboard when a substantial amount of brake fluid is lost, showing that a failure has occurred.

Master cylinder

The master cylinder is located under the hood on the driver's side, and can be identified by the large fluid reservoir on top. The master cylinder has separate primary and secondary piston assemblies for the front and rear circuits.

Combination valve and RWAL valve

All models without ABS have a combination valve and a RWAL valve. A pressure differential switch inside the combination valve is connected to the brake warning light on the dash. This switch monitors fluid pressure in the front and rear hydraulic brake circuits. A decrease or loss of fluid pressure in either circuit will cause the switch valve to move forward or backward in response to the change in pressure. When the valve moves, it pushes the switch plunger up, which closes the electrical circuit to the warning light. The switch valve will remain in this position until the hydraulic system is repaired.

A metering valve is used to balance the braking force between the front disc and the rear drum brakes. The metering valve holds off fully applied pressure to the front disc brakes until the rear drum brake shoes are in full contact with the drums. The valve is designed to maintain front brake fluid pressure between 3 and 30 psi until the hold-off limit of 117 is reached. At this point, the metering valve opens completely, allowing full fluid pressure to the front brakes.

Power brake booster

The power brake booster uses engine manifold vacuum to provide assistance to the brakes. It is mounted on the firewall in the engine compartment, directly behind the master cylinder.

Diesel engines, which have no manifold vacuum, are equipped with an auxiliary pump that provides vacuum to operate the power brake booster. This pump is half of an integral assembly that also includes the power steering pump.

Anti-lock brake systems

A Rear-Wheel Anti-Lock (RWAL) brake system is standard on all models. An all-wheel anti-lock brake system (ABS) is available as an option. Both systems are manufactured by the Kelsey-Hayes Corporation. The RWAL and ABS anti-lock systems are designed to prevent wheel lockup during periods of high wheel slip, in order to improve directional stability and control, during hard braking.

Parking brake

The parking brake mechanically operates the rear brakes only. The parking brake cables pull on a lever attached to the brake shoe assembly, causing the shoes to expand against the drum.

Precautions

There are some general precautions and warnings related to the brake system:

a) *Use only brake fluid conforming to DOT 3 specifications.*
b) *The brake pads and linings may contain asbestos fibers which are hazardous to your health if inhaled. Whenever you work on brake system components, clean all parts with brake system cleaner or denatured alcohol. Do not allow the fine dust to become airborne.*
c) *Safety should be paramount whenever any servicing of the brake components is performed. Do not use parts or fasteners which are not in perfect condition, and be sure all clearances and torque specifications are adhered to. If you are at all unsure about a certain procedure, seek professional advice. Upon completion of any brake system work, test the brakes carefully in a controlled area before driving the vehicle in traffic.*

If a problem is suspected in the brake system, don't drive the vehicle until it's fixed.

2 Disc brake pads - replacement

Refer to illustrations 2.3 and 2.4a through 2.4t

Warning: *Disc brake pads must be replaced on both front wheels at the same time - never replace the pads on only one wheel. Also, the dust created by the brake system may contain asbestos, which is harmful to your health. Never blow it out with compressed air and don't inhale any of it. An approved filtering mask should be worn when working on the brakes. Do not, under any circumstances, use petroleum-based solvents to clean brake parts. Use brake system cleaner only!*

1   Loosen the front wheel lug nuts, raise the front of the vehicle and support it securely on jackstands. Apply the parking brake. Remove the front wheels.

2   Remove about two-thirds of the fluid from the master cylinder reservoir and discard it.

3   Push the piston back into the bore with a C-clamp to provide room for the new brake pads **(see illustration)**. As the piston is depressed to the bottom of the caliper bore, the fluid in the master cylinder will rise. Make sure it doesn't overflow. If necessary, remove

2.3 Using a large C-clamp, push the piston back into the caliper bore - note that one end of the clamp is positioned against the flat end of the piston housing and the screw is pushing against the outer pad

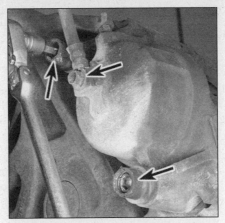

2.4a Before starting, wash down the brake disc and caliper assembly with brake cleaner

2.4b Unscrew the caliper Allen bolts (upper and lower arrows) and remove; don't remove the banjo bolt (center arrow) from the brake hose unless you plan to replace the hose or overhaul the caliper

2.4c Lift the caliper assembly off the brake disc

2.4d This step isn't necessary if you're holding the caliper assembly as you replace the pads, but anytime you aren't holding it, support it with a coat hanger or piece of wire as shown - allowing it to hang by the brake hose will damage the hose

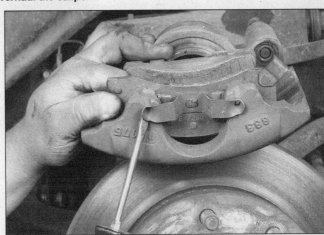

2.4e Pry the ends of the retaining clip out of the holes in the caliper frame . . .

some more fluid.

4   To replace the brake pads, follow the accompanying photo sequence, beginning with **illustration 2.4a**. Be sure to stay in order and read the caption under each illustration. Work on one brake assembly at a time so that you'll have something to refer to if you

get in trouble.

5   While the pads are removed, inspect the caliper for brake fluid leaks and ruptures in the piston boot. Overhaul or replace the caliper as necessary (see Section 3). Also inspect the brake disc carefully (see Section 4). If machining is necessary, follow the information in that

2.4f . . . and remove the outer pad

2.4g Pull the inner pad retaining clip loose from the piston and remove the pad

9

2.4h Remove the caliper mounting bolts

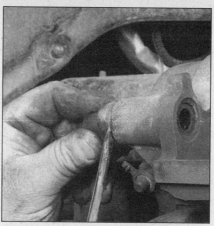

2.4i Pry off the caliper bolt dust boots and inspect them; if they're cracked or torn, replace them

2.4j Pry the seals out of the caliper bolt holes

2.4k Inspect the two small bushings inside each caliper bolt hole; if they're worn or damaged, replace them

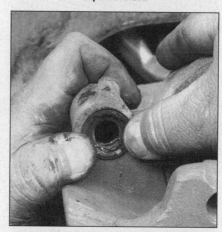

2.4l Wipe off the seals, lubricate them with multi-purpose grease and install them in the caliper bolt holes

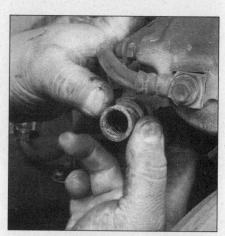

2.4m Install the caliper bolt dust boots

2.4n Apply multi-purpose grease to the upper sliding way of the caliper bracket . . .

2.4o . . . and to the lower way

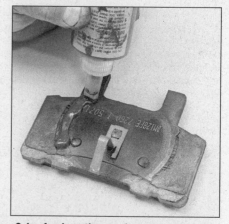

2.4p Apply anti-squeal compound to the back of both pads and let it dry for a few minutes

Section to remove the disc.

6   Before installing the caliper mounting bolts, clean them and check them for corrosion and damage. If they're significantly corroded or damaged, replace them. Be sure to tighten the caliper mounting bolts to the torque listed in this Chapter's Specifications.

7   Install the brake pads on the opposite wheel, then install the wheels and lower the vehicle. Tighten the lug nuts to the torque listed

in the Chapter 1 Specifications.

8   Add brake fluid to the reservoir until it's full (see Chapter 1). Pump the brakes several times to seat the pads against the disc, then check the fluid level again.

9   Check the operation of the brakes before driving the vehicle in traffic. Try to avoid heavy brake applications until the brakes have been applied lightly several times to seat the pads.

2.4q When you install the new inner pad, make sure the retaining clip is fully seated in the piston

2.4r Pop the outer pad onto the caliper; make sure that the pad is pressed all the way down and the ends of the retaining clip are fully engaged with the caliper

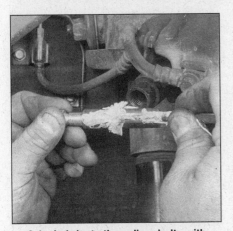

2.4s Lubricate the caliper bolts with multi-purpose grease . . .

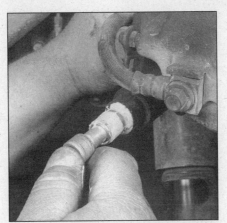

2.4t . . . insert them into the caliper bolt holes, install the caliper and tighten both bolts to the torque listed in this Chapter's Specifications

3.4 With a block of wood placed between the piston and caliper frame, use compressed air to ease the piston out of the bore

3   Disc brake caliper - removal, overhaul and installation

Note: *If an overhaul is indicated (usually because of fluid leaks, a stuck piston or broken bleeder screw) explore all options before beginning this procedure. New and factory rebuilt calipers are available on an exchange basis, which makes this job quite easy. If you decide to rebuild the calipers, make sure rebuild kits are available before proceeding. Always rebuild or replace the calipers in pairs - never rebuild just one of them.*

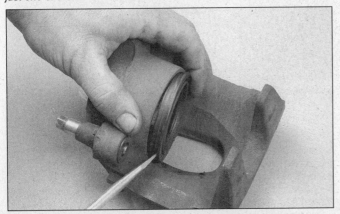

3.5 Carefully pry the dust boot out of the caliper

Removal

1   Loosen the front wheel lug nuts, raise the vehicle and support it securely on jackstands. Remove the front wheels.
2   Remove the brake hose-to-caliper banjo bolt and detach the hose from the caliper. (If the caliper is only being removed for access to other components, don't disconnect the hose.) Discard the two copper sealing washers on each side of the fitting and use new ones during installation. Wrap a plastic bag around the end of the hose to prevent fluid loss and contamination.
3   Remove the caliper following the first few steps of Section 2 (it's part of the brake pad replacement procedure), remove the brake pads, then clean the caliper with brake system cleaner. DO NOT use kerosene, gasoline or petroleum-based solvents.

Overhaul

Refer to illustrations 3.4, 3.5, 3.6, 3.10a, 3.10b, 3.10c, 3.11a, 3.11b and 3.12

4   Place several shop towels or a block of wood in the center of the caliper to act as a cushion, then use compressed air, directed into the fluid inlet, to remove the piston **(see illustration)**. Use only enough air pressure to ease the piston out of the bore. If the piston is blown out, even with the cushion in place, it may be damaged. **Warning:** *Never place your fingers in front of the piston in an attempt to catch or protect it when applying compressed air, as serious injury could occur.*
5   Pry the dust boot from the caliper bore **(see illustration)**.
6   Using a wood or plastic tool, remove the piston seal from the

9

groove in the caliper bore **(see illustration)**. Metal tools may cause bore damage.

7   Remove the bleeder screw.

8   Clean the remaining parts with brake system cleaner or clean brake fluid, then blow them dry with compressed air.

9   Inspect the surfaces of the piston for nicks and burrs and loss of plating. If surface defects are present, the piston must be replaced. Check the caliper bore in a similar way. Light polishing with crocus cloth is permissible to remove slight corrosion and stains. **Caution:** *If the caliper pistons are made of phenolic resin instead of metal, do NOT polish or sand them. And do NOT interchange metal pistons for plastic or vice-versa.*

10   Study the illustrations of the disassembled caliper **(see illustrations)**. Lubricate the new piston seal with clean brake fluid and position the seal in the cylinder groove using your fingers only **(see illustration)**. Make sure it isn't twisted.

11   Install the new dust boot in the groove in the end of the piston **(see illustration)**. Dip the piston in clean brake fluid and insert it squarely into the cylinder. Depress the piston to the bottom of the cylinder bore **(see illustration)**.

12   Seat the boot in the caliper counterbore using a boot installation tool or a blunt punch **(see illustration)**. Install the bleeder screw.

3.6 The piston seal should be removed with a plastic or wooden tool to avoid damage to the bore and seal groove (a pencil will do the job)

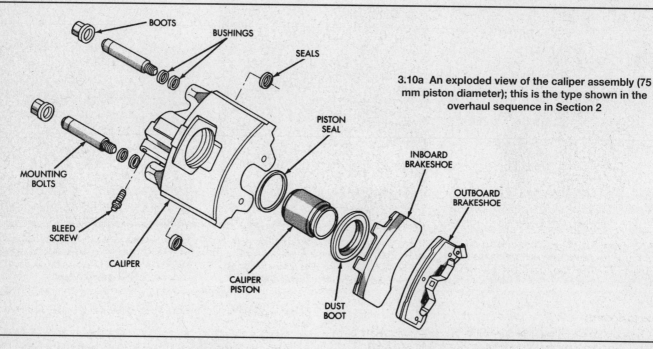

3.10a An exploded view of the caliper assembly (75 mm piston diameter); this is the type shown in the overhaul sequence in Section 2

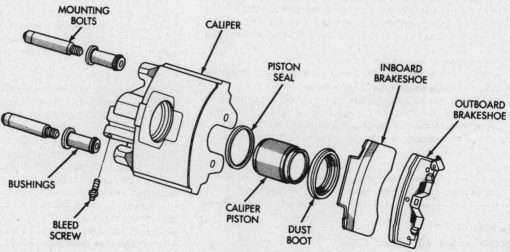

3.10b An exploded view of the caliper assembly (80/86 mm piston diameter); note the longer removable bushings - instead of two small ones in each bolt hole, and the absence of seals and boots for the bolt holes - slightly different than the unit shown in the Section 2 sequence

3.10c Position the new seal in the cylinder groove - make sure it isn't twisted

3.11a Slip the boot over the piston

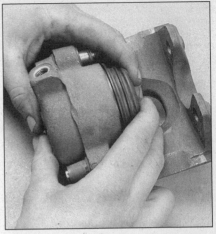

3.11b Push the piston straight into the caliper - make sure it doesn't become cocked in the bore

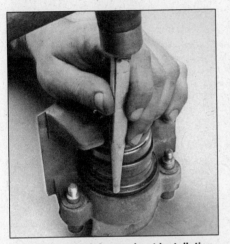

3.12 If you don't have a boot installation tool, gently seat the boot with a drift punch, working evenly around the boot

4.3 Use a dial indicator to check disc runout - if the reading exceeds the specified runout limit, the disc will have to be machined or replaced

4.4a On some models, the minimum thickness is cast into the inside of the disc - on others, it's located on the outside of the disc (typical)

Installation

13   Clean the sliding ways of the caliper bracket and lubricate them with high-temperature grease (see illustrations 2.4n and 2.4o).

14   Install the caliper and brake pads as described in Section 2.

15   Using new sealing washers on both sides of the brake hose banjo fitting, attach the hose fitting to the caliper and tighten the banjo bolt securely.

16   Bleed the brakes as outlined in Section 10.

17   Install the wheels and lug nuts. Lower the vehicle and tighten the lug nuts to the torque listed in the Chapter 1 Specifications.

18   After the job has been completed, firmly depress the brake pedal a few times to bring the pads into contact with the disc.

19   Check the operation of the brakes before driving the vehicle in traffic. Check the calipers, bleeder fittings and hose connections for leaks.

4   Brake disc - inspection, removal and installation

Inspection

Refer to illustrations 4.3, 4.4a and 4.4b

1   Loosen the wheel lug nuts, raise the front of the vehicle and sup-port it securely on jackstands. Apply the parking brake. Remove the front wheels.

2   Remove the brake caliper as described in Section 2, and support it with a piece of heavy wire so that it won't hang by the brake hose. Visually inspect the disc surface for score marks, hard spots and other damage. Light scratches and shallow grooves are normal after use and won't affect brake operation. Deep grooves require disc removal and refinishing by an automotive machine shop. Be sure to check both sides of the disc.

3   To check disc runout, place a dial indicator at a point about 1/2-inch from the outer edge of the disc (see illustration). Set the indicator to zero and turn the disc. The indicator reading should not exceed the runout limit listed in this Chapter's Specifications. If it does, the disc should be refinished by an automotive machine shop. Note: *Professionals recommend resurfacing the brake discs regardless of the dial indicator reading (to produce a smooth, flat surface that will eliminate brake pedal pulsations and other undesirable symptoms related to questionable discs). At the very least, if you elect not to have the discs resurfaced, deglaze them with sandpaper or emery cloth.*

4   The disc must not be machined to a thickness less than the spec-ified minimum thickness. The minimum (or discard) thickness is cast into the disc (see illustration). The disc thickness can be checked with a micrometer (see illustration) at several points around the circumfer-ence of the disc.

9

4.4b Use a micrometer to measure the thickness of the disc at several points

5.4a To remove the brake drum simply pull it straight off

5.5b If you can't pull off the drum fairly easily, apply some penetrating oil at the hub-to-drum joint and allow it to soak in, lightly tap the drum to break it loose . . .

Removal and installation

5   If you're working on a two-wheel drive model, refer to Chapter 1, Section 37, *Front wheel bearing check, repack and adjustment* for the disc removal and installation procedure.

6   If you're working on a four-wheel drive model, refer to Chapter 8, Section 23, *Hub bearing and front axleshaft (4WD models) - removal and installation*, as the hub and disc must be removed as a unit. To separate the disc from the hub on these models, the wheel studs must be driven out with a brass mallet.

5   Drum brake shoes - replacement

Refer to illustrations 5.4a through 5.4ww and 5.5
Warning: *Drum brake shoes must be replaced on both wheels at the same time - never replace the shoes on only one wheel. Also, the dust created by the brake system may contain asbestos, which is harmful to your health. Never blow it out with compressed air and don't inhale any of it. An approved filtering mask should be worn when working on the brakes. Do not, under any circumstances, use petroleum-based solvents to clean brake parts. Use brake system cleaner only!*

5.4c . . . then carefully tap around the outer edge of the drum to drive it off the studs - don't use excessive force!

Caution: *Whenever the brake shoes are replaced, the retractor and hold-down springs should also be replaced. Due to the continuous heating/cooling cycle that the springs are subjected to, they lose their tension over a period of time and may allow the shoes to drag on the drum and wear at a much faster rate than normal.*

1   There are two types of drum rear brakes on the vehicles covered by this manual; the 11-inch-diameter brakes used on 1500 models, and the 13-inch diameter brakes used on 2500 and 3500 models. The two systems are very similar in design, differing mainly in size and parking brake lever arrangement.

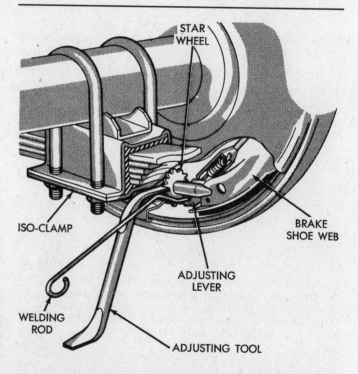

5.4d If the drum still can't be pulled off, the shoes have worn into the drum and will have to be retracted - this is done by inserting a screwdriver or piece of heavy wire into the slot in the backing plate to hold the adjusting lever away from the star wheel, then turning the star wheel with another screwdriver or a brake adjusting tool

2   Loosen the wheel lug nuts, raise the rear of the vehicle and support it securely on jackstands. Block the front wheels to keep the vehicle from rolling and release the parking brake.

3   Remove the wheel. **Note:** *All four rear brake shoes must be replaced at the same time, but to avoid mixing up parts, work on only one side at a time.*

4   Follow the accompanying illustrations for the inspection and replacement of the brake shoes. Be sure to follow the photo sequence and read each caption **(see illustrations)**. **Note:** *If the brake drum cannot be easily pulled off the axle and shoe assembly, make sure that the parking brake is completely released, then apply some penetrating oil at the hub-to-drum joint. Allow the oil to soak in and try to pull the drum off. If the drum still cannot be pulled off, the brake shoes will have to be retracted. This is accomplished by first removing the plug from the backing plate. With the plug removed, pull the lever off the adjusting star wheel with one narrow screwdriver while turning the adjusting wheel with another narrow screwdriver, moving the shoes away from the drum (see illustration 5.4d). The drum should now come off.*

5   Before reinstalling the drum it should be checked for cracks, score marks, deep scratches and hard spots, which will appear as small discolored areas. If the hard spots cannot be removed with fine emery cloth or if any of the other conditions listed above exist, the drum must be taken to an automotive machine shop to have it resurfaced. **Note:** *Professionals recommend resurfacing the drums whenever a brake job is done. Resurfacing will eliminate the possibility of out-of-round drums.* If the drums are worn so much that they can't be resurfaced without exceeding the maximum allowable diameter

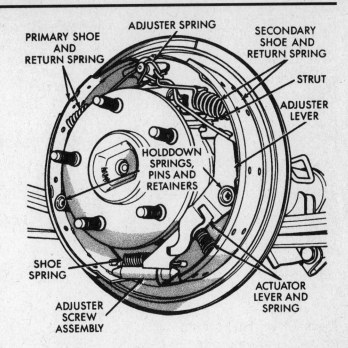

5.4e Details of the rear drum brake assembly (11-inch brake)

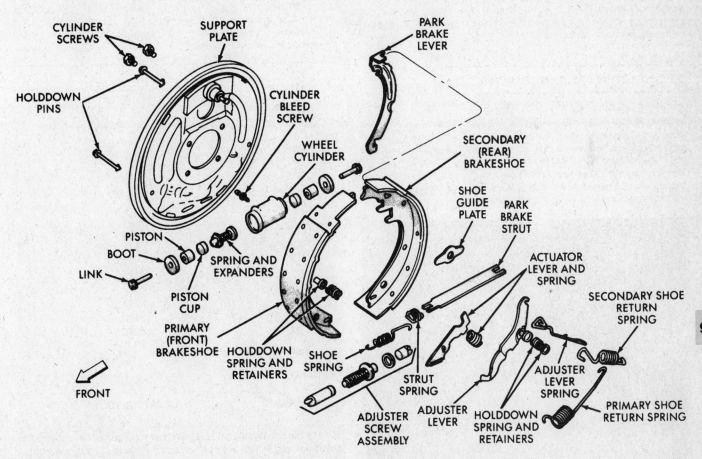

5.4f An exploded view of the 11-inch brake assembly

9

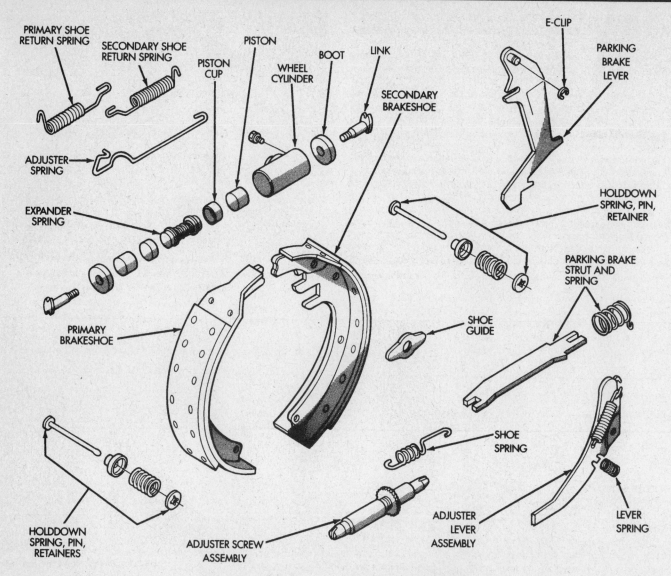

PRIMARY SHOE
RETURN SPRING

SECONDARY SHOE
RETURN SPRING

PISTON
CUP

PISTON

WHEEL
CYLINDER

BOOT

LINK

E-CLIP

PARKING
BRAKE
LEVER

SECONDARY
BRAKESHOE

ADJUSTER
SPRING

EXPANDER
SPRING

HOLDDOWN
SPRING, PIN,
RETAINER

PARKING BRAKE
STRUT AND
SPRING

PRIMARY
BRAKESHOE

SHOE
GUIDE

HOLDDOWN
SPRING, PIN,
RETAINERS

ADJUSTER SCREW
ASSEMBLY

ADJUSTER
LEVER
ASSEMBLY

SHOE
SPRING

LEVER
SPRING

5.4g An exploded view of the 13-inch brake assembly

**5.4h Before beginning work, wash away all traces of dust with
brake system cleaner - DO NOT use compressed air (rear axle
and hub removed for clarity)**

**5.4i Using a brake spring tool, disengage the secondary shoe
return spring from the anchor pin**

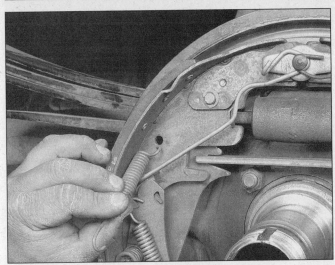

5.4j Unhook the other end of the spring from the secondary shoe and set the spring aside

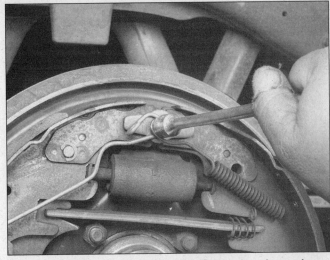

5.4k Using the brake spring tool, disengage the primary shoe return spring from the anchor pin

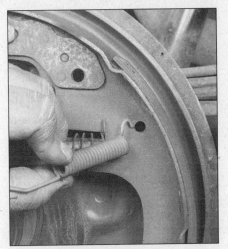

5.4l Unhook the other end of the spring from the primary shoe

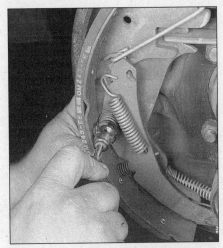

5.4m Using a hold-down spring tool, push in on the retainer and turn it 90-degrees . . .

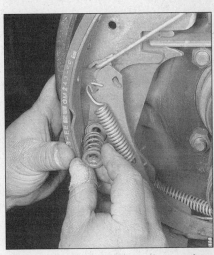

5.4n . . . and remove the retainer, spring and pin

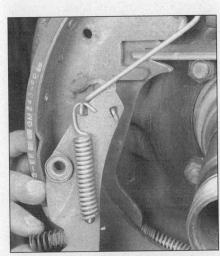

5.4o Remove the spring from the parking brake lever

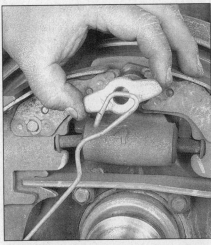

5.4p Remove the adjuster spring and the shoe guide

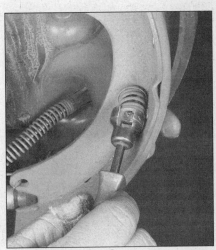

5.4q Using the hold-down spring tool, push in on the retainer and turn it 90-degrees . . .

9

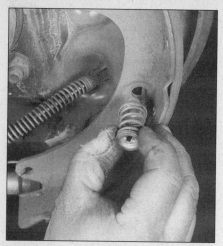

5.4r . . . and remove the retainer, spring and pin

5.4s Disengage the parking brake strut from the secondary shoe . . .

5.4t . . . then disengage the parking brake strut from the primary shoe; don't lose the strut spring - and don't forget where it goes (on the end of the strut that engages the primary shoe)

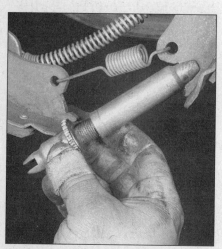

5.4u Remove the adjuster screw assembly

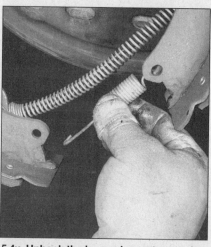

5.4v Unhook the lower shoe return spring from both shoes

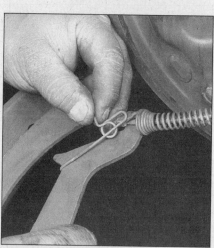

5.4w Move the parking brake cable retainer aside . . .

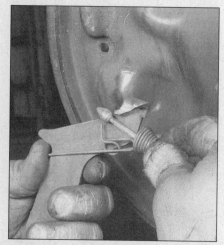

5.4x . . . then disengage the end of the parking brake cable from the parking brake lever

5.4y To separate the parking brake lever from the secondary shoe, remove this small E-clip retainer from the lever pivot pin (on 11-inch brakes the lever simply unhooks from the shoe)

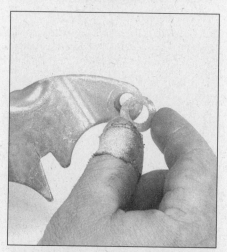

5.4z Note the washer that goes between the lever and the secondary shoe - don't forget to install this washer!

5.4aa Clean off the parking brake lever pivot pin, lube it with high temperature grease, install the washer, install the lever and pop the E-clip retainer into place with a pair of pliers

5.4bb Clean the backing plate, then lubricate all the points on the plate that support the shoes with a thin film of high-temperature grease

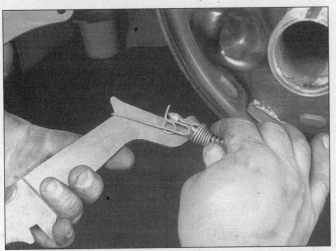

5.4cc Reattach the parking brake cable to the parking brake lever; make sure the wire retainer is returned to its original position to prevent the parking brake cable from coming off

5.4dd Install the secondary shoe and parking brake lever as shown; make sure that the crescent cutout in the shoe is fully seated against the anchor and the notch below it is engaged by the wheel cylinder pushrod

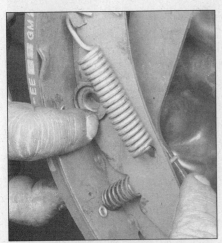

5.4ee Place the small adjuster lever spring in position between the lever and the secondary shoe

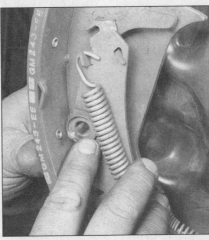

5.4ff Insert the secondary hold-down spring pin through the backing plate, install the spring seat . . .

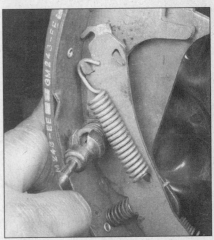

5.4gg . . . install the spring and retainer and twist the retainer to lock it into place

9

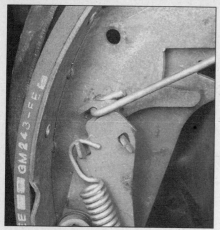

5.4hh Engage the lower end of the adjuster spring with the adjuster lever as shown

5.4ii Install the shoe guide on the anchor pin

5.4jj Hook the upper end of the adjuster spring over the anchor pin

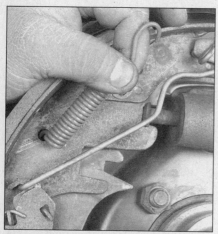

5.4kk Engage the lower end of the secondary return spring with the secondary shoe

5.4ll Using the brake spring tool, connect the upper end of the return spring with the adjuster spring

5.4mm Place the parking brake strut in the slot in the parking brake lever

5.4nn Place the primary shoe assembly into position; again, make sure the crescent cutout at the top of the shoe is fully seated against the anchor and the notch below is engaged with the wheel cylinder pushrod and, last but not least, that the parking brake strut and spring are properly engaged with the shoe

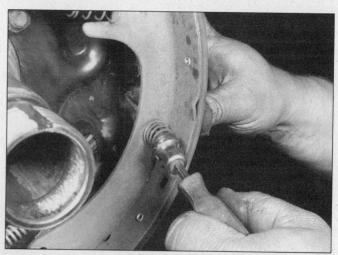

5.4oo When everything is as it should be, insert the primary shoe hold-down spring pin through the backside of the backing plate, install the spring seat, the spring and the retainer, and give the retainer a twist with a hold-down spring tool

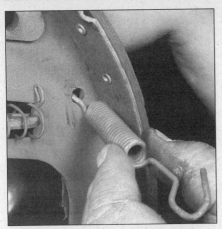

5.4pp Engage the lower end of the primary return spring with the primary shoe . . .

5.4qq . . . and hook the upper end of the spring over the anchor pin with a brake spring tool

5.4rr This is how it should look; the return springs must be installed in this order - with the primary return spring on top of the secondary return spring)

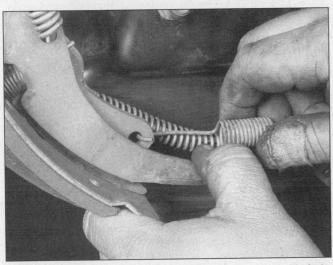

5.4ss Engage the long end of the lower return spring with the secondary shoe . . .

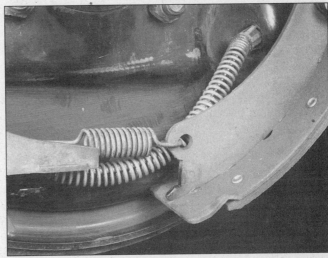

5.4tt . . . and the short end of the spring with the primary shoe

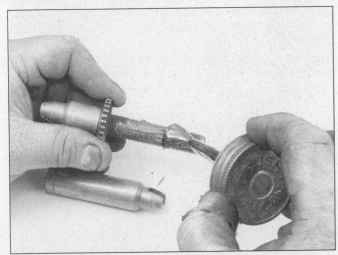

5.4uu Clean the adjuster screw, then lubricate the threads and the sliding surface of the button with high-temperature grease

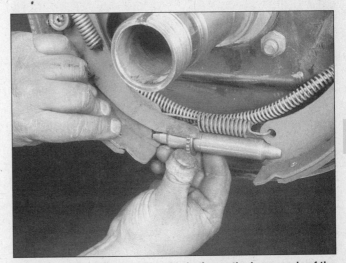

5.4vv Install the adjuster assembly between the lower ends of the shoes, then turn out the adjuster far enough to keep it in place (don't turn it out all the way or you won't be able to install the drum over the new shoes)

9

5.4ww This is how it should look when you're done (right side shown)

5.5 The maximum allowable inside diameter is cast into the outer edge of the drum

(stamped into the drum) **(see illustration)**, then new ones will be required. At the very least, if you elect not to have the drums resurfaced, remove the glazing from the surface with emery cloth or sandpaper using a swirling motion.

6   Install the brake drum. Turn the brake adjuster until the shoes rub on the drum as the drum is turned, then back-off the adjuster until the shoes don't rub.

7   Mount the wheel, install the lug nuts, then lower the vehicle.

8   Make a number of forward and reverse stops to adjust the brakes until satisfactory pedal action is obtained.

9   Check brake operation before driving the vehicle in traffic.

---

6   Wheel cylinder - removal, overhaul and installation

Removal

Refer to illustration 6.2

Note: *If an overhaul is indicated (usually because of fluid leakage or sticky operation) explore all options before beginning the job. New wheel cylinders are available, which makes this job quite easy. If you decide to rebuild the wheel cylinder, make sure a rebuild kit is available before proceeding. Never overhaul only one wheel cylinder. Always rebuild both of them at the same time.*

1   Remove the brake shoes (see Section 5).

2   Unscrew the brake line fitting from the rear of the wheel cylinder

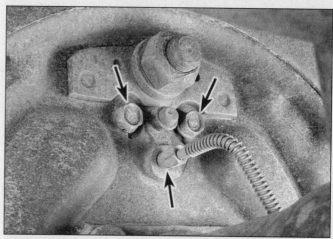

6.2 Disconnect the brake line fitting (lower arrow) with a flare-nut wrench, then remove the mounting bolts (upper arrows)

(see illustration). If available, use a flare-nut wrench to avoid rounding off the corners on the fitting. Don't pull the metal line out of the wheel cylinder - it could bend, making installation difficult.

3   Remove the two bolts securing the wheel cylinder to the brake backing plate.

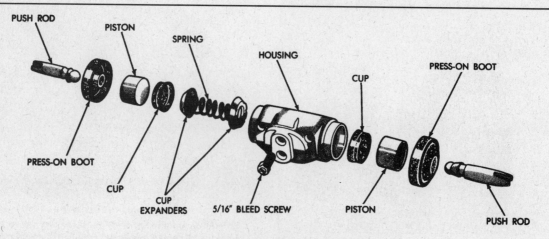

6.6 An exploded view of a typical wheel cylinder assembly

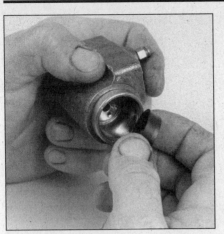

6.11 Install a piston cup with its open end (lips) facing in

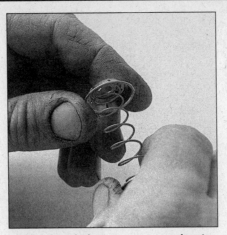

6.12a Attach the new cup expanders to the spring . . .

6.12b . . . then insert the expander/spring assembly into the other end of the cylinder, followed by the remaining piston cup

4 Remove the wheel cylinder.

5 Plug the end of the brake line to prevent the loss of brake fluid and the entry of dirt.

Overhaul

Refer to illustrations 6.6, 6.11, 6.12a, 6.12b and 6.13

6 To disassemble the wheel cylinder, first remove the rubber boot from each end of the cylinder and push out the two pistons, cups (seals) and spring expander **(see illustration)**. Discard the rubber parts and use new ones from the rebuild kit when reassembling the wheel cylinder.

7 Inspect the pistons for scoring and scuff marks. If defects are present, the pistons should be replaced with new ones. **Note:** *Most wheel cylinder overhaul kits include all components except the pistons and the pushrods. Use all of the parts included in the kit.*

8 Examine the inside of the cylinder bore for score marks and corrosion. If these conditions exist, the cylinder can be polished slightly with crocus cloth to restore it, but replacement is recommended.

9 If the cylinder is in good condition, clean it with brake system cleaner or brake fluid. **Warning:** *DO NOT, under any circumstances, use gasoline or petroleum-based solvents to clean brake parts!*

10 Remove the bleeder screw and make sure the hole at its inner end is clean.

11 Lubricate the cylinder bore with clean brake fluid, then insert one of the new rubber cups into the bore. Make sure the lip on the rubber cup faces in **(see illustration)**.

12 Attach the two cup expanders to the new expander spring, place

the assembly in the opposite end of the bore and push it in until it contacts the rear of the rubber cup **(see illustrations)**.

13 Install the remaining cup in the cylinder bore, and install both pistons **(see illustration)**.

14 Attach the rubber boots to the pushrods, then install the boots and pushrods.

15 The wheel cylinder is now ready for installation.

Installation

Refer to illustration 6.16

16 Chrysler recommends applying a thin coat of silicone sealant to the wheel cylinder mounting surface **(see illustration)** before installation. The sealant prevents road splash from entering the brake drum past the cylinder.

17 Installation is otherwise the reverse of removal. Attach the brake line to the wheel cylinder before installing the mounting bolts and tighten the line fitting after the wheel cylinder mountings bolts have been tightened. If available, use a flare-nut wrench to tighten the line fitting. **Note:** *It is recommended, especially on 4WDs and vehicles driven in off-road conditions, to apply some RTV sealant around the opening in the backing plate before bolting in the wheel cylinder. This will keep out water and dust.*

18 Bleed the brakes (see Section 10). Don't drive the vehicle in traffic until the operation of the brakes has been thoroughly tested.

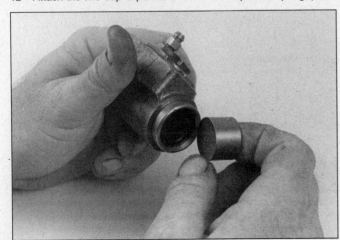

6.13 Install a cleaned piston into each end of the cylinder with the flat side toward the cup

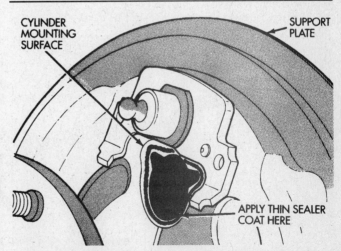

6.16 Apply a thin coat of silicone sealant between the brake backing plate and the wheel cylinder to prevent water from entering the brake drum assembly

CYLINDER MOUNTING SURFACE

SUPPORT PLATE

APPLY THIN SEALER COAT HERE

9

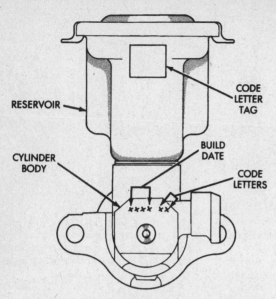

7.1 Identification code locations for master cylinder body and reservoir

7.3 Use a flare-nut wrench to loosen the brake line fittings, then remove the two master cylinder mounting nuts (arrow - other nut not visible in this photo)

7　Master cylinder - removal, overhaul and installation

Refer to illustration 7.1

1　Three different master cylinders are used on the various models covered by this manual. The differences concern reservoir size and cylinder bore diameter: the master cylinder unit in 1500 (1/2-ton) models has 1.125-inch bore; the unit in 2500 (3/4-ton) and 3500 (1-ton) models has a 1.252-inch bore. Although both versions of this unit have the same bore, the unit used in 3500 models has a longer stroke length and larger reservoir capacity. To verify that you have the right master cylinder, refer to the cylinder body code letters on the front end of the cylinder; the reservoir code letters are on an adhesive backed tag attached to the front face of the reservoir **(see illustration)**. On 1500 models, the code letters are NK; on 2500 models, the letters are NL; on 3500 models, the letters are NP. **Caution:** *Do NOT interchange master cylinders. Doing so will cause improper brake balance and diminished braking performance.*

Removal

Refer to illustration 7.3

2　Place rags under the brake line fittings and prepare caps or plas-tic bags to cover the ends of the lines once they're disconnected. **Caution:** *Brake fluid will damage paint. Cover all painted surfaces and avoid spilling fluid during this procedure. Brake fluid can be siphoned out of the reservoir using a squeeze bulb, but wear safety goggles.*

3　Loosen the flare nuts at the ends of the brake lines where they enter the master cylinder. To prevent rounding off the flats on these nuts, a flare-nut wrench, which wraps around the nut, should be used **(see illustration)**. Pull the brake lines away from the master cylinder slightly and plug the ends to prevent contamination.

4　Remove the two master cylinder mounting nuts. Remove the master cylinder from the booster, taking care not to kink the hydraulic lines **(see illustration 7.3)**.

5　Remove the reservoir cap(s), then discard any fluid remaining in the reservoir.

Overhaul and installation

Refer to illustrations 7.7, 7.8, 7.9, 7.10, 7.14, 7.15a, 7.15b, 7.15c, 7.15d, 7.16 and 7.17

Note: *Before deciding to overhaul the master cylinder, check on the availability and cost of a new or factory rebuilt unit and also the availability of a rebuild kit.*

6　Mount the master cylinder in a padded vise.

7　Remove the primary piston lock-ring by depressing the piston and prying the ring out with a screwdriver **(see illustration)**.

7.7 Push the primary piston in with a Phillips screwdriver and remove the lock-ring

7.8 Pull the primary piston and spring assembly out of the bore

7.9 To remove the secondary piston, tap the cylinder against a block of wood

7.10 Pry the reservoir out of the grommets

7.14 Lay the reservoir face down on a bench and push the master cylinder straight down over the reservoir fittings with a rocking motion

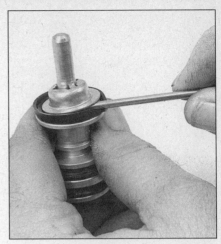

7.15a Pry the secondary piston spring retainer off with a small screwdriver, then remove the seal

7.15b Remove the secondary seals from the piston (some pistons have only one seal)

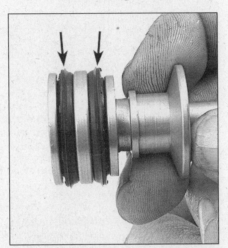

7.15c Install the secondary seals with the lips facing away from each other (on the single-seal design, the seal lip should face away from the center of the piston)

7.15d Install a new primary seal on the secondary piston with the seal lip facing in the direction shown

8   Remove the primary piston assembly from the cylinder bore **(see illustration)**.

9   Remove the secondary piston assembly from the cylinder bore. It may be necessary to remove the master cylinder from the vise and invert it, carefully tapping it against a block of wood to expel the piston **(see illustration)**.

10   Pry the reservoir off the body with a screwdriver **(see illustration)**. Remove the grommets.

11   Do not attempt to remove the quick take-up valve from the master cylinder body - it's not serviceable.

12   Inspect the cylinder bore for damage. If any damage is found, replace the master cylinder body with a new one, as abrasives cannot be used on the bore.

13   Lubricate the new reservoir grommets with brake fluid and press them into the master cylinder body. Make sure they're properly seated.

14   Lay the reservoir on a hard surface and press the master cylinder body onto the reservoir, using a rocking motion **(see illustration)**.

15   Remove the old seals from the secondary piston assembly and install the new secondary seals with the lips facing away from each other **(see illustrations)**. The lip on the primary seal must face in **(see illustration)**.

16   Attach the spring retainer to the secondary piston assembly **(see illustration)**.

9

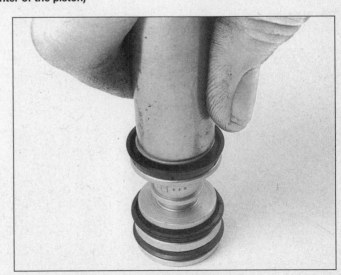

7.16 Install a new spring retainer over the end of the secondary piston and push it into place with a socket

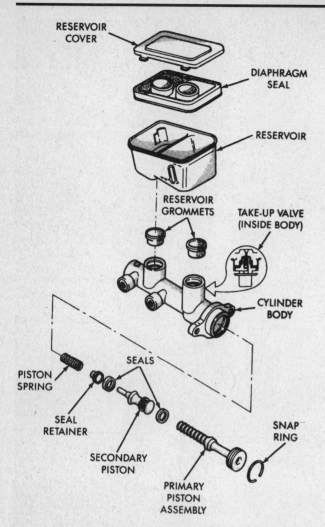

7.17 An exploded view of the master cylinder assembly

17   Lubricate the cylinder bore with clean brake fluid and install the spring and secondary piston assembly **(see illustration)**.

18   Install the primary piston assembly in the cylinder bore, depress it and install the lock-ring.

19   Inspect the reservoir cover and diaphragm for cracks and deformation. Replace any damaged parts with new ones and attach the diaphragm to the cover.

20   Whenever the master cylinder is removed, the entire hydraulic system must be bled. The time required to bleed the system can be reduced if the master cylinder is filled with fluid and bench bled (refer to Steps 21 through 23) before the master cylinder is installed on the vehicle.

21   Fill the reservoirs with brake fluid. The master cylinder should be supported so the brake fluid won't spill during the bench bleeding procedure.

22   Hold your fingers tightly over the holes where the brake lines normally connect to the master cylinder to prevent air from being drawn back into the master cylinder.

23   Stroke the piston several times to ensure all air has been expelled. A large Phillips screwdriver can be used to push on the piston assembly. Wait several seconds each time for brake fluid to be drawn from the reservoir into the piston bore, then depress the piston again, removing your finger as brake fluid is expelled. Be sure to put your fingers back over the holes each time before releasing the piston. When the bleeding procedure is complete, temporarily install plugs in the holes.

24   Carefully install the master cylinder by reversing the removal steps.

25   Bleed the brake system (see Section 10).

8   Parking brake cables - replacement

Front cable

Refer to illustrations 8.3a, 8.3b, 8.4, 8.5, 8.7, 8.8a, 8.8b, 8.8c, 8.8d and 8.8e

1   Remove the knee bolster (see Chapter 11).

2   Release the parking brake. Raise the vehicle and place it securely on jackstands.

3   Loosen the tensioner nut to create slack in the front cable and

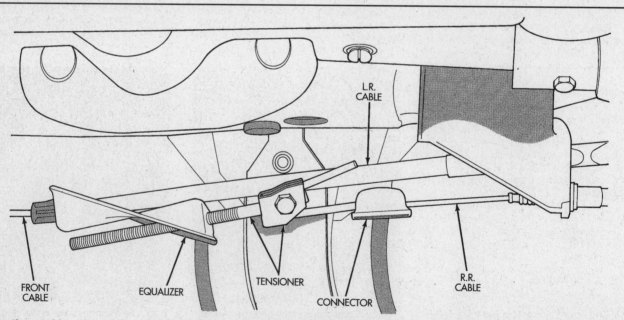

8.3a The three cables - front, left rear and right rear - join at the equalizer/tensioner assembly, underneath the left side of the vehicle, next to the frame rail

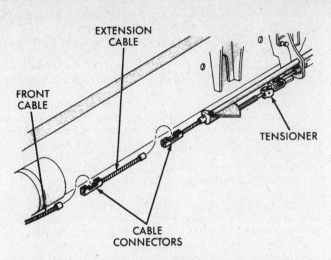

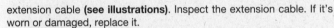

8.3b If you look carefully, you'll see that the front cable and the left rear cable are actually connected together, via the extension cable

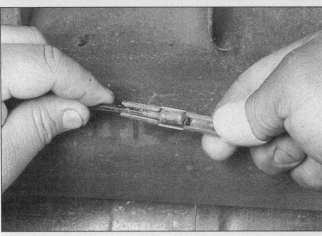

8.4 After loosening the tensioner nut to put some slack in the cable assembly, disengage the front cable from the extension cable connector (before you hook up a new front cable, have a look at the extension cable; if it's frayed or corroded, now is the time to replace it, while everything is apart)

extension cable **(see illustrations)**. Inspect the extension cable. If it's worn or damaged, replace it.

4   Disengage the front cable from the extension cable connector **(see illustration)**.
5   Detach the cable from the bracket **(see illustration)**.
6   Remove the jackstands and lower the vehicle.
7   Roll back the carpet and detach the cable grommet **(see illustration)** from the floor, then pull the cable up through the floor.
8   Disconnect the small cable that connects the parking brake release handle to the parking brake foot pedal assembly **(see illustration)**. Unbolt the parking brake foot pedal assembly and detach the front cable from the pedal **(see illustrations)**.
9   Installation is the reverse of removal. Be sure to adjust the parking brake when you're through (see Section 9).

Rear cable

Refer to illustration 8.12a, 8.12b, 8.12c, 8.13, 8.14a and 8.14b
10   Raise the vehicle and place it securely on jackstands.
11   Remove the secondary brake shoe and disconnect the parking brake cable from the parking brake lever (see Section 5).

8.5 To detach the front cable from this bracket, compress the locking fingers of the retainer and pull the cable through

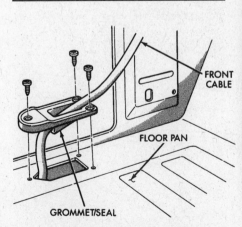

8.7 The grommet/seal for the front cable is attached to the floor by three small screws which must be removed

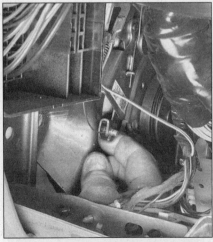

8.8a Detach this small cable from the parking brake pedal assembly before trying to remove the pedal from the kick panel bulkhead

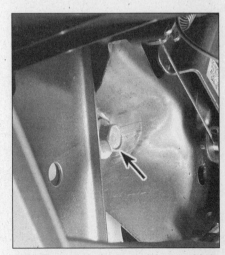

8.8b The parking brake pedal assembly is attached to the kick panel bulkhead by this bolt . . .

9

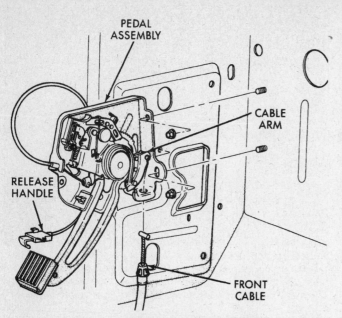

PEDAL ASSEMBLY

CABLE ARM

RELEASE HANDLE

FRONT CABLE

8.8c . . . and to the firewall by two nuts

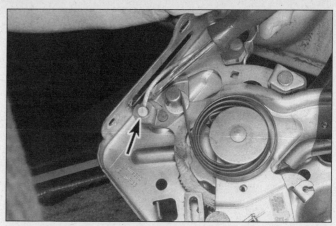

8.8d To disconnect the front cable from the parking brake pedal, pop out this plug on the end of the cable . . .

12 Remove the spring from the rear end of the cable, compress the locking fingers of the cable retainer and pull the cable through the brake backing plate **(see illustrations)**.

13 Remove the cable from the reaction bracket **(see illustration)** on the right rear frame rail.

14 Disengage the rear cable from the tensioner **(see illustrations)**.

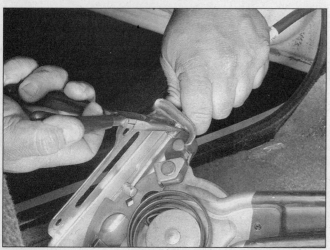

8.8e . . . then compress the locking fingers of the cable retainer and pull the cable through the bracket

8.12a To detach the rear parking brake cable from the brake backing plate, slide off the spring . . .

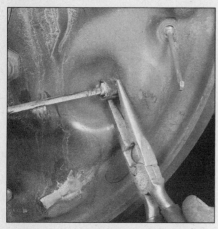

8.12b . . . compress the fingers of the retainer . . .

8.12c . . . and pull the cable through the backing plate

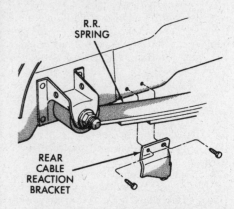

R.R. SPRING

REAR CABLE REACTION BRACKET

8.13 Mounting details of the rear parking brake cable reaction bracket

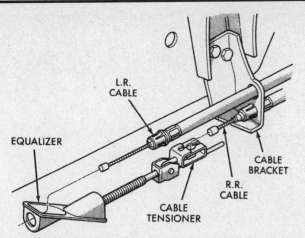

8.14a Parking brake cable tensioner assembly; to disconnect the left rear cable from the equalizer, disconnect the front end of the cable from the connector at the rear end of the extension cable (see illustration 8.4), compress the locking fingers of the retainer and pull the cable through the equalizer

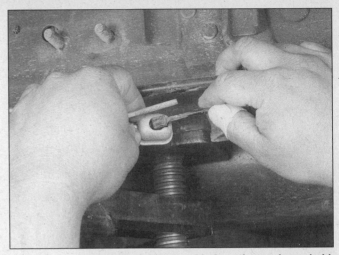

8.14b To disconnect the right rear cable from the tensioner, hold the tensioner and work the plug on the end of the cable out through this hole; then compress the fingers of the cable retainer and pull the cable through the bracket (shown in 8.14a)

15   Detach the cable from the frame bracket behind the tensioner.
16   Remove the cable.
17   Installation is the reverse of removal. Be sure to adjust the cable when you're through (see Section 9).

9   Parking brake - adjustment

Refer to illustration 9.10
1   The parking brake is pedal operated and is normally self-adjusting through the automatic adjusters in the rear brake drums. However, supplementary adjustment may be needed in the event of cable stretch, wear in the linkage or after installation of new components.
Note: *Before making any adjustment to the parking brake assembly, make sure the rear drum brakes are properly adjusted first.*
2   Raise the rear of the vehicle until the wheels are clear of the ground, support it securely on jackstands and block the front wheels. Release the parking brake pedal by pulling on the release lever.
3   The adjuster is located on the outside of the frame on the driver's side. Hold the cable from turning with locking pliers, then back off the cable tensioner adjusting nut **(see illustration 8.3a)** to create slack in the cables.
4   Remove the rear wheels and the rear brake drums (see Section 5).
5   Inspect the condition of the brake parts:
  a) *Inspect the condition of the rear brake assemblies and replace parts as necessary.*
  b) *Verify that the parking brake cables operate freely and are not binding or seized. Replace faulty cables (see Section 8).*
  c) *Adjust the rear brake shoes so that they drag on the drum slightly when the drum is turned, then back off the adjustment until there is no drag.*
6   Install the wheels, remove the jackstands and lower the vehicle. Tighten the wheel lug nuts to the torque listed in the Chapter 1 Specifications.
7   Fully apply the parking brake pedal.
8   Raise the vehicle again and place it securely on jackstands.
9   Mark the tensioner rod 1/4-inch from the edge of the tensioner bracket.
10   Tighten the adjusting nut at the equalizer until the mark on the tensioner rod moves into alignment with the tensioner bracket **(see illustration)**. **Caution:** *Do NOT loosen or tighten the tensioner adjusting nut after completing the adjustment.*
11   Release the parking brake pedal assembly and verify that the rear wheels rotate freely without drag.
12   Remove the jackstands and lower the vehicle.

10   Brake system - bleeding

Refer to illustration 10.10
Warning: *Wear eye protection when bleeding the brake system. If the fluid comes in contact with your eyes, immediately rinse them with water and seek medical attention.*
Note: *Bleeding the brake system is necessary to remove any air that's trapped in the system when it's opened during removal and installation of a hose, line, caliper, wheel cylinder or master cylinder.*
1   It will be necessary to bleed the system at the master cylinder and at all four brakes if air has entered the system due to low fluid level, or if the brake lines have been disconnected at the master cylinder.
2   If a brake line was disconnected only at a wheel, then only that caliper or wheel cylinder must be bled.
3   If a brake line is disconnected at a fitting located between the master cylinder and any of the brakes, that part of the system served by the disconnected line must be bled.
4   Remove any residual vacuum from the power booster (if equipped) by applying the brake several times with the engine off.
5   Remove the master cylinder reservoir cover and fill the reservoir with brake fluid. Reinstall the cover. **Note:** *Check the fluid level often during the bleeding operation and add fluid as necessary to prevent the fluid level from falling low enough to allow air bubbles into the master cylinder.*

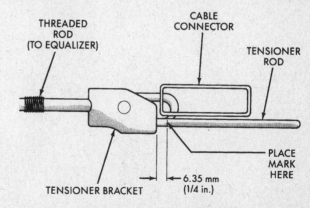

9.10 Tighten the adjusting nut at the equalizer until the mark on the tensioner rod moves into alignment with the tensioner bracket

9

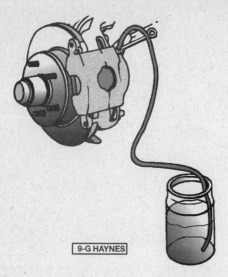

9-G HAYNES

10.10 When bleeding the brakes, a clear piece of tubing is attached to the bleeder screw fitting and submerged in brake fluid - the air bubbles can easily be seen in the tube and container (when no more bubbles appear, the air has been purged)

6   Have an assistant on hand, as well as a supply of new brake fluid, an empty clear plastic container, a length of 3/16-inch plastic, rubber or vinyl tubing to fit over the bleeder valve and a wrench to open and close the bleeder valve.

Rear Wheel Anti-Lock (RWAL) brake system

7   Bleed the brakes in the following sequence: master cylinder, combination valve, RWAL valve, right (passenger side) rear wheel, left (driver side) rear wheel, right front wheel and left front wheel.
8   To bleed the master cylinder, loosen the rear fitting on the master cylinder and have your assistant slowly push the brake pedal to the floor and hold it there. **Note:** *Be sure to place rags or newspapers underneath the fittings to absorb the fluid).* Tighten the fitting when the pedal reaches the bottom of its travel. Repeat this until the flow of fluid is free of air bubbles, then repeat the procedure on the front fitting. Top up the master cylinder reservoir with fluid.
9   Bleed the combination valve, followed by the RWAL valve, in a similar manner.
10   Move on to the right rear brake. Loosen the bleeder screw slightly, then tighten it to a point where it's snug but can still be loosened quickly and easily. Place one end of the tubing over the bleeder screw fitting and submerge the other end in brake fluid in the container **(see illustration)**.
11   Open the bleeder screw and have your assistant slowly push the brake pedal to the floor and hold it there. Watch for air bubbles to exit the submerged end of the tube. Tighten the fitting when the pedal reaches the bottom of its travel. Repeat this until the flow of fluid is free of air bubbles.
12   Proceed to the left rear wheel, the right front wheel and the left front wheel, in that order, and perform the same procedure. Be sure to check the fluid in the master cylinder reservoir frequently.

4-wheel Anti-Lock Brake System (ABS)

Warning: *The following procedure only applies to systems using the original front anti-lock valve. A special tool is required to properly bleed new front anti-lock valve and motor assemblies (and replacement of that component should be left to a dealer service department or other qualified repair shop anyway).*
13   Bleed this system following the above procedure, but in the following sequence: master cylinder, rear anti-lock valve, combination valve, front anti-lock valve, left (driver side) rear wheel, right (passenger side) rear wheel, right front wheel and left front wheel.

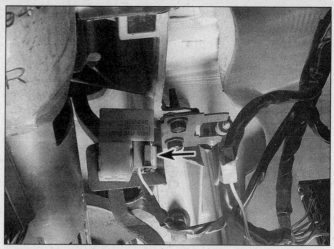

11.2 Electrical connector (arrow) for the brake light switch

RWAL and ABS systems

14   Never use old brake fluid. It contains moisture which will allow the fluid to boil when it heats up, rendering the brakes useless. When bleeding, make sure the fluid coming out of the bleeder is not only free of bubbles, but clean also.
15   Refill the master cylinder with new fluid at the end of the operation.
16   Check the operation of the brakes. The pedal should feel solid when depressed, with no sponginess. If necessary, repeat the entire process. **Warning:** *Do not operate the vehicle if you are in doubt about the effectiveness of the brake system.*

11 Brake light switch - check, replacement and adjustment

Check

Refer to illustrations 11.2 and 11.3
1   Remove the knee bolster (see Chapter 11).
2   Locate the brake light switch at the top of the brake pedal and unplug the electrical connector from the switch **(see illustration)**.
3   Pull the plunger all the way out to its fully extended position and attach the leads of an ohmmeter to terminals 5 and 6 **(see illustration)**.

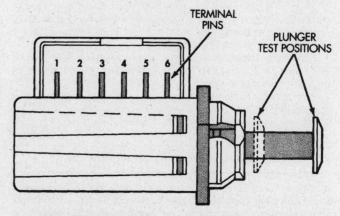

TERMINAL PINS

PLUNGER TEST POSITIONS

1 2 3 4 5 6

11.3 Brake light switch electrical connector terminal guide

Terminals 1 and 2 are for the RWAL/ABS module and PCM circuits
Terminals 3 and 4 are for the speed control circuit
Terminals 5 and 6 are for the brake light circuit

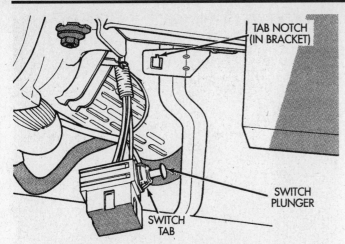

11.7 To release the brake light switch locking tab from its notch in the switch mounting bracket, rotate the switch counterclockwise 30-degrees and pull out the switch; to install the switch, align the tab on the switch with the notch at the top of the hole, insert the plunger through the hole, and rotate the switch 30-degrees clockwise

If there's continuity, proceed to the next step. If there isn't, replace the switch.

4   Push the plunger all the way into the switch to its fully retracted position and attach the ohmmeter test leads to terminals 1 and 2. If there's continuity, the switch is okay. If there isn't, replace the switch.

Replacement and adjustment

Refer to illustration 11.7

5   Remove the knee bolster (see Chapter 11).
6   Unplug the electrical connector and unbolt the switch and bracket assembly **(see illustration 11.2)**.
7   Press the brake pedal as far as it will go and hold it there, and rotate the brake light switch counterclockwise about 30-degrees to align the switch lock tab with its notch in the bracket **(see illustration)**.
8   Installation is the reverse of removal, except that the position of the switch plunger *must be preset* before the switch is installed (see next Step).
9   To preset the switch plunger, pull the plunger all the way out to its fully extended position, then push it in four detent positions (four clicks). The plunger should now extend about 0.55-inch out of the switch housing.
10   Plug in the switch electrical connector.
11   Press the brake pedal as far as it will go and hold it there, align the switch lock tab with its notch in the bracket **(see illustration 11.7)**, insert the lock tab through the notch and rotate the switch clockwise about 30-degrees to lock it into place.
12   Release the brake pedal, then lightly pull the pedal all the way to the rear. The pedal adjusts the switch plunger to its correct position as the pedal is moved to the rear.
13   Check the operation of the switch (see above) and verify that it works properly.
14   Install the knee bolster (see Chapter 11).

12   Brake hoses and lines - check and replacement

1   About every six months, with the vehicle raised and placed securely on jackstands, the flexible hoses which connect the steel brake lines with the front and rear brake assemblies should be inspected for cracks, chafing of the outer cover, leaks, blisters and other damage. These are important and vulnerable parts of the brake system and inspection should be complete. A light and mirror will be needed for a thorough check. If a hose exhibits any of the above defects, replace it with a new one.

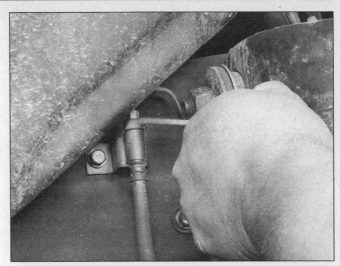

12.3 Disconnect the brake line from the hose fitting with a flare-nut wrench

Flexible hose replacement

Refer to illustration 12.3

2   Clean all dirt away from the ends of the hose.
3   Disconnect the brake line from the hose fitting **(see illustration)**. Be careful not to bend the frame bracket or line. If necessary, soak the connections with penetrating oil.
4   Disconnect the hose from the caliper, discarding the sealing washers on either side of the fitting.
5   Using new sealing washers, attach the new brake hose to the caliper, tightening the union bolt securely.
6   Pass the female fitting through the frame or frame bracket. With the least amount of twist in the hose, install the fitting in this position. **Note:** *The weight of the vehicle must be on the suspension, so the vehicle should not be raised while positioning the hose.*
7   Attach the brake line to the hose fitting and tighten the fitting securely.
8   Carefully check to make sure the suspension or steering components don't make contact with the hose. Have an assistant bounce the vehicle and also turn the steering wheel lock-to-lock during inspection.
9   Bleed the brake system (see Section 10).

Metal brake lines

10   When replacing brake lines, be sure to use the correct parts. Don't use copper tubing for any brake system components. Purchase prefabricated steel brake lines, with the tube ends already flared and fittings installed, from a dealer parts department or auto parts store. These lines are also sometimes bent to the proper shapes, but if you purchase straight steel tubing, be sure to use a bending tool to make kink-free bends.
11   When installing the new line make sure it's well supported in the brackets and has plenty of clearance between moving or hot components.
12   After installation, check the master cylinder fluid level and add fluid as necessary. Bleed the brake system (see Section 10) and test the brakes carefully before placing the vehicle into normal operation.

13   Power brake booster - check, removal and installation

1   The power brake booster unit requires no special maintenance apart from periodic inspection of the vacuum hose and the case.
2   Disassembly of the power unit requires special tools and is not ordinarily performed by the home mechanic. If a problem develops, it's recommended that a new or factory rebuilt unit be installed.

9

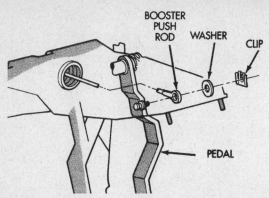

13.13 Attachment details of the power brake booster pushrod

13.14 Location of right-side power brake booster mounting nuts (arrows) left-side nuts not visible in this photo

Operating check

3   Depress the brake pedal several times with the engine off and make sure that there is no change in the pedal reserve distance.
4   Depress the pedal and start the engine. If the pedal goes down slightly, operation is normal.

Airtightness check

5   Start the engine and turn it off after one or two minutes. Depress the brake pedal several times slowly. If the pedal goes down farther the first time but gradually rises after the second or third depression, the booster is airtight.
6   Depress the brake pedal while the engine is running, then stop the engine with the pedal depressed. If there is no change in the pedal reserve travel after holding the pedal for 30 seconds, the booster is airtight.

Removal

Refer to illustrations 13.13 and 13.14
7   Unplug the electrical connectors from the RWAL valve and from the differential pressure switch on the combination valve.
8   Disconnect the brake line from the combination valve to the front brakes (or to the ABS valve).
9   Disconnect the brake line from the RWAL valve to the rear brakes.
10   Remove the master cylinder (see Section 7). It isn't necessary to detach the combination valve and RWAL valve from the master cylinder - remove the master cylinder and the two valves as a single assembly.
11   Disconnect the vacuum hose from the power brake booster.
12   Working inside the vehicle, remove the knee bolster (see Chapter 11).
13   Working under the dash, disconnect the power brake pushrod from the top of the brake pedal by prying off the clip **(see illustration)**.
14   Remove the nuts attaching the booster to the firewall **(see illustration)**.
15   Carefully lift the booster unit away from the firewall and out of the engine compartment.

Installation

16   To install the booster, place it into position and tighten the retaining nuts to the torque listed in this Chapter's Specifications.
17   Connect the booster pushrod to the brake pedal **(see illustration 13.13)**. **Warning:** *Make sure you use a new clip.*
18   Install the master cylinder (see Section 7) and the combination valve and RWAL valves (see Section 14).
19   Connect the brake lines to the master cylinder, combination valve and RWAL valve and tighten all fitting nuts securely.
20   Connect the vacuum hose to the brake booster assembly.
21   Bleed the brake system (see Section 10).
22   Carefully test the operation of the brakes before placing the vehicle in normal operation.

14   Combination valve - check and replacement

Check

Metering valve

Refer to illustration 14.1
1   To check the metering valve, have an assistant apply and release the brake pedal while you watch the valve stem (the small black button on the front of the combination valve) **(see illustration)**. If the valve is operating correctly, the stem will extend slightly when the brakes are applied and retract when the brakes are released. If the valve does not protrude slightly each time the brake pedal is applied, replace the combination valve.

Pressure differential switch

2   Raise the vehicle and place it securely on jackstands.
3   Connect a bleeder hose to a rear wheel cylinder and immerse the other end of the hose in a container partially filled with brake fluid **(see illustration 10.10)**. Loosen the bleeder screw slightly.
4   To check the pressure differential switch, have your helper sit inside the vehicle, apply the brake pedal, and watch the red brake warning light.
5   If the warning light comes on, the switch is operating correctly. Bleed the rear wheel cylinder to ensure no air was let into the system.
6   If the warning light doesn't come on, check the circuit fuse, the bulb and the wiring (see (Chapter 12). (One quick way to eliminate the fuse and bulb as the problem is to apply the parking brake; if the park-

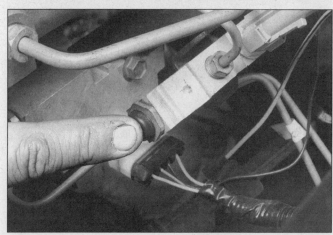

14.1 The metering valve stem (arrow) should protrude slightly when the brake pedal is applied

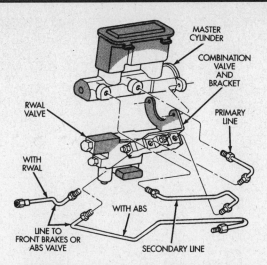

14.9 An exploded view of the hydraulic lines for the master cylinder, the combination valve and the RWAL valve

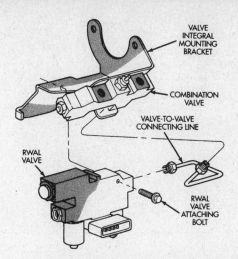

14.12 Mounting details for the combination valve and the RWAL valve

ing brake switch turns on the light, the fuse and bulb are okay). Repair the circuit or replace parts as necessary and retest the warning light switch. Don't forget to bleed the rear wheel cylinder to ensure no air was let into the system.

7   If, after making the necessary repairs and/or part replacements, the warning light still doesn't come on, the switch is faulty. Replace the combination valve.

Replacement

Refer to illustrations 14.9 and 14.12

8   Unplug the electrical connectors from the combination valve and RWAL valve **(see illustration 14.1)**.

9   Disconnect the brake lines from the combination and RWAL valves to the rear wheels, and the line connecting the master cylinder to the combination valve **(see illustration)**. Plug the ends of the lines to prevent loss of brake fluid and the entry of dirt.

10   Remove the master cylinder (see Section 7).

11   Remove the combination valve, valve bracket and RWAL valve as a single assembly.

12   Remove the brake line connecting the combination valve to the

RWAL valve **(see illustration)**.

13   Remove the bolt attaching the RWAL valve to the combination valve bracket, then separate the RWAL valve from the bracket.

14   Installation is the reverse of removal. Be sure to tighten all brake line fitting nuts securely.

15   Bleed the system (see Section 10) when you're done.

15   Power brake vacuum pump (diesel engine) - removal and installation

Refer to illustration 15.2, 15.3, 15.4, 15.5, 15.10 and 15.12

1   Disconnect the cable from the negative terminal of the battery.
Note: *If you're working on a 4WD model, it may be helpful to raise the vehicle, place it securely on jackstands, and work from below.*

2   Disconnect the vacuum hose from the vacuum pump **(see illustration)**.

3   Disconnect the oil feed line from the vacuum pump **(see illustration)**.

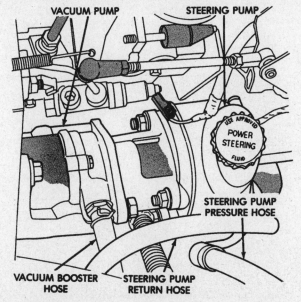

15.2 Detach the vacuum hose from the vacuum pump

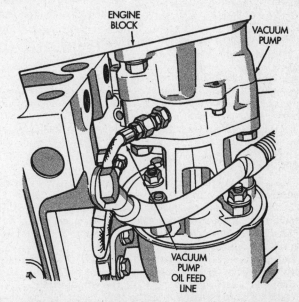

15.3 Disconnect the oil feed line from the vacuum pump

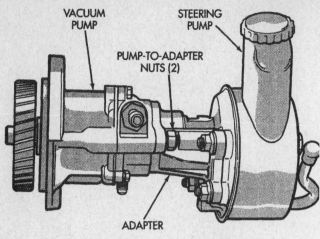

15.4 There are two pump-to-adapter nuts

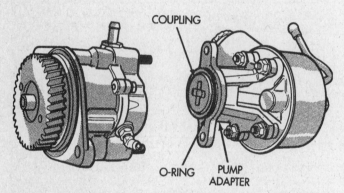

15.10 Inspect the adapter O-ring and, if it's worn or damaged, replace it (be sure to lubricate the new O-ring lightly with clean engine oil)

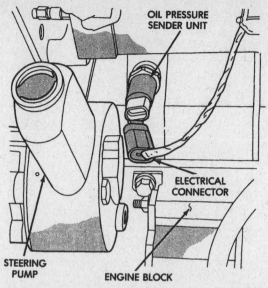

15.5 The oil pressure sender unit is mounted in the block right behind the power steering pump; at least unplug the connector and, if you want the extra room, remove the sender

15.12 These tangs on the vacuum pump must be aligned with the slots in the adapter coupling before tightening the pump-to-adapter nuts

4   Loosen the two nuts that attach the vacuum pump to the power steering pump adapter **(see illustration)**.

5   Unplug the electrical connector from the oil pressure sender unit, which is located right behind the power steering pump **(see illustration)**. It isn't absolutely necessary to remove the sender unit itself, but removing it will give you more room to work.

6   Remove the nut from the power steering pump-to-block bracket. It isn't necessary to disconnect the power steering hoses.

7   Unbolt the vacuum pump from the gear housing cover (two bolts).

8   Pull the vacuum pump and power steering pump to the rear to disengage the vacuum pump drive gear from the timing gears.

9   Remove the two nuts that attach the vacuum pump to the power steering pump adapter and remove the pump. If necessary, turn the pump gear back and forth to disengage the pump shaft from the coupling.

10   Inspect the pump adapter O-ring **(see illustration)**. If it's cut or torn, replace it.

11   Lubricate a new O-ring and install it on the pump adapter.

12   Note the position of the drive slots in the coupling. Rotate the drive gear to align the tangs on the vacuum pump with the slots in the coupling **(see illustration)**.

13   Make sure that the pump is properly seated into the adapter, then install the two pump-to-adapter washers and nuts and tighten them securely.

14   Installation is otherwise the reverse of removal. Be sure to tighten all fasteners securely.

16   Anti-Lock Brake System - general information

Rear Wheel Anti-lock (RWAL) brake system

1   The Rear Wheel Anti-Lock (RWAL) brake system is standard equipment on all models. It is designed to maintain vehicle maneuverability, directional stability and optimum deceleration under severe braking conditions on most road surfaces. RWAL does so by monitoring the rotational speed of the rear wheels and controlling the brake line pressure to the rear wheels while braking. This prevents the rear wheels from locking up prematurely during hard braking, regardless of the payload.

Components

Rear wheel speed sensor

Refer to illustration 16.2

2   A wheel speed sensor **(see illustration)**, mounted in the top of the rear differential housing, transmits speed and rate-of-deceleration

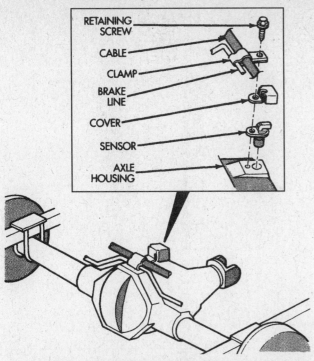

16.2 The RWAL speed sensor assembly is located on top of the rear differential

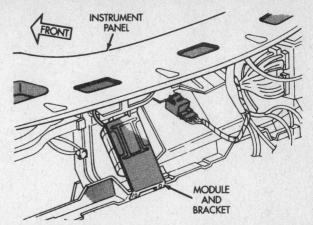

16.3 The RWAL electronic control module is mounted in the middle of the dash; you can get to it by removing the knee bolster under the steering column

inputs, in analog form (variable voltage signal), to the electronic control module. The sensor is actuated by an "exciter ring" pressed onto the differential case adjacent to the ring gear. The exciter ring is the "trigger mechanism;" as it rotates, the teeth on the ring interrupt the magnetic field around the sensor pole (the sensor is similar in construction and operation to a pick-up coil in an electronic distributor). The rate of interruption produces a variable voltage signal which is transmitted to the control module.

Electronic control module/Controller Anti-lock Brake (CAB)
Refer to illustration 16.3

3   The electronic control module (1994 and 1995 models) or Controller Anti-lock Brake (CAB) (1996 models) **(see illustration)** is mounted in the center of the dash (to access it, remove the knee bolster underneath the instrument panel; the module is just to the right of this area). The module inputs variable voltage signals from the rear wheel speed sensor, converts this analog signal into digital data, processes this data and controls the isolation and dump valves inside the RWAL valve, which modulates hydraulic line pressure to the rear wheel cylinders to avoid wheel lock-up. The module also has self-diagnostic capabilities which enable it to continuously monitor the system for malfunctions during vehicle operation.

RWAL valve

4   The RWAL valve **(see illustrations 14.9 and 14.12)** is located under the master cylinder. It contains a *dump valve* and an *isolation valve*. If the module senses that the rate of rear wheel speed deceleration exceeds the rate of vehicle deceleration, it energizes a solenoid which opens the isolation valve to prevent any further increase in driver-induced brake fluid pressure to the rear wheels. If this initial stage fails to prevent rear wheel lock-up, the module momentarily energizes a second solenoid which opens the dump valve to vent a small amount of "isolated" rear brake pressure to the accumulator. The movement of fluid to the accumulator reduces the isolated pressure at the wheel cylinders. This "dump cycle" (or pressure venting) is limited to very short time intervals (milliseconds). The module pulses the dump valve until rear wheel deceleration matches vehicle deceleration. The system switches back to normal operation as soon as the rear wheels are no longer locking up.

Warning light

5   If a problem develops within the system, the ABS warning light will glow on the dashboard. A diagnostic code will also be stored, which, when retrieved by a service technician, will indicate the problem area or component.

Diagnosis and repair
Refer to illustration 16.7

6   If the ABS warning light on the dashboard comes on and stays on, make sure the parking brake is not applied and there's no problem with the standard brake hydraulic system. If neither of these is the cause, the RWAL system is probably malfunctioning. Check the following:

a) *Make sure the brakes, calipers and wheel cylinders are in good condition.*
b) *Check the electrical connectors at the control module assembly.*
c) *Check the fuses.*
d) *Follow the wiring harness to the speed sensor and valve and make sure all connections are secure and the wiring isn't damaged.*

7   If the above preliminary checks don't identify the problem, you may wish to output any stored diagnostic trouble codes stored in the electronic control module. First, find the RWAL Service Diagnostic connector, which is clipped to the underside of the knee bolster **(see illustration)**.

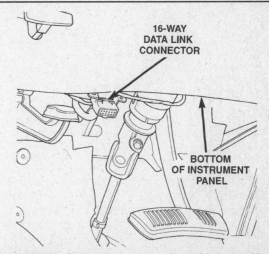

16.7 The RWAL diagnostic connector (arrow) is located behind the lower edge of the knee bolster - ground the black-wire terminal (no. 13) momentarily to output any stored codes

9

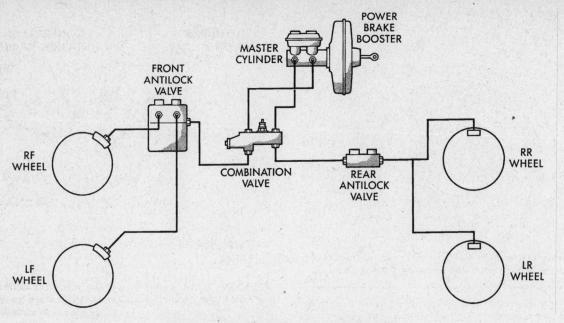

16.10 Hydraulic schematic for four-wheel ABS

8   Using a jumper wire, momentarily ground terminal 13 (the black wire terminal) of the diagnostic connector and watch the amber ABS warning light on the dashboard. Fault codes will be displayed (and the red BRAKE warning light will also go on) by a long flash, followed by a series of short flashes. Count the long and short flashes and compare to the following chart for diagnosis.

9   After the malfunction has been identified and repaired (most code-related problems will require dealership attention), the codes can be cleared from memory by disconnecting the battery for 30 seconds.

RWAL system fault codes

1	Not used
2	Open isolation valve wiring or bad control module
3	Open dump valve wiring or bad control module
4	Closed RWAL valve switch
5	Over 16 dump pulses generated in 2WD vehicles (disabled for 4WD)
6	Erratic speed sensor reading while rolling
7	Electronic control module fuse pellet open, isolation output missing, or valve wiring shorted to ground
8	Dump output missing or valve wiring shorted to ground
9	Speed sensor wiring/resistance (usually high reading)
10	Sensor wiring/resistance (usually low reading)
11	Brake switch always on, RWAL light comes on when speed exceeds 40 mph
12	Not used
13	Electronic control module phase lock loop failure
14	Electronic control module program check failure
15	Electronic control module RAM failure

Anti-Lock Brake System (ABS)

Description

Refer to illustration 16.10

10   The Anti-lock Brake System (ABS) prevents wheel lock-up under heavy braking conditions on virtually any road surface **(see illustration)**. Preventing the wheels from locking up maintains vehicle maneuverability, preserves directional stability, and allows optimal deceleration. How does ABS work? Basically, by monitoring the rotation speed of the wheels and controlling the brake line pressure to the calipers/wheel cylinders at each wheel during braking.

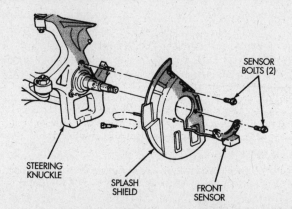

16.11a The front wheel speed sensors are attached to the brake backing plate

Components

Wheel speed sensors

Refer to illustrations 16.11a and 16.11b

11   A wheel speed sensor **(see illustration)** is mounted at each front wheel. A sensor ring, or "tone wheel," **(see illustration)** is pressed onto the backside of the disc. As the tone wheel turns, its teeth interrupt the magnetic field around the speed sensor (which is similar to a pick-up coil in an electronic distributor), producing a voltage signal that varies in proportional to the speed of rotation of each wheel. The analog outputs from the two front wheel speed sensors are transmitted to the ABS control module. A third wheel speed sensor, for the rear wheels, is located at the top of the differential housing. It's identical in function and operation to the rear wheel speed sensor previously described for RWAL systems.

ABS control module/Controller Anti-lock Brake (CAB)

Refer to illustration 16.12

12   The ABS control module (1994 and 1995 models) or Controller Anti-lock Brake (CAB) **(see illustration)**, which is located on the front of the ABS valve in the left rear corner of the engine compartment, monitors wheel speeds and controls the hydraulic control unit (front wheels) and the RWAL valve (rear wheels) to prevent wheel lockup.

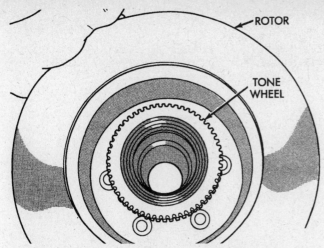

16.11b The tone wheels for the front wheel speed sensors are pressed onto the inner hub of the front brake discs

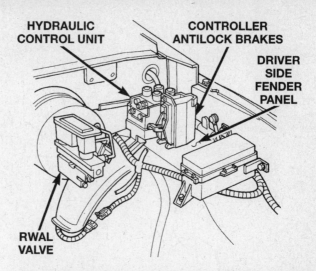

16.12 The Controller Anti-lock Brake (electronic control module) and the hydraulic control unit for the ABS system are mounted in the left rear corner of the engine compartment

The module receives three analog voltage signals (one from each front wheel speed sensor and one from the rear wheel speed sensor), converts these signals into digital data, processes this data and adjusts the solenoids inside the hydraulic control unit and the RWAL valve accordingly.

Hydraulic control unit

13   The Hydraulic Control Unit (HCU) **(see illustration 16.12)** is located in the engine compartment in the left rear corner of the engine compartment. The HCU contains the front anti-lock valve and the pump/motor assembly. The front anti-lock valve consists of a solenoid valve body with two-channel pressure control of the front brakes. One channel controls the left front brake unit; the other controls the right front. Each front brake unit is controlled independently. The solenoid-actuated valves are cycled on and off at a high rate of speed to prevent either wheel from slipping during rapid deceleration.

RWAL valve

14   The RWAL valve used with ABS is identical in function and operation to the rear RWAL valve previously described for RWAL systems.

Diagnosis and repair

15   The ABS system has self-diagnostic capabilities. Each time the ignition key is turned to On, the system runs a self-test. If it finds a problem, the ABS warning light comes on and remains on. If there's no problem with the system, the light goes out after a second or two.

16   If the ABS warning light comes on, and stays on during vehicle operation, there is a problem in the ABS system. Two things now happen: The controller stores a diagnostic trouble code (which can be displayed with a DRB II scanner at the dealer) and the ABS system is shut down. Once the ABS system is disabled, it will remain disabled until the problem is fixed and the trouble code is erased. However, the regular brake system will continue to function normally.

17   Although a DRB (a special electronic tester) is necessary to properly diagnose the system, you can make a few preliminary checks before taking the vehicle to a dealer:

a)   *Make sure the brake calipers are in good condition.*
b)   *Check the electrical connector at the controller.*
c)   *Check the fuses.*
d)   *Follow the wiring harness to the speed sensors and brake light switch and make sure all connections are secure and the wiring isn't damaged.*

18   If the above preliminary checks don't rectify the problem, the vehicle should be diagnosed by a dealer service department.

9

Notes

Chapter 10
Suspension and steering systems

Contents

Specifications

Torque Specifications

Ft-lbs (unless otherwise indicated)

Front Suspension

Independent front suspension (2WD models)

Balljoints	
Lower ballstud nut	55
Upper ballstud nut	55
Lower control arm bolts	
1994 and 1995	150
1996	
Wax-coat frame*	110
E-coat frame*	200
Shock absorbers	
Upper nut	30
Lower bolt	100
Stabilizer bar	
Link nut	25
Stabilizer bushing clamp bolts	
1994 and 1995	35
1996	
Wax-coat frame*	35
E-coat frame*	45
Upper control arm bolts	
1994 and 1995	180
1996	
Wax-coat frame*	150
E-coat frame*	200

4WD models

Balljoints	
Model 44 axle	
Upper ballstud nut	80
Lower ballstud nut	75
Model 60 axle	
Step 1	
Lower ballstud nut	35
Upper ballstud nut	70
Step 2 (lower ballstud nut)	140 to 160

10

Torque Specifications

Ft-lbs (unless otherwise indicated)

Front Suspension (continued)

4WD models (continued)
Shock absorber
Bracket	55
Lower bolt	100
Upper nut	30
Stabilizer bar	
Link lower nut	
1994	70
1995 and 1996	87
Link upper nut	27
Stabilizer bushing clamp bolts	
1994 and 1995	35
1996	
Wax-coat frame*	35
E-coat frame*	45
Track bar	
Ballstud nut	62
Track bar bolt	130
Upper suspension arms	
Arm-to-axle bracket nut	89
Arm-to-frame nut	
1994 and 1995	62
1996	
Wax-coat frame*	62
E-coat frame*	110
Lower suspension arms	
Arm-to-frame nut	
1994 and 1995	88
1996	
Wax-coat frame*	90
E-coat frame*	150
Arm-to-axle nut	
1994	170
1995 and 1996	110

Rear suspension
Shock absorber	
Lower nut	100
Upper nut	
1994 and 1995	70
1996	
Wax-coat frame*	70
E-coat frame*	110
Leaf springs	
U-bolt clamp nuts	
6,010 to 10,500 GVW	110
11,000 GVW cab-chassis	120
Front and rear eye nuts/bolts	
6,010 to 7,500 GVW	
1994 and 1995	100
1996	150
8,800 to 11,000 GVW	
1994 and 1995	140
1996	210

Steering
Airbag module retaining nuts	80 to 100 in-lbs
Drag link ballstud nuts (4WD)	65
Idler arm-to-frame bolts	
Regular bolts	80
Heavy-duty bolts	200
Power steering pump-to-adapter bracket nuts (diesel)	18
Steering wheel-to-steering shaft nut	45

Torque Specifications

	Ft-lbs (unless otherwise indicated)
Steering damper	
Damper-to-center link nut (2WD)	50
Damper-to-drag link nut (4WD)	50
Damper-to-frame nut	
1994 and 1995	50
1996	
Wax-coat frame*	50
E-coat frame*	65
Steering coupler	36
Steering gear mounting bolts	140
Pitman arm	
Pitman arm-to-steering gear nut	185
Pitman arm-to-center link nut	65
Tie rods	
Tie-rod ballstud nuts	65
Tie-rod adjuster clamp nuts	40
Wheel lug nuts	See Chapter 1

* *Refer to the 11th digit of the VIN number: If the 11th VIN digit is "J" (St. Louis), the frame uses an E-coat; if the 11th digit is an "S" (Dodge City), "G" (Saltillo, Mexico) or "M" (Lago Alberto, Mexico), the frame has a wax coat.*

1   General information

Front suspension

Refer to illustrations 1.1 and 1.2

2WD models **(see illustration)** are equipped with an independent front suspension system with upper and lower control arms, coil springs and shock absorbers. A stabilizer bar controls body roll. Each steering knuckle is positioned by a pair of balljoints in the ends of the upper and lower control arms.

4WD models **(see illustration)** utilize a solid front axle located by a pair of longitudinal suspension arms on either side. The front axle is suspended by a pair of coil springs and shock absorbers.

1.1   Front suspension and steering components (2WD models)

1 Stabilizer bar	4 Stabilizer bar link-to-	7 Steering gear	11 Inner tie rod
2 Stabilizer bar bushing	control arm nuts	8 Pitman arm	12 Tie-rod adjuster tube
clamps	5 Lower control arms	9 Center link	13 Tie-rod end
3 Stabilizer bar links	6 Coil springs	10 Idler arm	

10

1.2 Front suspension and steering components (4WD models)

1	Stabilizer bar	5	Pitman arm	9	Upper suspension arms
2	Stabilizer bar bushing clamps	6	Drag link	10	Lower suspension arms
3	Steering damper	7	Tie-rod	11	Tie-rod adjuster tube
4	Track bar	8	Coil springs	12	Drag-link adjuster tube

1.3 Rear suspension components (2WD model shown; 4WD models similar)

1	Leaf springs	3	Spring plates
2	Spring plate U-bolts	4	Shock absorbers

2.2 To disconnect the lower end of the track bar from the axle bracket, remove this bolt

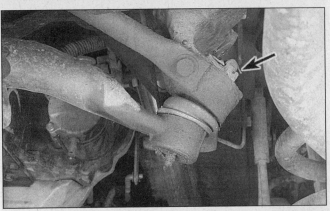

2.3 To disconnect the upper end of the track bar from the frame bracket, remove the cotter pin, loosen the nut, install a small two-jaw puller and press the ballstud out of the bracket (you can also use a picklefork, but it will damage the boot)

Rear suspension

Refer to illustration 1.3

The rear suspension **(see illustration)** consists of two shock absorbers and two leaf springs. Some models are also equipped with a stabilizer bar.

Steering

The steering column is designed to collapse in the event of an accident. A small U-joint connects the steering shaft to the steering gearbox. A power-assisted recirculating-ball type steering gearbox transmits turning force through the steering linkage to the steering knuckles. The steering linkage consists of a Pitman arm, an idler arm, a center link (2WD models) or drag link (4WD models) and a pair of tie rods. Each tie-rod assembly consists of an inner tie rod, an adjuster tube and an outer tie-rod. A steering damper between the frame and the center link or drag link reduces unwanted "bump steer" (the slight turning or steering of a wheel away from its normal direction of travel as it moves through its suspension travel).

Frequently, when working on the suspension or steering system components, you may come across fasteners which seem impossible to loosen. These fasteners on the underside of the vehicle are continually subjected to water, road grime, mud, etc., and can become rusted or "frozen," making them extremely difficult to remove. In order to unscrew these stubborn fasteners without damaging them (or other components), be sure to use lots of penetrating oil and allow it to soak in for a while. Using a wire brush to clean exposed threads will also ease removal of the nut or bolt and prevent damage to the threads. Sometimes a sharp blow with a hammer and punch is effective in breaking the bond between a nut and bolt threads, but care must be taken to prevent the punch from slipping off the fastener and ruining the threads. Heating the stuck fastener and surrounding area with a torch sometimes helps too, but isn't recommended because of the obvious dangers associated with fire. Long breaker bars and extension, or "cheater," pipes will increase leverage, but never use an extension pipe on a ratchet - the ratcheting mechanism could be damaged. Sometimes, turning the nut or bolt in the tightening (clockwise) direction first will help to break it loose. Fasteners that require drastic measures to unscrew should always be replaced with new ones.

Since most of the procedures that are dealt with in this Chapter involve jacking up the vehicle and working underneath it, a good pair of jackstands will be needed. A hydraulic floor jack is the preferred type of jack to lift the vehicle, and it can also be used to support certain components during various operations. **Warning:** *Never, under any circumstances, rely on a jack to support the vehicle while working on it.*

Whenever any of the suspension or steering fasteners are loosened or removed they must be inspected and, if necessary, be replaced with new ones of the same part number or of original equipment quality and design. Torque specifications must be followed for proper reassembly and component retention. Never attempt to heat or straighten any suspension or steering components. Instead, replace any bent or damaged part with a new one.

2   Track bar (4WD models) - removal and installation

Refer to illustrations 2.2 and 2.3

1   Apply the parking brake. Raise the front of the vehicle, if necessary, and support it securely on jackstands.

2   Disconnect the lower end of the track bar from the axle bracket **(see illustration)** on the right end of the axle.

3   To disconnect the upper end of the track bar **(see illustration)** from the frame bracket, loosen the nut, install a small two-jaw puller and separate the track bar ballstud from the bracket (a "picklefork" type balljoint separator will work too, but it will damage the boot).

4   Installation is the reverse of removal. Be sure to tighten both fasteners to the torque listed in this Chapter's Specifications.

3   Stabilizer bar and bushings (front) - removal and installation

2WD models

Refer to illustrations 3.2 and 3.3

1   Apply the parking brake. If necessary for working clearance, raise the front of the vehicle and support it securely on jackstands.

2   To disconnect the stabilizer bar links from the lower control arms, remove the lower link nut from the underside of each control arm **(see illustration)**.

10

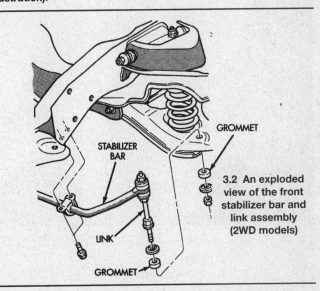

3.2 An exploded view of the front stabilizer bar and link assembly (2WD models)

3.3 To detach the stabilizer bar from the frame, remove the bolts from the two bushing clamps

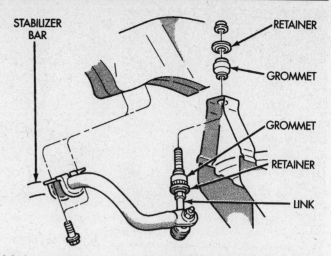

3.8 An exploded view of the front stabilizer bar and link assembly (4WD models)

3   Unbolt the stabilizer bushing clamps **(see illustration)** from the frame.
4   Remove the stabilizer bar and link assembly from the vehicle.
5   Pull the bushings off the stabilizer bar and inspect them for cracks, hardness and other signs of deterioration. Inspect the bushings in the lower ends of the links. Replace all damaged bushings.
6   Installation is the reverse of removal. Do not torque any fasteners until the vehicle has been lowered to the ground. After lowering the vehicle, tighten all fasteners to the torque listed in this Chapter's Specifications.

4WD models

Refer to illustration 3.8
7   Apply the parking brake. If necessary for working clearance, raise the front of the vehicle and support it securely on jackstands.
8   Disconnect the stabilizer bar links from the axle brackets **(see illustration)**.
9   Remove the nuts and retainers from the frame support brackets **(see illustration 3.3)**.
10   Remove the stabilizer bar and link assembly from the vehicle.
11   Pull the bushings off the stabilizer bar and inspect them for cracks, hardness and other signs of deterioration. Inspect the bushings in the lower ends of the links. Replace all damaged bushings.

12   Installation is the reverse of removal. Do not torque any fasteners until the vehicle has been lowered to the ground. After lowering the vehicle, tighten all fasteners to the torque listed in this Chapter's Specifications.

4   Shock absorber (front) - removal and installation

Refer to illustrations 4.2a, 4.2b, 4.2c, 4.3a and 4.3b
1   Loosen the wheel lug nuts, raise the vehicle and support it securely on jackstands placed under the frame rails. Apply the parking brake. Remove the wheel. Support the lower control arm with a floor jack.
2   Remove the upper shock absorber stem nut **(see illustrations)**. Use an open end wrench to keep the stem from turning. If the nut won't loosen because of rust, squirt some penetrating oil on the stem threads and allow it to soak in for a while. It may be necessary to keep the stem from turning with a pair of locking pliers, since the flats provided for a wrench are quite small. Remove the retainer and grommet and, on 4WD models, the upper mounting bracket (it's secured by three nuts) **(see illustration)**.
3   Remove the lower mounting bolt and nut **(see illustrations)**. On 2WD models, pull the shock absorber out from the wheel well. On 4WD

4.2a Shock absorber stem nut (arrow) (2WD models)

4.2b Shock absorber stem nut (arrow) (4WD models)

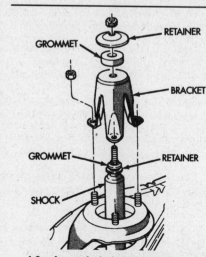

4.2c An exploded view of the shock absorber upper mounting bracket (4WD models)

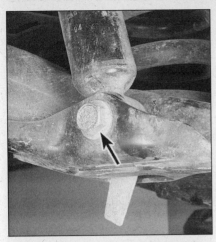

4.3a Remove the bolt (arrow) from the lower control arm (2WD models)

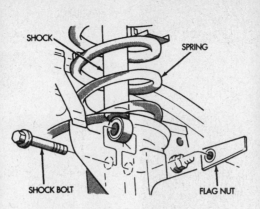

4.3b Shock absorber lower mounting details (4WD models)

SHOCK   SPRING

SHOCK BOLT   FLAG NUT

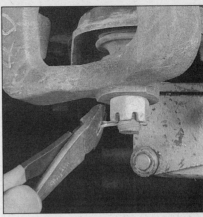

5.8a To separate the lower control arm from the steering knuckle, support the lower control arm with a jack, remove this cotter pin and back off - but don't remove - the ballstud nut . . .

models, pull the shock absorber up and out from the engine compartment. Remove the rubber grommets and washer from the top of the shock absorber.

4   Extend the new shock absorber as far as possible. Position a new washer and rubber grommet on the stem. On 2WD models, guide the shock up into the upper mount. On 4WD models, lower the shock into position from the engine compartment and install the upper mounting bracket.

5   Install the upper rubber grommet and washer and wiggle the stem back-and-forth to ensure the grommets are centered in the mount. Tighten the stem nut to the torque listed in this Chapter's Specifications.

6   Install the lower mounting bolt and nut and tighten but don't torque them yet.

7   Install the wheel and lug nuts. Lower the vehicle and tighten the lug nuts to the torque listed in the Chapter 1 Specification's. Tighten the shock absorber lower mounting bolts to the torque listed in this Chapter's Specifications.

5   Coil spring - removal and installation

2WD models

Refer to illustrations 5.8a and 5.8b

1   Loosen the front wheel lug nuts, raise the front of the vehicle and support it securely on jackstands placed under the frame rails.

2   Remove the wheels.

3   Disconnect the outer tie rod from the steering knuckle (see Section 14).

4   Disconnect the stabilizer bar link from the lower control arm (see Section 3).

5   Support the outer end of the lower control arm with a floor jack.

6   Loop a length of chain through the coil spring and bolt the ends together to prevent the spring from flying out if it slips. Make sure there is enough slack in the chain to allow the spring to fully extend.

7   Disconnect the lower end of the shock absorber from the lower arm (see Section 4).

8   Carefully separate the lower control arm balljoint from the steering knuckle **(see illustrations)**. Slowly lower the jack and allow spring pressure to release.

9   Remove the coil spring.

10   Check the spring for deep nicks and corrosion, which could cause premature failure. Replace the spring if these or any other questionable conditions are evident.

11   Installation is the reverse of removal. Make sure the upper insulator is in place on the spring, and be sure to tighten all suspension and steering fasteners to the torque listed in this Chapter's Specifications.

5.8b . . . then install a two-jaw puller and pop the ballstud loose from the knuckle

4WD models

12   Loosen the front wheel lug nuts, raise the front of the vehicle and support it securely on jackstands placed under the frame rails. Remove the wheels.

13   Support the end of the axle from which you're removing the spring with a floor jack.

14   Attach a coil spring compressor loosely to the coil spring to make sure it won't slip, fall off or fly out. If you don't have a spring compressor, at least chain the spring to the upper spring mount.

15   Remove the upper suspension arm and loosen the lower suspension arm nuts and pivot bolts (see Section 7). **Caution:** *Make sure you paint or scribe alignment marks on the lower arm cam, eccentric bolt and bracket before loosening the nut* **(see illustration 7.2).**

16   Mark and disconnect the front driveshaft from the front axle (see Chapter 8).

17   Disconnect the track bar from the frame rail bracket (see Section 2).

18   Disconnect the drag link from the Pitman arm (see Section 14).

19   Disconnect the stabilizer bar link from the axle (see Section 3).

20   Disconnect the shock absorber from the axle (see Section 4).

21   Lower the axle until the coil spring is free and remove the spring.

22   Installation is the reverse of removal. Make sure the marks you made on the lower suspension arm eccentric pivot bolt, cam and bracket match up. Be sure to tighten all fasteners to the torque listed in this Chapter's Specifications after the vehicle has been lowered to the ground.

10

6.3a To separate the upper arm from the steering knuckle, remove this cotter pin and loosen the castle nut . . .

6.3b . . . then use a small puller or a picklefork tool to separate the arm from the knuckle

6 Upper control arm (2WD models) - removal and installation

Refer to illustrations 6.3a, 6.3b and 6.4

1   Loosen the front wheel lug nuts. Raise the front of the vehicle and support it securely on jackstands placed under the frame rails. Remove the wheel.
2   Place a floor jack underneath the outer end of the lower control arm and raise the jack head until it touches the arm and moves it up slightly. the jack must remain in this position throughout the entire procedure.
3   Detach the upper control arm balljoint from the steering knuckle **(see illustrations)**.
4   Mark the relationship of the upper control arm pivot bar to the frame. Remove the nuts securing the pivot bar to the frame **(see illustration)** and remove the control arm.
5   Check the control arm for distortion and cracks. If the arm is damaged, replace it.
6   Inspect the bushings in the upper control arm for cracking, hardness and general deterioration. If the bushings are worn or damaged, take the arm to a dealer service department or an automotive machine shop to have them replaced.
7   Installation is the reverse of removal. Align the marks on the pivot

bar and the frame, then tighten the pivot bar nuts and the balljoint nut to the torque listed in this Chapter's Specifications.

7 Suspension arms (4WD models) - removal and installation

Refer to illustration 7.2, 7.3a, 7.3b and 7.4

1   Loosen the front wheel lug nuts. Raise the front of the vehicle and support it securely on jackstands. Remove the wheel.
2   If you're removing a lower suspension arm, paint or scribe alignment marks on the cam adjusters **(see illustration)** to ensure that the arm is installed correctly.

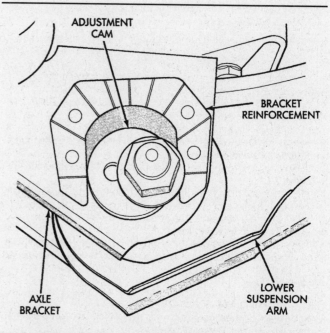

7.2 On 4WD models, the lower suspension arms are connected to the front axle with eccentric bolts and adjustment cams; the relationship of the lower arms to the axle is critical because it sets the caster angle, so be sure to mark the position of the bolt and cam in relation to the axle bracket to ensure that correct caster is maintained

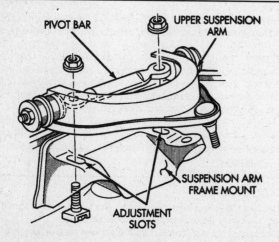

6.4 To detach the upper control arm from the frame bracket, remove the nuts securing the pivot bar to the frame

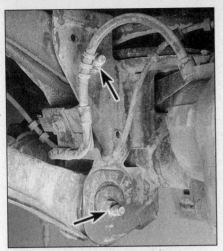

7.3 To detach a front suspension arm from the front axle, remove the nuts and knock out the bolts with a punch

7.4 To detach a front suspension arm from the frame bracket, remove one of these nuts (arrows) and knock out the pivot bolt (4WD models)

8.2 To detach the brake backing plate from the steering knuckle, remove these three bolts (arrows) (2WD model shown, 4WD similar)

3   Remove the lower suspension arm nut, cams and cam bolt from the axle (see illustrations).
4   Remove the suspension arm nut and pivot bolt from the frame bracket (see illustration).
5   Installation is the reverse of removal. Be sure to tighten all suspension fasteners to the torque listed in this Chapter's Specifications after the vehicle is on the ground.

8   Steering knuckle - removal and installation

2WD models

Refer to illustration 8.2
1   Loosen the wheel lug nuts, raise the vehicle and support it securely on jackstands. Remove the wheel.
2   Remove the disc brake caliper and disc (see Chapter 9). Disconnect the electrical connector from the ABS sensor and remove the sensor. Remove the brake backing plate (see illustration).
3   Disconnect the tie-rod from the steering knuckle (see Section 14).
4   Support the lower control arm with a floor jack. The jack must remain in this position throughout the entire procedure.
5   Separate the lower control arm from the steering knuckle (see illustrations 5.8a and 5.8b).
6   Separate the upper control arm from the steering knuckle (see Section 6).
7   Carefully inspect the steering knuckle for cracks, especially around the steering arm and spindle mounting area. Also inspect the balljoint stud holes. If they're elongated, or if you find any cracks in the knuckle, replace the steering knuckle.
8   Installation is the reverse of removal. Be sure to tighten all suspension fasteners to the torque listed in this Chapter's Specifications.

4WD models

Refer to illustration 8.14
9   Loosen the wheel lug nuts, raise the vehicle and support it securely on jackstands. Remove the wheel.
10   Remove the disc brake caliper and disc (see Chapter 9).
11   Remove the hub bearing and axle shaft (see Chapter 8).
12   Disconnect the tie rod or drag link from the steering knuckle (see Section 14).
13   Remove the ABS sensor wire and bracket from the steering knuckle.

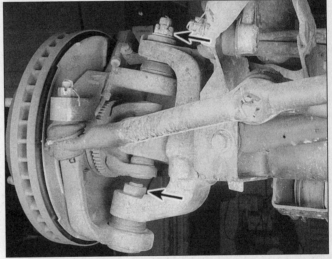

8.14 Location of the steering knuckle ballstud nuts (arrows) on a 4WD model

14   Remove the cotter pin from the steering knuckle upper ballstud nut and loosen both the upper and lower ballstud nuts (see illustration).
15   Separate the steering knuckle from the axle housing yoke. Use a brass hammer to knock it loose if necessary.
16   Installation is the reverse of removal. Be sure to tighten all suspension fasteners to the torque listed in this Chapter's Specifications after the vehicle has been lowered to the ground.

9   Lower control arm (2WD models) - removal and installation

Refer to illustration 9.5
1   Loosen the wheel lugs nuts. Raise the front of the vehicle and support it securely on jackstands. Remove the wheel.
2   Disconnect the stabilizer bar from the lower control arm (see Section 3).
3   Place a floor jack underneath the outer end of the lower control arm and raise the jack head until it touches the arm.

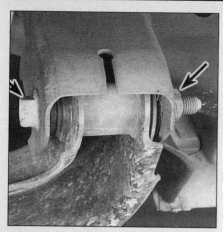

9.5 To detach the lower control arm from the frame, remove the nuts and pivot bolts (arrows) (rear shown, front similar)

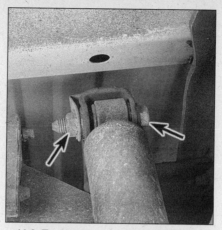

11.2 To detach a rear shock absorber from the frame, remove this nut and bolt (arrows)

11.3 To detach a rear shock from the axle, remove this nut and bolt

4   Remove the coil spring (see Section 5).

5   Remove the lower control arm nuts and pivot bolts **(see illustration)** and detach the control arm from the crossmember.

6   Inspect the bushings in the control arm for cracking, hardness and general deterioration. If the bushings are worn or damaged, take the control arm to a dealer service department or an automotive machine shop to have them replaced.

7   Installation is the reverse of removal. Be sure to tighten all suspension fasteners to the torque listed in this Chapter's Specifications after the vehicle is on the ground.

10   Balljoints - check and replacement

Check

1   Loosen the wheel lug nuts, raise the front of the vehicle and support it securely on jackstands. Remove the wheel.

Upper balljoint

2   On 2WD models, place a floor jack under the lower control arm and raise it slightly. Using a large screwdriver or prybar, pry up on the upper control arm and watch for movement at the balljoint. Any movement indicates a worn balljoint. Now grasp the steering knuckle and attempt to move the top of it in-and-out; if any play is felt, the balljoint will have to be replaced.

Lower balljoint

3   On 2WD models, place a floor jack under the lower control arm and raise it slightly.

4   Grasp the tire and attempt to move the bottom of it in-and-out; if any play is felt, the balljoint will have to be replaced. **Note:** *This check assumes that the wheel bearings are properly adjusted.*

Replacement

2WD models

5   Loosen the wheel lug nuts, raise the front of the vehicle and support it securely on jackstands. Remove the wheel.

6   If you're replacing a lower balljoint, remove the lower control arm (see Section 9).

7   If you're replacing an upper balljoint, remove the upper control arm (see Section 6).

8   Take the control arm to a dealer service department or to an automotive machine shop and have the old balljoint pressed out and a new one pressed in.

9   Installation is the reverse of removal. Be sure to tighten all fasteners to the torque listed in this Chapter's Specifications after the vehicle has been lowered to the ground.

10   The front end alignment should be checked, and if necessary, adjusted, by an alignment shop.

4WD models

11   Loosen the wheel lug nuts, raise the front of the vehicle and support it securely on jackstands. Remove the wheel.

12   Remove the steering knuckle (see Section 8).

13   Take the steering knuckle to a dealer service department or to an automotive machine shop and have the old balljoint pressed out and a new one pressed in.

14   Installation is the reverse of removal. Be sure to tighten all fasteners to the torque listed in this Chapter's Specifications.

15   The front end alignment should be checked, and if necessary, adjusted, by an alignment shop.

11   Shock absorber (rear) - removal and installation

Refer to illustrations 11.2 and 11.3
Note: *When replacing shock absorbers, remove and install only one shock absorber at a time.*

1   Loosen the wheel lug nuts, raise the rear of the vehicle and support it securely on jackstands placed under the frame rails. Remove the wheels and support the rear axle with a floor jack placed under the axle tube on the side being worked on. Don't raise the axle - just support its weight.

2   Remove the nut and bolt that attach the upper end of the shock absorber to the crossmember **(see illustration)**. If the nut won't loosen because of rust, apply some penetrating oil and allow it to soak in for awhile.

3   Remove the nut and bolt that attach the lower end of the shock to the axle bracket **(see illustration)**. Again, if the nut is frozen, apply some penetrating oil, wait awhile and try again.

4   Extend the new shock absorber as far as possible. Install new rubber grommets into the shock absorber eyes (if they are not already present).

5   Installation is the reverse of removal. Be sure to tighten the shock absorber mounting fasteners to the torque listed in this Chapter's Specifications after the vehicle is on the ground.

12   Leaf springs and bushings (rear) - removal and installation

Removal

Refer to illustrations 12.2a, 12.2b, 12.3 and 12.4

1   Loosen the wheel lug nuts, raise the rear of the vehicle and sup-

port it securely on jackstands placed under the frame rails. Remove the wheel and support the rear axle with a floor jack placed under the axle tube. Don't raise the axle - just support its weight.

2   Remove the nuts, U-bolts, spring plate, and spring seat that clamp the leaf spring to the axle **(see illustrations)**.

3   Remove the leaf spring shackle bolts and the shackle **(see illustration)**.

4   Unscrew the front bolt **(see illustration)** remove the leaf spring from the vehicle.

Installation

5   To install the leaf spring, position the spring on the axle tube so that the spring center bolt enters the locating hole on the axle tube.

6   Line up the spring front eye with the mounting bracket and install the front bolt and nut.

7   Install the rear shackle assembly.

8   Tighten the shackle bolt and the front bolt until all slack is taken up.

9   Install the U-bolts and nuts. Tighten the nuts until they force the spring plate against the axle, but don't torque them yet.

10   Be sure the auxiliary spring, if equipped, aligns with the main spring.

11   Install the wheel and lug nuts. Tighten the lug nuts to the torque listed in the Chapter 1 Specifications. Remove the jackstands and lower the vehicle.

12   Tighten the U-bolts, pivot bolts and shackle bolts to the torque listed in this Chapter's Specifications.

Bushing replacement

Note: *The leaf spring bushing (one piece eye) can be replaced with the spring installed in the vehicle. Use caution working around the vehicle suspension and make sure the frame is supported securely with heavy duty jackstands.*

13   Loosen the wheel lug nuts, raise the rear of the vehicle and support it securely on jackstands placed under the frame rails. Remove the wheel and support the rear axle with a floor jack placed under the axle tube. Don't raise the axle - just support its weight.

14   Remove the bolt and nut on the defective leaf spring bushing and remove the spring from the frame rail bracket or spring shackle.

15   Use a bushing press to force the bushing from the leaf spring eye. Install a new bushing.

16   Insert the end of the spring into the frame rail bracket or spring shackle.

17   Install the bolt and retaining nut. Do not torque the nut until the full weight of the vehicle is supported by the springs.

18   Remove the jackstands and tighten the nut to the torque listed in this Chapter's Specifications.

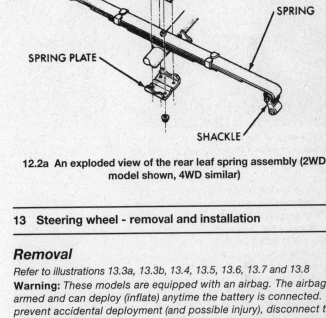

12.2a An exploded view of the rear leaf spring assembly (2WD model shown, 4WD similar)

13   Steering wheel - removal and installation

Removal

Refer to illustrations 13.3a, 13.3b, 13.4, 13.5, 13.6, 13.7 and 13.8

Warning: *These models are equipped with an airbag. The airbag is armed and can deploy (inflate) anytime the battery is connected. To prevent accidental deployment (and possible injury), disconnect the negative battery cable whenever working near airbag components. After the battery is disconnected, wait at least 2 minutes before beginning work (the system has a back-up capacitor that must fully discharge). For more information see Chapter 12.*

1   Park the vehicle with the front wheels in the straight-ahead position. **Warning:** *Do NOT turn the steering shaft before, during or after steering wheel removal. If the shaft is turned while the steering wheel is removed, a mechanism known as the clockspring can be damaged. The clockspring, which maintains a continuous electrical circuit between the wiring harness and the airbag module, consists of a flat, ribbon-like electrically conductive tape which winds and unwinds as the steering wheel is turned.*

2   Disconnect the cable from the negative terminal of the battery. Wait at least two minutes for the airbag capacitor to discharge before proceeding (see Warning above).

10

12.2b To remove the spring plate and U-bolts, remove these four nuts

12.3 To detach the rear end of the leaf spring from the shackle plates, remove the upper nut and bolt; to detach the shackle plates from the frame bracket, remove the lower nut and bolt

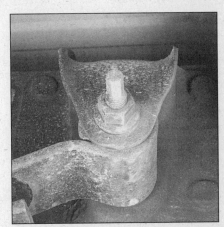

12.4 To detach the front end of the leaf spring from the forward bracket, remove this nut and bolt

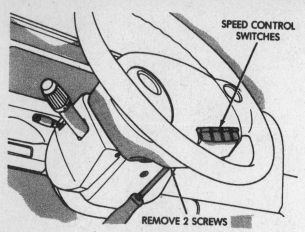

13.3a To detach the speed control switches, remove two screws from the backside of the steering wheel

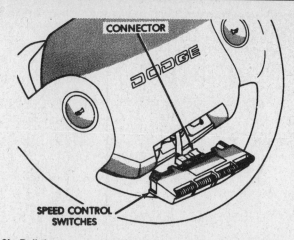

13.3b Pull the speed control switches out from the steering wheel and unplug the electrical connector

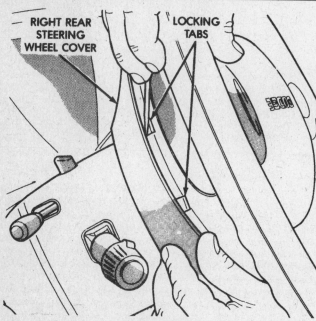

13.4 Pry off the right rear steering cover with a screwdriver, if equipped

3   If the vehicle is equipped with speed control, remove the speed control switch retaining screws (see illustration). Pull off the switches and unplug the electrical connector (see illustration).

4   If equipped, remove the right rear steering wheel cover using a small screwdriver (see illustration).

5   Remove the four nuts attaching the airbag module (see illustration). It will probably be necessary to turn the steering wheel to gain access to the nuts; just be sure to center the wheel after the nuts have been removed.

6   Lift off the airbag module and unplug the electrical connector (see illustration). When you set the airbag module down, make sure the airbag side is facing UP, so that if it accidentally deploys, it won't launch itself.

7   Remove the steering wheel retaining nut and mark the position of the steering wheel to the shaft (see illustration), if marks don't already exist or don't line up.

8   Use a puller to detach the steering wheel from the shaft (see illustration). Don't hammer on the shaft to dislodge the wheel.

Centering the clockspring

Refer to illustration 13.10

Note: If the front wheels are still pointed straight ahead and the steering shaft was not rotated while the steering wheel was removed, you can skip this Section and proceed to Step 13.

9   Place the front wheels in the straight-ahead position.

10   Depress the two plastic auto-locking tabs on the clockspring (see illustration) to disengage the locking mechanism.

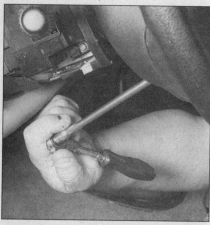

13.5 Remove the four airbag module retaining nuts

13.6 Unplug the electrical connector from the airbag module

13.7 After removing the nut, mark the relationship of the wheel to the shaft

13.8 Remove the steering wheel with a steering wheel puller

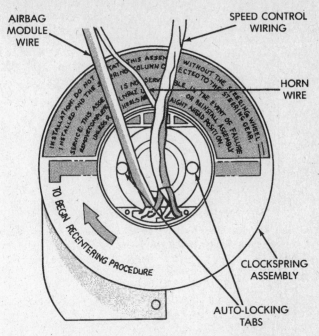

13.10 Details of the airbag system clockspring

11   While keeping the clockspring locking mechanism disengaged, rotate the clockspring rotor clockwise to the end of its travel. DO NOT apply excessive torque.

12   From the end of travel, turn the rotor two and one-half turns counterclockwise. The horn wire should end up at the top, and the airbag wire at the bottom.

Installation

13   Pull the speed control and airbag wires through the lower hole in the steering wheel. Pull the horn wire through the smaller hole at the top **(see illustration 13.7)**. Make sure the wires aren't pinched or tangled.

14   Align the mark on the steering wheel hub with the mark on the shaft and slide the wheel onto the shaft. Install the nut and tighten it to the torque listed in this Chapter's Specifications.

15   Plug in the electrical connectors to the horn buttons, speed control switch and airbag module. Make sure that the connector to the airbag module is latched securely beneath the module locking clip.

16   Install the airbag module, install the four nuts and tighten them to the torque listed in this Chapter's Specifications.

17   Connect the cable to the negative terminal of the battery.

18   To verify that the airbag system is working properly, turn the ignition key on and see if the airbag warning light comes on, then goes off. If the warning light stays on, take the vehicle to a dealer and have them diagnose the airbag system.

14   Steering linkage - inspection, removal and installation

Inspection

Refer to illustrations 14.1a and 14.1b

1   The steering linkage connects the steering gear to the front wheels and keeps the wheels in proper relation to each other. The linkage on 2WD models **(see illustration)** consists of a Pitman arm fastened to the steering gear shaft, which moves a center link back and forth. The back-and-forth motion of the center link is transmitted to the steering knuckles through a pair of tie rods. Each tie-rod assembly consists of a pair of inner and outer tie rods connected by a threaded adjuster tube. An idler arm, connected between the center link and the frame reduces shimmy and unwanted forces to the steering gear. The linkage on 4WD models **(see illustration)** consists of a Pitman arm, a drag link (the outer end of which doubles as the right tie rod), and a long tie-rod connecting the drag link to the left steering knuckle. A steering damper between the drag link and the frame dampens

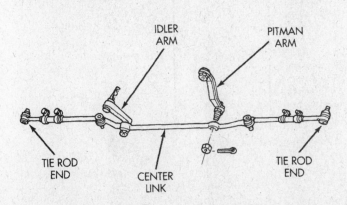

14.1a Steering linkage on 2WD models

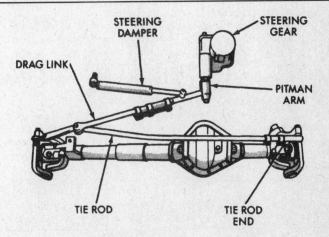

14.1b Steering linkage on 4WD models

10

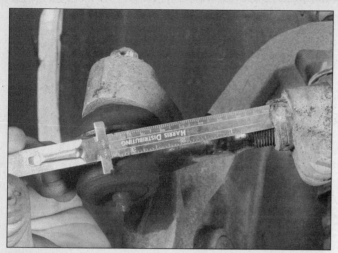

14.7 Before removing a tie-rod end, make sure you either count the number of exposed threads or measure the distance from the adjuster tube to the center line of the ballstud

14.8 Detach the tie-rod end from the steering knuckle with a small puller (this type of puller is useful for separating any of the balljoints used in the steering linkage)

unwanted oscillations in the steering linkage. Wheel toe adjustments are made at an adjuster tube on the tie-rod.

2   Set the wheels in the straight ahead position and lock the steering wheel.

3   Raise one side of the vehicle until the tire is approximately one inch off the ground.

4   Mount a dial indicator with the needle resting on the outside edge of the wheel. Grasp the front and rear of the tire and, using light pressure, wiggle the wheel back-and-forth and note the dial indicator reading. The gauge reading should be less than 0.108-inch. If the play in the steering system is more than specified, inspect each steering linkage pivot point and ballstud for looseness and replace parts if necessary.

5   Raise the vehicle and support it on jackstands. Check for torn ballstud boots, frozen joints and bent or damaged linkage components.

Removal and installation

6   Loosen the wheel lug nuts, raise the vehicle and support it securely on jackstands. Apply the parking brake. Remove the wheel.

Tie-rod end

Refer to illustrations 14.7 and 14.8

7   Count the number of threads showing and jot down this number to maintain correct toe-in during reassembly, or measure the distance between the adjuster tube and the center line of the ballstud **(see illustration)**. Loosen the adjuster tube clamp bolts.

8   Remove the cotter pin and loosen, but do not remove, the castle nut from the ballstud. Using a two-jaw puller, separate the tie-rod end from the steering knuckle **(see illustration)**. Remove the castle nut, and pull the tie-rod from the knuckle and unscrew it from the adjuster tube. **Caution:** *The use of a picklefork-type balljoint separator most likely will cause damage to the balljoint boot.*

9   Lubricate the threaded portion of the tie-rod end with chassis grease. Screw the new tie-rod end into the adjuster tube and adjust the distance from the tube to the ballstud by threading the tie-rod into the adjuster tube until the same number of threads are showing as before (the number of threads showing on both sides of the adjuster tube should be within three threads of each other). Or use the measurement you made before removing the tie-rod end. Don't tighten the adjuster tube clamps yet.

10   Insert the tie-rod ballstud into the steering knuckle. Make sure the ballstud is fully seated. Install the nut and tighten it to the torque listed in this Chapter's Specifications. If a ballstud spins when attempting to tighten the nut, force it into the tapered hole with a large pair of pliers.

11   Install a new cotter pin. If necessary, tighten the nut slightly to

align a slot in the nut with the hole in the ballstud.

12   Tighten the adjuster tube clamp nut to the torque listed in this Chapter's Specifications. The adjuster tube clamp bolt should be horizontal.

13   The above procedure depicts the tie-rod end of a 2WD tie-rod assembly, but it also applies to the tie-rod end on 4WD models.

14   Install the wheel and lug nuts, lower the vehicle and tighten the lug nuts to the torque listed in the Chapter 1 Specifications. Drive the vehicle to an alignment shop to have the front end alignment checked and, if necessary, adjusted.

Center link/drag link

15   Raise the front of the vehicle and support it securely on jackstands. Apply the parking brake.

16   Loosen, but do not remove, the nuts securing the center link (2WD models) or drag link (4WD models) ballstuds to the tie-rod assemblies, the idler arm (2WD), the steering damper (4WD) and the Pitman arm. Separate the ballstuds with a two-jaw puller, then remove the nuts.

17   If the tie-rod end on the drag link (4WD models) is in need of replacement, refer to Steps 7 through 12.

18   Installation is the reverse of the removal procedure. If the ballstuds spin when attempting to tighten the nuts, force them into the tapered holes with a large pair of pliers. Be sure to tighten all fasteners to the torque listed in this Chapter's Specifications.

Pitman arm

Refer to illustrations 14.19a and 14.19b

19   Loosen the Pitman arm nut **(see illustration)**. Mark the relationship of the Pitman arm to the shaft. Using a Pitman arm puller, separate the Pitman arm from the steering gear shaft **(see illustration)**. To separate the other end of the Pitman arm from the center link or drag link, use a small two-jaw puller.

20   Installation is the reverse of removal. Be sure to tighten the fasteners at both ends of the Pitman arm to the torque listed in this Chapter's Specifications.

Idler arm (2WD models)

Refer to illustration 14.22

21   Remove the cotter pin and loosen the idler arm ballstud nut. Unbolt the idler arm from the frame **(see illustration)**.

22   Separate the idler arm from the center link with a small two-jaw puller.

23   Installation is the reverse of removal. Be sure to tighten the fasteners to the torque listed in this Chapter's Specifications.

14.19a Remove the Pitman arm nut and mark the relationship of the arm to the shaft . . .

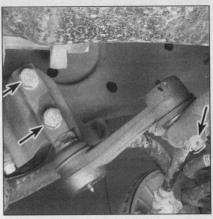

14.19b . . . then remove the Pitman arm with a puller

14.22 To replace the idler arm on 2WD models, remove the two mounting bolts and loosen the ballstud nut (arrows), then use a small puller to separate the idler arm ballstud from the center link

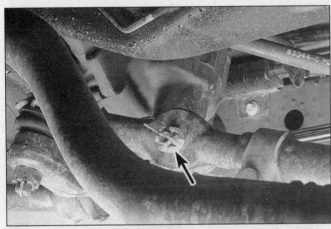

14.24 To replace the steering damper, remove this cotter pin (arrow), loosen the castle nut and use a small puller to separate the damper shaft ballstud from the drag link . . .

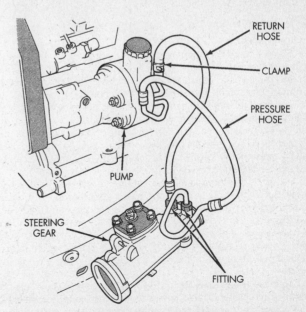

14.25 . . . then remove this bolt and nut from the frame bracket (4WD model shown, 2WD models similar)

Steering damper (4WD models and some 2WD models)

Refer to illustrations 14.24 and 14.25

24   To detach the steering damper from the center link (2WD) or drag link (4WD), remove the cotter pin **(see illustration)**, loosen the nut and use a small two-jaw puller to separate the damper shaft from the drag link.

25   To detach the damper from the frame bracket, remove the nut and bolt **(see illustration)**.

26   Installation is the reverse of removal. Be sure to tighten both fasteners to the torque listed in this Chapter's Specifications.

15 Steering gear - removal and installation

Caution: *Do not allow the steering wheel to rotate with the steering gear removed or damage to the airbag clockspring may occur.*

Refer to illustrations 15.2 and 15.3

1   Disconnect the cable from the negative battery terminal. Place the front wheels in a straight-ahead position. Lock the steering column and remove the ignition key. Raise the front of the vehicle and support it securely on jackstands. Apply the parking brake.

2   Place a drain pan under the steering gear. Unscrew the fittings and detach the hoses **(see illustration),** then cap the ends to prevent excessive fluid loss and contamination.

15.2 Typical power steering hose assembly (diesel shown, gasoline engines similar)

10

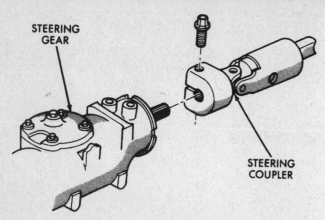

15.3 Mark the relationship of the steering coupler to the steering gear input shaft, then remove the pinch bolt

3   Mark the relationship of the steering coupler to the steering gear input shaft. Remove the steering coupler pinch bolt **(see illustration)**.
4   Detach the Pitman arm from the steering gear shaft (see Section 14).
5   Support the steering gear and remove the mounting bolts. Lower the unit, separate the intermediate shaft from the steering gear input shaft and remove the steering gear from the vehicle.
6   Raise the steering gear into position and connect the steering coupler to the steering gear input shaft. Be sure to match up the alignment marks.
7   Install the mounting bolts and washers and tighten them to the torque listed in this Chapter's Specifications.
8   Slide the Pitman arm onto the shaft. Make sure the marks are aligned. Install the washer and nut and tighten the nut to the torque listed in this Chapter's Specifications.
9   Install the steering coupler pinch bolt and tighten it to the torque listed in this Chapter's Specifications.
10   Connect the power steering hoses/lines to the steering gear and fill the power steering pump reservoir with the recommended fluid (see Chapter 1).
11   Lower the vehicle and bleed the steering system (see Section 17).

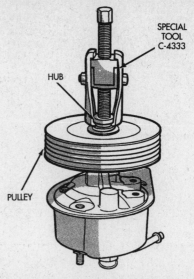

16.3 This special tool, designed for removing power steering pump pulleys, is available at most auto parts stores

16   Power steering pump - removal and installation

1   Using a suction gun, suck out as much power steering fluid from the reservoir as possible. Position a drain pan under the pump and disconnect the high pressure line and fluid return hose **(see illustration 15.2)**. Cap the ends of the lines to prevent excessive fluid leakage and the entry of contaminants.

Gasoline engines

Refer to illustrations 16.3, 16.4a, 16.4b, 16.5a and 16.5b
2   Loosen the serpentine belt and slip the belt off the pump pulley (see Chapter 1).
3   Remove the pulley from the shaft with a special power steering pump pulley removal tool **(see illustration)**. This tool can be purchased at most auto parts stores.
4   Remove the front attaching bolts **(see illustrations)** and the rear attaching bolts and nuts, then lift the pump and bracket from the engine. Remove the four mounting nuts to detach the pump from the bracket.
5   A special pulley installation tool is also available for pressing the pulley back onto the pump shaft **(see illustration)**, but an alternate tool can be fabricated from a long bolt, nut, washer and a socket of the

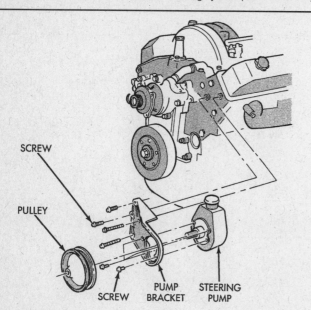

16.4a Mounting details of the power steering pump and bracket (V6 and V8 engines)

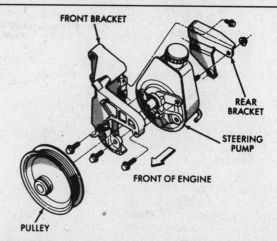

16.4b Mounting details of the power steering pump and bracket (V10 engine)

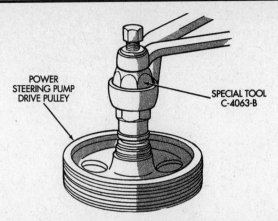

16.5a There's a special tool available for installing power steering pump pulleys, but . . .

16.5b . . . a long bolt with the same thread pitch as the internal threads of the power steering pump shaft, a nut, washer and a socket that is the same diameter as the pulley hub can also be used to install the pulley on the shaft

same diameter as the pulley hub **(see illustration)**. Push the pulley onto the shaft until the pulley hub is flush with the shaft. **Caution:** *Never drive the pulley onto the shaft with a hammer.*

6   Installation is otherwise the reverse of removal. Be sure to bleed the power steering system following the procedure in Section 17. **Note:** *After installation is complete, start the engine and see if the drivebelt squeaks. If it does, stop the engine, install the pulley removal tool and adjust the pulley outward approximately 1/64 to 1/32-inch. Run the engine again - if the noise is worse, stop the engine, install the pulley installation tool and press it on about 3/64-inch. Be careful not to push it on too far, as the pulley could contact the pump mounting bolts.*

Diesel engine

Refer to illustrations 16.8 and 16.9

7   Refer to Chapter 9, Section 15 (*Power brake vacuum pump - removal and installation*) and remove the vacuum pump and power steering pump as an assembly.

8   After separating the vacuum pump and power steering pump as described in Chapter 9, remove the adapter from the power steering pump **(see illustration)**.

9   Install the adapter on the new power steering pump (don't forget the spacers) and tighten the nuts to the torque listed in this Chapter's Specifications. Make sure the pump spacers and power steering

pump mate perfectly with the vacuum pump adapter bracket **(see illustration)**.

10   The remainder of installation is the reverse of removal (see Section 15, Chapter 9).

17   Power steering system - bleeding

1   Following any operation in which the power steering fluid lines have been disconnected, the power steering system must be bled to remove all air and obtain proper steering performance.

2   With the front wheels in the straight ahead position, check the power steering fluid level and, if low, add fluid until it reaches the Cold (C) mark on the dipstick.

3   Start the engine and allow it to run at fast idle. Recheck the fluid level and add more if necessary to reach the Cold (C) mark on the dipstick.

4   Bleed the system by turning the wheels from side-to-side, without hitting the stops. This will work the air out of the system. Keep the reservoir full of fluid as this is done.

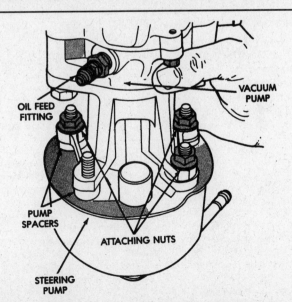

16.8 To separate the vacuum pump adapter bracket from the power steering pump, remove these nuts

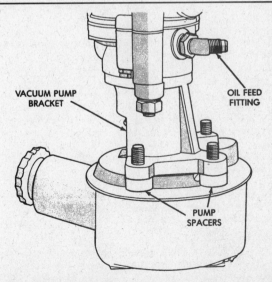

16.9 When installing the vacuum pump adapter bracket on the power steering pump, make sure the spacers are in place - do not tighten the nuts until everything mates perfectly

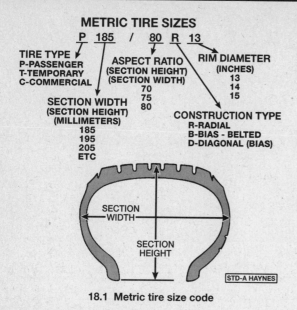

18.1 Metric tire size code

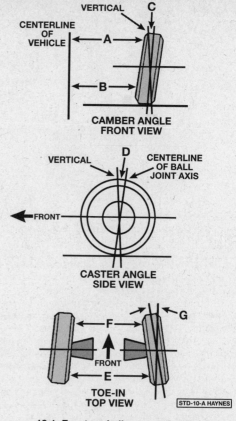

19.1 Front end alignment details

1   *A minus B = C (degrees camber)*
2   *E minus F = toe-in (measured in inches)*
3   *G - toe-in (expressed in degrees)*

5   When the air is worked out of the system, return the wheels to the straight ahead position and leave the vehicle running for several more minutes before shutting it off.
6   Road test the vehicle to be sure the steering system is functioning normally and noise-free.
7   Recheck the fluid level to be sure it is up to the Hot (H) mark on the dipstick while the engine is at normal operating temperature. Add fluid if necessary (see Chapter 1).

18   Wheels and tires - general information

Refer to illustration 18.1

Most vehicles covered by this manual are equipped with metric-sized fiberglass or steel-belted radial tires **(see illustration)**. Use of other size or type of tires may affect the ride and handling of the vehicle. Don't mix different types of tires, such as radials and bias belted, on the same vehicle as handling may be seriously affected. It's recommended that tires be replaced in pairs on the same axle. If only one tire is being replaced, be sure it's the same size, structure and tread design as the other.

Because tire pressure has a substantial effect on handling and wear, the pressure on all tires should be checked at least once a month or before any extended trips (see Chapter 1).

Wheels must be replaced if they are bent, dented, leak air, have elongated bolt holes, are heavily rusted, out of vertical symmetry or if the lug nuts won't stay tight. Wheel repairs that use welding or peening are not recommended.

Tire and wheel balance is important to the overall handling, braking and performance of the vehicle. Unbalanced wheels can adversely affect handling and ride characteristics as well as tire life. Whenever a tire is installed on a wheel, the tire and wheel should be balanced by a shop with the proper equipment.

19   Front end alignment - general information

Refer to illustration 19.1

A front end alignment refers to the adjustments made to the front wheels so they are in proper angular relationship to the suspension and the ground **(see illustration)**. Front wheels that are out of proper alignment not only affect steering control, but also increase tire wear. On 2WD models the camber, caster and toe-in can be adjusted. On 4WD models the only adjustments possible are toe-in and caster.

Getting the proper front wheel alignment is a very exacting process, one in which complicated and expensive machines are necessary to perform the job properly. Because of this, you should have a technician with the proper equipment perform these tasks. We will, however, use this space to give you a basic idea of what is involved with front end alignment so you can better understand the process and deal intelligently with the shop that does the work.

Toe-in is the turning in of the front wheels. The purpose of a toe specification is to ensure parallel rolling of the front wheels. In a vehicle with zero toe-in, the distance between the front edges of the wheels will be the same as the distance between the rear edges of the wheels. The actual amount of toe-in is normally only a fraction of an inch. On 2WD models, toe-in adjustment is controlled by the tie-rod end position on the tie-rod. On 4WD models toe-in is adjusted by turning the adjuster sleeve on the center link. Incorrect toe-in will cause the tires to wear improperly by making them scrub against the road surface.

Caster is the tilting of the top of the front steering axis from the vertical. A tilt toward the rear is positive caster and a tilt toward the front is negative caster. On 2WD models this angle is adjusted by altering the position of the upper control arm pivot bar on the frame (by moving the rear of the bar in or out, and moving the front of the bar slightly in the opposite direction. On 4WD models caster is adjusted by turning the cam bolts on the lower suspension arm.

Camber (the tilting of the front wheels from vertical when viewed from the front of the vehicle) on 2WD models is also adjusted by changing the position of the upper control arm pivot bar on the frame - moving it out increases the camber and moving it in decreases camber. On 4WD models, camber isn't adjustable - if the camber angle isn't correct, the components causing the problem must be replaced. **Caution:** *Never attempt to adjust the camber angle by heating or bending the axle or any other suspension component!*

Chapter 11 Body

Contents

1 General information

The vehicles covered by this manual are built with a body-on-frame construction. The frame is a ladder-type, consisting of two C-sectioned steel side rails joined by crossmembers. The frame is riveted, with the exception of the transmission crossmember, which is bolted in place for easy removal.

Certain components are particularly vulnerable to accident damage and can be unbolted and repaired or replaced. Among these parts are the doors, seats, tailgate, liftgate, bumpers and fenders.

Only general body maintenance practices and body panel repair procedures within the scope of the do-it-yourselfer are included in this Chapter.

2 Body - maintenance

1 The condition of your vehicle's body is very important, because the resale value depends a great deal on it. It's much more difficult to repair a neglected or damaged body than it is to repair mechanical components. The hidden areas of the body, such as the wheel wells, the frame and the engine compartment, are equally important, although they don't require as frequent attention as the rest of the body.

2 Once a year, or every 12,000 miles, it's a good idea to have the underside of the body steam cleaned. All traces of dirt and oil will be removed and the area can then be inspected carefully for rust, damaged brake lines, frayed electrical wires, damaged cables and other problems. The front suspension components should be greased after completion of this job.

3 At the same time, clean the engine and the engine compartment with a steam cleaner or water-soluble degreaser.

4 The wheel wells should be given close attention, since undercoating can peel away and stones and dirt thrown up by the tires can cause the paint to chip and flake, allowing rust to set in. If rust is found, clean down to the bare metal and apply an anti-rust paint.

5 The body should be washed about once a week. Wet the vehicle thoroughly to soften the dirt, then wash it down with a soft sponge and plenty of clean soapy water. If the surplus dirt is not washed off very carefully, it can wear down the paint.

6 Spots of tar or asphalt thrown up from the road should be removed with a cloth soaked in solvent.

7 Once every six months, wax the body and chrome trim. If a chrome cleaner is used to remove rust from any of the vehicle's plated parts, remember that the cleaner also removes part of the chrome, so use it sparingly.

3 Vinyl trim - maintenance

Don't clean vinyl trim with detergents, caustic soap or petroleum-based cleaners. Plain soap and water works just fine, with a soft brush to clean dirt that may be ingrained. Wash the vinyl as frequently as the rest of the vehicle. After cleaning, application of a high-quality rubber and vinyl protectant will help prevent oxidation and cracks. The protectant can also be applied to weatherstripping, vacuum lines and rubber hoses, which often fail as a result of chemical degradation, and to the tires.

11

These photos illustrate a method of repairing simple dents. They are intended to supplement *Body repair - minor damage* in this Chapter and should not be used as the sole instructions for body repair on these vehicles.

1   If you can't access the backside of the body panel to hammer out the dent, pull it out with a slide-hammer-type dent puller. In the deepest portion of the dent or along the crease line, drill or punch hole(s) at least one inch apart . . .

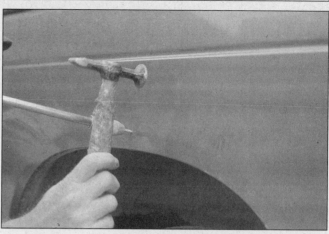

2   . . . then screw the slide-hammer into the hole and operate it. Tap with a hammer near the edge of the dent to help 'pop' the metal back to its original shape. When you're finished, the dent area should be close to its original contour and about 1/8-inch below the surface of the surrounding metal

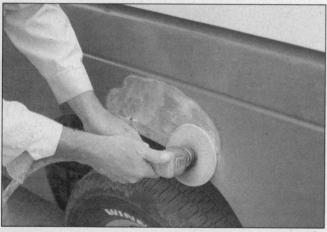

3   Using coarse-grit sandpaper, remove the paint down to the bare metal. Hand sanding works fine, but the disc sander shown here makes the job faster. Use finer (about 320-grit) sandpaper to feather-edge the paint at least one inch around the dent area

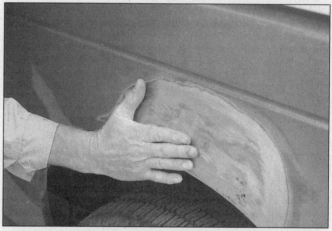

4   When the paint is removed, touch will probably be more helpful than sight for telling if the metal is straight. Hammer down the high spots or raise the low spots as necessary. Clean the repair area with wax/silicone remover

5   Following label instructions, mix up a batch of plastic filler and hardener. The ratio of filler to hardener is critical, and, if you mix it incorrectly, it will either not cure properly or cure too quickly (you won't have time to file and sand it into shape)

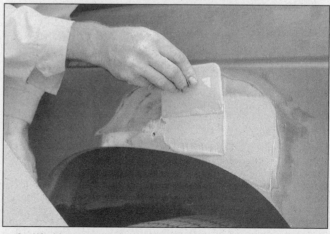

6   Working quickly so the filler doesn't harden, use a plastic applicator to press the body filler firmly into the metal, assuring it bonds completely. Work the filler until it matches the original contour and is slightly above the surrounding metal

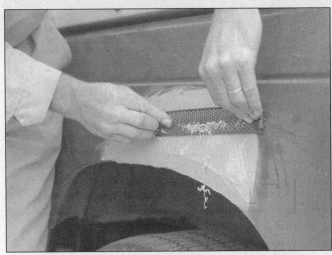

7   Let the filler harden until you can just dent it with your fingernail. Use a body file or Surform tool (shown here) to rough-shape the filler

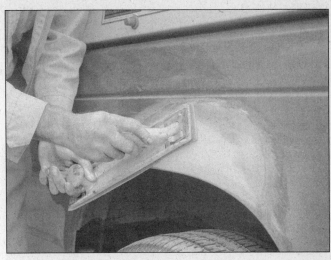

8   Use coarse-grit sandpaper and a sanding board or block to work the filler down until it's smooth and even. Work down to finer grits of sandpaper - always using a board or block - ending up with 360 or 400 grit

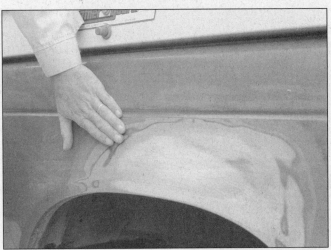

9   You shouldn't be able to feel any ridge at the transition from the filler to the bare metal or from the bare metal to the old paint. As soon as the repair is flat and uniform, remove the dust and mask off the adjacent panels or trim pieces

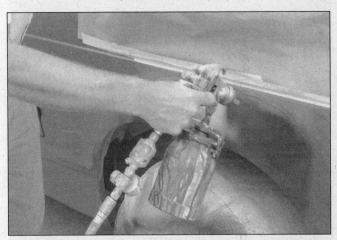

10   Apply several layers of primer to the area. Don't spray the primer on too heavy, so it sags or runs, and make sure each coat is dry before you spray on the next one. A professional-type spray gun is being used here, but aerosol spray primer is available inexpensively from auto parts stores

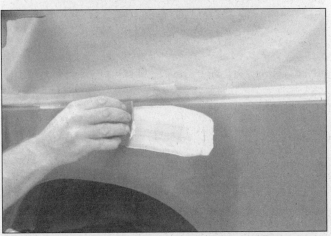

11   The primer will help reveal imperfections or scratches. Fill these with glazing compound. Follow the label instructions and sand it with 360 or 400-grit sandpaper until it's smooth. Repeat the glazing, sanding and respraying until the primer reveals a perfectly smooth surface

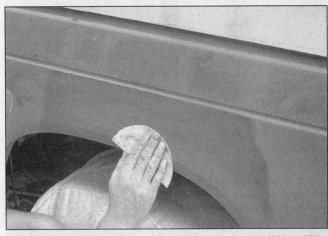

12   Finish sand the primer with very fine sandpaper (400 or 600-grit) to remove the primer overspray. Clean the area with water and allow it to dry. Use a tack rag to remove any dust, then apply the finish coat. Don't attempt to rub out or wax the repair area until the paint has dried completely (at least two weeks)

4   Upholstery and carpets - maintenance

1   Every three months remove the floormats and clean the interior of the vehicle (more frequently if necessary). Use a stiff whisk broom to brush the carpeting and loosen dirt and dust, then vacuum the upholstery and carpets thoroughly, especially along seams and crevices.

2   Dirt and stains can be removed from carpeting with basic household or automotive carpet shampoos available in spray cans. Follow the directions and vacuum again, then use a stiff brush to bring back the "nap" of the carpet.

3   Most interiors have cloth or vinyl upholstery, either of which can be cleaned and maintained with a number of material-specific cleaners or shampoos available in auto supply stores. Follow the directions on the product for usage, and always spot-test any upholstery cleaner on an inconspicuous area (bottom edge of a backseat cushion) to ensure that it doesn't cause a color shift in the material.

4   After cleaning, vinyl upholstery should be treated with a protectant. **Note:** *Make sure the protectant container indicates the product can be used on seats - some products make may a seat too slippery.* **Caution:** *Do not use protectant on vinyl-covered steering wheels.*

5   Leather upholstery requires special care. It should be cleaned regularly with saddlesoap or leather cleaner. Never use alcohol, gasoline, nail polish remover or thinner to clean leather upholstery.

6   After cleaning, regularly treat leather upholstery with a leather conditioner, rubbed in with a soft cotton cloth. Never use car wax on leather upholstery.

7   In areas where the interior of the vehicle is subject to bright sunlight, cover leather seating areas of the seats with a sheet if the vehicle is to be left out for any length of time.

5   Body repair - minor damage

Repair of scratches

1   If the scratch is superficial and does not penetrate to the metal of the body, repair is very simple. Lightly rub the scratched area with a fine rubbing compound to remove loose paint and built up wax. Rinse the area with clean water.

2   Apply touch-up paint to the scratch, using a small brush. Continue to apply thin layers of paint until the surface of the paint in the scratch is level with the surrounding paint. Allow the new paint at least two weeks to harden, then blend it into the surrounding paint by rubbing with a very fine rubbing compound. Finally, apply a coat of wax to the scratch area.

3   If the scratch has penetrated the paint and exposed the metal of the body, causing the metal to rust, a different repair technique is required. Remove all loose rust from the bottom of the scratch with a pocket knife, then apply rust inhibiting paint to prevent the formation of rust in the future. Using a rubber or nylon applicator, coat the scratched area with glaze-type filler. If required, the filler can be mixed with thinner to provide a very thin paste, which is ideal for filling narrow scratches. Before the glaze filler in the scratch hardens, wrap a piece of smooth cotton cloth around the tip of a finger. Dip the cloth in thinner and then quickly wipe it along the surface of the scratch. This will ensure that the surface of the filler is slightly hollow. The scratch can now be painted over as described earlier in this Section.

Repair of dents

See photo sequence

4   When repairing dents, the first job is to pull the dent out until the affected area is as close as possible to its original shape. There is no point in trying to restore the original shape completely as the metal in the damaged area will have stretched on impact and cannot be restored to its original contours. It is better to bring the level of the dent up to a point which is about 1/8-inch below the level of the surrounding metal. In cases where the dent is very shallow, it is not worth trying to pull it out at all.

5   If the back side of the dent is accessible, it can be hammered out gently from behind using a soft-face hammer. While doing this, hold a block of wood firmly against the opposite side of the metal to absorb the hammer blows and prevent the metal from being stretched.

6   If the dent is in a section of the body which has double layers, or some other factor makes it inaccessible from behind, a different technique is required. Drill several small holes through the metal inside the damaged area, particularly in the deeper sections. Screw long, self tapping screws into the holes just enough for them to get a good grip in the metal. Now the dent can be pulled out by pulling on the protruding heads of the screws with locking pliers.

7   The next stage of repair is the removal of paint from the damaged area and from an inch or so of the surrounding metal. This is easily done with a wire brush or sanding disk in a drill motor, although it can be done just as effectively by hand with sandpaper. To complete the preparation for filling, score the surface of the bare metal with a screwdriver or the tang of a file or drill small holes in the affected area. This will provide a good grip for the filler material. To complete the repair, see the Section on *filling and painting*.

Repair of rust holes or gashes

8   Remove all paint from the affected area and from an inch or so of the surrounding metal using a sanding disk or wire brush mounted in a drill motor. If these are not available, a few sheets of sandpaper will do the job just as effectively.

9   With the paint removed, you will be able to determine the severity of the corrosion and decide whether to replace the whole panel, if possible, or repair the affected area. New body panels are not as expensive as most people think and it is often quicker to install a new panel than to repair large areas of rust.

10   Remove all trim pieces from the affected area except those which will act as a guide to the original shape of the damaged body, such as headlight shells, etc. Using metal snips or a hacksaw blade, remove all loose metal and any other metal that is badly affected by rust. Hammer the edges of the hole on the inside to create a slight depression for the filler material.

11   Wire brush the affected area to remove the powdery rust from the surface of the metal. If the back of the rusted area is accessible, treat it with rust inhibiting paint.

12   Before filling is done, block the hole in some way. This can be done with sheet metal riveted or screwed into place, or by stuffing the hole with wire mesh.

13   Once the hole is blocked off, the affected area can be filled and painted. See the following subsection on *filling and painting*.

Filling and painting

14   Many types of body fillers are available, but generally speaking, body repair kits which contain filler paste and a tube of resin hardener are best for this type of repair work. A wide, flexible plastic or nylon applicator will be necessary for imparting a smooth and contoured finish to the surface of the filler material. Mix up a small amount of filler on a clean piece of wood or cardboard (use the hardener sparingly). Follow the manufacturer's instructions on the package, otherwise the filler will set incorrectly.

15   Using the applicator, apply the filler paste to the prepared area. Draw the applicator across the surface of the filler to achieve the desired contour and to level the filler surface. As soon as a contour that approximates the original one is achieved, stop working the paste. If you continue, the paste will begin to stick to the applicator. Continue to add thin layers of paste at 20-minute intervals until the level of the filler is just above the surrounding metal.

16   Once the filler has hardened, the excess can be removed with a body file. From then on, progressively finer grades of sandpaper should be used, starting with a 180-grit paper and finishing with 600-grit wet-or-dry paper. Always wrap the sandpaper around a flat rubber or wooden block, otherwise the surface of the filler will not be completely flat. During the sanding of the filler surface, the wet-or-dry paper should be periodically rinsed in water. This will ensure that a very smooth finish is produced in the final stage.

17   At this point, the repair area should be surrounded by a ring of bare metal, which in turn should be encircled by the finely feathered

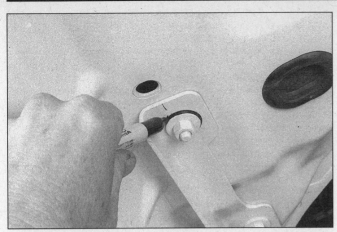

9.2 Use paint or a marking pen to draw a line around the hood mounting nuts

edge of good paint. Rinse the repair area with clean water until all of the dust produced by the sanding operation is gone.

18   Spray the entire area with a light coat of primer. This will reveal any imperfections in the surface of the filler. Repair the imperfections with fresh filler paste or glaze filler and once more smooth the surface with sandpaper. Repeat this spray-and-repair procedure until you are satisfied that the surface of the filler and the feathered edge of the paint are perfect. Rinse the area with clean water and allow it to dry completely.

19   The repair area is now ready for painting. Spray painting must be carried out in a warm, dry, windless and dust free atmosphere. These conditions can be created if you have access to a large indoor work area, but if you are forced to work in the open, you will have to pick the day very carefully. If you are working indoors, dousing the floor in the work area with water will help settle the dust which would otherwise be in the air. If the repair area is confined to one body panel, mask off the surrounding panels. This will help minimize the effects of a slight mismatch in paint color. Trim pieces such as chrome strips, door handles, etc., will also need to be masked off or removed. Use masking tape and several thickness of newspaper for the masking operations.

20   Before spraying, shake the paint can thoroughly, then spray a test area until the spray painting technique is mastered. Cover the repair area with a thick coat of primer. The thickness should be built up using several thin layers of primer rather than one thick one. Using 600-grit wet-or-dry sandpaper, rub down the surface of the primer until it is very smooth. While doing this, the work area should be thoroughly rinsed with water and the wet-or-dry sandpaper periodically rinsed as well. Allow the primer to dry before spraying additional coats.

21   Spray on the top coat, again building up the thickness by using several thin layers of paint. Begin spraying in the center of the repair area and then, using a circular motion, work out until the whole repair

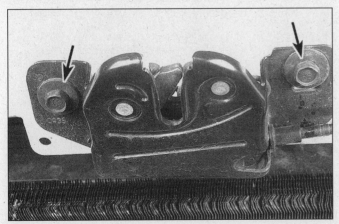

9.10 Loosen the hood latch bolts (arrows), then move the latch as necessary to adjust the hood closed position

area and about two inches of the surrounding original paint is covered. Remove all masking material 10 to 15 minutes after spraying on the final coat of paint. Allow the new paint at least two weeks to harden, then use a very fine rubbing compound to blend the edges of the new paint into the existing paint. Finally, apply a coat of wax.

6   Body repair - major damage

1   Major damage must be repaired by an auto body shop specifically equipped to perform body and frame repairs. These shops have the specialized equipment required to do the job properly.

2   If the damage is extensive, the body must be checked for proper alignment or the vehicle's handling characteristics may be adversely affected and other components may wear at an accelerated rate.

3   Due to the fact that all of the major body components (hood, fenders, etc.) are separate and replaceable units, any seriously damaged components should be replaced rather than repaired. Sometimes the components can be found in a wrecking yard that specializes in used vehicle components, often at considerable savings over the cost of new parts.

7   Hinges and locks - maintenance

Once every 3000 miles, or every three months, the hinges and latch assemblies on the doors, hood and trunk should be given a few drops of light oil or lock lubricant. The door latch strikers should also be lubricated with a thin coat of grease to reduce wear and ensure free movement. Lubricate the door and trunk locks with spray-on graphite lubricant.

8   Windshield and fixed glass - replacement

Replacement of the windshield and fixed glass requires the use of special fast-setting adhesive/caulk materials and some specialized tools and techniques. These operations should be left to a dealer service department or a shop specializing in glass work.

9   Hood - removal, installation and adjustment

Refer to illustrations 9.2, 9.10 and 9.11
Note: *The hood is heavy and somewhat awkward to remove and install - at least two people should perform this procedure.*

Removal and installation

1   Use blankets or pads to cover the cowl area of the body and the fenders. This will protect the body and paint as the hood is lifted off.

2   Scribe alignment marks around the hinge nuts to insure proper alignment during installation (paint or a permanent-type felt-tip marker also will work for this) **(see illustration)**.

3   Disconnect any cables or wire harnesses which will interfere with removal.

4   Have an assistant support the weight of the hood. Remove the hinge-to-hood nuts.

5   Lift off the hood.

6   Installation is the reverse of removal.

Adjustment

7   Fore-and-aft and side-to-side adjustment of the hood is done by moving the hood in relation to the hinge plate after loosening the bolts.

8   Scribe or trace a line around the entire hinge plate so you can judge the amount of movement.

9   Loosen the nuts and move the hood into correct alignment. Move it only a little at a time. Tighten the hinge nuts and carefully lower the hood to check the alignment.

10   Adjust the hood latch so the hood closes securely **(see illustration)**.

11

11   Adjust the hood bumpers on the radiator support so the hood is flush with the fenders when closed **(see illustration)**.

12   The safety catch assembly on the hood itself can also be adjusted fore-and-aft and side-to-side after loosening the bolts.

13   The hood latch assembly, as well as the hinges, should be periodically lubricated with white lithium-base grease to prevent sticking and wear.

10   Hood latch and cable - removal and installation

Refer to illustration 10.1

Warning: *These models are equipped with an airbag. The airbag is armed and can deploy (inflate) anytime the battery is connected. To prevent accidental deployment (and possible injury), disconnect the negative battery cable(s) whenever working near airbag components. After the battery is disconnected, wait at least 2 minutes before beginning work (the system has a back-up capacitor that must fully discharge). For more information see Chapter 12.*

Latch

1   Remove the bolts and detach the latch assembly. Unhook the spring and use a screwdriver to detach the cable end from the latch **(see illustration)**.

2   Installation is the reverse of removal.

Cable

3   Disconnect the cable from the latch **(see illustration 10.1)**. Detach the cable from the fasteners along the left inner fender.

4   Working in the passenger compartment, remove the screws and detach the hood release cable and handle assembly from the instrument panel.

5   Pull the cable through the firewall grommet into the passenger compartment.

6   Insert the end of new cable through the firewall grommet into the engine compartment.

7   Pull the cable through from the engine compartment side.

8   The remainder of installation is the reverse of removal.

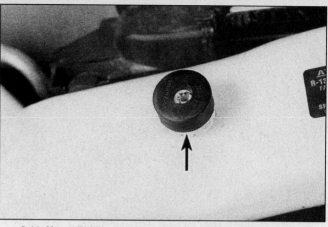

9.11 Use a Phillips-head screwdriver to thread the rubber bumper (arrow) in-or-out to make fine adjustments to the hood closed height

11   Radiator grille - removal and installation

Refer to illustrations 11.2 and 11.3

1   Open the hood.

2   Remove the mounting screws and nuts, then detach the grille assembly from the assembly bracket **(see illustration)**.

3   Remove the screws attaching the assembly bracket to the hood and lower it from the hood **(see illustration)**.

4   Installation is the reverse of removal.

12   Front fender - removal and installation

Refer to illustrations 12.4, 12.5, 12.6a, 12.6b and 12.6c

Warning: *These models are equipped with an airbag. The airbag is armed and can deploy (inflate) anytime the battery is connected. To prevent accidental deployment (and possible injury), disconnect the*

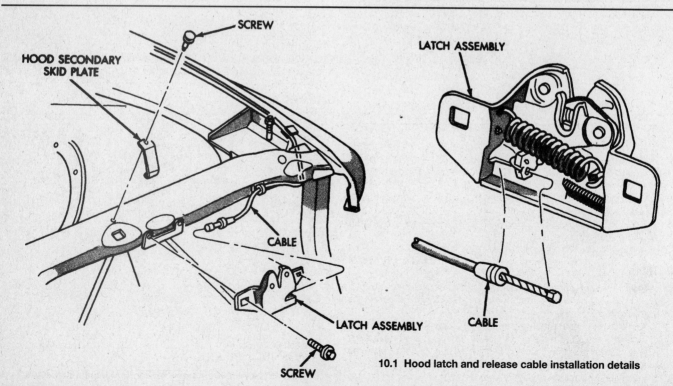

10.1 Hood latch and release cable installation details

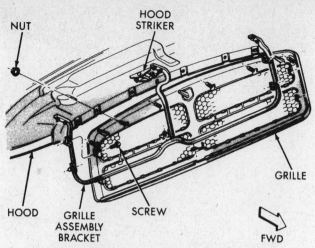

11.2 **Remove the screws and nuts, then detach the grille from the bracket**

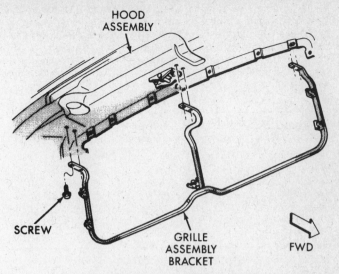

11.3 **Grille bracket assembly details**

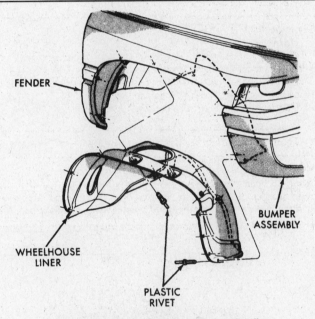

12.4 **Wheelhouse liner installation details**

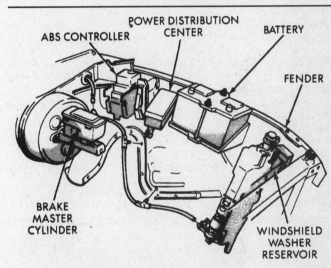

12.5 **Remove the bolts and detach components such as the ABS controller, power distribution center and battery from the fender**

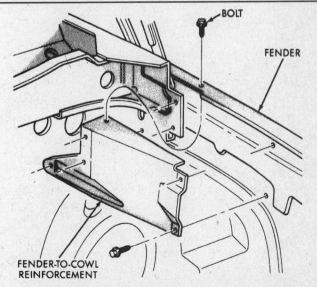

12.6a **Cowl reinforcement-to-fender installation details**

negative battery cable(s) whenever working near airbag components. After the battery is disconnected, wait at least 2 minutes before beginning work (the system has a back-up capacitor that must fully discharge). For more information see Chapter 12.

1   Open the hood, raise the vehicle, support it securely on jackstands and remove the front wheel.

2   Remove the composite headlight assembly, side marker and turn signal lamps (see Chapter 12).

3   Remove the front bumper assembly (see Section 13).

4   Pry out the plastic rivets and remove the inner fender liner **(see illustration)**.

5   Disconnect the antenna and all lighting system electrical connectors and other components that would interfere with fender removal **(see illustration)**.

6   Remove the fender mounting bolts **(see illustrations)**.

7   Detach the fender. It's a good idea to have an assistant support the fender while it's being moved away from the vehicle to prevent damage to the surrounding body panels.

8   Installation is the reverse of removal.

9   Tighten all nuts, bolts and screws securely.

11

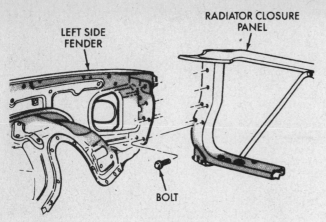

12.6b Fender-to-radiator panel installation details

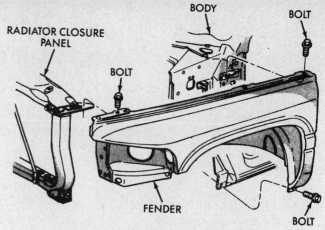

12.6c Fender-to-body installation details

13 Bumpers - removal and installation

Refer to illustrations 13.2 and 13.6
Warning: *These models are equipped with an airbag. The airbag is armed and can deploy (inflate) anytime the battery is connected. To prevent accidental deployment (and possible injury), disconnect the negative battery cable(s) whenever working near airbag components. After the battery is disconnected, wait at least 2 minutes before beginning work (the system has a back-up capacitor that must fully discharge). For more information see Chapter 12.*

Front bumper

1   Support the bumper with a jack or jackstand.
2   With an assistant supporting the bumper, remove the bolts, nuts and stud plates retaining the bumper to the frame **(see illustration)**.
3   Disconnect any wiring harnesses or any other components that would interfere with bumper removal and detach the bumper.
4   Installation is the reverse of removal. Tighten the retaining bolts/nuts securely.

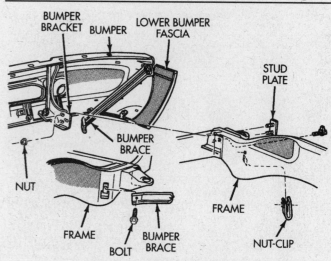

13.2 Front bumper and support brace installation details

13.6 Rear bumper installation details

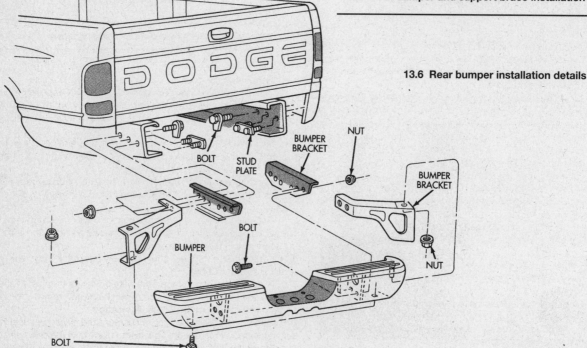

14.2a Use a Phillips screwdriver to remove the screws in the door pull

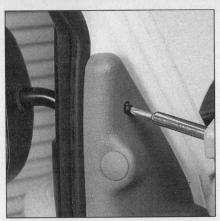

14.2b One of the door trim panel screws is located at the upper front corner

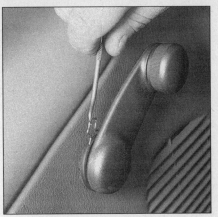

14.3 Use a hook-tool to remove the retaining clip, then detach the window crank handle

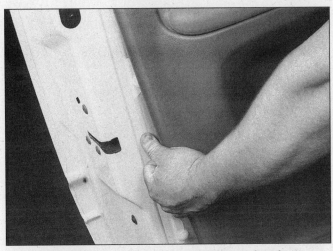

14.5 Pull the panel away from the door and unplug the electrical connectors

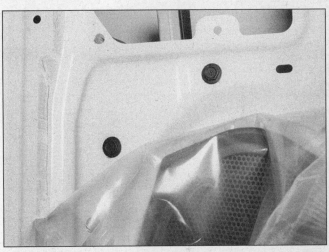

14.6 Peel the water deflector carefully away from the door, taking care not to tear it

Rear bumper

5   Support the bumper with a jack or jackstand.

6   With an assistant supporting the bumper, remove the bolts, nuts and stud plates retaining the bumper to the frame **(see illustration)**.

7   Disconnect license plate light.

8   Installation is the reverse of removal. Tighten the retaining bolts/nuts securely.

14.7 Pry out any retainers that remain in the door and install them in the trim panel before installation

14   Door trim panel - removal and installation

Refer to illustrations 14.2a, 14.2b, 14.3, 14.5, 14.6 and 14.7

1   Disconnect the negative cable(s) from the battery(ies).

2   Remove all door trim panel retaining screws and door pull/arm-rest assemblies **(see illustrations)**. If equipped with power mirrors, remove the switch knob by pulling it straight back and remove the switch retaining nut.

3   On manual window models, remove the window crank **(see illustration)**. On power window models, pry out the control switch assembly and disconnect the electrical connector.

4   Insert a putty knife between the trim panel and the door and disengage the retaining clips. Work around the outer edge until the panel is free.

5   Once all of the clips are disengaged, detach the trim panel, disconnect any wiring harness connectors and remove the trim panel from the vehicle **(see illustration)**.

6   For access to the inner door, carefully peel back the plastic water-shield **(see illustration)**.

7   Prior to installation of the door panel, be sure to reinstall any clips in the panel which may have come out during the removal procedure and remain in the door itself **(see illustration)**.

8   Connect the wiring harness connectors and place the panel in position in the door. Press the trim panel into place until the clips are seated.

9   Install the armrest/door pulls and the window crank. Connect the negative battery cable.

11

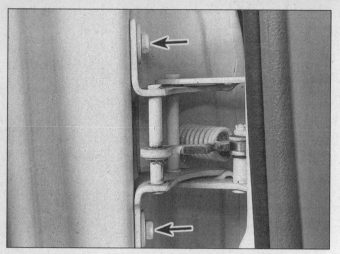

15.3 Mark their locations, then remove the door retaining bolts (arrows)

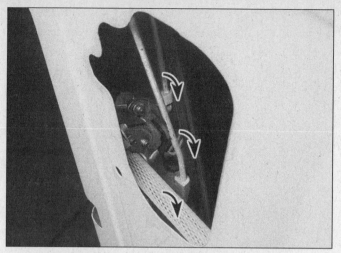

16.2 Rotate the plastic retaining clips off the rods, then detach the latch links

15 Door - removal, installation and adjustment

Refer to illustration 15.3

1   Remove the door trim panel. Disconnect any electrical connectors and push them through the door opening so they won't interfere with door removal.

2   Place a jack under the door or have an assistant on hand to support it when the hinge bolts are removed. **Note:** *If a jack is used, place a rag between it and the door to protect the door's painted surfaces.*

3   Scribe around the mounting bolt heads with a marking pen, remove the bolts and carefully lift off the door **(see illustration)**.

4   Installation is the reverse of removal, making sure to align the hinge with the marks made during removal before tightening the bolts.

5   Following installation of the door, check the alignment and adjust the hinges, if necessary. Adjust door lock striker, centering it in the door latch.

16 Door latch, lock cylinder and handles - removal and installation

Refer to illustrations 16.2, 16.3, 16.7, 16.8, 16.10 and 16.12

Latch

1   Raise the window completely and remove the door trim panel and wathershield (see Section 14).

2   Disconnect the link rods from the latch **(see illustration)**.

3   Remove the three Torx-head mounting screws (it may be necessary to use an impact-type screwdriver to loosen them), then remove the latch from the door **(see illustration)**.

4   Place the latch in position and install the screws. Tighten the screws securely.

5   Connect the link rods to the latch.

6   Check the door to make sure it closes properly. Readjust the latch (by loosening the screws and moving it) as necessary until the door closes smoothly (with the door handle flush with the door).

7   After installation, loosen the linkage adjusting screw by inserting a hex-head wrench through the adjustment hole in the end of the door, lift up on the door handle to remove all slack from the linkage, then tighten the adjusting screw **(see illustration)**.

Lock cylinder

8   Remove the outside door handle (see below). Disconnect the link, use a screwdriver to push the key lock cylinder retainer off and withdraw the lock cylinder from the door handle **(see illustration)**.

9   Installation is the reverse of removal.

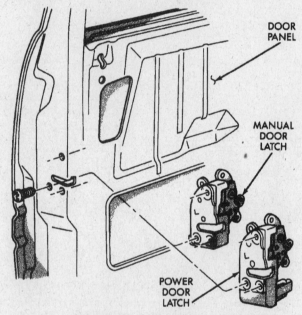

16.3 Door latch installation details

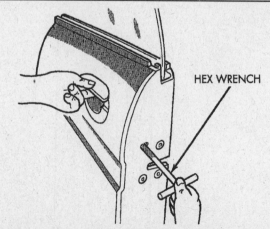

16.7 Insert a hex-head wrench into the adjustment hole, loosen the screw and lift up on the door handle to remove slack from the linkage

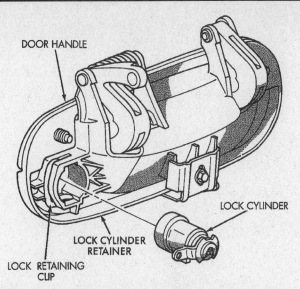

16.8 Remove the retaining clip and detach the lock cylinder from the outside door handle

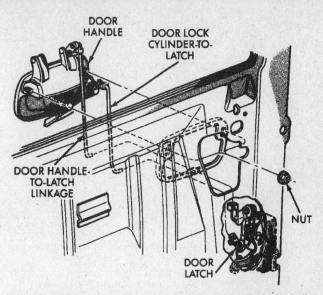

16.10 Outside door handle and latch linkage installation details

Outside handle

10   Disconnect the outside handle link from the latch, remove the mounting nuts and detach the handle from the door **(see illustration)**.

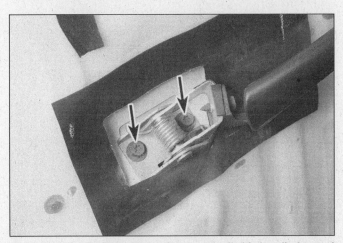

16.12 Remove the bolts (arrows), rotate the inside handle forward and disconnect the rods

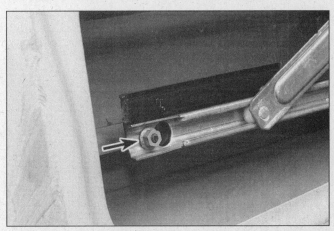

17.3 Pry the inner weather seal out of the door glass opening

11   Place the handle in position, attach the link and install the nuts. Tighten the nuts securely.

Inside handle

12   Remove the retaining bolts, rotate the handle forward and disconnect the links, then lift the handle off the door **(see illustration)**.
13   Installation is the reverse of removal.

17   Door window glass - removal and installation

Refer to illustrations 17.3 and 17.4

1   Remove the door trim panel and watershield (see Section 14).
2   Lower the glass.
3   Pry the inner weather seal out of the door glass opening **(see illustration)**
4   Remove the two nuts retaining the glass to the window regulator track. Slide the glass forward until the studs line up with the holes in the track, then detach the glass from the track **(see illustration)**.
5   Lift the glass up and out of the door through the glass opening.
6   To install, lower the glass into the door, slide it into position and install the nuts.
7   The remainder of installation is the reverse of removal.

17.4 Loosen the nut located at each end of the window regulator track (arrow), then slide the glass off the track and lift the glass out of the door

11

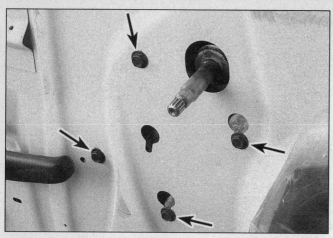

18.3a Door window regulator mounting bolt locations (arrows)

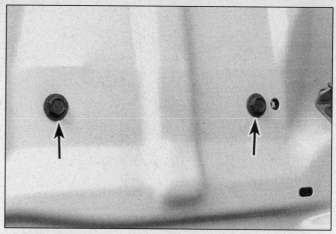

18.3b Door window regulator track bolt locations (arrows)

18   Door window regulator - removal and installation

Refer to illustrations 18.3a and 18.3b

Warning: *Do not remove the electric motor from the regulator assembly. The lift arm is under tension from the counterbalance spring and could cause personal injury if allowed to retract.*

1   Remove the door trim panel and watershield.
2   Remove the door window glass (see Section 17).
3   Remove the window regulator-to-door and track attaching bolts **(see illustrations)**.

4   On power window equipped models, unplug the electrical connector.
5   Remove the regulator from the door.
6   Installation is the reverse of removal.

19   Floor shift lever boot - removal and installation

Refer to illustration 19.3

1   Unscrew the shift knob from the lever.
2   Pull up the edge of the carpeting for access to the boot retaining screws.
3   Remove the screws, detach the boot and lift it up over the shift lever **(see illustration)**.
4   Installation is the reverse of removal.

20   Center console - removal and installation

Center console and seat cushion

Refer to illustration 20.1

1   Working under the seat cushion, remove the mounting bolts from the seat brackets **(see illustration)**.
2   Detach the console and lift it up.

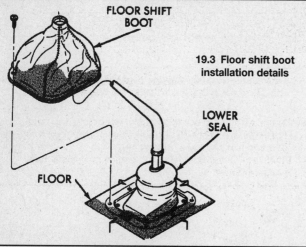

19.3 Floor shift boot installation details

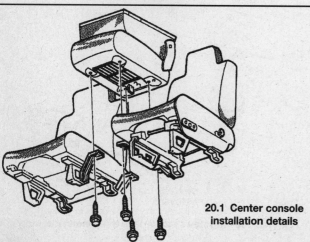

20.1 Center console installation details

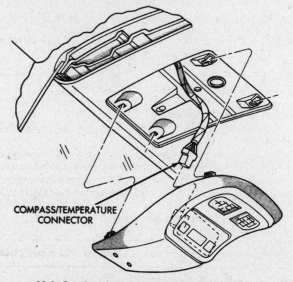

20.6 Overhead console installation details

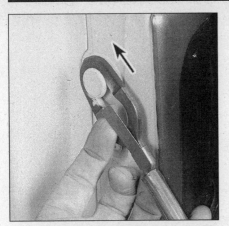

21.1 Lift the spring retainer up and slide the cable end off the pin

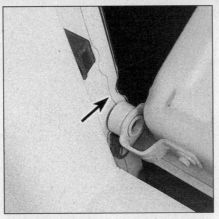

21.2 Align the flat on the right side hinge-pin with the slot in the hinge pocket and lift the tailgate off the vehicle

22.1a Use a small screwdriver to detach the escutcheon

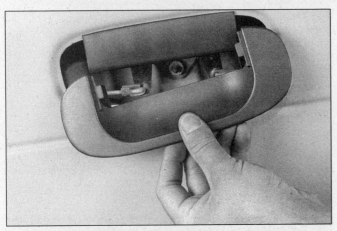

22.1b Lift the escutcheon out of the opening

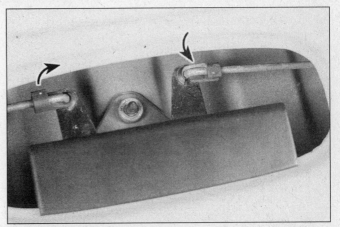

22.2 Rotate the plastic retaining clips off the control rods and detach the rods from the handle

3   Unplug any electrical connectors and remove the console from the vehicle.
4   Installation is the reverse of removal.

Overhead console

Refer to illustration 20.6
5   Disconnect the negative battery cable.
6   Remove the retaining screws at the front, pull the front of the console down and toward the rear to detach the clips. Unplug the compass electrical connector and lower the console **(see illustration)**.
7   Installation is the reverse of removal.

21   Tailgate - removal and installation

Refer to illustrations 21.1 and 21.2
1   Open the tailgate and detach the retaining cables **(see illustration)**.
2   Lower the tailgate until the flat on the right side hinge-pin aligns with the slot in the hinge pocket. Lift the tailgate out of the pocket **(see illustration)**. With the help of an assistant to support the weight, withdraw the left hinge pin from the body and remove the tailgate from the vehicle.
3   Installation is the reverse of removal.

22   Tailgate latch and handle - removal and installation

Refer to illustrations 22.1a, 22.1b, 22.2, 22.3 and 22.4
1   Use a small screwdriver to pry off the handle escutcheon **(see il-**

lustrations). Be very careful not to chip the paint.
2   Rotate the plastic retaining clips off the control rods and detach the rods from the handle **(see illustration)**.
3   Remove the retaining screws and detach the handle from the tailgate **(see illustration)**.

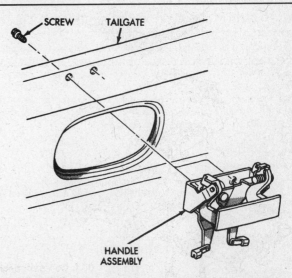

22.3 Remove the screws and detach the handle assembly

11

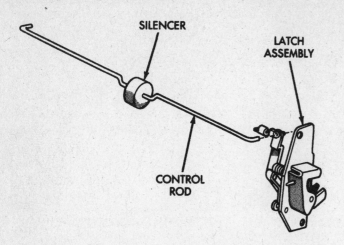

22.4 Remove the screws, pull the latch assembly off the tailgate and detach the control rod

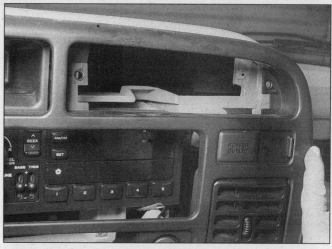

23.2 Grasp the cluster bezel securely and pull out sharply to detach the clips

4   Remove the screws and withdraw the latch assembly from the end of the tailgate **(see illustration)**.
5   Installation is the reverse of removal. Tighten all fasteners securely.

23   Instrument cluster bezel - removal and installation

Refer to illustration 23.2
Warning: *These models are equipped with an airbag. The airbag is armed and can deploy (inflate) anytime the battery is connected. To prevent accidental deployment (and possible injury), disconnect the negative battery cable(s) whenever working near airbag components. After the battery is disconnected, wait at least 2 minutes before beginning work (the system has a back-up capacitor that must fully discharge). For more information see Chapter 12.*
1   Remove the cup holder and ashtray (see Section 24).
2   Grasp the bezel securely and pull out sharply to detach the retaining clips from the instrument panel **(see illustration)**.
3   Disconnect the electrical connector from the cigar lighter and auxiliary power outlet.
4   Installation is the reverse of removal.

24   Instrument panel trim bezels - removal and installation

Warning: *These models are equipped with an airbag. The airbag is armed and can deploy (inflate) anytime the battery is connected. To prevent accidental deployment (and possible injury), disconnect the negative battery cable(s) whenever working near airbag components. After the battery is disconnected, wait at least 2 minutes before beginning work (the system has a back-up capacitor that must fully discharge). For more information see Chapter 12.*

Cup holder

Refer to illustration 24.2
1   Pull the cup holder out for access to the retaining screws.
2   Remove the two screws and detach the cup holder **(see illustration)**.
3   Installation is the reverse of removal.

Ashtray

Refer to illustration 24.5
4   Pull the ash tray out for access to the retaining screws.
5   Remove the two screws and detach the ashtray **(see illustration)**.
6   Installation is the reverse of removal.

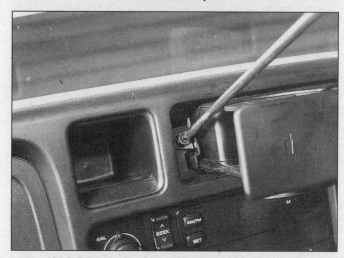

24.2 Remove the two cup holder retaining screws

Knee blocker

Refer to illustrations 24.7 and 24.8
7   Remove the screws and detach the anti-theft plug (if equipped) **(see illustration)**.

24.5 Remove the two ash tray retaining screws

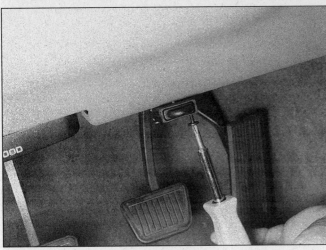

24.7 Remove the two screws and detach the anti-theft plug from the instrument panel

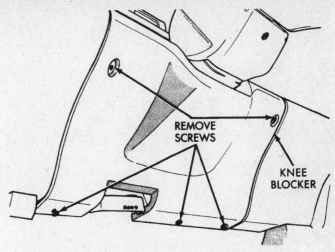

24.8 The knee blocker is held in place by five screws

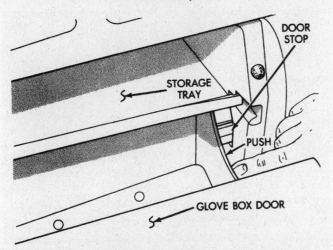

24.11 Push on the side of the glove box door until the door stop clears the instrument panel

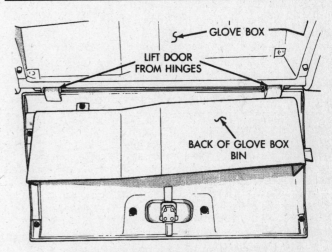

24.12 Lift the glove box bin off the hinges

8   Remove the Phillips-head screws and lower the knee blocker from the instrument panel **(see illustration)**.
9   Installation is the reverse of removal.

Glove box

Refer to illustrations 24.11 and 24.12
10   Open the glove box door.
11   Detach the glove box bin by pushing on the right side until the door stop clears the opening **(see illustration)**.
12   Press on the stem of the retaining strap button and remove the strap. Lift the glove box bin from the hinges and remove it from the vehicle **(see illustration)**.
13   Installation is the reverse of removal.

25   Instrument panel - removal and installation

Refer to illustrations 25.1, 25.7, 25.8, 25.10, 25.11, 25.12a, 25.12b, 25.13a and 25.13b
Warning: *These models are equipped with an airbag. The airbag is armed and can deploy (inflate) anytime the battery is connected. To prevent accidental deployment (and possible injury), disconnect the negative battery cable(s) whenever working near airbag components. After the battery is disconnected, wait at least 2 minutes before beginning work (the system has a back-up capacitor that must fully discharge). For more information see Chapter 12.*

1   Remove the right and left side cowl trim panels **(see illustration)**.
2   Remove the knee blocker, cup holder and ashtray (see Section 24).
3   Remove instrument cluster bezel (see Section 23). Remove the instrument cluster (see Chapter 12).

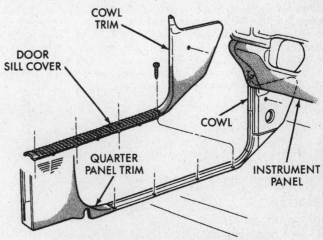

25.1 Cowl trim and door sill installation details

11

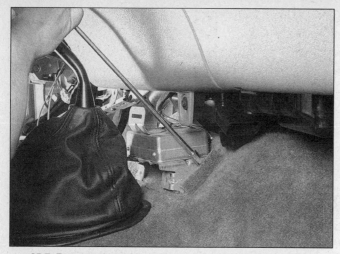

25.7 Remove the airbag control module mounting screws

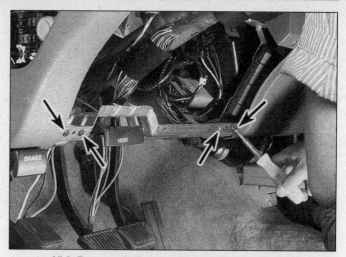

25.8 Remove the lower left side instrument panel support screws (arrows)

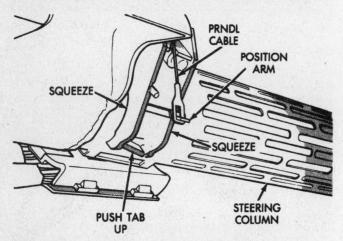

25.10 Detach the PRNDL cable from the position arm, push the cable retainer tab up, squeeze the sides together and remove the retainer

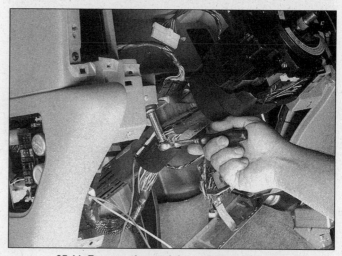

25.11 Remove the retaining nuts and lower the steering column down

4   Remove the screws and detach hood release and parking brake handles from the instrument panel.
5   Remove steering column covers (see Section 26).
6   Disconnect the electrical connector from the multi-function switch.

7   Remove the airbag control module mounting screws **(see illustration)**. Disconnect the module electrical connector, remove the module from the vehicle and store it in a safe place.

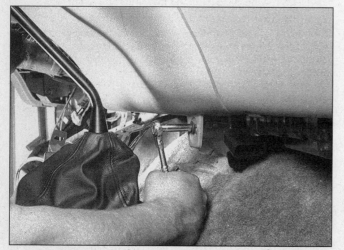

25.12a Remove the bolts along the lower edge of the instrument panel

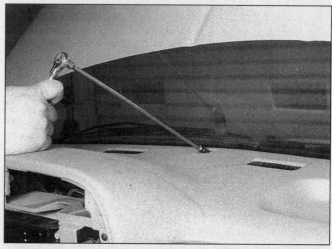

25.12b Use a socket and extension to reach the bolts along the top edge of the instrument panel

25.13a Loosen the hinge bolts at each end of the instrument panel

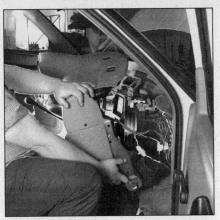

25.13b Rotate the instrument panel back and lift it off the hinge bolts

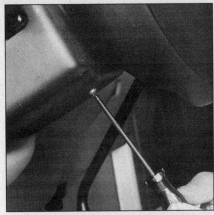

26.1a The steering column cover is retained by Torx-head screws, remove the screws . . .

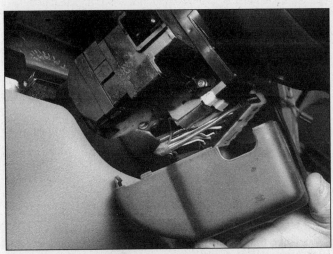

26.1b . . . and detach the lower steering column cover

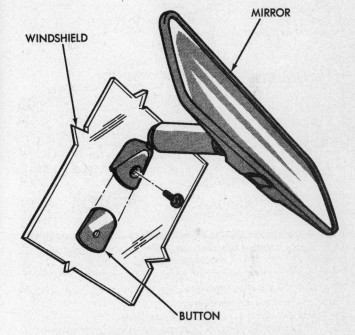

27.1 Windshield mounted mirror installation details

8   Remove the screws and detach the lower left side instrument panel support **(see illustration)**.

9   Disconnect the airbag connector, located under the left side of the instrument panel.

10   On column shift models, pull the shift selector indicator (PRNDL) cable down and detach it from the position arm **(see illustration)**. Remove the cable retainer.

11   Remove the steering column retaining nuts **(see illustration)**. Lower the column down and allow it to rest on the seat. If necessary, loosen the toe-plate nuts.

12   Remove the bolts along the bottom and top edges of the instrument panel **(see illustrations)**.

13   Loosen the pivot bolts at each end, then rotate the interment panel back and lift it off the pivot bolts **(see illustrations)**.

14   Disconnect any remaining electrical connectors. Disconnect the heater/air conditioning vacuum harness from the control panel and disconnect the temperature control cable from the heater core housing.

15   Remove the instrument panel from the vehicle.

16   Installation is the reverse of removal.

26   Steering column covers - removal and installation

Refer to illustrations 26.1a and 26.1b

Warning: *These models are equipped with an airbag. The airbag is armed and can deploy (inflate) anytime the battery is connected. To prevent accidental deployment (and possible injury), disconnect the*

negative battery cable(s) whenever working near airbag components. After the battery is disconnected, wait at least 2 minutes before beginning work (the system has a back-up capacitor that must fully discharge). For more information see Chapter 12.

1   Remove the screws and detach the lower half of the steering column cover **(see illustrations)**.

2   Unscrew the steering column tilt lever (if equipped) and remove the upper half of the cover.

3   Installation is the reverse of removal.

27   Rear view mirrors - removal and installation

Refer to illustrations 27.1, 27.5 and 27.7

Windshield mounted mirror

1   Use a Phillips-head screwdriver to remove the set screw, then slide the mirror up off the button on the windshield **(see illustration)**.

2   Installation is the reverse of removal.

11

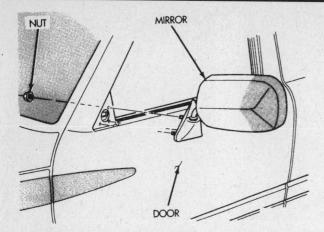

27.5 Standard door-mounted mirror installation details

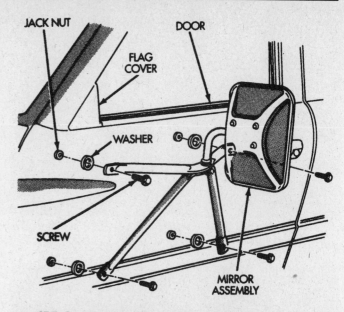

27.7 Camper-style mirror assembly installation details

Standard door-mounted mirror

3   Remove the door trim panel (see Section 12).
4   On power mirrors, unplug the electrical connector.
5   Remove the nuts and detach the mirror from the door **(see illustration)**.
6   Installation is the reverse of removal.

Camper-style mirror

7   Remove the bolts and detach the mirror assembly from the door **(see illustration)**.
8   Installation is the reverse of removal.

28   Cowl grille - removal and installation

Refer to illustrations 28.3a and 28.3b
1   Mark the position of the windshield wiper blades on the windshield with a wax marking pencil.
2   Remove the wiper arms.
3   Remove the plastic cowl grille retainers, disconnect the windshield washer hoses and detach the cowl grille from the vehicle **(see illustrations)**.
4   Installation is the reverse of removal. Make sure to align the wiper blades with the marks made during removal.

29   Seats - removal and installation

Refer to illustrations 29.2a and 29.2b
1   Remove the center console and seat cushion (see Section 20).

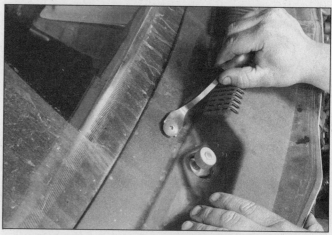

28.3a Using a trim panel clip removal tool, pry off the plastic cowl grille fasteners

2   Remove the seat retaining bolts and nuts, then lift the seat from the vehicle **(see illustrations)**.
3   Installation is the reverse of removal.

28.3b Detach the washer hose from the cowl grille

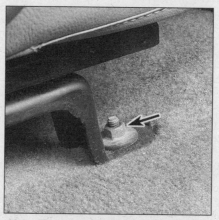

29.2a The seats are attached to the floor with either a nut . . .

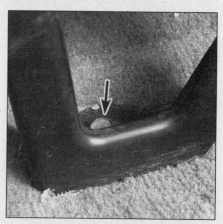

29.2b . . . or a bolt at each corner

Chapter 12
Chassis electrical system

Contents

1 General information

The electrical system is a 12-volt, negative ground type. Power for the lights and all electrical accessories is supplied by a lead/acid-type battery which is charged by the alternator.

This Chapter covers repair and service procedures for the various electrical components not associated with the engine. Information on the battery, alternator, distributor and starter motor can be found in Chapter 5.

It should be noted that when portions of the electrical system are serviced, the negative cable(s) should be disconnected from the battery(ies) to prevent electrical shorts and/or fires.

2 Electrical troubleshooting - general information

A typical electrical circuit consists of an electrical component, any switches, relays, motors, fuses, fusible links or circuit breakers related to that component and the wiring and connectors that link the component to both the battery and the chassis. To help you pinpoint an electrical circuit problem, wiring diagrams are included at the end of this book.

Before tackling any troublesome electrical circuit, first study the appropriate wiring diagrams to get a complete understanding of what makes up that individual circuit. Trouble spots, for instance, can often be narrowed down by noting if other components related to the circuit

12

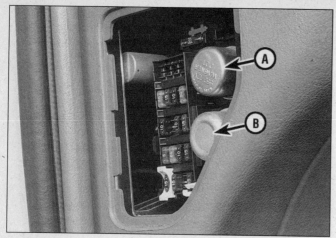

3.1a The fuse block is located in the left end of the instrument panel under a cover - it also contains the hazard (A) and turn signal (B) flasher units

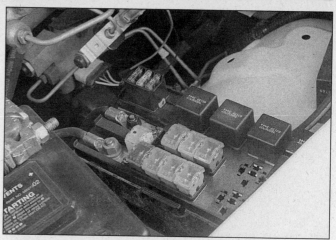

3.1b The power distribution center in the engine compartment contains fuses and relays

are operating properly. If several components or circuits fail at one time, chances are the problem is in a fuse or ground connection, because several circuits are often routed through the same fuse and ground connections.

Electrical problems usually stem from simple causes, such as loose or corroded connections, a blown fuse, a melted fusible link or a bad relay. Visually inspect the condition of all fuses, wires and connections in a problem circuit before troubleshooting it.

If testing instruments are going to be utilized, use the diagrams to plan ahead of time where you will make the necessary connections in order to accurately pinpoint the trouble spot.

The basic tools needed for electrical troubleshooting include a circuit tester or voltmeter (a 12-volt bulb with a set of test leads can also be used), a continuity tester, which includes a bulb, battery and set of test leads, and a jumper wire, preferably with a circuit breaker incorporated, which can be used to bypass electrical components. Before attempting to locate a problem with test instruments, use the wiring diagram(s) to decide where to make the connections.

Voltage checks

Voltage checks should be performed if a circuit is not functioning properly. Connect one lead of a circuit tester to either the negative battery terminal or a known good ground. Connect the other lead to a connector in the circuit being tested, preferably nearest to the battery or fuse. If the bulb of the tester lights, voltage is present, which means that the part of the circuit between the connector and the battery is problem free. Continue checking the rest of the circuit in the same fashion. When you reach a point at which no voltage is present, the problem lies between that point and the last test point with voltage. Most of the time the problem can be traced to a loose connection. **Note:** *Keep in mind that some circuits receive voltage only when the ignition key is in the Accessory or Run position.*

Finding a short

One method of finding shorts in a circuit is to remove the fuse and connect a test light or voltmeter in its place to the fuse terminals. There should be no voltage present in the circuit. Move the wiring harness from side-to-side while watching the test light. If the bulb goes on, there is a short to ground somewhere in that area, probably where the insulation has rubbed through. The same test can be performed on each component in the circuit, even a switch.

Ground check

Perform a ground test to check whether a component is properly grounded. Disconnect the battery and connect one lead of a self-powered test light, known as a continuity tester, to a known good ground. Connect the other lead to the wire or ground connection being tested.

If the bulb goes on, the ground is good. If the bulb does not go on, the ground is not good.

Continuity check

A continuity check is done to determine if there are any breaks in a circuit - if it is passing electricity properly. With the circuit off (no power in the circuit), a self-powered continuity tester can be used to check the circuit. Connect the test leads to both ends of the circuit (or to the "power" end and a good ground), and if the test light comes on the circuit is passing current properly. If the light doesn't come on, there is a break somewhere in the circuit. The same procedure can be used to test a switch, by connecting the continuity tester to the switch terminals. With the switch turned On, the test light should come on.

Finding an open circuit

When diagnosing for possible open circuits, it is often difficult to locate them by sight because oxidation or terminal misalignment are hidden by the connectors. Merely wiggling a connector on a sensor or in the wiring harness may correct the open circuit condition. Remember this when an open circuit is indicated when troubleshooting a circuit. Intermittent problems may also be caused by oxidized or loose connections.

Electrical troubleshooting is simple if you keep in mind that all electrical circuits are basically electricity running from the battery, through the wires, switches, relays, fuses and fusible links to each electrical component (light bulb, motor, etc.) and to ground, from which it is passed back to the battery. Any electrical problem is an interruption in the flow of electricity to and from the battery.

---

3   Fuses - general information

Refer to illustrations 3.1a, 3.1b and 3.3

The electrical circuits of the vehicle are protected by a combination of fuses, circuit breakers and fusible links. The fuse block is located in the end of the instrument panel under a cover **(see illustration)**. There is also a fuse and relay block, called the power distribution center, located on the right side of the engine compartment **(see illustration)**.

Each of the fuses is designed to protect a specific circuit, and the various circuits are identified on the fuse panel itself.

Miniaturized fuses are employed in the fuse block. These compact fuses, with blade terminal design, allow fingertip removal and replacement. If an electrical component fails, always check the fuse first. A blown fuse is easily detected with a test light - if voltage is available on one side of the fuse but not the other, it's blown (the circuit must be energized for this check). You can also visually inspect the element for evidence of damage.

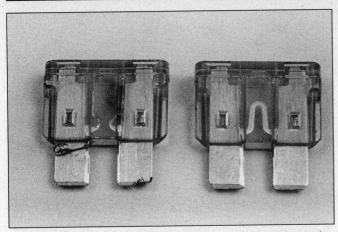

3.3 The fuse on the left is blown, the one on the right is good

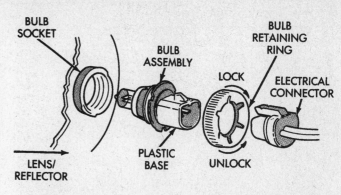

8.4 Disconnect the connector and unscrew the plastic collar, then grasp the bulb assembly and pull it out of the housing

Be sure to replace blown fuses with the correct type. Fuses of different ratings are physically interchangeable, but only fuses of the proper rating should be used. Replacing a fuse with one of a higher or lower value than specified is not recommended. Each electrical circuit needs a specific amount of protection. The amperage value of each fuse is molded into the fuse body.

If the replacement fuse immediately fails, don't replace it again until the cause of the problem is isolated and corrected. In most cases, the cause will be a short circuit in the wiring caused by a broken or deteriorated wire.

4 Fusible links - general information

1   Some circuits are protected by fusible links. The links are used in circuits which are not ordinarily fused, such as the ignition circuit.
2   The fusible links on these models are similar to fuses in that they can be visually checked to determine if they are melted. The fusible links are located in the power distribution block in the engine compartment.
3   To replace a fusible link, first disconnect the negative cable from the battery. Disconnect the burned-out link and replace it with a new one (available from your dealer or auto parts store). Always determine the cause for the overload which melted the fusible link before installing a new one.

5 Circuit breakers - general information

Circuit breakers protect components such as power windows, power door locks and headlights. Some circuit breakers are located in the fuse box.

Some circuit breakers reset automatically, so an electrical overload in a circuit breaker protected system will cause the circuit to fail momentarily, then come back on. If the circuit does not come back on, check it immediately. Once the condition is corrected, the circuit breaker will resume its normal function.

6 Relays - general information

Several electrical accessories in the vehicle use relays to transmit the electrical signal to the component. If the relay is defective, that component will not operate properly.

The various relays are grouped together in the distribution center, as well as in other locations **(see illustration 3.1b)**.

If a faulty relay is suspected, it can be removed and tested by a dealer service department or an auto repair shop. Defective relays must be replaced as a unit.

7 Turn signal and hazard flashers - check and replacement

Turn signal flasher

1   The turn signal flasher, a small canister-shaped unit located in the fuse block, flashes the turn signals **(see illustration 3.1a)**.
2   When the flasher unit is functioning properly, an audible click can be heard during its operation. If the turn signals fail on one side or the other and the flasher unit does not make its characteristic clicking sound, a faulty turn signal bulb is indicated.
3   If both turn signals fail to blink, the problem may be due to a blown fuse, a faulty flasher unit, a broken switch or a loose or open connection. If a quick check of the fuse box indicates that the turn signal fuse has blown, check the wiring for a short before installing a new fuse.
4   To remove the flasher, simply pull it out of the fuse block.
5   Make sure that the replacement unit is identical to the original. Compare the old one to the new one before installing it.
6   Installation is the reverse of removal.

Hazard flasher

7   The hazard flasher, a small canister-shaped unit located in the fuse block, flashes all four turn signals simultaneously when activated.
8   The hazard flasher is checked in a fashion similar to the turn signal flasher (see Steps 2 and 3).
9   To replace the hazard flasher, pull it from the fuse block **(see illustration 3.1a)**.
10   Make sure the replacement unit is identical to the one it replaces. Compare the old one to the new one before installing it.
11   Installation is the reverse of removal.

8 Headlight bulb - replacement

Refer to illustration 8.4

Warning: *Halogen bulbs are gas-filled and under pressure and may shatter if the surface is scratched or the bulb is dropped. Wear eye protection and handle the bulbs carefully, grasping only the base whenever possible. Don't touch the surface of the bulb with your fingers because the oil from your skin could cause it to overheat and fail prematurely. If you do touch the bulb surface, clean it with rubbing alcohol.*

1   Disconnect the negative cable from the battery.
2   Open the hood.
3   Remove the battery.
4   Reach behind the headlight assembly, disconnect the electrical connector, unscrew the collar, grasp the bulb base and pull it straight out of the headlight housing **(see illustration)**.
5   Insert the new bulb into the housing, secure it with the collar and plug in the connector.

12

9   Headlights - adjustment

Refer to illustrations 9.1 and 9.3

Warning: *The headlights must be aimed correctly. If adjusted incorrectly, they could temporarily blind the driver of an oncoming vehicle and cause an accident or seriously reduce your ability to see the road. The headlights should be checked for proper aim every 12 months and any time a new headlight is installed or front end body work is performed. The following procedure is only an interim step to provide temporary adjustment until the headlights can be adjusted by a properly equipped shop.*

1   Headlights have two spring-loaded adjusting screws **(see illustration)**.

2   This procedure requires a blank wall, masking tape and a level floor.

3   Position masking tape vertically on the wall in reference to the vehicle centerline and the centerlines of both headlights **(see illustration)**.

4   Position a horizontal tape line in reference to the centerline of all the headlights. **Note:** *It may be easier to position the tape on the wall with the vehicle parked only a few inches away.*

5   Adjustment should be made with the vehicle parked 25 feet from the wall, sitting level, the gas tank full and no unusually heavy load in the vehicle.

6   Starting with the low beam adjustment, position the high intensity zone so it's two inches below the horizontal line and two inches to the right of the headlight vertical line. Adjustment is made by turning the top adjusting screw clockwise to raise the beam and counterclockwise to lower the beam. The adjusting screw on the side should be used in the same manner to move the beam left or right.

7   With the high beams on, the high-intensity zone should be vertically centered with the exact center just below the horizontal line. **Note:** *It may not be possible to position the headlight aim exactly for both high and low beams. If a compromise must be made, keep in mind that the low beams are the most used and have the greatest effect on driver safety.*

8   Have the headlights adjusted by a dealer service department or service station at the earliest opportunity.

10   Composite headlight housing - removal and installation

Refer to illustration 10.3

Warning: *These models are equipped with an airbag. The airbag is armed and can deploy (inflate) anytime the battery is connected. To prevent accidental deployment (and possible injury), disconnect the negative battery cable whenever working near airbag components. After the battery is disconnected, wait at least 2 minutes before beginning work (the system has a back-up capacitor that must fully discharge). For more information see Section 23.*

1   Open the hood.

2   Remove the park and turn signal lamp (see Section 11).

3   Remove the retaining screws, pull the housing out and disconnect the electrical connector **(see illustration)**.

4   Installation is the reverse of removal. After you're done, check the headlight adjustment (see Section 9).

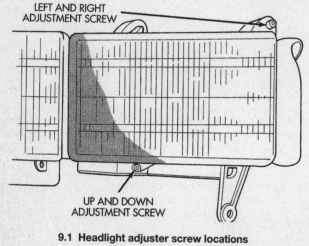

9.1   Headlight adjuster screw locations

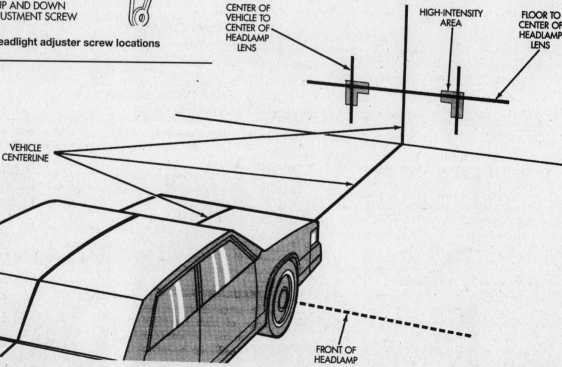

9.3   Headlight adjustment screen details

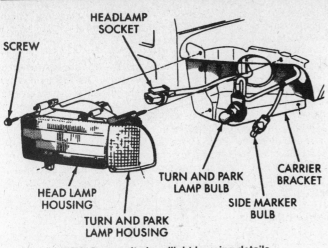

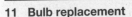

10.3 Composite headlight housing details

11.1 Remove the Phillips head screw and detach the turn signal light housing

bulb straight out **(see illustrations).**
3   Installation is the reverse of removal.

11 Bulb replacement

Turn signal/parking/side marker lights

Refer to illustrations 11.1, 11.2a and 11.2b
1   Remove the screw that secures the turn signal/parking light housing, then rotate the housing out for access to the bulb holders **(see illustration).**
2   Turn the bulb holder counterclockwise to remove it and pull the

Tail light

Refer to illustrations 11.4a, 11.4b, 11.5a and 11.5b
4   Remove the screws and detach the tail light housing **(see illustrations).**
5   Rotate the bulb holder counterclockwise and remove it from the back of the housing **(see illustration).** Press the tabs and pull the bulb from the holder **(see illustration).**
6   Installation is the reverse of removal.

11.2a Rotate the bulb holder and lift it out

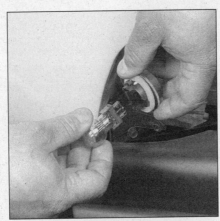

11.2b Remove the bulb by pulling straight out

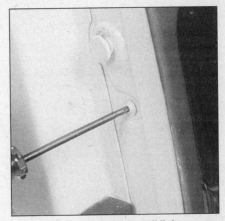

11.4a Remove the tail light housing screws

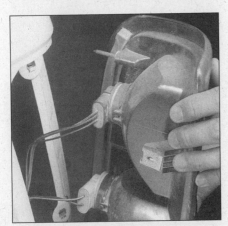

11.4b Detach the tail light housing by pulling it straight back

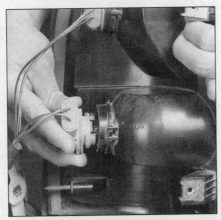

11.5a Rotate the bulb holder and pull it out to remove it

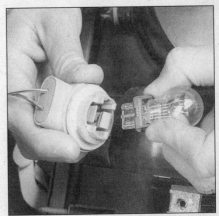

11.5b Squeeze the clips and pull the bulb straight out of the holder

12

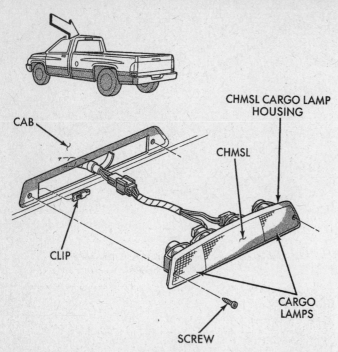

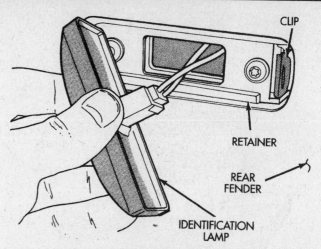

11.7 Remove the screws and pull the Center High-Mounted Stop Light housing out

Center High-Mounted Stop Light (CHMSL)/cargo lamp

Refer to illustration 11.7

7   Standing in the truck bed, remove the two Phillips-head screws and withdraw the lamp housing from the cab **(see illustration)**.
8   Facing the cab, rotate the bulb holder 1/4-turn clockwise and withdraw it away from you, then replace the bulb by pulling it straight from the holder.
9   Installation is the reverse of removal.

Side identification lamp

Refer to illustration 11.11

10   The side identification lamp must be replaced as a unit.
11   Use a small screwdriver detach the housing, then disconnect the electrical connector **(see illustration)**.
12   Installation is the reverse of removal.

11.11 Pry out the side identification lamp with a small screwdriver

Instrument cluster lights

Refer to illustration 11.14

13   To gain access to the instrument cluster illumination lights, the instrument cluster will have to be removed (see Section 16). The bulbs can then be removed and replaced from the rear of the cluster.
14   Rotate the bulb counterclockwise to remove it **(see illustration)**.
15   Installation is the reverse of removal.

License plate light

Refer to illustration 11.16

16   Remove the Torx-head screws, detach the bulb cover, then pull the bulb straight out of the holder **(see illustration)**.
17   Installation is the reverse of removal.

Interior lights

Refer to illustrations 11.18 and 11.20

18   Pry the dome light lens off, then replace the bulb by pulling it straight out **(see illustration)**.
19   Installation is the reverse of removal.
20   Use a small flat-bladed screwdriver to the pry off the overhead console light lens **(see illustration)**. Detach bulb from the terminals. It may be necessary to pry the bulb out - if this is the case, pry only on the ends of the bulb (otherwise the glass may shatter).
21   Seat the new bulb in the terminals. Hold the lens level and press it into place.

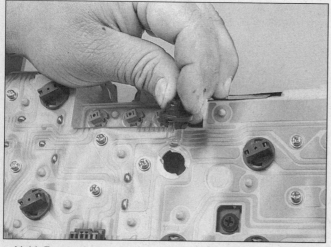

11.14 Rotate the instrument cluster bulb housing and lift it out

11.16 Remove the screws and detach the license bulb cover for access to the lamp bulbs

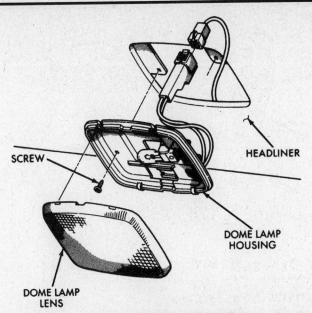

11.18 Dome lamp bulb details

SCREW

HEADLINER

DOME LAMP
HOUSING

DOME LAMP
LENS

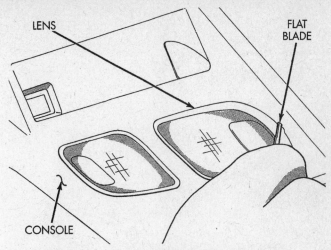

LENS

FLAT
BLADE

CONSOLE

11.20 Pry out the overhead console light lens with
a small screwdriver

12.2a Remove the bolts and pull the radio out

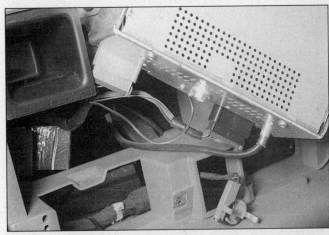

12.2b Disconnect the connectors from the back of the radio

12 Radio and speakers - removal and installation

Refer to illustrations 12.2a and 12.2b
Warning: *These models are equipped with an airbag. The airbag is armed and can deploy (inflate) anytime the battery is connected. To prevent accidental deployment (and possible injury), disconnect the negative battery cable whenever working near airbag components. After the battery is disconnected, wait at least 2 minutes before beginning work (the system has a back-up capacitor that must fully discharge). For more information see Section 23.*

Radio

1　Remove the instrument panel center bezel (see Chapter 11).
2　Remove the mounting bolts, pull the radio out of the instrument panel, disconnect the connectors, then remove it from the vehicle **(see illustrations)**.
3　Installation is the reverse of removal.

Door Speakers

Refer to illustration 12.5
4　Remove the door trim panel (Chapter 11).
5　Remove the screws and detach the speaker **(see illustration)**. Pull the speaker out of the door, disconnect the electrical connector and remove the speaker from the vehicle.

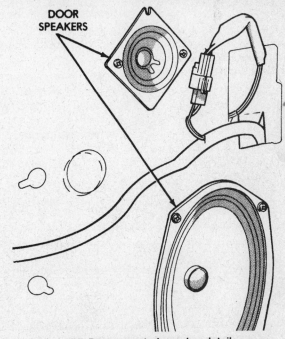

DOOR
SPEAKERS

12.5 Door-mounted speaker details

12

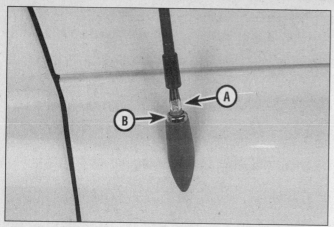

13.2 Pull the plastic cover up out of the way then unscrew the antenna mast (A) with a small wrench and remove the nut (B) with needle-nose pliers

13 Antenna - removal and installation

Refer to illustration 13.2

1   Disconnect the negative battery cable.
2   Use a small open-end wrench to unscrew the antenna mast, then remove the cap nut and lift off the upper adapter and gasket **(see illustration)**. Be very careful - the tools could slip and scratch the fender. It's a good idea to surround the base of the antenna with rags to prevent against scratching.
3   Working in the passenger compartment. remove the five screws and detach the right side kick panel/sill cover. Detach the radio end of the antenna cable. Connect a long piece of string or thin wire to the antenna cable.
4   Install the antenna mast temporarily and push the antenna down far enough so that you can grasp the cable end through the fender opening.
5   Push the cable through the fender, into the engine compartment, then pull it from the passenger compartment.

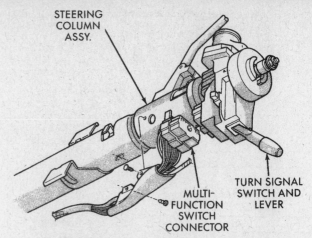

14.2 Disconnect the multi-function switch connector

6   Push the new cable end up through the fender, then install the adapter, cap nut and antenna mast.
7   Connect the string or wire to the radio end of the new cable and pull it through into the passenger compartment and connect it.
8   Install the right side kick panel/sill cover and connect the battery negative cable.

14 Multi-function switch - check and replacement

Warning: *These models are equipped with an airbag. The airbag is armed and can deploy (inflate) anytime the battery is connected. To prevent accidental deployment (and possible injury), disconnect the negative battery cable whenever working near airbag components. After the battery is disconnected, wait at least 2 minutes before beginning work (the system has a back-up capacitor that must fully discharge). For more information see Section 23.*

1   The multi-function switch is located on the left side of the steering column. It incorporates the turn signal, headlight dimmer and windshield wiper/washer functions into one switch.

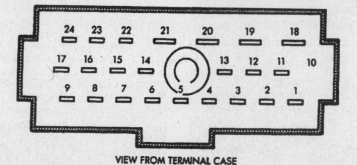

VIEW FROM TERMINAL CASE

SWITCH POSITIONS		
TURN SIGNAL	**HAZARD WARNING**	**CONTINUITY BETWEEN**
NEUTRAL	OFF	12 AND 14 AND 15
LEFT	OFF	15 AND 16 AND 17
LEFT	OFF	12 AND 14
LEFT	OFF	22 AND 23 WITH OPTIONAL CORNER LAMPS
RIGHT	OFF	11 AND 12 AND 17
RIGHT	OFF	14 AND 15
RIGHT	OFF	23 AND 24 WITH OPTIONAL CORNER LAMPS
NEUTRAL	ON	11 AND 12 AND 13 AND 15 AND 16

14.3a Turn signal and hazard flasher terminal guide and continuity chart

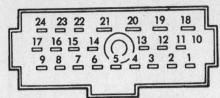

MULTIFUNCTION SWITCH PINS

SWITCH POSITION	CONTINUITY BETWEEN
OFF	PIN 6 AND PIN 7
DELAY	PIN 8 AND PIN 9
	PIN 2 AND PIN 4
	PIN 1 AND PIN 2
	PIN 1 AND PIN 4
LOW	PIN 4 AND PIN 6
HIGH	PIN 4 AND PIN 5
WASH	PIN 3 AND PIN 4

*RESISTANCE AT MAXIMUM DELAY POSITION SHOULD BE BETWEEN 270,000 OHMS AND 330,000 OHMS.

*RESISTANCE AT MINIMUM DELAY POSITION SHOULD BE ZERO WITH OHMMETER SET ON HIGH OHM SCALE.

14.3b Windshield wiper/washer terminal guide and continuity chart

VIEW FROM TERMINAL SIDE

SWITCH POSITION	CONTINUITY BETWEEN
LOW BEAM	18 AND 19
HIGH BEAM	19 AND 20
OPTICAL HORN	20 AND 21

14.3c Headlight dimmer switch terminal guide and continuity chart

Check

Refer to illustrations 14.2, 14.3a, 14.3b and 14.3c

2   Remove the steering column covers and the knee blocker for access (see Chapter 11). Disconnect the multi-function switch connector **(see illustration)**.

3   Use an ohmmeter or self-powered test light and the accompanying diagrams **(see illustrations)** to check for continuity between the switch terminals with the switch in each position.

Replacement

Refer to illustration 14.4

4   Remove the multi-function switch bolts (this will require a special anti-theft Torx head tool), then detach the switch from the steering column **(see illustration)**.

5   Installation is the reverse of removal.

15   Headlight switch - replacement

Refer to illustrations 15.3a, 15.3b and 15.4

Warning: *These models are equipped with an airbag. The airbag is armed and can deploy (inflate) anytime the battery is connected. To*

14.4 Disconnect the multi-function switch electrical connector (A), remove the three Torx-head tamper-proof screws (B) and detach the switch

prevent accidental deployment (and possible injury), disconnect the negative battery cable(s) whenever working near airbag components. After the battery is disconnected, wait at least 2 minutes before beginning work (the system has a back-up capacitor that must fully discharge). For more information see Section 23.

1   Disconnect the negative cable(s) at the battery(ies).

2   Remove the instrument cluster bezel (see Chapter 11).

3   Remove the retaining screws, pull the switch out and disconnect the electrical connector **(see illustrations)**.

15.3a Remove the headlight switch retaining screws (arrows)

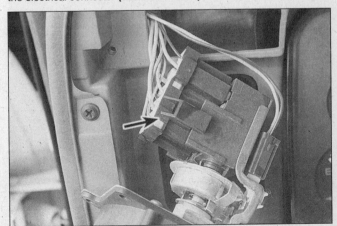

15.3b Disconnect the electrical connector (arrow)

12

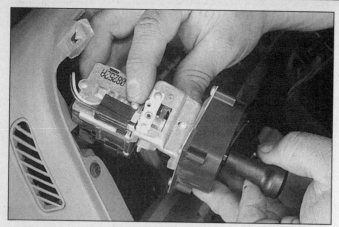

15.4 Depress the release button on the bottom of the switch, then withdraw the knob and shaft

4   Press the release button on the bottom of the switch and withdraw knob and shaft **(see illustration)**.
5   Installation is the reverse of removal.

16   Instrument cluster - removal and installation

Refer to illustrations 16.3, 16.4a and 16.4b
Warning: *These models are equipped with an airbag. The airbag is armed and can deploy (inflate) anytime the battery is connected. To*

16.4a Use a Phillips-head screwdriver to remove the four cluster retaining screws

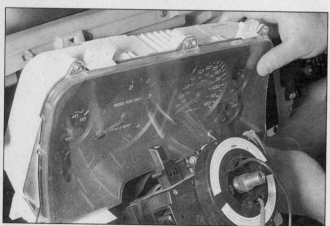

16.4b Pull the cluster out and disconnect the connectors

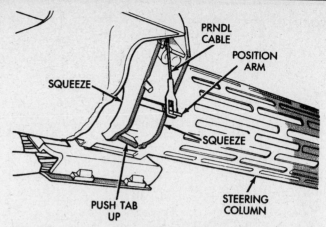

16.3 Disconnect the gear indicator (PRNDL) cable and retainer from the steering column

prevent accidental deployment (and possible injury), disconnect the negative battery cable(s) whenever working near airbag components. After the battery is disconnected, wait at least 2 minutes before beginning work (the system has a back-up capacitor that must fully discharge). For more information see Section 23.
1   Disconnect the negative cable(s) from the battery(ies).
2   Remove the instrument cluster bezel and the knee blocker (see Chapter 11).
3   Remove the gear indicator cable from the position arm, push the release tab on the retainer up, squeeze the sides together and remove the retainer from the steering column **(see illustration)**.
4   Remove the screws and pull the cluster out for access, reach behind the cluster and disconnect the electrical connectors and remove the cluster **(see illustrations)**.
5   Installation is the reverse of removal.

17   Horn - check and replacement

Check

1   Remove the cover from the power distribution center **(see illustration 3.1b)** and check the horn fuses and relay, replacing any faulty components.
2   Disconnect the electrical connector from the horn.
3   Have an assistant press the horn button and use a voltmeter to make sure there is battery voltage at the dark green/red wire of the connector. If the relay is good and there's no voltage at the horn, the wire (which leads to the relay) has a fault.

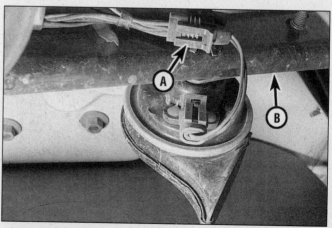

17.6 Disconnect the horn connector (A) and remove the retaining bolt (B)

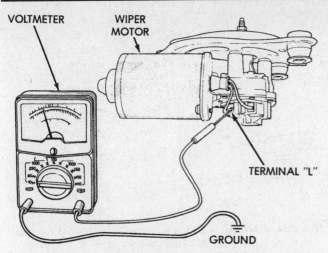

18.4 Check for voltage between the windshield wiper motor L terminal and ground

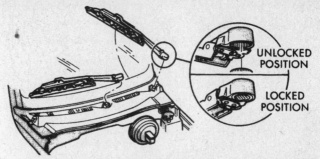

18.8 Use a screwdriver to unlock the wiper arm, the grasp the arm and use a rocking motion to detach it from the step

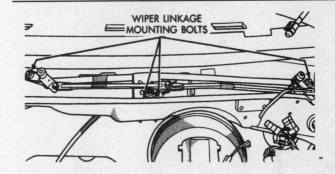

18.10 Remove the wiper linkage mounting bolts

4   Use an ohmmeter to measure the resistance between the wiring connector black wire and a good ground. The should be zero ohms.
5   If there's voltage at the horn and the wiring circuits are good, the horn is faulty and must be replaced.

Replacement

Refer to illustration 17.6
6   Disconnect the electrical connector, remove the mounting bolt and detach the horn **(see illustration)**.
7   Installation is the reverse of removal.

18   Windshield wiper motor - check and replacement

Refer to illustrations 18.4, 18.8, 18.10, 18.11 and 18.12

Check

1   If the wiper motor doesn't run at all, first check for a blown fuse (see Section 3).
2   Check the wiper switch (see Section 14).
3   Turn the ignition switch and wiper switch On.
4   Connect a voltmeter between the terminal L of the wiper motor and ground **(see illustration)**. If there is less than one volt, move the negative test lead to the battery negative pole. If the voltage increases, there is a bad ground connection at the motor mount.
5   If, after a ground check and repair there is still no voltage, there is

an open circuit in the wiper switch or harness.
6   A voltage of less than three volts means the motor is faulty and must be replaced.

Replacement

7   Disconnect the negative cable from the battery.
8   Mark the positions of the wiper arms on the windshield, then remove the wiper arms **(see illustration)**.
9   Remove the cowl grille (see Chapter 11).
10   Working through the cowl opening, remove the wiper linkage mounting bolts **(see illustration)**.
11   Remove the assembly, turn it over and disconnect the wiper motor electrical connector **(see illustration)**.
12   Pry off the drive link with a screwdriver, hold the motor drive crank with a wrench, remove the nut and detach the crank, then remove the three screws and detach the motor **(see illustration)**.
13   Installation is the reverse of removal.

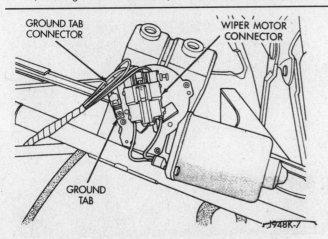

18.11 Disconnect the electrical connector from the back of the motor

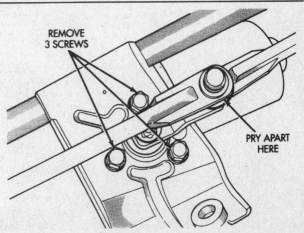

18.12 Pry off the links, remove the nut and detach the wiper arm, then remove the three bolts and detach the motor

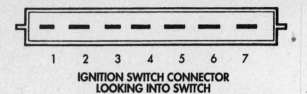

IGNITION SWITCH CONNECTOR
LOOKING INTO SWITCH

SWITCH POSITION	CONTINUITY BETWEEN
START	PIN 3 AND GROUND PIN 1 AND PIN 7 PIN 2 AND PIN 7
RUN	PIN 4 AND PIN 5 PIN 2 AND PIN 7 PIN 6 AND PIN 7
ACC	PIN 6 AND PIN 7

19.3 Ignition switch terminal guide and continuity chart

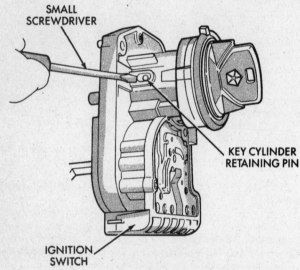

19.8a On 1994 models, push the retaining pin in to unseat the lock cylinder

19   Ignition switch/key lock cylinder - check and replacement

Refer to illustrations 19.3, 19.7, 19.8a, 19.8b, 19.9a, 19.9b and 19.10
Warning: *These models are equipped with an airbag. The airbag is armed and can deploy (inflate) anytime the battery is connected. To prevent accidental deployment (and possible injury), disconnect the negative battery cable(s) whenever working near airbag components. After the battery is disconnected, wait at least 2 minutes before beginning work (the system has a back-up capacitor that must fully discharge). For more information see Section 23.*

1   The ignition switch is located on the right side of the steering column and is held in place by three Torx T-20 tamper-proof screws which require a special tool (available at auto parts stores) for removal.

Check

2   Remove the switch (see Steps 5 and 6).
3   Use an ohmmeter or self-powered test light and check for continuity between the indicated switch terminals in each switch position **(see illustration)**.
4   If the switch does not have the correct continuity, replace it.

19.7 The ignition switch is held in place by three Torx-head tamper-proof screws (arrows) (the lower screw is located under the cover)

19.8b On 1995 and later models, remove the tamper-proof screw

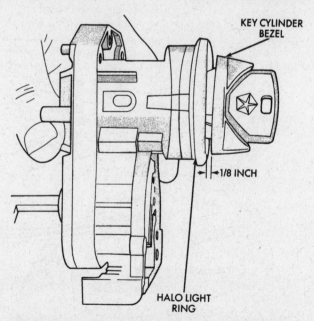

19.9a The lock cylinder will protrude about 1/8-inch from the switch once it's unseated - don't try to remove it until you rotate it to the Lock position and remove the key

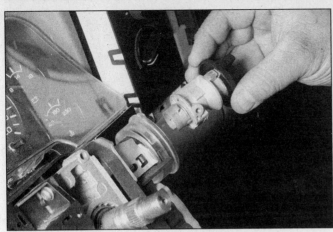

19.9b With the lock cylinder in the Lock position, it will pull out easily

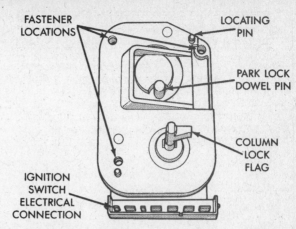

19.10 Make sure the switch column lock flag is parallel with the electrical connection before installation

Replacement

5   Disconnect the negative battery cable(s).

6   Remove the steering column covers (see Chapter 11).

7   Remove the tamper-proof screws and detach the switch from the steering column. Disconnect the electrical connector and remove the switch **(see illustration)**.

8   If it's necessary to remove the lock cylinder, insert the key and turn it to the Lock position. On 1994 models, press the retaining pin in with a small screwdriver until it is flush with the surface **(see illustration)**. On 1995 and later models, the retaining pin is replaced with a theft-proof screw which must be removed to release the lock cylinder **(see illustration)**.

9   Turn the key clockwise to the Off position, which will unseat the lock cylinder, but don't try to remove it yet **(see illustration)**. With the cylinder unseated, rotate the key counterclockwise to the Lock position, remove the key, then remove the lock cylinder from the ignition switch **(see illustration)**.

10   Installation is the reverse of removal. As the switch is engaged to the column park-slider linkage, make sure the column lock flag on the switch is parallel with the electrical connectors **(see illustration)**.

11   Insert the lock cylinder in the Lock position until it bottoms in the switch. While pushing the lock cylinder in, insert the key and turn it clockwise to the Run position. On 1995 and later models, install the theft-proof retaining screw.

20 Cruise control system - description and check

Refer to illustrations 20.6 and 20.7

1   The cruise control system maintains vehicle speed with a computer-controlled vacuum actuated servo motor located in the engine compartment, which is connected to the throttle linkage by a cable. Listed below are some general procedures that may be used to locate common problems.

2   Locate and check the fuse (see Section 3).

3   Have an assistant operate the brake lights while you check their operation (voltage from the brake light switch deactivates the cruise control).

4   If the brake lights don't come on or don't shut off, correct the problem and retest the cruise control.

5   Inspect the control linkage between the speed control servo and the throttle linkage.

6   Visually inspect the vacuum hoses and wiring harness connected to the cruise control servo and replace as necessary **(see illustration)**.

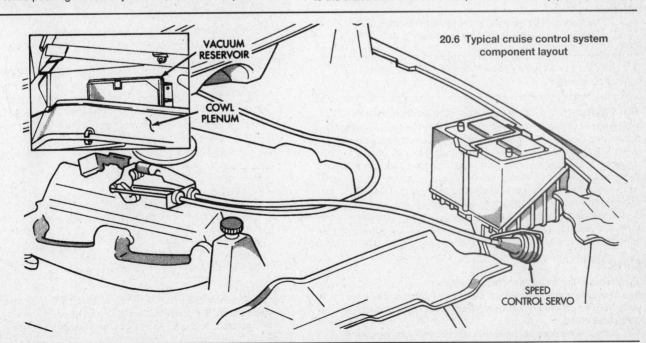

20.6 Typical cruise control system component layout

7   The cruise control system relies on the vehicle speed sensor pickup is located at the transmission. Inspect the sensor wiring for damage **(see illustration)**. Refer to Chapter 6 for more information on the speed sensor.

8   Test drive the vehicle to determine if the cruise control is now working. If it isn't, take it to a dealer service department or an automotive electrical specialist for further diagnosis and repair.

21   Power door lock system - description and check

1   The power door lock system operates the door lock actuators mounted in each door. The system consists of the switches, actuators, relays and associated wiring. Diagnosis can usually be limited to simple checks of the wiring connections and actuators for minor faults which can be easily repaired.

2   Power door lock systems are operated by bi-directional solenoids located in the doors. The lock switches have two operating positions: Lock and Unlock. These switches activate a relay which in turn connects voltage to the door lock solenoids. Depending on which way the relay is activated, it reverses polarity, allowing the two sides of the circuit to be used alternately as the feed (positive) and ground side.

3   Always check the fuse first (see Section 3).

4   Operate the door lock switches in both directions (Lock and Unlock) with the engine off. Listen for the faint click of the relay operating.

5   If there's no click, check for voltage at the switches. If no voltage is present, check the wiring between the fuse block and the switches for shorts and opens.

6   If voltage is present but no click is heard, test the switch for continuity. Replace it if there's no continuity in both switch positions.

7   If the switch has continuity but the relay doesn't click, check the wiring between the switch and relay for continuity. Repair the wiring if there's no continuity.

8   If the relay is receiving voltage from the switch but is not sending voltage to the solenoids, check for a bad ground at the relay case. If the relay case is grounding properly, replace the relay.

9   If only one lock solenoid operates, remove the trim panel from the affected door (see Chapter 11) and check for voltage at the solenoid while the lock switch is operated. One of the wires should have voltage in the Lock position; the other should have voltage in the Unlock position.

10   If the inoperative solenoid is receiving voltage, replace the solenoid.

11   If the inoperative solenoid isn't receiving voltage, check for an open or short in the wire between the lock solenoid and the relay.

Note: *It's common for wires to break in the portion of the harness between the body and door (opening and closing the door fatigues and eventually breaks the wires).*

22   Power window system - description and check

1   The power window system operates the electric motors mounted in the doors which lower and raise the windows. The system consists of the control switches, the motors, glass mechanisms (regulators) and associated wiring.

2   The windows can be lowered and raised from the master control switch by the driver or by remote switches located at the individual windows. Each window has a separate motor which is reversible. The position of the control switch determines the polarity and therefore the direction of operation. Some systems are equipped with relays that control current flow to the motors.

3   Each motor is equipped with a separate circuit breaker in addition to the fuse or circuit breaker protecting the whole circuit. This prevents one stuck window from disabling the whole system.

4   The power window system will only operate when the ignition switch is ON. In addition, when activated the window lockout switch at the master control switch disables the switches at the passenger's

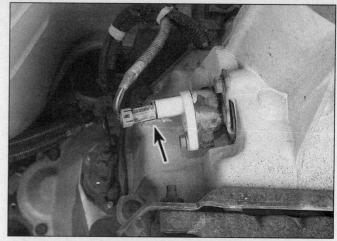

20.7 Check the vehicle speed sensor wiring and electrical connector (arrow) for damage

window also. Always check these items before troubleshooting a window problem.

5   These procedures are general in nature, so if you can't find the problem using them, take the vehicle to a dealer service department.

6   If the power windows don't work at all, check the fuse or circuit breaker.

7   Check the wiring between the switches and fuse panel for continuity. Repair the wiring, if necessary.

8   If only one window is inoperative from the master control switch, try the other control switch at the window. **Note:** *This doesn't apply to the drivers door window.*

9   If the same window works from one switch, but not the other, check the switch for continuity.

10   If the switch tests OK, check for a short or open in the wiring between the affected switch and the window motor.

11   If one window is inoperative from both switches, remove the trim panel from the affected door and check for voltage at the motor while the switch is operated.

12   If voltage is reaching the motor, disconnect the glass from the regulator (see Chapter 11). Move the window up and down by hand while checking for binding and damage. Also check for binding and damage to the regulator. If the regulator is not damaged and the window moves up and down smoothly, replace the motor. If there's binding or damage, lubricate, repair or replace parts, as necessary.

13   If voltage isn't reaching the motor, check the wiring in the circuit for continuity between the switches and motors.

14   Test the windows after you are done to confirm proper repairs.

23   Airbag system - general information

Refer to illustration 23.1

These models are equipped with a Supplemental Restraint System (SRS), more commonly called an airbag system. This system is designed to protect the driver from serious injury in the event of head-on or frontal collision. It consists of an airbag module in the center of the steering wheel, two crash sensors mounted at the front of the vehicle and an Airbag Control Module (ACM) which contains a safing sensor and is located inside the passenger compartment **(see illustration)**.

Airbag module

The airbag module contains a housing incorporating the cushion (airbag) and inflator unit. The inflator assembly is mounted on the back of the housing over a hole through which gas is expelled, inflating the bag almost instantaneously when an electrical signal is sent from the system. The specially wound wire that carries this signal to the module

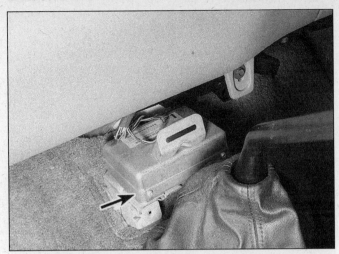

23.1 The airbag control module (arrow) is located under the center of the instrument panel - do not tamper with the yellow connectors attached to it

is called a clockspring. The clockspring is a flat, ribbon-like electrically conductive tape which is wound so it can transmit an electrical signal regardless of steering wheel position.

Sensors

The system has three sensors: two crash sensors at the front of the vehicle mounted along the inner fender panels behind the grille opening reinforcement and a safing sensor in the Airbag Control Module (ACM) located under the instrument panel, on the transmission hump.

The front crash sensors are basically pressure sensitive switches that complete an electrical circuit during an impact of sufficient G force. The electrical signal from the crash sensors is sent to the safing sensor in the ACM, which then completes the circuit and inflates the airbags.

Airbag Control Module (ACM)

The ACM contains the safing sensor, a capacitor that maintains electrical system power if the battery is damaged and an on-board microprocessor which monitors the operation of the system. It checks this system every time the vehicle is started, causing the AIRBAG light to go on, then off, if the system is operating properly. If there is a fault in the system, the light will go on and stay on and the ACM will store fault codes indicating the nature of the fault. If the AIRBAG light does go on and stay on, the vehicle should be taken to your dealer immediately for service.

Disabling the airbag system

Whenever working in the vicinity of the steering wheel, steering column or near other components of the airbag system, the system should be disarmed. To disarm the system perform the following steps:

a) *Turn the ignition switch to the Off position.*
b) *Disconnect the cable from the negative battery terminal (both batteries on diesel models).*
c) *Wait at least two minutes for the backup power supply to be depleted before beginning work.*

Enabling the system

To enable the airbag system, perform the following steps:

a) *Turn the ignition switch to the Off position.*
b) *Connect the cable(s) to the negative battery terminal(s).*
c) *Turn the ignition switch to the On position. Confirm that the airbag warning light glows for 6 to 8 seconds, then goes out, indicating the system is functioning properly.*

24 Power seats - description and check

1   Power seats allow you to adjust the position of the seat with little effort. These models feature a six-way seat that goes forward and backward, up and down and tilts forward and backward. The seats are powered by three reversible motors mounted in one housing that are controlled by switches on the side of the seat. Each switch changes the direction of seat travel by reversing polarity to the drive motor.
2   Diagnosis is a simple matter, using the following procedures.
3   Look under the seat for any object which may be preventing the seat from moving.
4   If the seat won't work at all, check the circuit breaker in the fuse block.
5   With the engine off to reduce the noise level, operate the seat controls in all directions and listen for sound coming from the seat motors.
6   If the motor doesn't work or make noise, check for voltage at the motor while an assistant operates the switch.
7   If the motor is getting voltage but doesn't run, test it off the vehicle with jumper wires. If it still doesn't work, replace it.
8   If the motor isn't getting voltage, remove the switch and check for voltage. If there's no voltage at the switch, check the wiring between the fuse block and the switch. If there's battery voltage at the red/light blue wire of the switch, check the circuit breaker. Check the black/orange wire and replace the switch if there's no continuity. If the switch is OK, check for a short or open in the wiring between the switch and motor.
9   Test the completed repairs.

25 Electric rear view mirrors - description and check

Side mirror

1   The electric rear view mirrors use two motors to move the glass; one for up and down adjustments and one for left-right adjustments.
2   The control switch has a selector portion which sends voltage to the left or right side mirror. With the ignition ACC position and the engine OFF, roll down the windows and operate the mirror control switch through all functions (left-right and up-down) for both the left and right side mirrors.
3   Listen carefully for the sound of the electric motors running in the mirrors.
4   If the motors can be heard but the mirror glass doesn't move, there's probably a problem with the drive mechanism inside the mirror. Remove and disassemble the mirror to locate the problem.
5   If the mirrors don't operate and no sound comes from the mirrors, check the 15 amp fuse in the fuse block located in the left side of the dash (see Section 3).
6   If the fuse is OK, remove the switch bezel (see Chapter 11) for access to the back of the mirror control switch without disconnecting the wires attached to it. Turn the ignition ON and check for voltage at the switch. There should be voltage at one terminal. If there's no voltage at the switch, check for an open or short in the wiring between the fuse panel and the switch.
7   If there's voltage at the switch, disconnect it. Check the switch for continuity in all its operating positions. If the switch does not have continuity, replace it.
8   Re-connect the switch. Locate the wire going from the switch to ground. Leaving the switch connected, connect a jumper wire between this wire and ground. If the mirror works normally with this wire in place, repair the faulty ground connection.
9   If the mirror still doesn't work, remove the mirror and check the wires at the mirror for voltage. Check with ignition ON and the mirror selector switch on the appropriate side. Operate the mirror switch in all its positions. There should be voltage at one of the switch-to-mirror wires in each switch position (except the neutral "off" position).
10   If there's not voltage in each switch position, check the wiring between the mirror and control switch for opens and shorts.
11   If there's voltage, remove the mirror and test it off the vehicle with jumper wires. Replace the mirror if it fails this test.

12

COLOR CODE	COLOR	STANDARD TRACER COLOR	COLOR CODE	COLOR	STANDARD TRACER CODE
BL	BLUE	WT	OR	ORANGE	BK
BK	BLACK	WT	PK	PINK	BK OR WT
BR	BROWN	WT	RD	RED	WT
DB	DARK BLUE	WT	TN	TAN	WT
DG	DARK GREEN	WT	VT	VIOLET	WT
GY	GRAY	BK	WT	WHITE	BK
LB	LIGHT BLUE	BK	YL	YELLOW	BK
LG	LIGHT GREEN	BK	*	WITH TRACER	

26.4a Wire color code chart

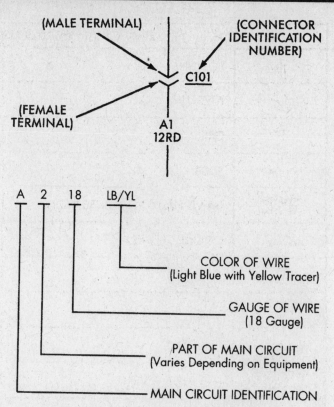

26.4b Wire code and connector identification chart

Automatic/day night mirror

12　To reduce glare, the automatic day/night mirror adjusts the amount of light reflected according to conditions. This is achieved with two photocell sensors, one facing forward and one facing rearward, that darken or lighten the thin layer of electrochromic material incorporated into the mirror glass.

13　Disconnect the electrical connector from the mirror. With the ignition On, the cavity with the brown/light green wire should have battery voltage.

14　With the ignition Off, the cavity with the black wire should have continuity to ground. If not, there is a loose ground connection in the circuit.

15　With the shift selector in Reverse and the ignition switch On, place the mirror switch in the On position. The connector cavity with the violet /black wire should have battery voltage. If not there is a fault in the backup lights circuit.

17　With the shift selector in Neutral and the ignition switch On, place the mirror switch in the On position.

18　Cover the forward facing sensor, shine a light into the rear facing sensor, make sure the glass darkens, then shift the transmission into reverse and make sure it lightens. If it doesn't replace the mirror (see Chapter 11).

26　Wiring diagrams - general information

Refer to illustrations 26.4a, 26.4b, 26.4c and 26.4d

Since it isn't possible to include all wiring diagrams for every year and model covered by this manual, the following diagrams are those that are typical and most commonly needed.

Prior to troubleshooting any circuits, check the fuse and circuit breakers (if equipped) to make sure they're in good condition. Make sure the battery is properly charged and check the cable connections (see Chapter 1).

When checking a circuit, make sure that all connectors are clean, with no broken or loose terminals. When disconnecting a connector, do not pull on the wires. Pull only on the connector housings themselves.

Refer to the accompanying charts for an explanation of the wiring diagrams and the wire color codes applicable to your vehicle **(see illustrations)**.

CIRCUIT	FUNCTION
A	Battery Feed
B	Brake Controls
C	Climate Controls
D	Diagnostic Circuits
E	Dimming Illumination Circuits
F	Fused Circuits (Secondary Feed)
G	Monitoring Circuits (Gauges)
H	Open
I	Not Used
J	Open
K	Powertrain Control Module
L	Exterior Lighting
M	Interior Lighting
N	ESA Module
O	Not Used
P	Power Option (Battery Feed)
Q	Power Options (Battery Feed)
R	Passive Restraint
S	Suspension/Steering
T	Transmission/Transaxle/Transfer Case
U	Open
V	Speed Control, Washer/Wiper
W	Open
X	Audio Systems
Y	Open
Z	Grounds

26.4c Circuit code identification chart

LEGEND OF SYMBOLS USED ON WIRING DIAGRAMS

Symbol	Name	Symbol	Name
+	POSITIVE		BY-DIRECTIONAL ZENER DIODE
−	NEGATIVE		MOTOR
	GROUND		ARMATURE AND BRUSHES
	FUSE	C100	CONNECTOR IDENTIFICATION
	GANG FUSES WITH BUSS BAR		MALE CONNECTOR
	CIRCUIT BREAKER		FEMALE CONNECTOR
	CAPACITOR		DENOTES WIRE CONTINUES ELSEWHERE
Ω	OHMS		DENOTES WIRE GOES TO ONE OF TWO CIRCUITS
	RESISTOR		SPLICE
	VARIABLE RESISTOR	S100	SPLICE IDENTIFICATION
	SERIES RESISTOR		THERMAL ELEMENT
	COIL	TIMER	TIMER
	STEP UP COIL		MULTIPLE CONNECTOR
	OPEN CONTACT		OPTIONAL WIRING WITH / WIRING WITHOUT
	CLOSED CONTACT		"Y" WINDINGS
	CLOSED SWITCH	88:88	DIGITAL READOUT
	OPEN SWITCH		SINGLE FILAMENT LAMP
	CLOSED GANGED SWITCH		DUAL FILAMENT LAMP
	OPEN GANGED SWITCH		L.E.D. — LIGHT EMITTING DIODE
	TWO POLE SINGLE THROW SWITCH		THERMISTOR
	PRESSURE SWITCH		GAUGE
	SOLENOID SWITCH		SENSOR
	MERCURY SWITCH		FUEL INJECTOR
	DIODE OR RECTIFIER		

26.4d Wiring diagram symbol legend

12

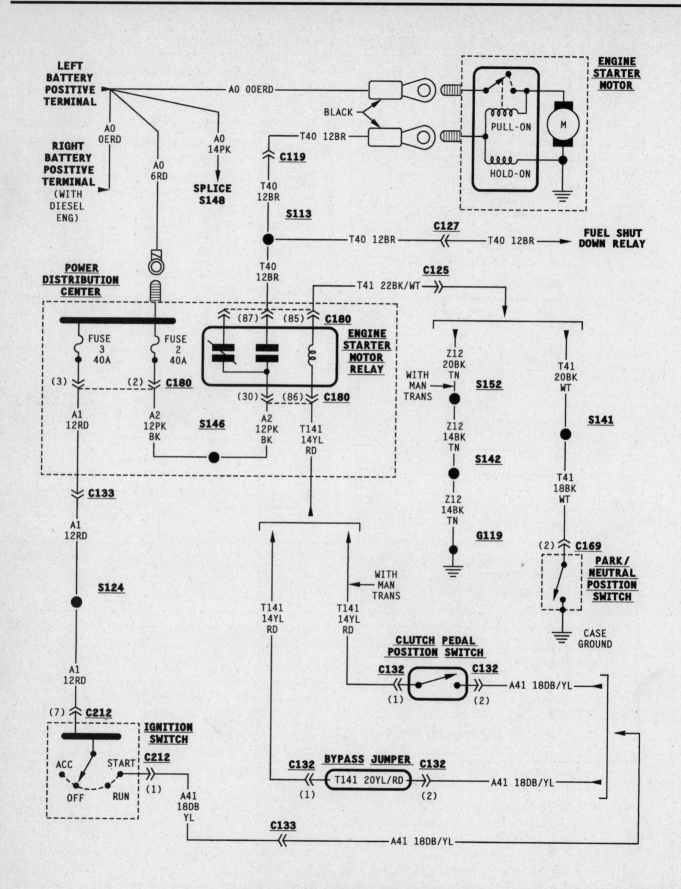

Typical engine starting system wiring diagram

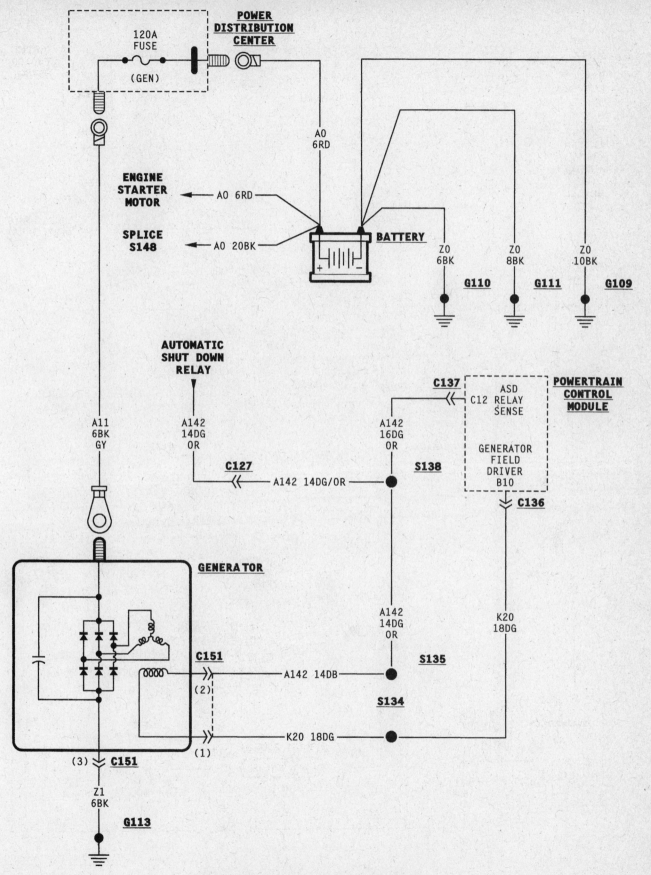

Typical engine charging system wiring diagram

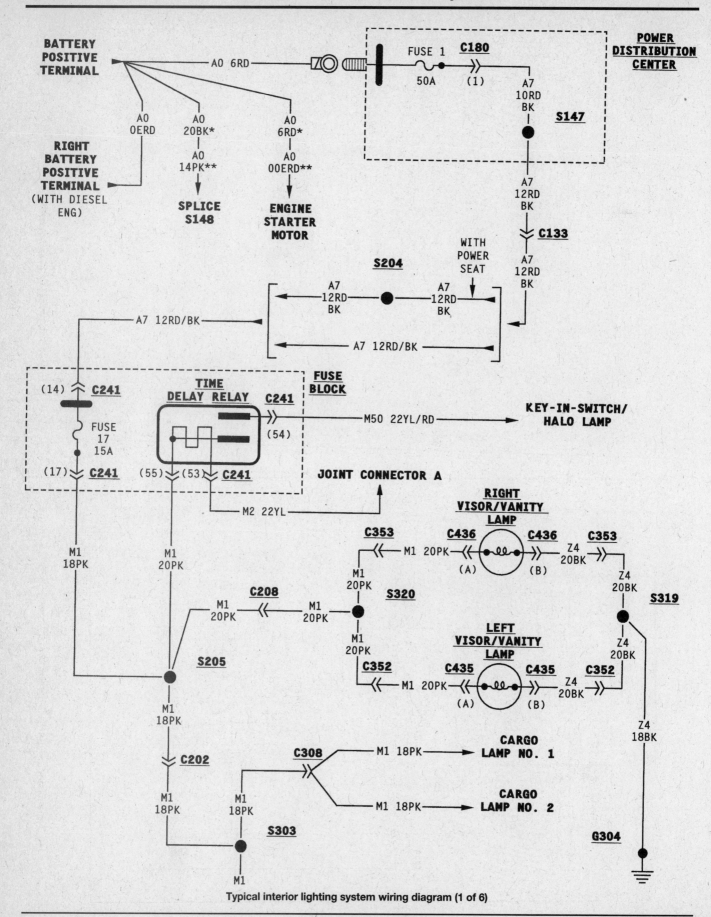

Typical interior lighting system wiring diagram (1 of 6)

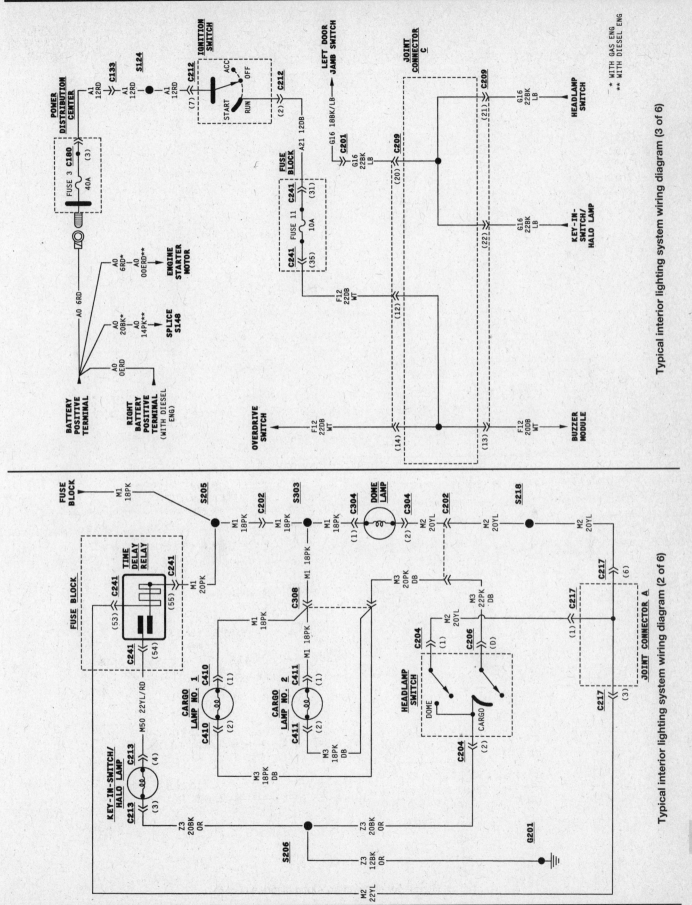

Typical interior lighting system wiring diagram (3 of 6)

Typical interior lighting system wiring diagram (2 of 6)

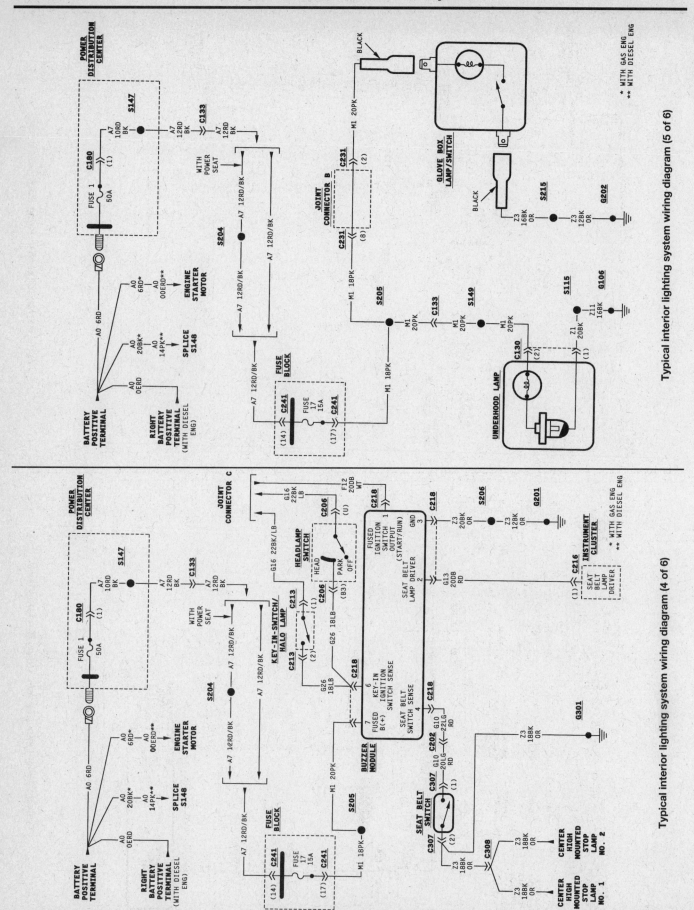

Typical interior lighting system wiring diagram (5 of 6)

Typical interior lighting system wiring diagram (4 of 6)

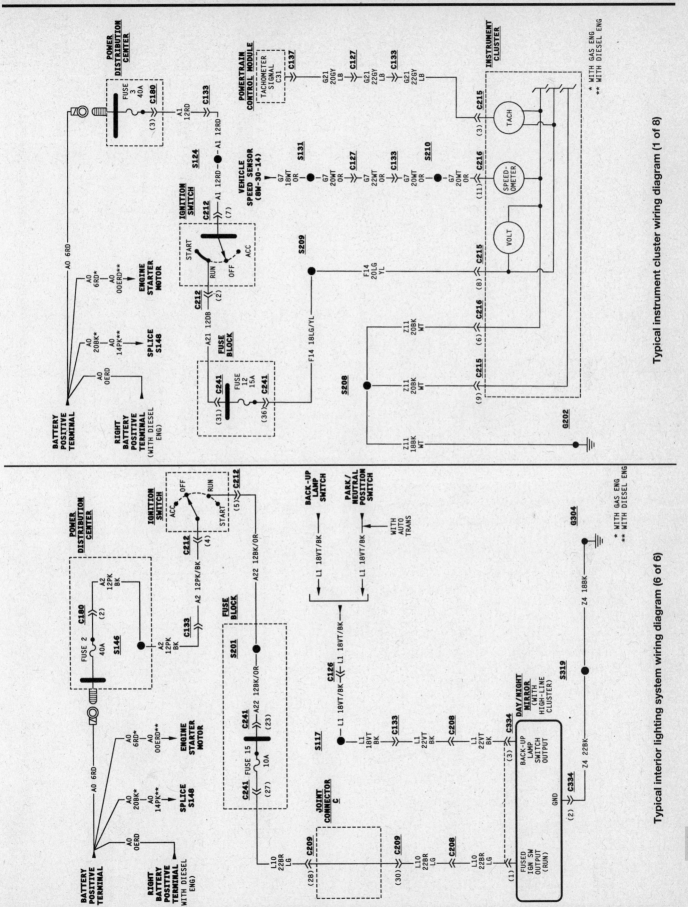

Typical instrument cluster wiring diagram (1 of 8)

Typical interior lighting system wiring diagram (6 of 6)

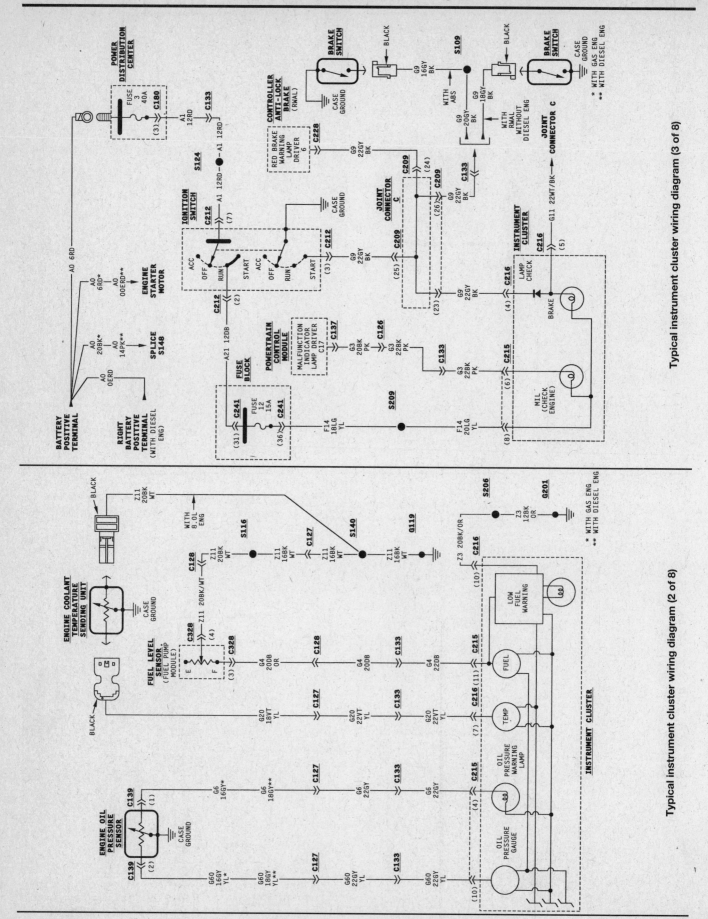

Typical instrument cluster wiring diagram (3 of 8)

Typical instrument cluster wiring diagram (2 of 8)

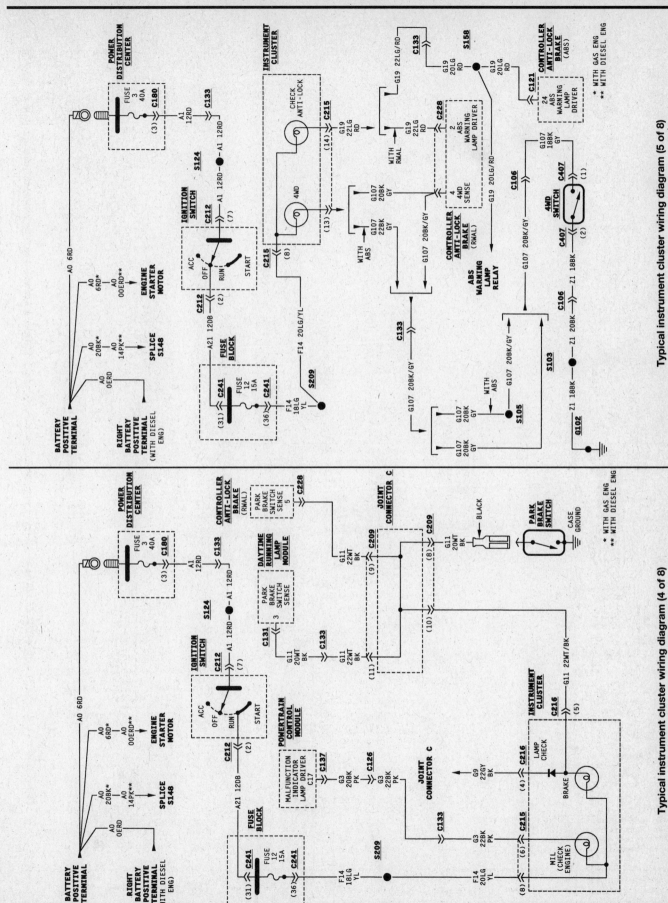

Typical instrument cluster wiring diagram (5 of 8)

Typical instrument cluster wiring diagram (4 of 8)

12

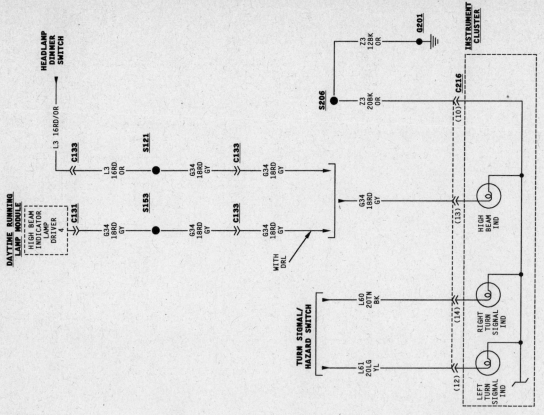

Typical instrument cluster wiring diagram (7 of 8)

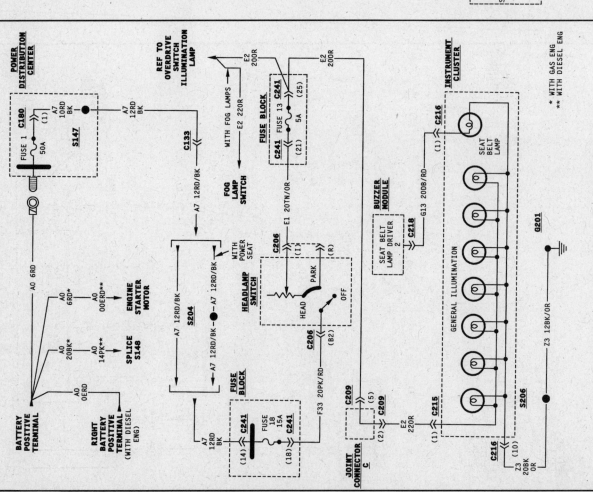

Typical instrument cluster wiring diagram (6 of 8)

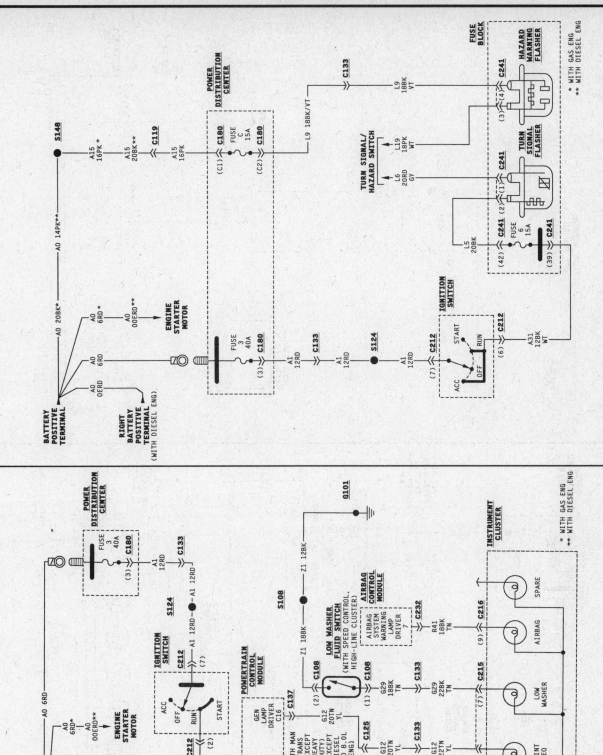

Typical turn signal wiring diagram (1 of 4)

Typical instrument cluster wiring diagram (8 of 8)

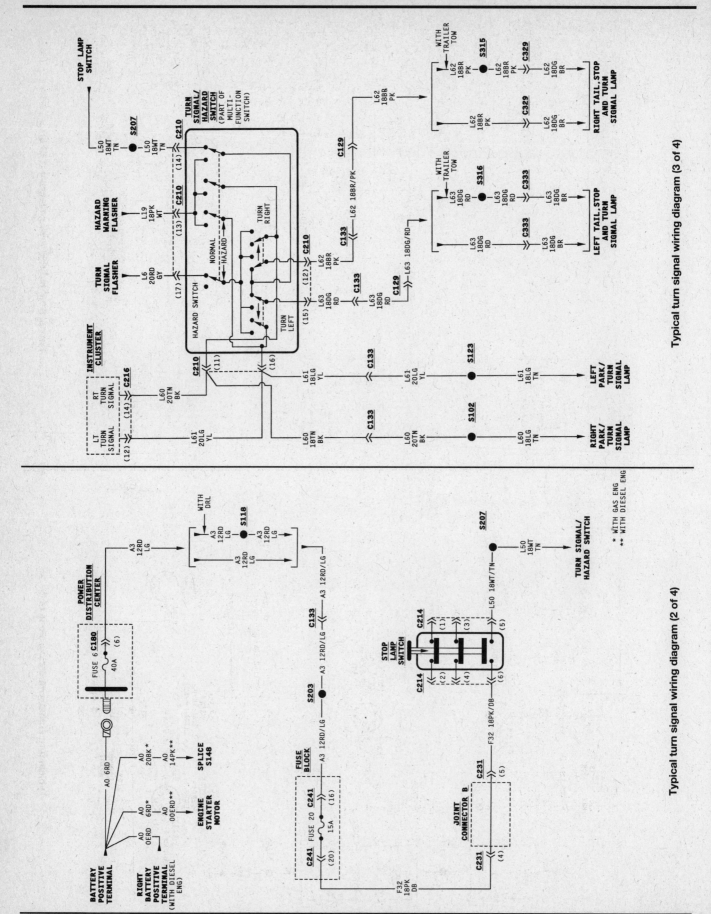

Typical turn signal wiring diagram (3 of 4)

Typical turn signal wiring diagram (2 of 4)

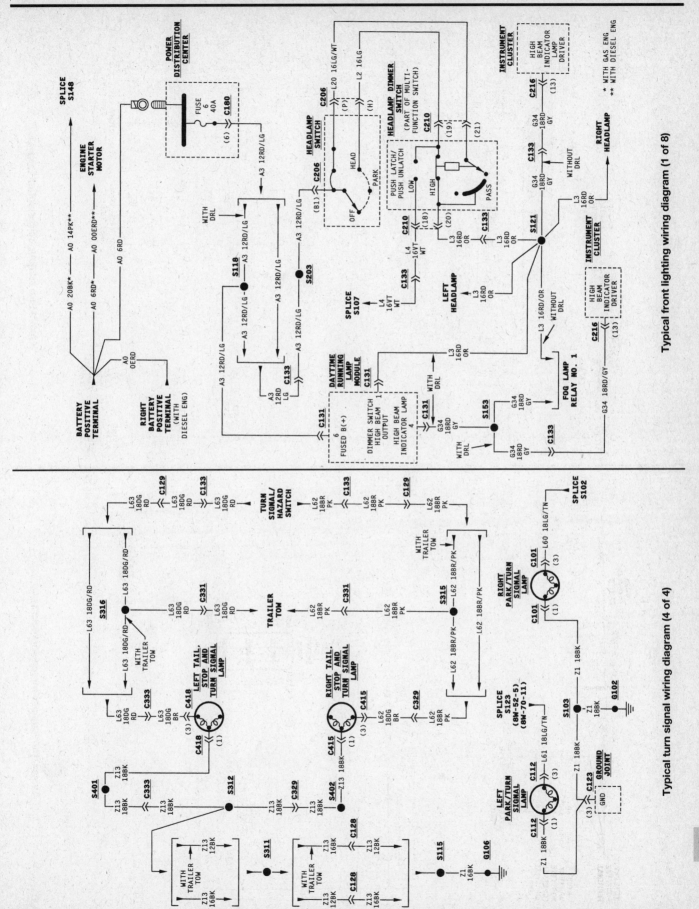

Typical front lighting wiring diagram (1 of 8)

Typical turn signal wiring diagram (4 of 4)

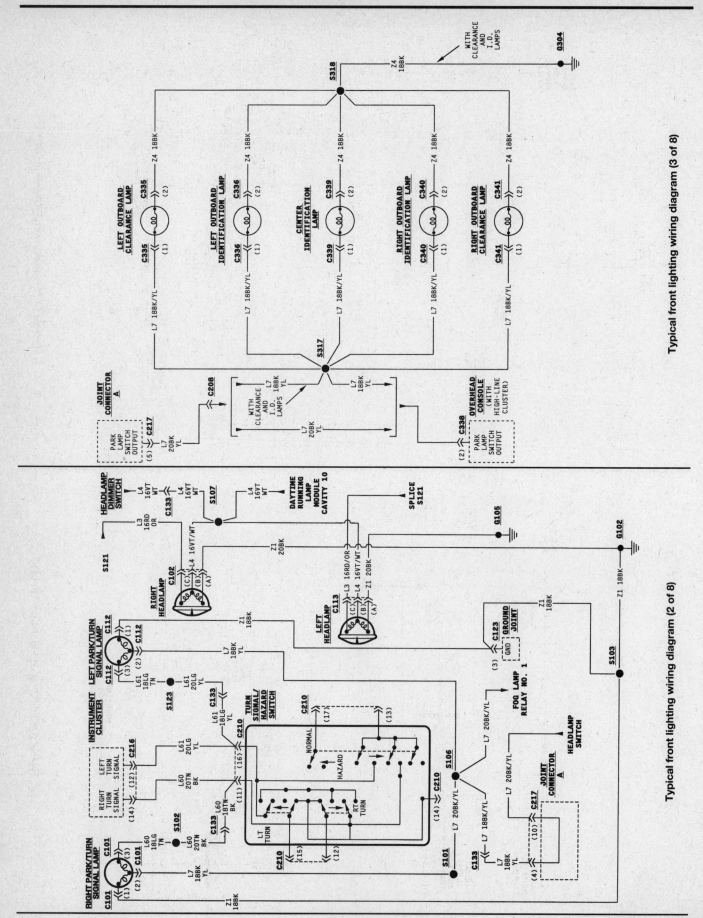

Typical front lighting wiring diagram (3 of 8)

Typical front lighting wiring diagram (2 of 8)

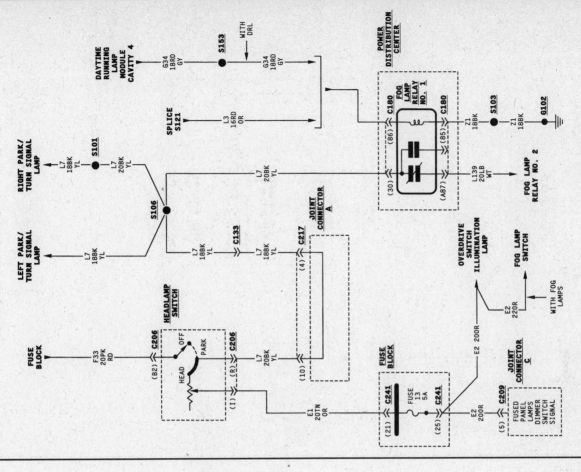

Typical front lighting wiring diagram (5 of 8)

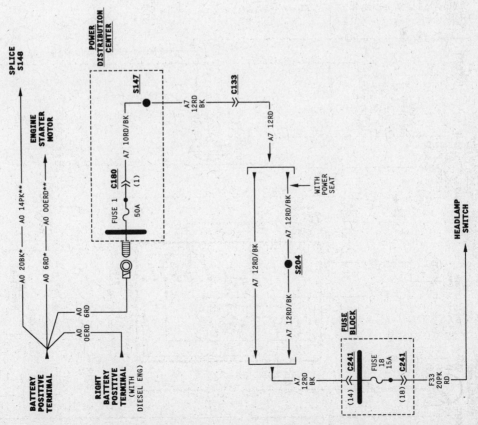

Typical front lighting wiring diagram (4 of 8)

12

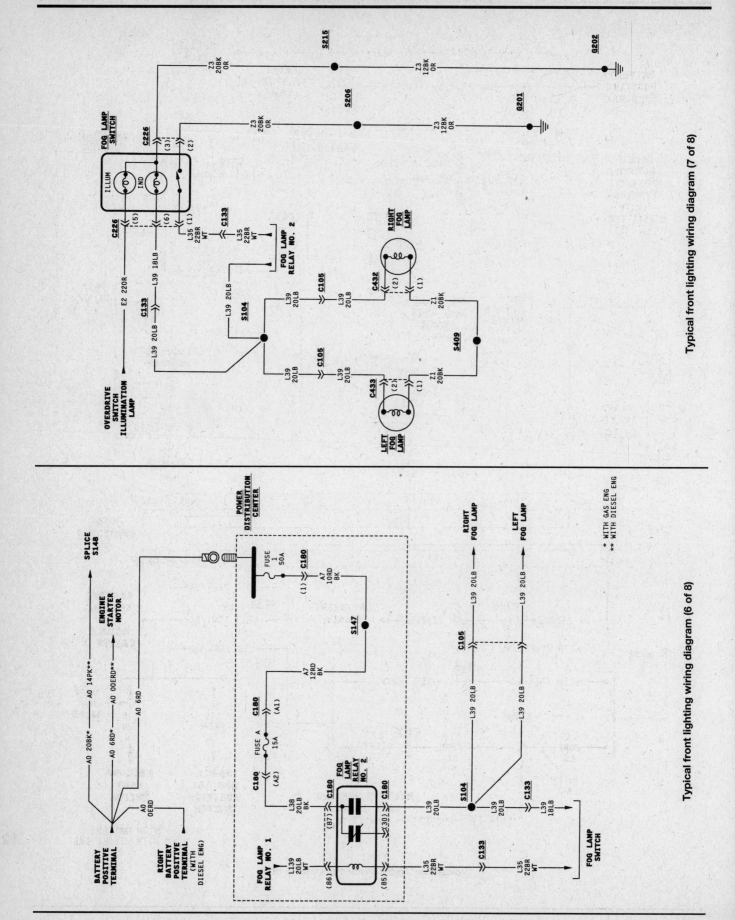

Typical front lighting wiring diagram (7 of 8)

Typical front lighting wiring diagram (6 of 8)

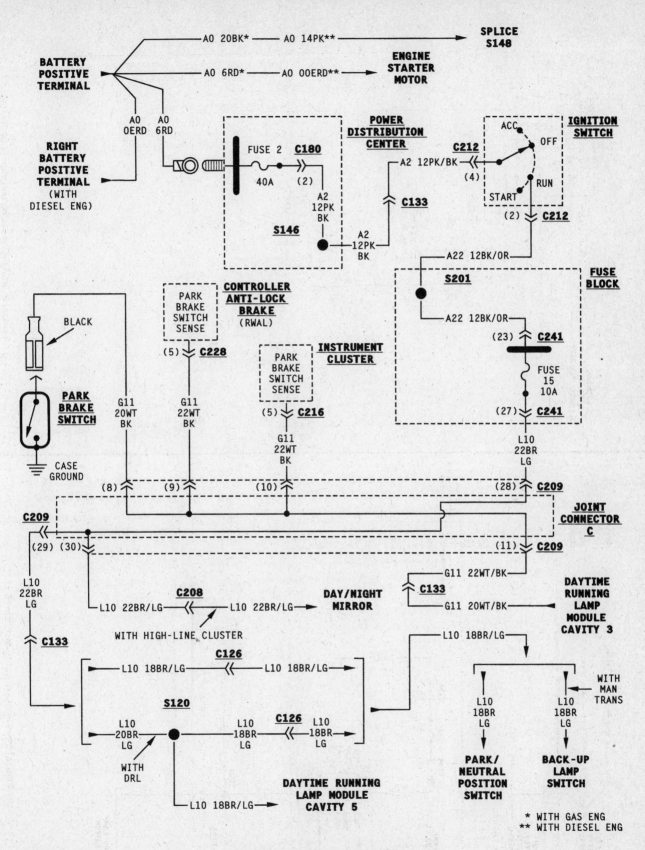

Typical front lighting wiring diagram (8 of 8)

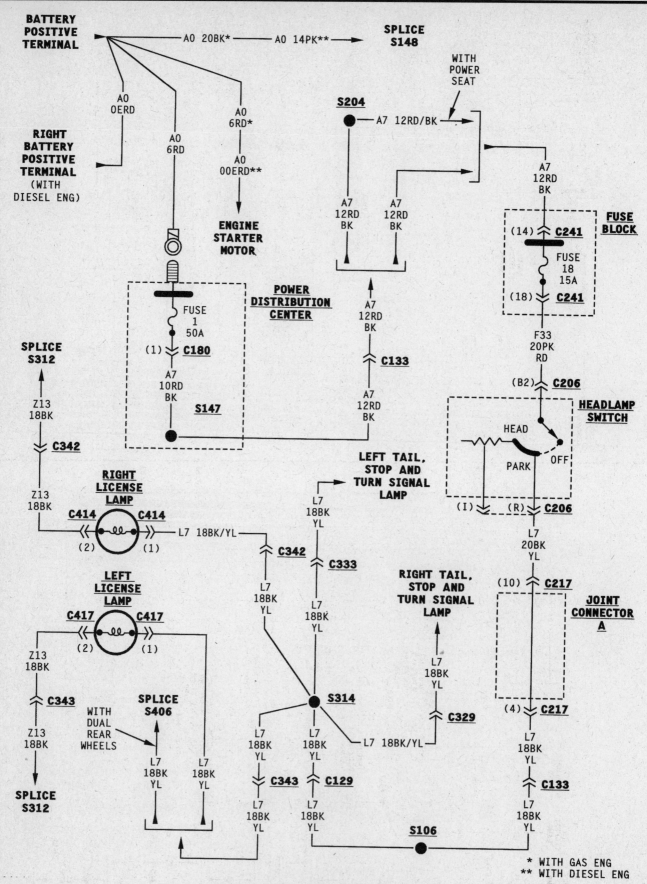

Typical rear lighting wiring diagram (1 of 6)

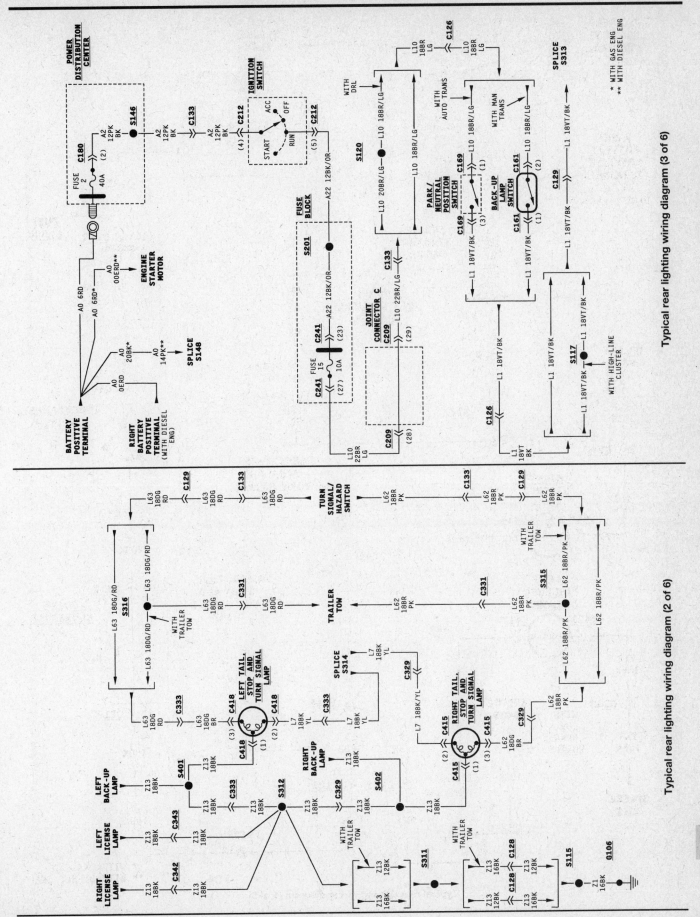

Typical rear lighting wiring diagram (3 of 6)

Typical rear lighting wiring diagram (2 of 6)

12

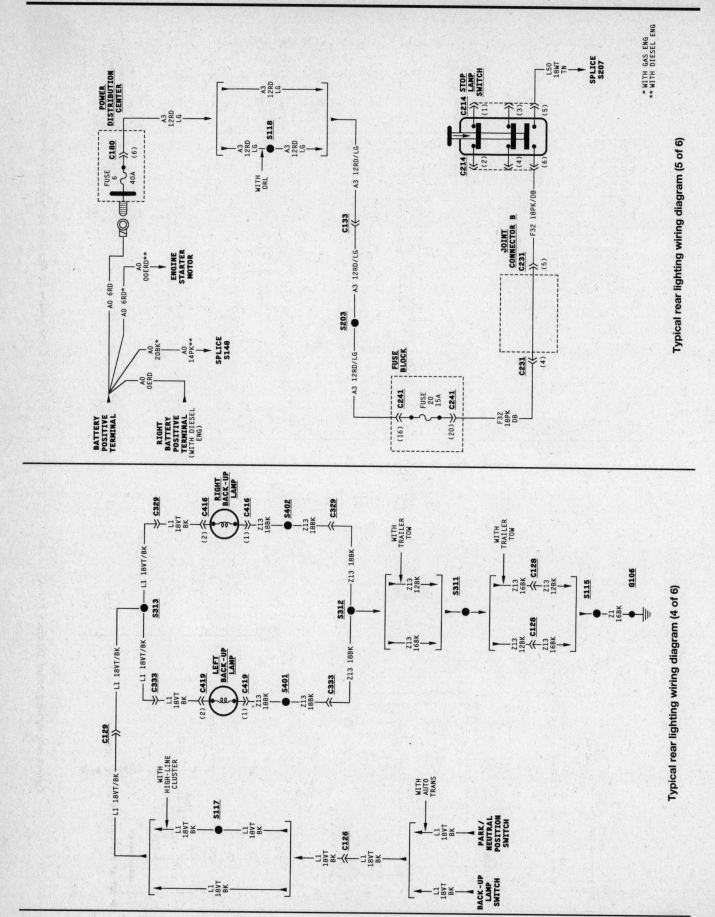

Typical rear lighting wiring diagram (5 of 6)

Typical rear lighting wiring diagram (4 of 6)

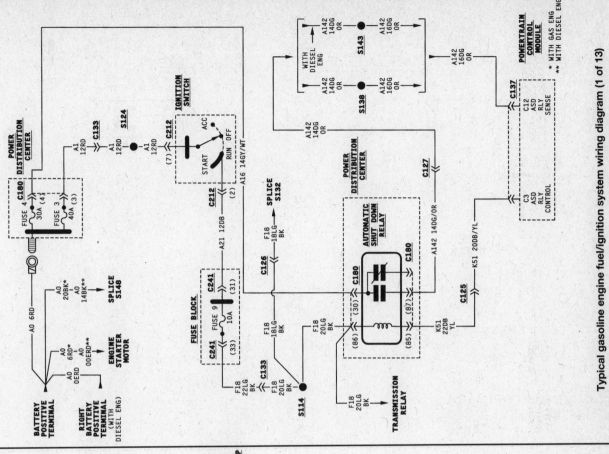

Typical gasoline engine fuel/ignition system wiring diagram (1 of 13)

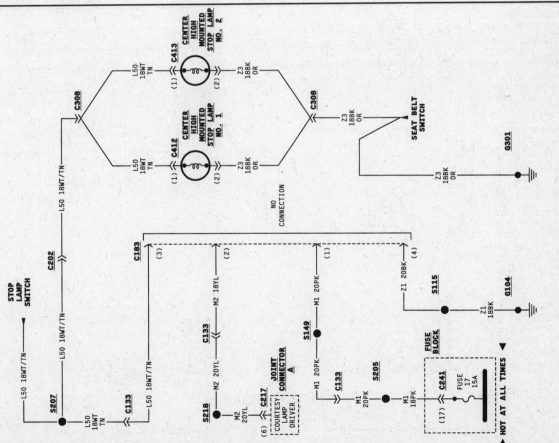

Typical rear lighting wiring diagram (6 of 6)

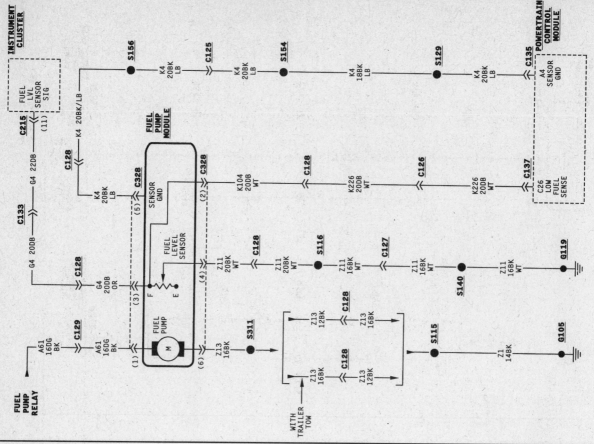

Typical gasoline engine fuel/ignition system wiring diagram (3 of 13)

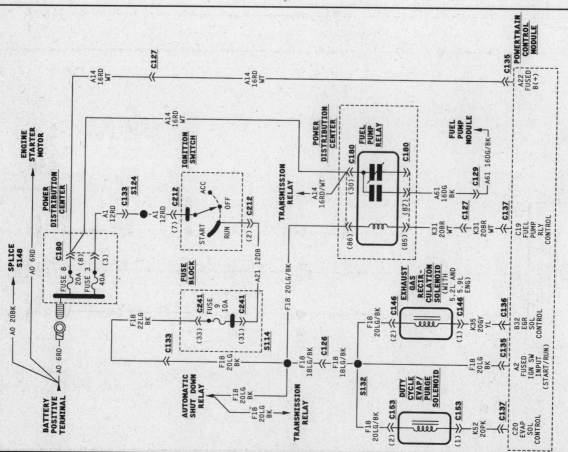

Typical gasoline engine fuel/ignition system wiring diagram (2 of 13)

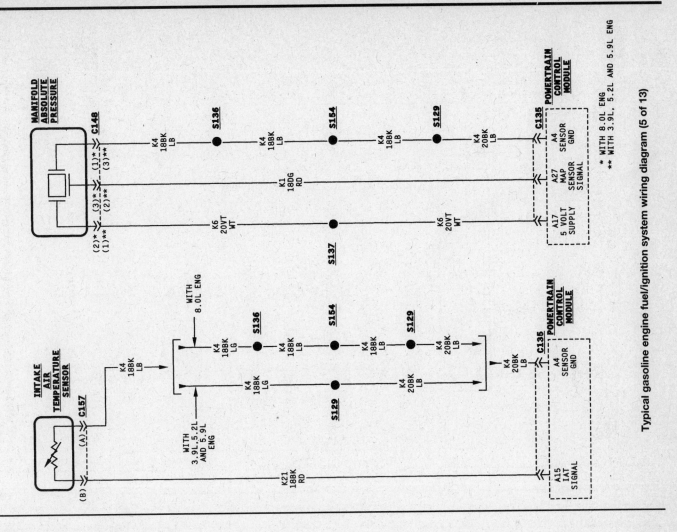

Typical gasoline engine fuel/ignition system wiring diagram (5 of 13)

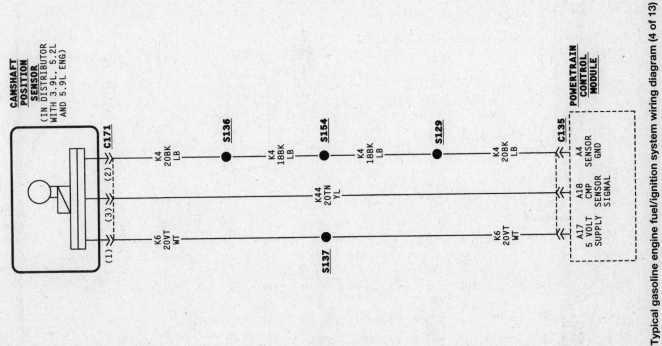

Typical gasoline engine fuel/ignition system wiring diagram (4 of 13)

12

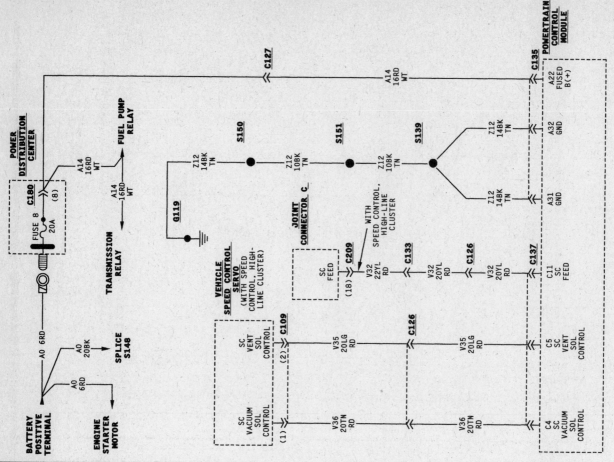

Typical gasoline engine fuel/ignition system wiring diagram (7 of 13)

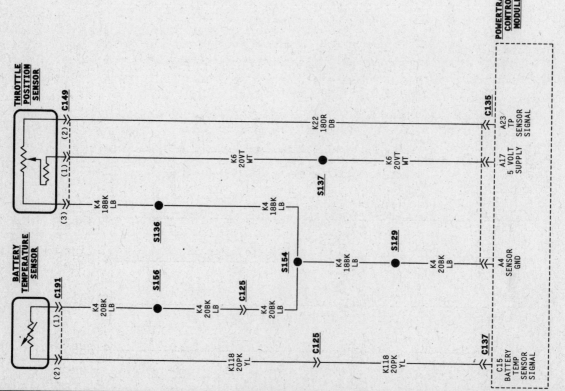

Typical gasoline engine fuel/ignition system wiring diagram (6 of 13)

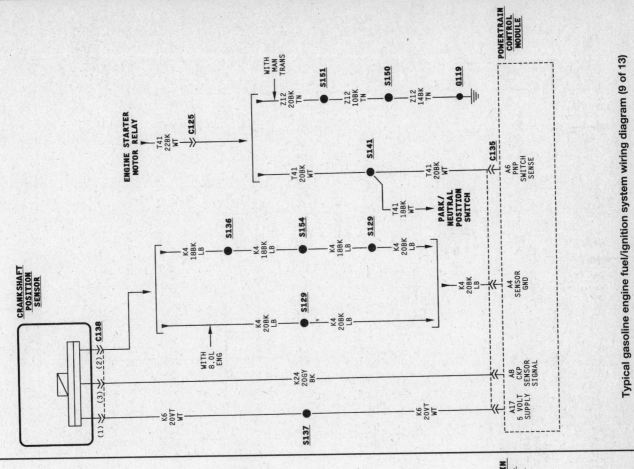

Typical gasoline engine fuel/ignition system wiring diagram (9 of 13)

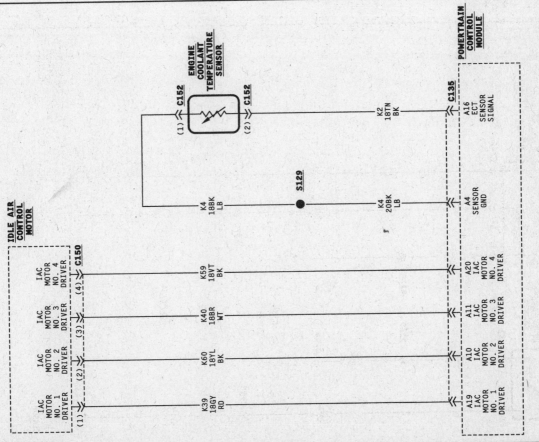

Typical gasoline engine fuel/ignition system wiring diagram (8 of 13)

12

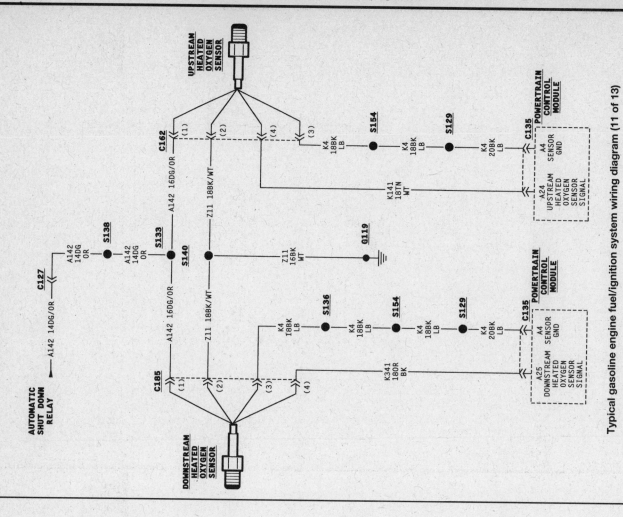

Typical gasoline engine fuel/ignition system wiring diagram (11 of 13)

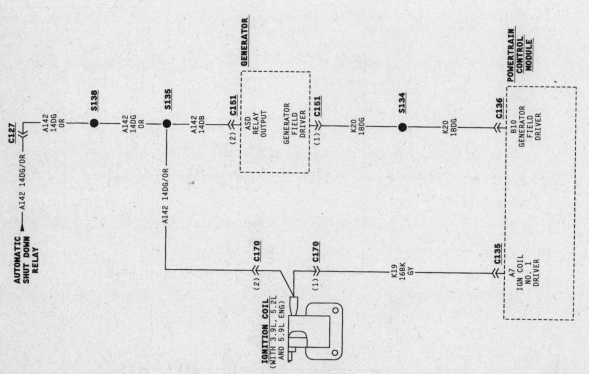

Typical gasoline engine fuel/ignition system wiring diagram (10 of 13)

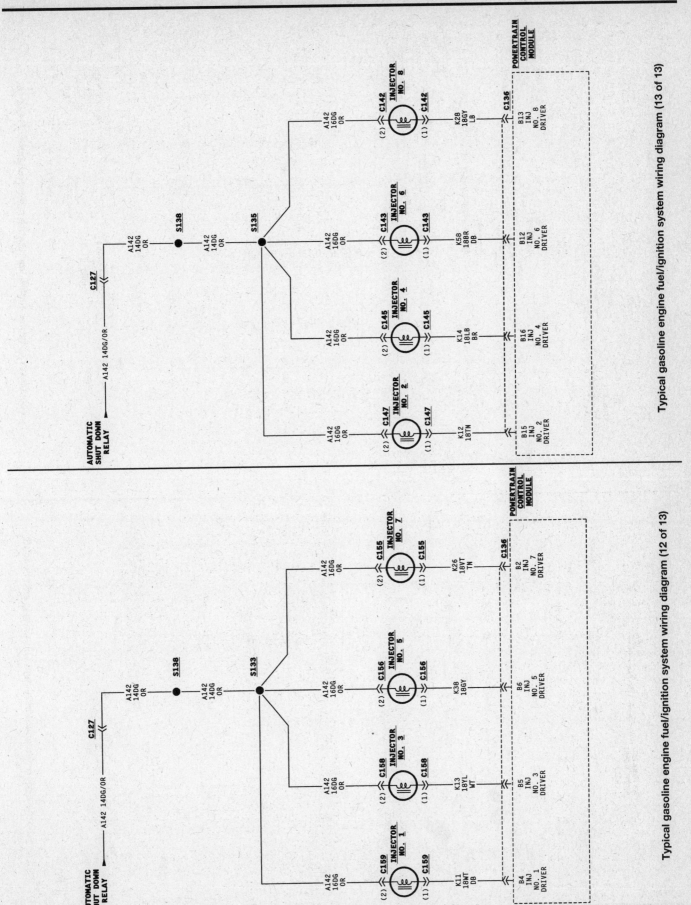

Typical gasoline engine fuel/ignition system wiring diagram (13 of 13)

Typical gasoline engine fuel/ignition system wiring diagram (12 of 13)

12

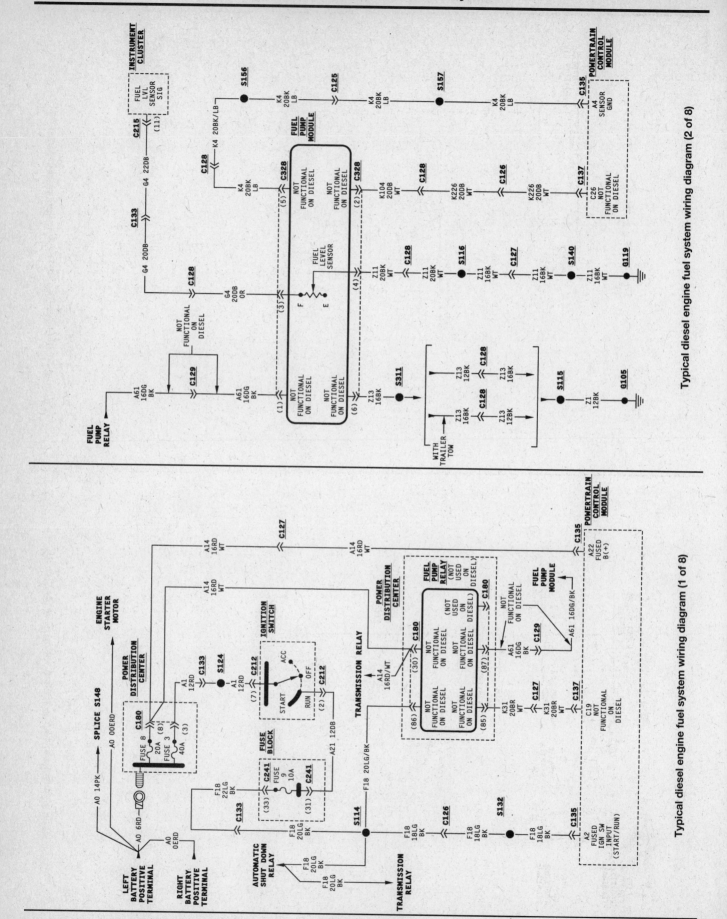

Typical diesel engine fuel system wiring diagram (2 of 8)

Typical diesel engine fuel system wiring diagram (1 of 8)

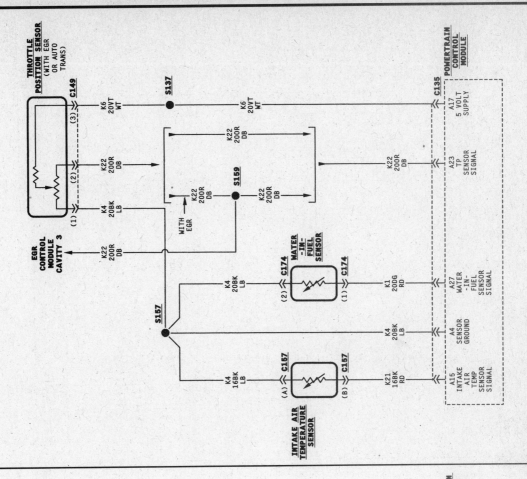

Typical diesel engine fuel system wiring diagram (4 of 8)

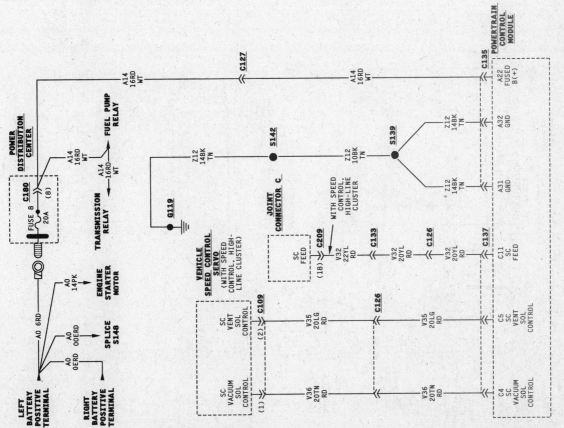

Typical diesel engine fuel system wiring diagram (3 of 8)

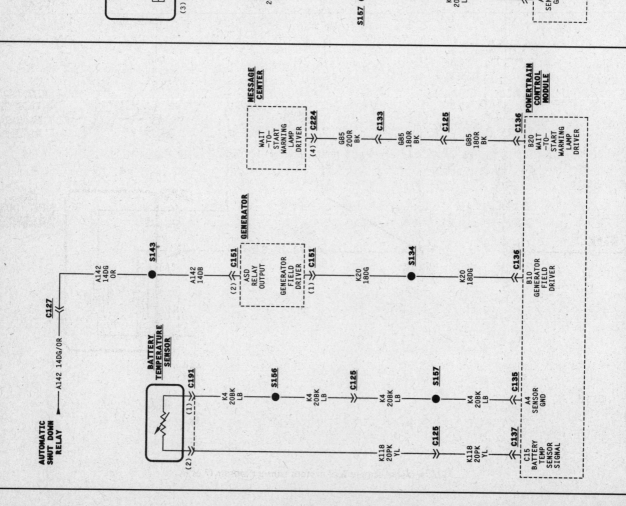

Typical diesel engine fuel system wiring diagram (6 of 8)

Typical diesel engine fuel system wiring diagram (5 of 8)

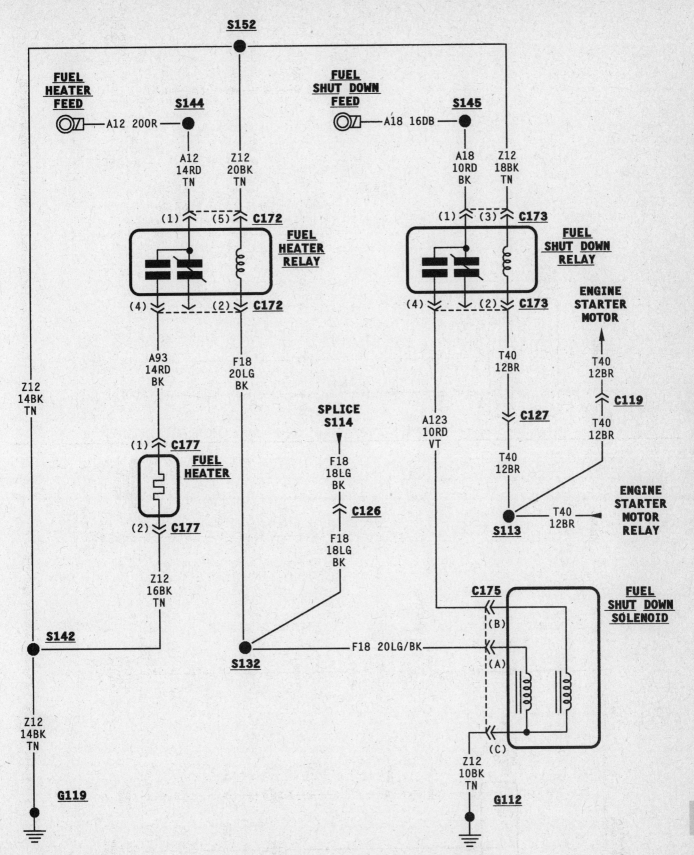

Typical diesel engine fuel system wiring diagram (7 of 8)

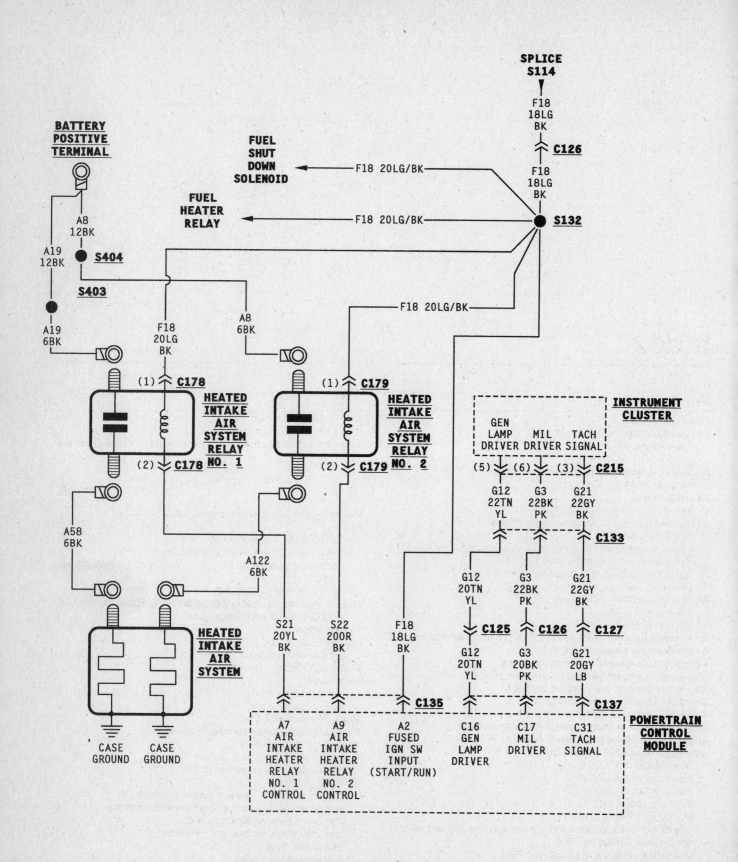

Typical diesel engine fuel system wiring diagram (8 of 8)

Index

Haynes Automotive Manuals

NOTE: New manuals are added to this list on a periodic basis. If you do not see a listing for your vehicle, consult your local Haynes dealer for the latest product information.

ACURA
*1776   **Integra & Legend** all models '86 thru '90

AMC
    Jeep CJ - see *JEEP (412)*
694   **Mid-size models,** Concord, Hornet, Gremlin & Spirit '70 thru '83
934   **(Renault) Alliance & Encore** all models '83 thru '87

AUDI
615   **4000** all models '80 thru '87
428   **5000** all models '77 thru '83
1117   **5000** all models '84 thru '88

AUSTIN
    Healey Sprite - see *MG Midget Roadster (265)*

BMW
*2020   **3/5 Series** not including diesel or all-wheel drive models '82 thru '92
276   **320i** all 4 cyl models '75 thru '83
632   **528i & 530i** all models '75 thru '80
240   **1500 thru 2002** all models except Turbo '59 thru '77
348   **2500, 2800, 3.0 & Bavaria** all models '69 thru '76

BUICK
    Century (front wheel drive) - see *GENERAL MOTORS (829)*
*1627   **Buick, Oldsmobile & Pontiac Full-size (Front wheel drive)** all models '85 thru '95
    Buick Electra, LeSabre and Park Avenue; Oldsmobile Delta 88 Royale, Ninety Eight and Regency; Pontiac Bonneville
1551   **Buick Oldsmobile & Pontiac Full-size (Rear wheel drive)**
    Buick Estate '70 thru '90, Electra'70 thru '84, LeSabre '70 thru '85, Limited '74 thru '79
    Oldsmobile Custom Cruiser '70 thru '90, Delta 88 '70 thru '85, Ninety-eight '70 thru '84
    Pontiac Bonneville '70 thru '81, Catalina '70 thru '81, Grandville '70 thru '75, Parisienne '83 thru '86
627   **Mid-size Regal & Century** all rear-drive models with V6, V8 and Turbo '74 thru '87
    Regal - see *GENERAL MOTORS (1671)*
    Skyhawk - see *GENERAL MOTORS (766)*
    Skylark '80 thru '85 - see *GENERAL MOTORS (38020)*
    Skylark '86 on - see *GENERAL MOTORS (1420)*
    Somerset - see *GENERAL MOTORS (1420)*

CADILLAC
*751   **Cadillac Rear Wheel Drive** all gasoline models '70 thru '93
    Cimarron - see *GENERAL MOTORS (766)*

CHEVROLET
*1477   **Astro & GMC Safari Mini-vans** '85 thru '93
554   **Camaro V8** all models '70 thru '81
866   **Camaro** all models '82 thru '92
    Cavalier - see *GENERAL MOTORS (766)*
    Celebrity - see *GENERAL MOTORS (829)*
625   **Chevelle, Malibu & El Camino** all V6 & V8 models '69 thru '87
449   **Chevette & Pontiac T1000** '76 thru '87
550   **Citation** all models '80 thru '85
*1628   **Corsica/Beretta** all models '87 thru '95
274   **Corvette** all V8 models '68 thru '82
*1336   **Corvette** all models '84 thru '91
1762   **Chevrolet Engine Overhaul Manual**
704   **Full-size Sedans** Caprice, Impala, Biscayne, Bel Air & Wagons '69 thru '90

    Lumina - see *GENERAL MOTORS (1671)*
    Lumina APV - see *GENERAL MOTORS (2035)*
319   **Luv Pick-up** all 2WD & 4WD '72 thru '82
626   **Monte Carlo** all models '70 thru '88
241   **Nova** all V8 models '69 thru '79
*1642   **Nova and Geo Prizm** all front wheel drive models, '85 thru '92
420   **Pick-ups '67 thru '87** - Chevrolet & GMC, all V8 & in-line 6 cyl, 2WD & 4WD '67 thru '87; Suburbans, Blazers & Jimmys '67 thru '91
*1664   **Pick-ups '88 thru '95** - Chevrolet & GMC, all full-size pick-ups, '88 thru '95; Blazer & Jimmy '92 thru '94; Suburban '92 thru '95; Tahoe & Yukon '95
*831   **S-10 & GMC S-15 Pick-ups** all models '82 thru '93
*1727   **Sprint & Geo Metro** '85 thru '94
*345   **Vans - Chevrolet & GMC,** V8 & in-line 6 cylinder models '68 thru '95

CHRYSLER
2114   **Chrysler Engine Overhaul Manual**
*2058   **Full-size Front-Wheel Drive** '88 thru '93
    K-Cars - see *DODGE Aries (723)*
    Laser - see *DODGE Daytona (1140)*
*1337   **Chrysler & Plymouth Mid-size** front wheel drive '82 thru '93
    Rear-wheel Drive - see *Dodge Rear-wheel Drive (2098)*

DATSUN
402   **200SX** all models '77 thru '79
647   **200SX** all models '80 thru '83
228   **B - 210** all models '73 thru '78
525   **210** all models '78 thru '82
206   **240Z, 260Z & 280Z** Coupe '70 thru '78
563   **280ZX** Coupe & 2+2 '79 thru '83
    300ZX - see *NISSAN (1137)*
679   **310** all models '78 thru '82
123   **510 & PL521 Pick-up** '68 thru '73
430   **510** all models '78 thru '81
372   **610** all models '72 thru '76
277   **620 Series Pick-up** all models '73 thru '79
    720 Series Pick-up - see *NISSAN (771)*
376   **810/Maxima** all gasoline models, '77 thru '84
    Pulsar - see *NISSAN (876)*
    Sentra - see *NISSAN (982)*
    Stanza - see *NISSAN (981)*

DODGE
    400 & 600 - see *CHRYSLER Mid-size (1337)*
*723   **Aries & Plymouth Reliant** '81 thru '89
1231   **Caravan & Plymouth Voyager Mini-Vans** all models '84 thru '95
699   **Challenger & Plymouth Saporro** all models '78 thru '83
    Challenger '67-'76 - see *DODGE Dart (234)*
236   **Colt** all models '71 thru '77
610   **Colt & Plymouth Champ** (front wheel drive) all models '78 thru '87
*1668   **Dakota Pick-ups** all models '87 thru '93
234   **Dart, Challenger/Plymouth Barracuda & Valiant** 6 cyl models '67 thru '76
*1140   **Daytona & Chrysler Laser** '84 thru '89
*545   **Omni & Plymouth Horizon** '78 thru '90
*912   **Pick-ups** all full-size models '74 thru '91
*556   **Ram 50/D50 Pick-ups & Raider and Plymouth Arrow Pick-ups** '79 thru '93
2098   **Dodge/Plymouth/Chrysler** rear wheel drive '71 thru '89
*1726   **Shadow & Plymouth Sundance** '87 thru '93
*1779   **Spirit & Plymouth Acclaim** '89 thru '95
*349   **Vans - Dodge & Plymouth** V8 & 6 cyl models '71 thru '91

EAGLE
    Talon - see *Mitsubishi Eclipse (2097)*

FIAT
094   **124 Sport Coupe & Spider** '68 thru '78
273   **X1/9** all models '74 thru '80

FORD
*1476   **Aerostar Mini-vans** all models '86 thru '94
788   **Bronco and Pick-ups** '73 thru '79
*880   **Bronco and Pick-ups** '80 thru '95
268   **Courier Pick-up** all models '72 thru '82
2105   **Crown Victoria & Mercury Grand Marquis** '88 thru '94
1763   **Ford Engine Overhaul Manual**
789   **Escort/Mercury Lynx** all models '81 thru '90
*2046   **Escort/Mercury Tracer** '91 thru '95
*2021   **Explorer & Mazda Navajo** '91 thru '95
560   **Fairmont & Mercury Zephyr** '78 thru '83
334   **Fiesta** all models '77 thru '80
754   **Ford & Mercury Full-size,** Ford LTD & Mercury Marquis ('75 thru '82); Ford Custom 500,Country Squire, Crown Victoria & Mercury Colony Park ('75 thru '87); Ford LTD Crown Victoria & Mercury Gran Marquis ('83 thru '87)
359   **Granada & Mercury Monarch** all in-line, 6 cyl & V8 models '75 thru '80
773   **Ford & Mercury Mid-size,** Ford Thunderbird & Mercury Cougar ('75 thru '82); Ford LTD & Mercury Marquis ('83 thru '86); Ford Torino,Gran Torino, Elite, Ranchero pick-up, LTD II, Mercury Montego, Comet, XR-7 & Lincoln Versailles ('75 thru '86)
*654   **Mustang & Mercury Capri** all models including Turbo. Mustang, '79 thru '93; Capri, '79 thru '86
357   **Mustang V8** all models '64-1/2 thru '73
231   **Mustang II** 4 cyl, V6 & V8 models '74 thru '78
649   **Pinto & Mercury Bobcat** '75 thru '80
1670   **Probe** all models '89 thru '92
*1026   **Ranger/Bronco II** gasoline models '83 thru '93
*1421   **Taurus & Mercury Sable** '86 thru '94
*1418   **Tempo & Mercury Topaz** all gasoline models '84 thru '94
1338   **Thunderbird/Mercury Cougar** '83 thru '88
*1725   **Thunderbird/Mercury Cougar** '89 and '93
344   **Vans** all V8 Econoline models '69 thru '91
*2119   **Vans** full size '92-'95

GENERAL MOTORS
*829   **Buick Century, Chevrolet Celebrity, Oldsmobile Cutlass Ciera & Pontiac 6000** all models '82 thru '93
*1671   **Buick Regal, Chevrolet Lumina, Oldsmobile Cutlass Supreme & Pontiac Grand Prix** all front wheel drive models '88 thru '95
*766   **Buick Skyhawk, Cadillac Cimarron, Chevrolet Cavalier, Oldsmobile Firenza & Pontiac J-2000 & Sunbird** all models '82 thru '94
38020   **Buick Skylark, Chevrolet Citation, Olds Omega, Pontiac Phoenix** '80 thru '85
1420   **Buick Skylark & Somerset, Oldsmobile Achieva & Calais and Pontiac Grand Am** all models '85 thru '95
*2035   **Chevrolet Lumina APV, Oldsmobile Silhouette & Pontiac Trans Sport** all models '90 thru '94
    General Motors Full-size Rear-wheel Drive - see *BUICK (1551)*

GEO
    Metro - see *CHEVROLET Sprint (1727)*
    Prizm - see *CHEVROLET Nova (1642)*
*2039   **Storm** all models '90 thru '93
    Tracker - see *SUZUKI Samurai (1626)*

GMC
    Safari - see *CHEVROLET ASTRO (1477)*
    Vans & Pick-ups - see *CHEVROLET (420, 831, 345, 1664)*

(Continued on other side)

* Listings shown with an asterisk (*) indicate model coverage as of this printing. These titles will be periodically updated to include later model years - consult your Haynes dealer for more information.

Haynes North America, Inc., 861 Lawrence Drive, Newbury Park, CA 91320 • (805) 498-6703

Haynes Automotive Manuals (continued)

NOTE: New manuals are added to this list on a periodic basis. If you do not see a listing for your vehicle, consult your local Haynes dealer for the latest product information.

HONDA
- 351   **Accord CVCC** all models '76 thru '83
- 1221   **Accord** all models '84 thru '89
- 2067   **Accord** all models '90 thru '93
- 42013   **Accord** all models '94 thru '95
- 160   **Civic 1200** all models '73 thru '79
- 633   **Civic 1300 & 1500 CVCC** '80 thru '83
- 297   **Civic 1500 CVCC** all models '75 thru '79
- 1227   **Civic** all models '84 thru '91
- *2118   **Civic & del Sol** '92 thru '95
- *601   **Prelude CVCC** all models '79 thru '89

HYUNDAI
- *1552   **Excel** all models '86 thru '94

ISUZU
- *1641   **Trooper & Pick-up**, all gasoline models Pick-up, '81 thru '93; Trooper, '84 thru '91

JAGUAR
- *242   **XJ6** all 6 cyl models '68 thru '86
- *478   **XJ12 & XJS** all 12 cyl models '72 thru '85

JEEP
- *1553   **Cherokee, Comanche & Wagoneer Limited** all models '84 thru '93
- 412   **CJ** all models '49 thru '86
- 50025   **Grand Cherokee** all models '93 thru '95
- *1777   **Wrangler** all models '87 thru '94

LINCOLN
- 2117   **Rear Wheel Drive** all models '70 thru '95

MAZDA
- 648   **626 Sedan & Coupe (rear wheel drive)** all models '79 thru '82
- *1082   **626 & MX-6 (front wheel drive)** all models '83 thru '91
- 267   **B Series Pick-ups** '72 thru '93
- 370   **GLC Hatchback (rear wheel drive)** all models '77 thru '83
- 757   **GLC (front wheel drive)** '81 thru '85
- *2047   **MPV** all models '89 thru '94
-   **Navajo**-see Ford Explorer (2021)
- 460   **RX-7** all models '79 thru '85
- *1419   **RX-7** all models '86 thru '91

MERCEDES-BENZ
- *1643   **190 Series** all four-cylinder gasoline models, '84 thru '88
- 346   **230, 250 & 280 Sedan, Coupe & Roadster** all 6 cyl sohc models '68 thru '72
- 983   **280 123 Series** gasoline models '77 thru '81
- 698   **350 & 450 Sedan, Coupe & Roadster** all models '71 thru '80
- 697   **Diesel 123 Series** 200D, 220D, 240D, 240TD, 300D, 300CD, 300TD, 4- & 5-cyl incl. Turbo '76 thru '85

MERCURY
- **See FORD Listing**

MG
- 111   **MGB** Roadster & GT Coupe all models '62 thru '80
- 265   **MG Midget & Austin Healey Sprite** Roadster '58 thru '80

MITSUBISHI
- *1669   **Cordia, Tredia, Galant, Precis & Mirage** '83 thru '93
- *2097   **Eclipse, Eagle Talon & Plymouth Laser** '90 thru '94
- *2022   **Pick-up & Montero** '83 thru '95

NISSAN
- 1137   **300ZX** all models including Turbo '84 thru '89
- *1341   **Maxima** all models '85 thru '91
- *771   **Pick-ups/Pathfinder** gas models '80 thru '95
- 876   **Pulsar** all models '83 thru '86

- *982   **Sentra** all models '82 thru '94
- *981   **Stanza** all models '82 thru '90

OLDSMOBILE
-   **Bravada** - see CHEVROLET S-10 (831)
-   **Calais** - see GENERAL MOTORS (1420)
-   **Custom Cruiser** - see BUICK Full-size RWD (1551)
- *658   **Cutlass** all standard gasoline V6 & V8 models '74 thru '88
-   **Cutlass Ciera** - see GENERAL MOTORS (829)
-   **Cutlass Supreme** - see GM (1671)
-   **Delta 88** - see BUICK Full-size RWD (1551)
-   **Delta 88 Brougham** - see BUICK Full-size FWD (1551), RWD (1627)
-   **Delta 88 Royale** - see BUICK Full-size RWD (1551)
-   **Firenza** - see GENERAL MOTORS (766)
-   **Ninety-eight Regency** - see BUICK Full-size RWD (1551), FWD (1627)
-   **Ninety-eight Regency Brougham** - see BUICK Full-size RWD (1551)
-   **Omega** - see GENERAL MOTORS (38020)
-   **Silhouette** - see GENERAL MOTORS (2035)

PEUGEOT
- 663   **504** all diesel models '74 thru '83

PLYMOUTH
-   **Laser** - see MITSUBISHI Eclipse (2097)
-   *For other PLYMOUTH titles, see DODGE listing.*

PONTIAC
-   **T1000** - see CHEVROLET Chevette (449)
-   **J-2000** - see GENERAL MOTORS (766)
-   **6000** - see GENERAL MOTORS (829)
-   **Bonneville** - see Buick Full-size FWD (1627), RWD (1551)
-   **Bonneville Brougham** - see Buick (1551)
-   **Catalina** - see Buick Full-size (1551)
- 1232   **Fiero** all models '84 thru '88
- 555   **Firebird** V8 models except Turbo '70 thru '81
- 867   **Firebird** all models '82 thru '92
-   **Full-size Front Wheel Drive** - see BUICK Oldsmobile, Pontiac Full-size FWD (1627)
-   **Full-size Rear Wheel Drive** Oldsmobile, Pontiac Full
-   **Grand Am** - see GENER
-   **Grand Prix** - see GENER
-   **Grandville** - see BUICK
-   **Parisienne** - see BUICK
-   **Phoenix** - see GENERA
-   **Sunbird** - see GENERA
-   **Trans Sport** - see GEN

PORSCHE
- *264   **911** all Coupe & Targa Turbo & Carrera 4 '65
- 239   **914** all 4 cyl models '6
- 397   **924** all models includi
- *1027   **944** all models includi

RENAULT
- 141   **5 Le Car** all models '7 Alliance & Encore - s

SAAB
- 247   **99** all models includin
- *980   **900** all models includi

SATURN
- 2083   **Saturn** all models '91 t

SUBARU
- 237   **1100, 1300, 1400 & 1**
- *681   **1600 & 1800** 2WD & 4

SUZUKI
- *1626   **Samurai/Sidekick and** all models '86 thru '95

TOYOTA
- 1023   **Camry** all models '83 thru '91
- 92006   **Camry** all models '92 thru '95
- 935   **Celica Rear Wheel Drive** '71 thru '85
- *2038   **Celica Front Wheel Drive** '86 thru '92
- 1139   **Celica Supra** all models '79 thru '92
- 361   **Corolla** all models '75 thru '79
- 961   **Corolla** all rear wheel drive models '80 thru '87
- *1025   **Corolla** all front wheel drive models '84 thru '92
- 636   **Corolla Tercel** all models '80 thru '82
- 360   **Corona** all models '74 thru '82
- 532   **Cressida** all models '78 thru '82
- 313   **Land Cruiser** all models '68 thru '82
- *1339   **MR2** all models '85 thru '87
- 304   **Pick-up** all models '69 thru '78
- *656   **Pick-up** all models '79 thru '95
- *2048   **Previa** all models '91 thru '93
- 2106   **Tercel** all models '87 thru '94

TRIUMPH
- 113   **Spitfire** all models '62 thru '81
- 322   **TR7** all models '75 thru '81

VW
- 159   **Beetle & Karmann Ghia** all models '54 thru '79
- 238   **Dasher** all gasoline models '74 thru '81
- *884   **Rabbit, Jetta, Scirocco, & Pick-up** gas models '74 thru '91 & Convertible '80 thru '92
- 451   **Rabbit, Jetta & Pick-up** all diesel models '77 thru '84
- 082   **Transporter 1600** all models '68 thru '79
- 226   **Transporter 1700, 1800 & 2000** all models '72 thru '79
- 084   **Type 3 1500 & 1600** all models '63 thru '73
- 1029   **Vanagon** all air-cooled models '80 thru '83

VOLVO
- 203   **120, 130 Series & 1800 Sports** '61 thru '73
- 129   **140 Series** all models '66 thru '74
- *270   **240 Series** all models '76 thru '93
- 400   **260 Series** all models '75 thru '82
- *1550   **740 & 760 Series** all models '82 thru '88

TECHBOOK MANUALS
- 2108   **Automotive Computer Codes**

* Listings shown with an asterisk (*) indicate model coverage as of this printing. These updated to include later model years - consult your Haynes dealer for more

Haynes North America, Inc., 861 Lawrence Drive,